For the People
A History of St Francis Xavier University

In *For the People* James Cameron charts the institutional development
of St Francis Xavier University from 1853 to 1970, illustrating how the
college has become an integral part of the region's history and culture
through its tradition of service to the people of eastern Nova Scotia on
both the mainland and Cape Breton Island. Basing his research on documentary and oral sources, Cameron describes the early nineteenth-century
migration of the Highland Catholic Scots, the settlement and development
of their communities, and the founding of St.F.X. as a means of religious,
economic, and social advancement in eastern Nova Scotia.

Among broad developments in administration, faculty, students, curriculum, finances, and facilities which Cameron examines, the formation of the
Extension Department, Xavier Junior College (now University College of
Cape Breton), and the Coady International Institute stand out as pivotal
events in the history of St.F.X. and demonstrate its attunement to the
changing needs of its constituency. The move to broaden the curriculum
by including extension education and the promotion of various forms of
economic cooperation to stimulate development in regional and international communities exemplify the unifying theme "for the people" at
St.F.X.'s foundational core.

For the People presents an engaging account of the fascinating personalities who administered and staffed the institution, its successes and failures
during the nineteenth century, and its expansion and progress in the twentieth century. The title of this institutional biography appropriately captures
the spirit of St.F.X. and its commitment to community service.

JAMES D. CAMERON is professor of history at St Francis Xavier University.

FOR THE PEOPLE

A History of St Francis Xavier University

JAMES D. CAMERON

Published for St Francis Xavier University by

McGILL-QUEEN'S UNIVERSITY PRESS

Montreal & Kingston • London • Buffalo

© St. Francis Xavier University 1996
ISBN 0-7735-1385-X
Legal deposit second quarter 1996
Bibliothèque nationale du Québec

Printed in Canada on acid-free paper

Canadian Cataloguing in Publication Data

Cameron, James, 1953–
    For the people: a history of St. Francis Xavier University
    Includes bibliographical references and index.
    ISBN 0-7735-1385-X
    I. St. Francis Xavier University – History.
    I. St. Francis Xavier University. II. Title.
    LE3.S315C26 1996   378.716'14   C95-900946-9

Typeset in Old Style 7 11/13 by Caractéra inc., Quebec City.

*This volume is respectfully dedicated
to all members of the
Xaverian family, past, present, and future.*

Contents

Illustrations

Unless otherwise noted, all photographs by kind permission of the St Francis Xavier University Archives.

Acknowledgment

We wish to acknowledge the support of The Eaton Foundation and the Eaton Family in making possible the research, writing, and publication of *For the People: A History of St Francis Xavier University*.

At the time of the founding of the University in 1853, Timothy Eaton had just arrived in Canada from Ireland to join his brothers and sisters in beginning a new life in a new country.

As St Francis Xavier University has stressed service to one's community throughout our long history, Timothy Eaton and subsequent generations have participated in the development of Canada and in supporting our social welfare infrastructure. In addition to providing employment opportunities for hundreds of thousands of Canadians, The Eaton Foundation, the Eaton Group of Companies and the Eaton Family have contributed very generously to Hospitals, Universities, Scholarship programs, Art Galleries, Museums, and Social Welfare programs across Canada.

St Francis Xavier University is proud to be associated with the Eaton Family. Together, we have helped to build Canada.

Foreword

The history of St Francis Xavier University is a story of remarkable achievement. Despite its humble origins in a remote village in north-eastern Nova Scotia, this university has gained a national and international reputation.

From its earliest days three things have distinguished St Francis Xavier University: concern for social justice, the development of strong ties with its students and alumni, and the role its graduates continue to play in public life.

Concern for social justice takes many forms and is most apparent in the philosophy of the Antigonish Movement, brought to fruition in the university's Extension Department and the Coady International Institute. This concern continues to permeate the campus today and finds expression through student organizations, chaplaincy, and voluntary commitment to helping others.

The strong ties of students, alumni, and alumnae to *their* university find expression in "The Xaverian Family." The relationship of student to student, student to faculty, and faculty to faculty quickly becomes apparent to campus visitors. Taken together, the concern for social justice and bonding to the Xaverian Family form part of what is commonly referred to as "the X Spirit."

Its founders saw the university as a means to provide leaders for the community and especially for the local church. Soon the university was providing leaders for the entire region and beyond: within the church, within the labour movement and social organizations, and at the highest levels of public life. In recent years graduates of St Francis Xavier University have occupied simultaneously the roles of prime minister of Canada, deputy leader of the opposition, leader of the senate, and leader of the opposition in senate, while many others served as members of parliament, senators, premiers, deputy premier, ministers of the crown, provincial legislators, and senior judges.

One may speculate how a small rural university, remote from the corridors of provincial and national power and far from the centres of commerce and wealth, could make such an impact on the country and on the world and also develop such a strong network of alumni. Dr James D. Cameron's history provides us with keen insights for addressing this question.

The Eaton Foundation supported the preparation of this book and St.F.X. owes its gratitude to the generosity of Mr George Eaton, whose friendship with one of our illustrious graduates led to the commission of this history.

David J. Lawless, PH D
President and Vice-Chancellor
St Francis Xavier University
1995

Preface

The motto of St Francis Xavier University (St.F.X.) is taken from St Paul's letter to the Philippians and counsels its readers to reflect on "whatsoever things are true" (4:8). This historical study of St.F.X. aims at the truth about its past; therefore it is not a promotional piece, adorned with hagiography – the celebration of great presidents, world-renowned faculty, and famous alumni. On the contrary, it is about real human beings, largely eastern Nova Scotia Roman Catholics of modest means and mostly average capabilities, and their efforts from 1853 to 1970 to provide themselves with adequate opportunities in higher education. Father Jimmy Tompkins, a central figure in the history of St.F.X. from 1902 to 1922, stated in the *Xaverian* of March 1917 that a history of the university should "give tone, direction and unity to present endeavour and prevent a spirit of drift which is likely to take hold of any institution that forgets its purpose and the inspiration that gave it being." This first full-scale history of the university, covering the period from its founding to 1970, should help Xaverians and others take stock of the institution's historical pilgrimage, legacy, and contribution.

In this study I chronicle and interpret the development of the university's principal phases – administration, faculty, students, philosophy, curriculum, mission, finances, and facilities, and chart the pivotal events in its history. I also consider it critical to show the changing relationship between St.F.X. and the Roman Catholic Church, the government, and its constituency. As well, I attempt to place the St.F.X. story within the changing context of life in eastern Nova Scotia. My mandate required a "scholarly" history covering "all phases and departments of the university"; this I try to achieve while also producing a thorough and critical, yet readable and sympathetic, narrative. I write for a general audience; the specialist will find elaboration and critical concerns addressed in many of the endnotes.

The history of St.F.X. properly begins in two places: the Scottish Highlands and Rome. The late eighteenth- and early nineteenth-century Highland emigrations to eastern Nova Scotia and the beliefs and traditions of Roman Catholicism profoundly shaped the institution. After surveying this background, the study describes how Bishop Colin F. MacKinnon in 1853 founded St.F.X. in Cape Breton and then transferred it two years later to mainland Antigonish County. In 1855 St.F.X. was only one of several denominational colleges which had recently been founded in the Maritime provinces by the Anglicans, Baptists, Methodists, and Roman Catholics. In the twentieth century, I have given special attention to the debate over university federation in the 1920s, to the beginnings in 1928 of an innovative and dynamic extension program, to the establishment in 1951 on Cape Breton of Xavier Junior College (now called the University College of Cape Breton), to the formation of the Coady International Institute in 1959, and to the dramatic changes at St.F.X. between 1945 and 1970. The St.F.X. Extension Department and the Coady International Institute are not treated in depth or comprehensively; both these projects are of such importance that they really deserve separate written histories. While I have described the founding of the affiliated College of Mount St Bernard, located adjacent to St.F.X., I have only dealt with its history from the viewpoint of the university and as "The Mount" intersected with it at the point of college-level courses. Mount St Bernard is owned and operated by the Congregation of the Sisters of Notre Dame, whose motherhouse is located in Montreal and whose local administration remained entirely separate from St.F.X. A thorough history of the Mount from the Mount's perspective awaits a historian expert in the traditions and sources of this congregation, and commissioned by them to research and write it. Neither are St.F.X.'s considerable athletic achievements herein systematically narrated. The comprehensive history of sport at St.F.X. awaits a historically inclined sports enthusiast who will fill out the sketch provided here and supplement John McFarland's *Seventy-Five Years of Hockey* (1971).

The idea of "for the people" is a unifying theme in the history of St.F.X. I borrow the phrase from a pamphlet published in 1921 by Father Jimmy Tompkins called *Knowledge for the People*. My emphasis on this theme does not imply that St.F.X. has an unbroken record of institutional altruism or that the church revealed no self-interest by sponsoring the college. However, a persisting official and actual concern with service to the people of eastern Nova Scotia has characterized St.F.X.; only the confirmed cynic can ignore it. The bishop of the diocese, Colin F. MacKinnon, established St.F.X. to develop a professional Catholic leadership in order to foster the spiritual and social progress of the descendants of the Scottish Highland emigrants in eastern Nova Scotia. Yet, as an offspring of the universal church, he wanted his college to span ethnic boundaries by also serving the

Acadian and Irish Catholics. At the end of the nineteenth century, St.F.X. broadened its curriculum to meet the changing needs of its constituency; and then, during the first two decades of the twentieth century, it began experimenting with extension education. These experiments culminated in 1928 with the formation of an Extension Department which gave new meaning to the theme "for the people." With this work, St.F.X. added to its mandate the responsibility to serve its constituency by stimulating the social and economic development of communities in the region. In 1951 it belatedly fulfilled its responsibility to serve more adequately the people of the industrial area of Cape Breton by establishing Xavier Junior College, which eventually became the University College of Cape Breton. Finally, the founding of the Coady International Institute in 1959 shifted the St.F.X. theme "for the people" from a regional to an international key. Thus "for the people" has been an important theme in St.F.X.'s past.

The following narrative history is based on documentary and oral sources which are referenced in the endnotes. I also used student and faculty alumni surveys to recapture the more recent experience of these two groups. The sources for the first fifty years of St.F.X. history are scanty indeed, for there exists nearly a complete absence of administrative and student records. However, selected government, newspaper, and ecclesiastical records provided enough information to chart the college's main lines of development through these years.

Many people willingly helped me during this research project. I begin by gladly acknowledging their contributions: Father Gregory MacKinnon, past president of St.F.X., for appointing me in 1990 to the position of university historian; Dr David Lawless, president and vice chancellor, for continued support and interest; Dr Raymond MacLean, for wise counsel, timely encouragement, and scholarly insight; Kathleen MacKenzie, university archivist, for her endless patience, cooperation, and expertise in the university records; other members of my advisory committee – Revs. Msgr Cyril H. Bauer, chair, Malcolm MacDonell, the late Charles Brewer, the late Msgr Malcolm MacLellan, Roderick B. MacDonald, and Dr J.J. MacDonald and J. Thomas Langley; the congenial, cooperative, and expert staff of the Angus L. MacDonald Library; Brian MacDonald and staff of the department of university development; Bishop Colin Campbell for access to the diocesan archives and the assistance of Chancellor Regis Halloran; the late Father Angus Anthony Johnston, whose published and unpublished sources on the history of the Diocese of Antigonish, many of them collected from archives in Quebec, Scotland, and Rome, have been an indispensable foundation for much of my work; and the late Father

William Edwards, whose collection of documents and notes on the first fifty years of St.F.X. history I have found useful.

Other St.F.X. staff, as well as local residents, also contributed in important ways to this work: Dr Winston Jackson, sociology; Dr Leo P. Chiasson, biology; Dr Leonard Pluta, economics; Dr Steve Baldner, philosophy; Leah Duffy, assistant registrar; Drs Ronald J. MacKinnon, Alexander MacEachern, and Gerhard Dueck, mathematics and computing sciences; Judith MacLean; Sisters Irene Doyle, May Mulvihill, and Roderick McMullin of the Sisters of St Martha; Dr John Hamilton; Zita Cameron; Ellen Arsenault; Kay Desjardin; Bruce Nunn; and Sister Margaret MacDonell, CND. I am also indebted to those who read parts or all of the manuscript and helped improve it: Dr Al Balawyder, Rev. Dr Donald F. Campbell, Ronald A. MacDonald, A.G. Mac-Donald, Dr A.A. MacDonald, and Kathleen MacKenzie, as well as the members of the advisory committee acknowledged above.

In addition, I have profited from the assistance of staff at the Public Archives of Nova Scotia, the National Archives of Canada, the Beaton Institute of Cape Breton Studies (especially Dr Robert Morgan and Kate Currie), the Archives of the Archdiocese of Halifax, Giovanni Pizzorusso and Mateo Sanfilippo at the Canadian Academic Centre in Italy, and from the work and advice of other historians – Peter B. Waite, William Westfall, John G. Reid, Paul Axelrod, and G. Edward MacDonald. Those members of the St.F.X. community who so kindly permitted me to interview them or who submitted written recollections and documents I have acknowledged in an appendix list at the end of this study.

Two anonymous readers for McGill-Queen's University Press indicated weaknesses and omissions in the manuscript and the Canadian Catholic Historical Association, *Historical Studies*, kindly permitted me to include material from an earlier article entitled "'Erasing forever the brand of social inferiority': St Francis Xavier University and the Highland Catholics of Eastern Nova Scotia" (vol. 59, 1992.)

Special thanks to my wife, Patsy, and our children, Rachel, Adrian, Daniel, Stephen, and Julian, who have had to put up with a husband and father preoccupied with Xaverian affairs, past and present. Patsy also worked part-time as a research assistant through much of the project as did Shelley Kyte through its final year.

Finally, the Eaton Foundation has been the sole patron of the History of St.F.X. Project from start to finish. Without their generous support St.F.X. would not now have a written history.

While thankful for the help of so many, I remain fully responsible for the selection, organization, presentation, and interpretation of the material herein contained, along with the inevitable errors and omissions.

For the People

Introduction:
Of Scotland and Rome

St Francis Xavier University (St.F.X.) is located in the town of Antigonish, eastern Nova Scotia, Canada. Yet its history, especially the first fifty years, is best understood against the backdrop of the Scottish Highlands and Rome, for the founding fathers of the institution were descendants of Highland Roman Catholics; their aims, aspirations, and achievements in higher education in Nova Scotia can only be understood in the context of their earlier cultural experience.

The Scottish Highland Background
The Scottish Catholics who clambered onto the rugged shores of eastern Nova Scotia during the late eighteenth and early nineteenth centuries hailed from the highlands and islands of Scotland. They christened their new communities with old country names, such as Lochaber, Moidart, Keppoch, Arisaig, Strathglass, and Inverness. They also proudly bore the names of their ancient clans, names such as Beaton, Cameron, Campbell, Gillis, MacDonald, Chisholm, and MacNeil. For centuries they had lived a Spartan existence among the rocks and heather as an oppressed minority, marginalized in a Protestant English-speaking country by their Roman Catholic–Gaelic culture.[1] Most Highlanders were impoverished tenant farmers and farm labourers who nonetheless possessed a rich oral culture and clan tradition. Since the tumultuous sixteenth century, when the Reformed faith had replaced Catholicism as the established religion of Scotland, the Catholic remnant had lived in peril. From 1560 prohibitory legislation threatened the Catholic faithful with severe civil disabilities, punishment, and even execution. Persecution of Catholics, commonly led by rabid anti-Catholic Presbyterian ministers, waxed and waned through the centuries. This disposed Catholics, during the seventeenth and eighteenth centuries, to support the ill-starred Jacobite cause which tried to restore the Catholic Stuarts to the throne. After the final defeat of the movement at Culloden in 1746, the British government acted

immediately to pacify the Highlands and eradicate Jacobitism. It disarmed clans, eliminated the ancient juridical rights of the clan chiefs, confiscated Catholic estates and installed alien factors to administer them, and prohibited Highland dress and bagpipes. In some instances, Catholic homes and chapels were torched. Toward the end of the eighteenth century, relief for the Catholic minority (perhaps 3 per cent of the overall population) from the trial of religious intolerance gradually materialized.[2] The British government passed a Relief Bill in 1793 which allowed for freedom of worship, the right to inherit and purchase property, and access to employment in the public service. Nonetheless, traces of discrimination, abuse, and mistrust remained; the Highland Catholics rediscovered it when they crossed the Atlantic. Britain did not officially grant Catholics full political rights until 1829 when Parliament passed the Emancipation Bill.

The culturally rooted subjugation of Catholics in Scotland made them nearly invisible in the educational and intellectual life of the nation.[3] Ironically, educational opportunities for Catholics were few in a country which became known for its democratic system of schooling.[4] Apparently, Catholic parents in some areas were content to have their children educated in the Protestant schools as long as teachers did not force their young to imbibe Protestant doctrine.[5] At times, some Highland Catholics operated covert or undercover Catholic schools. Native Catholics who wanted to serve the Scottish Catholic mission as priests had few higher educational opportunities; most had to attend seminaries on the continent, usually at the Scots colleges in France, Spain, or Rome.[6] Since Catholics had such restricted access to education, few of them contributed to the astonishing intellectual achievements of eighteenth century Scotland.[7]

Pilgrimage Overseas
The grim social, religious, and economic outlook for Scottish Catholics in the eighteenth and nineteenth centuries rendered emigration to the New World an attractive prospect. Those who opted to leave joined a massive westward movement of population – nearly one million emigrated from the British Isles to British North America between 1800 and 1850 alone.[8] Large numbers flocked from the western Highlands and islands.[9] Of these, a "vastly disproportionate" number were Roman Catholics, frequently with a clergyman at their head.[10] For a time in the late eighteenth century the Roman Catholic Church appeared ready to develop St John's Island (renamed Prince Edward Island in 1798) as a refuge for Scottish Catholics; however, from 1790 the church became more passive toward emigration and, at times, outright resentful and hostile.[11] Nonetheless, the Catholic exodus to

4

the New World continued, and its substantial size was confirmed by later census figures; these reveal that, by mid-century, Scottish Catholics composed a majority of the population of eastern Nova Scotia.[12] Passenger lists show that most emigrants were farmers, labourers, or tradesmen accompanied by their wives and children.[13] The economic lot of the pre-1815 emigrants was, in general, better than that of the emigrants who came afterwards. A complex interplay of social and economic trends – the dissolution of the clan system, clearances of land for sheep grazing, increasing rents, overpopulation, famine, and the collapse of the kelp industry – fuelled the emigration.[14] As well, the promise of the New World, especially its abundant land, often romanticized by self-interested emigration agents, exerted a strong pull on those who hoped to preserve their traditional way of life or to take advantage of expanded opportunities in British North America.[15]

New Homeland in Eastern Nova Scotia
The main British North American destinations for migrating Highlanders were Glengarry in Ontario, Prince Edward Island, and eastern Nova Scotia.[16] By the Treaty of Utrecht in 1713, Britain had obtain mainland Nova Scotia from France, and Cape Breton came into its possession in 1763. Catholic Highlanders began landing on the shores of northern Nova Scotia in the 1780s; on the recommendation of Father Angus Bernard MacEachern of Prince Edward Island, they commonly trekked eastward along the Gulf Shore, some even crossing over to Cape Breton Island before finding suitable places to homestead. Their settlements edged inland along rivers and intervales as the superior shore lands were filled up.[17] The immigrants immediately confronted the arduous task of pioneering. The earliest settlers had the best choice of land; this advantage contributed to differences in agricultural prosperity, but proximity to markets, background agricultural experiences, and cultural traditions also played their part.[18] In contrast to Scotland, the farms were larger, the standard of living higher, and the houses more substantial. Generally, a nuclear family worked the land within a homogeneous ethnic and religious community with kith and kin located nearby. At first, church and government influences were weak and roads non-existent; however, a new society was in the making.

By the 1850s, this transplanted Highland community, the largest part of the future constituency of St.F.X., had experienced considerable demographic, economic, social, political, and religious development; its pioneer phase was fading into the past.[19] The Highlanders were scattered through the seven counties of eastern Nova Scotia – Pictou, Antigonish, Guysborough, Richmond, Inverness, Victoria, and Cape Breton – embraced by the Roman Catholic Diocese of Arichat. The diocesan population had reached nearly 105,000 and most were native born.[20] A substantial majority were Scots: 67 per cent by 1871.[21] But other ethnic groups were also part of the St.F.X. constituency: 14,989 Acadians (11 per cent of the diocese), 14,977 Irish (11 per cent), 11,835 English (8 per cent), and 735 natives (0.5 per cent).[22] Catholics composed about 45 per cent of the population and formed majorities in Antigonish, Inverness, Richmond, and Cape Breton counties.[23] Most people inhabited the countryside and farmed or fished; domestic production and small manufacturing had begun to grow as millers, craftsmen, and merchants appeared. Developments within the colony of Nova Scotia overall benefited its eastern inhabitants. Trade thrived as a large merchant fleet maintained links with Britain, New England, and the West Indies.[24] The colony, its capital located in Halifax, had been granted an elected assembly in 1758; in 1848 political reformers had won responsible government. As early as the 1820s, Catholics were sitting in the provincial legislature and by 1830 the British parliament had fully dismantled the penal laws which had restricted the rights of Catholics since the Reformation.[25] In spite of the continuing thorn of anti-Catholicism, at times pressed deep by militant Protestants threatened by the growth of "Popery," Catholic prospects brightened.[26] By 1860, seven years before the confederation of the British North American colonies, the bishop of the diocese exuded optimism: "The growing importance of the Catholic body in numbers and influence is sure to tell upon, and command, the respect of the Protestant government under which we live."[27]

The Rome Connection
Since the Highland descendants who founded St.F.X. were Roman Catholics, their allegiance to Rome profoundly influenced the history of the institution and its constituency. By mid-century, Maritime Catholicism had emerged from an earlier stage, during the pioneering period, of organizational infancy and dependence on Quebec to become "one of the region's major social institutions."[28] Rome had carved the Diocese of Arichat out of the Diocese of Halifax in 1844 because of population increases and ethnic tensions; by 1852 the new diocese embraced nineteen large parishes and as many missionary priests who served a flock of about fifty thousand faithful.[29] As the pioneers prevailed in their fight for survival and security, the literate element of the population, notably the clergy,[30] promoted learning; the inhabitants, prodded by educational reformers, gradually developed formal educational institutions (common schools, academies, grammar schools, and a normal school) within an emergent state educational

system administered centrally by a council of public instruction and a superintendent.[31]

The Vatican appointed Father William Fraser, a native of Inverness County, Scotland, and vicar apostolic of Nova Scotia from 1827,[32] the first bishop of the new Diocese of Halifax in 1842. Then two years later it transferred the pioneering prelate to the newly created Diocese of Arichat (renamed the Diocese of Antigonish in 1886).[33] While the official seat of the diocese remained in Arichat, Cape Breton, Bishop Fraser preferred to live among his countrymen in Antigonish until his death in October 1851. His successor was Rev. Colin Francis MacKinnon, a native-born son of the Parish of St Ninian's, Antigonish and founder of St Francis Xavier University. MacKinnon acceded to the episcopate during the spiritual reign of Pope Pius IX (1846–1876), who defined the doctrine of the Immaculate Conception and convened in 1869 the First Vatican Council, which enunciated the doctrine of Papal Infallibility.[34]

The Urban College
The Sacred Congregation for the Propagation of the Faith (hereafter the Propaganda Fide or the Propaganda) – the congregation charged with overseeing the far-flung missionary work of the church – best sustained the bond between Rome and the Diocese of Arichat.[35] During the nineteenth century, a succession of select student seminarians from the diocese, including Bishop MacKinnon, travelled to the congregation's Urban College in Rome to be prepared for orders within the church; thereafter they swore to report regularly to the congregation's prefect, as all missionary priests did, on their priestly activities in far-off eastern Nova Scotia.[36] Pope Urban VIII had founded the famous College in 1627 to prepare secular, missionary priests for the mission territories within the jurisdiction of the congregation.[37] Since many of the students from foreign lands had limited or no access to higher education, the Urban College curriculum necessarily covered the liberal arts as well as the advanced levels of philosophy and theology.[38] Its papal founder had granted the college power to confer the doctorate in philosophy and theology.[39] There existed nowhere else in the world a college which drew its students from such diverse points on the globe and offered them such a rich cosmopolitan experience. Rev. Dr John Schulte, the first rector of St.F.X., wrote of his Rome experience: "the students, being talented young men chosen from every quarter of the globe, afforded an excellent opportunity of studying the various traits of human nature and becoming acquainted with the character and institutions of the nations of the world."[40] Colonials educated there

testified that the experience did much to erase their own parochialism and to uproot western chauvinism.[41]

The founding and historical development of St.F.X. have been closely bound up with the lives of the people of eastern Nova Scotia, especially those from Scotland. Their background as Highlanders and their faith as Roman Catholics defined their new institution of higher learning in the New World.

PART ONE

Origins of Catholic Higher Education in Eastern Nova Scotia, to 1877

· I ·

Predecessors and Beginnings

Tuesday, 18 September 1855 marked the official opening of St Francis Xavier College/Seminary[1] in the village of Antigonish, its permanent home. Yet the college/seminary had actually operated for the preceding two years in the southeastern Cape Breton village of Arichat. Even before that, several Scotch and Irish clerics had tried to set up advanced schools in the region. Unfortunately, these pioneering educational efforts proved either futile or short-lived. The college in Antigonish was the latest attempt by the Highland descendants to supply their own needs for higher education. It symbolized their cultural growth, and, along with other sectarian colleges, reinforced the denominational nature of higher education in colonial Nova Scotia.

The Dearth of Priests
The region's pioneering priests desired advanced schools so they could better care for the spiritual needs of the Catholic settlers and their descendants. Ever since the Highlanders' large-scale immigration to the Maritimes in the late eighteenth and early nineteenth centuries, a tiny band of clerical leaders had decried the dearth of priests for their people. Frequently they appealed to the Old Country or to Quebec for help. Unfortunately, the burgeoning Catholic population in the Maritimes urgently required priests when the vast Diocese of Quebec was ill prepared to respond to its need. The British Conquest of New France in 1760 had precipitated a priestly exodus from the colony and the new rulers forbade religious orders to recruit. Not until the 1790s did the diminished Canadian priesthood begin to recover. In Halifax, lay Catholics sought for clergy overseas, but clerical shortages persisted as "the Maritimes still lacked an effective method of ensuring a continuous supply of reliable priests."[2] Entwined with the issue of clerical supply was the problem of priestly quality. Terrence Murphy identified the dilemma: "An area such as the Maritimes, desperately in need of clergy but far removed from the immediate supervision of a bishop,

11

was very vulnerable to irregular clergy who were searching for a place to establish themselves."[3] Evidently, a regional seminary would be the only permanent solution to the cry for priests and the problem of "clerical adventurers."

Certain prelates discussed, even attempted, the local training of clerics in the Maritimes decades before any permanent seminary was founded. Father Angus Bernard MacEachern, who had arrived on Prince Edward Island in 1790, almost immediately voiced his concern for local training; Catholics purchased a two-hundred-acre Island farm in 1794 with this as one of its ultimate aims.[4] But the poverty of MacEachern's flock meant hope deferred. Father Edmund Burke proposed a seminary in Halifax in 1802, yet, among other difficulties, the supply of teachers proved inadequate; by 1808 the proposal was abandoned.[5] Not until 1818 was Burke, appointed vicar apostolic of Nova Scotia the year before, able to train seminarians in his Halifax residence. Six of these were eventually ordained and placed in Nova Scotian parishes.[6] In 1816 Burke and MacEachern conceived a joint plan to open a regional seminary at St Margaret's Parish, Arisaig, the oldest Highland Catholic mission in Nova Scotia, centrally located on its gulf shore. Apparently the Catholics of Arisaig even bought two hundred acres of land for the planned seminary which the prelates hoped to open in the summer of 1820. Unfortunately, Burke was called to his eternal reward in the fall of that year and the seminary dream came to naught.[7]

Yet MacEachern on Prince Edward Island remained deeply troubled that the enormous Maritime Catholic population lacked schools for raising native pastors.[8] Finally, in 1831, two years after he was made bishop of the new Diocese of Charlottetown, MacEachern opened St Andrew's College at the head of Hillsborough River on Prince Edward Island.[9] His school amounted to "a sort of high school/ junior college" to prepare boys for seminary training. Some of its students did eventually become priests, but the college languished and closed in 1844; scarcity of funds was the cause.[10]

William Fraser, an immigrant priest from the Highlands and vicar apostolic of Nova Scotia from 1827 who resided in Antigonish County, was a friend of MacEachern's and cooperated his St Andrew's venture. Fraser shared the same sense of a pressing need for priests. In 1831 he sent five students to the Island and tried to support the college financially.[11] The St Andrew's Board of Trustees listed him as a member, although it is doubtful he ever attended their meetings.[12] MacEachern found it surprising that Fraser had not acted before him to establish a preparatory school on mainland Nova Scotia; the site would have been more central and the resources greater. Apparently Fraser did maintain a few students at his Antigonish residence.[13]

Actually, Fraser played a minimal role in founding institutions of higher learning, either in the Diocese of Halifax or Arichat, even though he obtained a substantial bequest in the late 1830s for just that purpose and had eight years of experience as professor-administrator of a tiny college in Scotland.[14] The Catholic Church wardens in Halifax were the ones who opened the Seminary of St Mary's on 1 January 1840 after a period of frustration with Fraser's lack of interest.[15] But a harsh judgment of Fraser's apparent apathy in matters educational should be tempered by these considerations: the general poverty of his diocese, the rudimentary state of its educational institutions, his heavy episcopal and missionary duties, and his dislike of business and administration.[16] Moreover, unlike his successors Bishop Colin F. MacKinnon and Bishop John Cameron, Fraser apparently did not support the emerging Nova Scotia pattern of denominational colleges. He, along with many others in March 1844, petitioned the legislature for one non-sectarian college on the grounds of economy, toleration, efficiency, and protection from narrow interests.[17] For some years he had been an inactive trustee of Pictou Academy.[18] Fraser remained, right up to his death in 1851, essentially a missionary priest; educational pioneering he left to his priests and laity.

First Schools of Higher Studies, Diocese of Arichat
Father William B. MacLeod, the first native priest of the Diocese of Arichat, not Bishop Fraser, is rightly called its first "pioneer of higher education."[19] MacEachern appointed him in 1824 to the Bras d'Or Lake Mission, which included East Bay and Grand Narrows. Gradually, MacLeod gathered some young men around him to prepare them for seminary studies; when a school was readied at East Bay, he placed his students there under the tutelage of Malcolm MacLellan, a good classical scholar who was a recent emigrant from Scotland. The late diocesan historian, Rev. A.A. Johnston, has underscored the importance of MacLeod's school: "it was a minor seminary and the first institution in the present Diocese of Antigonish in which young men were given their preliminary training for the ecclesiastical state."[20] The school's most celebrated alumnus was the successor to Bishop Fraser, Bishop Colin MacKinnon.[21] The East Bay College, as it has been called, was a important pioneering educational effort. Lamentably, it was short-lived and likely closed about 1828.[22]

Two other important educational experiments in the diocese preceded the founding of St.F.X. Father John Chisholm, a native of Scotland but brought with his family to the new world, began in the busy seaport of Arichat an academy which lasted from November 1833 to 1841. Father Chisholm incurred considerable debt for his efforts; in trying to defray expenses, he obtained farm produce to sell in New-foundland, but perished at sea when his ship was lost. The academy reopened in 1853 in conjunction with the beginnings of St.F.X.[23] And Father Colin MacKinnon in 1838, shortly after returning from his studies in Rome to the mission of St Andrews, a district of considerable agricultural industry and activity, established a grammar school there. Fourteen years later he recalled, "when I arrived home in 1837 from the Propaganda in Rome, I found that there was not one Catholic School in the place in which the classics were taught. To obviate this evil, and found a nursery for such of our young men as intended to dedicate themselves to the service of the Church, a grammar school was founded in the vicinity of my parochial church, in the Township of St Andrews, County of Sydney." Several missionary priests received their classical education there, under the tutelage of, among others, the MacLellan brothers, John and Malcolm, who had taught at East Bay; in 1852 ten to twelve "young men" were studying Latin.[24] The school soon earned a reputation for high-quality instruction and successful alumni.[25]

Bishop Colin F. MacKinnon, Father of Diocesan Higher Education
When MacKinnon succeeded Fraser on the latter's death in October 1851, he brought new dynamism to the leadership of the diocese. Fortunately, the first phase of his episcopate coincided with improving economic conditions; Maritime trade was bolstered by Reciprocity with the United States (1854–66), the Crimean War, and the American Civil War (1861–65). Frantic railway construction in the colonies also contributed to the economic upswing.[26] The novice bishop had been born 20 July 1810 of Highland Catholic parentage at Williams Point, a rural area close to Antigonish. After classical studies at Father MacLeod's East Bay College 1824–28, MacKinnon, at Bishop Fraser's direction, travelled to the Urban College in Rome. There he studied from 1829 to 1837, earned a PH D and DD, and became thoroughly "imbued with the spirit of Rome."[27] The young Nova Scotian was ordained to the priesthood by Cardinal Fransoni on 4 June 1837; after the long and arduous trek back to Nova Scotia, his bishop assigned him as the first resident pastor to St Andrews.[28] MacKinnon soon won the reputation of outstanding priest of the diocese; hence, when Bishop Fraser's health began to decline in 1850, Bishop Walsh of Halifax pleaded with Cardinal Fransoni in Rome to have MacKinnon, "whose merit is so universally acknowledged," appointed coadjutor.[29] He wrote: "[MacKinnon] is grave and respectable in his appearance, priestly in his dress and habits, a good linguist, not only preaches well and writes well in English but also in Gaelic for the Scotch which is

Rev. Dr Colin F. MacKinnon, founder of
St Francis Xavier University and second bishop of the
Diocese of Arichat 1851–77

a most desirable qualification in any Bishop of Arichat."[30] Roman authorities must have been convinced; MacKinnon was mitred on 11 November 1851. His diocese was then composed of nineteen congregations led by the same number of missionary priests. Most of his Catholic people were Highlanders, Acadians, Irish, and Micmacs; they were farmers, fishermen, or "poor tradesmen." To adequately meet their spiritual needs, the new bishop decided he needed at least twelve more priests.[31]

This need for priests was the central reason why Bishop MacKinnon promoted education for his Catholic flock. In his first pastoral letter as bishop, February 1852, he expressed his firm intention to establish a seminary: "A Diocesan Seminary, even on a small scale, is among the first cares of a Bishop: consequently it will receive our earliest and most serious attention."[32] By then MacKinnon had seen enough to be convinced of the crying need for a steady supply of dependable and locally trained native priests. Clerical candidates had to travel far away to Quebec or Rome at great expense and risk to complete their studies.[33] And the shortage of priests made dependence on "clerical adventurers" all too common. MacKinnon lamented: "The reception of clerical adventurers into the missions of this country has been the bane of religion in our province. Catholicism has suffered more from the bad conduct of such men than from all other obstacles put together."[34] MacKinnon's anxiety about a diocesan seminary, therefore, was rooted in his need for priests to be effective pastors to his people.

The Origins of St Francis Xavier University
On the southern shore of Isle Madame in the village of Arichat next to the Notre Dame de l'Assomption Church stands a lonely monument, a solitary witness to the distant, misty origins of St Francis Xavier University in the county of Richmond just off the southern coast of Cape Breton Island. It announces: "At Arichat under the leadership of Right Reverend Colin F. MacKinnon the first classes of Saint Francis Xavier University began on July 20, 1853."[35] These "first classes" were enthusiastically announced to the public on 28 July 1853 by the Antigonish *Casket*: "We have much pleasure in announcing to our readers that His Lordship Dr MacKinnon has, on Wednesday last, opened a Seminary at Arichat, on a principle which is likely to produce a new era in the history of Literature in this Diocese."[36] Two weeks before the opening, MacKinnon had explained his plan in a Pastoral Letter: the new seminary would train youth for the priesthood and provide "lay-youth" with a sound education so they would benefit their country as Christians in the "various grades of civil life."[37] While MacKinnon's foremost concern was the development of an indigenous priesthood,

his vision also encompassed the educational advancement of the Catholic laity.

MacKinnon made it clear from the start that the Arichat location on Isle Madame would be temporary; Antigonish would be the permanent home of the infant college/seminary. But his buildings at Antigonish were unfinished in 1853, so Arichat, the official seat of the diocese and centrally positioned within it, was the most reasonable interim location.[38] The town was a busy seaport with over one thousand inhabitants and more vessels registered in it than any other Nova Scotia seaport except for Halifax.[39] Water was then the best means of travel. About four thousand Catholics peopled the Island, most of them Acadians.[40] Mariners and fishermen abounded, but a sizeable number of farmers worked its fields. There MacKinnon would be able to keep a watchful eye over the seminary, since he himself had moved to Arichat from St Andrews in May 1853. Moreover, a "grand old house"[41] was available for rent; it was known as "old Hubert's big house" and commanded a lovely view of the ocean. MacKinnon took it for two years.[42]

The Problem of Funding

Financing this educational venture was probably the bishop's number one headache. One year before, he had pleaded with the cardinal prefect of the Propaganda to lay the "destitute" state of his diocese before the congregation.[43] Simultaneously he had decided to request alms from the French lay missionary society called the Association for the Propagation of the Faith.[44] The needy bishop arranged the first annual diocesan collection for the association in 1852 and received from it 20,000 francs in May 1853.[45] Thus began a long, and for the diocese, financially fruitful relationship.[46] A decade later MacKinnon acknowledged his debt to the association: "Whatever we have been able to do for the common good, for the progress of religion, for education and for humanity, we must attribute it all humanly speaking, to this renowned and holy society established for the propagation of the faith."[47] The good works supported by the association included aid to poor missions, the creation of the seminary, the purchase of valuable land for church purposes, and contributions to the public school in Arichat.[48]

MacKinnon also had his eye on the public treasury as a source of funds for the new seminary. He wrote to the provincial secretary, Joseph Howe, in early July 1853, informing him of the imminent opening of the seminary and carefully noting that it would carry out the functions of an academy – indeed, it would be the Arichat Academy resurrected, but with a name change.[49] The Academy in its first life had, from 1835, received an annual government grant of one hundred pounds. MacKinnon hoped this information would be an instructive precedent for Howe, since the new academy/seminary would likewise fulfil the provisions of the School Act relating to academies and thus would also qualify for the grant.[50] MacKinnon's lobby, along with a petition of certain Arichat citizens, persuaded the civil authorities in Halifax; the government coffers were promptly opened to the tune of one hundred pounds annually.[51] The resurrected academy, now combined with a seminary, had found another source of financial aid.

The First Rector and Staff

A new seminary, MacKinnon was well aware, required much more than adequate funding; its success would depend too on competent administration and teachers. Here the young bishop also revealed a solicitous care for his new educational venture. On Thursday, 14 July he convened a group in Arichat called "the friends of the Seminary" who nominated certain "gentlemen" as "very fit persons" to be trustees of the new seminary. The nominees were Henry Martell, Simon Donovan, Thomas Lenoir, John Fuller, senior, and Captain Babin. Martell represented the Township of Arichat in the provincial legislature and Fuller had sent the petition for a renewal of the Arichat Academy grant to the assembly. These "friends" apparently accepted their nominations, for they remained the official trustees until 1855.[52] Their responsibilities included hiring staff and supervising the affairs of the fledgling institution.

MacKinnon had been searching for a dedicated scholar-rector to lead his college/seminary. The studious John Cameron from the district of St Andrews Nova Scotia was a potential candidate, but in 1853 he had not yet completed his studies in Rome, where Bishop Fraser had sent him in 1844. Meanwhile, MacKinnon heard, probably through Cameron, of another outstanding student at the Urban College: a Prussian named John Schulte who hoped to serve in North American missions. Roman officials agreed to MacKinnon's request that Schulte be ordained and sent to his diocese. Schulte arrived, in late January 1853, a neophyte priest in a foreign land.[53]

The Prussian priest-professor became a fascinating and central figure during the founding years of St.F.X. As its first rector, then director of studies, he would be the backbone of the nascent institution for almost a decade.[54] Only twenty-seven when he arrived, he had already displayed exceptional talent and piety. His birthplace was Arnsberg, Westphalia, in Prussia. There he had received his classical training under the guidance of a learned Catholic priest. Afterwards, in 1846, at a time when certain famous Oxford Tractarians, like John

18

Rev. Dr John Schulte, St.F.X.'s first rector,
1853–54

Henry Newman (later cardinal), were marching to Rome, Schulte had entered its cosmopolitan Urban College. A brilliant academic performance in philosophical and theological studies earned him both a PH D (1849) and a DD (1852). By this time he had astonishing facility in five languages – German, Italian, English, Latin, Greek, and Hebrew. Bishop MacKinnon in Nova Scotia was most gratified to receive such a scholarly and dedicated priest, and he ardently thanked Cardinal Fransoni for directing young Schulte to his diocese. He informed the prefect: "I am giving him charge of the Seminary, and I have every hope that, under the direction of a man of such zeal and learning, the students will make great progress in study and piety."[55] Before the seminary opened, Schulte had opportunity to experience life first-hand in his new diocese: he assisted MacKinnon at St Andrews Parish from January to March 1853, and afterwards pastored in the town of Pictou for several months.[56] When the college/seminary finally opened in Arichat, Schulte was there as rector, spiritual director, and professor of theology, philosophy, and Italian.

Bishop MacKinnon's other pioneer faculty members at the Arichat college during its first year included Rev. Hubert Girroir, Roderick MacDonald, and John Fuller. Girroir was twenty-eight, one year older than Schulte, and a native of Tracadie, Nova Scotia. He had studied at St Mary's College, Halifax and had completed his theology at the Grand Seminary in Quebec. MacKinnon had earlier appointed him assistant priest at Arichat, so Girroir was a convenient choice to teach Christian doctrine and French at the local seminary. In February 1854, he became rector of the cathedral in Arichat, and was distinguished as the first native Acadian priest of the diocese.[57] Roderick MacDonald, an austere twenty-seven-year-old Scot, originally from Margaree, Cape Breton, taught mathematics, Latin, and Greek. Earlier he had studied in Antigonish and then Pictou Academy.[58] Reports circulated that his progress in physics and mathematics had been "exceptionally brilliant." By the close of his St.F.X. career in 1877, MacDonald would be known as an "exact and painstaking instructor."[59] Finally, John Fuller, a native of Arichat, taught elementary English in the academy; he was the only member of the first year's staff who remained for the 1854–55 term.[60] The founding faculty exhibited quite a mix: a Prussian, an Acadian, a Scot, and an Anglo.

By the late summer of 1854, Bishop MacKinnon found it necessary to send Schulte back to the Pictou mission. While gratified with his performance, the bishop needed a priest in Pictou, and Schulte had already served there for a few months in the spring of 1853.[61] The damp climate in Arichat had also aggravated Schulte's asthmatic condition. Back in December his delicate health had required him to seek relief for a short time in Antigonish,[62] so he probably welcomed the transfer to Pictou. At the first year's conclusion, Roderick Mac-Donald also retired from Arichat to Antigonish because of the climate.[63] Thus, after only one year, the college/seminary staff, apart from the English teacher, John Fuller, who really taught academy-level courses, had to be fully replaced.

Rev. Dr John Cameron

Fortunately, MacKinnon was able to gather sufficient staff to continue the seminary for another year in Arichat. His key appointment was of the twenty-seven-year-old Rev. Dr John Cameron to the rectorship recently vacated by Schulte. Cameron, a native of the South River district of St Andrews, had been among the first pupils at MacKinnon's grammar school there. Bishop Fraser, impressed by this scholarly youth, had sent him on the long pilgrimage to the Urban College, where, after ten years' work, he had been ordained; he then returned to rural Nova Scotia bearing doctoral degrees in philosophy and divinity.[64] The Rome experience deeply influenced Cameron. Two years after he had arrived there, Pius IX was made pope, and Cameron became strongly devoted to him.[65] Of his years in Rome, Cameron's biographer writes: "That decade was to shape his thinking, and later that of his diocese, moulding a Catholicism which obediently followed the leadership of Rome."[66] In addition to nurturing his studious habits, extending his amazing facility with languages,[67] and establishing his academic credentials, Rome had produced a most loyal and devout son of the church.

Roman officials were impressed by Cameron's piety and his devotion to his studies. They assigned him residence prefect and in 1853 appointed him librarian in the Propaganda; in 1854 he served temporarily as secretary to Cardinal Barnabo (secretary of the Propaganda Fide) and as assistant to the vice-rector of the Urban College.[68] One official concluded he showed "good promise as a missionary."[69] Back in Nova Scotia, Cameron also soon won the admiration of church officials and laity. Just four months after he arrived at the seminary in Arichat, MacKinnon offered this epigrammatic assessment of his protégé: "He is a first rate scholar, but what is better, he is a good man."[70] Cameron's teaching career at the seminary and his parish labours strengthened his reputation. Indeed, he would eventually succeed MacKinnon as bishop of the diocese and become a revered and widely known Canadian churchman.[71]

Through the second year at Arichat, Cameron shared the teaching load at "Old Hubert's Big House" with three other teachers and one student: John Fuller remained as teacher of English; Dr Alexander

MacIntyre arrived in November to replace Roderick MacDonald – his subjects were mathematics and navigation;[72] a mysterious D. Villeroy[73] taught French; and Charles Martell of Arichat instructed in the art of singing. By the spring of 1855, Bishop MacKinnon judged that this tiny band of teachers had done well under the "steady guidance" of the new rector, John Cameron.[74]

First Students in Arichat

From the beginning, the youthful pedagogues at Arichat energetically fostered the academic and spiritual progress of their eager scholars.[75] By December 1853, MacKinnon had reported twelve ecclesiastical students in residence at the seminary; he expected four more in early spring who would begin the course in theology. St Andrews Grammar School and its fine classical scholar Malcolm MacLellan had trained several of these seminarians.[76] In August the students were studying rhetoric and the classics; they supposedly undertook philosophy and theology a little later. Apparently Schulte, for reasons unknown, also proposed the study of Italian, and the students decided "to make a trial of it twice a week." One student, Martin Gillis, mused that the inspiration among his comrades for studying Italian arose from the opportunity to compete with their instructor of Christian doctrine, Father Girroir, who would also be their classmate. No one recorded how the classroom rivalry between the cleric and his upstart lay competitors ended.

Student life in the "Big House" at Arichat was confined but not excessively regimented. The school day opened at 10:00 a.m., students had an hour and a half of free time after dinner, and further free time from 6:00 p.m. until supper. Student societies and organized sports were non-existent. The theological apprentices were allowed to visit friends at first vacation, but not during subsequent holidays. According to one boarder, student life had its lighter side: "Although we are much confined here, yet at Recreation hours, we will be quite merry; from sources which would appear quite insipid and immaterial we, when together, can extract much matter." Sarcastic but friendly remarks were frequently aimed at the cook, a Mr Brennan who was originally from Prospect, Nova Scotia. Earlier he had been cook at St Mary's College in Halifax, then had entered the Trappist monastery at Tracadie, Nova Scotia, for four or five years before moving on to the college/seminary at Arichat. Brennan's cleanliness and bread-baking skills left much to be desired; therefore the students made easy prey of him. Yet Gillis conceded: "On the whole, we are very much attached to him for he is always well-disposed toward us and is very pious and spiritual."[77] Evidently even the cook agreed that "man does not live by bread alone" and thus tried to care for more than the mere physical needs of his daily guests.

A successful first year at Arichat culminated in early July 1854 with the send-off of four young gentlemen to theological studies at the Grand Seminary, Quebec. Kenneth MacDonald, Thomas Sears, William Chisholm, and Martin Gillis had received minor orders from Bishop MacKinnon on 25 June. Then, on 4 July: "all the students and scholars of the seminary, with their reverend president [Dr Schulte] at their head, attended by the teachers of the institution, came to the wharf to bid their departing friends and companions a hearty farewell." Bishop MacKinnon and his staff at the infant institution were doubtless gratified by this promotion to higher studies of "the first fruits of our ecclesiastical seminary." He believed the students were so advanced already that they would at once be able to undertake the study of dogmatic and moral theology.[78] Tragically, the careers at the Grand Seminary of three of these students were plagued by ill health: Gillis died within three months; Sears was committed to hospital for an extended period; and Chisholm barely made it back to Arichat alive. Eventually Sears and Chisholm made a complete recovery and progressed further toward the priestly estate; indeed, they would be St.F.X.'s first gifts to the priesthood.[79]

A slightly larger number of young scholars registered at the college/seminary during its second year: fifteen students attended in November 1854 and about forty or more were in the common school and academy.[80] The seminarians generally boarded in the "Big House."[81] Aside from the regimentation and confinement, and the inevitable diseases which periodically ravaged the student body, a scholar's life in Arichat could be pleasant; for some, it was a welcome change from the physical rigours of farm life. Daniel MacGregor, a precocious youth who later became a colourful professor at St.F.X., feared that student life would become increasingly regulated once the bishop moved the college/seminary to Antigonish. He wrote, "On our going to Antigonish, I believe that the rules will become more rigorous, for as yet, they have not the full stability or regularity of an old established college."[82] Professors Cameron and Girroir sometimes played hurley with the students, a Highland game resembling field hockey. One student commented that Rector Cameron was "courteous, pious, respectable in manners, and not at all arbitrary."[83] MacGregor, a year later when he was teaching at St Andrews, reminisced that his work was not nearly "so pleasant as the pastimes and sport, that we were accustomed to have in the college."[84] In addition to the drudgery of learning, student life at the Arichat college/seminary evidently had its charms.

Although the school was situated in Acadian territory, the roots and race of its students were mostly Scottish. In the second year, five seminarians hailed from Cape Breton and about nine from mainland Nova Scotia. In the fall of 1854, no Acadians were enrolled, although Cameron expected a few shortly.[85] Acadians who aspired to advanced education were handicapped by the use of English in the classrooms of the region.[86] Three students were Irish. Two of these from Margaree, MacGregor reported, were "peculiarly rich in the native brogue of their county"; he admired their academic prowess and predicted they would "take the shine out of all the Scotch boys except two."[87] Given the strong ethnic identities of the time, some ethnic rivalry was, no doubt, part of the atmosphere of the college/seminary, yet no evidence of conflict remains. Of the Arichat seminarians, eleven became priests, and of these, one was eventually appointed a vicar apostolic and another a bishop.

Transfer from Arichat To Antigonish
The college/seminary was moved from Arichat in 1855. Bishop MacKinnon had readied new facilities in Antigonish, so transferred the institution there, minus the academy, in the late summer.[88] From the start, the rented quarters in Arichat had only been temporary; some of the staff and students, moreover, had found even two years of the foggy, damp climate too much. On the mainland MacKinnon hoped to make Antigonish "the centre of a compact Catholic county"[89] where over 80 per cent of the population was Catholic. To him, it also made most sense to centre the college/seminary in an area fertile with priestly vocations. Very practical considerations likewise impelled the move: the diocese owned a bishop's residence in Antigonish, a most convenient and inexpensive place to house seminarians; rent for "Old Hubert's Big House" in Arichat had been steep, as had been the necessities of life. MacKinnon had also concluded that many in the diocese wanted the change of location.[90] Finally, the young bishop was haunted by a rumour that the diocesan boundaries might be changed and the three mainland counties fused with the Diocese of Halifax. This unsettling prospect likely furthered his resolve to relocate his higher educational enterprise on the mainland; such a move would bolster his claim to all seven counties of eastern Nova Scotia.[91] For these several reasons, Antigonish became the permanent home of the fledgling college/seminary, later to be named St Francis Xavier University.

The Significance of Beginnings
The Arichat college/seminary was a modest beginning, but beginnings are essential. Its founder, Bishop MacKinnon, had conceived of the

school to meet what he believed were the urgent sacred and secular needs of his people. Then, with the help of rectors Schulte and Cameron, he had organized the small institution, hired staff, planned a curriculum, instituted some semblance of order and discipline, and tapped into important funding sources. And last, but not least, his seminary had educated a small band of scholars to an advanced level where, even after the first year, they could pursue theological studies at an established, major seminary. The misty origins of St.F.X. at Arichat were fleeting and temporary; however, the educational architect and his little institution had accomplished "sound and serious work" there.

For the Highland Catholic descendants in eastern Nova Scotia, Bishop MacKinnon's experiment in higher education symbolized their rising standard of economic and social maturity, and marked a turning point for them. Barely a century separated the Highland progeny from the hopelessness and despair of defeat at Culloden; fewer years lay between their painful pilgrimages overseas and the arduous work of developing a new homeland in Nova Scotia. A people once subjugated by religious intolerance, racial bigotry, and economic oppression now had their own college/seminary, a promising means to advance their religious, social, and economic interests in a new, freer, and more hospitable land.

For the province, the inception of St.F.X. at Arichat in 1853 further strengthened the pattern of denominational colleges, and from a centralist's perspective, fragmented even more the higher educational efforts of Nova Scotians. Ever since Loyalist Anglicans had established King's College at Windsor in 1789, the trend, in spite of efforts by Rev. Thomas McCulloch (Pictou Academy, 1816) and Lord Dalhousie (Dalhousie University, 1820) to establish non-denominational institutions of higher learning, had been toward small, regional, church-sponsored colleges.[92] The Baptists had opened Acadia College at Wolfville in 1839, Halifax Catholics had begun St Mary's College in 1840, and the Methodists in 1843 had started the Wesleyan Academy just across the border in Sackville, New Brunswick. Powerful religious, ethnic, and sectional loyalties ensured, in W.S. MacNutt's words, "a judicious division of scarcity" in the development of nineteenth-century Nova Scotia higher education.[93] St Francis Xavier University began as a child of its time and place.

·2·

Institutional Foundations, 1855–64

Opening in Antigonish

The College[1] of St Francis Xavier formally opened in Antigonish, on 18 September 1855. Rather incongruously, the German priest, Dr John Schulte, rose to address the audience of hopeful students and Antigonish respectables; they had assembled at the corner of College and Main streets in the freshly constructed two-storey college and public school building. The native-born priest, Dr John Cameron, was there too, adding to the scholarly grace and priestly tone of the occasion. Cameron was now rector of the seminary perched up on St Ninian's Street in the newly renovated bishop's residence. Except for the absence of Bishop MacKinnon, en route to Rome on his first *ad limina* visit, the college's inaugural ceremony gratified the participants. A correspondent for the *Halifax Catholic* mused that Schulte's lecture "for beauty, comprehensiveness and style ... could seldom be eclipsed."[2] Another enthusiast described the new edifice as "the finest house in the Province of Nova Scotia."[3] Evidently the villagers found impressive their stately new institution directed by articulate European-trained scholars like Cameron and Schulte. Catholics in Halifax already had their own college – St Mary's (established 1838) – as did those on Prince Edward Island – St Dunstan's (established January 1855). Now Antigonish and the Diocese of Arichat were opening their very own institution of higher learning.

However, what the new institution promised for the future religious, social, and educational improvement of the Catholics of colonial eastern Nova Scotia probably most gratified the celebrants of the opening. The church, many hoped, would be supplied with a body "of efficient and pious native priests," a door would be opened to the "learned professions," and the schools would gain better-prepared Catholic teachers.[4] Those present at the opening were no doubt euphoric; in hindsight they were justified, for St.F.X. would eventually fulfil what it promised and belie magnificently its inauspicious start in the village of Antigonish on that Tuesday in 1855.

A Request for Government Funding

Eight months before, on 5 February 1855, the solicitor-general of Nova Scotia and representative for the County of Antigonish, William Alexander Henry,[5] presented to the house a petition of Bishop Colin MacKinnon and the trustees of the college at Antigonish requesting an annual government grant of 250 pounds. Through this petition MacKinnon hoped to ensure financial support for the college even before he relocated it from Arichat to Antigonish.[6] But he was not overly sanguine that the petition would succeed; in view of the prevalence of virulent anti-Catholicism in the colony,[7] he anticipated that "a strong current of opposition will set in against the accomplishment of our views."[8] So MacKinnon marshalled all the arguments he could to convince the legislators that his college deserved public support: a considerable sum of money had already been spent on new buildings; in October last a public school had been opened in the new college building; other like "seminaries of learning" in the west and central part of the province were receiving grants; the institution promised to greatly benefit the population of nearly one hundred thousand in the eastern counties; and enrolments would likely exceed one hundred students in the summer of 1855. MacKinnon also urged support of his petition in letters to Joseph Howe and James W. Johnston, leader of the Conservative opposition and a member of the legislative committee on education.[9] Doubtless to MacKinnon's surprise, the committee on 24 March recommended "to the favourable consideration of the house" his grant petition; it had concluded: "The effort of Dr MacKinnon to furnish [the Catholics of eastern Nova Scotia] with the means of acquiring a liberal education is very creditable and ought to be encouraged."[10] The house and council accepted the committee's advice (other collegiate institutions, such as King's, St Mary's, and the Wesleyan Academy in Sackville were already receiving grants) and supported the bishop's educational project at Antigonish; they would do so for the next twenty-five years.

In his petition, MacKinnon stated that he had spent 1700 pounds, raised earlier by voluntary subscription, on the needed buildings. The new college edifice required the greatest outlay.[11] It was already under construction at the corner of Main and College streets in July 1854. The architect and builder was Alexander MacDonald, known locally as "Sandy the Carpenter," the designer of several other impressive town structures. His handiwork produced a two-storey wooden building

Original St.F.X. classroom building, built 1854 and located on College Street, behind the present town office; moved later to Court Street; burned in 1943

with basement and six large classrooms. MacDonald patterned his work on the improved plans which the superintendent of education, John William Dawson, had published in 1850.[12] The youngest scholars would be taught in the basement,[13] the older ones on the ground floor, and the college students in the upper storey.[14] Out-of-town students who were not "priestly candidates" would have to board with Catholic families in Antigonish. The priestly candidates, in MacKinnon's plan, would stay at the late Bishop Fraser's residence on St Ninian's Street. The villagers had built it for Fraser in 1846 and nicknamed it the "Big House"; after extensive renovations inside and out, the ecclesiastical seminary was also ready for use.[15] The combination college-seminary establishment was then opened, but not before MacKinnon had laid in supplies and had acquired bells to regulate college life.[16]

Catholic-Protestant Competition
The prospect in 1854 of a new Catholic educational establishment in Antigonish aroused some local Protestants to fresh educational endeavours. Hugh Cameron, a Catholic, recalled much later,

The construction of the college in 1854, stimulated an opposition to it which built a large and well-equipped school house near the Presbyterian Church, in the centre of the village, which was in operation and very largely attended before the opening of the College in 1855. It was conducted by a young man from Pictou, named MacDonald, who ingratiated himself with the people before Saint Francis Xavier College was opened in September 1855.[17]

Daniel MacDonald's school was, at first, "very largely attended," for in 1855-56 fifty-eight scholars were enrolled – forty-seven male and eleven female – and fourteen of these were studying classics, mathematics, algebra, and agricultural chemistry.[18] The trustees of the school tried unsuccessfully to capture the St.F.X. Academy grant and the grant to St Andrews Grammar School for their own enterprise.[19] This development was not the first occasion for Catholic-Protestant educational rivalry in Antigonish; for decades Catholics had been dissatisfied with alleged Protestant control over local schooling.[20] But from 1855 on, Protestant efforts would be eclipsed by the new, formidable Catholic educational establishment.

Actually, the formation of St.F.X. signalled a strengthening Catholic presence in a town which had long been a Protestant, "English-speaking enclave" of merchants and tradesmen surrounded by an expanding sea of Gaelic-speaking Catholic farmers.[21] By 1861, about 2800 people lived in the district of Antigonish, most of them native-born; farmers and farm labourers were predominant throughout the county, but

29

considerable numbers of tradesmen – blacksmiths, carpenters, millers, etc. – also practised their arts. Fishermen and mariners clustered with their families along the coastline in small settlements like Arisaig, Livingstone's Cove, and Ballantyne's Cove.[22] Of course the first inhabitants of the district had been the Micmac. But the original European settlers were Loyalists, followed by other newcomers, mostly Protestant and from New England. By mid-century, however, the impact of earlier Highland Catholic settlement was pronounced.[23]

During the 1850s the district and its shire town participated in the relative prosperity of the region. Antigonish witnessed the founding of a Catholic weekly called the *Casket* in 1852; the telegraph and semi-weekly mail delivery arrived that same year. And in mid-decade, two substantial building projects along the main street were completed: a new courthouse and St.F.X. College.[24] In 1861 local Presbyterians built an attractive new Presbyterian church and that same year citizens organized permanently the Highland Society of the County of Sydney. No doubt these advances fuelled the confidence of local people in the mid-Victorian assumption of unending material progress.

Early College Organization and Staff
At its beginning in Antigonish, the College of St Francis Xavier was divided into two separate departments – the clerical seminary and the public schools. The ecclesiastical students at the seminary on St Ninian's Street lived under "Rules of Domestic Discipline" and the watchful eye of Rector John Cameron, who superintended the literary and disciplinary functions of the combined establishments.[25] He did more: Bishop MacKinnon also appointed him parish priest of St Ninian's, and professor and bursar in the college. In the classroom, Cameron instructed in moral theology daily, in church history three times weekly, and in Sacred Scripture twice weekly. He complained, understandably, that his "weak shoulders" could scarcely bear the strain.[26] MacKinnon recalled Schulte from Pictou Parish, where he had gone from Arichat in 1854, to join Cameron in administering the college.[27] Schulte became director of studies, overseeing the academic program and the progress of each student.[28] His massive teaching load (about fifty-six hours a week compared to Cameron's thirteen, states an early college report) included dogmatic theology, logic and metaphysics, ethics and natural law, Hebrew, Greek, Latin, and religious instruction.[29] Such a burden was a strain on his delicate health and exacted a heavy toll.

Also involved in college administration were seven trustees – three priests and four laymen. The three clerics – Rev. William B. MacLeod, first native-born priest of the Diocese of Arichat, founder of the East Bay College, and pastor at Arisaig, Rev. Ronald MacGillvray of St

Andrews, and Rev. Alexander MacSween, parish priest at Pictou – would remain trustees for the next decade. The four laymen were Duncan Grant (a wealthy local merchant), Dougald Cameron from Middle South River and a cousin of the rector John Cameron, Alexander M. Chisholm of Antigonish Harbour, and Archibald McGillvray from Morristown (trustee for only one year).[30] The exact role of these founding trustees is unclear, but the School Act of 1845 suggests their duties: the provision of a schoolhouse, the hiring of teachers, reporting to government on finances, enrolments, courses, etc. – in all, to ensure that the school was satisfying the requirements of the School Act.[31] These first college trustees were unincorporated; therefore, the recently incorporated Roman Catholic Episcopal Corporation of Arichat held title to the college property and received the government grant.[32]

Cameron and Schulte were flanked by several other teachers that first year in Antigonish: Roderick MacDonald (natural philosophy or the sciences, mathematics, Latin poets, English composition, and navigation), Hugh Cameron, and five advanced students – William Chisholm (Latin and religious instruction), Thomas Sears (religious instruction), Charles Martell (Gregorian chant), Ronald MacDonald (Latin), and Ronald MacGillvray (Latin). Roderick MacDonald, a very competent scholar, would stay with St.F.X. right through until 1877.[33] Young Hugh Cameron had studied under MacDonald, but immediately before coming to St.F.X. had been teaching at St Andrews. His teaching duties in the English department included English, geography, globes, arithmetic, bookkeeping, writing, and reading.[34] A brief staffing controversy swirled around Cameron when Schulte and MacDonald offered him a position which the trustees simultaneously tendered to certain female teachers. The embarrassing conflict was resolved in Cameron's favour.[35] For the second year of instruction at St.F.X., Hugh Cameron pressed for the appointment of another Cameron. He maintained, perhaps boasted, that, in spite of the opening of the rival Protestant school run by the Pictonian Daniel MacDonald, his English department at St.F.X. was overflowing with students. Therefore, he recommended the trustees divide the English department into a high school department and a common school department, and hire Duncan Cameron – in his view, the best available teacher for the common school level. The trustees agreed and added a third Cameron to the staff of the infant college.[36]

College Aims and Program
Bishop MacKinnon, through his new college, wanted to form a Scottish Catholic leadership for eastern Nova Scotia which would preserve the faith and elevate the religious tone, educational level, and social

standing of his diocese. This goal would be achieved, he anticipated, using a classical curriculum with English, not Gaelic, as the central language of instruction, and in a safe Catholic atmosphere, where the doctrinal purity and moral rectitude of his scholarly charges could be carefully protected and nurtured. An educational program which stressed the unity of knowledge, solid academic standards, discipline, and character formation would produce, thought the bishop, the kind of Catholic graduate best equipped to pursue the middle-class professions – the ministry, medicine, law, and teaching.[37] Education for the professions at St.F.X. was highly selective; family finances, academic opportunity at the preparatory levels, scholastic ability, religious and moral conformity, and aptitude for the classical languages determined who advanced to the higher levels. Only a small number did so. Frequently, recruitment and encouragement by parish clergy, financial and otherwise, also determined who made it to college or seminary.

The absence of the Highlander's native tongue of Gaelic at St.F.X. reveals the pragmatic bent of the bishop's vision for collegiate education and his social aspirations for his youthful countrymen. In colonial Nova Scotia, English was the language of commerce, politics, and the professions; hence, expert facility in its use was essential to the preparation of socially mobile graduates. Highland culture and traditions were not a priority; social advancement and integration were.[38] Bishop MacKinnon apparently shared a widespread attitude: in general, the Gaels of eastern Nova Scotia did not want their children to "waste time" on their native tongue, but instead to learn English so "they could succeed in the world."[39] Moreover, Highland Catholics, with their recent background in poverty, illiteracy, and oppression, often felt a sense of social inferiority, as they compared themselves to their Presbyterian neighbours in Pictou County,[40] or to people in the urban centres of Nova Scotia and New England.[41] Long into the twentieth century, some Highland descendants would remain ashamed and embarrassed by the memory of the economic and social plight of their forebears.[42] This attitude surely revealed the extent to which the contemporary social and cultural standards of the dominant society had been internalized by the Highland descendants. St.F.X. was established to help at least some of these descendants to achieve those standards, and thereby to elevate the social standing of the entire ethnic community and of the Irish and Acadian Catholics. The college was both a tool and a symbol of an emerging "culture of aspiration" among the Highland Catholics in eastern Nova Scotia.[43]

Since Dr Schulte was "the backbone"[44] of St.F.X. through its founding years, his educational views, undoubtedly shaped by his long Rome experience, were of great consequence for the college.[45] In his opening lecture to the students in 1860, he affirmed that education should prepare a student to become "useful"; this end would be most efficiently achieved, he proposed, through the pursuit of three immediate aims: "to become a good Christian, to develope [sic] the healthy physical constitution of the body, and to acquire useful knowledge."[46] Schulte eloquently argued these three latter points, always stressing the fundamental importance of Christian doctrine and virtue, but not neglecting to underscore the need for robust health and the acquisition of knowledge. To neglect the ancient truth, claimed Schulte, that "the fear of the Lord is the beginning of wisdom" would result in unruly passions and an understanding which had lost its true point of view. Classical studies, central to all liberal education at nineteenth-century colleges and preparatory to the study of the sciences and theology, would cultivate the understanding and refine the taste through the examination of ancient languages and texts.[47] Another lecturer, Rev. Ronald MacDonald, also affirmed the central place of the classics but cautioned, too, that pagan authors had to be "baptized" or "placed under subjection to Christian truth."[48] In his view, history and the classics were a means of mental training and a source of "indispensable knowledge" about "worthies of the past, their wisdom, their follies, their language and their deeds."[49]

Philosophy, maintained Father MacDonald, was likewise important, for it gave the student a comprehensive view of truth. It functioned as a conciliator, guarding the freedom of the sciences and protecting the domain of revealed truth. Finally, Christian doctrine in the St.F.X. curriculum answered the questions of eternity. God is the end of all knowledge, the truth that encompasses, unifies, and completes all.[50] MacDonald concluded that a religious education "harmonizes all opposites, the creature with the creator, the natural with the supernatural, the individual with the race, social duties with religious obligations, order with liberty, authority with freedom, the immutability of dogma with the progress of intelligence, and conservatism with reform."[51]

In theory at least, the early teachers at St.F.X. did not appear to advocate passiveness and the mere memorization of facts. Schulte, for one, stressed active attention, individual initiative, private studies, and thorough understanding; he eschewed dogmatism and authoritarianism. Of textbooks, he advised, "They should not be mere catechisms, especially in science." Memorizing such "catechistical" textbooks "would keep the mind in an infantile condition and would lead to a dogmatizing disposition." Schulte encouraged the students to learn how to think. For him, the insistence on the word of any human authority in education was "destructive of science and injurious to the development of the human mind." All sciences, human or divine, had

33

to be subjected to the canons of reason.[52] His comments revealed an immense confidence that reason rightly exercised would never contradict revealed truth. This confidence was surely the only grounds on which he was able to advocate such unfettered critical thought within a bastion of Catholic orthodoxy.

Dominant Influences at Early St.F.X.

The St.F.X. founders, Drs MacKinnon, Cameron, and Schulte, absorbed their Catholic approach to education – the college's philosophy of education, its organization of studies, its methods of teaching, and its seminary discipline – from the arrangements established in the Catholic colleges of continental Europe where they had been educated.[53] No doubt Dr Schulte also instituted some of the practices he had observed in the schools of Prussia, his native country.[54] Hence, the formative influences on the St.F.X. foundations of education included the interests and traditions of the Roman Catholic Church, the social aspirations of the Catholics in the diocese, especially those of their leaders, vocational requirements, and the admission standards of the seminaries in Rome and Quebec. The curriculum drew on traditions springing from medieval scholasticism, with its confidence in the harmony of faith and reason, and from Renaissance humanism, which stressed the value of the classical languages and texts. Overall, St.F.X.'s educational emphasis paralleled that of other nineteenth-century colleges where "traditional forms of religious belief involving the willing suspension of critical judgement ... occupied a greater place than did the fine-tuning of the intellect for the purpose of discovering new forms of objective truth."[55]

Open for Business

After all the groundwork was complete, St.F.X. opened for business in September 1855. The first term in Antigonish continued until some time in December. From then on until at least 1858 the scholastic year ran from 7 January to 21 December with a mere six weeks off in July and August. The admission policy was avowedly broad: "The College is open to all Denominations. No offence is ever given to parents or pupils on account of their religious persuasions. But religious instructions and exercises of piety are given to Catholic pupils, separately, several times during the week, which Protestant pupils are not bound to attend and even could not attend without particular permission from their parents and the superior of the college."[56] However, in spite of this public declaration, few Protestants attended the college; at least one even actively campaigned against Protestant youth enrolling.[57] Nonetheless, about thirty-eight students registered in the college and seminary (at least twelve of them had started in Arichat) and close to forty-five in its public schools for a total of eighty-three. In comparison to the town's past, when with a degree of regularity schools had appeared and vanished,[58] the inauguration of St.F.X. ushered in a golden age of educational activity and opportunity in Antigonish.

The College's Name
The newly opened college came to be known popularly as St Francis Xavier's College, named after the famous Jesuit missionary to the Far East, St Francis Xavier (1506–1552). It was a logical christening, but why it came about is somewhat doubtful. In 1853 Bishop MacKinnon had promised that the college would be called the "Seminary of Saint Ninian's" because "the institution will take this name of St Ninian's of Antigonish, where it is to be permanently located after a year or two."[59] During its Arichat sojourn, contemporary writers used names such as "Arichat School of Higher Studies," "Arichat Seminary," "Arichat College," and "Arichat Academy."[60] A comment in 1888 by Bishop John Cameron perhaps provides a clue to the college's permanent name; he claimed "the privilege of christening" it.[61] While a student at the Urban College, Rome, he had come to admire his Jesuit instructors. He then wrote, "The superiors who are Jesuits please me extremely well."[62] Two years before returning to assume the rectorship of the college in Nova Scotia, he had witnessed the festivities surrounding the tercentenary of St Francis Xavier's death. Finally, the saint had been a missionary, and Nova Scotia was designated a Catholic mission territory.[63]

Early College Traditions
A school creates its own traditions and practices; St.F.X. was no exception. From the start a public lecture was held on opening day when a professor would wax eloquent on an educational theme. Then the college rules would be "read and emphasized," and a printed copy presented to each student. Early in its history Xaverians began observing the festival of their patron saint, Francis Xavier. The observance soon earned special significance. In the 1860s, the feast day on 3 December was commonly celebrated with "eclat and honours." The ecclesiastical students prepared for it with a three-day spiritual retreat conducted by the bishop. The feast day itself would begin with a pontifical high mass which included a discourse on the significance of the festival; the "joyful day" would close with public prayers and a solemn benediction of the blessed sacrament.[64] Examinations, the bane of students and professors alike, were scheduled twice a year: a three-day public examination including one day of recitations, demonstrations, dialogues, and musical

concerts at the end of June[65] and a private examination before the professors and trustees in December. Shortly thereafter, parents received "testimonials concerning the conduct and proficiency" of their young. By 1861, the scholastic year no longer paralleled the calendar year but instead ran from late August to late June. In June of 1861, St.F.X. began the practice of publicly conferring academic prizes. Bishop MacKinnon believed such recognition would create a "powerful stimulus to exertion" among the young scholars and "a laudable ambition for literary honours."[66]

The Early Student Experience at St.F.X.

Within the constraints of their meagre resources, the early St.F.X. masters strove to provide their disciples with a solid teaching program. Dr Schulte tried to adapt the course of study to the goals of individual students; each received about five hours of "actual teaching or training each day," which might include lectures, repetitions, recitations, debates, translations, and compositions. The college classrooms were stocked with standard teaching aids like blackboards, maps, charts, and globes.[67] In February 1856, Rector Cameron and the trustees acquired a one-hundred-pound grant from the legislature toward the purchase of "physical apparatus" for teaching natural philosophy (science) and practical or agricultural chemistry.[68] By the way, natural philosophy was an important part of the nineteenth-century liberal arts curriculum. It sought to understand "the unifying principles and laws that governed the natural world."[69] Before the end of the 1850s, St.F.X. students also had a philosophy debating club.[70]

The St.F.X. student body exhibited some diversity during the founding years. Daniel MacGregor, a student from Lismore, gave a noteworthy description of its early composition to his uncle:

I assure you that it is really interesting to see the number of students and day scholars now attending the College. Such a medley of Scotch and Irish, Nova Scotians and Cape Bretoners, English and French, Protestants and Catholics thus thrown into the society of one another without the least anterior acquaintance, cannot but have a good effect in removing prejudices (if any such there be) which the natives of our country might have toward those of another country.[71]

Prejudices of various kinds did lurk just below the surface. For example, Hugh Cameron reported that as a student at St.F.X. in 1854–55 he "had to contend with powerful opposition" because of "Highland feuds." Whether college life successfully rooted them out is uncertain.[72] Anyway, 68 per cent of the total enrolments in 1856–57 of 130 were of

Scottish lineage, about 14 per cent were Irish, and the remaining were English and Acadian. About one-third lived in Antigonish and more than four-fifths came from within the county itself; a small band of eight students had trekked from Cape Breton. Only twenty of the "fairer sex" enrolled that year, all at the public school level; they would not be admitted to the college level until 1894.[73] Overall, St.F.X. students appeared contented with their circumstances and scholarly challenges.[74]

Tuition fees posed a dilemma for many students. Most of them came from farming and fishing families with modest incomes. The diocese was generally poor and many families lacked hard cash. Poverty created two problems in student attendance at early St.F.X.: delayed starts and interrupted studies. Dr Schulte, in both the *Casket* announcements of college openings and in lectures, sounded a perennial warning: "Students, especially those of the Higher Branches, should enter the College at the beginning of the term, as the systematic teaching observed in the College will enable them to make greater progress."[75] Not only were there late starters, but students were commonly forced to interrupt their studies so they could replenish their resources and repay their debts. Dr John Cameron lamented that few St.F.X. students could afford to "attend steadily and continuously" throughout the college curriculum; frequently they had to teach in the common schools during the summer term.[76] These attendance problems did little to enhance the quality of instruction and learning at the college; neither did they increase the young institution's financial stability. In 1857 college authorities tried to relieve the financial hardship of the ecclesiastical students and reduce salary expenses by releasing Hugh and Duncan Cameron, the English Department teachers, and replacing them with minimally paid student instructors.[77] For some reason, they soon abandoned the experiment.[78]

Early College Finances
Tuition fees remained a significant but uneven source of income for the college. The government grant of 250 pounds became the most important source. Furthermore, the priest-professors, Drs Cameron and Schulte, worked for a pittance and established a long-standing tradition of unselfish clerical service to the college which substantially reduced its expenses.[79] In the words of a later priest, clergy were willing to take their "payment in the currency of the Kingdom that is not of this world."[80] Sometimes the parishes, in addition to rendering an annual contribution to the French Association for the Propagation of the Faith, an offering supplemented by that benevolent society and returned to the diocese, made direct donations to the college. For

example, St Margaret's Parish, Arisaig, contributed "110 bushels of wheat, and a large quantity of other grains" to the diocesan seminary in early 1857.[81] Thus began another long-standing tradition of parish support for the diocesan college.

By the fall of 1856, Bishop MacKinnon claimed that nearly five thousand pounds had been spent by the diocese on its new literary institutions in Antigonish. He held up for special praise the donation of two early bachelor benefactors, Samuel and Angus MacDonald of nearby Meadow Green. In August 1855, they had granted, out of their extensive landholdings, four hundred acres located on the north side of Antigonish Harbour, about three miles from town.[82] How much this gift benefited St.F.X. during its early years is hard to tell. The Mac-Donald brothers might have hoped that the students, through daily work on the farm, could earn their board.[83] An editorial in the *Casket*, 18 November 1858, claimed the soil and location were excellent: "[the farm] proves of incalculable value to his Lordship in supporting the infant institution for the benefit of which its former generous owner[s] intended it to be applied." But a later comment by Bishop MacKinnon, in 1860, revealed that the farm had been of little use until then, although he was optimistic: "This farm when properly cultivated will be of invaluable aid to our Diocesan Seminary."[84] However, MacKin-non would sell the land in 1869 for $2000.[85]

The Ryan Legacy was also of uncertain benefit to the founding of St.F.X. John Ryan, a native of Halifax, had attended the Urban Col-lege, Rome in the 1830s, but died there in 1836. And a tragic death it was, for he was only twenty years old. Ryan generously bequeathed about 2700 pounds and his personal library to the Vicariate Apostolic of Nova Scotia, then under Fraser's jurisdiction, for the erection of a seminary.[86] After the separation of Arichat from the Diocese of Halifax in 1844, the legacy remained in the possession of Bishop William Fraser, who failed to divide it evenly with Halifax, as he had prom-ised.[87] Bishop MacKinnon received Ryan's library of about one thou-sand books (mostly ecclesiastical) at Fraser's death, and by 1857, also the funds which had been held in trust.[88] How much was actually obtained and applied to the construction and improvement of St.F.X. is uncertain, for the administrators exacted a commission and the bishop himself had used some for purposes other than Ryan had directed.[89]

Ryan's library, along with book contributions from other "gentle-men," formed the core of the original St.F.X. library. An early college report described the holdings: "A Library was established since the opening of the Institute by the munificence of the Right Rev. Doctor MacKinnon. This Library has been increased by the private Library of the late Rev. Alexander McLeod of Arisaig, bequeathed by him to the College and by donations of several other Gentlemen, so that it contains at present over one thousand volumes."[90] In future years, the collection would gradually expand through the donations of bishops, priests, and friends.[91]

Bishop MacKinnon's Move to Antigonish

A newcomer arrived at the college in 1858: Bishop MacKinnon. The bishop had concluded that his relocation from Arichat to the seminary on St Ninian's Street, Antigonish would benefit his school and seminarians, and better promote "the general good of religion."[92] No doubt he would feel more at home there, close to his birthplace and among his Scottish countrymen. He remained there until his episcopal resignation about twenty years later, even though he had assured the Catholics of Arichat that church law required his move be temporary.[93] MacKinnon's entry onto the Antigonish scene had two consequences. First, it was another step in the gradual shift of the administrative centre of the diocese away from Arichat to Antigonish. Second, it signalled a reduction in Dr John Cameron's role at St.F.X. From the beginning, of course, Cameron had worn the hats of rector, professor, bursar, and parish priest. Such an excessive workload made MacKinnon rightly fear for his priest-professor's health; thus he limited Cameron's involvement with the college to two hours a day[94] and appointed another priest to one of his missions. The bishop himself became rector.[95] The scholarly Schulte, whose educational work was always highly regarded by MacKinnon, henceforth served as rector in the latter's absence.[96]

A Female School

One year before Bishop MacKinnon moved to Antigonish, he had purchased land directly north of the college; his intent was to begin a female convent and academy,[97] as he had done at Arichat in 1856. He believed that Christianity had emancipated women, and therefore, he must provide for the education in the diocese of "the fairer portion of mankind."[98] But the project failed; sisters to staff the proposed convent were unavailable.[99] This failure probably led him to establish a "female school" in the college building.[100] Its opening was announced in the *Casket* in early November 1858: "We learn that a female school has been opened in the lower story of the College in this village. It is under the direction of Miss Hooper, who, together with all the branches of a good, sound English education, will also teach French, Italian and the Piano-forte if required. Young ladies, avail yourself of this opportunity."[101] Narcissa Hooper, a non-Catholic who would conduct the female department until her replacement by a Mrs Cunningham in 1861, enrolled some boys as well as girls.[102] The label "female" was inspired, apparently, more by the sex of the teacher than by that of her pupils.[103] The bishop's dream of a convent in Antigonish for the fairer sex would not be realized in his lifetime. However, it symbolized a long-standing concern in the diocese for the education of women which would eventually bear fruit.

Early Growth and Changes

Since the seminary had once again become a bishop's residence in 1858, and the number of seminarians was expanding, MacKinnon decided to renovate.[104] His plea for funds to the Society for the Propagation of the Faith succeeded and he added a third storey as sleeping quarters for about sixteen boarders;[105] it gained a reputation for being distinctly cool, if not downright frigid, during the winters.[106] He also appointed a prefect to enforce quiet during study times and to accompany the seminarians on their walks. Students shared the duty of reading a work of edification during mealtimes in the refectory.[107] Bishop MacKinnon also completed a new chapel "principally designed for the benefit of the ecclesiastical students." The charming, diminutive sanctuary had four stained glass windows within the chancel, a neatly decorated but simple altar, several beautiful pictures, a carpeted floor, and a few rows of pews. The bishop, staff, and students fittingly dedicated the little church in honour of the patron saint of the college, St Francis Xavier.[108]

The founding staff and trustees at St.F.X. remained relatively stable through its first five years. Some changes occurred in the English Department and a graduate, Rev. Ronald MacDonald (ordained in October 1859), was hired to teach the Greek and Latin classics, which he did for three years. This talented alumnus from Maryvale was one of the earliest St.F.X. success stories: he eventually became bishop of Harbour Grace, Newfoundland after a distinguished career as a parish priest.[109] Two new trustees, from South River, Dr Alexander MacIntosh and Hugh MacDonald, were appointed in 1860 and remained trustees for the next decade. MacIntosh had been a student in the Arichat days; subsequently he studied medicine in Philadelphia, then returned to Antigonish as a physician. MacDonald, another St.F.X. alumnus, studied law and pursued politics. He would become an avowed anticonfederate, then an MP for Antigonish (1867–73), and finally, the first Roman Catholic to become judge of the Supreme Court of Nova Scotia.[110] Bishop MacKinnon expressed pride that mostly native talent manned and administered his college: "It is a singular, yet very encouraging circumstance," he mused, "that all the gentlemen, clerical and lay, connected with the College of St Francis Xavier, with one solitary exception, viz., the director of studies, are natives of Nova Scotia."[111]

Not only were mostly native-born people associated with the work of the college, but they were becoming increasingly associated with the wider work of the diocese, thanks to St.F.X. Gradually it was realizing MacKinnon's plan to build up a home-grown priesthood. In the fall of 1861, Dr Cameron could proudly report to Rome that eleven students had been ordained and were working within the diocese.[112] Yet tragically, in 1860, one of the young aspirants to the priesthood became the first St.F.X. student to die. Allen MacKinnon, twenty-two, of North Grant and a nephew of the bishop, succumbed to that pervasive killer, consumption. Priests, professors, and students sadly attended his funeral in St Ninian's Church where the Rev. Dr Schulte gave "a highly appropriate and pathetic funeral discourse for a young man who had shown high promise."[113]

A Shocking Apostasy

The college received a second blow within one year of the death of Allen MacKinnon. In January 1861, Dr Schulte had opened the term with an excellent public lecture, later published under the title "How to Study." He dedicated it to Bishop MacKinnon "as a token of filial devotion and sincere respect for his Lordship's commitment to the cause of learning and Christian education."[114] With seven years of prominent service to the college and community, Schulte appeared as a solid and secure pillar of the growing Catholic educational establishment in Antigonish. Then sometime late in the autumn, he vanished mysteriously without warning. His distressed bishop eventually learned that Schulte had gone to Boston (probably by water, then the easiest means of travel to New England), and might not return. He reported in December to the Propaganda: "While he was with us he acted as a very good priest and a very learned man."[115] By August 1862, MacKinnon had learned more, and what he had heard shocked him: Schulte had "turned" – apostatized! MacKinnon's update to the Propaganda was considerably less charitable than his first report: Schulte had "slyly and with great deception" concealed the true state of his faith from his colleagues while in Antigonish. Furthermore, speculated MacKinnon, "the root of his evil seems to have been intemperance." At this point the bishop was planning to go to Canada for medical advice (his eyesight was failing), where he hoped to corral the wayward priest, who had moved there from Boston, and bring him "back to sanity" and Antigonish.[116] But Schulte never returned.

Almost thirty years later, Schulte described the spiritual pilgrimage that had precipitated his sudden, unannounced departure from

Antigonish. His "doubts and mental conflicts," apparently, had begun early in his theological studies, but his "religious transmutation was slow, gradual and sure, until finally the distinctive doctrines of Rome ceased to satisfy."[117] What he called "the sacrifice of the mass" and Rome's "intense and absolute priestism" especially troubled him. Gradually his studies led him to abandon his belief in the "inerrancy of the Church"; then his "whole mental life was turned upside down." His memories of the anguish, conflict, and pain were especially poignant, since he had felt constrained to leave the church "which I dearly loved and in which I had spent the best part of my life."[118] Evidently his troubled decision to leave the church arose from personal experience and reflection; it had nothing to do with intemperance as Bishop MacKinnon alleged.[119] And while his internal religious revolution occurred during his time in Antigonish, Schulte tried to preserve his spiritual integrity by administering the sacraments as infrequently as possible.[120]

Schulte's unannounced exit from St.F.X. and the village was anything but graceful and courteous. He must have judged that, given the solid Catholic tone of the area and his own prominence, it would be easier for him, personally, if he slipped away quietly to more religiously congenial surroundings. Apart from some initial outrage and bitterness when the news broke in town that he had entered the Anglican priesthood,[121] the separation of "the old deserter"[122] and Catholic Antigonish has been viewed graciously by both sides. Schulte always retained a sense of gratitude and respect for his "Roman Catholic Brethren,"[123] and Catholics have held his work and memory in high regard.[124] In Ontario Schulte married, served in several Anglican parishes, taught for short stints at Huron College, London, and Alma College, St Thomas; quite suddenly, he died, on 15 December 1895 at the age of sixty-nine.[125] The Schulte episode marred what would be an otherwise unassailable record of loyalty to Rome by the college's priest-presidents.

Schulte's rude departure from St.F.X. in 1861 marked the beginning of the end of its founding era. He left a gaping hole in the ranks of the staff. Surprisingly, Bishop MacKinnon enlarged the hole in 1863 by moving Dr John Cameron from St Ninian's in Antigonish to Arichat.[126] The bishop's reasons for transferring him appear inscrutable, for the joint loss of Schulte and Cameron dealt a fatal blow to the seminary program; it was not resumed to any extent until 1865 when a St.F.X. alumnus, Rev. Dr Daniel MacGregor, returned from Rome as a professor of theology. Through the interim, ecclesiastical students travelled, by necessity, either to Rome or to Quebec to complete their training.[127] Furthermore, in 1862 the bishop, after much anguish, reluctantly transferred his capable professor of Latin and Greek, Rev.

Ronald MacDonald, to the Pictou mission, where he replaced its ailing pastor.[128] All these staff changes altered the original college-seminary level programs at St.F.X. But the institutional foundations had been laid and a substantial Catholic educational beachhead established in Antigonish. Moreover, the college had shown some capacity for fulfilling the purposes for which it had been founded. However, the survival of the young college through its next fifteen years was anything but assured.

·3·

Advancement and Regression, 1865–77

In September 1865, the start of St.F.X.'s second decade in Antigonish, about fifty students were registered at the college and seminary levels. By December there were twenty seminarians, of whom five were far advanced in their theological studies.[1] These aspiring scholars found colourful personalities within the college walls.[2] Three of these characters would constitute its greatest strengths and weaknesses; eventually each would help to place in question the very survival of the institution. A public discussion of a central university and the establishment of the University of Halifax would also add to the uncertainty.

The Faculty

First, there was Rev. Dr Daniel MacGregor, age twenty-eight, fresh from five years of graduate studies at the Urban College in Rome, where he had been ordained after earning the PH D and DD. MacGregor conducted courses in English, rhetoric, logic, and theology. Like Schulte before him, he would gain local prominence through his learned public orations, popular preaching, and distinguished position at the college. This Lismore native had been a first student at Arichat, then later a student and assistant teacher at Antigonish.[3] The bishop's application for MacGregor's admission to the Urban College described him as "a talented and very industrious young man";[4] one of his Rome masters came to agree with the assessment.[5] MacGregor returned from Rome armed with degrees and settled convictions, at least on matters scholastic. A lecture he delivered in September 1866, before a "numerous assemblage of the highly respectable people of the town and its vicinity," revealed a serious, idealistic scholar who advocated exacting academic standards – thoroughness, comprehensiveness, and a careful cultivation of the mind; he had entitled his speech "The Evils of a Superficial Education."[6] About ten years later, his bishop would admit that MacGregor had endeared himself to a multitude of students through his urbanity and gentlemanly conduct.[7] A student remembered that his teaching excellence lay in that most useful gift: the power of "simplified illustration."[8] But the professor would also gain a reputation for something which hindered his usefulness and contributed to the decline of the college: MacGregor was "very fond of his droppie;"[9] it was his Achilles Heel.

Then there was the fifty-five-year-old bishop of the diocese and college rector,[10] Colin MacKinnon. His was a solid, stately, serious presence at St.F.X., a model of earnestness and duty who lived by the rule: "In all situations endeavour to improve on all matters coming within the sphere of your official duties."[11] Justly esteemed as the major pioneer educator of the diocese, he lavished special care on his most valued educational project, the college. Although a man of intense discipline and immense energy, failing eyesight plagued him and year by year made reading and writing more difficult and painful.[12] Such a debility, along with bouts of mental instability which intensified during the late 1870s,[13] would unfortunately make MacKinnon, like his prominent professor MacGregor, an increasing liability to the very institution he had founded.

Others likewise taught at the college in 1865. Peter Fiset, a native of Quebec, had come two years before to finish his theological studies while teaching French and the higher classics. MacKinnon ordained him on 3 December 1864, the Feast of St Francis Xavier, and then appointed him in September 1865 to the pastorate of Havre Boucher.[14] Roderick MacDonald, then discharging administrative duties as secretary and treasurer, also continued in mathematics and the sciences, as did Archibald McGillvray in English. By September 1865, Eunice MacKinnon had replaced Mrs Cunningham in the female department.[15] Two years before, the bishop had appointed the young cleric Hugh Gillis (ordained May 1860)[16] director of studies, as well as parish priest of St Ninian's. Gillis, and Bishop MacKinnon, Dr Alexander Chisholm, and Roderick MacDonald, would be the most enduring figures at St.F.X. for the next twelve years. A native of Middle South River, Gillis had been a student at St.F.X. since its inception in Arichat. He replaced Rev. Alex MacSween as a trustee in 1865.[17] Unlike Dr John Cameron, who served St Ninian's Parish immediately before him, Father Gillis did not teach at the college. Alexander MacKinnon's long tenure with the English Department began in 1865. He was a nephew of Roderick MacDonald in mathematics.[18] To ease the burden of Dr MacGregor's teaching duties at the advanced levels,[19] the bishop placed Rev. Dr Alexander Chisholm at St.F.X. His was a crucial appointment, for this native of Marydale and graduate of the Urban College would serve St.F.X. for an extended period, even into the early years of the twentieth century. Chisholm had earned the PH D and DD

Rev. Dr Daniel M. MacGregor, professor 1865–68,
ca Jan 1872–77

Rev. Dr Alexander Chisholm, professor 1866–67,
1868–75, 1877–81, 1885–95, 1904–7

after an eight-year sojourn in Rome (1858–66). He was only twenty-three when he arrived at St.F.X.;[20] six years later Bishop MacKinnon judged him to be, like Dr Schulte before, "the backbone of the college."[21] One admirer found him to be "naturally amiable and charitable and his character mild and gentle;"[22] officials in Rome had come to a similar conclusion and had noted his "aptitude for teaching."[23]

The College Charter

In the same year Dr Chisholm arrived, an important event occurred in the history of St.F.X.: the Nova Scotia government accorded it powers to grant degrees.[24] Bishop MacKinnon's petition for a charter was presented to Charles Tupper's Conservative government on 28 April 1866. In it, MacKinnon paraded before the House all the college's strong points and accomplishments – its "spacious and commodious buildings," the staff of "highly efficient professors," the "high" attendance that year of fifty-eight scholars in the classical, philosophical, and theological departments, and the anticipation of even greater numbers in the future. Further, he reminded the politicians that his college was the only educational institution in eastern Nova Scotia teaching "the sciences of logic, metaphysics, ethics, and moral and dogmatic theology," along with the branches of an English, mathematical, and classical education. Moreover, its alumni had performed successfully in other institutions and the college had a "first class" male and female common school associated with it. For all these compelling reasons, argued the bishop, his college should be empowered to grant degrees.[25] The politicians agreed; the legislature and council passed without debate a university bill which received royal assent on Monday, 7 May.[26]

The charter was worded as follows:

Saint Francis Xavier's College, at Antigonish, shall be held and taken to be an University, with all and every the usual privilege of such an institution, and that the students in the said College shall have the liberty and privileges of taking the degrees of Bachelor, Master, and Doctor in the several Arts and Faculties, at the appointed times; and shall have power within themselves, of performing all scholastic exercises necessary for the conferring of such degrees, as shall be directed by the statutes, rules, and ordinances of the said College.[27]

This chartering of St.F.X. substantially boosted its standing and probably gratified all with an investment in its future well-being. No doubt the bishop coveted a charter to increase St.F.X.'s credibility and that of its graduates. Furthermore, other denominational colleges in the region had gained charters. Finally, confederation of the British

North American colonies was imminent in 1866. Laurence K. Shook claims, "Everyone felt that Confederation would tend to freeze the educational arrangements of the various provinces and that it would be wise to enter the new era in as firm and healthy a situation as possible."[28] Therefore, St.F.X., along with four other Catholic colleges in Ontario, strove that year to advance their legal standing through university charters or acts of incorporation.[29]

That such a small, upstart institution had achieved with apparent ease the legal status of a university within about ten years is somewhat surprising. The government made no careful evaluation of its academic standards, worth, and integrity; the politicians seemed remarkably generous and confident in the bishop's report about St.F.X. Maybe the student enrolment or the breadth of its curricular offerings impressed them. Maybe they were impressed by the academic credentials of its staff, or perhaps the academic and professional track record of the alumni. Or maybe it was because the bishop of Arichat's brother was a member of Tupper's executive council, or because the legislature had established a precedent by granting university powers to other denominational colleges.[30] It was also likely that Premier Tupper found the petition for a charter a happy opportunity to indulge some of the Catholics of his province in order to mitigate their bitterness – he had recently withheld their legal right to separate, publicly funded common schools. The bishop's request and the government's generous response were timely in more ways than one.

Free State-Sponsored Schools
From 1864 to 1866, Tupper's government had enacted important and controversial school legislation which had established a free state-sponsored school system financed by compulsory assessment.[31] Evangelical Presbyterian educational reformers, many from Pictou County immediately west of Antigonish, likely had much to do with shaping public opinion supportive of state schooling.[32] One bill provided for the inculcation "by precept and example respect for religion and the principles of Christian morality;"[33] but this minimal provision was far from protecting separate denominational schools. John MacKinnon, the brother of Bishop MacKinnon, threatened to resign from Tupper's cabinet over the issue, but did not.[34] Archbishop Thomas L. Connolly of Halifax apparently swallowed Tupper's bitter educational pill after the premier assured him that "The Council of Public Instruction, being the cabinet, would always contain Roman Catholic representatives and, therefore, Catholic interests would be safeguarded."[35] In spite of the "gentlemen's agreement," denominational religion had been officially

48

expelled from the public schoolhouse curriculum in Nova Scotia; Catholics were dismayed.[36]

Tupper's educational agenda, at least in some respects, was especially galling for Bishop MacKinnon. He had long wanted Catholic schools;[37] to provide them for his flock was one reason he had founded St.F.X. In 1856, one year after the government founded the provincial normal school in Truro under the principalship of Dr Alexander Forrester, a Free Church evangelical Presbyterian, MacKinnon concluded that it was essentially closed to Catholic teachers;[38] therefore, he had urged the government to recognize and fund his college in Antigonish as the normal school for the Diocese of Arichat. In fact, St.F.X. already functioned as such, affirmed the bishop. His request failed.[39] Given his devotion to Catholic education, it was no surprise that he developed, in 1868, a very lengthy petition to request that Premier William Annand's Liberal government, which had replaced the Conservatives in November 1867, amend the recently passed School Act in order to protect the "rights of religion" in education.[40] The petition also failed. The many schools scattered through the bishop's diocese (in 1860 there were about 150 common schools, 18 grammar schools, and several academies) would remain legally non-sectarian. However, the actual fate of religion in particular schools was another matter.[41]

A Standardized College Program

Degree-granting powers for St.F.X. did more than bolster its academic status and credibility; the charter also compelled the institution to standardize more explicitly its program. Previously, pupils undertook a course of studies judged by the head professors to prepare them for their chosen profession or for advanced sacerdotal studies in Quebec or Rome. But the charter forced college authorities to decide more permanently on specifics: examination topics, length of courses, and required mastery. Two years after attaining the charter, the staff were still struggling to define a standard course of studies necessary for graduation; only three degrees had been granted by then.[42] The uneven preparation of matriculants entering from schools vastly differing in quality, of course, did little to help. Up to that point, a degree was conferred on a student at the "united request of the professors."[43] But the college staff were expecting that "a period of four years for him who is possessed of ordinary talents and industrious habits ought to suffice, provided that his common English preparatory education were exact and comprehensive."[44] By 1871, St.F.X. had conferred nine BA degrees and by the end of the decade nineteen;[45] degrees in programs other than the liberal arts were nowhere on the horizon.

49

Confederation and a New Cathedral

On 1 July, one year after St.F.X. had acquired university status, Nova Scotia joined a confederation of the British North American colonies which included Ontario, Quebec, and New Brunswick. The confederation question had been highly controversial in the Maritimes, but strong pressures and fears, as well as hopes, rendered it attractive to many political leaders. The deed itself, made legal by Britain's passage of the British North America Act in March 1867, promoted the political, economic, and religious integration of the Maritimes with central Canada.[46] The bishop of Arichat had earlier addressed his diocesan clergy and laity on this momentous issue, recommending confederation to them as the best means to retain British aid in warding off the external threat of republicanism from the south; confederation alone, he argued, would preserve domestic peace and freedom.[47] No records exist which show how the St.F.X. college community responded to the issue.

That same year, MacKinnon initiated a project which would soon pose an internal threat to the meagre financial resources of his diocese, and therefore, to his beloved college. On 29 June 1867, he laid the cornerstone for a new and ambitious St Ninian's Cathedral built next to his residence-seminary in Antigonish. Seven years later, when the cathedral was finally completed, the bishop would be feeling the severe financial squeeze of the burdensome debt he had incurred.[48] His sources of revenue had never been lucrative. Fortunately, the Association for the Propagation of the Faith annually contributed 10,000 to 20,000 francs.[49] In the year of confederation, the government decided to increase the provincial college grant from $1000 to $1400; the extra $400 to St.F.X. was an evident boon. But the increase was partially offset by a decline in paid tuition during the 1870s and economic depression which "created immense hardship throughout the region."[50] Through these years, college authorities were forced to defer regular maintenance and improvements to their buildings; the bishop had few funds to divert from his hefty construction project.[51]

Internal Difficulties and Decline

Shortly after returning in 1870 from the first Vatican Council in Rome,[52] MacKinnon complained to the Urban College about another problem which had occasionally distressed him: the behaviour of one of his priest-professors. He had moved Rev. Dr Daniel MacGregor from St.F.X. to the Arichat Academy for the 1868–69 scholastic year, and then from there to his home parish of Lismore; Rev. Dr Alexander Chisholm had remained as head professor at the college. MacKinnon's

1871 complaint to Rome about MacGregor ran thus: "He has already passed through all the duties and priestly charges wherein he could be employed in the diocese; and in every case he fell down on the job completely. The root and source of the evil is intoxification."[53] MacGregor's "falls" seriously affected his work and the students at St.F.X. where he was head professor. MacKinnon's successor would later report to the Canadian Apostolic Delegate that MacGregor might be seen "reeling in a state of intoxification during a full half of the class hours."[54] MacKinnon removed him while also exhorting him to retreat temporarily to the Trappist monastery for personal help. Apparently, his problems with "intoxification" were sporadic, for after MacGregor returned to college duties from Lismore around January 1872, MacKinnon could inform Rome that he was "doing better."[55] But alas, by mid-January of the year following, MacGregor was "again unfit to be a professor in the College."[56] This time, for reasons unknown, his bishop left him there;[57] he remained until MacKinnon's successor, Dr John Cameron, decided his fate five years later.

The combination of financial demoralization, building deterioration, Bishop MacKinnon's declining health and mental instability, and MacGregor's drinking bouts probably explains why enrolments declined at St.F.X. in the late 1860s and early 1870s. Fifty-eight students had been registered in the higher branches in 1865; by 1870 the number had dropped to eighteen.[58] Changes in the diocese also likely affected the registration figures. While the provincial population from 1851 to 1871 had increased by 110,946 to 387,800, the Diocese of Arichat's share of the total had decreased from 38 to 36 per cent. Within the diocese, the County of Antigonish grew more slowly than other counties: since 1851 it had increased by only 3000 to 16,512, although it retained its high Catholic proportion of almost 85 per cent.[59] Outmigration from eastern Nova Scotia, indeed from the whole region, had become a problem. Because of the region's traditional trade links with New England, many Maritimers became aware of attractive employment opportunities there, especially in the economically expansive Boston area. Thus an increasing number of them began moving to the favoured destinations of New England and later western Canada. People of Scottish and Irish lineage, and especially the young and active, were prominent in the migration.[60] Nevertheless, the Scots remained the dominant ethnic group throughout the diocese, although their native Gaelic tongue was vanishing.[61] The college's constituency remained essentially Scottish, rural, and poor. In spite of drooping registrations, the staff and students plodded along through their educational exercises.

The College Question
Sometime in the summer or fall of 1874, during its time of increased vulnerability and distress, St.F.X. received a perplexing, perhaps unsettling, invitation from the Dalhousie University board of governors in Halifax. The said invitation requested the college authorities attend a conference about establishing a central teaching university in Nova Scotia. Apparently a new Dalhousie board member had convinced its governors to undertake a mission to "combine the resources of all the colleges" in one university.[62] The circular invitation was also sent to the other denominational colleges in Nova Scotia – Acadia, Kings, St Mary's – and Mount Allison in New Brunswick.[63] When they all refused to attend the proposed conference, Dalhousie promptly memorialized the government for a larger grant and an increased board membership. The government granted these requests and also gave the board power to affiliate other colleges or schools in arts, theology, law, and medicine. Sister institutions in Nova Scotia viewed the Dalhousie move as "an overt attempt to assert supremacy over the other colleges of the province"; therefore they responded vigorously with petitions for a fairer distribution of the denominational grants.[64]

The Dalhousie proposal showed that forces of change threatening to the denominational college status quo were afoot. Of course, attacks on it had been mounted before, but without success. Peter B. Waite aptly states: "The college question was a little like measles or whooping cough, breaking out every now and then in the body politic of Nova Scotia."[65] As recently as March 1867, the Congregational Union of New Brunswick and Nova Scotia had petitioned the Nova Scotia legislature not to grant money to denominational schools and colleges.[66] Over fifty years before, in 1818, Dalhousie University itself had been founded as an alternative to the Anglican exclusivism of King's College in Windsor; and ever since, there had been champions of non-sectarianism and centralization in Nova Scotia higher education.[67] But religious interests, ethnicity, and geography were the first factors which had resisted the challenge of the educational dissenters; tradition was the last. Nova Scotia's superintendent of education rightly observed in 1875: "the denominational system is now rooted and grounded in the convictions and affections of its numerous and influential adherents."[68] By the 1870s, the denominational college status quo was unlikely to crumble quickly.

The University of Halifax
Nonetheless, St.F.X. and its sister colleges were entering a new era. Premier P.C. Hill's Liberal government judged in 1876 that the "fullness of time" had arrived for a new arrangement in higher education.

Hence, the provincial secretary introduced into the House on 8 March two bills "which constituted one measure." One bill provided for denominational college grants, but for only five more years, enough time to allow the colleges to "set their houses in order and to prepare for the contingency that at the end of that time these grants would cease and never be renewed." During the interim, St.F.X. and St Mary's would annually receive $1500 each, Dalhousie $3000, King's $2400, Acadia $2400, and Mount Allison $2400.[69] The ultimate object of the University Bill was "to establish a central university free from denominational control and at the same time do justice to existing institutions."[70] The bill named the new institution the University of Halifax and modelled it after the University of London. The government's explicit aim was to raise the standard of higher education in the province and allow anyone who desired, including people who lacked the opportunity to follow a regular college program, "to obtain academical degrees." The University of Halifax would be merely an examining and degree-granting body until further legislative notice.[71] "Young men of ability," the government hoped, would go up to this Provincial Examining Board in Halifax to get their degrees. At the end of five years the government believed it would be justified in perfecting "a measure which might establish a teaching body."[72] Such, at least, were the government's objects, expectations, and hopes.

There were critics of the scheme. The opposition leader, Simon Hugh Holmes, charged that the government had revealed a contemptible lack of will in drafting the university legislation. It had created, he declared, merely "a University upon paper." Holmes predicted that the measure would fail; the government had foolishly not withdrawn the degree-granting powers from the affiliated colleges. They would surely not suspend such powers voluntarily.[73] Other commentators echoed Holmes's cogent criticism and prophecy. Some believed that the curriculum standards were "most exorbitant and ill-considered" for Nova Scotia; and if the government was not going to retract the colleges' degree-granting powers, then it should make the annual grants depend on acceptable reports from "Inspectors of Colleges."[74] Of course, Dalhousie was critical of the scheme, being already a central, nonsectarian university. However, the government no doubt knew that the colleges would not send their students to Dalhousie; thus it gave birth to another, rather peculiar educational offspring.[75]

Despite criticism, the legislature enacted the government bills and incorporated the University of Halifax with a chancellor, vice-chancellor, and twenty-four fellows who together constituted the senate. Rev. George W. Hill, Anglican clergyman at St Paul's, Halifax, brother of Premier P.C. Hill, and the inspirer of the drive at Dalhousie in 1874 to draw all the colleges together into one central university, was appointed chancellor; F.C. Sumichrast became the registrar. St.F.X., with King's, Dalhousie, St Mary's, Acadia, and Mount Allison, was affiliated with the new university. This gave any student who had completed a course of study at one of these institutions the right to be admitted as a candidate for a degree from the University of Halifax.[76]

The affiliation of St.F.X. with this new examining board, and Sumichrast's comment, in December 1877, that "The affiliated colleges have nearly all evinced a desire to assist in promoting the aims of the University," imply that college authorities in Antigonish had some sympathy with its agenda.[77] Sumichrast even reported that St.F.X. and St Mary's were planning "to assimilate their courses of study to the University."[78] The university senate was empowered to appoint examiners. In 1877, it selected Rev. Ronald MacDonald, an alumnus of St.F.X. and parish priest in Pictou, and Rev. Dr Alexander Chisholm, professor at the college, to be members of the board of examiners.[79] Chisholm, along with a professor at Dalhousie, became examiner in classics. He developed the classics examination, but served for only one year.[80] Rev. Ronald MacDonald's role in the university was much more significant. Appointed a founding member of the senate from 1876 to 1880, he attended the organizational meetings which determined finances, curricula, the selection of examiners, the establishment of committees, and the by-laws. MacDonald also became examiner in logic in 1877, and in mental and moral philosophy from 1878 to 1880.

The founding of the University of Halifax did not immediately threaten the survival of St.F.X. The government was moving slowly, testing the waters and hedging its bets. For the present, the grant to the college continued and its degree-granting powers remained secure. And the government's expedient dispensation of five years gave St.F.X. officials time to speculate on the possible consequences of the withdrawal of the grant and on what the spectre of a central teaching university implied for Catholic higher education in Nova Scotia. Meanwhile, threats enough to the college's strength and survival arose on the home front.

Threats to St.F.X.'s Survival

By 1876 the financial condition of the Diocese of Arichat posed one imminent danger to St.F.X. In an appeal to that trusty French society, the Association for the Propagation of the Faith, Dr John Cameron, coadjutor to Bishop MacKinnon since 1870, described the deplorable state of the diocese and underscored the "danger imminent que la religion en souffre beaucoup dans ce pays."[81] A depression of two years' standing had apparently restricted the contributions of the faithful;[82]

and this at a critical time, for the crushing debt incurred by Bishop MacKinnon's construction of the cathedral continued to exact a heavy toll.[83]

The bishop himself, then sixty-six years old, posed a second danger to the college. Dr Cameron reported that the debt on the cathedral had "taken away much of his gentleness." He worked day and night, and was apparently "indulgent toward others but severe on himself." Those around him expressed special concern about his mental instability.[84] Cameron informed the Propaganda in September 1876 that MacKinnon "breaks out in shrieks, hitting whatever is in his way. I was an eye witness last week and Hugh Gillis tells me that evident signs already of this in 1874 and MacKinnon's last visit to Cape Breton has made this common knowledge."[85] Such behaviour did not reassure and settle those students living above the bishop in the seminary. And, of course, the word had spread.

By then, Cameron observed that St.F.X. had lost all credibility with the public[86] and he anticipated that it would soon lose its $1500 government grant.[87] The following year, Father Hugh Gillis of St Ninian's Parish would overhear people as far away as Truro declare "it shameful that an institution like St Francis Xavier receive Provincial allowance."[88] But blame for the college's regression did not rest on the bishop's shoulders alone; Professor MacGregor's known fondness for "the droppie" had done little to inspire confidence in the institution. And apparently, that stalwart of the mathematics and science department, Roderick MacDonald, now fifty years old and a St.F.X. veteran of twenty-three years, had also become a liability because of drink.[89] These problems had been slowly taking their toll on enrolments, especially in the seminary where the bishop lived. For during the scholastic year 1876–77, only five ecclesiastical students were brave or tolerant or dedicated or desperate enough to stay in the "big house."[90] And finally, both the college and seminary buildings by then obviously and urgently needed repair.[91]

A New Bishop and His College Problems
Dr John Cameron, still rector of the Cathedral in Arichat, worked to reverse the trend of deterioration in diocesan affairs. On 19 January 1877, Rome appointed him apostolic administrator of the diocese, which accorded him full powers to govern the diocese in place of MacKinnon. In April, he wrote the Propaganda and reminded them of the bishop's poor health and the deplorable state of the seminary. He suggested to Rome that the title "Bishop of Arichat" be taken from MacKinnon and that he be ordered to leave the seminary.[92] But the old bishop disliked the plan and informed Father Gillis that he expected

Bishop John Cameron, second rector of St.F.X. 1854–58 and third bishop of the Diocese of Arichat 1877–1910

to stay right where he was. Twenty ecclesiastical students would be coming in the fall of the year, he predicted, and he had planned to paint the "big house" and build a road from it to the new cathedral.[93] MacKinnon's attachment to his seminary residence remained firm.

Meanwhile Bishop Cameron had some difficult decisions to make about his professors. For reasons unknown, Dr Alexander Chisholm had been appointed to a parish in May 1875; MacKinnon had replaced him with Rev. Donald Chisholm, an alumnus of St.F.X. who only remained for one year. After his departure, Rev. Dr Angus Cameron arrived and became vice-rector. Like his new associate at the college, Dr MacGregor, Angus Cameron had undergone the rigours of travel to the Urban College, where he obtained the PH D and DD after eight years of study.[94] These faculty changes had not resolved the serious difficulties posed for the college by Dr MacGregor and Roderick Mac-Donald. Bishop Cameron eventually arrived at the painful conclusion that both would have to go. He penned a curt letter of dismissal to MacGregor on 5 July 1877: "With heartfelt regret I have to inform you that your services as professor in St.F.X.'s College shall be henceforth dispensed with, and that, in consequence of a serious failing which I need not specify you cannot be entrusted with the care of souls in any mission of the diocese."[95] Cameron believed MacGregor's intemperance had inflicted disgrace and near ruin upon the "once honoured College of St Fr. Xavier."[96] While acknowledging the positive qualities of character MacGregor had displayed during his professorship, Cameron was determined not to allow him another trial – he had failed too many before. The bishop hoped his severance from St.F.X. would induce MacGregor to join a religious order and to live under rule. At some point in that distressing summer of 1877, Cameron also dismissed the senior member of the staff, Roderick MacDonald, who had been professor of mathematics and science for nearly twenty-five years. Father Hugh Gillis had recommended the move, but counselled his bishop to give MacDonald "timely notice."[97] Apparently the deed was done; however, no record of it remains. Within the course of a few short months, therefore, two veterans of St.F.X. had gone.[98] Yet there still remained the delicate and disturbing problem of the unstable Bishop MacKinnon, whose presence in the seminary had become so awkward and troublesome.

The Removal of Bishop Mackinnon

On the suggestion of Cameron, the work of uprooting MacKinnon from the seminary devolved upon the bishop's old and trusted friend Michael Hannan, the archbishop of Halifax.[99] He had replaced Archbishop Connolly, who had died the year before. Hannan arrived at

Antigonish to perform the unpleasant task on Tuesday, 17 July, armed
with letters from Cardinal Franchi of the Propaganda and Bishop
George Conroy, apostolic delegate to Canada, which authorized him
to elicit MacKinnon's resignation of the diocese and cooperation in
moving from the seminary. In return, MacKinnon was promised the
title of Archbishop of Amida.[100] Hannan's secretary, Rev. Edward
Murphy, and two diocesan priests – Hugh Gillis and Ronald Mac-
Donald – helped the archbishop's mission succeed. MacKinnon agreed
to resign and, before 1 September, "to remove from my present residence in the Seminary at Antigonish and leave buildings, furniture and
other things hitherto used by the professors or seminarians as they
have hitherto so used." There was one condition: Bishop Cameron had
to guarantee him an annual pension of $800.[101] Hannan feared that
MacKinnon would change his mind after he signed the agreement;
therefore, immediately after leaving the interview with MacKinnon,
he wisely mailed the documents to his Halifax address. The next
morning MacKinnon reportedly flew into a rage when he discovered
that Hannan no longer had the fateful documents. The archbishop
lamented later: "I have, I fear, lost the esteem and friendship of an old
– my oldest – friend in the Episcopacy. The mission was on that
account very painful and trying to me."[102]

Even after this distasteful task, Hannan's work was still not quite
complete, for MacKinnon found it most painful to contemplate leaving
the seminary which he had founded and subsequently nurtured with
paternalistic solicitude for nearly twenty-five years. In early August,
he informed Father Gillis that, after consulting some friends, he had
decided to defy church authorities and remain where he was and
wanted to be. "We have five boys already," he stated, "and we can
accommodate twenty and things can go on very well." Gillis sadly
reported this news to Bishop Cameron and commented, "It pains me
to think that an episcopacy so fruitful in good works should be clouded
by contumacy at its close."[103] But MacKinnon's "contumacy" was
short-lived. Archbishop Hannan wrote a strong letter to him and by
the end of the month he was gone.[104] MacKinnon himself informed
Bishop Cameron of his move: "The big house is free, waiting for a
Rector, Professors, and students." Perhaps with a touch of legitimate
pride, he continued: "I hope you will attend to it and for the next
twenty-five years give out as many pastors of souls as it has given
under our superintendence."[105] Shortly thereafter Hugh Gillis moved
from the glebe house on Main Street to the seminary and became the
fourth rector of St.F.X.[106] With MacKinnon's move, the college was
relieved of its third veteran in one summer. Like the other two, he had
once been an important asset to the institution; but by the fateful

summer of 1877 the founder of St.F.X. had become its most serious liability.

MacKinnon died two years later. Notwithstanding the personal difficulties which had tainted the conclusion of his episcopate, he had made an immense contribution to the progress of the diocese. At the beginning of his reign twenty-five years earlier, he had nineteen active priests of whom nine were native-born; he left behind sixty secular priests of whom forty-seven were native-born. He had begun with sixteen missions; with the assistance of priests and laity, he left behind forty-three parishes with about eighty-one churches.[107] MacKinnon's educational leadership was especially outstanding; he had founded three noteworthy institutions – St Andrews Grammar School, the Arichat Academy, and St Francis Xavier College – and had attempted to start a female convent and academy. In his oration at the bishop's funeral in September 1879, Rev. Ronald MacGillivray underscored MacKinnon's contribution to his flock of Scotch, Irish, and Acadian faithful: "They belonged chiefly to the poor and illiterate class. At the time, Catholics had but few, if any representative men. But the reproach has been removed from us by the educational zeal of Bishop MacKinnon." Education for the professions, especially the priesthood, and social advance – this was the bishop's "most noble and enduring work" for the Catholics of eastern Nova Scotia.[108] The college at Antigonish, which he had founded, staffed, chartered, and fostered, had been the main instrument for his "most noble and enduring work."

PART TWO

The Bishop and His College, 1877–97

·4·

Institutional Renaissance, 1877–90

When Colin MacKinnon resigned as bishop of the diocese in the summer of 1877, St.F.X teetered on the brink. In the words of a later rector, "the college had reached a very low ebb [and] was becoming moribund."[1] Fortunately, the enfeebled bishop's successor, Dr John Cameron, first rector of the college in Antigonish (1855–58), shared with MacKinnon a deep commitment to education. Therefore, he immediately began work to restore St.F.X.'s earlier vigour and reputation. In a few short years early signs of promise appeared; by the end of the 1880s the new bishop and his successive rectors had orchestrated an educational renaissance at the college in Antigonish. Around the old seminary on St Ninian's Street, a bustling campus began to develop, and close by a school for the education of females. Observers might have been surprised at the brightening prospects, for economic slump plagued certain areas of the diocese.

The College Context
During the 1880s, the region and local community witnessed important social, economic, and political changes. The national policy of Sir John A. Macdonald's Conservative government in Ottawa promoted economic development through tariffs and an intercontinental railway. Industry appeared in some of the larger urban centres, and many country people (farmers remained the largest occupational group) were drawn to the cities by the promise of a better life. Yet staples production and trade tended to stagnate, even though, in 1876, the Intercolonial Railway connected the Maritimes with central Canada. Maritimers had little sense of collective identity and interprovincial cooperation was rare. Overall, Atlantic Canada was "a society challenged in the 1880s by increased urbanization, emigration, industrialization and class conflict."[2] In Nova Scotia the high American tariff hurt fisheries exports and shipbuilding declined. The new Liberal

63

government, elected in 1884 and led by W.S. Fielding, even threatened secession from the Canadian federation.

Within the County of Antigonish, the population had reached a nineteenth-century high of 18,060. The County Incorporation Act of 1879 and the Towns' Incorporation Act of 1889 provided for elected local government and taxation. Antigonish itself had grown substantially by 1881 – the population hovered around two thousand and included at least twenty-two merchants and many craftsmen. Through the early 1880s, town and county folk were kept informed by two newspapers – the *Aurora* and the *Casket* – both Catholic in outlook. The Eastern Extension railway snaked toward Antigonish from New Glasgow in the late 1870s, and in 1880 connected Antigonish to Mulgrave on the Strait of Canso. By 1891, the tracks had even stretched from Port Tupper on the Cape Breton side of the strait to Sydney. Economic development in the cities and improved rail transportation facilitated outmigration; simultaneously these advances enlarged the college's constituency and made it easier for youth to get to Antigonish.[3]

Changes in College Personnel and Finances
Within this setting, Bishop Cameron's immediate commitment to resuscitating the college arose from his fear of losing the important government grant and his concern for the welfare of his people. As step one, he appointed a rector, since he himself resided in Arichat, the seat of the diocese. Cameron's choice, a logical one, was Father Hugh Gillis, parish priest for St Ninian's, ardent apostle of temperance, and long-time associate of St.F.X.[4] He was conveniently on hand in Antigonish, and had assisted the ailing Bishop MacKinnon since 1863 in the supervision of the college, both as the director of studies and as a college trustee. Indeed, his relation to St.F.X. had been long and intimate, for he had studied first under Schulte, and then Cameron, at the Arichat Seminary from 1853 to 1855; next, he followed the college to Antigonish and pursued his studies there until his ordination in 1860. Gillis was numbered among that small group of ecclesiastical students at early St.F.X. who prepared for orders exclusively within the diocese. Moreover, he would be the only St.F.X. rector in the nineteenth century not educated in Rome.[5] In the fall of 1877, he moved from the glebe house on Main Street into the seminary on the hill to take up the reins of college administration. His contribution to St.F.X. largely remained that of administrator and spiritual adviser to the students.[6] In both roles students found him tactful and earnest; his reward was popularity and respect. While apparently "zealous and hardworking," he still found the two mantles of priest and rector, in

his words, "to say the least very tiresome."[7] His bishop, John Cameron, had found the same two decades before.

The bishop's reform of St.F.X. had included the dismissal of two faculty members, Father MacGregor, who had taught theology, church history, and rhetoric, and Roderick MacDonald, the instructor in mathematics and science. They had to be replaced. Rev. Angus Cameron, who had arrived in July 1876, became vice-rector and professor of Latin, the Greek classics, and English. Then, in 1877, the bishop transferred Rev. Alex Chisholm back to the college and appointed him director of studies and professor of theology, mental philosophy, and Latin; already, he had seven years of experience at St.F.X. On the recommendation of Father Hugh Gillis, Bishop Cameron hired A.G. MacDonald, a native of River Denys, Cape Breton, as instructor of mathematics and science. A competent and experienced instructor, MacDonald had a reputation for literary ability and "moral firmness."[8] He turned out to be an excellent choice, for his career proved him an efficient and dynamic instructor, and dedicated friend of the college. A local druggist, J.D. Copeland, lectured in chemistry from 1878 and two advanced students, Angus Chisholm and Alexander MacDonald (later bishop of Victoria), assisted in mathematics and Latin. Alexander MacKinnon, who had been hired in 1866, carried on with the advanced classes of the town public schools. If alcohol had plagued some staff members before, chronic ill-health became the new trial, for both lead professors, Fathers Chisholm and Cameron, complained of weakened constitutions.[9]

This renewed faculty taught the St.F.X. staples: the classical languages and literature, modern languages such as French and English, mathematics, a sprinkling of science, Christian doctrine, and philosophy. These courses composed a program of either four or five years; the freshman year was equivalent to the later Nova Scotia high school grade twelve.[10] In 1878–79 seven students commenced theological studies, but the college could only offer such courses intermittently.[11] Some murmurs of discontent circulated about the Christian doctrine class, which brought together all levels of Catholic students once a week for the purpose of religious training and edification.[12] The full-time college faculty of only three, however, were restricted in what they could provide. Overwork and, therefore, unsatisfactory work would be a perennial difficulty for faculty at St.F.X., a problem which sometimes, no doubt, short-changed the students.

To renew the teaching staff was only one challenge faced by Bishop Cameron in his attempt to revive the college. His predecessor, Bishop MacKinnon, had bequeathed him a staggering debt of over $42,000 incurred through an ambitious program of church construction such as the impressive stone cathedral in Antigonish.[13] The new bishop declared war on this debilitating burden. In spite of several obstacles,[14] which included a serious economic slump in the diocese, Cameron wiped out the debt by about 1883. He performed the administrative miracle through a combination of the following: alms from the Association for the Propagation of the Faith,[15] contributions from his own monies, donations from benefactors,[16] diocesan collections, and low salaries at his college.[17]

A Proposal for the Merger of Maritime Catholic Colleges
While Bishop Cameron contemplated the demoralized state of his diocesan college in early 1877, a proposal hailing from the archbishop of Halifax gave him pause for serious consideration. Hannan, the alienated friend of the retired Archbishop MacKinnon, faced a crisis at St Mary's College in Halifax; in April of the year past, the Christian Brothers, who had run the school, withdrew to Montreal. Hannan wrote to Cameron: "It strikes me that your Lordship, who I learn is reorganizing St Francis Xavier's, might suggest or have in mind some plan or prospect in which I could cooperate or meet you half ways."[18] The plan, perhaps partly engendered by the new University of Halifax and the fear of a central non-sectarian university, turned out to be for a amalgamated Maritime Catholic college. Bishop Peter McIntyre of Charlottetown was enthusiastic when approached about the scheme, but the bishops of Chatham and Saint John, New Brunswick were uninterested; the archbishop's plan, therefore, slipped into hibernation for the next two years.[19]

Archbishop Hannan revived the proposal in early 1879. By then the details of his scheme had ripened. He thought that the two dioceses of Halifax and Antigonish should go it alone – although he wanted to consult Bishop McIntyre again – that a religious order like the Jesuits should be invited to run the college,[20] and that St Mary's should be closed and its government grant diverted to the new college. He wondered, furthermore, if Father Ronald MacDonald's partially constructed convent building in the town of Pictou could be hijacked for the proposed united Catholic college.[21] In spite of his own plans, and professed indifference and pessimism about this new one, Father MacDonald proved to be accommodating, for he wrote to Bishop Cameron: "I am disposed to place no obstacle to whatever scheme His Grace and your Lordship may in your wisdom devise for the education of the Catholic young men of this Province." But there were conditions: he would surrender the property and title to it if he received credit for having given $8000, the cost of the site and building, toward the proposed college fund.[22]

Since the decision to merge St.F.X. in a larger united college at Pictou was a major one, Cameron thought it best to consult his priests. Most of them were alumni of the diocesan college in Antigonish and their opinions were divided. The supporters of the scheme dreamed of increased financial resources and improved staff, and hence, a program superior to anything then offered at a Maritime Catholic college. But the nay-sayers reminded Bishop Cameron that St.F.X. had been built at considerable sacrifice to the diocese, that its benefits were widely manifest, and that shortly it promised to enter a flourishing state. Moreover, some of the Scottish priests feared Irish control from Halifax or at least a spirit of "national bigotry" which would place the two dioceses on a collision course. Finally, the dissidents contended that Pictou was "too densely Protestant" for a Catholic college.[23] Cameron pondered the advice of his priests, but left the final decision to Hannan.

In August of that year Archbishop Hannan appeared to abandon the proposition. The reasons he gave Bishop Cameron were financial – he could not meet the conditions laid down by Cameron and Father Ronald MacDonald in Pictou. Cameron expected Hannan to assume one-half the bill of $27,000 which would be required to complete the building, to accept Father MacDonald's claim of $8000 for the original cost of construction, and to pledge his support to a religious order, if it assumed control of the college. Hannan acknowledged the reasonableness of these conditions; yet given his straitened economic circumstances, he was only prepared to divert the provincial subsidy of $1500 from St Mary's and to proffer his "earnest support and sympathy." The disappointed archbishop summed up for Bishop Cameron his final judgment about the scheme: "I am sincerely sorry that I can only regard the project now as one to be abandoned for the present."[24] Thus the proposal for a united Catholic college in the Maritimes died; but the matter was not quite at an end. The idea of strength in Catholic unity cast a potent spell over some, and this charm would aid its rebirth in the late 1890s.

Recovery and Growth

In 1880, with the proposal for an amalgamated Maritime college discarded, Bishop Cameron pressed ahead with further changes at St.F.X. He replaced Father Gillis as rector with Rev. Dr Angus Cameron, the vice-rector of four years' standing. Cameron, a nephew of the bishop and a native of Lower South River, had earlier followed his uncle's trail to Rome for further studies. There he earned the two most advanced degrees; unfortunately typhoid fever broke his health. Perhaps his weakened constitution helps to explain the lacklustre image of his college administration. Nevertheless, he was reputedly broad-minded, prudent, and intellectually capable, as well as somewhat withdrawn.[25] Notwithstanding his health difficulties, his college experienced significant recovery and growth during his four-year rectorship.[26] Dr Angus Cameron's responsibility for this progress is now impossible to determine.

Physical expansion was one element of that progress. In the summer of 1880, a three-storey brick wing (eighty feet by thirty-eight feet and oriented north to south), which could board nearly fifty students and provide increased classroom space and offices, was built to the east of, and attached to, the old seminary on St Ninian's Street. This was the first brick structure and it would become, a century later, the oldest part of the university.[27] The bishop found himself driven to undertake this enlargement to accommodate an expanding student body, to increase the supply of Catholic teachers for schools within the diocese,[28] and to rehabilitate the college's reputation. The bishop also hired workers to repair the foundation and flue of the old seminary building; by then it was thirty-four years old. This work, he claimed, was "vraiment providentielle," as it "saved the old building and perhaps its inmates from destruction." Little did St.F.X. students know about the real dangers of pursuing higher education in Antigonish! The foundation was in a "ruinous state" and one flue exposed the building to imminent destruction by fire.[29] The construction and restoration cost $12,000.[30]

On completion of the new addition in 1881, authorities transferred classes from the College Street building which they sold to the dominion government in 1882; it renovated the old college into a post office.[31] The common school children shifted into the new Main Street School, and the high school and college students moved to the enlarged edifice on the hill.[32] From then on, the college was consolidated in one location on the south border of the town, where it would remain permanently. These changes also marked the origins of an expanded residential life at St.F.X. which had earlier been restricted to seminarians. St.F.X. began to develop as a residential college because of the distances students travelled to attend (it was no coincidence that the first residence was built soon after the railway reached Antigonish), the young age of some of the scholars and their need for supervision, and the lack of housing in the local community. Residence life gave rise to the system of *in loco parentis* where the faculty supervised and counselled in the place of parents, an arrangement common to all nineteenth century residential colleges. It also created the necessary conditions for the development of a strong and enduring tradition of close community at St.F.X. symbolized by the perennial phrase "Xaverian family."

First brick wing of Xavier Hall (built 1880) attached to the old seminary
(built 1846)

Like the college students, the bishop of the diocese also made a move in 1881. After receiving permission from Rome, and citing the support of the archbishop of Halifax, of the other Maritime bishops, and of the diocesan clergy for his relocation, Bishop Cameron moved from Arichat into the seminary at Antigonish in late September 1880.[33] He would remain there until a new, separate bishop's residence was readied in 1883. Cameron's move from Arichat signified the final and conclusive shift of the diocese's centre from there to Antigonish.[34] The transfer of the see would be made official in 1886 by pontifical decree.[35]

St.F.X. and the University of Halifax

Shortly after this first expansion of St.F.X., certain legislative developments at the provincial capital had decisive repercussions for the college. In 1876, the Liberal government had created the University of Halifax, intending that it eventually become a provincially supported teaching university instead of merely an examining board; it had also decreed that the denominational college grants would be withdrawn after five years. Two years later S.D. Holmes's Conservatives had defeated the Liberals. By 1881 the new government saw clearly that the University of Halifax scheme lacked public support. It had examined only fifty-seven students; seventeen of these had failed.[36] Holmes's prophecy in 1876 that the "Paper University" would come to naught had apparently been fulfilled. Chancellor Hill believed optimistically that the university had done much good in directing attention to higher education, improving the quality of college instruction, facilitating the exchange of views among leading educators, and providing an opportunity for people of limited means to acquire a degree.[37] But even he admitted that all the affiliated colleges, with the exception of Mount Allison, had refused to cooperate with the University of Halifax over the four years of its experimental existence. The regional, ethnic, and religious rivalries and commitments which manifested themselves in Nova Scotia's pattern of denominational colleges seemed insurmountable.[38]

As an affiliate of the University of Halifax, St.F.X. was rightly indicted by the chancellor's gloomy conclusion. Since the founding of the University, only two St.F.X. students had written its first bachelor of arts examination; both had failed.[39] The chemistry examination did them in because a failure in one subject virtually meant complete failure; as yet the authorities had made no provision for supplemental examinations. The examiners felt discomfort with the St.F.X. students' predicament, so they unanimously memorialized the senate to provide supplementals for them and for any others who might discover themselves in a similar plight.[40] The chancellor supported the memorial, and, in a letter to Professor Alexander Chisholm, praised the scholarship of the students while noting that they could hardly be blamed for a low performance in a subject "for which there is no special provision" at St.F.X.[41] But the main point was that St.F.X. had given almost no support to the University of Halifax. Rev. Ronald Macdonald, an alumnus of St.F.X. and member of the University of Halifax senate, felt it a humiliation that in five years St.F.X. had not sent up to the university "one young man fit even to matriculate."[42]

Bishop Cameron's attitude to the university was mostly responsible for his college's lack of support. While he seconded concerns to raise the standards and efficiency of the denominational colleges, he considered the University of Halifax an "expensive, pretentious, and unprofitable institution."[43] Moreover, uniform, written examinations, he believed, encouraged "cram" and would reduce education to the mere acquisition of knowledge instead of the development of men's faculties. In addition, an institution like St.F.X., established for the Catholic people of eastern Nova Scotia and thus one which had work "peculiarly its own to perform," needed to live and move and have its being where individuality, thoroughness, and freedom could flourish. Cameron also rightly contended that St.F.X. suffered serious disadvantages because it was situated in the most recently settled part of the province, had no large town or wealthy Catholics to back it, and "few schools fit to duly qualify young men for its halls." Such hindrances made it unfair to place St.F.X. in competition with older and better-endowed institutions.[44] Finally, the bishop feared the spectre of a central teaching university patterned after the University of Toronto. He utterly opposed "nonsectarian" education and showed little reserve in his judgment of it: "Godless education is a fiendish monster which ought to be exposed in all its hideous and soul-destroying deformity."[45] Not only would such a university be "soul-destroying" and subject, he predicted, to excessive Presbyterian control, but the taxation of Catholics to support such an institution would be a violation of their civil liberties. In Cameron's view, the discussions with Archbishop Hannan during these years about a united Catholic college held more promise. For these manifold and compelling reasons, the bishop and his college had maintained a decidedly passive stance toward the University of Halifax, an attitude which had helped to ease its decline into oblivion.

The University of Halifax, during its five-year existence, appeared to have little impact on St.F.X. It did arouse fears of a central, nonsectarian teaching university among leading Catholics of eastern Nova Scotia, and perhaps sharpened their sense of what was at stake for Catholic higher education. Moreover, St.F.X. at least "evinced" a desire to support the aims of the university and to adjust its course of study to it.[46] But whether this actually happened is difficult to say. The experience of the only two St.F.X. students examined by the University of Halifax shows that, in the sciences, the college's curriculum was not assimilated and probably could not be under its stringent circumstances. And the bishop's attitude toward the university revealed that St.F.X. felt little inclined to follow its lead.[47] If anything, St.F.X. had a tempering effect on the standards of the University of Halifax, and made it adjust a little to the realities of Nova Scotia higher education. The failure, in 1879, of the two St.F.X. students in chemistry prompted the board of examiners to request supplementals and probably gave rise to the registrar's recommendation to the senate that chemistry be removed from the list of compulsory subjects at the first bachelor of arts examination. Sumichrast noted that not all the colleges had laboratories or chairs of chemistry, a circumstance which restricted the preparation they provided their students in this subject. The senate passed his recommendation.[48]

The Demise of the University of Halifax

Premier Holmes, a man strongly in favour of one central university for Nova Scotia, circularized the affiliated colleges in February 1881, asking if each would surrender its degree-granting powers to a general examining board composed of college representatives. In this way he hoped to bolster the University of Halifax scheme to establish province-wide standards. St.F.X., St Mary's, and Mount Allison agreed to suspend – but not surrender – their powers, as long as the government continued the college grants.[49] But Dalhousie, King's, and Acadia were recalcitrant.[50] For the University of Halifax, the handwriting was on the wall. Holmes lamented that, because of the increased grants made in 1876 to the denominational colleges – under a Liberal administration, he noted – they had "struck their roots more deeply into the soil than had previously been the case; in other words, they were stronger, better equipped, more determined to live than they were in 1876."[51] His government yielded to the petitions urging the continuation of the grants. Thus it sponsored a colleges bill which abolished the University of Halifax and made the grant of $1400 to each college conditional on an annual visitation and a good report from the superintendent of education.[52]

The Fight to Retain Government Funding

Meanwhile, Bishop Cameron marshalled his own forces within the diocese and legislature to ensure the renewal of the grants. In November 1880, a close and astute political friend had advised him to petition the government, but to let his Protestant allies enter the field first in order to pre-empt the "Catholic Cry." It was wise counsel and he heeded it.[53] A petition signed by 6935 ratepayers from within the diocese was forwarded to the assembly in March 1881.[54] By the end of January, the bishop had also elicited the commitment of the MPPs for Cape Breton, Richmond, Guysborough, and Inverness counties to vote for the grants.[55] And finally, he successfully campaigned to bring his leading clergy on side and urged their "respective representations in behalf of the renewal of the college grants." In fact, all the clergy, with one prominent exception,[56] supported the bishop's campaign. By February 1881, Cameron expressed confidence that the denominational colleges would succeed in obtaining continued government support.[57]

Bishop Cameron's close and astute political friend was John S.D. Thompson, a convert to Catholicism and a talented Halifax lawyer.[58] Thompson, standing for the Conservatives in a provincial by-election in Antigonish County in 1877, was elected through the powerful assistance of Cameron, who saw his candidacy as a golden opportunity to gain a credible and highly competent Catholic voice in public life.[59] From then until Thompson's untimely death in 1894 while he was serving as the first Catholic prime minister of Canada, they maintained a close relationship, "almost like that of son to father."[60] After the Conservative win in 1878, Thompson joined Holmes's cabinet as attorney-general. The promotion gave Cameron a Catholic ally who then occupied a strategic position at the provincial capital. This was immensely convenient when the college grants were threatened, for the bishop armed Thompson so he could defend the Catholic position in the legislature.

Thompson undoubtedly contributed to the passage of the government's colleges bill in the assembly, where it gained overwhelming approval in late March. But the victory was short-lived; in the legislative council disgruntled members convinced their colleagues, by a majority of one, to kill the bill.[61] Cameron was surprised and dismayed by this development; the councillors, he thought, dared not block the bill. However, informers had told him that "Chancellor Hill and his Dalhousie friends [were] hard at work canvassing the old fogies to resort to such an extreme measure."[62] He later declared that the defeat of the grants "removed from our legislation the last practical token of recognition of Christianity in our schools"; it meant, in his view, that the "Sectarianism of infidelity" had won.[63] Nevertheless, the deed had been done; the subsidy withdrawn. The denominational colleges would wait eighty-two years before the province would re-enter the field of college subsidies.[64]

Financial Crisis and Resolution

The withdrawal of the grant precipitated the second financial crisis for St.F.X. within five years. But Bishop Cameron, who had wisely prepared himself for the worst, had an emergency plan ready: to apply for the government academy grant to sustain his high school preparatory department at St.F.X., and also, to create a permanent endowment fund for the college. The school act of 1866 had provided for an academy grant of $600 for each county; any academy which had been built and organized in accordance with the directions of the council of public instruction could apply for it.[65] Shortly after the cessation of grants, Attorney-General John Thompson informed Cameron that the council would likely offer it to St.F.X. without insisting that the college become strictly an academy.[66] With Thompson's assistance, therefore, St.F.X. did obtain this grant for its preparatory department; apparently it was the only college which did so.[67] One year later, David Allison, the superintendent of education, reported that the St.F.X. preparatory department was doing work "considerably more advanced" than that done in most Nova Scotia academies.[68] Doubtless St.F.X. was fortunate to retain at least some government support, and therefore to survive the withdrawal of the college grants. St Mary's in Halifax was not so lucky; it was forced to close in 1881 and remained so until 1903.[69]

Endowment Fund and Incorporation

Bishop Cameron was determined to create an endowment fund in order to compensate for the loss of the government grant; this would make St.F.X., in his inimitable words, "independent of the whims of politicians and the malice of bigots."[70] Through an appeal to the diocese, he hoped to collect a total of $30,000 in three annual instalments. Since the diocese was poor and investments would be slow to yield interest, Cameron moved rapidly to begin his canvass. In May he issued a pastoral letter which forcefully reminded the faithful of their duty to support Christian education; it also promised that a mass would be "offered to God in perpetuity" for all who contributed.[71] Moreover, the bishop again made good use of his key Halifax contact, John Thompson, who approached Catholic friends in the capital about the college's needs; he soon had a subscription list which totalled over $1000.[72] To the bishop's chagrin, the endowment fund drive only produced one-half of its stated objective by the fall of 1883. Nonetheless, these funds had begun to yield interest of more than $600 a year; by 1886 over $21,000 had been invested in municipality debentures, private ventures, and mortgages.[73]

Cameron felt uneasy about authorizing on his own the investment of the endowment funds, so acting on the advice of Thompson, he moved to incorporate the trustees of St.F.X. and place the responsibility on their shoulders.[74] He had Thompson, still attorney-general for the government, draft an act of incorporation and a set of by-laws.[75] The legislature approved the bill on 10 March 1882, two months before Holmes resigned as leader of his troubled government and was replaced as premier by Thompson. The new premier's Conservative administration was short-lived, for it went down to defeat at the hands of the Liberals in the June election.[76] Until the incorporation of a board of governors, the bishop and his rectors had discharged St.F.X.'s primary administrative duties. But the growth of the college assets convinced Bishop Cameron of the need to regulate legally such resources.[77]

The new act incorporated Bishop Cameron and his successors, and Rev. John Shaw, Rev. Neil McNeil, William Girroir, and Colin McIsaac under the name "the Governors of Saint Francis Xavier's College, Antigonish." All members, except the bishop, were to hold office until death, resignation, permanent removal from the province, or removal from the Roman Catholic Church. The board was to fill vacancies by election, with the proviso that any appointees be Catholic and approved by the bishop. Except for the bishop, and perhaps Girroir, the founding members were St.F.X. alumni. Vice-rector McNeil would become the rector in 1884. MacIsaac was a local barrister and would later represent Antigonish County as a Liberal at both the provincial and federal levels.[78] Girroir was a justice of the peace and father of (later Senator) Edward Lavin Girrior, who would succeed him on the board around 1902.

The incorporation bill conferred important powers on the new board while reserving veto authority for the bishop. The governors assumed power to accept, purchase, sell, and convey real and personal property, but they could not hold real estate exceeding $50,000. Their first purchase – a substantial one amounting to $15,000 paid to the Roman Catholic Episcopal Corporation – was of fifty acres of land which extended south from and included the college buildings.[79] Finally, the new corporation was empowered to make "statutes, rules, and ordinances" for the management of the college and its funds and property, and for the appointment and removal of faculty and the regulation of their salaries; all such acts were subject, of course, to the approval of the bishop.[80] The university charter powers granted to St.F.X. in 1866 remained in force.

In a way, the withdrawal of the government grant was a blessing in disguise. First, it focused attention on the college's financial needs and required the diocese to take full responsibility for them. Moreover, it acted as a catalyst which stimulated the incorporation of a board, and therefore, made possible a broader involvement of people in college administration.[81] The formation of the board, furthermore, amounted to a first step in the administrative separation of St.F.X. from the church, although Bishop Cameron retained veto power over appointments and decisions, and, of course, final authority over the rectors and lead professors who were his priests. Finally, by including two laymen on the founding board – Girroir and MacIsaac – the bishop recognized the potential value of the laity, along with that of the priests, to the administration of St.F.X.

A Female Convent in Antigonish

Since Bishop Cameron's financial plight showed improvement by the fall of 1881, he decided to press ahead with another cherished educational project – a female convent for his people. It was slated to open in 1883 and would be located to the east of the college, with St Ninian's Cathedral intervening. In less than twelve years, the convent would begin a long, close, and fruitful association with St.F.X. From the start, there would be mutual respect, including material and spiritual assistance. Twenty-four years earlier, Bishop MacKinnon had unsuccessfully tried to provide "female education" in Antigonish. Now his successor cited "a loud cry" in the town for a convent staffed by the Congregation of the Sisters of Notre Dame (CNDs). Cameron praised the choice in a letter to his friend John Thompson: "During my seventeen years sojourn at Arichat I was able to appreciate the immense good achieved by these admirable Christian women."[82] The respect and confidence was mutual; in 1880, the superior-general of the congregation had asked Cameron to intercede with Rome in a conflict over certain customs which they practised.[83] The community had been founded in Montreal, over two centuries before, by Marguerite Bourgeoys as an uncloistered congregation dedicated to the work of education. As the first religious order of women founded in North America, it had quickly become famous for its educational work.[84] By the nineteenth century, the CNDs had long been at work within the Diocese of Arichat. Their earliest assignment had been at Fort Louisbourg in the mid-1700s; by 1880, three years before Bishop Cameron opened the convent in Antigonish, they were conducting schools in Arichat, West Arichat, and Pictou.[85]

The motherhouse in Montreal acceded to Bishop Cameron's request for teachers; thus, CNDs staffed the new convent in Antigonish when it finally opened.[86] The building, completed by the end of October 1883 at a cost of over $8000, was made large enough to accommodate boarders.[87] The institution was called "St Bernard" in honour of the superior-general, Mother St Bernard, who was celebrating her golden

Mount St Bernard College established in 1883 by the Congregation of the Sisters of Notre Dame

jubilee that year.[88] Sister St Zephyrin, with twenty years' experience as head of the Arichat Convent, became superior of St Bernard and would remain so until 1894. Five other CNDs composed the founding staff: St Mary of the Incarnation, St Alexandrine, St John the Baptist, St Joseph, and St Ovid. The convent made an agreement with the local school trustees to share in the town's common school work and draw the provincial grant.[89] On Monday, 5 November 1883, Bishop Cameron officially opened the new school with a blessing of the building and celebration of mass in the convent chapel. Eighty-six lively students bustled about.[90] The sisters offered courses, from grades one to at least eight, which reflected the philosophy that education involved the training of the whole person – body, will, and intellect. Their curriculum, designed to give a "thorough female education," included the French and English languages, writing, arithmetic, bookkeeping, algebra, geometry, geography, use of the globes, ancient and modern history, rhetoric, botany, philosophy, chemistry, music, drawing, painting, and needlework.[91] The sisters also believed it their duty to encourage the students in habits of order, simplicity, economy, conscientiousness, and Christian devotedness. Such characteristics would, they believed, "make and mark the true woman."[92]

The Convent of St Bernard soon vindicated again the reputation of the CNDs for excellence in education. In 1886, after a visit from the superintendent of education, it qualified for government support as an academy, teaching, in addition to the common school grades, those from nine to twelve; hence it was renamed "St Bernard's Young Ladies Academy."[93] The county inspector of schools reported glowingly that year: "The excellent character of the work done in St Bernard's Convent, Antigonish is well-known, – a thorough training, polished education, and gentle manners, distinguish its graduates."[94] "The Mount," as it came to be known, would continue until 1955 teaching both the elementary and high school levels.[95]

Staff Changes and the Appointment of a New Rector
One year after the founding of St Bernard's, Bishop Cameron made three crucial staff changes next door at St.F.X. In the fall of 1884, he appointed the rector, Angus Cameron, to the parish of Sydney Mines. The rector may have been moved for health reasons, but it is now impossible to assess his performance at the college or to determine his bishop's cogitations. Rev. Alexander MacDonald, fresh from the Urban College, Rome and armed with both a PH D and DD, as well as a reputation for superior piety and obedience,[96] became prefect of studies at St.F.X. and professor of Latin, English, and philosophy; he would remain as one of the leading professors for nearly twenty years,

becoming known for his allegiance to St Thomas Aquinas in all things philosophical, and for his antipathy to Charles Darwin and his theory of evolution, a theory which created controversy in the nineteenth-century colleges from both the scientific and religious perspectives.[97]

The most significant staff change was the bishop's appointment of Rev. Dr Neil McNeil to the rectorship. McNeil, the son of an Inverness County blacksmith, had come to the college in 1880 as professor of science and Latin; he had also served as vice-rector for four years. In 1882, the bishop selected him as a founding member of the board of governors. A biographer described McNeil as "young [he was then thirty-three years old] and of good physique, medium small in stature, with a serene face and deep blue eyes."[98] That McNeil was highly capable and talented his subsequent distinguished career as a prominent Canadian churchman would prove beyond all doubt. The Urban College, his *alma mater*, had conferred on him doctorates in divinity and philosophy. Unlike earlier eastern Nova Scotia Catholic pilgrims to Rome, young McNeil had taken a detour on the way home: at the University of Marseilles, in France, he had pursued postgraduate studies in astronomy and higher mathematics;[99] he also learned to speak French.

At St.F.X., McNeil kept several irons in the fire – he taught, he administered, and he wrote. This latter activity included editing a weekly Catholic journal called the *Aurora*, which Bishop Cameron had founded in 1881 as a diocesan organ to propagate Christian doctrine and defend the rights of Catholics in education.[100] McNeil seemed to thrive on the challenges, for he continued as rector until 1891.[101] In later years, he would reflect that one weakness of his rectorship had been his openness to the influence of others and his inability "to take a determined stand and stick to it."[102] One year after McNeil's appointment to the rectorship, A.G. MacDonald, who had been a respected instructor in mathematics and science since 1877, departed the college to become inspector of schools for the County of Antigonish.

Further Expansion
McNeil presided over an ambitious building program in 1887–88. From 1880 to 1887 enrolments at the college had more than doubled to over one hundred. The bishop had encouraged his priests "to emphatically discountenance" parents sending their children "to godless or heretical schools at home or abroad."[103] By 1888 demand far exceeded supply – there was no room for even one-half the boarders who applied, no infirmary, and no space for recreation, for professors' offices, or for clergy retreats.[104] Already five years before, Bishop Cameron had moved out of the old seminary, and into his own residence perched on

Rev. Dr Alexander MacDonald,
professor of philosophy 1884–1903

Rev. Dr Neil McNeil, rector 1884–91. Eventually
became archbishop of Toronto 1912–34

the brow of the incline to the south of the Cathedral, so space would be freed up for more students.[105] Then he began a hunt for monies to supplement his meagre budget and establish a building fund. Using a judicious combination of boasting, flattery, cajolery, begging, and high principle, Bishop Cameron appealed to the good will and generosity of both the Association for the Propagation of the Faith, which he obtained, and his own flock.[106] Meanwhile, McNeil borrowed money from individuals and bursary funds.[107]

The first building to go up was a wooden gymnasium in 1887.[108] But the most impressive and enduring structure was a large addition to the existing wing. In 1888 the old wooden seminary of Bishop Fraser vintage was detached from this brick wing and moved a few hundred feet to the west.[109] At a cost of about $30,000 it was replaced with a main wing (ninety feet by thirty-nine feet), extending from east to west and boasting a central bell tower, and, in the interests of symmetry, with a west wing (eighty-three feet by thirty-eight feet) aligned from north to south. The whole was two-storey brick with dormitories on the third level. The lower levels contained rooms for classes, study, reception, and offices; they also had a chapel, assembly hall, refectory, library, and museum. By mid-October it was nearly complete. The bishop claimed that it was "excellent in every respect" and that local people were immensely proud of it.[110] The parishioners of St Ninian's had particular reason to be gratified; some of them had laboured hauling stone for the new buildings and had subscribed a handsome sum to the cost of construction.[111]

The College Renaissance Reviewed

By the end of the 1880s, friends and associates of St.F.X., especially Bishop Cameron, could peer back over the decade with a deep sense of satisfaction. St.F.X. had not only been saved from collapse, but it had been vastly improved. Student enrolments, partly because of the inauguration of rail service, had more than doubled from about 50 in 1879-80 to 109 in 1889-90.[112] And in origins, the student body had become much more diverse than during the 1850s and 1860s: scholars had been attracted from outside the limits of the diocese and the province, and even from the United States (about ten students).[113] Most still came from eastern Nova Scotia – Antigonish town (11 per cent), Antigonish county (42 per cent), and Cape Breton (34 per cent). More than one-half the students were of Scottish descent; Acadians accounted for only 6 per cent.[114] The students' families most often farmed or fished, but as Nova Scotia became more socially and eco- nomically diverse, students came with increased frequency from the homes of miners, merchants, and professionals. The threat of a central

Xavier Hall. The central wing and the one to its right were added in 1888.

university had receded, and through the formation of an endowment fund, the college had achieved limited financial independence. A newly incorporated board of governors, a crucial constitutional development, provided more effectively for the administration of St.F.X. New and commodious brick buildings had been constructed, and a new female convent had expanded and improved educational opportunities for young Catholic women in the town and region. A strengthened faculty offered a more diverse curriculum with varied offerings in the sciences – physics, chemistry, physiology, botany, geography, and astronomy.[115] In all, St.F.X. through the 1880s experienced a renaissance which redeemed its reputation.

The college had partly bred its own success. Bishop Cameron stated in 1888 that St.F.X. had already been "largely instrumental in giving a bishop and sixty-four priests to the church, and in preparing a still larger number of edifying and intelligent laymen for the learned professions."[116] Many of these alumni had been integrated into Maritime society; they had improved the political and economic clout of Catholics[117] and proved loyal to their *alma mater*. Catholic numbers in the diocese had also increased – in 1877, around 65,000 Catholics lived in the diocese and, in spite of outmigration, by 1887 there were 73,000. That year forty churches, thirty-six missions, and two convents had been reported; a decade later there were eighty-five churches and seven convents.[118] In spite of a languishing economy in the diocese, the college's constituency had been noticeably strengthened.[119]

Bishop Cameron's leadership and support had been crucial to St.F.X.'s progress through the 1880s. He had the vision, the contacts, the authority, the administrative skill, and the will which brought about a "second spring" or an "educational renaissance" at the college; it was no exaggeration to call him its "second founder."[120] But the next decade would be a somewhat different story: some of the bishop's activities would inflict damage on his flourishing diocesan college and detract from its service to the Catholics of eastern Nova Scotia.

·5·

Political Controversy and Expansion, 1891–97

Bishop Cameron's politics were Conservative. His unswerving loyalty to the party acted as a two-edged sword, in some ways benefiting his college and diocese, in other ways harming them. For St.F.X., the disadvantages of the bishop's partisanship for the federal Conservative party appeared unmistakable during the 1890s. A swirl of politically inspired media controversy enveloped the college in 1891 and again in 1897; both times the hue and cry about the bishop's political cunning had damaging consequences for the college. Nonetheless, the school continued to build on the growth Cameron and his rectors had initiated during its "second spring" in the 1880s; the 1890s was a busy decade. Indeed, the whole nation was busy and expansive. Wilfrid Laurier's Liberals finally unseated the Conservative government in 1896. His aggressive minister of the interior, Clifford Sifton, recruited new immigrants for western Canada. Foreign trade increased and ambitious railway projects were undertaken. Canada's cities burgeoned with more people, more commerce, and more industry.

Bishop and Rector Collide

Rev. Dr Neil McNeil, rector of St.F.X. since 1884, became editor of the *Casket* in 1890; Michael Donovan, a newcomer to Antigonish, had assumed management of it early in the year.[1] The bishop hoped that under Donovan's ownership it would be "a Catholic and Conservative journal";[2] however, by March he had agreed, under pressure from some of the clergy,[3] to permit the exclusion of all party politics from the paper in order to prevent the mischief of political provocation.[4] In April the *Casket* announced its future editorial policy: "It is now both a relief and a pleasure to be able to tell our readers, that, owing to the kind indulgence of leading Liberal-Conservative friends, we are today in a position to inform the public that the *Casket* will henceforth observe strict neutrality as to the merits or demerits of any political party which will not infringe on the rights of the Church."[5] The interpretation of the last phrase – "the rights of the Church" – would prove controversial. The announcement added that the journal was not the organ of the bishop of the diocese; yet it hoped for his continued goodwill. The hope would soon be dashed.

Controversy erupted in December 1890 only months before the federal election set for 5 March 1891. Editorials appeared as far afield as Winnipeg and Ottawa accusing Bishop Cameron of undue influence in both the election of 1885, when his friend John Thompson entered federal politics, and again in the federal election of 1887 (Thompson, representing Antigonish, actually won all three elections). Such public allegations impelled the bishop to attempt a self-defence. He tried to resort to the columns of the *Casket* but quickly discovered that his rector, McNeil, intended to stick by the editorial policy announced back in April. Cameron was scandalized and accused McNeil of being decidedly rude and offensive; the obstructive rector, he believed, was part of a Grit or Liberal conspiracy in arms against him.[6] McNeil did publish a letter from Archbishop Cornelius O'Brien of Halifax, written on behalf of Cameron and defending a bishop's right to participate in public affairs; but, in the interests of neutrality, McNeil likewise allowed the local provincial Liberal member, Angus MacGillivray, a lawyer and Roman Catholic, to publish a critique of it. Again, Cameron showed outrage that the *Casket* would publish what he considered an attack on the church; it further dismayed him that his three Urban College alumni at St.F.X. – Drs Neil McNeil, Alex Chisholm, and Alex MacDonald – supported MacGillivray's position.[7]

Bishop Cameron exhibited admirable intellectual gifts, but his reaction to McNeil's editorial policy revealed the power of his political loyalties; they seduced him into abandoning reason for prejudice. His charge of "Grit conspiracy," his conviction that McNeil's actions were "calculated to foment a spirit of insubordination to ecclesiastical authority," and his avowal that he complained about the *Casket* from a "purely religious standpoint" can only be explained on the grounds of political bias.[8] For Cameron, an editorial policy of strict neutrality in political affairs had become a "Grit conspiracy" designed to block Tory access to the media. Moreover, it was nigh ludicrous for the bishop to suggest that McNeil's editorial actions aimed at encouraging insubordination to his bishop. Finally, Cameron's objection to *Casket* policy was evidently not purely religious. To claim such clearly appeared as an attempt to cloak a political salvo in sacred garb and hope that everyone was gullible enough to mistake the disguise.

In November 1891, the besieged rector corresponded with Rome. McNeil explained his view of the controversy in order to forestall any suspicion that he had disobeyed his bishop. As editor, he had tried to avoid political partisanship, especially at times of elections, since his Catholic subscribers supported both parties. During the recent federal election of March 1891, he reported, Bishop Cameron had been deeply committed to the success of one candidate, John Thompson. When attacked in the media, he had wanted McNeil to come to his defence. But McNeil refused for these reasons: "not only because I did not want to alienate the subscribers," he stated, "not only because many of the bishop's arguments I could not sincerely defend, but especially because I believed and still do that clergy should not get mixed up in these political affairs when the defense of the church or moral principles does not require it."[9] McNeil, in this frank confession to Rome, revealed his fundamental disagreement with Bishop Cameron over the proper relation of clerics to politics.

The Demise of a Rectorship
The disagreement was one of substance, and Bishop Cameron did not plan to be the loser in the dispute. In the *Casket*, 13 August 1891, a brief notice appeared: Rev. Dr McNeil had been transferred to the Parish of West Arichat. In spite of the pleadings of a lay Catholic deputation which had lobbied the bishop to retain him as rector, McNeil was gone by early September. Cameron's official explanation for the move claimed that "the scarcity of French-speaking priests in the Diocese" required it.[10] But the real reasons were self-evident: McNeil was being punished for his supposed "anti-episcopal" editorial stance and was being forced to surrender his editorship of the *Casket*. Political passion had blinded the bishop's judgment; the loss of a gifted rector was the injurious result for St.F.X. McNeil's attempt to undermine the bishop's tactic by continuing his editorial work from West Arichat failed. In early February 1892, the bishop gloated, in a letter to Thompson: "Dr McNeil's grip of the *Casket* is relaxing, and one of these days, the man who undertook to create and lead an anti-episcopal party, shall be quietly brought down to his level. After that the *Casket* will cease to be your enemy or mine, and the discomfited Doctor shall have been taught a lesson salutary to himself and others."[11]

Bishop Cameron's prediction came to pass, for a little later in February he received a private apology from his chastised rector.[12] By late March, he granted a pardon, but one accompanied by several stinging barbs: "I must not, however, appear to forget that the domineering and offensive attitude you thought proper to assume towards me began years before you had any connection with the *Casket*, and was simply the product of the conceit you had of your own superiority." The bishop attributed McNeil's scorn for his own political stance "to pride alone." And in a disingenuous backhanded rebuke, Cameron confessed to McNeil that he had "spoilt" him "by exceeding partiality in word and deed" and had, therefore, "nobody now so much to blame as myself for your conceit." McNeil's penitence was prudent, given the authority Bishop Cameron wielded over him; unfortunately, the young priest's commitment to principle had cost him the rectorship of the college.

The bishop's judgment of McNeil's contribution to St.F.X. was poisoned by the rector's intransigence as editor of the *Casket*. But a Protestant student of McNeil's believed the rector occupied a class alone, "a Catholic possessed of a large Catholicity and charm." On McNeil's transfer from St.F.X. to West Arichat, he reflected: "It seemed to me such a pity to bury the brilliant professor in such an obscure corner."[13] A colleague believed MacNeil's editorial columns had reflected great honour on the college and diocese.[14] In August 1891, shortly before McNeil left for West Arichat, town delegates expressed regret at his imminent departure; they praised the "zeal, energy, and public spirit" which he had displayed during his eleven years of work in Antigonish, and the "high state of efficiency to which higher education had been raised."[15]

McNeil had set himself the goals, as rector of St.F.X., to elevate the status of the college, increase the efficiency of its teaching staff, and expand its usefulness. The threefold increase in enrolment since the beginning of his rectorship provided one measure of his success. After leaving, McNeil continued interested and active in St.F.X. affairs, and later he gained fame as one of its most celebrated alumni. Beginning in 1895, Rome granted him a series of important appointments: vicar apostolic of St George's, Newfoundland (1895–1904),[16] first bishop of St George's (1904–10), archbishop of Vancouver (1910–12), and finally, archbishop of Toronto (1912–34).[17] McNeil's reputation in the diocese remained high, for in 1904 seven priests, all graduates of the Urban College, asked the Propaganda to appoint him coadjutor to the aging Bishop Cameron. McNeil was utterly unacceptable to Bishop Cameron because of their tangle in 1890–91 over politics and editorial policy at the *Casket*.[18]

A Changing of the Guard

McNeil's replacement as rector in 1891 was Rev. Dr Daniel A. Chisholm, a thirty-two-year-old native of North Intervale, Guysborough County.[19] Chisholm possessed strong academic ability, as his studies at St.F.X. and Rome had proved. At his return in 1888 from the Urban College, Cameron had forthwith placed him at the college as professor of logic, Latin, and Greek.[20] Chisholm appeared physically delicate, and his unassuming manner accorded with his rather feeble frame. A

Rev. Dr Daniel A. Chisholm, rector 1891–98

colleague would later venture, "Beneath a cold and austere, but always courteous exterior, he possessed a warm and gentle heart."[21] Xaverians nicknamed him "Dr Dan"[22] and tended to see him as a thorough disciplinarian; however, the discipline began with himself. As rector, he worked tirelessly, apparently with little regard for his delicate health, to discharge the exhausting responsibilities imposed on him by a flourishing institution.[23]

Faculty changes early in Dr Chisholm's rectorship strengthened and expanded the college's program. Dr Alexander MacDonald remained as professor of Latin, English, and philosophy; and Rev. Dr Alexander Thompson returned, in September 1891, after six years in Rome, to be instructor in physics and higher mathematics, as well as vice-rector.[24] Under his later rectorship, St.F.X. would be significantly altered. Like Dr McNeil's work before him, Thompson's courses revealed and stimulated a rising interest in the sciences at St.F.X. Thomas Horrigan of Peabody, Massachusetts replaced Rev. Dr Angus J. Chisholm after the young priest's tragic death from typhoid during his first year of teaching at St.F.X.[25] Horrigan, who arrived in September 1893, taught English literature, Latin, and elocution (voice training).[26] A student described him as "a large imposing man" who "carried himself with studied dignity."[27] Possessing exceptional gifts for public speaking and singing, he would contribute much to the college's cultural life and public events. Moreover, on summer vacations he energetically recruited New England Catholic students for St.F.X.[28] J.E. Layton, a graduate of Mount Allison Conservatory, taught instrumental music from September 1892,[29] and a graduate of the Truro School of Agriculture arrived the year before to teach agriculture. Donald MacAdam, a St.F.X. alumnus who studied science at McGill and Harvard before attending the Grand Seminary of Montreal, was ordained in 1893 and then appointed professor of chemistry, botany, and geometry.[30]

In spite of the formidable atmosphere of classical studies at St.F.X., young Father MacAdam, through the next seven years, promoted the language and literature of the Celts by giving courses in Celtic studies and by organizing a Gaelic Society.[31] The *Casket* announced in the fall of 1894: "The more loyal sons of the heather are just now jubilant over the fact that they have succeeded, despite the strong classic atmosphere of St.F.X., in getting a class in their own beloved Gaelic started and that as a consequence they are able to inhale pure Celtic air three times a week."[32] This marked the first time such courses were taught at St.F.X.; it was through the enthusiasm of this young Cape Bretoner and native of East Bay who would later found the Scottish Catholic Society of Canada.

Rev. Donald M. MacAdam, professor of science
1893–1900 and keen promoter of Celtic traditions

By this time the bishop's selection of priest-professors and administrators had established a definite pattern at St.F.X.[33] Most were of Highland Catholic background and from strong Catholic rural homes. They were a privileged group, usually academically capable, and often encouraged toward further studies by their parish priests. At the college, the bishop had selected them for advanced degrees, usually at the Urban College, Rome, with the intention of assigning them to St.F.X. when the need arose. Diocesan educational levels were low by later standards, so rural communities viewed their highly trained priests with considerable pride. At the college, the priest-professors, who composed the bulk of the small faculty, carried an exacting load of teaching and administrative duties; this circumstance, along with a lack of financial resources and the primarily educational goals of the institution, largely excluded ongoing scholarship. The use of minimally paid priest-professors from eastern Nova Scotia enabled St.F.X. to survive; it also furthered the religious aims of the college, which were those of the church. Faculty were hired for their ability to cultivate character, personal piety, and orthodox Catholic belief among the students. The "open market-place of academic competition for posts" would be a twentieth-century invention.[34]

The First Graduate Program
The expansion and strengthening of the St.F.X. curriculum was evident in another new offering: the Master of Arts degree (MA). The 1890–91 calendar stated the requirements: "A Bachelor of Arts, of at least three years standing and of good reputation, who produces a thesis satisfactory to the Faculty on a literary, scientific or philosophical subject, is entitled to the Degree of Master of Arts."[35] At this time, only A.J.G. MacEchen of North Sydney, later a St.F.X. college professor of English, had earned the MA. But by 1897, a total of four St.F.X. graduates had earned the master's degree. This offering of a graduate degree revealed the staff's growing confidence in their academic resources and their desire to give students a chance to gain higher academic credentials.[36]

Life as a Student at St.F.X.
Chisholm and his colleagues organized student life at St.F.X. in order to form the ideal Catholic leader – a liberally educated, intelligent, mature, devout, and loyal Catholic gentleman[37] who would aid in the strengthening and propagation of Catholicism and the social and economic uplift of the Scottish, Irish, and Acadian Catholics of eastern Nova Scotia. Even to be admitted to St. F.X., a student had not only to meet the academic standards but also to present "a certificate of

good moral character from a responsible person."[38] A student departed the college with degree in hand only if he had satisfied the established course requirements and had been judged "of good character."[39] Assuming a fallen human nature, and recognizing the immaturity of many of their charges, the faculty believed that this ideal person was formed most effectively in a protected setting through externally imposed discipline. Discipline was easiest to ensure where there was a maximum of control and a minimum of unsupervised liberty and distraction. Protection from immorality and doctrinal heresy had also to be guaranteed. Thus, the priestly authorities provided residential facilities and strongly encouraged all students to use them.[40] Most did. There they submitted, quite willingly, to the faculty's serious paternalistic efforts to civilize them according to the Catholic ideal.[41]

The college functioned *in loco parentis*. The administration, the faculty, and the student prefects were "to take the place of parents" for the residential students.[42] Discipline was strictly enforced. The authorities monitored, policed, corrected, punished, and reported behaviour which departed from the established norms. They likewise carefully regulated personal habits. The consumption of alcohol on the campus was utterly forbidden, and staff frequently exhorted the students to take the total abstinence pledge.[43] Rules against profanity and "immodesty of language" were publicized. Under Chisholm, all reading materials required the approval of the vice-rector, and even personal correspondence was "subject to the inspection of the Rector." The administration charged students for any damage they did to the college property.[44] Students' relations with the opposite sex were to consist of nothing more than admiration from a distance, and excursions into town were carefully restricted. Rector McNeil had not allowed students to attend theatrical and other performances in the 1880s; Rector Chisholm eased up a little – he granted them permission to attend lectures or literary entertainments. Students were only allowed to go downtown on Thursdays, by twos, and only with permission; on other days, a student appointed as a porter ran errands for those who needed things in town. The college advised parents not to give their sons pocket money, but instead, to place it on deposit with the rector for distribution at his discretion.[45] The college regimen was modelled, evidently, after rules which regulated seminary life.

Although the practice of initiation was frowned on, it reared its head anyway. When it began is impossible to know; but in 1894 the practice was in vigorous health. The "ceremonies" for the new students were performed in the evenings as they arrived. First, the unsuspecting student meandered from the Antigonish train station up to the college, where the rector interviewed and registered him. But he was not yet "one of the boys"; upper class men required him to enter the recreation hall in "blissful ignorance" where, to his horror, "violent hands are immediately laid upon him and he is once, twice, thrice, hurled into mid-air, returning each time to the outstretched arms of loving friends, open to receive him." If the student struggled "like a caged lion," the ceremony was repeated. Apparently, certain "venerable and dignified" newcomers at times tried desperately, with the aid of college authorities, to outlaw the "affectionate upheavals." But the custom prevailed.[46] The perpetrators considered initiation a required rite for group membership. At best, it created a sense of group consciousness while also giving the newcomer a rude first lesson in existing student status relations and hierarchy.[47]

The Organization of an Alumni Association
After nearly forty years of educational work with the youth of the diocese, the college naturally began to look at its growing and prospering list of alumni with both a sense of pride and an eye for opportunity. Already in 1890, the idea of forming an alumni association had been publicly aired.[48] Then, in September 1893, Dr Chisholm and his staff took the initiative: they invited previous students and alumni to an organizational meeting at St.F.X. on 11 and 12 October. The *Casket* announcement confessed: "The Alma Mater needs the help of her own sons in carrying on the great work of imparting a sound Christian education." It artfully appealed to a sense of indebtedness, pride, and nostalgia in its alumni.[49] By 1893, St.F.X. could and did boast of the following alumni: two bishops, sixty-three priests, three supreme court judges, twenty-three barristers, twenty-four doctors, one county court judge, one federal senator, four MPs, ten college professors, two public school inspectors, fifteen teachers, eleven students of theology, seven law students, ten medical students, and a host of others to over three hundred. Here was a well-placed, solid, and valuable constituency indeed; it would be folly to leave it uncultivated. The college's appeal to its graduates suggested that the proposed association "bind themselves by some living tie to the life of the College, by some tie that will make them feel an active interest in the working of the College machinery." The suggested possibilities included the election of several college governors, the establishment of an alumni chair in some discipline, the creation of alumni bursaries or prizes, or some involvement in college sports.[50]

About fifty enthusiastic alumni attended the organizational meeting on 11 October and signed the association roll as founding members.[51] Twenty-eight of these were priest alumni. The assembly elected Bishop Cameron chairman, appointed a constitution committee, heard an oration by Rector Chisholm, and, in the evening, enjoyed a convivial dinner and entertainment with music, skits, speeches, and toasts. The following day, the association adopted its new constitution and elected its first officers: Senator William MacDonald, president, Rev. James Quinan, vicar-general to Bishop Cameron, vice-president, Judge Angus MacIsaac, vice-president, and Joseph A. Wall, barrister, secretary-treasurer. Laity outnumbered the clergy nine to two on the founding executive.[52] The constitution and by-laws placed the new Alumni Association under the patronage of his lordship, the bishop, and stated its object as "the promotion of the interests of St.F.X. College." The by-laws made provision for both ordinary membership – graduates and professors – and associate membership – all others. Membership dues amounted to two dollars a year or twenty dollars for life. The association could elect annually two representatives to the St.F.X. board of governors.[53] Its constitution called for one annual association meeting to be held in the college hall during closing exercises.[54] And the pleasure of renewing old friendships was not to be neglected: "To accentuate the social aspect of the meeting of old students, it was resolved to make an annual Alumni Dinner a feature of each yearly gathering."[55]

The new association was duly incorporated in 1894.[56] At that year's annual meeting, seventy members gathered. They happily elected Sir John Thompson, member of parliament for Antigonish and, by then, prime minister of Canada, an associate member. Within one year, the new association had done a solid job of organization. Yet only ninety-three members out of a total of over three hundred graduates had enrolled – close to 45 per cent of these were clerics.[57] Nonetheless, the Alumni Association's formation marked an event of considerable importance for St.F.X. As a *Casket* correspondent so aptly put it: "The Institution has received a quickening impulse, a fresh accession of life and vigor to prosecute its work."[58]

The Early Contributions of the Alumni Association
The newly organized alumni began work immediately to further the college's interests through public promotion, fund-raising, and student recruitment. They urged that the college hold a public closing each year; St.F.X. held its first one in June 1894, which gained full coverage in the *Casket*.[59] Beginning that year, and continuing for five more, the association voted $100 annually toward Thomas Horrigan's salary, American professor of English and elocution. In 1901–2, it would grant $40 of prize money for worthy students.[60] A fund-raising committee reported in 1899 that alumni had subscribed $3180 for the college.[61] In addition to financial contributions, the association also encouraged

its members "to contribute annually some specimen or object of interest to the College Museum, some work to the College Library, or
something to the Laboratory, the Gymnasium, or College Athletic
Association."[62] Such donations – and they were many – were gratefully
acknowledged in the annual college calendars.[63] Generous alumni likewise gave money and medals for academic prizes. The college's minimal efforts required to organize and foster an association of alumni
began to pay handsome dividends.

By organizing its alumni, St.F.X. gave them a formal means to
influence college policies and plans. They took advantage of it: at their
annual meeting in 1896, the association formed a committee to determine "the best means of enlarging the usefulness of the College and
extending its influence."[64] Being beneficiaries of a college education
which had equipped them for positions of social leadership, the alumni
realized the critical role of colleges and universities in the "progress of
civilization," and for preparing well-trained leaders. St.F.X., they
believed, had to keep pace with rapid strides in social change and
developments in the arts and sciences. To do so it had to develop and
maintain modernized buildings, broad library holdings, and up-to-date
laboratories and equipment. In official statements, the alumni sounded
progressive and optimistic about the future. An emergent note of
triumphalism characterized their declarations: St.F.X. and its alumni
had successfully overcome great economic and social disabilities; they
felt well equipped to meet the vast challenges of a new century.[65]

Based on written submissions from the alumni in 1897, Rector
Chisholm drafted an ambitious and expansionist report which proposed that St.F.X. become the Catholic University of Liberal Arts for
the Maritimes and Newfoundland. He praised the advantages of the
St.F.X. campus – its central location, its rural setting, its easy access
by rail, the prospects of industry-generated wealth in the diocese, its
growing endowment fund, and its unique ability to serve Catholic
women through its affiliated ladies' academy. This alumni-inspired
report revealed the optimism which had been generated by two
decades of college growth and countless alumni career successes. The
earlier proposal of 1877 for a federated Maritime Catholic college had
been an idea born of desperation; the proposal of 1897 was the offspring of expansion and optimism. However, both schemes shared the
same fate: they never materialized.[66]

The First Honours Programs
At the initiative of the alumni, St.F.X. offered its first honours courses
within a decade of commencing master's-level courses. College authorities advertised an English honours course in 1897–98 and planned to

offer similar courses in modern languages, classics, mathematics, science, and philosophy. Several "energetic members" of the association drafted syllabi for the courses and collected money for prizes. Outside examiners offered to assist the faculty. A.J.G. MacEchen, a North Sydney lawyer, was the architect behind the English honours course. He even set the exams and marked them. Any graduate or senior student could apply to the honours program; the candidate had to acquire his bachelor of arts first, and then sit a rigorous set of examinations in order to obtain the honours certificate. St.F.X. hoped "to encourage more advanced work in Higher Studies" by providing these honours level courses.[67]

The Convent and College Affiliate

St Bernard's Ladies' Academy also became interested in advanced-level studies. By 1890, when student enrolment had reached forty-six, and within seven years of its founding, the school had apparently qualified sixty-seven of its students for provincial teaching licences.[68] Three years before, the Ladies' Academy had professors from the college, especially in the sciences, conduct regular classes and experiments for their female students. Since St.F.X. students accompanied the professors, these qualify as the first higher-level coed classes in Antigonish. Academy pupils also used the college laboratory facilities.[69] However, these were makeshift arrangements, exceptions made necessary by a lack of faculty resources and equipment; the ideal in Catholic Antigonish remained separate education for males and females. The convent's curriculum, by 1894, had evolved into three distinct levels: the elementary, intermediate, and senior or academic courses. The senior-level students received lectures from St.F.X. professors in English literature, physics, and chemistry. At the end of their third year at the senior level, successful students obtained diplomas.[70]

In 1894, St Bernard's Academy affiliated with St.F.X. This gave female students the opportunity to take a college-level program and obtain a bachelor of arts degree.[71] The affiliation effected a noteworthy expansion of higher educational opportunities for the region's Catholic women. The new arrangement was made under Sister St Maurice – a daughter of Francis Collins of patriot and Reform fame in Upper Canada – who replaced Sister St Zephyrin as superior that year. A year or two before, a young Protestant woman had apparently asked to be admitted to the BA program. She was directed to Dalhousie; but a like request from a Catholic woman could not be resolved so easily.

Pressures did mount locally for college-level courses for women equivalent to those available to men at St.F.X. A social trend of more women pursuing higher education was apparent both regionally and elsewhere.[72] The academy students, moreover, had demonstrated good academic ability. Several CNDs – Sisters St Maurice (the superior), St Margaret of the Cross, and her own sister, St Leonard – responded to the pressures; Sister St Margaret of the Cross might have been the driving force.[73] Bishop Cameron supported the affiliation agreement. Earlier he had shown his solicitude for women when he had acted as an advocate for the CNDs and had also supported the Sisters of Charity in Halifax through their nasty dispute with Archbishop Hannan from 1880 to 1882.[74] Bishop Cameron, expressing a widespread Victorian assumption, stated that women had "a keener sense of Christian faith and morality" than men. Opportunities in church and society required they not be restricted to the nursery.[75] Given his effort to establish the convent in 1883, and his convictions about the role of women and the dangers of non-sectarian education, he was no doubt strongly in favour of the extension of higher educational opportunities to women within the diocese. The example of other Maritime universities, the church's stress on women's nurturing function in society and family, and the rising numbers of women who sought to teach were also factors which contributed to the new affiliation.[76]

The First Female Graduates
The closing exercises at the academy in June 1897 established a landmark in female Catholic higher education. The *Casket* announced the event: "For the first time, so far as we know, in the history of Catholic Education in America, the degree of Bachelor of Arts was to be conferred on a class of young ladies by a Catholic College." Three years before, St Bernard's Academy had been affiliated with St.F.X.; now four young women had completed the college course of studies with "marked success" and had passed the required examinations.[77] The editors of the St.F.X. student journal lauded the "excellent abilities" of their female counterparts, and also underscored the historic nature of the occasion.[78] St Bernard's Academy, in affiliation with St.F.X., rightly won a certain distinction with this first; two more years would pass before another Catholic college in North America conferred the BA on female graduates.[79]

The Origins of the Sisters of St Martha
Another important development in the 1890s concerned Catholic women of the diocese and its college, St.F.X. Apparently, domestic help for the college had become a critical problem by then because of transiency and incompetence.[80] After unsuccessfully investigating the chances of acquiring nuns trained for domestic work from other Catholic colleges, Bishop Cameron and the college authorities decided to

First female graduates, June 1897: Florence MacDonald (left),
Mary E. Bissett, Lillian E. MacDonald, and Margaret F. MacDougall

establish, themselves, an auxiliary order of sisters for this purpose.[81] In late May 1894, the diocesan clergy received a circular from the bishop explaining his plan. By then, he had arranged with Mother Bonaventure, superior of the Sisters of Charity, Halifax, to have postulants trained at Mount St Vincent.[82] The Sisters of Charity had already organized an auxiliary order to do domestic work in their own institutions; the bishop wanted his diocesan candidates to train with them and then return to establish a convent at St.F.X.[83] He announced that the order "would perform the domestic duties of educational and charitable institutions, – our College to be given a preferential place." Bishop Cameron urged the clergy to comb their congregations for worthy candidates and to explain to them "the great spiritual and even temporal advantages of life to be had by the Sisters of St Martha." Recruits had to be virtuous, robust, and industrious; generally, only those between eighteen and twenty-six years of age would be accepted.[84] The first recruits for the novitiate in Halifax left Antigonish in September.[85] Cameron hoped they would return fully trained in 1896, but there would be a one-year delay.

Building Expansion and Improvements
Because of the impending entry of an auxiliary order of sisters, and increasing student registrations (combined high school and college numbers had reached 134), new facilities had to be built.[86] In 1894, Chisholm and his faculty planned a series of expansions at St.F.X. – an enlarged kitchen, a convent for the new congregation of sisters, and an additional storey for the college building. Chisholm, who was secretary-treasurer of the board of governors, presented these plans, as a five-year building program which would cost about $20,000, to the board, and urged that all debts be paid off and construction begun immediately.[87] At this time, the endowment fund totalled $27,546; the college's regular sources of income included a $1500 annual provincial grant for the academy department,[88] tuition fees, endowment fund investment interest, and alms from the Association for the Propagation of the Faith. Over the next few years, St.F.X. financed its building expansion with loans[89] and gifts made to its building fund.

The first phase of the expansion began in May 1895. A new matching brick wing (sixty feet by forty feet), aligned from east to west, was attached to the west wing erected seven years before (currently it connects Aquinas to St Augustine). In obedience to their rector, Father Gillis, the parishioners of St Ninian's once again trekked to the quarry and hauled stone to the college grounds.[90] The new wing, finished before winter at a cost of $8500, had a basement, two storeys, and a mansard. The first floor housed a new kitchen facility, a bakery, and a small dining room for the college farm hands.[91] A laundry, pharmacy, and small workmen's dormitory occupied the second floor; on the third was the college infirmary.[92] Rector Chisholm and his aids completed other college improvements over the next two years – plumbing and hot water heating in both college and convent in 1896, and full electrification by the fall of 1897.[93] Afterwards, a wit commented in the student paper: "Everyone is delighted with Alec Tricity. We have been anxiously awaiting his arrival for some time, and now that he has arrived it is to be hoped that he will remain with us a long time as we need him."[94] "Alec Tricity" never left.

The Entry of the Marthas

By the summer of 1897, a three-storey brick residence, about forty-eight feet square and designed to accommodate twenty-five Sisters of St Martha, had been finished at a cost of $25,000. This "handsome structure" on St Ninian's Street was placed directly west of the new St.F.X. kitchen facility and connected to it by a structure thirty-four feet by twenty-four. The convent was later named Augustine Hall. To prepare for the move of the first sisters from Halifax to Antigonish, Mother Fidelis, the new superior at Mount St Vincent's, made final arrangements with President Chisholm. She appeared less enthusiastic about the Martha venture than her predecessor Mother Bonaventure had been – she might have had good reasons. Vocations to the auxiliary order had been slow, perhaps because of the prospect of exhausting and heavy work. Chisholm confidently assured her that once the new sisterhood had seized the "popular imagination" there would be an avalanche of postulants. Furthermore, he agreed to make things easier for the Marthas by installing a laundry plant at St.F.X. so there would be, in his words, "not a particle of heavy work."[95]

However, Mother Fidelis was not so easily reassured and mollified. She claimed that the Sisters of Charity had trained the Marthas at their own expense; therefore, she felt under no obligation to the college. Fidelis informed Chisholm that the Marthas had not originated with the college's needs in 1894; instead the Sisters of Charity had received Archbishop O'Brien's permission to found such an auxiliary order the year before to undertake the domestic management of their own schools. Apparently, four sisters were then in training at the Sisters of Charity Motherhouse in Wellesley, Massachusetts.[96] The arrangement with St.F.X., she told Chisholm, "has been to me a veritable cold bath ever since I felt it had to be encountered."[97] In spite of these eleventh-hour strains in the negotiations between St.F.X. and the Sisters of Charity in Halifax, and Mother Fidelis's misgivings about her end of the bargain, the agreement survived. In July 1897, ten Marthas –

Original motherhouse of the Sisters of St Martha; now St Augustine's Hall, built in 1897

One of the Marthas at work

professed and novices – under the supervision of three Sisters of Charity, moved into the new convent on the campus and began their arduous work of cooking, washing, mending, cleaning, and nursing. The St.F.X. convent would remain a mission of the Sisters of Charity for the next three years.

The entry of the Marthas marked a new era in hygiene and comfort for the St.F.X. students. Certainly, living conditions in the residences had gradually improved since 1880: a new brick wing had been completed in 1881; a gym erected in 1887; then a second wing had been added in 1888; a further wing, which housed a new kitchen, laundry, and nursing facilities, had been built in 1895; plumbing and hot-water heating had been installed in 1896; and full electrification had been completed in 1897. But the Marthas dramatically transformed the domestic regimen and atmosphere. The "neatness and home-like appearance of the dormitories" and the refectory's "excellent table" revealed their dedication and skill.[98] They ministered effectively to the students in times of sickness and tragedy. The students were especially vulnerable to contagious disease. In a way, the college was a clearinghouse for disease as students, returning from vacation, frequently introduced what they had contacted in their communities. In January 1890, thirty-six cases of the flu had been reported at the college.[99] Student deaths, while infrequent, profoundly moved the small, intimate student body. Two deaths occurred in 1894 – the first ones in twenty-five years – and then one each in 1896, 1899, and 1904.[100] The presence of the Marthas, who quickly gained a reputation for compassion and generosity, helped Xaverians adjust to such harsh realities.

The Appearance of Student Societies
Around the mid-1890s, student societies appeared at St.F.X. From the start, St.F.X. students had no doubt enjoyed the popular activities of drama, debating, and sports. But formally organized and enduring societies, usually supervised by faculty, did not begin until this decade; from then on they remained a staple and prominent part of student life. Professor Horrigan formed the St Cecilia Music Society and Dramatic Association in 1893, and began to train a college choir.[101] A Debating Society appeared. Those interested in Gaelic and their Scottish Highland roots were delighted by Rev. Donald M. MacAdam's Celtic course and his Heather Society (Commun an Fhroaich) which appeared in 1896. Its "sacred mission" was to preserve and venerate "the noble traits of the Gael" and to foster "the tongue in which most of its members first learned to lisp the sacred name of mother."[102] Sometimes it jointly sponsored activities with the supportive Highland

Society of Antigonish, an association which had been formed at least as early as 1861 to preserve and promote the Celtic heritage.[103]

These early student societies at St.F.X., during Chisholm's regime, dealt mainly with the mind and the soul; but the body was not neglected. The Athletic Association probably originated in 1892; its purpose: to provide and organize "the games which constitute the physical exercise of the students."[104] Even local residents and businesses contributed to its fund, which supported sports at St.F.X. The association's early subcommittees sponsored activities such as baseball, lawn tennis, rugby, handball, croquet, and cricket.[105] The first St.F.X. field day was held on the college grounds immediately before the closing exercises in June 1897. Organizers intended it to be "a grand public outdoor exhibition of athletics"; activities included traditional Highland games, baseball, and tug-of-war.[106] By the end of the decade, St.F.X. teams would be competing with teams from the surrounding towns and other Maritime colleges; an intercollegiate hockey league would be established by 1906.[107] Undoubtedly, sports competitions provided entertainment, bolstered college morale and loyalty, and gave the students opportunities to develop athletic skills and prowess.

The student societies offered Xaverians a number of benefits. Academic tensions often ran high and the societies granted a diversion and a means of releasing these pressures.[108] As well, they satisfied the human need for conviviality and the desire to perform and compete. Undoubtedly, they also enriched the educational program of the college by providing opportunities for the students to develop skills in leadership and the arts. Finally, high faculty involvement in the societies' executive positions reinforced the college's paternalism and its close teacher-student relations, which contributed to strong community life.

The Beginning of College Journalism at St.F.X.
It is difficult to measure the vigour and dimensions of student intellectual life at St.F.X. in the 1890s. The main influences on them were the professors, some of whose intellectual, moral, and spiritual stature was formidable, the academic program, and Roman Catholic orthodoxy. In addition to the Debating Society, the students acquired another independent forum for expression and discussion with the inauguration, in October 1896, of a monthly student newspaper, the *Excelsior*.[109] Before this, some students had written an "occasional squib" for the local paper, but, perhaps because of their treatment by "neighboring weeklies," they decided to publish a paper of their own.[110] After the appearance of the first edition, the *Casket* congratulated the rookie editors on their "modest monthly" and judged that it was "quite a promising production"; in a friendly, paternalistic tone, it advised

Mock parliament, 1893

them not to make the student paper a channel for material to be found in the "journalistic sewers of neighboring towns."[111]

Apparently the first student editors, M.A. McAdam and J.W. McIsaac, needed no such advice, as their choice for the journal's title indicated. The tone of their paper would be high and lofty; they would seek to promote noble ideals. Politics would be avoided, since they had concluded that political morality was decadent and such topics would stir up partisanship on campus. The editors stated the paper's main purposes as follows: "the development of literary composition among the students, the uniting more closely of the students of former years with those of the present time, the chronicling of college doings in and out of class and general news."[112] The paper aimed not only for a high and lofty tone but also for a serious and scholarly one. Countless articles appeared on the classics, religion, philosophy, science, major world events, education, and Canadian history. However, the lighter side of life was not overlooked. For example, graduates became the object of gentle satire, and sometimes humour seasoned the *Excelsior*'s pages. Pranks, usually attributed to imaginary societies, like the Society for the Prevention of Useless Appendages and the Society for the Prevention of the Violation of the Laws of Nature as Regards the Removal of Hair, were also chronicled.[113] The student writers generally grappled with issues which were at the forefront of discussion in society. These included topics such as imperial federation, the morality of war, university federation, the role of women, the relation between science and religion, and the place of religion in education. Most often, St.F.X. students echoed the opinions of their Catholic elders, especially if the issues they wrote about had religious implications.

In 1903 the editors of *Excelsior* would change its name to *Xaverian*. By then, they believed that the name "Excelsior" was being devalued in public discourse; it had become, they concluded, "a cheap appellation ... unhappily applied to almost every new patent." Moreover, to them, the new name was "a more fitting representative of the college from which it issued."[114]

Political Controversy Renewed

Shortly before graduation exercises in 1897, the college found itself dragged into a disagreeable media brawl over politics. It followed close on the heels of the provincial election of 20 April, which George Henry Murray's Liberal party had won. The *Eastern Chronicle*, a Liberal organ published in New Glasgow, precipitated a caustic and clever exchange with the rector and the *Casket* by accusing St.F.X. of aiding the Tories in the election campaign. The editor charged that, from

1881, St.F.X. and its preparatory department, which were essentially one, had been receiving a government grant through the generosity of the Liberal party. This exceptional arrangement had been made immediately after the withdrawal of government grants to the denominational colleges, when the Conservatives still held power; no other college received government support in Nova Scotia.[115] The Liberals, who had replaced the Conservatives that year and would remain in power until 1925, had honoured the singular treatment of St.F.X. Yet, in the recent election, the ungrateful college, charged the *Eastern Chronicle*, had sent, or at least allowed, one of its instructors to aid the Tories. Moreover, the bishop and three of his professors were "Tory of the deepest dye"; professors of Liberal stripe had not even dared to cast their votes for fear of losing their positions. It was no secret, the editor continued, that "any of the professors who differed from the political views of the Head of the College [Bishop Cameron] felt the displeasure of this Head by either dismissal or a sort of boycotting. The ablest educationists in the college were quietly sent away or frozen out." Evidently Liberals in the region had carefully marked the Bishop Cameron–Rector McNeil affair of 1891. The editor even claimed that those who borrowed money from the College Endowment Fund – and the numbers were considerable – felt obliged to support the Conservatives. Finally, he alleged that clerical interference in Antigonish represented only one instance of a broader problem, which had been highlighted in the federal election of 1896 when the whole Canadian Catholic hierarchy had challenged the legality of the elimination of separate Catholic schools in Manitoba.[116]

This political artillery fire, which originated in Protestant Pictou County, aroused the fierce ire and indignation of Rector Chisholm.[117] He dissected, attacked, ridiculed, and dismissed the charges of the *Eastern Chronicle*. Professors at the college had a recognized right to their own political opinions; he asserted vigorously that they were not all of one political stripe. And the religious and political sensibilities of the students were always protected, he claimed. Neither was the college indebted to one political party. The editor of the *Eastern Chronicle*, declared the rector, was nothing less than an "inspired idiot" playing party politics.[118] Chisholm wryly offered him one year's free tuition in the St.F.X. preparatory department so he could learn to write "passibly intelligible English" and meditate on the divine commandment: "Thou shalt not bear false witness against thy neighbour." In Chisholm's mind, the opinions of a rabidly anti-Catholic journal like the *Eastern Chronicle* could not be taken seriously. For his part, Bishop Cameron curtly denied that politics ever affected his treatment of the staff at St.F.X.[119] The intensity of indignation expressed by the bishop and rector showed that the Pictou County editor had struck a raw nerve in Antigonish.

The dispute between the college administration and the *Eastern Chronicle* waned and finally petered out. The antagonists had accomplished little; there were no victors. But the controversy shows that St.F.X. paid a price for the political entanglements of its bishop and certain faculty. A.G. MacDonald, a professed Liberal who taught at St.F.X. from 1877 to 1885 and eventually became a Normal School instructor in Truro, told Rector Chisholm in May that St.F.X. had a reputation for rabid Toryism: "the college had in years gone by the name of being a nursery for political machinations against the Grits. No liberal in the diocese of any prominence believed otherwise. I know personally that schemes were concocted when I was on staff to injure, if not ruin me." MacDonald claimed that certain students even assailed him in the columns of the *Casket* for his Liberal sympathies.[120] The Tory reputation of the college was likely strengthened during the federal election of 1896 when Rev. Dr Alexander MacDonald, professor of philosophy and later bishop of Victoria, read a circular on behalf of Bishop Cameron before the parishioners in neighbouring Heatherton.[121] The result was startling: when Dr MacDonald was about to read the circular, which told the faithful it was their duty to vote for the Conservative candidate, sixty of them, later nicknamed the "Heatherton Stampeders," sprang to their feet and bolted from the church.[122] Such periodic machinations by the bishop in favour of the Tory party probably made diocesan Catholics of Liberal persuasion reluctant to send money or offspring to his college, a place many perceived as a Tory stronghold.

The Conclusion of Another Rectorship

Early the next year, in February 1898, Dr Chisholm had to leave the college for an extended trip south; his failing health demanded it.[123] He expected it to be a temporary leave for rest and recuperation. However, the leave became permanent, for when he returned to Nova Scotia in the spring, the bishop appointed him to St Joseph's Parish, North Sydney. The circumstances surrounding his exodus from St.F.X. were not entirely happy. The rector's health was in decline and Bishop Cameron probably wanted to ease the strain caused by heavy administrative duties.[124] One student later claimed that the rector had left St.F.X. "already marked for the tomb."[125] However, Chisholm himself alleged that his superior had plans to remove him from St.F.X. even before his illness because some enemy had successfully assailed his character and administration.[126] His declining health gave the bishop a chance to retire him, and he seized it at once, complained Chisholm.

While he was in Florida, reports of staff changes and "startling departures in discipline" at St.F.X. had distressed him. From these, he
inferred that the bishop had appointed a new rector.[127] For whatever
reasons, Chisholm's rectorship was over. Unfortunately, he only lived
until 1905, when he died at the age of forty-six.[128]

Eulogists claimed that Dr Chisholm had undermined his feeble
health by unremitting work and heroic self-sacrifice at the college;
perhaps they were right.[129] From 1891 he had laboured ceaselessly as
rector, professor, business manager, and college apologist. And his
contributions, with the aid of his bishop and faculty, were significant:
a substantial building program, arrangements for a new congregation
of sisters to care for the college's domestic needs, the impetus for a
new Alumni Association, an expanded course of studies, an ambitious
proposal to consolidate Maritime Catholic higher education at St.F.X.,
and an affiliation agreement with St Bernard's Academy which opened
college-level courses to women. Furthermore, enrolments had continued to mount. At the conclusion of Chisholm's rectorship, some admir-
ers believed St.F.X. had become "the foremost Catholic centre of
advanced education in the Maritime provinces"; in their view, this
achievement was largely to his credit.[130] The growth at St.F.X. had
generated rising ambitions and great optimism. Certainly it had been
a busy, expansive, and, in some ways, controversial decade; and it was
not quite over yet.

PART THREE

The College Goes Progressive, 1898–1921

·6·

New Departures, 1898–1906

Bishop Cameron appointed Vice-Rector Alexander M. Thompson to replace the ailing Rector Chisholm. The new rector would remain at the head of St.F.X. for nearly nine years. He would choose, for compelling reasons, to set a decidedly new course for the college, a course some would laud and others would attack. The college, during Thompson's rectorship, suffered severe growing pains. At times, the cross-fire was deadly as combatants debated how St.F.X. should develop as the new century dawned. Nonetheless, Thompson and his supporters instituted and defended significant new departures, even though some people, both at the college and in its constituency, found them startling.

A New Rector and His Staff
Rev. Dr Thompson, only thirty-two at his appointment to the rectorship, had already taught at St.F.X. for seven years while serving as vice-rector for six. His range of scholarship and teaching spanned the arts, divinity, science, and mathematics; such a breadth of learning preserved him from the tunnel vision of the specialist. He shunned scholars of limited vision and once wondered aloud "which of the two is the greater sinner in this respect, the shallow scientist or the narrow theologian."[1] Thompson emerges as a man of conviction; after he had determined on a course of action or a policy, little could deter him from it. When his appointment was finally announced in June 1898, the *Casket* praised the appointee's scholarship and ability, and judged him a worthy successor to Chisholm.[2] His rectorship was the first exception, since Schulte's (1853–54), to the rule of the Scots at St.F.X. Moreover, Thompson was the first of two priests from Cloverville, a rural community located immediately north of Antigonish, who, in succession, would lead St.F.X. for the next thirty-eight years.

As Thompson assumed the rector's chair, the faculty was shuffled and increased. Thompson and Rev. Dr Alex MacDonald, professor of philosophy and other arts courses since 1884, provided necessary

Rev. Dr Alexander M. Thompson, rector
1898–1906 and founder of the school of
applied science

Rev. Dr Dugald Gillis, professor of philosophy

continuity and stability. Rev. Dr Dugald C. Gillis, a graduate of the Urban College, arrived in 1897 as vice-rector and professor of philosophy, Latin, and Greek. Following a three-year absence (1903 to 1906), Gillis would remain at St.F.X. for nearly two decades.[3] Another Rome-educated alumnus, Rev. Dr Ronald MacDonald of East Bay, Cape Breton, became professor of mathematics in September 1898 and later inherited the vice-rectorship from Gillis.[4] Rev. Lauchlin MacPherson of Cloverville came in 1898 to teach French and history and be the students' spiritual adviser.[5] The next year, Rev. D.V. Phalen was appointed to the college as professor of English literature. Phalen had a knack for journalism and contributed to the *Casket* as writer and editor from 1900 to 1909.[6] Professor Horrigan, the Massachusetts native who had served the college for seven years and had contributed so much to its cultural life, resigned in the spring of 1900 to become an itinerant lecturer.[7] Finally, two other people "from away" added a certain cosmopolitan ambience to college life from 1899 to 1901: Rev. Joseph Defoy, a graduate of the Quebec Académie de Musique, was professor of music, and Professor Heinrich Schonenburger, from St Michael's College, Zug, Switzerland, taught French and German.[8]

Curricular Adjustments

Rector Thompson began to chart a new institutional direction, remarkable, among other things, for its novel departures in program offerings. He planned to expand the curriculum beyond the strictly classical into professional and commercial programs. This strategy, he believed, was demanded by the changing social context, and by his discovery that some students were unsuited for rigorous classical training. Diversification of curricula was a general trend at other colleges in Nova Scotia. Undergraduates enrolled in college arts programs remained dominant in 1900 – there were 522; however, already, 48 had enrolled in science, 84 in medicine, 71 in law, and 63 in theology.[9]

The colleges, by expanding their programs, were responding to broad social changes and to more exacting academic standards demanded by the professions. During most of the nineteenth century the professions of law and medicine had largely supplied their own training independently of the universities. However, gradually the universities did assume responsibility for professional training. In Ontario medical faculties appeared at the University of Toronto in the late 1880s and at Queen's University, Kingston in 1892.[10] At Dalhousie in Nova Scotia, a law faculty was established in 1883 and one in medicine in 1889.[11]

The professional opportunities of St.F.X. graduates expanded with the changing social and economic structure. Critical regional developments had been under way which were deeply affecting the Highland descendants and their Irish and Acadian counterparts. During the final two decades of the nineteenth century, places like Halifax, Yarmouth, New Glasgow, Amherst, and Sydney rapidly industrialized.[12] This development stepped up urbanization in the region, altered the material appearance of the growing towns, and created new institutional demands and social problems.[13] By 1900, Sydney, with its new steel plant, was the most important town in the Diocese of Antigonish. The growth of Nova Scotia's towns and cities promoted further social differentiation and institutional development. Urban expansion created a "more complex social structure to encompass the various gradations of life and work within such towns."[14] New churches, schools, and hospitals appeared, managed by an elite of new professional administrators, financial experts, clerics, lawyers, doctors, and engineers.[15] In 1861, the *Census of Nova Scotia* reported 385 clergymen, 147 lawyers, 205 physicians and surgeons, 86 engineers, and 864 teachers. By 1911 the numbers had vastly increased: 652 clergymen, 249 lawyers, 408 physicians and surgeons, 279 engineers, and 3423 teachers.[16] Such rapid growth in the professions was paralleled by higher enrolments at St.F.X. and demands for new programs.

Therefore, the college announced in 1899 several supplements to its main course of classical study. The faculty offered a new four-year bachelor of letters program which gave students the choice of French or Greek in place of Latin.[17] That same year staff organized a Department of Law. Rector Thompson arranged for three local barristers to give one lecture a week in key areas of jurisprudence – Honourable A. MacGillivray taught constitutional history, C.E. Gregory covered international law, and Joseph A. Wall lectured on contracts. Thereafter, a senior student at St.F.X. could gain credit from the Barristers' Society of Nova Scotia for one year of law school if he satisfied these three conditions: (1) articled with a barrister; (2) attended the lectures in law at St.F.X., and; (3) passed the prescribed examinations.[18] This new curricular excursion into jurisprudence added an important new program which remained in place until the Dalhousie Faculty of Law discontinued its affiliation with Maritime colleges in 1922; from then on law students in Nova Scotia could only acquire their professional training in Halifax.

The Faculty of Applied Science
Together with the bachelor of letters course and the Department of Law, Thompson sponsored another major departure from the curricular status quo: a Faculty of Applied Science or School of Engineering.[19] Nova Scotia's industrial development, he believed, required St.F.X. to provide a course of practical value for students interested in science,

engineering, and technology. Thompson outlined his thinking to Andrew Carnegie, the famous and wealthy American industrialist-philanthropist who, the rector hoped, would aid his new project: "It seemed to us most deplorable that the young men of Nova Scotia ... should lack the opportunities for the technical training which is necessary for their taking a prominent part in the industrial development of their own country, owing to the neglect of their universities to supply them with anything beyond a classical curriculum of studies."[20] To supply this need, Thompson marshalled the necessary resources – staff, money, equipment, and facilities. By the spring of 1899, he was fully convinced of the soundness of his new venture and confided in a friend: "I feel myself urged on so forcibly to the undertaking that I am beginning to regard the impulse as something supernatural."[21] Such a heightened level of conviction gave Thompson the fortitude necessary to overcome all obstacles on the path to curricular reform.[22]

The new applied science program really built on the increasing emphasis which some faculty had placed on science at St.F.X. during the 1880s and 1890s. Science had earlier been taught as a cultural subject through readings, lectures, and demonstrations.[23] During the first decades at St.F.X. one professor had taught a little of every science (then called natural philosophy), largely "by the book"; but gradually a trend of specialization took shape. When Thompson set up the Department of Applied Science, science was to be practised at St.F.X. as well as taught, and primarily for its evident usefulness to society.[24] The new science program offered an amazing array of courses: mathematics, chemistry and analysis, surveying, civil engineering and applied mechanics, descriptive geometry and drawing, mechanical engineering, zoology, geology and mineralogy, botany, physics, and electrical engineering. New science students had to embark on a daunting four-year journey through these fields of study, under the direction of a handful of instructors.

Rector Thompson became the first dean of the Faculty of Applied Science and also its professor of physics. Rev. D. MacAdam, who had been teaching chemistry, botany and geometry at St.F.X. since 1893, left in 1900; he was replaced by Rev. Dr Hugh MacPherson, professor of chemistry and mining. MacPherson would be associated with St.F.X., astonishingly, for the next fifty years, and would come to be known familiarly as "Little Doc Hugh." He had earned a DD and PH D in Rome, and then, on Thompson's recommendation, had studied for another year at the Industrial School connected with the University of Lille in France.[25] Dr Ronald MacDonald became professor of geology and mineralogy; civil engineering and applied mechanics were taught by a local engineer, C.C. Gregory. T.M. Phalen covered mathematics

Rev. Dr Hugh MacPherson ("Little Doc Hugh"),
professor of engineering and geology 1900–50

and mechanical engineering, and G.A. Bernasconi taught descriptive geometry.[26] Thompson also hired George Macdonald of Moncton, a respected electrical engineer, to teach that subject.[27] None of the faculty had specialized undergraduate or postgraduate degrees in science. However, they furthered their expertise in science and technology at summer schools and could draw on considerable practical experience in their fields.

A New Science Building and the Problem of Financing
Of course, Thompson urgently needed larger facilities and technical equipment for the ambitious new science and engineering program. So he decided to erect a three-storey brick wing (ninety feet by forty-five feet) to the south of the existing west wing of the college. It ran north-south and had a connection to the older section and on the opposite end a brick boiler house.[28] The third floor contained rooms for professors and students, the first and second provided classroom space, and the basement housed heavy equipment – engines and dynamos, etc. – and science laboratories.[29] The new structure cost $14,000.[30]

Such costs raised the perennial difficulty of financing. The college's annual income from endowments, revenues, tuition, and government grants totalled about $12,000. St.F.X. commonly obtained some monies with bold appeals in the *Casket* and through fund-raising forays into the parishes by the priest-professors.[31] The low revenues had normally been sufficient for the operation of the college, partly because the teaching clergy were given the most meagre salaries.[32] However, the new programs instituted at Rector Thompson's initiative placed heavy demands on the budget. In 1901, college authorities raised the annual tuition and board to $160, from $130 the year before.[33] In addition, Bishop Cameron appointed one priest to canvass full-time for the college. Father Neil MacDonald, pastor at Arisaig, solicited throughout the diocese[34] and beyond into the New England states; he even approached Andrew Carnegie.[35] The bishop himself donated $3000 to his college.[36] The Alumni Association as well schemed and planned for their *alma mater.*[37] In 1903 a special committee petitioned the bishop to have an annual "College Sunday" collection in the diocese for St.F.X. The committee hoped the yearly offering would become a "popular and effective means of securing the present and future prosperity and prestige of Saint Francis Xavier College."[38] Both bishop and clergy supported the scheme,[39] and, in its first year, they collected about $4300.[40]

In spite of being frequently reminded that St.F.X. was important to their progress, power, prestige, and dignity, Catholics in eastern Nova Scotia did not support the college as Rector Thompson thought they should.[41] He expressed surprise that, considering the quality of work done at St.F.X., it should "nevertheless be so little prized or estimated at its true worth by our own people." He even wondered if the lack of support resulted from a sense of inferiority on the part of the Irish and Highland Scots who had long been oppressed, and had come to think that their "more triumphant adversaries" were intrinsically superior. Such oppressed peoples, he reasoned, came to view things "home-made" as inferior to what the "dominant nation can produce." Thompson himself humbly viewed St.F.X. as the best college in the Maritimes and believed its constituency, instead of neglecting it, should "boom" it on every possible occasion.[42]

Notwithstanding the withdrawal of the college grants in 1881, the government had remained an important source of revenue for St.F.X. since its founding in 1853. Given this fact, as well as his conviction that the new Department of Engineering would provide a public service, Thompson decided to lobby the province for support. A deputation travelled to Halifax in March 1901 with a petition, "largely signed" in the mining districts of eastern Nova Scotia, for a grant of $6000.[43] The petition argued that the development of mining was vital to Nova Scotia, that Antigonish occupied a convenient location, and that facilities had already been readied in the town.[44] The petitioners also vigorously opposed proposals for the construction and endowment of a central engineering school; the anticipated expense, they predicted, would be outrageous and local jealousies would certainly be aroused. They underscored the undoubted fact that Nova Scotia's diverse educational institutions had firmly rooted themselves in the sympathy and confidence of its various peoples.[45] To clinch the case in favour of St.F.X., they maintained that it had already qualified itself to carry forward advanced scientific instruction; therefore, it had first claim on the largesse of the legislature.

The government stalled. An impatient Rector Thompson told Premier George H. Murray, a Victoria County Presbyterian who was premier from 1896 to 1923, that he suspected the denominational connection at St.F.X. was giving his Liberal government cold feet. So he reminded the premier of two things: first, that denominationalism had "no formal connexion" with the school of applied science, and second, that government support for St.F.X. would gain for it a favourable political effect in eastern Nova Scotia. Thompson also feared that his college's move into technical education would elicit competition from other schools which would quickly enter the field.[46]

Affiliation with the Nova Scotia Technical College
The rector's fears were well founded. After failing to obtain government support, Dalhousie organized a School of Mining Engineering

in 1902, and King's, in 1905, started a School of Engineering in Sydney.[47] Mount Allison and Acadia were offering two years of engineering, a program which could be completed at McGill. The universities were responding to a growing chorus of reformers demanding more practical, useful education so Nova Scotians could capitalize on their abundant natural resources, stimulate economic growth, and reduce outmigration.[48] But the new utilitarian programs, which had also been appearing at the major universities in Ontario,[49] placed Premier Murray and his Liberals in an awkward position. The government could ill afford to support all the applied science schools; nor could it risk favouring one, as St.F.X. pleaded.[50] Eventually, members of the Nova Scotia Mining Society proposed a compromise: the colleges should teach the first two years of a technical program and a central, government-sponsored college in Halifax should provide the last two years.[51] St.F.X., by then under the administration of a successor to Thompson, with the other Nova Scotia colleges, accepted the compromise as "in the interest of all, and of the country at large."[52] The government passed the Technical Education Act of 1907, which authorized it to establish the Nova Scotia Technical College at Halifax.[53] From 1909, when the new college opened under the principalship of F.H. Sexton, the St.F.X. applied science program was scaled down from a four-year to a two-year course; through its affiliation with the college at Halifax, St.F.X. students from then on could complete the engineering program there.[54] Subsequent negotiations between St.F.X. and McGill, in 1914, would give students the further option of finishing their engineering program in Montreal.[55]

The first St.F.X. graduates to obtain the bachelor of science degree completed their programs in 1904.[56] Thereafter, very few science degrees were awarded – only about five more by 1920; most students followed the engineering course, which they had to complete at the Nova Scotia Technical College. The students had little apparent interest in science for its own sake. However, the establishment of the Department of Applied Science marked the end of the monopoly held by the traditional liberal-classical education at St.F.X. which had been constructed in the nineteenth century. Now it had to share an expanding curricular field with the sciences and technical subjects. Economic utility was becoming an important educational emphasis at St.F.X., as it was elsewhere in Nova Scotia.[57] The college began to participate in a national trend discovered by Patricia Jasen: "from now on, the wants of society, not the dictates of a metaphysical system, would openly determine the content and structure of higher education."[58]

The Rector's Plans for the St.F.X. High School

Rector Thompson was also attracted by the idea of introducing more diversity into the high school curriculum in response to the changing social and economic conditions of Nova Scotia. In February 1902, the *Casket* announced the opening of a school of manual training situated in the former St.F.X. gymnasium. Boys from the town schools – 193 during the first half-year – were scheduled in for a few hours each week.[59] Thompson, the promoter of the project, ensured that the manual training school was fully equipped and competently run. He hired Alexander Sutherland, a graduate of the MacDonald Manual Training School recently founded in Truro. This school had been named after Sir William C. MacDonald, a Canadian philanthropist and advocate of manual training for boys. Such training, apparently, was meant to serve several purposes: to promote literary studies through regular, refreshing diversions from them, to promote the mental and moral powers of the child through training of the hand, to prepare students for further studies in technology, and "to divert the flow of young people from the overcrowded professions into the various useful trades."[60] Manual training did not amount to technical education; rather it involved exercises in simple activities like woodworking and drawing.[61] Thompson, the local Antigonish school board, and many of the town's parents were sold on the idea; together they obtained a small government grant to finance it.[62]

The St.F.X. rector introduced a second supplement into the high school course of studies in 1902 and formalized it in 1903. This was a department of commerce. J.M. Almon, a non-Catholic and the late principal of the Nova Scotia Business College in Yarmouth, was hired to supervise the department.[63] It aimed to provide "a first-class business education for boys and young men destined for commercial pursuits." The college announced that the program was a response to "a long-felt want, and in accordance with the suggestion of some of the best business men in our constituency." Two different courses of study were offered by the department: a shorthand course, which included, predictably, shorthand, typewriting, correspondence, penmanship, and orthography (spelling), and a business course, which consisted of bookkeeping, commercial arithmetic, penmanship, correspondence, commercial law, orthography, business practice, and banking. Almon's new department emphasized the practical; its motto advised: "Let the search light of practice illuminate the dark places of theory." St.F.X. high school students could complete the commercial program in four to eight months; if they passed a final examination, their reward was either a business or a shorthand diploma.[64]

For unknown reasons, the St.F.X. Academy or Preparatory Department began to acquire more formal status or distinctness during Thompson's rectorship. A new name appeared – "The Collegiate School of St John the Baptist" – and soon afterwards a calendar separate from the St.F.X. prospectus.[65] Grades nine to eleven had been retained by St.F.X. after its move from College Street to the campus on St Ninian's Street in 1881; thereafter, the high school had achieved academy status. The academy staff had never been fully distinct from the college faculty, and its supervision had always been subsumed under the general administration of the college. From 1900, Rev. H.D. Barry replaced M.A. MacAdam as headmaster of the Collegiate School.[66] Antigonish townspeople profited financially and educationally by having St.F.X. run the academy, for the institution shared the buildings owned by the college corporation; furthermore, selected courses were taught by its highly trained faculty.[67] Of course, providing and controlling a preparatory department also benefited the college both financially and academically. After 1881, it had obtained and then retained the government's county academy grant; the St.F.X. high school, moreover, provided a steady supply of adequately and evenly prepared freshmen for the college program.

The Collegiate School at St.F.X. essentially encompassed a three-year course of study, grades nine to eleven. Any student who successfully completed the course and final examination achieved university matriculation in arts or applied science at St.F.X. The school tried to accept only those students prepared for the first year of high school, but from 1894–95 authorities felt compelled to form classes for grades seven and eight.[68] The school administration then adopted the policy of placing boys less than thirteen years of age under the supervision of the Marthas. Thompson explained why: "we found it impossible to have very small children attend to the neatness of their person, etc., unless they were under the supervision of women. One of the sisters is always on hand to see that they are kept clean and that their clothing is attended to."[69] The Marthas evidently worked, not only as domestics at St.F.X., but also as surrogate mothers.[70] The high school students lived mostly in residence. According to college authorities, their emulation of the older college students was, at times, misplaced. Certain college students acted as bad examples, chewing tobacco and holding the college rules in contempt. Student prefects were sometimes accused of bullying, even abusing, the younger students.[71] Sixty-one boys enrolled in 1903–4 and only twenty-one of these came from the town; the rest hailed from throughout the diocese, and even from Halifax, Saint John, the Magdalen Islands, and Ontario.[72]

St.F.X. High School, class of 1904

The Marthas Separate from the Charities

By 1900, St.F.X. had benefited from the domestic service of the Sisters of St Martha for three years. Thompson and the clergy of the diocese expressed great satisfaction with their performance.[73] Their work – sweeping, dusting, bed-making, laundering, cooking, baking, nursing, and mothering – and their "feminine touch" undoubtedly created "a more homelike atmosphere at the university."[74] One Martha later reflected, "eventually the College, from being a little better than barracks, became more homelike, more orderly and by far a better place to live in … On the whole there was a striking contrast between the 'old order' and the 'new.'"[75] The new order was created through exhausting work poorly rewarded; the Marthas' vows of poverty, chastity, and obedience gave St.F.X. a great financial advantage and would continue to do so for over fifty years.

Although Mother Fidelis, the superior of the Sisters of Charity (the Charities) in Halifax, was disgruntled with the low number of new postulants to her auxiliary order, a total of thirty-one had gone from the Diocese of Antigonish between 1894 and 1900.[76] Since she had sent only seven to Antigonish, and unfortunately appeared reluctant to send more, Bishop Cameron decided to establish an order of Marthas independent from the Halifax Charities and their auxiliary order.[77] When the end of the Marthas' probationary period arrived in July 1900, Bishop Cameron offered those at Mount St Vincent the opportunity to join an independent order or to remain with the Halifax Charities. Apparently thirteen decided to leave and move to Antigonish.[78] By the end of July, the Marthas held their first provisional election for a superior; Sister Mary Innocentia MacNamara was chosen. St Martha's convent at St.F.X. became the motherhouse and opened a novitiate. The three Charities, who had supervised the work at St.F.X. from 1897, returned to Mount St Vincent.

The new community also adopted a constitution which affirmed their specific devotion to the work at St.F.X. As well, it placed the community, in temporal matters, under the authority of the St.F.X. board of governors and the bishop; a council, composed of the rector, the vice-rector, and another college priest, were granted the power to decide the eligibility of applicants to the community and to give permission for novices to make profession. For its part, the college was responsible for full financial support of the community. Each sister was allowed a monthly wage of $2. By the end of 1902, the Marthas had grown to thirty-four, including postulants.[79] Their work would very soon expand beyond the college walls – even far outside the diocese – into health care, education, and other forms of social service;[80] and as this happened, the young congregation would press for and achieve by

1920 administrative independence from St.F.X. However, from the college's dire domestic needs had arisen the initial impulse to form the community, and the Marthas had given these needs "a preferential place."[81] Because of this early close association, a special and enduring bond developed between the Marthas and St.F.X. In a way, the college had been "the cradle" of the congregation.[82]

Attack on Thompson's "New Departures"

The new order created at St.F.X. by Rector Thompson and his allies did not please everyone; on the contrary, the departures were distressing to some – they felt impelled to challenge them. Rev. Dr Alex MacDonald, a fellow Urban College alumnus and a seventeen-year St.F.X. veteran who had served as prefect of studies and professor of Latin, English, and philosophy, emerged as the leading dissident. MacDonald was Thompson's senior by seven years, and in 1900 had become the bishop's vicar-general. He was a formidable opponent and appeared to fire the first weighty shot at the rector in June 1901. In a long and caustic letter, which concluded with a threat of resignation if things remained unchanged, he appealed to Bishop Cameron and laid before him a series of damaging charges. These attacked Thompson's novel regime: college discipline, coeducation, St.F.X.'s *raison d'être*, its financial management, and the rector's administrative style.

MacDonald asserted that Thompson imposed little discipline on the students, who were allowed, he claimed, to run rampant through the college buildings at recreation times, and to enter the town at will. Under Chisholm's rule, the boys had only been permitted to go to town on Thursdays if they had specific business to discharge. Moreover, MacDonald attacked Thompson's innovative practice of having girls from Mount St Bernard take regular classes with the boys at the college. Again, during Chisholm's rectorship, a few professors had taught selected courses at the convent, and some of the boys in the higher grades had even been allowed to attend; but MacDonald did not think the desire to reduce salaries and eliminate the duplication of classes justified the new "abuses." He also charged that the natural sciences had been receiving more than their proper share of the interest, solicitude, and monies of the college.[83] This trend, combined with lax discipline and coeducation, was eroding the primary object of St.F.X. In MacDonald's mind, this always was and should always remain the preparation of young men for the priesthood. He called for a return to the old order.[84]

MacDonald's criticisms were not exhausted by these issues alone. He described Rector Thompson as "a full-fledged autocrat, arbitrary and whimsical, who seeks counsel of no one and brooks no opposition to his imperious will." Thompson, maintained MacDonald, utterly disregarded the board of governors and the members of his staff. The new regime of loose discipline, coeducation, expanded facilities, and curricular expansion into the applied sciences had been imposed unilaterally from above; there had been no consultation. Moreover, Thompson had instituted tuition hikes which would make St.F.X. into an elitist school for the sons of the wealthy; and his practice of allowing boys who could afford it to rent private rooms introduced undesirable distinctions between the poor and the wealthy students. MacDonald demanded the end of "one-man rule," the development of a council of priests to investigate his charges against the rector, and the formation of a senate to administer college funds, control discipline, and report regularly to the board of governors.[85]

To what extent Rector Thompson, his antagonist MacDonald, and the other professors had personal exchanges on these issues is now apparently impossible to know. But the tensions must have, at times, made the atmosphere electric in the college. Other key faculty members, like the vice-rector, Rev. Dr Ronald MacDonald, Rev. Dr Dugald Gillis, Rev. Ronald Beaton, and Rev. D.V. Phalen, appeared to share MacDonald's discontent.[86] And it seems that Dr Alex MacDonald, who was elected president of the Alumni Association in 1902, at least had its backing for regular meetings of the board of governors.[87] The news of the new departures at the college, and rumours of the controversies that swirled around them, also spread throughout the diocese and were, no doubt, embellished. In 1902, a disturbed alumnus in Sydney wrote to Thompson: "startling stories are being whispered around about the discipline – or want of discipline – prevailing in the college during the past two or three years." The stories were of students sneaking away from the college, of intoxification, and of "clandestine meetings" with the opposite sex.[88] Such stories were bound to mar the reputation of the college and perhaps erode its financial base. Some parish priests, it seems, were so opposed to Thompson's regime at St.F.X. that they advised prospective students to boycott it and attend college outside the diocese.[89]

The Rector's Defence
However, Thompson was not easily deterred from the course he had set for St.F.X.; on the contrary, he defended his actions vigorously. In retrospect, he confessed that, at times, he even gave evidence of his Irish ancestry.[90] When he heard that accusations were being made against him at Rome, Thompson was especially aroused. He asked that Propaganda officials investigate through the appropriate channels or directly present him with the complaints of each accuser. He wrote:

"You can see how difficult it is to defend oneself against hidden accusers and against accusations I know nothing about."[91] Sometimes he seemed to think there was a plot or a conspiracy against him, or some in the diocese who were intent, for whatever reasons, to ruin the reputation of the college. In 1903, he told a friend, "There is a certain element in this Diocese that regards it not only justifiable but even commendable to resort to lying and any other means diabolical in order to ruin the characters of their fellow men so long as by doing so they may have a chance of reflecting on the College."[92]

Thompson's way of reacting to attacks on his rectorship was no doubt rooted in the idiosyncrasies of his own personality. But his college policies were based on firm convictions, and these convictions he articulated and defended. St.F.X. must, he declared, expand into science and technology to meet the requirements of changing times and thus better serve the people of the diocese. Furthermore, the classics were not the sole means of intellectual training and development: "Experience teaches us that many whose minds seem specially fitted for a study of the sciences find in the Classics but little stimulus for mental exertion, and vice versa."[93] And Thompson argued that his administrative style had not been chosen arbitrarily either, but on the basis of careful thought. He believed his rectorship was democratic in the proper way, namely, that the board of governors had elected him and it had the power to remove him at will. But once chosen as rector he should then be granted the power to administer routine college affairs and to stamp "his own personality upon the work in which he is engaged." Thompson thought that an annual report and answers to direct queries from the board were sufficient; indeed, he claimed the board had disapproved of the procedure of calling them together when he faced either a minor or a major decision.[94] He noted, "the binding of a college president to consult the members of the Board of Governors tends to cripple his powers in furthering the interests of the college." When he consulted the long-time president of Harvard, Charles Eliot, for his views on the proper relation between the university administration, faculty, and board, however, Thompson received little confirmation of his own approach.[95] Eliot's heavyweight opinion must have given Thompson pause; it is uncertain whether it convinced him to become more collegial and consensual in administrative style.

On the issue of student discipline, Thompson was definitely not prepared to retreat from his more light-handed approach. If it appeared lax to hard-liners, then so be it. In a letter to a concerned parent, Thompson frankly stated his own sentiments on discipline, and those which governed his relations to the students: "There are little defects in a college of boys, for which the remedies suggested by some are worse than the diseases which they are intended to cure. Such remedies constitute what is called the French discipline, a system which will never be introduced into this college so long as I am its rector. Boys who need such discipline should be sent to a convent, not to a college." He later referred to this approach as the "French spy system" and continued, "keeping a boy in a cradle or putting him under strict espionage until he reaches manhood does not suit our English speaking boys. What we endeavour to do here is steer between the lawlessness of some modern colleges on the one hand and on the other, that mean espionage which almost inevitably results in forming either ninnies or toughs."[96] Thompson evidently thought of himself as an advocate, in discipline, of the golden mean.

The contention of Thompson's contemporaries that he was an innovator in discipline implies that something similar to the so-called "French spy system" was in vogue at St.F.X. before his rectorship. Rector Chisholm, his predecessor, had been known as a firm disciplinarian; all student reading material had to be approved by college authorities and personal correspondence was "subject to the inspection of the Rector."[97] When Thompson travelled from St.F.X. to Rome as a student of theology in the late 1880s, he heard of a different system and found it much more congenial.[98] This was the approach which had been developed by Don Bosco, the Italian founder of the Salesians, an order he had started in Italy in 1859; it had then spread worldwide. The Salesians dedicated themselves to the Christian education of youth. Bosco's educational approach, called the Salesian preventive system of education, forbade corporal punishment and minimized the temptation to sin by placing youths in appropriate surroundings. E.F. Fardellone writes, "Frequent confession and Communion, thorough catechical training, and fatherly guidance were the pillars of this system of the spiritual life of youths with their study, work, and play." The system appeared to stress the norms of reason, religion, amiability, and fatherliness. Bosco also required that youth be taught trades; this apparently made him a "pioneer in modern vocational training."[99] Thompson's initiation of vocational training at St.F.X., and his new system of discipline, show he was a disciple of Bosco. Indeed, while in Rome, he had tried to see Bosco and considered him "one of God's most chosen saints." It was to Bosco's educational philosophy that he appealed in the controversy over student discipline at St.F.X.[100]

The Rector's Victory

It appears, at least from the side of those opposed to Thompson's new order at St.F.X., that the disputes which erupted reached an unsatisfactory conclusion. No evidence exists that the besieged president backed down on any of his new departures or that he was converted to a different administrative style. Presumably, neither the board of governors nor Bishop Cameron intervened to force his hand. Neither is there evidence that his detractors had the general support of other lay and clerical staff. Apparently the controversy cooled, but did not vanish altogether, as the advocates of the "ancien régime" were gradually transferred away from the college; Thompson outstayed nearly all of them. The vice-rector, Ronald MacDonald, had found his partnership with Thompson uncomfortable, and, from his new parish in 1902, complained to Thompson of his "unceremonious dismissal" from the college.[101] Rev. D.V. Phalen left in 1901, and Rev. Dr D.C. Gillis two years after.[102] The chief spokesman for the dissidents, Rev. Dr Alex MacDonald, submitted his resignation in 1902, but the bishop, for reasons unknown, delayed one more year before transferring him to a parish.[103] Thompson, the primary cause of the turn-of-the-century tempest at St.F.X., remained rector until November 1906.

Celebration of St.F.X.'s Jubilee
In the fall of 1905, the same year Alberta and Saskatchewan in the west joined confederation and before Thompson's exit, St.F.X. celebrated in grand style its fiftieth anniversary.[104] The town, college, convent, and cathedral were lavishly decorated for the influx of hundreds of enthusiastic visitors and the convivial events – processions, speeches, sermons, receptions, presentations, suppers, and entertainments – planned for 6 and 7 September. The sudden crowd of guests caused the small town to stagger under the heavy demand for accommodation. The celebration provided a marvellous opportunity for all concerned to reminisce, to boast, and to affirm their loyalty and enthusiasm for the triumphant college. The campus rink was "festooned with the national and papal colors" for a major event in the afternoon of the 6th, when Rector Thompson addressed a large crowd of alumni, students, residents, and prominent guests. At the end of his speech, degrees were awarded to seventeen graduates; twenty-one honorary doctor of laws degrees were conferred on an elite cast which included Dr A.H. McKay, the Nova Scotia superintendent of education, George H. Murray, the premier of Nova Scotia, Robert L. Borden, the leader of the federal Conservatives and future prime minister, Rev. Dr Falconer, principal of Pine Hill Divinity College (Presbyterian), Rev. Dr Forrest, president of Dalhousie University, Rev. Dr Emery, rector of Ottawa University, and the Right Rev. Dr James Morrison, vicar-general of the Diocese of Charlottetown. Superintendent McKay would later report to the Nova Scotia legislature that St.F.X. had celebrated its golden jubilee "in splendid form" and with

the "harmonious cooperation of its sister universities." He believed the occasion was both "an epoch-making event in the development of interdenominational courtesy"[105] and the first "fraternal meeting of the representatives of our universities."[106] The presence of such an august body of administrators and public men surely gratified the aging Bishop Cameron and flattered the college administration; it was a very public stamp of approval on the conquests and accomplishments of their small diocesan college.

Thompson's rectorial address was marked by a spirit of both triumphalism and eulogy.[107] He eloquently underscored the great odds overcome by the college: the penurious circumstances of its birth before confederation and its roots among the Scots, Irish, and Acadians, people who had faced and overcome intense suffering and hardship. "The leaders of this brave and faithful people," he declared, "saw the necessity of a seat of learning. The marks left by the shackles of oppression had not yet completely disappeared, and no surer means could there be of erasing forever the brand of social inferiority than the college." It had become their "glory and ... pride." Thompson was convinced, in 1905, that his beloved college had succeeded in removing the Highland Scottish, Irish, and Acadian legacy of poverty, oppression, and inferiority.[108]

Undoubtedly the college, founded and maintained through sacrifice and effort, had done much for the Catholics of eastern Nova Scotia – especially those of Highland descent – and had fulfilled, beyond expectation, the hopes and dreams of its founder and supporters. Moreover, it was probably partly true that the accomplishments of its graduates redounded to the glory and increased prestige not only of the college but also of the entire diocese. Yet many Catholics in eastern Nova Scotia would have viewed with scepticism the golden jubilee celebration of social mobility and broadened influence. Poverty continued to plague many, and the flow of migrants away from the diocese remained unabated. The forte of the college's classical curriculum had been the preparation of a fortunate minority for the learned professions. Finally, social advance and respectability had been achieved at some cultural cost. The drive to obtain economic prosperity and social equality had eroded the rich legacy of Highland tradition and the strong sense of ethnic identity among the Scots of eastern Nova Scotia.[109] But in 1905, few descendants of the Highlanders lamented this erosion of their distinct culture; most appeared willing to exchange it for the promises and rewards of assimilation.[110] For in this way, they could erase forever "the brand of social inferiority" and become more than mere "hewers of wood and drawers of water for their non-Catholic neighbors."[111]

Old Bishop Cameron sat with the platform party during the rector's speech, and Thompson extravagantly honoured him as the "father of this institution," the one who resurrected it from a near-moribund state, and the one who was responsible for its present standing.[112] Likewise, he praised the faithful support of the clergy and the laity. Surveying the college's past progress, and the dedication of its supporters, he prophesied that providence had a "brilliant future" in store for it.[113]

Commencement exercises at Mount St Bernard followed the event at the rink; then, at last, supper and musical entertainment. At eight in the evening in St Ninian's Cathedral, Rev. Dr James Morrison, vicar-general of Charlottetown, sermonized on Ecclesiasticus 44: "Let us now praise men of renown and our fathers in their generation ..."[114] The busy and exciting day concluded with a reception hosted by Bishop Cameron on the lawn of Mount St Bernard College. Apparently, the scene was beautiful and "fairy-like"; Chinese lanterns illuminated the grounds, the crowd milled to and fro, bands "enlivened the air with their sweet and soul-stirring melodies," and the college building was ablaze in outline from lights specially mounted for the grand occasion. The next day included a meeting of the Alumni Association, who used the jubilee to raise funds for the college,[115] and then, finally, adulatory speeches in the rink from those leading men whom St.F.X. had awarded honorary degrees.[116] For the participants, the golden jubilee festivities had been a success in every way. The *Casket* reported: "Antigonish put on its best attire on Wednesday and proceeded to cull out a holiday such as can be enjoyed only once in fifty years."[117]

The Achievements of Fifty Years
In spite of a rough ride at frequent points along the way, St.F.X. had accomplished much in its short fifty-year pilgrimage. It had provided the Catholics of eastern Nova Scotia, male and female, with expanded opportunities in higher education and with a growing body of socially mobile graduates who had entered both the professions and public life. An incomplete alumni list for the institution's first fifty years appeared in 1905; it recorded 1238 names.[118] Of these, at least 58 per cent were of Highland descent.[119] One hundred and eighteen had entered the religious ministry, sixty-two had become lawyers, and seventy-five had established medical practices. The college had educated no fewer than eight Scottish Catholics who served in the provincial legislature; several more had become MPs.[120] Moreover, among the elite graduates there were two bishops, three supreme court judges, one county court judge, one dominion senator, and more than ten professors.[121] The list

shows that the college's work had introduced significant differences in economic and social standing into the Highland Catholic community of eastern Nova Scotia, differences apparently based largely on "professional occupation rather than entrepreneurial activity."[122] Moreover, the college had furthered the interests of the Roman Catholic Church by training an indigenous body of priests and lay Catholic teachers for the diocese. Locally, it had enriched the cultural life of the town of Antigonish, and its demands for food, supplies, and labour had benefited the local economy. By the time of its jubilee celebration in 1905, a larger faculty taught a much more diversified curriculum in more ample and efficient buildings. The original, primary object of preparing students for the priesthood had slowly been eclipsed by the need to develop lay leaders for secular work.[123] The college's endowment fund was slowly growing, and its domestic needs were confidently and efficiently cared for by the new Sisters of St Martha. The student body had increased and was more diverse in origin. People had become more conscious of academic degrees and the first ones had been granted to Catholic women. Thus, real substance underlay the celebratory rhetoric of the jubilee events in 1905.[124]

The Harried Rector's Departure

Rector Thompson remained at St.F.X. little more than one year after the 1905 jubilee celebrations. For several years, he had been pressing Bishop Cameron for a transfer to parish life. Finally, the bishop, who viewed Thompson, rightly or wrongly, as a "victim of cruel persecution," reluctantly capitulated and moved him to St Anne's Parish, Glace Bay in November 1906; he would remain there for the next eighteen years.[125] His controversial nine-year rectorship had substantially altered the St.F.X. ethos: the disciplinary regimen had been relaxed and the curriculum broadened to include programs in law, applied science, manual training, and commerce.[126] The students profoundly regretted that their warm-hearted and progressive rector had to leave.[127] They felt he had related to them as "a gentleman to gentlemen" and had kept St.F.X. abreast of the times through new buildings and programs.[128] A *Xaverian* editor claimed that Rector Thompson had "greatly stimulated the power of this institution and widened its beneficent influence upon life in these Provinces."[129] However, Thompson insisted on being removed from the front line.

·7·

Soaring Ambitions,
1906–14

Wilfrid Laurier, Liberal prime minister of Canada 1896–1911, predicted that the twentieth century would be Canada's century. That optimism seemed to infuse St.F.X. through the century's opening decade and beyond, even surviving the ordeal of war. After Thompson's rocky rectorship, the controversies evoked by his new departures subsided. And in 1906, St.F.X. acquired a new president[1] who helped to inaugurate a long era of relative stability and incremental change.[2] He would be assisted by a dynamic vice-president, ambitious for the college and ardent for progress and advance. Indeed, to a considerable extent, the new vice-president inspired the college's optimistic tone for the next fifteen years. He would enliven the sentiment of "for the people" and give it fresh meaning.

Administrative Shuffle
Thompson's successor, a tall, stately, endearing priest who shared his predecessor's convictions about student discipline, was Rev. Dr Hugh P. MacPherson of Cloverville, Antigonish County (not to be confused with "Little Doc Hugh" MacPherson, the chemist who had come in 1900). MacPherson, a St.F.X. alumnus, had graduated from the Grand Seminary, Quebec. In May 1892, his bishop, urgently needing a priest for Arichat, had recalled him to the diocese before the completion of his theological course. The young MacPherson had then remained in parish work for the next fourteen years. In October 1906, with little teaching background, and lacking the usual Urban College experience which most earlier rectors had, Bishop Cameron appointed him president of St.F.X. Cameron considered him to be the "most competent person available" to replace Thompson.[3] MacPherson was just thirty-nine years old at his debut as college president in Antigonish. The Grand Seminary, at Bishop Cameron's request, had recently conferred on him an honorary doctorate – in Cameron's view, a fitting symbol of rank for his new college president. Visitors and correspondents alike

Rev. Dr Hugh P. MacPherson
("the Old Rector"), rector 1906–36

soon found MacPherson a charming, hospitable, witty, and humorous individual. Some were delighted with his talents as a fiddler and songster. MacPherson was a character, and his peculiar habits, especially his absent-mindedness, and his exceptionally long tenure as president, fuelled innumerable anecdotes about him, many scarcely believable. His personality and scholarly bent – he had a superb knowledge of philosophy, theology, and the classics, as well as marked ability in modern languages – appeared to qualify him well for his new assignment.[4]

Shortly after MacPherson's transfer to the college, Father Jimmy Tompkins became vice-president.[5] This was a key promotion. Tompkins had been placed at St.F.X. on his return in 1902 from graduate studies in Rome. A native of Margaree, Cape Breton, he had, with great determination, worked his way through college by alternate study and teaching. While he was making good progress in his program at the Urban College, the delicate state of his health forced him to return to Nova Scotia before acquiring the usual doctoral degrees.[6] Although a rather frail, diminutive individual, with a pale complexion, thin face, and grey eyes, Tompkins was a most capable, intense, dynamic young priest who showed great promise; physically and intellectually he remained constantly on the move. As vice-president, he was responsible for fund-raising; before long, he also assumed the added duties of director of studies.[7]

President MacPherson and Vice-President Tompkins, along with Rev. Ronald Beaton, Michael J. McIntyre, and Rev. John H. MacDonald, covered the courses in ancient and modern languages. Dr Dugald Gillis, back at St.F.X. after several years in parish work, delivered weighty lectures in the philosophical disciplines. Courses in English were taught by Joseph A. Wall, a local lawyer. Rev. D.J. MacIntosh, also bursar, gave the religion course called Christian doctrine. Town talent continued to teach the several courses in law: Honourable Judge MacGillivray, C.E. Gregory, E. Lavin Girroir (later senator), and Allan MacDonald. Students in the sciences, mathematics, and engineering had Dr Hugh MacPherson, Clarence M. Allen, Michael J. McIntyre, J.J. Cameron, MD, and Walter Shea. Thomas Horrigan, the New England import, returned from his lecture circuit to teach elocution for two years. Of this faculty of about fifteen full- and part-time professors and lecturers, only two had earned doctorates, six had masters' degrees, and the remaining had bachelors' degrees. The staff was exclusively male; about one-half were of Scottish background, and around the same proportion were priests.

Xaverian Scholars

The new MacPherson-Tompkins administration and staff supervised and taught a student body which had grown substantially since the founding of St.F.X. over fifty years before. The main characteristics of the students and the features of their college life had changed in important ways. Most students still came from Catholic homes in eastern Nova Scotia; however, "Capers" and those from outside the diocese – even from outside the province – had increased in proportion. The college's constituency was expanding.[8] Of a total enrolment in 1885–86 of sixty-one, about one-half came from Antigonish County and only 28 per cent from Cape Breton. Twenty years later, 115 students attended St.F.X. Then, only 29 per cent came from within the county while 36 per cent journeyed from Cape Breton.[9] At least two factors account for this trend. First, the rail connections between Antigonish and the Strait of Canso (1880), and from Sydney to the strait (1891), helped Islanders get to St.F.X. Second, industrialization, centred around coal mining and steel manufacture in the Sydney–Glace Bay region, had spurred substantial urban growth there. The population of Cape Breton in 1891 was 34,244; by 1901 it had jumped to 49,166, and the populations of both Sydney, the largest town in the diocese, and Glace Bay had more than doubled in the same decade. That area received a stream of immigrants from Russia, Scandinavia, the British Isles, the United States, southeastern Europe, and Newfoundland anxious to find work in the mines and steel industry.[10] In contrast, during the same ten-year period, the population of Antigonish County declined from 16,114 to 13,617.[11] These shifts in the distribution and concentration of people within the diocese affected the origins of St.F.X. students.

The upswing by 1906 in the numbers of non-diocesan students and non–Nova Scotians was probably related to the college's growing reputation, the informal recruitment of new students by St.F.X. alumni, regional improvements in roads and rail, and outmigration. This last factor might have been the key. In 1904–5, 11 per cent of the St.F.X. student body were from Nova Scotia outside of the Diocese of Antigonish, 16 per cent were New Brunswick natives, and small numbers came from Prince Edward Island, Ontario, Quebec, and the New England states.[12] Many of these latter were drawn to St.F.X. because their families had roots in eastern Nova Scotia. Decades before, whole families and young singles had started a massive exodus from the Maritimes.[13] Andrew Clark estimates, "Between 1871 and 1921 the emigration of native-born from the three Maritime Provinces amounted to some four hundred thousand people."[14] In the early 1880s, a well-travelled correspondent had written to an Antigonish newspaper, claiming that "Natives of Cape Breton are becoming as ubiquitous as the black crow of common nationality."[15] Of all the ethnic groups in Nova Scotia, those of Scottish background most often travelled down the road.[16] Through recruitment, nostalgia, or loyalty, the sons or friends of these expatriates sometimes made their way back to the college in Antigonish; their presence created at St.F.X. a more cosmopolitan atmosphere.

Diverse motivations brought the young scholars to the doors of St.F.X. The highest aspiration of many Catholic families was to give a son to the church. Others recognized the scholarly capabilities of a child, and hoped that this early demonstration of intellectual promise would bear fruit. No doubt some diocesan young people and their parents craved social status; they likely saw the college as a means to overcome the "brand of social inferiority" bequeathed to them by circumstance, ethnicity, and religion. To others, higher education was nothing more than a door of escape from the grinding poverty and arduous labours of farm life. And there were also the realists; they confronted, in Paul Axelrod's words, "the reality of declining rural life by seeking new opportunities as middle class professionals in the emerging industrial world."[17] The college itself offered certain incentives: tuition rates were low, and it was a safe religious haven for Roman Catholic young people. Families or individuals probably decided for the college out of a complex mix of such motivations and incentives.

St.F.X. students were an elite group, but usually from modest social and economic backgrounds. Their privilege was most often founded on above-average academic interest and ability. Of course, many academically capable eastern Nova Scotia youth were unable to join the elect, for the family farm depended on their labour, or cash was too scarce. Of those privileged to enrol at the college, their academic levels often widely differed because educational opportunities within the diocese were uneven. High schools were not accessible for many students, unless they moved to towns like Sydney, Baddeck, Pictou, Antigonish, or Port Hood. School sections frequently closed for long periods of time.[18] As well, the quality of education was often adversely affected by unfit buildings, lack of equipment, irregular attendance, and the itineracy and poor qualifications of teachers.[19] Into the twentieth century, the student body had remained male, although from 1890 female students from the convent had begun to use the college laboratory;[20] certain professors had also taught mixed classes. The female presence at St.F.X. had been bolstered by the entry of the Marthas in 1897. So from the 1890s on, the exclusivity of the male preserve had begun to erode. Student ages ranged widely from the early teens into the twenties. The youngest were those who studied in the preparatory department; the oldest were generally ecclesiastical students who sometimes stayed at St.F.X. to take their first year of theology. Almost all the students were Catholic and most were from Scottish background (almost 60 per cent); however, Protestants occasionally registered, and there was a steady but small attendance of Irish, English, and Acadians. Finally, St.F.X. students were generally poor; frugality was a requirement. In 1906, tuition and board, set at $160 annually, were payable at the beginning of each term; only pauper students were granted the privilege of deferring full payment of their fees until they could afford them.[21] Penury forced many students to teach in the summer; moreover, some occasionally interrupted their studies to work, or even abandoned them, if their finances so dictated.

The Force of Religion
Student life at St.F.X. was permeated and enfolded by religion. Daily religious rituals, like mass and prayers, were practised, the church year was observed, priest-professors conducted most classes, and the religious community of Marthas was omnipresent. The stately St Ninian's Cathedral, built by Bishop MacKinnon, stood adjacent to the college, to the east of that was Mount St Bernard, run by the Sisters of the Congregation of Notre Dame, and on a prominence a short distance to the south stood the bishop's residence, superintending the whole. The symbols and reminders of religion met the student's gaze at every turn. The college authorities pledged to give the "utmost attention" to each pupil's spiritual and moral welfare.[22] Shared religious beliefs and daily corporate worship, undergirded by Scottish ethnicity, strengthened the sense of community and intimacy among the students captured by the enduring phrase "Xaverian family." In addition, the conventions of religious practice and belief no doubt resisted the trend to secularization and preoccupation with the material; this trend coalesced in the cities because of industrialization, urbanization, and new intellectual challenges to faith.[23] There appeared at St.F.X. no unsettling religious debates like those unleashed at some Canadian Protestant colleges, such as Victoria College, Toronto (Methodist) and McMaster University, Hamilton (Baptist), by the higher criticism of scripture and theological modernism.[24] The Catholicism of the college offered the students a spiritual anchor stone and a world view or cosmic vision of life. Finally, it reminded them of the fundamental issues of life and death, and held before them exalted standards of Christian conduct. Undoubtedly, St.F.X. was then a sheltered Catholic

enclave with an emphasis on compliance with the community in religious thought and practice.

Daily Regimen and Regulation

All students participated in the daily regimen. At 6:00 a.m. they would rise; between 6:30 and 8:00 a.m., when classes began, they attended mass in the chapel, next they had fifteen minutes each of study and recreation, and then they ate breakfast in the refectory. They visited the chapel again at noon for the recitation of the Angelus, then had dinner, which was followed by one hour of recreation. At 3:30 p.m., classes ended and students made a short visit to the blessed sacrament, followed, before supper, by about one hour of recreation. Study time and prayers in the chapel also preceded supper. A little more recreation came after supper, then study, and final prayers in the chapel at 9:30; lights were out by 10 p.m.[25] Weather permitting, students took a daily "time honored walk" to the cemetery.[26] Thursday was mostly a free day, although Catholic students attended a class in Christian doctrine, and the faculty held regular classes on Saturday. The entire academic community observed important feast days, such as All Saints, St Francis Xavier's Day, the Immaculate Conception, Christmas, New Year, Epiphany, and Easter. It became traditional to hold a Triduum leading up to St Francis Xavier's Day on 3 December, and another, brief spiritual retreat, which ended on Easter.[27]

Surprisingly, at least from a later standpoint, the rigour of the discipline and regulation at St.F.X., although tempered under both Presidents Thompson and MacPherson, aroused little student dissent. Issues of student power, individual freedom, and nonconformity were a world away. The rule was acquiescence and there were few exceptions to it.[28] Student acceptance of the regimen was probably rooted in a hierarchical social, family, and religious structure which deferred to authority.[29] As well, the authoritarianism was tempered by a paternalistic, human face which moderated its affront. The college authorities, moreover, had powers of expulsion, and control over marks, degrees, and recommendations, a not insignificant tool of social control. Finally, the regimen was not all rigid control and authoritarianism; outlets existed for the students at recreation and vacation times, as well as through student organizations. For example, a student reporter described, in 1896, the antics, songs, and hilarity of the students from the college's west wing – the "western boys" – as they left for Christmas vacation: "Never before did the outlets of their imprisoned hilarity take as wild a flight as it did on Dec. 23."[30] Although students rarely challenged the *status quo*, they sometimes made their accommodation by temporarily defying it through quiet subversion –

The first rink, called "the Cigar Box." Built in 1901 and replaced in 1921

by using candles long past the "lights out" deadline, by contriving and performing pranks, or by breaking loose off campus, e.g., raiding nearby orchards. Not all the youthful energy at St.F.X. could be channelled into behaviours acceptable to the adult authorities.

A New College Farm

St.F.X. students participated in a college community undergoing inevitable change. From 1907 to 1909, St.F.X. witnessed three tightly linked developments which concerned its property, finances, and constitution. In June 1907, the college purchased from C. Ernest Gregory, a local barrister and lecturer in contracts at St.F.X., his 280-acre farm called "Fernwood," located on the northeast border of the town.[31] The farm included a palatial home, which had been built in 1879, and farm buildings perched on the crest of a steep-sloped hill which overlooked Antigonish and its harbour; behind it to the north loomed Sugar Loaf Mountain. The college officials hoped the farm would supply it with basic foodstuffs and a surplus income; however, its layout and low-grade, rocky soil made it enduringly inefficient. At the diocesan clergy retreat in early August, Bishop Cameron suggested another use for Fernwood: the farm home could serve as a refuge for aged and infirm priests. The clergy agreed, proposed that the retirement home be managed by the Marthas, recommended that the farm be renamed "Mount Cameron" in the bishop's honour, and subscribed $40,000 to the new project.[32] St.F.X. took possession of the farm, assigned Rev. Moses Doyle to manage it, and in November 1907, signed an agreement with the diocese to provide a rest home and hostelry there for clerics; St.F.X. had tackled the business of farming and retirement services in earnest. The set-up of Mount Cameron, and the agreement between the board of governors and the diocese, formalized the college's then existing practice of supplying a place of retirement for some diocesan priests.[33] A few years later, the college purchased, through the aid of a friend, another property from C.E. Gregory, a cottage located about fifteen kilometres north of Antigonish at Jimtown on St George's Bay. St.F.X. hoped to use it for summer visitors and as a resort and retreat for overworked staff.[34]

Another Endowment Fund Campaign

The development related to college finances was the lay-initiated plan for an endowment fund campaign, heartily supported by Bishop Cameron,[35] and organized by diocesan delegates at an enthusiastic conference in the Sydney Lyceum on 30 November 1907.[36] The conference formed an endowment fund association and aimed to raise at least $100,000.[37] Campaign propaganda stressed the need for low tuition fees so that St.F.X. could remain "truly a college for the people" and for monies to upgrade the college facilities. A pamphlet declared, "This is an age of progress, and Catholics and Catholic institutions must be up-to-date and responsive to the new demands of industry and science."[38] The canvass for an endowment fund was only the second in the institution's history; the first had been conducted twenty-five years before in 1882. The campaign was closely associated with the Alumni Association drive to endow a chair of English, a project inspired by the first appointee to the chair, A.J.G. MacEchen. He was president of the Alumni Association and a lawyer from Sydney who would remain at St.F.X. for five years.[39] Ten years before, he had initiated, planned, and supervised the first honours course at St.F.X.

Ambitious Plans
The purchase of Mount Cameron farm, along with the endowment fund campaign, led MacPherson and the St.F.X. board to make, in 1909, the first substantial revision to its act of incorporation – constitution.[40] Besides perpetuating its incorporation and rights to operate a residential degree-granting college, their new constitution enlarged the board from seven to thirteen (three had to be diocesan priests), limited terms of office to three years, and retained sweeping veto powers for the bishop. The board, to be composed of Catholics only, had powers to contract and make regulations, to manage the St Francis Xavier's endowment fund, then being created, and to maintain a home for aged and infirm priests at Mount Cameron farm. Control of the retirement home was given to the bishop, the college president, and a committee of five other diocesan priests. The act also clearly distinguished between the board's responsibilities and those of the faculty of arts composed of the president, the vice-president, and the professors. The board was to manage the college properties and "temporalities"; the arts faculty was responsible for instruction, courses of study, examinations, and the granting of degrees. Another most significant section, perhaps the brain-child of Vice-President Jimmy Tompkins, permitted the college to establish new departments, schools, and faculties, and to conduct, in connection with St.F.X., other schools, including summer schools and university extension work. This revised act of incorporation, along with the Mount Cameron Farm purchase and the $100,000 endowment fund campaign, signalled rising institutional ambitions among the college leadership.

Certain curricular proposals and experiments in the years following the appointments of MacPherson and Tompkins also signalled heightened aspirations at the college. In 1909, authorities discussed expanding the one-year law course, begun by Thompson in 1899, into a full-fledged law program. MacPherson dreamed of training Catholic law- yers who would influence public life. In a fund-raising letter to Senator William Miller, he modestly declared that St.F.X. was "nearer being a real University than any other English-speaking Catholic institution in Canada, and its future is by far the most promising of any of them."[41] The law school proposal, however, failed to materialize, prob- ably because of insufficient moral and financial support. A less ambi- tious curricular offering, and one made before, called for a course in Celtic studies. Certain Highland descendants in eastern Nova Scotia continued to press for the preservation of their rich cultural heritage.[42] A *Casket* article of 13 February 1906 claimed that over one-half of the approximately eighty thousand Catholics in Antigonish Diocese were Gaelic-speaking. In 1907, and for the next three years, St.F.X. hired Rev. Alexander MacLean Sinclair, described as "a Kelt from toe to tonsure," to teach the Celtic heritage. Rev. Sinclair was a retired Presbyterian minister, and, to that time, the only Protestant cleric ever to teach at the Catholic college. He was grandson of the famous Bard MacLean of Glenbard, Antigonish County, and a foremost Gaelic scholar and proponent.[43] Sinclair lectured one semester of each aca- demic year at Dalhousie and St.F.X. to relatively small classes, labour- ing to pass on the venerable Gaelic language, and the literature, customs, and history of the Celtic race.[44]

The MacPherson-Tompkins administration soon made three other program changes. First, in 1907–8, they added one extra year to the three-year arts course;[45] at the end of that academic year, the gradu- ating class was invited to return for one more year – about one-half did.[46] A St.F.X. announcement warned parents that the St.F.X. high school did not do common school work, and only students who had successfully completed theirs would be admitted to the college high school program.[47] Then, in 1909, St.F.X. advertised surprisingly ambi- tious masters' and doctoral programs in arts and sciences. The PH D regulations required candidates to write preliminary and final exami- nations, devote at least two years to full-time postgraduate studies, and submit a dissertation; the program could be completed in residence or *in absentia.*[48] The PH D offering was undoubtedly a naïve gesture, for it reached far beyond the financial and academic means of the small college; although several people inquired about the program, no can- didates fulfilled its requirements and it was wisely withdrawn within a decade.[49] Its appearance did reveal that St.F.X. was aware of the growing influence of the German research ideal at the major American and Canadian universities, an ideal which inspired the founding of Johns Hopkins University and the development of doctoral programs at the University of Toronto.[50]

First St.F.X. summer school, 1909

The First Summer School

The recently revised constitution allowed St.F.X. to establish special schools and conduct extension work. College authorities decided in 1909 to take advantage of this provision by offering a five-week summer school. The *Xaverian* described this third program innovation as "an experiment in University Extension."[51] The regular faculty, aided by prominent visiting lecturers which included three judges, offered a wide range of arts and science courses, as well as evening lectures on popular topics. Some of these lecturers discussed Catholic social theory and action, and contemporary social issues. About seventy students enrolled, many of them teachers. The calendar outlined the college's rationale for the summer school: "to bring within reach of the largest possible number some of the advantages of higher education, to give special aid to teachers and others who desire to qualify themselves for higher positions," and to aid those preparing for examinations.[52] This summer school, held again in 1910, marked the college's first formal experiment in university extension work, a type of work for which it would one day gain renown. The *Casket* described the experiment as "a grand success."[53] Along with the curricular ventures into applied science, law, and commerce effected under Rector Thompson, and the college's support for an anti-tuberculosis campaign in eastern Nova Scotia (1909–), the summer school revealed the college's growing sensitivity to the increasingly diverse needs of its constituency.[54]

Wealthy Friends and New Buildings

The contributions of two key benefactors, and really the first substantial ones in the history of St.F.X., both resident in Massachusetts, helped to sustain and realize, for the next decade, the college's rising educational ambitions. Together these men, applauded by the *Casket* as "the militant friends" of St.F.X.,[55] largely funded between 1910 and 1920 the construction of five new buildings on the campus. A science hall, the only permanent structure containing classroom space which would appear on the campus for over fifty years, was built in 1910 through the generosity of Neil McNeil of Boston. McNeil was a Cape Breton expatriate who had followed the late-nineteenth-century tide of outmigration to Boston where, in spite of little formal schooling, he became a successful and wealthy building contractor. By the time of his large donation in 1910, at the age of about sixty-eight years, he had already made several small gifts to St.F.X. At Tompkins's request he had given $1000 for the cottage at Jimtown; furthermore, he had paid the St.F.X. tuition fees for several nephews. Now, toward the end of an astonishing career, he began to take an intense interest in the well-

Neil McNeil, wealthy building contractor
and St.F.X. benefactor

Science Hall — St. F. X. College, Antigonish, N. S.

MacNeil Science Hall, built in 1910

being and advance of the college.[56] His gift of about $40,000 paid for the new building which was named in his honour.[57] The college located it between the cathedral and the main building, facing north on St Ninian's Street.[58] McNeil's Boston firm contracted and supervised the construction of an impressive Anglo-Gothic two-storey brick structure which measured about one hundred by fifty feet. The college calendar boasted that it contained the latest equipment and accommodated the biology, physics, chemistry, and geology laboratories.[59] Along with Thompson's engineering hall, built ten years before, the new and commodious science hall was material evidence that St.F.X. had moved into technology and the sciences.

On 24 August 1911, the day St.F.X. dedicated the new MacNeil Science Hall,[60] it laid the cornerstone for a new chapel. Retired rector Rev. Dr Alex Thompson used the opportunity in his guest sermon at the cathedral to stress the symbolism of the joint celebrations; in his view, they revealed the Catholic conviction that "the truth of divine faith and the findings of human reason proceed from the same source, the infinite and eternal wisdom of God."[61] Thompson, in the face of stiff opposition, had placed science on a firmer basis at St.F.X. with the founding in 1899 of a department of applied science; it was appropriate that he preach at the dedication ceremony, and understandable that his sermon revealed a mood of self-vindication. President MacPherson, who continued to receive criticism about the new directions at St.F.X. which had been initiated by Thompson, had also invited the Canadian apostolic delegate, Most Reverend Donatus Sbarretti, to be present at the dedication. He wrote, "We are most anxious to have the highest ecclesiastical dignitary in Canada visit us, become personally acquainted with our work and aims, and judge of us according to our deserts."[62] The college wanted its new departures legitimized with the *imprimatur* of high ecclesiastical authority.

McNeil's Boston firm also supervised construction of the new chapel, an imposing red brick, Anglo-Gothic structure which could seat about five hundred worshippers. The chapel was placed west of the main building, in which the old chapel had been located, facing north on St Ninian's Street.[63] The bulk of its funding came from Dr John Somers, a friend of Neil McNeil and another expatriate Nova Scotian who had won a degree of medical fame and fortune for himself in the "Boston States." Somers was a native of Antigonish, a St.F.X. alumnus, as well as an honorary graduate (1905); he avowed that his gift had been prompted by a sense of indebtedness to St.F.X. and enthusiasm for its broad, Catholic educational approach.[64] Like McNeil's, Somers's support and friendship bred heady optimism and exhilaration at St.F.X. Both men had been carefully courted by Father

Dr John Somers, medical doctor and early St.F.X. benefactor

Tompkins and President MacPherson,[65] a wise tactic for a cash-strapped but ambitious college.

The Death of Bishop Cameron and His Successor's Appointment
Meanwhile, as the college strengthened its relations with McNeil and Somers and enjoyed the first fruits of their largesse, certain diocesan events had direct repercussions for St.F.X. Bishop Cameron, whose health had been sliding for several years, died on 6 April 1910. He was eighty-three. The college community was deeply moved by his death; he had shown it great solicitude since his administration began after the resignation of Bishop MacKinnon thirty-three years before. Moreover, Cameron had given critical support to the controversial changes instituted by Rector Thompson. Now his long and sometimes rocky relation to certain members of the college staff was over.[66] Rome had not selected a successor to Bishop Cameron before his death, so the administration of the extensive diocese landed temporarily on the shoulders of MacPherson, the college president. Actually Bishop Cameron had wanted President MacPherson to succeed him, but the consistorial congregation in Rome, responsible for the appointment of a new bishop, received contradictory information and opinions about him which gave them pause. Some of the representations had originated in the diocese.[67] Meanwhile, MacPherson, for two and one-half years, was fated to struggle along wearing two hats. Not only did he inherit the delicate and controversial problems which were part of the legacies of Bishop Cameron and Rector Thompson, but the reputation of his college was now tied closely to his performance as diocesan administrator.[68]

President MacPherson was happily relieved of the distracting burden of diocesan administration by the arrival of a new bishop in September 1912. Rev. Dr James Morrison, a native of Prince Edward Island, former rector of St Dunstan's College, Charlottetown (1892 to 1895), and administrator of the Diocese of Charlottetown, was the new man. His episcopate would be the longest one in the history of the Diocese of Antigonish – nearly thirty-eight years. Morrison's experience as rector of St Dunstan's College undoubtedly gave him sensitivity to the special problems faced by a small diocesan college. He became a resolute supporter of St.F.X., and a close friend of President MacPherson. In time, he would gain a reputation among his new flock for caution, prudence, orthodoxy, conservatism, and aloofness. Unlike Cameron, Morrison wisely avoided the dangerous minefield of political entanglements. He expected the same of St.F.X.: in 1921 he would caution two priest-professors accused of campaigning for the Farmer candidate, "At all costs the College must be kept out of mere party

James Morrison, bishop of the Diocese of Antigonish
1912–50. "A canny Scot"

politics directly and indirectly."[69] Vice-President Tompkins had this first impression of his new superior: "He is about six feet two inches in height and quite ascetic and intellectual looking. I should take him withal to be a 'canny Scot' which will not do him any particular harm in his line of business in these parts."[70] Tompkins's assessment of Morrison as a "canny Scot" was accurate, a fact Tompkins would later learn from bitter personal experience. The faculty and students at St.F.X. expressed great satisfaction that their new bishop and chancellor was "an ardent and experienced educationist"; they assured him of their confidence that the college's future under his wise guidance would rival its "eminently useful past."[71]

Diocesan Factionalism

Bishop Morrison was soon introduced to some of the factionalism and controversy which continued to simmer and sometimes swirl around the college.[72] By 1913, the endowment fund campaign, begun in 1907, had failed to garner much more than one-quarter of its targeted $100,000, despite special pleading by the *Casket* on behalf of the college.[73] While some people explained the failure on the grounds of labour strife in Sydney, a smallpox epidemic in Cape Breton, and the death of Bishop Cameron – reportedly the "chief spirit in the movement"[74] – others informed the novice Bishop Morrison that dubious new directions at St.F.X. had seriously undermined Catholic confidence in the institution. Rev. Ronald MacDonald, parish priest in Pictou, volunteered this assessment to the bishop: Rev. Dr Alexander MacDonald (then bishop of Victoria), he claimed, had spoken for most of the priests of the diocese in 1902[75] when he had firmly critiqued Rector Thompson's new emphasis on science at St.F.X. and his lax disciplinary regime. Father Ronald and others also believed the college had overtaxed its financial and intellectual resources because of its romantic aspiration to become a university.[76] Rev. A.H. Cormier, a disgruntled member of the college staff who taught French, judged the MA and PH D offerings a pretentious farce, and he complained that Vice-President Tompkins took advantage of a weak President MacPherson and patronized and manipulated the staff.[77]

The fairness of Cormier's charges against Tompkins is difficult to judge. However, Tompkins was plainly the main driving force behind the soaring ambitions and "pretensions" of the college. A *Casket* editorial once described him as "a veritable human dynamo in educational matters."[78] Since his sojourn in Rome, his health had continuously improved;[79] by 1911 he was even hoping to acquire for himself a PH D from Laval. President MacPherson thought it would mean "a good deal for St Francis Xavier's College that one holding the position which

Father Tompkins holds should have a University degree."[80] Tompkins was a visionary, preoccupied with progress and modernization. His frequent travels forced him to compare St.F.X. and eastern Nova Scotia to the wider world. He often expressed contempt for those who stood in the way of change. Once he reported to Neil McNeil of Boston, "You know that down here there are so many little pinheaded fellows that they are likely to make a man as small as themselves and keep him back unless he possesses a very unusual fund of enthusiasm."[81]

Father Tompkins and the Forward Movement

Tompkins himself possessed a most unusual "fund of enthusiasm." He was a central proponent of the Forward Movement in Antigonish County, where leading citizens collaborated to improve the town, attract settlement to the county farms, revitalize local business and manufacturing, and reform agriculture.[82] The Antigonish Forward Movement, part of a "progressive impulse" which swept through the Maritimes and the rest of North America, began in the fall of 1913.[83] Its champions were responding to the demoralization of the county caused by economic depression and outmigration. From 1901 to 1911, the population of Antigonish County had dropped from 13,617 to 11,962.[84] The decline and backwardness sensed by local leaders was probably made more poignant by promising advances in neighbouring Pictou County, where industrial development had strengthened the economy, created employment opportunities, and expanded agricultural markets.[85] A *Casket* article – sounding like vintage Tompkins – stated: "We have to restore faith in our county and its possibilities; we have to bring back our departed population; to set the wheels of industry humming in our midst; and to bring our Town up to the standard of modern industrial and aesthetic progress, in order that it may become a worthy nucleus for such a community as we want Antigonish County to be."[86] Enthusiasm for the Forward Movement would persist for some years in Antigonish; the *Casket* ceaselessly and energetically promoted it, religiously reporting its advances and victories;[87] and Tompkins, joined by other college professors like Drs Moses Coady and Hugh MacPherson, continued to be a central driving force behind it.[88]

Upgrading the Faculty

In his zealous campaign for modernization, Tompkins best succeeded in upgrading St.F.X.'s faculty and academic standards. He had concluded that faculty were ill prepared and poorly qualified, not only at St.F.X. but at all Canadian Catholic colleges. The vice-president complained that Catholics remained about twenty-five years behind the times; and he was convinced they occupied few higher positions in Canadian public life because "there is no such thing as Catholic Higher Education in the country."[89] Tompkins ridiculed the lack of specialization: "Take the majority of our so-called colleges and look over the list of professors. Rev. Robert Brown, S.T.B., PH.D., Professor of Latin, Physics, Geometry, English, Geography, Music and Penmanship. Some genius! Have these people ever heard of specialization?"[90] Evidently Tompkins had, and he believed Catholics would only progress in higher education if they followed the lead of the bigger universities into specialization and research.

Tompkins was no defeatist; on the contrary, he was a fervent activist, and, together with President MacPherson, determined that St.F.X. would lead the way to real Catholic university education as he envisioned it. By 1910 they had recruited six talented St.F.X. graduates as prospective professors whom they had sent to study at prominent universities: Patrick J. Nicholson at Johns Hopkins in Baltimore, James Boyle at the University of Louvain, Belgium, Rev. Cornelius J. Connolly at the University of Munich, Germany, Moses M. Coady and Hugh MacDonald at the Urban College, Rome, and Rev. Roderick K. MacIntyre, who was joined by Rev. Daniel J. MacDonald in 1910, at the Catholic University of America in Washington.[91] St.F.X. established a very satisfactory relation with the latter graduate university.[92] Many St.F.X. professors would be trained there, and three of its future presidents; for its part, the college would supply the Catholic University with several prominent scholars.[93] All seven of these alumni would return to join the St.F.X. faculty; several of them would profoundly shape its future direction and reputation. President MacPherson expressed this hope in 1912: "The policy of getting our professors educated in the most celebrated universities of Europe and America will soon have us supplied with men whose standing cannot be disputed and whose names will be an advertisement for us all over the country."[94] He clearly had a desire for an improved public image.

In addition to recruiting its own graduates, the St.F.X. administration also sought graduates from Oxford and Cambridge in order to boost further the college's program and standing. Tompkins, who had established contacts in the British Isles when he attended in 1912 the Congress of Empire Universities in London, travelled to England in the spring of 1914 to interview several candidates; three were hired.[95] Two were Cambridge graduates – W.H. Bucknell, professor of English and history, and H.R. Howard, professor of mathematics – and the third, H.R.W. Smith, a classicist, was an Oxford graduate.[96] Another facet of the St.F.X.-British connection also revealed the college's efforts to lift itself up during this period. Authorities gained affiliations

Rev. Dr Cornelius J. Connolly, professor of biology 1911–22, 1923–24

with Oxford University (1915) and Cambridge University (1917);[97] this recognition apparently meant that X-graduates accepted by these universities would be exempt from preliminary examinations and probations.[98]

Review of College Progress

By 1914, St.F.X. had substantially upgraded itself. It had acquired a more specialized and qualified faculty; out of sixteen staff members, seven had doctorates and three had masters' degrees. In spite of a weak response to the 1907 financial campaign, and an abortive $300,000 campaign in 1913 which had been proposed by the Alumni Association,[99] a dynamo fund-raiser had been found in Tompkins, who had successfully courted two generous benefactors; these good Samaritans had financed the construction of two impressive new buildings: a science hall and a chapel. The college then offered a relatively broad program encompassing the arts, sciences, religion, engineering, and law. After updating its constitution, St.F.X. had made its first experiment with extension work. Student enrolments at the college level had steadily increased from about 90 in 1901 to 145 in 1913. A young, new bishop had been appointed to the diocese; he had pledged his full support to the work of St.F.X. and its aspirations to become "the great Catholic University of Canada."[100]

These happy developments coalesced to inspire optimism in the hearts of the college staff and its alumni and supporters.[101] The administration judged prospects so bright that they even hired, in 1912, a Boston landscape designer, who advised them on the best ways to expand the campus.[102] The resulting campus plan was an ambitious one which called for a most elaborate group of building extensions, sports facilities, and dormitories, including a seminary.[103] Predictably, the first college song, penned in 1913, exuded optimism; its chorus rhapsodized:

> Xavier's, look not backwards. The future is thy goal.
> A new world lies before thee. Strong in its fierce young soul!
> Xavier's, thy quest is onward. 'Mid Empire newly born.
> 'Tis thine to move a people's heart, To greet a nation's morn![104]

Unfortunately, a dark cloud loomed on the horizon of the "nation's morn"; it was the dark cloud of war.

·8·

War and Resurgence,
1914–21

Britain's declaration of war on Germany in August 1914 immediately committed Canada to the cause. Eventually she would send over six hundred thousand young men to the killing fields in Europe; more than sixty thousand would never return. On the home front, war created unprecedented ethnic tensions among Canadians. It also had immense consequences for the universities. At St.F.X., as elsewhere, the campus became militarized in appearance and mentality, enlistments thinned the ranks of students and faculty, financial resources dwindled, and authorities sponsored a hospital unit to assist the protracted war effort overseas. In spite of the distraction and apprehension caused by the war, college leaders pressed ahead with improvements. When the ordeal and anguish of the Great War ended, the college struggled to recover lost momentum. The administration laboured to reduce a substantial debt, experimented with new programs, and updated its constitution. Behind most of the innovations stalked the restless and intense figure of Father Jimmy Tompkins.

Mobilizing for War
Some years before the war, military drill had been conducted on the St.F.X. campus.[1] But only with the onset of hostilities in 1914 did serious military organization begin. At the initiative of President MacPherson, St.F.X. formed, by the summer of 1915, a company of the Canadian Officers' Training Corp (COTC).[2] In early February, a military official had addressed the students about forming a COTC. The *Casket* reported "great enthusiasm" among the students – a mood reflecting that of English-speaking Canada – and at least sixty-three students agreed to join.[3] The college assured nervous parents that participation was strictly voluntary, that it entailed no obligation to serve in the regular army, and that training was only for purposes of defence.[4] The department of militia and defence, under Conservative Prime Minister Robert Borden's "devout" militarist Sam Hughes,

provided the college with an instructor and supplies.[5] The COTC gave students elementary military training so they could apply for commissions in the active militia. Although its function is uncertain, the faculty, which numbered about sixteen, also formed a committee of military education.[6] The president, moreover, helped to organize a local branch of the Canadian Patriot Fund, a federal government reserve created to assist the dependants of military personnel.

St.F.X. students enrolled at the college from before the outbreak of war expressed dismay at the rapid military transformation of their campus. In 1916 a *Xaverian* editor lamented, "Today the College is a veritable Valcartier. Our commodious reception room and assembly hall have been transformed into drill sheds. Our campus is no longer the resort of ball-players, but the drill field of our sons in Khaki. How changed, indeed, of old!"[7] Furthermore, students recoiled at the horror of war and were distraught by its magnitude. Yet they seemed, like most other Canadian university students, unflinching in their loyalty to the British cause, and supported its professed aim "to defend civilization and humanity against the onslaughts of a ruthless militarism." Some Xaverians expressed astonishment that, after centuries of Christian influence, such a tragedy should sweep over Europe.[8]

Military Recruiting and College Enrolments
The escalation of the war and its murderous consequences increased the need for men. To the consternation of some parents, a recruiting officer established his headquarters at St.F.X. in 1916.[9] Professor Bucknell, an Englishman and popular public lecturer, occasionally helped him recruit throughout the area.[10] College enlistments were substantial. By the spring, two hundred students or alumni and four faculty had engaged in active service.[11] Of course, student enlistments decreased tuition revenues and faculty enlistments created a shortage of professors. The following faculty heeded the call to arms: H.R.W. Smith, professor of classics, Allan MacDonald, lecturer on law and Shakespearean literature, W.F. Chisholm, instructor of applied science, and Rev. Miles N. Tompkins, manager of Mount Cameron Farm.[12] The absence of Father Miles Tompkins, who served overseas as a military chaplain along with over ninety other Roman Catholic chaplains,[13] was a disaster for the college farm. Since President MacPherson found no competent person to replace him, Mount Cameron reported alarming deficits in the priest-farmer's absence.[14]

The war hurt college enrolments. There were 218 students at St.F.X. in 1913; by 1918 the number had dropped precipitously by 97 to 121.[15] Student enlistments appeared to peak through the first months of 1918.[16] Enrolment levels would have been even more disastrous if a

French-English fracas had not broken out at the University of Ottawa during the war. Vice-President Tompkins alleged, "The French have monopolized the University and all the English are leaving."[17] It was a characteristic exaggeration; but some English did leave, and from 1915 to 1918, about ten to twelve students each year trekked east to Antigonish. Laurence Shook claims that the University of Ottawa, then a small, Catholic, bilingual, liberal arts institution, had often been "racked by nationalist problems" and it remained at a low ebb from 1905 to 1920.[18] Its loss was St.F.X.'s gain, and it was a timely gain. Neither were the advertising and fund-raising possibilities in Ontario lost on the vice-president. Most of "the Ottawa boys," stated Father Tompkins, were "well-connected" upper class men who had "considerable cash."[19]

Wartime Building Construction
Providence appeared operative in another connection with the entry of the Ottawa contingent. St.F.X. had just completed a new dormitory shortly before the Ottawa students arrived in the fall of 1915. It was a most welcome addition to the existing row of buildings along St Ninian's Street. As enrolments had mounted from less than 100 in 1900 to 218 in 1914, St.F.X. had faced shortages of dormitory space. The college's Boston patron, Neil McNeil, had prepared plans for the new building, and, along with Dr John Somers, paid more than one-half the cost of about $39,000.[20] At the insistence of both McNeil and the college officials, the new residence was named after another somewhat affluent contributor, Captain Patrick Mockler of Brule, Nova Scotia.[21] Mockler, a Catholic and retired sailor-shipbuilder, had become a friend of the college. The plain, rectangular building which bore his name was made of brick and stone, measured 110 feet by 42 feet, consisted of four storeys and a basement, and was situated a short distance to the southwest of Somers Chapel. A later professor of English affectionately declared it "a styleless hulk of brick."[22] The hall provided accommodation for over one hundred students and was equipped with modern heating and plumbing.[23]

Wartime construction at St.F.X., a surprising phenomenon considering the institutional stress caused by the war, included two other buildings begun soon after Mockler Hall. A gymnasium and library appeared on the campus, again through the initiative and aid of Dr John Somers, who had paid, five years earlier, for the new chapel. Somers, a doctor, had concerns about the health of the St.F.X. students; he gave $20,000 to pay for the new gymnasium completed in 1918.[24] At his untimely death in July of that year, St.F.X. expressed its indebtedness to him; as its benefactor, he was responsible for three new

Captain Patrick Mockler, early St.F.X.
benefactor and retired sea captain

Mockler Hall residence, built 1916

buildings on campus, a $24,000 endowed chair of classics, and a final $10,000 bequest.[25] Of the civic-minded philanthropist, President MacPherson wrote, "he proved the truest of friends and contributed with an astounding generosity to the needs of the institution."[26] Judged against the backdrop of the general poverty of the college's constituency, the president's eulogy was no exaggeration.

Somers's offer to pay for the gymnasium had been conditional; it required St.F.X. to raise $25,000 for the construction and maintenance of a library.[27] Such a condition was onerous in the extreme, given the financial demands of war on the college's constituency. Nonetheless, the money was found and the library built between Mockler Hall and Somers's Chapel by the summer of 1918. Construction flaws, as well as the need for shelving and a trained librarian, delayed its use until 1921. The college's library collection, which had been slowly growing through the periodic contributions of bishops, priests, alumni, and friends, was moved – the librarian reported "tossed" – into the new library after a fire, in 1919, damaged the oldest section of the administration building. The college hired its first full-time librarian, May C. MacDonald (the daughter of former professor A.G. MacDonald), the year following.[28]

The St.F.X. No. 9 Stationary Hospital

The building projects certainly placed an extra burden on the college's war-depressed finances; another major wartime project did not. St.F.X. officials, with the blessing of the board of governors, decided in early 1916 to form a stationary hospital unit as part of the Canadian Army Medical Corp, a project also undertaken by other universities such as McGill, Toronto, Queen's, and Dalhousie.[29] The idea apparently originated with a Dr J. Stewart Carruthers, and was then promoted by his father-in-law, Senator A.B. Crosby of Halifax.[30] The formation of such units was logical: a field of potential recruits was at hand on the campuses, and the units could capitalize on student and alumni cohesion rooted in both a love for *alma mater* and a desire to promote her honour.[31] The minister of militia authorized the St.F.X. plan in January 1916, and organization on campus began in March under Commanding Officer Roderick C. MacLeod, a fifty-one-year-old native of Margaree, Cape Breton, and a graduate of both St.F.X. and the University of New York Medical School.[32] At the end of March, the *Casket* reported that close to one hundred men could be seen drilling daily on the campus; they were gradually being outfitted with all the necessary equipment.[33] After little more than two months' training at St.F.X., the unit moved to Halifax.[34] By the time it embarked from Halifax for England on 19 June 1916, it was 156

Old gymnasium, now Bauer Theatre, built in 1916

strong; 12 of its staff were medical officers, 26 were nursing sisters, and 118 were non-commissioned officers and men.[35] Apparently, about sixty of them were St.F.X. students and alumni.[36] There had been some controversy over the leadership of the unit and difficulty recruiting doctors.[37] Unlike most other universities which formed hospital units, and to its serious disadvantage, St.F.X. did not have a medical faculty.

From the beginning, President MacPherson and Vice-President Tompkins showed immense enthusiasm for the hospital unit project. MacPherson thought it fitting that St.F.X., as the "foremost institution for English-speaking Catholics in Canada," should, along with other "great colleges," send a unit to the front.[38] It would be a fine contribution to the war effort and a credit to Catholics, he believed. Tompkins rejoiced that the government would pay all expenses, while St.F.X. got "all the glory" and its name "blazed" from the Atlantic to the Pacific.[39] Authorities also believed a St.F.X. hospital unit would protect Catholic youth who joined it from "grave moral as well as physical dangers," threats they would be exposed to if scattered among different battalions.[40]

The overseas experience of the St.F.X. No. 9 Stationary Hospital was not entirely satisfactory. On arrival in England, its personnel were dispersed to different hospitals.[41] At certain times over the next eighteen months, the unit's continued existence was threatened; moreover, some members, frustrated at the delay in reaching the front in France, joined other units.[42] Then, on 4 January 1917, less than one year after the formation of the hospital unit, Commanding Officer MacLeod died suddenly of anthrax infection.[43] He was replaced by Major Henry E. Kendall, a Protestant and a graduate of Mount Allison and McGill.[44] Finally, the unit travelled to France, where it arrived in early February 1917. A German air attack the following May killed two and wounded twelve of its personnel; at the time, the hospital mercifully had no patients.[45] The unit was mostly inactive during the summer of 1918, and in August, Major Ronald St John MacDonald, a St.F.X. alumnus and experienced doctor, replaced Kendall as the commanding officer. After the war, MacDonald became associate professor of public health and preventive medicine at McGill. His sister was Margaret C. Mac-Donald, matron-in-chief of the Canadian Nursing Service.[46] For some months (February to April 1919) the unit operated a venereal disease hospital for Canadian soldiers before finally returning to Canada in July 1919, and then formally disbanding on 15 November 1920. By this time, only about 37 of the 150 staff had been original members of the No. 9 Stationary Hospital.[47]

The St.F.X. No. 9 Stationary Hospital apparently earned a good reputation for effectively discharging its sporadic assignments, in spite

Officers and nursing sisters of the St.F.X. Hospital Unit No. 9, Bramshott,
England, 1916

of the difficulties it faced – the division of the unit, the loss of personnel to other duties, the sudden death of its commanding officer, and a German air attack.[48] The project was another clear indication of the college's mounting ambitions, which the war had not entirely quenched. But the unit was really too ambitious for such a small college, and one which lacked a faculty of medicine. In contrast to other units, such as Dalhousie's Stationary Hospital No. 7,[49] St.F.X. students formed only a minority of the staff; thus the hospital, throughout its existence, had little more than a tenuous connection to the college.[50] Brian Hogan, historian of the unit, rightly concluded, "the St Francis Xavier Stationary Hospital was neither a University unit nor a functioning Stationary Hospital for much of its existence."[51] Finally, its assignment as a venereal disease hospital was probably distasteful to a unit associated with a Catholic college.

College Constituency and the War Effort
St.F.X.'s overall war effort was bound up with that of the diocese. The bishop of the diocese and chancellor of the university, Right Rev. Dr James Morrison, championed the allied cause.[52] Pro-British war propaganda was present on every hand – in the semi-official diocesan journal, the *Casket*, in the public school classrooms, in the college, in the pulpits, in the bishop's circulars, and in recruiting rallies.[53] The diocesan honour roll, completed soon after the conclusion of the war, stated, "The Catholic clergy of the diocese, from pulpit and platform, constantly led the way for their people in staunch support of the Allied Cause."[54] For example, Father Jimmy Tompkins's fund-raising magic, which was by then proverbial,[55] had been put to good use.[56] Authorities appointed him chairman of the Victory Loan Campaign for Antigonish County in October 1917, and he led it to surpass its target of $300,000 by over $100,000.[57]

Tompkins's fund-raising responsibilities at the college were made more onerous and urgent by the war. Declining enrolments and pre-war-level tuition fees increased the college's annual deficits and required it to borrow heavily. Such poverty had even forced the release of three professors by the end of the war – George Humphrey in ancient history and classics, H.R. Howard in mathematics, and T. Hay in drafting.[58] By 1920 St.F.X. had borrowed $11,000 from the episcopal corporation of Antigonish and close to $50,000 from parish priests.[59] Wartime, in the president's words, was "a period of retrogression" for St.F.X.[60] In early 1917, Tompkins was directed to "hit up" certain wealthy Americans – ones who were making money in the war industry – in order to help the college through the pinch.[61] From all appearances, the "hit up" failed; however, St.F.X. did receive promises of, or actual endowments for, chairs in history and geology in 1917. These gifts brightened the dreary financial picture a little.[62] And Bishop Morrison tried to enhance it even more by reviving the annual college collection, which had been instituted at the urging of alumni in 1903; unfortunately, the annual offering had declined in usefulness by 1914.[63] But a post-war recession which saw the down-turn of industrial activity in the Sydney–Glace Bay and New Glasgow areas did nothing to stimulate a fresh flow of cash into the college coffers.[64]

The armistice of 11 November 1918 brought great relief and rejoicing on the St.F.X. campus. In December, the *Xaverian* declared, "Right has triumphed over might, the soul of civilization over the sword of Prussia."[65] It was time to celebrate the college's contribution to the war effort and to honour its dead. Both students and faculty did this with a touch of extravagance. They extolled the college's patriotic efforts, its recruitment of hundreds of students and alumni, the enlistment of four professors, the successful fund-raising campaigns it had assisted, and the formation of a hospital unit.[66] The record was undoubtedly creditable, but one shrouded with anguish and tragedy. About 340 students and alumni had enlisted; 34 of these were reported killed or missing.[67] And beyond the campus there had been the further tragedies of the Halifax Explosion,[68] post-war riots, and the Spanish influenza epidemic of 1918. Moreover, the veterans whom fate permitted to return from the battlefields of Europe received little government help for resettlement and retraining.[69]

The Carnegie Chair of French
French-English relations in Canada had been severely strained in 1917 when Robert Borden's Union government instituted conscription for military service. At this time, about 23,400 Acadians lived within the Diocese of Antigonish; they represented 25 per cent of the population of 92,800 Catholics.[70] In the Maritimes the Acadians had been the "most visible" opponents of conscription, yet they had not been uniformly anti-war. However, the issue of conscription "decisively sharpened perceptions of the cultural and political gap between anglophones and Acadians in the region."[71] The collective memory of the Acadians included the tragic deportations of the 1750s. Tompkins, who had taught in the Acadian town of Cheticamp as a young man, and who had a special sensitivity for the plight of minorities, thought St.F.X. should do more to improve the educational status of the Acadians; the college would thus make an "amende honorable" on behalf of the English for past wrongs.[72] Therefore, he solicited the Carnegie Corporation of New York, the famous philanthropic foundation which administered part of the immense legacy of the wealthy industrialist

Andrew Carnegie, for an endowment of a chair in French.[73] The language had always been taught at St.F.X., and Acadians had been present in small numbers on staff and among the student body from the beginning. For example, between 1891 and 1921 they represented about 6 per cent of enrolments.[74] But Tompkins wanted to attract more of them through bursaries and high-quality French instruction. He wanted St.F.X. to say to young Acadians, "Come to our college and learn the best English and Science we can give you. That you may feel we are not trying to rob you of your language or traditions, we shall provide suitable and satisfactory instruction in French language and literature."[75]

Tompkins had been sizing up the Carnegie Corporation since 1914.[76] He knew that its British Dominions and Colonies Fund had been supporting selected educational projects in the Maritimes since 1911.[77] The diminutive priest from Nova Scotia made a good impression on key members of the corporation, and developed an enduring friendship with them which would be very fruitful indeed for St.F.X. He admired their expertise in educational affairs and their broad spirit open to all creeds.[78] In November 1919, the Carnegie Corporation generously offered $50,000 to endow a French chair and to provide four bursaries if St.F.X. raised an equal sum for scholarships and a lectureship in education.[79] In the *Casket*'s view, this gesture was "probably the greatest tribute of praise ever paid to St Francis Xavier's, because it is well-known that the directors of the Carnegie Corporation are educational experts of the highest order who bestow their funds on first class institutions only."[80] The following year the college fulfilled its part of the agreement and then hired in 1921, as the first Carnegie Professor of French, René Gautheron, a graduate of the University of Paris, former professor of French at the University of Montreal 1912–19,[81] and fellow of the University of France. The *Xaverian* claimed that this latter honour was "the highest qualification any French professor can possess."[82] Through the *Casket*, St.F.X. assured its Catholic constituency that the Carnegie Corporation was not a godless institution, but distributed its largesse irrespective of race and creed. The new French chair at St.F.X., predicted one professor, would promote a "bonne entente" between the races.[83]

The announcement of a chair of French propelled into action those Gaels loyal to their own cultural heritage. The Antigonish Highland Society, which had been formed in 1861 to preserve and promote Scottish culture,[84] was provoked by the alleged "lifting of the Gaul above the Gael" at the college;[85] it urged the college to establish a chair of Gaelic along with the chair of French.[86] The society underscored the importance of the "Highland element" in founding and developing

St.F.X.; and it did not want this element to play "second fiddle" to any other nationality.[87] Little had been done for Celtic culture since Rev. A. MacLean Sinclair had lectured at the college from 1908 to 1912. Unfortunately, St.F.X. just then found it impractical to endow a chair of Gaelic, even though it tried and had a promise of conditional support.[88] However, some stirrings, stimulated by a reported Gaelic revival overseas in Scotland and Ireland, were beginning in the local Celtic soul. A meeting of Scots in Sydney petitioned the government for Gaelic in the public schools, and some zealots formed the Scottish Catholic Society of Canada in the summer of 1919.[89] At St.F.X. a class in Gaelic was formed in early 1919, the Highland Society donated $100 to the effort the following year, a Gaelic column began appearing in the *Casket*, and the first Gaelic article appeared in the *Xaverian* in 1921.[90] But these efforts failed to satisfy some. A *Xaverian* contributor in 1925 lamented the "Anglicization" of the Gael in Canada and attacked the low priority given Scottish language and culture at St.F.X. He recommended more courses in Gaelic and Celtic history, and declared they would be of more value to Scottish students than "much of the useless Greek history and mythology we have to study."[91] From 1875 the enrolment of students of Scottish descent had been declining at St.F.X., but they still composed 46 per cent of the student body in 1925, and remained its single largest ethnic group.

Economic and Social Distress in the Region
Pressures other than ethnic tensions brought about program innovations at St.F.X. after the war. Rural depopulation and outmigration had emerged as a serious problem. For example, the population in Antigonish County had dropped from 18,060 in 1881 to 11,518 by 1921;[92] most other counties in the diocese, except for Cape Breton and Pictou Counties, had also lost substantial portions of their people as the young, and sometimes entire families, deserted the farms and fishing villages for more promising opportunities in the region's towns or cities, or in urban centres south of the Canadian border. Many Maritime leaders expressed alarm at the region's economic and political decline; in response they campaigned for "Maritime Rights" within the federation.[93]

The bishop and priests of the Diocese of Antigonish saw the rural demoralization at first hand, and some went on the prowl for solutions. Rev. Dr Hugh MacPherson and Rev. Miles Tompkins, a St.F.X. graduate with a B SC in agriculture from the University of Toronto,[94] even before the war had encouraged the area farmers to begin cooperative enterprises and to adopt "scientific methods" of agriculture.[95] But after the war, it was Father Jimmy Tompkins who became the central driving force in the search for answers. He had heard fascinating ideas about university extension in 1912 at the Congress of Empire Universities in England.[96] Tompkins had also been influenced by the teachings of Bishop O'Dwyer of Ireland, a church leader who stressed the connection between Catholic poverty and education, and by Archbishop Neil McNeil of Toronto, who was seeking to broaden the Christian concept of charity. Moreover, Right Rev. A.S. Barnes, chaplain at Cambridge University, had described the social work of the Catholic Social Guild in England and had urged St.F.X. to lead the way in doing a similar work when he received an honorary degree from St.F.X. and addressed convocation in June 1917.[97] No doubt Tompkins had also been exposed to the thinking of Pope Leo XIII, whose encyclical *Rerum Novarum* (1891) on the plight of the poor had been issued only a few years before he arrived in Rome as a student.[98] Donald F. MacDonald, a renowned geologist from Pictou County, similarly encouraged the college to make applied science information available to the farmers through extension work.[99]

Tompkins was convinced. He believed the control of industry and finance in the Maritimes had been centralized in Toronto and Montreal; he asserted, "Industrially and financially we are living under a despotism."[100] But along with others, Tompkins was optimistic that Maritimers were on the verge of real progress.[101] His fellow priest, President MacPherson, believed the people of eastern Nova Scotia had been shaken from their lethargy, backwardness, and isolation by the war. He was certain that the military crusade had been "a great electric shock" which showed the people what they were capable of doing for their own social and economic regeneration.[102]

Father Tompkins Spearheads Reform
Tompkins, with the cooperation of other concerned priests and laymen, developed two means to stimulate thinking and test ideas about regional social and economic problems. In early 1918 he began a weekly column in the *Casket*, called "For the People."[103] He recruited writers to submit articles examining current issues and proposing new ways to revitalize community life; the contributions dealt mostly with social, economic, and educational affairs, and topics included study clubs, farming, labour, and cooperation. Tompkins's columnists stressed themes of efficiency, progress, advancement, and success; they also called for greater efforts in Catholic higher education.[104] The St.F.X. professor Rev. Dr D.J. MacDonald composed many articles on economics. Another major contributor to Tompkins's "For the People" column was Henry Somerville, a Catholic sociologist he had recruited from England for Archbishop McNeil of Toronto in 1915.[105] Somerville

Rev. James J. Tompkins, professor and
administrator 1902–22

came from a working-class background; he had attended Ruskin College, Oxford and had become an authority on social and labour questions in England. At the request of the archbishop of Toronto, Somerville would become editor of the *Catholic Register*, an appointment he would hold until his death in 1953. With pen and tongue, he introduced Canadian Catholics to new social, economic, and political ideas, and helped to bring about approval, in the 1930s, of Catholic participation in the Cooperative Commonwealth Federation.[106] Somerville actually lectured at St.F.X. through 1918-19 on reform movements and Catholic social action.[107]

Tompkins was also the major inspiration behind the organization from 1918 to 1921 of educational and social conferences at St.F.X. which were attended largely, but not exclusively, by diocesan clergy.[108] Speakers at these assemblies presented papers on topics like the reform of rural education, advances in agriculture, housing, labour unions, and leadership training.[109] Sometimes renowned scholars, such as Rev. Dr John A. Ryan, a sociologist at the Catholic University of America and a supporter of "progressive social action," addressed the conferences.[110] In concert with pressure from lay people, the conferences focused the attention of St.F.X. faculty on the social and economic problems of the region and underscored the urgent need for some form of university-sponsored extension work.[111] Neil McArthur, a Sydney lawyer and St.F.X. alumnus, wrote to Tompkins in 1920: "A chain of schools throughout the industrial centres of Cape Breton and Pictou Counties under the direction and supervision of the University, with the assistance and support of local organizations in the various communities, would to my mind not only serve a very useful purpose for the public generally, but also develop a feeling of friendship towards the College, which would be of very great advantage."[112] This suggestion for "a chain of schools" did not materialize; however, certain other ideas did.

St.F.X.'s First People's School

Tompkins penned a famous pamphlet in 1920 which marshalled weighty arguments for extension work by St.F.X. *Knowledge for the People* was, in the words of his biographer, a "key statement of his life" which attacked the concept of the university as an "isolated eminence" serving only an elite group seeking professional careers.[113] He pronounced such an approach "a worn-out tradition."[114] The pamphlet, widely circulated in eastern Nova Scotia, exhorted St.F.X. to carry education and training to a knowledge-thirsty public, to the farmer, the fishermen, the miner, and the "average citizen." Tompkins was convinced that medical and law schools should be left to the

First people's school, 1921

"Dalhousies"; St.F.X. was especially equipped to bring knowledge to the people.[115] He reviewed experiments in extension work being carried out in Scotland, England, the United States, and other Canadian provinces, and then urged the college "to serve 100 per cent of the constituency" from which came its money and students.[116] In his inimitable and excited style he wrote to the editor of the *Casket*: "I didn't know much about the subject when I started studying but I find that a wonderful case can be put up for extension teaching, and if I am any judge of public opinion, the hour has struck when St.F.X. must get into the field."[117] The *Casket* gave a front-page summary of the striking pamphlet.[118]

At Tompkins's urging, these ideas were tried out in a people's school held at St.F.X. from 17 January to 12 March 1921. The *Casket*, by now solidly under the control of the bishop and clergy,[119] again acted as the propaganda arm of the college; it advertised the innovation far and wide.[120] Fifty-two adults, mostly from Antigonish County, registered in the school; of these, about thirty were farmers and the remainder included carpenters, clerks, miners, fishermen, and railway workers. Only one was a woman. All were over seventeen years of age, and most had achieved a grade school level anywhere from six to eleven. St.F.X. set no requirements for admission to its people's school.[121] The regular faculty taught the following academic and practical subjects: arithmetic, English language and literature, economics, chemistry, physics, business and finance, public speaking, and agriculture – stock breeding, feeding farm animals, soils and crops, veterinary hygiene, biology, and natural resources. Tompkins modelled this school after the Danish people's schools started in 1845 by Bishop Grundtvig. Two years before, Tompkins had praised these schools extravagantly and had recommended one for every county in Nova Scotia. However, he was willing to settle for less: "If we cannot have one in every county let us give it a trial and get one at least in the province."[122]

The school was so successful that it was repeated in 1922 with an even higher enrolment,[123] and in 1923 and 1924 organizers ran one in Glace Bay, Cape Breton.[124] The Glace Bay people's schools operated in the evenings under the direction of Rev. Dr Thomas O'R. Boyle, a St.F.X. philosophy professor who had been hired in September 1921.[125] Local teachers and St.F.X. staff taught a wide range of cultural and practical subjects. Attendance reached as high as 250 in 1923.[126] For a time, at least, the people's school fulfilled Tompkins's hope of putting St.F.X. "on the map." Even regular students at the college praised the effort to expand education beyond the "exclusive privilege of a favoured few"; they also had been impressed by the wealth of talent and experience which the adults brought to the campus.[127] Warm commendations appeared in the *Casket*, the *Sydney Post*, and the Halifax papers.[128] The faculty evidently thought of their people's school experiment as only the first step in extension work; their ambitious plans for the future contemplated community centres, itinerant lecturers, and travelling libraries.[129]

The Financial Campaign of 1920

The post-war resurgence of optimism which fuelled this extension experiment also convinced St.F.X. authorities, urged on by the faculty, to undertake a major financial campaign during the summer of 1920.[130] They set an ambitious target of $500,000 with these intentions: "to place the College on a footing of equality with other institutions of its kind," to eliminate the war-incurred deficit of nearly $75,000, to improve the physical plant, to establish scholarships, to meet the matching requirements of the Carnegie Corporation endowment for a chair of French, to keep tuition low, and to form a general development fund for future curricular and faculty expansion.[131] Officials also stressed, no doubt with the recent Russian communist revolution and the Winnipeg general strike in mind, the need for the "steadying influence of Catholic principles ... to counteract the radical and revolutionary forces at work in society today."[132]

The board hired a professional fund-raiser, Ward Systems of New York, to conduct the campaign. Individuals and corporations in the diocese, in the New England states, and in the Canadian west were canvassed. Some of the campaign propaganda claimed that St.F.X. had "set its face toward the people" through the work of certain faculty members in agriculture (Dr Hugh MacPherson) and the fisheries (Dr C.J. Connolly).[133] The *Casket* enthusiastically promoted the campaign and pleaded *ad nauseam* for its generous support by the Catholics of eastern Nova Scotia.[134] The Alumni Association also placed its weight behind the drive.[135] The provincial council of CNDs, on behalf of Mount St Bernard College, likewise offered to help with the campaign and share in the take on the grounds that Catholic women of the diocese deserved to attain standards of intellectual development equivalent to those of men.[136] The total subscription came to $565,000 and most of this originated from within the diocese;[137] however, a depression in 1921 slowed the payment of subscribed funds. By June 1927, about $420,000 had been collected.[138] The campaign of 1920 was the most ambitious and successful of any undertaken by St.F.X. to then. The organizational skills and experience of Ward Systems must have been largely responsible, for the diocese had recently suffered the twin crises of war and recession.

The campaign of 1920 was likely responsible for the entry at St.F.X. of the university's so-called "First Lady," that is, the hiring of the first full-time female lay employee. Her name was Rebecca MacLean.[139] She was a local lady, a single Catholic who would eventually serve three successive presidents while assisting countless other Xaverians, staff and students alike. As female support staff, her profile was low; however, this revealed nothing about her importance to the daily operations of the institution. In a quiet, dignified, unassuming, and lively manner, she earned the respect and gratitude of all.[140] At her retirement thirty-four years later, another devoted female Xaverian would state that, as a veteran university employee, MacLean "had rendered invaluable help to countless numbers of the staff, the students, and the faculty members."[141] MacLean initiated a pattern at St.F.X. of long-term devotion rendered by single female support staff. Their roles would be crucial to St.F.X. and would help define the institution for all Xaverians.

Neil McNeil and the Boston Properties

The financial status of the college was also bolstered in the early 1920s by an injection of revenue from its trusty college benefactor, Neil McNeil of Boston. From 1910, McNeil had been a close friend of St.F.X. authorities, a generous donor, and an expert adviser on building construction and alterations. In 1919 he decided to deed his extensive Boston properties, forty-three in all, to St.F.X.; they were worth from $500,000 to $600,000. The college community was euphoric at the news. President MacPherson praised it as "the biggest thing ever done by a Catholic for Catholic education, as far as I know."[142] The terms of the trust deed required all net income over $5000 from the estate be paid to McNeil until his death. The principal from the sale of properties was to be held in a Neil McNeil Endowment Fund and its revenues to be used at the discretion of the college.[143] McNeil died in December 1921.[144] Shortly thereafter, certain disgruntled relatives went after a share of his substantial estate.[145] Their strategy, it seems, was to contest the validity of McNeil's will on the grounds that President MacPherson, Father Tompkins, and others had exercised undue influence on an old man who was allegedly unstable and alcoholic; once they accomplished this, they could then also attack the validity of the trust deed.[146] The charges were ultimately judged false and the contestants failed to undermine the validity of McNeil's will or his trust deed.[147]

McNeil's trust deed was a mixed blessing for St.F.X. It did augment the college's revenues. From 1921 to 1925, for example, the college received a net benefit of about $49,000.[148] However, during his final years, McNeil had allowed the Boston properties to deteriorate; therefore, the college was forced to expend considerable sums to restore them.[149] Moreover, the subsequent litigation with McNeil's chagrined relatives and its expense was distasteful. For years, relatives and friends occasionally petitioned St.F.X. for a share of the estate income. Finally, the administrative burden and legal costs of managing the Boston properties were considerable.[150] Thus college authorities gradually sold the properties off and reinvested the money in securities.[151] Perhaps the large McNeil bequest was as important for its positive psychological impact on post-war St.F.X. as it was for the material assistance it rendered the college.

The Post-War Campus Scene
A.B. McKillop writes, "The world ushered in by the Great War appeared like the world of Alice – bewildering, disproportionate, seemingly out of control."[152] Evidences of this general disorder appeared at St.F.X. in the post-war period of reconstruction. Enrolments had dropped precipitously during the war; yet they rose steadily after the war from 121 in 1918 to 225 in 1921. The ethos of this post-war student body seemed different from the pre-war. The students were generally older; some were war veterans.[153] And women had become a larger minority which then accounted for about 15 per cent of enrolments.[154] College authorities felt compelled to allow returned soldiers to board outside the college so they might have "all the freedom they wished."[155] Students appeared less acquiescent and more ready to register complaints. Decades before it became a popular cause, one advocated more democracy in college life; he criticized the enforced "penal laws" at St.F.X., and recommended student participation in the college's academic and disciplinary administration in order to bring certain professors down from their isolation on "mighty Olympus" and to enkindle an "esprit de corps" at St.F.X.[156] In 1921, the entire student body made "serious complaint" to the board of governors about the declining quality of food, poor lighting, and the "increasing indifference" among faculty about overall student activities.[157] Moreover, on several notable occasions, students appealed disciplinary measures against fellow students. Indeed, the senior class, in February 1922, threatened to leave the college if its officials expelled a certain classmate; the faculty relented and reinstated the student, allegedly because the class had been "particularly satisfactory."[158] The practice of hazing, which had earlier vanished, reappeared at St.F.X. about this time. A faculty member in 1925 attacked this upper class reception of freshmen as "degrading, unjust, and un-Christian."[159]

Xavier Hall (east wing) shortly after 1919 fire

Power plant and Memorial Rink, both built in 1921

Condemning the practice was one thing; effectively abolishing it was another matter indeed.

Then, in September 1919, a mysterious fire inflicted considerable damage on the old east wing of the administration building and its resident library collection.[160] It also seriously injured one fire-fighter, Alex McNaughton. College authorities suspected an arsonist in their midst; they were right. With the help of a Halifax detective and a cunning set-up by two fellow students, the "fire-bug" confessed to the crime, was arrested, tried, and found guilty, to the great relief of the Xaverian community.[161] Of course, he was promptly expelled.[162] The president reported later that the incendiary was plotting to raze the college with dynamite in order to make a complete job of it.[163] In the words of the *Casket*, it was "a deliberate plot to destroy the institution."[164] What provoked the student's destructive behaviour is now uncertain; it would be over fifty years before another St.F.X. student would attempt to torch his *alma mater*.

On a more salutary note, two years later, St.F.X. students undertook a timely, war-related project when they set out on their own to finance a new rink to be dedicated as a memorial to the college's war dead.[165] The old rink, called the "Cigar Box" and built in 1901, had become a safety hazard. Furthermore, at least one professor thought a replacement would help to lift the slumped morale of the student body.[166] Back in 1914, students had already raised $5000 for a new rink, but the war brought their efforts to an abrupt halt and foiled their plans for recreational improvements. Construction began in November 1921; the final cost was about $36,000. The president hoped the new Memorial Rink would be a "noble inspiration" to subsequent generations of students at St.F.X.[167] It certainly became an important centre of athletic and social life for future Xaverians.

The First World War had been a trial by fire for both St.F.X. and its eastern Nova Scotia Catholic constituency. It had wrought change, some harsh, damaging, and difficult to surmount. The soaring ambitions evident among college officials at the turn of the century had been tempered by the war experience, but the generous financial support of Neil McNeil and Dr John Somers for new buildings, the successful people's school, the effective campaign of 1920, and the large McNeil gift of 1919 aroused a resurgence of ambitions and plans. Moreover, the college's vice-president, Father Jimmy Tompkins, proved irrepressible. However, St.F.X. would soon be embroiled in another crisis, one which harboured the potential for a complete change of the denominational college *status quo* in Nova Scotia.

PART FOUR

University Reform and Depression,
1921–36

·9·

The Challenge of
University Federation, 1922–23

In 1922 St.F.X. was nearly seventy years old. By then, the small liberal arts college of about 245 students and faculty had become a venerable institutional fixture of the Diocese of Antigonish. The 92,800 Catholics of eastern Nova Scotia,[1] many of Highland Scottish descent, were grateful that it had protected the faith of their youth and had granted them a standing in the public, professional, and commercial affairs of the country. Any plan for educational reform which threatened fundamental alteration of their college was bound to pierce to the quick of Catholic loyalties and arouse passionate controversy. Such a scheme forced itself into public consciousness with special urgency in 1922 when the prestigious Carnegie Corporation of New York released a provocative study of Maritime education which proposed a federated university for the region to be located in Halifax.

A Perennial Debate
The idea of a centralized, unified educational effort in Halifax was long-standing; advocacy for such a plan had become a Nova Scotian tradition.[2] A provincial university was Lord Dalhousie's motive for founding his nondenominational college in 1818.[3] Subsequent schemes had included the King's-Dalhousie union proposals of 1823 and 1884–85, the ill-starred University of Halifax experiment in the late 1870s,[4] a joint proposal by King's College, Windsor and Dalhousie University, Halifax in 1902 for Maritime university consolidation,[5] and, in 1909, a suggestion by the Nova Scotia superintendent of education that the University of Halifax be revived.[6] Maritime Catholics had regarded such proposals with suspicion; cooperation with their own kind – mooted in the 1870s and occasionally since then – had much greater appeal but no more success.[7] The Carnegie proposal in 1922 merely signalled the latest round, although a critical one, in a perennial debate about the *status quo* in Maritime higher education.

The Carnegie Investigation and Report

With its report, Carnegie had "struck while the iron was hot." University federation had a most powerful allure in 1922. First, the wealthy New York corporation promised money to back its recommendation. For some years, Carnegie philanthropy had been extending northeast to the Maritime colleges. St.F.X. itself had received $50,000 in 1919 for the endowment of a chair in French. All the colleges, lacking government funding since 1881 (the University of New Brunswick excepted), had incurred staggering wartime debts followed by burgeoning enrolments. Acadia College in Wolfville and King's in Windsor had recently suffered the loss of buildings through fire. In addition, trends of academic specialization and professionalization, generated by the needs of an industrial state devoted to utility and efficiency, were creating new and more exacting demands in education, demands for new programs, more faculty, and more elaborate facilities and equipment.[8] And finally, there remained the plague of outmigration rooted in economic underdevelopment which was lamented by the Maritime Rights Movement.[9] Not surprisingly, the Carnegie Corporation found itself besieged by requests for grants from Maritime colleges. Carnegie officials, therefore, decided to survey educational conditions in the region; the information obtained would be used in future granting decisions and would, they hoped, help them to avoid encouraging "injudicious forms of competition."[10] In May 1921, two officials – Dr William S. Learned, a member of the Carnegie staff, and Kenneth C.M. Sills, president of Bowdoin College, Maine – were commissioned to survey the region's educational institutions; they did so in October and November.

The results of the Learned and Sills survey became public in May 1922. The commissioners identified three central weaknesses in Maritime higher education: underfunding, inadequate facilities, and fragmented efforts. Their assessment of St.F.X. was moderately positive. They acknowledged the generally excellent qualifications of its faculty and the recent modern development of the campus;[11] overall, they thought, it was "a very genuine institution."[12] The successful financial campaign of 1920, concluded Learned and Sills, demonstrated that St.F.X. had a strong grip on the Catholics of eastern Nova Scotia. Finally, they praised the college's sense of responsibility for its constituency, as demonstrated by its training of rural school teachers, and its extension of education to the masses through its people's school.

Nevertheless, all the colleges were indicted in the Learned and Sills critique of the *status quo*. They recommended that the existing set-up be replaced, not by a specialization of function in each college, or by the selection of one college for special development, but instead by a federated Maritime university at Halifax composed of constituent denominational colleges which would hold their degree-granting powers in abeyance. The denominational character of Maritime society, argued Learned and Sills, required a central university organized internally on denominational lines; only this design would rally the population to unite behind it.[13] The central advantages of federation would be a unification of educational effort and high standards of academic excellence. The amalgamation of the colleges would leave the present campuses free to conduct high school work, a function they already provided. At Halifax, the constituent colleges would build their own residences, chapels, and lecture halls. All students would be required to register in one of the colleges. Learned and Sills believed such a scheme would be a superb way of organizing a large student body, in contrast to the American mega-universities, where students were virtually adrift.[14]

Their report anticipated the objection that religion would be slighted or eliminated in the federated university. Elsewhere, it argued, federation had worked to "stimulate, clarify, and conserve the denominational ideal and vigour in its colleges rather than weaken it."[15] "The best reason for the existence of the denominational college," affirmed the report, "lies in its endeavour to surround intellectual life with the high aspirations and illuminated motives that true religion is capable of generating."[16] Learned and Sills contemplated one united Catholic college in the federation for all Maritime Catholics. They appealed to precedents, such as the University of Toronto pattern, to buttress their case for a new arrangement in the Maritimes. Like the University of Toronto, their scheme did not represent the elimination of religion from higher education, but instead its recognition. In the words of C.B. Sissons, federation would be "a fusion of the interests of church and state."[17] The ambitious and radical scheme would be financed, they suggested, through existing college endowments, tuition fees, and government funding. The Carnegie Corporation itself eventually promised to contribute $3 million to finance the proposed reform. Its officials hoped that the Maritime colleges would discuss the federation scheme recommended by Learned and Sills and thereby develop a plan acceptable to all concerned.

A Champion of University Federation at St.F.X.

At St.F.X., Vice-President Tompkins became an outspoken champion of university federation and campaigned vigorously and widely in its favour. He was probably responsible, at least among Catholics, for much of the momentum in its favour. By this time in his life, Tompkins had gained extensive experience as a campaigner, and these skills, combined with his unfettered enthusiasm, optimism, and energy, made him a force to be reckoned with. In April 1922, he temporarily revived, in the local newspaper, a column called "For the People" which he had edited several years before; in it he reprinted articles which hailed the Carnegie proposal as a great solution to Maritime problems in higher education.[18]

Tompkins's zealousness for federation was partly rooted in his high regard for the educational expertise of the Carnegie people; on their side, Carnegie officials had grown to respect and admire the dynamic, persistent priest-reformer from the Maritimes. Furthermore, Tompkins and Dalhousie officials (also key proponents of federation) had mutual admiration for one another, symbolized by two events: Tompkins's acceptance of an honorary degree from Dalhousie in 1919 for his efforts to promote and improve education, and his suggestion in 1920 that St.F.X. collaborate with Dalhousie in a united financial campaign.[19] Tompkins, moreover, had ceaselessly laboured for educational progress – higher staff qualifications and specialization – at St.F.X. and, to him, the Carnegie scheme promised for Catholics a giant leap forward. For years he had been scathingly critical of Catholic efforts and attitudes in higher education. He confided in Learned that he was "intensely interested" in the movement because in it he saw "the realization of fifteen years of dreadful uphill work and against terrible odds of all kinds."[20]

Tompkins coveted not only improved Catholic educational standards through federation but also the economic and social uplift of the masses. John Reid rightly claims that, for Tompkins, "the federation scheme represented a final opportunity for the Maritime provinces to regain their prosperity through self-help." For him, as for other supporters, the "economic argument" was central.[21] In Tompkins's vision of the plan, all groups would benefit: Maritime Catholics would gain better-quality education by combining their efforts at Halifax; the Acadians, for whom he had earlier revealed a special solicitude, would, he anticipated, eventually have a constituent college;[22] the United Mine Workers of America, who were organizing educational clubs in Cape Breton with the plan of forming a labour college, would instead join it to the federation;[23] and, finally, the masses would benefit from federation because colleges, like St.F.X. and St Dunstan's in Charlottetown, would become people's schools. In other words, after the strictly academic programs had been moved to Halifax, these schools would be freed to "do for the whole people what they have in part been doing for one-half of one percent of the people."[24]

Father Tompkins's Supporters and Opponents
Tompkins was emboldened in his federation campaign by support from high-ranking Catholic authorities. Moral support and information

useful as propaganda came from Henry Carr, the superior of St Michael's College at the University of Toronto,[25] and also from the archbishop of Toronto, Neil McNeil, a former professor and rector of St.F.X.[26] Two British professors on staff, H.R.W. Smith and W.H. Bucknell, also drafted statements which described the positive experience of Catholics at the universities of Cambridge and Oxford.[27] Armed with such weighty authority and support, Tompkins was probably responsible for persuading the faculty to pass unanimously a resolution in January 1922 which supported university federation; Learned was most gratified by this early commendation of his proposal.[28] And Tompkins predicted that, in a short time, St.F.X. would be "a centre of red-hot enthusiasts for the scheme."[29]

But even then, Tompkins sighted opposition, an opposition he would condemn ever more bitterly as the enemy of all things liberal and progressive. His early antagonist was the St.F.X. president, H.P. MacPherson, for whose administrative abilities and educational ideas Tompkins had little esteem.[30] MacPherson had a long-standing antipathy to the idea of one grand Maritime university. In his view, such an institution would be inaccessible to many Maritime youth, and would be restricted in its ability to influence character and inculcate ideals.[31] Like Tompkins, MacPherson energetically canvassed Catholic leaders for their opinions on university federation. He was especially troubled by rumours about the Canadian apostolic delegate's alleged support for federation. However, on inquiry he discovered Peter Di Maria's prudent diplomacy: he only favoured such a scheme if it strengthened Catholics and was appropriate to the circumstances. Di Maria recommended that the critical question of federation be deferred to the collective wisdom of the Maritime bishops.[32]

President MacPherson summed up his own sentiments about university federation this way: "Personally, I dread this scheme."[33] It would ruin the faith of Catholics, he was convinced, and would reduce their influence in Maritime affairs. Furthermore, under his administration, St.F.X. had modernized and expanded its campus, developed a more highly qualified staff, endowed several chairs, and conducted in 1920 a successful financial campaign. In addition, he anticipated considerable revenues from the substantial Boston properties which Neil McNeil had recently willed to the college.[34] In MacPherson's view, St.F.X. had the confidence of the Catholics of eastern Nova Scotia, and he felt confident and optimistic about its future. To him, the Carnegie proposal was a distraction; in June he lamented, "The people are very much agitated over this merger question, and the division is going to do harm to St.F.X., whatever may be the outcome of the merger."[35]

The Maritime Universities Confer

At the initiative of King's College, joint discussions of university federation began on 7 July with an unofficial conference of university representatives held at Halifax.[36] Mount Allison University in Sackville, New Brunswick attended, along with Dalhousie and Acadia.[37] Two unofficial delegates from St Mary's College, Halifax (run by the Irish Christian Brothers) represented the Catholic Archdiocese of Halifax. At President MacPherson's request, J.A. Walker, a personal friend and Halifax lawyer, unofficially represented St.F.X. MacPherson was moving cautiously; he had only recently obtained the Learned and Sills report, and had not heard from the Maritime bishops who were yet to examine the scheme.[38] This first conference discussed, in a preliminary way, the Learned and Sills proposal, formed several committees to examine financial and constitutional issues, and scheduled a general conference when these committees would report.[39]

Bishop James Morrision's Opposition

Before this next conference, several crucial meetings were held at St.F.X. and by the Maritime Catholic hierarchy. At the annual diocesan clergy retreat in July, Tompkins discovered, to his dismay, that he would not be given a free hand to advertise his views. Already he had found President MacPherson's attitude frustrating; in June he lamented that "vicious propaganda" against federation was being circulated in Antigonish by the ignorant and misinformed. At the retreat he had to reckon with Bishop Morrison. According to Tompkins, the bishop refused to allow public discussion of the issue – an opportunity Tompkins was keenly anticipating – until an earnest lobby by three priests caused him to relent. Then, reported Tompkins, he "set himself up as the sole spokesmen" and invited questions. Tompkins was denied the right to be heard and later privately attacked Bishop Morrison as "autocratic" and "backward." He claimed that most of the one hundred priests at the retreat were "disgusted" by the bishop's actions and opinions.[40] However, later in July, Bishop Morrison did invite both President MacPherson and Tompkins to present their views before a meeting of Catholic representatives in Halifax.[41]

Bishop Morrison, quite characteristically, had slowly and cautiously formed his own convictions about university federation, and, as chief shepherd of the Catholics of eastern Nova Scotia, had decided how the crucial issue should be handled in the diocese. In early June he professed openness about federation, but he had misgivings about what he described as the "Protestant mentality."[42] First, he was leery of educational cooperation with Protestants, since, in his view, their neutrality in education was suspect. Certain de facto Catholic schools in the

184

diocese, especially in Pictou County, had been denied public funding by local school boards, in spite of their qualified staff and compliance with department of education curricular requirements. Catholics deplored the alleged Presbyterian intolerance and the injustice of double taxation; they even collected money in other parts of the diocese to lighten the financial burden weighing on their Pictou brethren.[43] Closer to home, indeed right in Antigonish itself, Bishop Morrison, about five years before, had blamed Protestant bigotry for blocking Catholic educational advance. Then he had accused Mayor D. Grant Kirk (1917–18) and the school inspector of keeping Catholic boys in a "squalid old building that was a disgrace to the community" and of attempting to prevent Catholics from building a new school.[44] Furthermore, Bishop Morrison had witnessed the treatment received by Catholic chaplains in the First World War at the hands of a "denominationally-biased" Canadian chaplaincy service.[45] So the bishop's misgivings about Protestants were rooted in his own bitter experience. Second, Morrison thought the Catholic Church would oppose a merger with Protestants; he wanted the Maritime hierarchy's opinion and the Vatican's consent before taking further steps.[46] Meanwhile, Morrison wished all propagandizing within the diocese to cease before irreparable damage had been inflicted on the reputation of the college. He urged the *Casket* editor not to publish material on the contentious issue. Some diocesan matters, ventured the bishop, should not be "ventilated through the Catholic press," but instead should be "referred to those whose special duty it is to deal with them."[47] The editor, Robert Phalen, would censor the controversial issue from his newspaper's columns until the end of October.

A Divided Catholic Hierarchy
In July and August two meetings convened which propelled Catholic developments further along. Archbishop Edward J. McCarthy of Halifax invited the Maritime and Newfoundland hierarchy to a conference in late July. Among other things, the conference directed Bishop Morrison to ask for Rome's view of the federation scheme; for unknown reasons he delayed for over three months.[48] Then, on 1 August, the St.F.X. board of governors met and appointed committees to study the "merger proposition" and report periodically on developments. President MacPherson composed the committee on education, and, along with board members Rev. H.D. Barry, Archibald A. McIntyre, and Neil McArthur, also the one on finance.[49] The board moved that, if he "deem it advisable," the bishop delegate representatives to attend joint conferences on the federation scheme.[50]

The Maritime and Newfoundland bishops, again at the request of Archbishop McCarthy, convened a second time at Halifax. The meeting, held on 19 October, was noteworthy, for it revealed a definite split in the Catholic episcopal ranks over university federation. The archbishop's invitation was the first indication to Bishop Morrison that trouble lay ahead: "I am convinced," asserted McCarthy, "that University Federation has far-reaching possibilities for the promotion of Catholic interests and the advancement of the Church in the Maritime provinces."[51] In reply, Morrison coldly informed McCarthy that the vast majority of his Catholics opposed merging St.F.X. in the proposed federation; he restated his conviction that the issue should be settled quickly, and hence removed from "the field of irresponsible propaganda which can only prove detrimental to the best Catholic interests."[52]

The Halifax conference included Archbishop McCarthy, Bishop Morrison, Bishops Edward-Alfred Leblanc and Patrick Chaisson of New Brunswick, and Bishop Much, who represented the archbishop of St John's, Newfoundland. At the conference table, McCarthy and Much argued for university federation if the morals of Catholic boys would be protected; but Bishops Morrison, Leblanc, and Chaisson were opposed.[53] Morrison made the longest plea for the *status quo*, contending that federation promised to undermine the goal of Catholic character formation, reduce vocations to the priesthood, and weaken relations between faculty and students in the several Catholic colleges. The prelates, reflecting widespread differences of opinion among Canadian Catholics over acceptable relations with Protestants in higher education,[54] eventually agreed to a compromise resolution which revealed internal tensions. Their joint resolution stated that the Carnegie scheme appeared detrimental to Catholic interests; thus the hierarchy could not commend it to the Catholics of the Maritimes and Newfoundland. They resolved to inquire of Rome before taking further steps. However, they favoured means to promote efficiency in education "with proper safeguards of conscience." This compromise position surely left all the bishops dissatisfied. A statement on university federation from a higher authority became even more urgent.[55] Bishop Morrison was again directed to submit the question to Rome.

St.F.X. Opts Out

At Morrison's request, the St.F.X. board of governors held a special meeting immediately after the Maritime and Newfoundland hierarchy conference.[56] The meeting was fateful. Several days before, President MacPherson had urged the bishop not to allow the passage of a resolution approving federation. Perhaps he was apprehensive about the possible actions of board member Rt Rev. William Foley of Halifax, a professed mergerite who had recommended a central educational hall for Catholics in his address to the St.F.X. graduating class in May

1921.[57] And MacPherson had reminded Morrison that Tompkins had spread abroad the false impression that the whole diocese supported the merger proposal.[58] Foley attended the meeting, along with eleven others. As chancellor, Bishop Morrison chaired the special session. He called on the secretary to read a committee report which condemned federation. Then Morrison himself reported on the bishops' conference which had met the day before in Halifax; he claimed that the bishops had decided against Maritime Catholic colleges entering federation. Actually, this gave their statement more finality than was warranted; the bishops had resolved not to take further steps until Rome had spoken. Nonetheless, the board, whose most influential members were anti-merger, resolved "That St Francis Xavier College do not enter the proposed Federation of Maritime Universities" and that it send no delegates to the federation conference scheduled for 23 and 24 October.[59] Even though the Holy See had not yet revealed its mind about Maritime university federation, St.F.X. authorities had decided to stand aloof from such a scheme, no matter what. Any mergerites at the board meeting were apparently given no quarter. Bishop Morrison, the day after the decisive meeting, expressed his hope that "in the not very distant future the best minds of the Maritime Provinces will bless us for having saved to Christianity the educational culture of our rising generation."[60]

The committee report on federation read before the board had been largely drafted by a faculty member and later president, Rev. Dr D.J. MacDonald.[61] It was a disorganized and repetitive attack on federation, from both the pedagogical and religious standpoints, and strongly advised college authorities not to place their heads "in the merger noose."[62] The report maintained that federation would fragment Catholic educational purposes, eliminate the central element of Christianity in the formation of leaders, close down a college that was doing admirable work, wipe out recent gains made in the curriculum, and bring about the loss of endowments and Catholic sources of revenue. Big is surely not necessarily better, declared the report, and a good liberal arts college need not have "expensive equipment, large libraries, and heavy endowments."[63] By quoting from modern college textbooks, MacDonald tried to demonstrate that much of the teaching of a central university would be pervaded by dangerous evolutionist, materialist, relativist, and anti-religious doctrines. He presented copious quotations from church authorities on the desirability of religious education. After critiquing the rhetoric of the mergerites, and counselling loyalty to the educational project of St.F.X.'s founding fathers, the author warned, "The Catholics of the Maritime Provinces are forbidden by common sense and the natural law to give up their distinctively

Catholic liberal arts work for a diluted, semi-Catholic, semi-pagan course of instruction in this proposed non-sectarian university."[64] How widely his report was circulated and what influence it had are hard to judge.[65] Bishop Morrison did send a copy to the apostolic delegate and encouraged him to send it to Rome.[66] Undoubtedly, it expressed the sentiments of at least Bishop Morrison, President MacPherson, and selected board members.

A Divided Catholic Camp

Since the Maritime and Newfoundland bishops had decided to appeal to Rome, the sentiments of diocesan priests, laity, and faculty toward university federation were essentially irrelevant to the outcome of the discussions. Furthermore, few reliable indicators of the extent of support for merger remain; no vote was taken among Catholics, as was done in 1924–25 by Presbyterians over church union in Canada. The *Casket* columns were closed to debate, although not to anti-mergerite arguments. Its editor had concluded that most laity admitted to little knowledge of the merger question and were pleased to defer to the bishop.[67] On the other hand, Tompkins claimed that almost everyone – faculty, governors, students, clergy, and laity – supported federation; but he was hardly an objective commentator. In his opinion, and it was probably overstated, six professors left that year in disgust over the bishop's handling of the proposal.[68] True, several professors left St.F.X. in the summer of 1922, but their reasons for doing so appear diverse.[69] There were advocates and antis among leading Catholic laity and priests in the diocese, just as there were elsewhere among Canadian Catholics generally. The Catholic camp was divided.

As developments progressed in the fall, Bishop Morrison and President MacPherson became ever more anxious for a prompt ruling from Rome. University representatives and government leaders from eastern Canada – about fifty of them – held a general conference at Halifax in Province House on 24 October. They expressed a distressingly complex tangle of opinions about naming the proposed university "Dalhousie"; however, at the end of the day, federationists had cause for hope.[70] Delegates from the archdiocese claimed that most Catholics in Nova Scotia advocated federation. With support from the archdiocese of Newfoundland, they read the following resolution: "Be it resolved, that we, the representatives of the Archdiocese of Halifax and Newfoundland, endorse such Federation, provided that Catholic rights and interests be safeguarded in entirety."[71] The media, of course, reported the conference proceedings; it seems Halifax federationists concluded that Antigonish had acted in a narrow, parochial, and isolationist fashion.[72] For their part, the bishop and college president in Antigonish deeply regretted that divisions among Maritime Catholics had been made public. Bishop Morrison, moreover, charged that the archbishops of Halifax and St John's had violated their agreement, made at the conference of 19 October, to take no further steps until they had received a judgment from Rome.[73] President MacPherson even supposed that Archbishop McCarthy's poor health in old age had undermined his ability to judge rightly.[74] Bishop Morrison became convinced that he was "scarcely able to think for himself" and was in the treacherous hands of pro-merger clerics in Halifax.[75]

The Casket Speaks Out

At this point, the *Casket* editor felt compelled to enter the theatre of combat in defence of his bishop and college. After the Maritime hierarchy conference on 19 October, and the St.F.X. board's negative decision, Phalen had pronounced the question closed for the Diocese of Antigonish; he had then resolved to remain silent on the issue.[76] But by the end of November, presumably with the blessing of Bishop Morrison, who had earlier directed him to expurgate federation material from the *Casket*, he opened fire on mergerites outside the diocese; he charged them with ignoring their bishops and ridiculing and maligning those opposed to federation. He spent his anti-mergerite ammunition in a series of ten articles which stated, then restated, and then stated again, the anti-merger position.[77] Moreover, in response to a *Sydney Post* writer – one who had been refused space in the *Casket*[78] – claiming that four Maritime bishops favoured federation, Phalen wrote directly to all eight members of the hierarchy; in January, he published their replies on the front page of the *Casket*.[79] His somewhat wily telegram had asked each if he still supported the joint resolution of 19 October. Only Archbishops Roche and McCarthy clearly affirmed their support for university federation.

Meanwhile, on 12 December, Maritime college and government representatives appointed a committee to present a memorandum, unanimously supported, to the Carnegie Corporation in New York. It outlined a scheme for the federation at Halifax of constituent colleges which would hold their degree-granting powers in abeyance. All denominational colleges were urged to enter the new university (to be called Dalhousie) so that government support would be ensured.[80] As expected, the Carnegie Corporation responded positively with a generous grant offer of $3 million when governments and interested institutions had achieved a formal agreement.[81] Soon thereafter King's, Mount Allison, and Dalhousie accepted the proposal.

Bishop Morrison Acts

In Antigonish, Vice-President Tompkins continued to campaign for federation, while some antis in the diocese pressed President MacPherson to remove the "two or three avowed mergerites" at St.F.X. or suffer loss of sympathy and support for the college.[82] Bishop Morrison was forced to act. He belatedly referred the question of university federation to Rome, as he had been asked to do by the Maritime hierarchy, first in July, and then again on 19 October. His appeal of 11 November was for swift disapproval of federation. He noted the earlier unanimous decision of the Maritime bishops and the definite refusal of St.F.X. to enter the merger. Morrison charged that Halifax interests were "trying to give effect to the confederation of the higher institutions of learning." The federation issue, to him, was a question of college accessibility for young Catholics, as well as one of safeguarding their faith and morals. The Carnegie scheme, a scheme which had originated with non-Catholic Americans and called for a "neutral" university with Catholics united in one constituent college, would render them a minority with little influence. He bewailed the disruptive impact of the Halifax propagandists and submitted, "if the Holy See should decide to send a letter disapproving this project as far as the Catholic colleges are concerned, it would settle the question and remove it from the field of discussion, so that our Catholic colleges could go on with their work and not be subjected to the unsettling effects of newspaper propaganda."[83]

Morrison's most dramatic and notorious move against the Catholic mergerites came in early December when he removed Vice-President Tompkins from the college and consigned him to the remote parish of Canso.[84] By then Morrison had concluded that Tompkins was "the prime mover among Catholics" for the "deadly proposition" of college merger and believed his position of vice-president "greatly aggravated the situation." The bishop later explained his action thus: "in order to safe-guard Catholic education for our young men, and to retain the confidence of the Catholic public in St.F.X. College, I felt obliged to remove him from the vice-rectorship of the college, and so appointed him to Canso."[85] For Tompkins, the transfer was a massive body blow; he had given himself heart and soul to the cause of St.F.X.'s progress and development for twenty years. However, Tompkins acted recklessly in his defiance of the formidable combined authorities of bishop and college board; he might have predicted that exile would be the penalty for even covert propaganda.[86] Although he kicked about the transfer, and threatened to leave the diocese, Tompkins eventually submitted and left quietly, in order, he claimed, to inspire his friends to work harder for the cause of federation. Perhaps to comfort himself, he believed his exile infused the federation movement with added impetus.[87] Seven years later Tompkins would still be hopeful that some form of federation was imminent.[88]

During his twenty-year college tenure, Tompkins had made important contributions to St.F.X. He had pressed unremittingly for higher standards, specialization, and improved faculty qualifications, along with the extension of university teaching to the masses. His success at fund-raising had become proverbial. A contemporary faculty member later recalled "Father Jimmy" as "the driving force of the University in those far off days and indefatigable on the trail of any and every prospective benefactor for his beloved College."[89] Tompkins had also quickly spotted talent and inspired and directed it. He was an effective and persistent prod, a man who afflicted the comfortable and complacent, a priest-reformer and a visionary.[90] However, certain limitations of character reduced his effectiveness. He expressed disdain for those who failed to see his visions or contemplated different ones. He was also of a "restless disposition" and provocative nature. Allowing for exaggeration, an element of truth resided in Bishop Morrison's claim that the priest was "forever in search of some novel or startling idea which he supposes will be the final permanent remedy for some of the world's ills."[91] This lack of stability and perseverance seemed evident in his request for successive posts at the college – librarian, vice-president, principal of the high school, prefect of studies, and registrar. By 1922, President MacPherson was predictably unwilling to admit that Tompkins had been a success in any one of these positions.[92] But this was the surly judgment of a disaffected colleague.

The Rome Lobby

Bishop Morrison was not the only Maritime prelate to petition Rome. His intransigence on federation impelled Archbishops McCarthy of Halifax and Roche of St John's to do likewise.[93] McCarthy thought a decision by Rome would "free the atmosphere and lift the cloud that certain persons see hovering over those who speak in favour of federation."[94] McCarthy's report on federation to the Congregation of Seminaries and Universities, the congregation of cardinals responsible for a ruling on the issue, strongly commended the scheme based on the alleged mediocrity of the current disparate college efforts, the supposed unnecessary duplication of educational resources, the precedents set by Oxford, Cambridge, and the University of Toronto, the guaranteed safeguards to faith and morals enshrined in the Learned and Sills proposal, and the dangers for Catholics of being left out of the central university.[95]

However, Bishop Morrison's lobbying of authorities in Rome was the most aggressive. Periodically, through the winter of 1922–23, he urged the Canadian apostolic delegate and Rome officials to act promptly on the question.[96] St.F.X. authorities, he reported, were being "abused and insulted" in the public press by Catholics and non-Catholics alike for not agreeing to the merger, an intolerable circumstance which he blamed largely on Archbishops McCarthy and Roche.[97] In February, Morrison warned a Roman official that Archbishop Neil McNeil of Toronto had left for Rome; he asked the official to counterbalance the influence of this prelate who had "liberal views" on federation and who would be acting in the interests of Halifax parties, while also attempting to justify the St Michael's set-up at the University of Toronto.[98] McNeil did exactly what Morrison suspected he would do;[99] he found in Rome "a rather strong current of opposition to Maritime federation" but received assurances that no ruling would be made to forbid federation with universities already established.[100]

The Vatican's Ruling on University Federation

Shortly thereafter it became clear whom Rome had found most persuasive on the question of Maritime university federation. At a meeting held on 22 March 1923, the Congregation of Seminaries and Universities considered the following question: "Whether the plan of forming a Federation of all the Colleges both Catholic and non-Catholic into one non-denomination University can be approved, permitted or tolerated?" They decided in the negative and their ruling was ratified and confirmed by Pope Pius XI.[101] Bishop Morrison was both relieved and elated by the news; he circulated a copy of the Holy See's decision to all his clergy and had it published in the *Casket*. The bishop rejoiced that "the attitude of the diocese was such as to be found consonant with the final decision of the Holy See."[102] For him, the matter was closed and should be settled now for all Catholics. He expressed the hope to the apostolic delegate that Catholics would "never again be tormented with such a question in regard to our Catholic educational endeavours."[103] On the other hand, Morrison's chief antagonist, Tompkins, had a deep, even bitter sense of a marvellous opportunity lost for Catholics, although he continued to promote the scheme and to hope that some form of federation would be realized.[104] He regretted that the question (whose terms he believed Bishop Morrison had wrongly presented to Rome) had ever been referred to Rome and commented, "We know more about our business than Rome does."[105] Almost thirty years later, shortly after the death of Bishop Morrison, Dr Coady would echo Tompkins's claim that the scheme had been misrepresented in Rome. He commented, "The blackest mark against the crowd who were against the merger is the trickery and bad faith shown in the question they asked."[106]

Nevertheless, Rome had ruled and many believed, like Bishop Morrison, that its decree placed an insurmountable blockade in the path of Catholic mergerites. Even if Rome had approved of federation, or had left the decision to individual bishops, it is doubtful that all Maritime Catholics would have been lured into the scheme. Bishop Morrison and his college opted out decisively as early as October 1922, and St.F.X. was the lead player on the stage of Maritime Catholic higher education in 1922-23. Moreover, the New Brunswick bishops opposed federation.[107]

The Ambiguity of Rome's Decree
Rome's decree undoubtedly added momentum to the Catholic anti-mergerite tide in the Maritimes; but it was certainly not decisive for Catholic-Protestant relations in Canadian higher education. First, it did not condemn the University of Toronto–St Michael's arrangement. Bishop Morrison wished it had, and in 1924 lamented that the Ontario model was being used as a justification for "all kinds of [Catholic] educational associations with Protestant institutions."[108] Second, Rome's declaration had only rejected one type of Catholic-Protestant cooperative arrangement in higher education, one which had not even been contemplated by the Learned and Sills Report; it had rejected, not a federation where individual denominational identities could be preserved, but a complete amalgamation and merging of institutions into a "nondenominational" or neutral university.[109] That other Catholic-Protestant institutional arrangements were acceptable to Rome soon became clear.

The archbishop of Edmonton, Henry J. O'Leary, helped to resolve the contentious issue of a Catholic institutional presence on state campuses.[110] O'Leary, who had been trained in canon law and had been influenced in his views on federation by Tompkins,[111] wanted to establish a Catholic college in affiliation with the University of Alberta.[112] He did not ask the Vatican if he could found a Catholic college on the campus of a local state university, but "whether it was permissible to protect and strengthen the religious faith of Catholics attending the university for which purpose he would need a Catholic college."[113] Rome, in 1926, replied in the affirmative. O'Leary believed the ruling was critical: "This decision," he declared, "is of the utmost importance as it legalizes institutions of this kind such as St Michael's College of Toronto and many others."[114] The ruling probably also explains why Rome granted Archbishop McCarthy, in 1927, permission to affiliate St Mary's with Dalhousie (the negotiations came to naught), a permission which deeply troubled Bishop Morrison in Antigonish, who lobbied Rome to "veto the affiliation."[115]

The Collapse of the Federation Scheme
The Maritime Protestant denominational colleges reacted diversely to the Carnegie proposal of 1922. In the fall of 1923, King's College, Windsor transferred to Halifax and associated with Dalhousie.[116] Baptist Acadia in Wolfville conclusively rejected federation in February 1923. Mount Allison, in Sackville, New Brunswick was slower to decide; some leading officials were sympathetic, and the question of a national church union between Canadian Methodists, Presbyterians, and Congregationalists interposed itself. But ultimately it also withdrew.[117] University of New Brunswick officials early indicated their plan to remain independent. By the summer of 1923, the handwriting was on the wall: the Learned and Sills proposal had failed to win full Protestant and Catholic support.

The Carnegie Corporation's offer of financial backing for a federated university at Halifax remained on the table until 1929.[118] Officials were disappointed that their reform proposal was generally repudiated.[119] But by 1926, after further experience with the region and with the advantage of hindsight, Carnegie authorities expressed more realism about Maritime affairs. After a visit to Atlantic Canada that year, the secretary to the president concluded, "An unconscionable sum of money was tied up in pursuit of an ideal without adequately taking into account the vested interests, economic and sentimental, the lines of religious division, the inherited traditions, and all the human factors which made the ideal, to say the least, extremely unlikely of realization."[120]

The Legacy of the University Federation Debate
Meanwhile, the corporation decided not to negotiate over funding with individual institutions; instead it proposed the formation of a central advisory committee which would express the general judgment of the Maritime universities on problems affecting higher education, and would encourage a coordinated and unified educational effort.[121] St.F.X., after some hesitation, joined the Central Advisory Committee on Education in the Maritime Provinces and Newfoundland, which included delegates from Acadia, Dalhousie, King's, the Nova Scotia Technical College, Pine Hill, the University of New Brunswick, and St Joseph's College.[122] The advisory committee's subsequent work was substantial; it supported selected grant applications to the corporation – for example, the successful application from Newfoundland for help to form a junior college at St John's – formed a Newfoundland and

Maritime examining board,[123] and regularly discussed topics of general concern, such as teacher training, matriculation standards, tuition fees, graduate studies, adult education, and the high school curriculum. Even though the movement for university federation failed, the corporation, through the advisory committee, did succeed in furthering higher educational cooperation in the region and in encouraging a broader perspective among the participating institutions.[124]

St.F.X.'s Opposition Interpreted

The Carnegie proposal in 1922 for university federation had been a serious challenge for St.F.X. In the end, the college and its bishop were major players in the subversion of the proposed reform, at least for Catholic colleges. The college leadership believed that St.F.X. had secured a firm place in the affections of its constituency: in the face of frightful obstacles, it had preserved and strengthened the faith of the Catholics in eastern Nova Scotia, and had granted their sons standing in the public and professional affairs of the country.[125] For many, St.F.X. had become "the rallying point and intellectual centre" of the Diocese of Antigonish.[126] If the college was transferred to Halifax, the diocese would lose its heart.

In addition, Catholics had historical and contemporary reasons for questioning Protestant motives. Past Catholic-Protestant conflicts over education and the chaplaincy service in the First World War, along with the current difficulty in obtaining government funding for Catholic-run schools in Pictou County, had created a legacy of latent and manifest suspicion. Authorities in Antigonish, moreover, continued to believe that Dalhousie was "supposedly undenominational but mainly Presbyterian."[127] Therefore, they harboured genuine fear that their distinctive and cherished Catholic approach to education would be co-opted by association with Dalhousie and other Protestant colleges. Furthermore, St.F.X. conservatism was rooted in a lively optimism about the college's future prospects. Since 1910, it had expanded and modernized, the faculty had specialized and upgraded its qualifications, and several new chairs had been endowed. The Catholics of eastern Nova Scotia had subscribed beyond the target of $500,000 in the financial campaign of 1920, and the bequest of a large Boston estate promised a substantial increase in college revenues. Finally, since the war, student enrolments had climbed consistently. These were the critical factors in the Diocese of Antigonish which inhibited mergerite sentiment during the convulsive Maritime university federation debates of 1922 and 1923.

· 10 ·

Between War and Depression:
the 1920s

By the spring of 1923, the university federation proposal was a dead issue for St.F.X., rendered so with finality by the Vatican's veto. The chancellor and college authorities, no doubt, felt relief that the unsettling question had been closed and the future of St.F.X. ensured. The years ahead, until close to the end of the decade, would be quite placid for their institution. Its staff would remain relatively stable and only a few significant curricular changes would be made – one would be the termination of high school work. Student enrolments would change little, although life on campus continued ever active and interesting.

However, the placidness of college life between the Great War and the Depression of the 1930s was, to an extent, misleading. For persistent and deepening economic and social problems plagued eastern Nova Scotia and troubled many diocesan clergy and laity. By the end of the 1920s, St.F.X. itself would be forced to confront these issues and become less of an "isolated [academic] eminence."[1] The problems it would face were those which heightened regional protest in the country at large. The cry for "Maritime Rights" revealed eastern discontent while the rise of the Progressive party on the prairies showed the depth of western alienation. The national political parties – Mackenzie King's Liberals and Arthur Meighen's Conservatives – were forced to grapple with these strains in the national fabric. In Nova Scotia, Premier George H. Murray's long reign came to a close, and successive Liberal and Conservative premiers – Ernest H. Armstrong (1923–25) and Edgar N. Rhodes (1925–30) had to deal with the province's deepening economic and social problems.

The "Old Rector" and His Administration
In the fall of 1923, Rev. Dr H.P. MacPherson remained in the institutional driver's seat. By then he was a veteran of several college crises and a seasoned administrator. His tall, stately figure, fascinating nervous habits, and human warmth were fixed in the memories of

generations of St.F.X. alumni.[2] They would remember him affectionately as "The Old Rector." Moreover, he had achieved some standing
in the province as a public-spirited individual and would serve on
Royal Commissions in 1926, 1930, and 1932.[3] Federal and provincial
politicians alike occasionally received from him recommendations of
Catholic appointees to important positions in the public service, for,
like most Catholics, he believed religious bigotry continued to restrict
them from equal participation in the public affairs of the country.[4]

MacPherson had formed, by then, a clear conception of St.F.X.'s
purpose, a purpose which deviated little from the college's founding
inspiration. Through liberal arts training it aimed to form the character
of young Catholics who would later become important shapers of
public opinion in Nova Scotia and beyond. The development of reason,
asserted MacPherson, was critical, but reason had to be guided by
ethical standards and imbued with religion. He advised one graduating
class, "The education which overlooks the moral faculty in man is
pitifully lop-sided. The pursuit of knowledge is indeed worthy of our
best efforts, but the true goal of human endeavour, is to be good."[5]
Quite expectedly, the president viewed with scepticism purely secular
education which left out of account God, the immortality of the soul,
and the future alternatives of bliss or misery. On his return from a visit
to McGill University in 1921, he lauded it as "a progressive institution,"
but reflected, "In some respects I much prefer our own St.F.X. College.
We have religion, supervision over the boys and the true faith. These
things, after all, are the important ones."[6]

Several capable individuals, all clerics, assisted MacPherson in his
administration of the college. Rev. Hugh J. MacDonald served as vice-
president and master of discipline. He was a graduate of St.F.X. and
the Urban College, Rome, and a classmate of Dr Moses Coady's who
had been at the college since September 1911. MacDonald taught Latin
and Italian; his keen sporting interests and fairness in enforcing discipline made him popular with the students.[7] The official librarian and
faculty secretary was Rev. Dr D.J. MacDonald, who replaced Hugh J.
MacDonald as vice-president in 1925. D.J. MacDonald had been educated in Rome, too, and at the Catholic University of America, where
he had applied himself to both English and economics. His support of
the anti-mergerite forces opposed to university federation marked him
as a St.F.X. loyalist; he remained at the college from 1912 to 1944.[8]

The director of studies and professor of chemistry (1917–36), Rev.
R.K. McIntyre, was of distinguished physical stature; he had also
followed the well-beaten graduate path from St.F.X. to the Catholic
University of America. One student remembered him as "a large kindly
man, an ideal priest, and an excellent teacher."[9] Finally, the professor

of physics, Rev. Dr Patrick J. Nicholson, was registrar. Like D.J. MacDonald, he would have a long, outstanding career at St.F.X., extending from 1916 to 1954. Nicholson was already known for his love of music, cinema, and Celtic history. He was a devout, almost puritanical individual, a tremendous worker, although a rather poor teacher.[10] Along with a priest-bursar, Rev. D.C. MacKay, and the assistant librarian, May MacDonald, these scholars, all of Scottish lineage, filled the college's administrative posts.

The St.F.X. Faculty in 1923

Seventeen individuals composed the St.F.X. faculty in 1923. Two of them were part-time lecturers, the remainder full-time; eight possessed doctorates, five had masters' degrees, and thirteen were priests. Fourteen were St.F.X. alumni, and over one-half were descendants of Highland immigrants. The teaching career of one faculty member, Rev. Dr Dugald C. Gillis, concluded in the spring of 1924 when Bishop Morrison appointed him chaplain at Bethany, Antigonish, the new motherhouse of the Sisters of St Martha.[11] Gillis had taught philosophy at St.F.X. for almost twenty-five years. One student remembered him as "a rare bird, an aging, sturdy, stocky, thick-set, wrestler-like hunched-shouldered clergyman." His teaching method – he apparently only used one – had a deadening effect on his student victims; it amounted to the dictation of notes in Latin and sometimes English with a rule against discussion and disapproval of the impertinence of questions.[12] Bishop Morrison replaced him with two younger priests, Rev. Thomas O'R. Boyle and Rev. Dr Moses Coady. He directed these young professors to stress Thomistic philosophy as much as possible. He hoped that, under new management, the philosophy department would excel: "The many pronouncements of the Supreme Pontiffs for the encouragement of the study of Thomistic Philosophy should stimulate us all to make this department a very prominent one in the arts course," stated Morrison. To better prepare prospective seminarians, he requested that Latin be the sole medium of communication in the philosophy classes.[13]

Father Boyle would teach the first year philosophy course. Originally from Newfoundland, he had been raised in Sydney, Cape Breton. After he had graduated, first from St.F.X. in 1915, and then from the Grand Seminary, Quebec, the bishop had placed him at the college in 1921, where he proved to be a fine teacher. In 1923 and 1924, he had conducted the people's schools in Glace Bay,[14] and, in subsequent decades, he would become a leading advocate for higher education in Cape Breton. Unfortunately, his bishop would be compelled to remove him from St.F.X. in 1930 because of scandalous incidents of public drunkenness.[15]

Dr Moses Coady

Dr Coady, by then an experienced educator, taught the upper level philosophy courses, along with courses in education. Coady had come from Northeast Margaree, Cape Breton to St.F.X., where he graduated in 1905; his next move was overseas to the Urban College, Rome and finally, after five years' labour, he obtained the prized PH D and DD degrees.[16] After returning to St.F.X. in 1910, he taught Latin, mathematics, apologetics, history, and education. Coady had a keen interest in education and believed the preparation of competent teachers to be an important means to revitalize the region's rural communities. He was a tall, rugged, optimistic individual with an immense capacity for work, a lively imagination, and a healthy sense of humour. From 1916 to 1925 he served as principal of the St.F.X. high school. In 1920, he helped to reorganize the moribund Nova Scotia Teachers Union, became its secretary for four years, and edited the Nova Scotia *Teachers' Bulletin*.[17] Students found Coady to be a superb teacher, dynamic, enthusiastic, compassionate, and persuasive.[18] He would leave a defining mark on the institution and on grassroots eastern Nova Scotia unequalled before or since.

Long- and Short-Term Recruits

While the faculty remained relatively stable during the 1920s, six young priest-professors did appear on the college scene. These men would be associated with St.F.X. for long periods of time, and, like Coady, would achieve prominence in its collective memory. They included Revs. Jerome C. Chisholm, biology (1926–51), R.V. Bannon, English (1924–31 and 1933–72), Leo B. Sears, Latin (1926–41), Hugh J. Somers, history (1928–29 and 1933–64), Leo G. McKenna, mathematics (1924–49), and Malcolm MacEachern, philosophy (1930–51). MacEachern, who eventually earned a DD at the University of Montreal and a PH D from Louvain, Belgium, would become bishop of Charlottetown (1954).

In 1923 instruction in French was given by Gabriel Bonno and Rev. Joseph Raiche. The Carnegie Chair in French, arranged for 1919–20, had been filled first by René Gautheron (1921–22) and then by Bonno (1923–26). Both teachers came from France. In 1929 President MacPherson claimed that the men from France (by then four of them had served on staff) were of "the highest scholarship" and mostly graduates of L'Ecole Normale Supérieure, a highly acclaimed French school.[19] Father Raiche came from Quebec, although he was a St.F.X. alumnus; he taught at the college from 1913 to 1934. Students remembered him as a mediocre teacher, an "easy going genteel type of man, always immaculately dressed."[20] By 1935 St.F.X. would have hired five

Rev. Joseph F. Raiche, professor of French 1913–34

scholars from France to conduct the French program. A later president opined in 1944: "that group individually seemed more interested in making their position here a stepping stone to some more preferable position than in making a success of their teaching." College authorities anxiously sought to stabilize instruction in French.[21]

Four priests – Revs. P.J. Nicholson, R.K. McIntyre, C.J. Connolly, and Hugh MacPherson – had prime responsibility for the sciences at St.F.X. in 1923. Nicholson and McIntyre have been introduced already. Connolly revealed superb academic ability, first at St.F.X., then through theological training at the Grand Seminary, Quebec, and finally at the University of Munich, where he acquired a PHD in biology. From 1911 to 1925 he taught biology at St.F.X., although in 1922–23 and in 1924–25 he received leaves to conduct research in the United States. The superior scholarly facilities and opportunities south of the border were too much for Connolly to resist; in 1924 he embarked on a distinguished career in psychology and anthropology at the Catholic University of America, where he would remain until 1953.[22] Father Hugh MacPherson taught engineering and geology. Here was a man of surprisingly broad intellectual competence who, by 1923, had already traced an interesting path. Bishop Cameron had placed him at the college in 1900 after his training in theology and applied science in European universities. From 1907 to about 1915 "Little Doc Hugh," as he was called, had been principal of the St.F.X. High School, then government agricultural representative for Antigonish County (1914–20), and simultaneously manager of Mount Cameron Farm from 1915 to 1919; there he sustained a tractor accident injury which left him with a permanent limp. MacPherson had pioneered in local agricultural cooperatives and would remain associated with St.F.X. for about three more decades.[23]

The St.F.X. Curriculum in the 1920s
This St.F.X. faculty taught a curriculum in the mid-1920s whose core continued to be the bachelor of arts program. It encompassed required courses in ancient and modern languages, economics, history, philosophy, religion, mathematics, and science. A few courses in the final three years were elective, but overall it was curricular prescription with a vengeance. The bachelor of science program included studies in physics, biology, chemistry, geology, and mathematics, along with a smattering of arts courses – modern languages, philosophy, and religion. A three-year diploma course in engineering continued to be offered, as well as a one-year master of arts program in several standard disciplines.[24] By 1931, about one-quarter of the degree students were graduating in the sciences and the remainder in the arts. Nine masters'

degrees were conferred that year. Thirteen students obtained teaching diplomas and thirty-eight students were studying engineering.[25]

The college made several important alterations in program offerings during the 1920s. In 1922 Dalhousie discontinued its affiliation with the other Maritime universities, and required law students to take their entire program in the Dalhousie Faculty of Law. Thereafter, St.F.X. dropped its one-year law program, which had been initiated by Rector Thompson in 1899, but continued to offer selected law courses.[26] From about 1927, all degree candidates were required "to give evidence of ability as a public speaker" by participating in debates, drama, or elocution.[27] Officials of St.F.X. and the local St Martha's Hospital affiliated in 1926 to offer a five-year degree course in arts and nursing which required two years of college studies and three years at the hospital.[28] Its purpose was to provide a broad education and "to qualify nurses who desire to fit themselves for teaching and supervision in schools of nursing and for public health nursing service."[29] By this time the Marthas had grown considerably and had assumed control of their own affairs independent of St.F.X. and subject to the bishop alone.[30]

The affiliated women's college of Mount St Bernard offered a number of courses – art, music, oral expression, and physical culture – which could be taken as electives by students in the degree programs. As well, the CNDs, in response to growing pressures for such offerings, provided a two-year diploma course in secretarial science as well as a one-year certificate or two-year diploma course in household arts.[31] By 1930–31 students could work toward a bachelor's degree of household science. The stimulus for establishing the program had been student requests in 1926 for a degree in the area of household economics. The superior at MSB, Sister St Margaret of the Cross, thereupon decided to qualify two staff members for teaching in this area; she also requested that St.F.X. open such a department "thereby giving to Catholic girls of the Maritime Provinces advantages equal to those now offered by Acadia and Mount Allison."[32] By 1936, fifteen degrees and six diplomas had been granted in home economics.[33]

After the war, social pressures had been exerted on women "to return to the traditional security of home, hearth, and husband."[34] During the 1920s increasing numbers of women attended university, yet nineteenth-century ideas about the appropriate sexual division of labour persisted. McKillop states, "Notions that university women were really mothers-in-waiting or that they should enrol in programs suitable to such 'inherent' attributes as nurturing or care-giving were ones that many talked about and a good number of women still believed in. Teaching and forms of social service continued to be the professional separate spheres of many university women."[35] The new nursing, secretarial, and household science programs at St.F.X.-MSB were local instances of common attitudes about the proper occupations for women, for they were exclusively women's programs.

Father Coady, in 1923, assumed, along with his upper level courses in philosophy, responsibility for teaching the principles of education and educational psychology.[36] Teacher training became more clearly formalized at St.F.X. three years afterwards when a department of education was established through the encouragement of Henry Munro, the provincial superintendent of education. He offered the Nova Scotia colleges "the privilege, on conditions, of training their students, graduate and undergraduate, in professional studies which, if satisfactory to the education office, will qualify him [sic] for a license to teach without further requirements, professional or academic"; henceforth, students would not have to attend the provincial Normal School in Truro to obtain the highest professional standing as teachers.[37] Munro suggested a number of courses in general arts and education, but granted much discretion to the universities. The universities themselves obtained the right, on behalf of each education student, to recommend the level of licence to be conferred by the education office. To accept the government offer, each university had to create its own department of education with a full-time instructor, and to make practice-teaching arrangements with local schools.[38] St.F.X., along with other provincial universities, found the scheme agreeable.[39] In 1920, it had endowed a chair of education for $50,000 as part of its agreement with the Carnegie Corporation for an equivalent grant to establish a chair in French.[40] From 1927, aspiring teachers at St.F.X. could qualify for a bachelor of arts or science degree and a provincial teacher's licence, if they fulfilled the additional education course requirements.[41]

The Termination of High School Work
The college in 1927 signalled the demise of its high school program and its replacement with a less ambitious preparatory department.[42] By 1929 the high school had formally ended.[43] It had been a constituent part of St.F.X. for almost forty years, operating under successive names such as the County Academy, the Collegiate School of St John the Baptist, St Francis Xavier's Academy and Preparatory School, and the St.F.X. High School. The majority of its students had lived in residence and were from outside Antigonish county. For decades, certain priests and faculty had expressed dissatisfaction with the high school program. As early as 1907, Rev. Dr Alexander Thompson had recommended that the academy work be separated from the college and transferred to the recently purchased Mount Cameron farm.[44] A majority of staff in 1920 believed the high school was failing to satisfy the needs of the

diocese; they advocated its severance from the college, but economic difficulties barred the way.[45] St.F.X. had gradually curtailed the high school program by dropping the lower level courses; for example, from 1907 only grades ten and eleven were offered. Through the 1920s, enrolments declined until by 1925–26 only sixty-one students attended. By the end of the 1920s, college officials decided that high school work did not justify its expense; moreover, they argued that, by then, the public school system had matured to the stage where equivalent high school programs were generally available elsewhere.[46] Placing the high school program on the chopping block meant the loss of the government grant, which had ranged from $600 to nearly $800 annually.[47]

President MacPherson's administration replaced the high school with a one-year preparatory department leading to university matriculation. This compromise program was an accommodation by St.F.X. to persistent unevenness in the quality and availability of eastern Nova Scotia high school facilities. The department was designed largely for conditioned students, i.e., those who failed to completely satisfy matriculation requirements. Moreover, older students who wanted to return to school were frequently embarrassed to enrol with younger classmates; thus, the St.F.X. preparatory department offered them an alternative, if they had already taken at least two years of high school.[48]

The Students and Campus Life
College-level enrolments at St.F.X. hovered around two hundred throughout the 1920s. By 1931, students of Scottish background composed about 40 per cent of the student body, English 25 per cent, Irish 17 per cent, and French 7 per cent. Females by then made up one-fifth of the student population. They attended classes with the males, but continued to live at the Mount in a separate women's sphere. Over 35 per cent of students came from mainland Nova Scotia, about 30 per cent from Cape Breton Island, 7 per cent from the United States, about 4 per cent each from Quebec and Newfoundland, and 14 per cent from New Brunswick.[49]

Perhaps university youth in the United States during the 1920s inaugurated "a 'revolution of manners and morals' characterized by social experimentation and a preoccupation with every passing fad or craze."[50] But at St.F.X. tradition reigned. First, students faced the ever-difficult problem of financing their education. The war-incurred college debt, which was still being paid off in 1924, forced board and tuition hikes from $176 in 1913 to $319 by 1931.[51] To help out, the college and outside benefactors made available a number of bursaries and scholarships. For example, from twelve to fourteen St.F.X. students annually held Knights of Columbus scholarships, valued at $200 a year.[52] In addition, four French-speaking students held $200 scholarships each year under the Carnegie-endowed Chair of French agreement. However, most bursary money at St.F.X. was designated for "young men intending to study for the priesthood."[53] In 1932, President MacPherson complained that St.F.X. each year had trouble collecting student fees.[54] By then, of course, the Depression had hit student financial resources even harder, but the decade of the 1920s itself had been one of economic stress for the region.[55]

In spite of penury, students entered and exited the St.F.X. campus with steady regularity through the 1920s. The *Xaverian* editors frequently tongue-lashed the student body for their lack of gregariousness. It was a perennial complaint. In one lashing, an editor asked: "When have we gathered together socially as human beings and not as compendiums of book-knowledge and windbags devoid of any true Christian spirit of mutual partnership? We, the students are the sufferers. From the standpoint of learning, our years here are fairly well spent; but from the standpoint of a full living existence, they are parched, wizened, atrophied, and devoid of all use."[56] To overcome such "sordid intellectualism," the gadfly recommended the formation of a glee club. In 1921 another editor was similarly dismayed by the decline in student societies and celebrations.[57] He too berated the students and lamented the alleged languishing of college spirit.

However, some societies were perennial favourites, come what may. These included the Debating Society, the *Xaverian*, the Dramatic Club, and the Athletic Association.[58] Periodically, of course, but never often enough for the *Xaverian* editors, the debating and sports teams made headline wins. Several British debating teams visited the campus during the 1920s.[59] In 1930, one even debated St.F.X. on the important resolution: "Resolved that maidens like moths are mostly caught by glare."[60] The class of 1924 was a definite exception to the supposed prevailing rule of student apathy. It was noteworthy, along with the class of 1925, for composing the first St.F.X. yearbook, an impressive production called the *Nexus*.[61] The class of 1924 even organized itself into a society and kept a minute book which revealed their vigour and spirit. Their unique class yell was this: "Slim Slam Jim Jam, Salaman Jalaman Gee, Rickety Rackety Clickety Clackety, Jimity Jamity Gingeree, Riffety Raffety Rizety Roar, We are the Class of '24."[62] In addition to the enthusiastic class of '24, the erection of a "wireless receiving antenna" on the roof of the Main Building in early fall, 1922, injected some excitement into student life in the early 1920s. The physics students undertook the project to capture nightly broadcasts and to interest college scholars in "practical radio electricity."[63] Of course, the decade of the 1920s saw the spread of such modern conve-

Xaverian Weekly staff, 1928–29

niences as radio, telephones and automobiles. Student societies and other organized activities at St.F.X. undoubtedly provided occasions for socializing, for diversions from the academic grind, for personal development, and for venting pent-up energies.

The Advent of Boxing

A new student activity appeared in 1930 that was especially effective for venting pent-up energies: boxing. Its introduction to the campus dismayed some of the priest-professors. The veteran president, H.P. MacPherson, had become a boxing enthusiast after attending a heavyweight match at Madison Square Gardens; he then spearheaded the development of his new "obsession" among the students. MacPherson designated Harvey Steele, a Sydney student who would later become widely known as a champion of social justice, as the trainer.[64] The Old Rector obtained all the necessary equipment and even required the Marthas to serve a special table for his aspiring boxers. The cream of the new boxing crop participated in the first Maritime intercollegiate boxing meet that year and St.F.X. went on to make a name for itself in the "manly sport."[65] Yet faculty opposition to the punishing sport persisted. Dr Nicholson, the godly, devout professor of physics, considered it unfit for a Catholic college. In 1950, when he was president and shortly after the Old Rector had died, he convinced the faculty to proscribe boxing at St.F.X.[66]

College Discipline and Religion

The daily lives of the students followed the long-established routine from the wake-up bell at 6:45 in the morning to "lights out" in the evening at 10 p.m. The regular activities included chapel, breakfast, classes, dinner, recreation breaks, evening prayers, supper, and study hall. Classes were scheduled for Saturday morning, and on Sunday there was a class in religion, to be attended by Catholic students in addition to the normal religious services. The routine was structured and rigid, undoubtedly for the sake of administrative efficiency, and also to inculcate habits of regularity and method.[67] A student in 1920 commented on the bell in the old Main Building: "The booming sound of this bell rang every morning to awaken the community and its ringing controlled practically all the comings and goings of the institution."[68] The dormitories in the main building had, by this time, acquired colourful appellations: "Broadway," "The Gardens," "Middle Dorm," "Pie Alley," and "Pig Alley."

Priest-prefects, stationed in each dormitory wing, supervised the college routine, enforcing adherence to schedules and regulations. A head prefect bore responsibility for discipline overall. By 1927, students

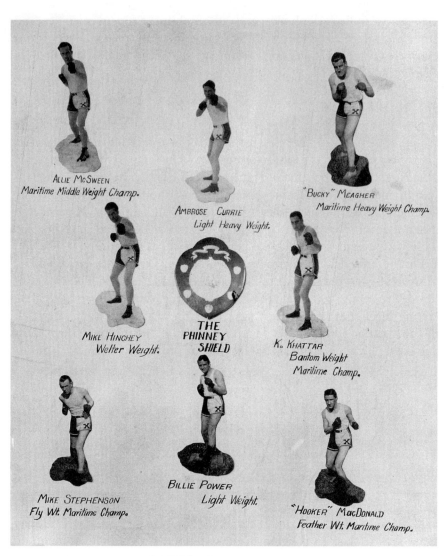

ALLIE McSWEEN
Maritime Middle Weight Champ.

AMBROSE CURRIE
Light Heavy Weight.

"BUCKY" MEAGHER
Maritime Heavy Weight Champ.

MIKE HINCHEY
Welter Weight.

THE
PHINNEY
SHIELD

K. KHATTAR
Bantom Weight
Maritime Champ.

MIKE STEPHENSON
Fly Wt. Maritime Champ.

BILLIE POWER
Light Weight.

"HOOKER" MacDONALD
Feather Wt. Maritime Champ.

St.F.X. boxing team, c. 1932

had to sign a promise to obey the rules of the college, to accept penalties attached to their violation, and to refrain from participating in initiation or hazing activities.[69] Campus opinion remained perennially divided about this latter ritual. Freshmen students found the practice "scary." One recalled having his face blackened, being sent up before a high court, and then being sentenced and roughed up by upper class men.[70] President MacPherson described hazing as of "a rather mild and harmless character." Yet he acknowledged that the faculty planned to abolish it.[71] Dr Nicholson, the critic of boxing, also despised initiation rites. He denied that initiation was a "time-hallowed tradition" at St.F.X.[72] and argued the evil of "perpetuating an atmosphere in which educated Christian gentlemen grow to believe that it is right to inflict pain on their fellow man in order to gratify what is low in human nature."[73] Incoming students in the fall of 1927 no doubt felt relieved that a new ruling had banned initiation.[74] By 1930 it had been replaced by a reception of new students which involved official greetings from college authorities, spirited speeches by the upper class students, entertainment, and "good fellowship."[75] However, this was by no means the end of initiation at St.F.X.

Apparently through bitter experience, President MacPherson had come to insist on official permissions for students who wanted to leave the campus at night. He admitted that the rule appeared severe, but stated, "leniency in this matter in former years has done the College great harm."[76] It had done certain students considerable damage, too. Associating with the wrong crowd, drinking and carousing, and causing public scandal were the chief problems. The college, of course, continued to enforce prohibition. The president, in 1930, even persuaded the Nova Scotia Liquor Board to locate a new liquor store for Antigonish further from the campus rather than nearer.[77] However, official regulation and student practice remained two different things. In spite of the routine and regulation, President MacPherson claimed, "We have reduced the number of our regulations to a minimum since we believe that a boy's character is better developed by placing a student on his own responsibilities; but at the same time, we insist upon strict observance of the few that remain."[78]

In 1925, President MacPherson declared that the whole St.F.X. program was "permeated with the Catholic spirit."[79] And so it appeared to be. Voluntarily, but at the faculty's strong urging, students frequented the chapel in the mornings, in the evenings, and on Sunday for the rosary and benediction of the blessed sacrament. They regularly received the sacraments of penance and the eucharist. Those students whose chapel attendance was irregular were "campused" or prohibited from leaving the college grounds. Students learned to chant the mass;

they also joined religious societies, like the Knights of the Blessed Sacrament, organized in 1921 to promote frequent reception of the blessed sacrament.[80] College officials organized special devotions during holy seasons, and scheduled two retreats annually – a one-day retreat early in the first term, and a longer one (three to four days) during holy week.[81] Priests from outside the diocese usually led the retreats. President MacPherson instructed one retreat master to focus on "honesty, temperance, the necessity of work, the desirability of deciding vocations before the end of the junior year, and most particularly, the duty of educated men towards the institutions of the country."[82] The student retreats were designed to further spiritual introspection, strengthen the will, and inspire the mind with noble motives.[83] Dr Nicholson was appointed, about 1926, to direct religious activities on campus by outlining and supervising all courses in religion, drawing up a program of Sunday sermons, and providing for confession and other religious exercises.[84] Nicholson also compiled the first St.F.X. prayer book in 1927.[85] The Catholic viewpoint permeated classes on Christian doctrine, apologetics, philosophy, English literature, and history. Finally, the Marthas provided excellent care for the students and reinforced the prevalent religious aura.

Harsh Regional Realities

While St.F.X. students were enmeshed in the routine, the regulation, and the scholastic regimen through the 1920s, events in the economic and social life of the region began to shake the complacency of the campus and awaken its authorities from their dogmatic slumbers. Viewed from a distance, one of the best indicators of serious regional problems was the Maritime Rights movement. An analyst of the movement discovered its roots in demographic, political, and economic decline, early-twentieth-century Maritime trends which were exacerbated by the post-war recession. The broadly based movement to reverse the decline relative to central Canada was "a spontaneous expression of the economic and social frustrations of the Maritime people."[86] Another signal of regional difficulties was the royal commissions formed to investigate general economic problems (1925), the coal industry (1926), and the fisheries (1927). Tariff reductions weakened protection of Maritime industry, freight rates increased on the Intercolonial, and the international demand for steel and coal declined.

During the 1920s, a period of crisis faced people employed in the fisheries, forestry, mining, agriculture, and manufacturing.[87] For example, the numbers occupied in agriculture decreased from 140,000 in 1880 to 96,000 in 1941; through the same period, a 45 per cent drop occurred in the number of occupied farms in the region.[88] Grave labour-management difficulties also developed in Nova Scotia mining communities like Sydney and Glace Bay. Labour radicalism exerted an ever-stronger appeal as unemployment and wage cuts inflamed the hard-pressed workers, who engaged in bitter and recurring strikes.[89] The "metal towns" in Pictou County, such as Trenton and New Glasgow, which had developed rapidly after 1900, also declined during the 1920s.[90] The general difficulties stimulated a more rapid exodus from the region. Apparently, about 147,000 people moved from the Maritimes between 1921 and 1931; and among the emigrants were "a high proportion of the more productive elements in society."[91] The "near destitution" of many people in the region happened without the security of later government aid programs, such as unemployment insurance and social assistance. In Antigonish County, St.F.X.'s home district, where the population decrease had been especially pronounced (from 16,114 in 1891 to 10,073 in 1931),[92] people had a keen sense of economic and social decline. President MacPherson reported dejectedly in 1926, "Business is slack and the people are leaving one by one for the United States. A spirit of pessimism [exists] among the people, and really the outlook is not at all bright."[93]

In spite of the appearance of stability and continuity at St.F.X. after the controversy about university federation in 1922–23, these harsh social and economic changes in the region were portents of a new era for the college. Indeed, some staff members, as well as parish priests in the diocese, had already started to grapple with the issues that were affecting their people. By the end of the 1920s, the college verged on a great new experiment which would substantially alter its character, broadcast its reputation far and wide, and infuse the old St.F.X. theme "for the people" with new meaning.

· I I ·

A New Agenda:
The Beginnings of Extension Work

The St.F.X. board of governors appointed Dr Moses Coady in 1928 to establish a department of extension. It was a watershed development for Coady and the small Catholic college of eastern Nova Scotia which would eventually catapult them both to fame.[1]

By then the St.F.X. faculty knew something of the concept of university extension. From 1900, college authorities had expanded the curriculum and had made temporary experimental forays into extension work. After 1899, Rector Thompson had moved beyond the classical into the professional, technical, and commercial areas by forming departments of applied science, law, and commerce. Before his "exile" to Canso, Father Jimmy Tompkins had often harangued, prodded, and pressed St.F.X. to break out of its elitist strait-jacket and take knowledge to all the people; his pet projects had included the summer school sessions of 1909–10, the "For the People" *Casket* column in 1918, the 1920 pamphlet challenge *Knowledge for the People*, and the people's schools of 1921–22.[2] Dr Hugh MacPherson, professor of science at St.F.X., had urged and organized agricultural cooperatives in the county from 1914 to 1919 while he was an agriculture representative for the province. He, along with Rev. Miles Tompkins, were the college's pioneer cooperators. Then Dr C.J. Connolly, professor of biology, had also grappled with practical problems in the fisheries.[3] During the war, Professor Bucknell had given extension lectures in Saint John, New Brunswick and had offered correspondence courses at St.F.X.[4] Moreover, in 1927 the Sisters of St Martha had begun local field-work in household arts and crafts.[5] But the board's critical decision of 1928 to form an extension department marked a deep and permanent commitment by St.F.X. to adult education. "For the people" would now be given a wider meaning.

The Diocesan Rural and Industrial Conferences
The board's action was a surrender to pressures internal and external which had been building through the 1920s. The diocesan rural con-

ferences, held annually from 1923, acted as one important source of pressure.[6] The conferences addressed serious economic and social problems, both rural and urban, which distressed the lives of many eastern Nova Scotians. Most frequently they were held at St.F.X. with the joint participation of faculty, clergy, and laity. Participants presented, debated, and discussed papers on vital topics, such as rural schools, rural depopulation, agricultural methods, housing, collective bargaining, unemployment, and cooperation. Certain clerical leaders – for example, Revs. Moses Coady, Michael Gillis, John R. MacDonald, James Boyle, Thomas O'R. Boyle, and Jimmy Tompkins – who shared similar convictions about social problems and reform, used the conferences to develop and promote a reformist agenda in the diocese.[7] The conferences had Bishop Morrison's blessing, and he warmly commended his clergy's tradition of working for the diocese's economic and social improvement. Although a cautious and prudent administrator, he nonetheless tried to make room for the initiatives of his priests, and either backed them or, like Gamaliel of old, waited to see if their undertakings "were of God."[8] While progressive reformism in the region might have been undermined by the post-war recession and the beginnings of de-industrialization, these conferences apparently preserved some spirit of reform at least in the Diocese of Antigonish.[9]

The conference participants tried to step beyond mere talk to concrete action. In 1924, for example, participants established, for five years, a scholarship fund to permit twenty-five men annually to attend the winter agricultural course at Truro.[10] The conference, two years later, unanimously supported work by the Marthas in rural education and home economics.[11] Several resolutions and papers called strongly for St.F.X. to undertake the training of leaders in community development and cooperation. For example, Rev. Thomas O'R. Boyle in 1924 successfully moved: "this Conference requests the College authorities to form a department of extension work, which will organize People's Schools in the central points of the Diocese, and direct Study Clubs in all sections."[12] The 1927 conference issued a similar challenge when it adopted the theme of extension education and, following its precedent set three years before with agricultural scholarships, set up twelve scholarships for young fishermen to attend the fisheries school in Halifax.[13] The conference in 1928 heard a paper by A.B. Mac-Donald, St.F.X. alumnus and county school inspector, on cooperative marketing and the need for vocational schools and colleges to prepare cooperative managers and rural leaders for the "progress and prosperity" of the country. That meeting pledged support to the organization best equipped to enter the field of adult education in the Maritimes and it authorized Father Jimmy Tompkins to generate interest in the proposal.[14] Evidently the social and economic difficulties of the 1920s had gained the attention of diocesan leaders; and their conference proceedings began to focus the pressures building for action.

The Scottish Catholic Society of Canada
The Scottish Catholic Society of Canada also pressed St.F.X. authorities to form an extension department. A later commentator put it this way: "They kept throwing pebbles at the windows of the ivory tower asking those within to rise to the task."[15] Scottish Catholic enthusiasts had formed the society in 1919 to preserve Catholicism among the Scots, to propagate Scottish history, language, and tradition, and to advance the educational and social standing of all Scottish Catholics.[16] The clergy supported the society and many local councils formed throughout the diocese during the following decade. The society even produced its own journal, called *Mosgladh* (*The Awakening*). Participants at its tenth annual convention in July 1928 pledged to raise $100,000 over five years to educate farmers and fishermen in cooperative and self-help movements.[17] Coady later recollected that this decision "scared" the bishop and the president of St.F.X. into action.[18] University, Alumni Association, and society delegates held several joint meetings. When extension work was definitely initiated in 1930, the Scottish Catholic Society concluded, "it was mainly through the activities and efforts of our Society that this Extension department started."[19] By then it had abandoned its ambitious fund-raising campaign and had agreed to support the proposed extension work at St.F.X. It gave $2000 to the college in the early 1930s.[20] Thus, the Scottish Catholic Society gave extension advocates both moral and financial support. Prominent members, like A.B. MacDonald and Revs. John R. MacDonald and Michael Gillis (secretary of the society 1921–25), were also leading participants in the rural conferences; A.B. MacDonald and Gillis themselves would eventually serve on the St.F.X. extension department staff.[21]

Father Gillis emerged as a key proponent of social action in the diocese and was, perhaps, most responsible for the extension department at St.F.X. Apparently in the 1910s he had urged the appointment of government agricultural representatives, the scientific training of farmers, and later, the education of women in home economics. In the 1920s he urged the Scottish Catholic Society to support the education of youth in rural science.[22] Coady described Gillis as "the creative mind behind all these movements, the dynamic leader and inspirer" who had pressured older leaders like Tompkins and Dr Hugh MacPherson into action.[23] For decades after extension began, Gillis stayed in close touch

Rev. Michael Gillis, parish priest and leading advocate
for social justice

with its leaders, forever advancing new ideas, offering constructive criticism, and furnishing moral support.

The St.F.X. Alumni Association

While the Scottish Catholic Society plotted and planned to advance rural education, the St.F.X. Alumni Association in 1928, under the presidency of Sydney lawyer Neil McArthur,[24] directly lobbied the board of governors to establish a department of extension.[25] At Coady's suggestion in 1927, the association had petitioned the board to form a committee on the question of extension work.[26] By then, Coady had become increasingly critical of the "philosophy of grand isolation" among the universities; he charged them with neglecting the masses, hand-picking the country, then training and exporting its brains.[27] In his view, education had become an "escape mechanism" or "trap door" through which the "bright and vigorous few" from among the masses could go into the higher professions and join the "elite of the nation."[28] At its next annual meeting, the association appointed Revs. Michael Gillis, John R. MacDonald, Hugh J. MacDonald, Jimmy Tompkins,[29] and school inspector A.B. MacDonald a committee to write a brief proposing "a chair or chairs in Rural Education and Rural Sociology" and to confer with the board of governors.[30] The committee presented its crucial report to the board on 17 August 1928; the board then held a special meeting on 19 November to discuss the proposal thoroughly.

It was a sharp summons, as well as a basic charter, for a program of social action in eastern Nova Scotia. Such a program, the report asserted, should be directed toward the three main sections of the working population – farmers, fishermen, and miners – who suffered the most under the existing dire social and economic conditions. In a direct appeal to institutional self-interest, the committee proposal claimed that extension work would establish securely the good will and support of the common people, and "render indisputable [St.F.X.'s] position as an institution essential to the Catholics of Nova Scotia and to the province at large." Neither did the committee neglect to set forth effectively the social teachings of the Catholic Church. These doctrines, they concluded, demanded efforts to solve the region's great problems, which had been publicly disclosed by the recent Royal Commissions on the coal industries (1926) and the fisheries (1927). The committee, therefore, urged the college to appoint staff to study "the underlying principles of sane Catholic social action" and the advances made along such lines in other countries. Its report declared in closing, "The Department of Social Action, or the Department of Extension, which is herein suggested, could do much to bring about the realization of more happy conditions, and to train leaders among the people themselves to help point the way towards their social, economic and educational improvement. The relation between this improvement and their spiritual welfare is so potent as not to require emphasis at this time."[31] The college governors, composed of nineteen members, of whom eleven were priests and over one-half from Cape Breton, were convinced by the Alumni Association committee that they had to act; thus, they granted Dr Coady leave from St.F.X. in January 1929 to study extension work in Canada and the United States.[32]

Preparations for the New Extension Program
Coady, by then a forty-eight-year-old St.F.X. faculty member of nearly twenty years' standing,[33] used his extended trip to places like Toronto, Ottawa, Guelph, western Canada, Wisconsin, and the Carnegie Foundation in New York as a scavenger hunt for techniques of adult education.[34] He met countless people concerned with the problems of the masses, but found no institution, he claimed, which had started anything really useful. Coady concluded that Maritime people would have "to work out their own salvation"; and the college could best help, he believed, through schools for adults, libraries, radio broadcasting, correspondence courses, study clubs, and the promotion of economic organizations.[35] However, before initiating extension work at St.F.X., and after attending a teachers' summer school in 1929 run by the college,[36] he was asked by the department of fisheries to organize the fishermen of eastern Canada.[37] With characteristic energy and optimism, Coady undertook the massive assignment, which extended from September 1929 to June 1930; his efforts culminated with a convention in Halifax to tie the 168 locals into one association called the United Maritime Fishermen.[38] From the gruelling experience involving extensive travel, Coady gained further knowledge about regional problems and techniques of community organization, and established for himself numerous local contacts and an expanding reputation.[39]

While Coady laboured among the fishermen, the St.F.X. board met in January 1930 and decided, after more urging and a promise of financial support from the Scottish Catholic Society, to shift the extension department into action.[40] Angus B. MacDonald was hired to assist in its commencement.[41] MacDonald, like Coady, was a striking figure, tall and physically impressive. A native of Antigonish County and a graduate of St.F.X., he had been encouraged by Tompkins over a decade before to pursue agriculture.[42] Therefore, he trained at both the Truro and Ontario agricultural colleges, and then, in the early 1920s, threw himself into educational work among farmers, first in Nova Scotia and then afterwards in Ontario. There he also studied education at the University of Toronto and the Ontario School of Education. In

1925 MacDonald became school inspector of Antigonish and Guysborough counties, and through the next five years earned a high reputation for excellent work. Then St.F.X. lured him into its orbit in January 1930.[43] By then, MacDonald, thirty-six years old, was well prepared for educational field-work; moreover, he had pressed, along with others, for his *alma mater*'s move into adult education.

The Extension Department Blueprint

In 1930 the new director of extension, Dr Moses Coady, and his assistant director, Angus B. MacDonald, forged a plan of action. The purpose of extension, they decided, was "the improvement of the economic, social, educational and religious conditions of the people in eastern Nova Scotia." Their social vision contemplated a cooperative society where all people would have equal access to the "good and abundant life."[44] All major primary producers in the region – farmers, fishermen, miners, and lumbermen – would be targeted. From the first, both visionaries planned to cooperate with government and other social agencies.[45] Moreover, they wanted the diocesan rural conferences expanded to embrace all community leaders and to provide their nascent work with inspiration, counsel, and direction.[46] Coady and MacDonald outlined the following possible extension activities: cultural and vocational short courses (both on and off campus), leadership courses, correspondence courses, study clubs, radio courses, technical and folk schools, night schools, lectures, library services, publishing, debates, community centre programs, and rural and town improvement competitions.[47]

The Launching of Extension Work

The central thrust of the work which they actually launched in the fall of 1930 among communities in the region was a program of adult education through economic cooperation. Their key tool of adult education was the study club, a method which embodied the idea of self-help, taught cooperation in learning, and encouraged the individual discipline of study and self-improvement.[48] As well, it capitalized on the innate human urge for companionship, the experience and wisdom of local community members, and the material interests of club participants. The study clubs brought interested people together for regular meetings through the fall and winter. Social conditions favoured such local activities, since television did not exist, cash was scarce, and travel often difficult.[49] Coady and MacDonald developed a list of promising study club leaders in the region's communities, and then mailed them materials on the purpose, formation, and conduct of such clubs.[50]

Dr Moses Coady, first director of St.F.X.
extension department 1930–52

A.B. MacDonald, first assistant director
of extension 1930–44

Extension had an agenda for the clubs. They designed the first lessons to help the farmers and fishermen grasp the general background and circumstances of their economic plight and to begin thinking about solutions. Coady and MacDonald's recipe for economic and social uplift was, first, knowledge of social conditions; next, a vision of the possible; finally, action through economic cooperation, with a hefty dosage of optimism leavening the whole. They allowed the clubs some election of study topics, but wanted their interests guided by the fundamental aim of solving current, practical, local difficulties. Most of the early clubs studied the business side of farming, especially marketing; others examined crop and livestock production.[51]

The study clubs were usually organized after what Coady described as "an intellectual bombing operation" at a mass meeting in a local community.[52] Before speaking in a community, Coady would ferret out all the information he could about its setting, economic background, and major problems and defects. Then he would try to "explode the dynamite that will pave the way for reconstruction."[53] His speeches at these meetings, often based on only a few scribbled notes, were delivered with power and conviction under titles like "Straight Thinking and the Nation," "The Way Out for Producers," and "Education as the Release of Human Energy."[54] Afterwards, extension workers organized those people inspired by Coady's powerful rhetoric into study clubs to begin striving toward better future possibilities.

The Need for Appropriate Study Materials
Extension workers soon confronted the problem of supplying the clubs with appropriate study materials and sustaining them over the long haul. Coady and MacDonald, both effective organizers and administrators, encouraged links between the clubs through combined monthly rallies, inter-club debates, and public speaking contests. Staff quickly discovered a dearth of useful written materials for the study clubs – many of the first texts they distributed were weighty, impenetrable volumes by American authors on subjects like rural sociology and cooperative democracy. Hence they were forced to produce "simple material in accordance with the psychology of the people of eastern Canada."[55] Thus the college made its first substantial venture into journalism and publication. The mimeographed study materials distributed to the early study clubs soon transmigrated into the bimonthly *Extension Bulletin* edited by George Boyle, which was not long in achieving a circulation of around seven thousand.[56] The *Extension Bulletin* served as a propaganda tool of about seven to eight pages which had sections devoted to fishermen, farmers, labourers, women,

Study club session

and banking and money. Some material was reprints of articles and speeches, and some was produced by extension staff themselves. By 1940 extension had produced at least twenty-two pamphlets, four books, and numerous journal and newspaper articles. The diocesan paper, the *Casket*, which had for years been promoting cooperative enterprises,[57] gave generous and celebratory coverage to all extension developments; from 1933 it included an extension column devoted exclusively to study club news and cooperative articles.[58] Furthermore, in the fall of 1930, extension formed travelling or circulating libraries and placed them at the disposal of the study clubs.[59] The books were packed in boxes which also served as book shelves. By 1934 twenty-five travelling libraries circulated; the extension office supplemented this service with an open shelf library which provided individual titles by mail.

The Centre of Action
The St.F.X. extension department itself was the powerhouse which spread and propelled the movement. It functioned as a coordinating, energizing, and nurturing centre. Undoubtedly it was then the most innovative and dynamic department at St.F.X.; its staff was imbued with an evangelical sense of mission. Moreover, extension was the first department where women made direct and major contributions to a formal program.[60] The first secretary, Kay Thompson, and two Sisters of St Martha – Marie Michael Mackinnon and Irene Doyle – found themselves responsible for all manner of tasks, clerical and otherwise – writing, speaking, listening, hosting, typing, planning, organizing, critiquing, and generating ideas. The extension office in the 1930s was a stimulating, exciting place to work. The office staff developed a strong spirit of family and of cooperation. And Coady, who valued the opinions and contributions of all, male and female, regularly appeared in a state of excitement and exhilaration over the latest ideas discovered. The enthusiasm he had was infectious.[61] Moreover, he was grateful for the contributions of others. When Kay Thompson moved to the Sydney extension office in 1941, Coady wrote, "Providence was kind to us. Almost without designing it we assembled a happy, and I think very competent group of people."[62]

The Annual Short Courses
Extension formed another support for the clubs by conducting annual short courses for community leaders. The first short course was held in 1933.[63] It distinctly resembled the people's school experiments of a decade before, although the purpose was focused more definitely on community development. In fact, Tompkins himself, along with other

Sister Irene Doyle (Sister Mary Anselm),
early extension department office staff

Sister Marie Michael MacKinnon, first director of the extension department's
women's program

St.F.X. faculty, taught at the first short course.[64] Its stated purpose was "to train men to direct the social and economic endeavours of the rural and industrial workers." The adult participants pondered the following: business arithmetic, English, bookkeeping, civics, elementary economics, history and principles of cooperation, cooperative business practices, and community organizations and programs.[65] By 1935, Coady had added a course entitled "Contemporary Social Movements" which gave students an introduction to socialism, communism, fascism, capitalism, and the cooperative movement as an instrument of democracy.[66] The short course lasted only four to six weeks, so the emphasis was "inspirational in character and designed to aid the students to continue their studies at home."[67] One field-worker recollects that it gave ample time "for a thorough discussion of local problems in co-operative enterprises and for the exposition of the whole program of adult education."[68] No admission requirements debarred those with little formal education, but extension staff preferred people who had leadership potential, either male or female. Coady sometimes asked the diocesan priests to help recruit promising parish members for the courses.

From 1932 to 1940, the short-course enrolments varied from 39 to 145. Most students were male, although the female minority expanded as the decade progressed. They gathered at St.F.X., usually early in the new year, from throughout the diocese; by 1940 substantial numbers were also coming from New Brunswick, Prince Edward Island, and a handful from the Magdalen Islands and Newfoundland. Many were fishermen who came on department of fisheries grants.[69] The students were often hard-nosed realists; they frequently challenged the staff with difficult, practical questions – for example, about the agenda of the new Cooperative Commonwealth Federation, the workability of cooperative organizations, interprovincial inequities, the lack of markets, low prices, and the resistance of local merchants to budding cooperative enterprises.[70] These adults measured extension propaganda against their own experience and were sometimes sceptical.

Extension Work among Women
The rural conference of 1931 called for extension to organize study clubs among women, and for leaders to cooperate with existing women's agencies, like the Catholic Women's League and the Women's Institutes, in order to promote adult education among women.[71] However, two years passed before the department organized a women's division. Coady placed the new program under the direction of a Martha, Sister Marie Michael MacKinnon.[72] Within one year, about

three hundred women's study clubs had examined problems in home-making, health, rural recreation, handicrafts, and cooperative organizations.[73] Most of the women's clubs were organized in farming and fishing communities, a fact which revealed the department's rural orientation; but it also formed some in industrial centres like New Glasgow and Sydney.[74] In order to help these new groups, the *Extension Bulletin* devoted a page to women's concerns.[75] Extension also made contact with women through mass meetings, field work, rural and industrial conferences, and direct correspondence.[76]

Although the study clubs were usually born in a community amid an explosion of optimism detonated by the dynamic Dr Coady, not all of them were successful. Some failed to promote the education of their members or advance the social and economic interests of their communities. Illiteracy was a serious hurdle in some areas, and extension staff had to develop methods to teach people rapidly how to read and write.[77] Clubs sometimes lacked good leadership and degenerated into bickering or gossip sessions; others harboured uncooperative members, unwilling to accept responsibilities or sceptical about the value of education. Local feuds and rivalries in some places also took their toll on the clubs. And those members who naïvely expected immediate results frequently lost heart and failed to persevere. Finally, local proprietors threatened by the unwelcome spectre of competition at times succeeded in demoralizing study club members.

The Promotion of Cooperative Organizations
The study club was the first pillar of extension. The second pillar was economic cooperation, a form of economic organization which attracted Canadians, both in the Maritimes and on the Prairies, wrestling with the impact of urbanization and industrialization.[78] Consumer cooperatives had begun to appear in Nova Scotia mining districts between 1861 and 1900. However, cooperativism became most firmly rooted in Canada between 1900 and 1914. In 1909 the Co-operative Union of Canada had formed, producing a journal called the *Canadian Co-operator.*[79] Coady and MacDonald wanted their study club members rapidly to receive economic rewards from their intellectual labours; cooperative action seemed to hold the most promise. This was the wily idea of starting at the people's point of most intense concern, namely their anxiety about economic security and advance. Later, Coady would reflect on the wisdom of starting something which demonstrated that thinking pays: "This is necessary," he maintained, "to attract the common people to a program of study." He added sardonically that it was also true for "the so-called elite at the top of the social heap."[80] By January 1931, extension had established a central

purchasing committee for interested farmers of Antigonish County which organized bulk farm purchases of fertilizer, flour, and seed.[81] Shortly thereafter, Coady was urging the farmers of St Andrews, a nearby community, to manufacture their own clothing, harness, and other domestic supplies.[82]

The work of extension grew by leaps and bounds in the early years of its lively existence. By the end of 1932, it had hired two extra part-time field-workers – Revs. James Boyle and Michael Gillis – and had opened an office in Glace Bay, an area which had been rife with labour strife for decades.[83] A.S. MacIntyre, a convert from Cape Breton industrial radicalism, worked in the industrial areas.[84] By the fall of 1932, 183 study clubs had been formed among farmers and fishermen, and 24 among miners. The spin-off into cooperative organizations included eight lobster factories and nine credit unions.[85] Credit unions, which extension began promoting in 1932 after receiving help from Roy F. Bergengren,[86] a successful American credit union organizer, developed most rapidly, probably because of the urgent need for credit and their relatively simple organization.[87] Extension staff were instrumental in having credit union legislation enacted in 1932;[88] six years later enough credit unions organized in Nova Scotia to form a credit union league.[89] Moreover, extension spread credit unionism to other parts of English-speaking Canada. In 1935 extension hired the first female field-worker – Ida Delaney.[90] By 1940, the department boasted 355 credit unions, 42 stores, 34 fisheries cooperatives, and 20 other types of cooperative associations in the three Maritime provinces of Nova Scotia, New Brunswick, and Prince Edward Island. Apparently around thirty thousand people were involved in study clubs.

By that year the extension department staff had expanded to eleven full-time and seven part-time workers. The year before, fifteen "fisheries fieldsmen" had begun work, under the supervision of extension, in communities designated by the federal department of fisheries in Nova Scotia, New Brunswick, Prince Edward Island, and the Magdalen Islands.[91] Extension's federally sponsored fisheries program became an important and long-term one. Three credit union leagues had been formed, one each in Nova Scotia, New Brunswick, and Prince Edward Island. The United Maritime Fishermen union had grown, and three wholesales had been established: the Canadian Livestock Co-operative in Moncton, New Brunswick, with its two branches in Nova Scotia – the Canadian Livestock Co-operative in Sydney, and Eastern Co-operative Services in Antigonish.[92] The 1930s had truly been glory days for St.F.X.'s extension department.

Early credit union, product of the extension program

Increasing Renown and Influence

Not only did the Antigonish Movement grow quickly in its early years, but also news of its successes rapidly migrated far beyond the Diocese of Antigonish. The news was broadcast in a multitude of ways: word of mouth, written correspondence, peripatetic extension staff, media reports, and migrant laity and clergy who spread out across the "Catholic network" of regional and national institutions.[93] For example, for several weeks in late 1933, Coady visited the new Clandonald farm colony of Highland settlers in Alberta; in October 1934 he addressed the congress of the Co-operative League of the United States which met in Chicago.[94] On a three-month Carnegie-sponsored trip to Washington, DC and to other points in the United States in 1936, Coady reportedly made a "great impression" and "spread the gospel of cooperation in all directions."[95] He soon developed close connections with prominent cooperative, credit union, and adult education leaders throughout the United States and Canada; many of these made pilgrimages to Antigonish in search of extension's magic formula for success. Both Coady and A.B. MacDonald supported the Canadian Association of Adult Education which formed in the mid-1930s, and they inspired its director, Edward A. Corbett.[96] In 1936, the Catholic Women's League of Canada adopted the study club technique and some of their clubs used materials produced by the St.F.X. extension department.[97] St Dunstan's College in Charlottetown announced in 1935 the beginnings of extension work along St.F.X. lines.[98] The following year, a St.F.X. graduate began to organize Newfoundland fishermen cooperatively.[99] The Credit Union movement and other organizations in the United States also borrowed techniques and exchanged ideas with Antigonish extension leaders.[100] From 1937 to 1940 the Co-operative Union League of the United States, a fan of St.F.X. extension, organized annual tours to eastern Nova Scotia; it brought along noted college men, church leaders, and cooperators so they could examine the incipient Antigonish Movement first hand. Media reports with titles like "A New Order," "Blazing the Road for Cooperation," and "A Maritime Miracle" likewise did their share to spread fact and fiction about the Antigonish Movement. Perhaps the ultimate commendation for Catholic extension workers came in 1936 when the Vatican warmly praised its work.[101] By the end of the 1930s, some international interest was appearing, and extension developed links with inquirers in places like New Zealand, China, India, the Philippines, and South Africa.[102] Representatives from Puerto Rico and Jamaica attended the rural and industrial conferences in the late 1930s and surveyed extension's work among the people of eastern Nova Scotia.

The Roots of Extension Success

Extension's early, arresting successes and its widespread appeal were undoubtedly related to the general harsh social and economic conditions of the Depression. George Boyle, who edited the *Extension Bulletin*, declared in 1934: "The depression has created the most attentive audience the world has ever known."[103] Another observer claimed that the Depression "made all men social-minded" and gave great impetus to extension efforts.[104] Since the Depression was universal, outmigration was no longer an easy solution to economic want. Ian MacPherson claims that the young who remained in the Maritimes "were particularly receptive to the moderate reformism of the Antigonish Movement."[105]

Of course, the enthusiasm, optimism, ability, and experience of both Dr Coady and A.B. MacDonald, as well as the extension machinery and techniques which they developed, were likewise critical to the movement's spread. A later assistant director of extension maintained that "no movement owes more to its personalities."[106] The leading personalities were impressive and persuasive; they commanded a high level of respect in the Maritime communities. Coady was a priest, and thus a member of that profession directly linked, for Catholics, with the moral and spiritual authority of Rome. Moreover, he was reputed as a superb teacher with the highest academic credentials. But Coady, and MacDonald too, came from among the working people of eastern Nova Scotia. Thus their inspirational oratory – and oratory was fundamental to the movement – was tailored to circumstances. When Coady spoke, the people saw a man of authority and prestige, and heard language permeated with optimism and hyperbole, replete with vivid images and snappy memorable phrases, and delivered with gusto and conviction. They saw and heard a man who was on their side, someone who was wrestling with their problems, and someone who gave them a vocabulary with evocative phrases – "the good and abundant life," "the vested interests," "the democratic formula," and "a fair share of the national income"; these helped them grasp their own situation and aim for a new day.[107]

The extension office staff, the field-workers, and voluntary community leaders – clergy, teachers, and others – were also critical to the effectiveness of the extension program. Of the diocesan clergy, Coady declared: "the majority ... had the movement so much at heart that they were from the beginning practically on the staff of the university in this work."[108] An observer described the supportive parish clergy as "mostly younger men who have fallen under the Tompkins-Coady spell, either as friends and associates or as former pupils."[109] Neither should one overlook the cooperation of government officials and workers in helping the extension program succeed.

Opposition, Criticism, and Difficulties

The extension movement did not sweep all before it; the staff's agenda aroused opposition and criticism. Some of it originated from within Coady's own priestly caste. First, there were the uncooperative priests, those who failed to enlist in the cause because of alleged selfish concern with their own comfort and security.[110] Coady reserved his harshest words for priests he believed were aligned with the "vested interests," although he recognized the temptation to be co-opted by social and economic power as "an ancient and natural weakness of human nature."[111] Some priestly detractors tossed out scripture verses like "The poor you have always with you," and levelled the charge of materialism against the Antigonish Movement. Coady judged such clerics, who dwelt in the high places of "rarefied spirituality," guilty of a "monstrous hypocrisy," since they desired modern homes, decent salaries, and comfortable pensions.[112] He often reminded his critics that modern totalitarian regimes had their ominous origins in the unrelieved suffering of the masses. Materialistic atheism, he insisted, attracted people because their spiritual leaders were found "among the base and subservient apologists of powerful economic masters."[113] "Fixing up the economic," asserted Coady, "is a main way and perhaps the only way to ensure law and order and decency and religion in the world."[114] Indeed, he had concluded that poverty tended to destroy faith; conversely, economic progress disposed people to religion.[115] Extension workers believed economic democracy was a "natural consequence" of the Christian faith and rooted in the church's social teachings.[116] Cooperation, they believed, was the embodiment of charity in economics and thus harmonized with the Fatherhood of God and the brotherhood of man. They would allow for no dichotomy between religious faith and economic life.

Merchants and politicians in the local communities and towns were frequently antagonistic toward the extension agenda. In some places they evidently profited by dominating the local economy; therefore, they contemplated with dismay and disfavour the prospect of competition from cooperative enterprise and possible loss of profits and control.[117] Coady did not expect otherwise; such people, he believed, would not "commit economic suicide for the sake of their less fortunate brethren," and he identified in their attitude a deceitful assumption that they were "commissioned by God as trustees of their weaker brethren."[118] However, Coady himself did not oppose private enterprise and did not believe economic cooperation to be a full solution to society's problems. Cooperative organizations could "act as an effective governor on a mixed society in which private ownership, some socialization and an area – perhaps a large area – of private profit, trail-blazing enterprise exists."[119]

In general, the governments of the Maritime provinces were sympathetic toward extension work. They had for years attempted to spread technical information to the people – for example, through agricultural representatives. However, certain government members were aligned with the "vested interests" and opposed St.F.X. extension.[120] Others were involved themselves in production or merchandising and for that reason wanted to thwart the St.F.X. adult education program. A.B. MacDonald wrote, "It often happens that people high up in government circles are engaged in the sale and processing of farm produce and they, through selfish motives, place every obstacle possible in the way of the development of ... co-operatives."[121] Coady's policy, when confronted with opposition and obvious exploitation, was to avoid violent counter-attacks. He thought the people themselves partly responsible, by default, for their own condition, a point he clearly argued in his book *Masters of Their Own Destiny*.[122] Thus, to encourage them in attacks on their exploiters would not elicit their best efforts, or provide an enduring impulse to work for the betterment of their own circumstances.[123]

Other difficulties, too, inhibited the spread and unification of cooperativism. Ethnic divisions between Acadian and English Canadians sometimes spawned conflicts. Indeed, extension would occasionally be criticized for neglecting Acadian communities by failing to provide French field-workers and literature.[124] Moreover, some Protestants identified the Antigonish Movement as a dangerous Roman Catholic program in spite of Coady's efforts to downplay its Catholicism.[125] Ian MacPherson concludes that Maritime cooperativism has been handicapped by localism, "provincial boundaries, metropolitan rivalries, personal animosities, complex historical backgrounds, institutional conflicts, religious divisions, and ethnic differences."[126]

Early Impact of Extension Work
In spite of the backlash of opposition and the hurdles thrown up by social divisions, the impact of early extension work in Nova Scotia was substantial. Undoubtedly it eroded the appeal of political radicalism in the industrial towns of the diocese; its Glace Bay proponent, A.S. McIntyre, was one prominent example of that. Bishop Morrison considered extension the centre of resistance to Communism in the region.[127] Coady believed the Communist coal miners and steel workers of eastern Nova Scotia formed "the spearhead of communism in Canada."[128] In 1935, McIntyre reported, "Communism is on the

advance ... in our Cape Breton towns and among our Catholic people."[129] Over a decade later, Coady claimed that the extension program "licked them," not so much by "a frontal attack on Communism as by a positive program of giving enlightenment, leadership and life to thousands among the proletariat and the primary producers."[130] He expressed deep concern about the relation of the church to the working classes; he was convinced that the Antigonish Movement did much to "dignify churchmen in the eyes of the people" and inoculate them against radicalism.[131]

More positively, extension efforts frequently elevated the tone of community life by fostering local leadership, provoking debate and discussion, and encouraging cooperation and sociability.[132] There was more knowledge among the people, more independence, more self-confidence, more literacy, and more understanding between Catholics and Protestants; on the other hand, people experienced less despair and demoralization. In addition, many improved their economic lot in communities and towns where they were able to found successful producer or consumer cooperatives.[133]

However, Coady's ultimate aim for the people of the "full and abundant life" was obviously not achieved in any complete or final way. He hoped adult education would go beyond economic revitalization and local control: "Through credit unions, co-operative stores, lobster factories and sawmills, we are laying the foundation for an appreciation of Shakespeare and grand opera."[134] While Coady had started at the ground floor of basic economic self-interest, his sights were set high. But people responded most energetically to a program of adult education rooted in their own urgent economic needs; the celebrated rewards of higher culture did not seem so compelling.

Extension's Internal Influence
The founding of the extension department at St.F.X. affected the internal life of the college itself. Students, at a stage in their lives most susceptible to idealism, were frequently inspired with fresh concerns about social justice. In the fall of 1930 the students formed the Students' Cooperative Society to give themselves knowledge and experience in cooperativism. The society ran a successful students' supply company or book store which sold stationery, books, tobacco, and confectionery.[135] A social economics club began in 1931; its purpose was to help students "develop a real social philosophy of life."[136]

Occasionally the *Xaverian Weekly* castigated the student body for its alleged ignorance of what the extension department was up to; it would be a perennial reproof. One reprimand in 1935 concluded with the plea: "Find out about the Extension Department! Learn the meaning of Christian Cooperation! Organize!"[137] Evidently, being a student at St.F.X. in the 1930s did not automatically turn one into a cooperator; neither would it automatically inspire a sense of social responsibility in future generations of Xaverians. However, some alumni would later attest that Dr Coady and extension either awakened or bolstered their concern for social justice.[138] That same year, 1935, Coady and MacDonald started a weekly study club in the extension offices located in the old administration building; the popular meetings excited students who wrestled with the central principles and issues faced by the extension movement.[139] The club even tried to organize Maritime university students into a Maritime Students' Cooperative League to help them explore the cooperative philosophy; unfortunately, the plan foundered.[140]

Financing Extension

Extension work aggravated St.F.X.'s ever-troublesome problem of financing. Of course, world depression in 1930 intensified the difficulty even more, for it deepened the economic slide of the region. Moreover, extension, in contrast to the regular college program, had a special financial handicap: it could not support itself through tuition revenues. At the start, Coady and MacDonald estimated for the board of governors that the new department would require annually about $10,000 to run effectively; the largest expenses would be salaries and travel.[141] In the founding years, extension leaders fortunately discovered several funding sources.

The most lucrative support came from the Carnegie Corporation of New York, who ten years before had advocated university federation in the region. In the strange ways of Providence, the wealth of a paradigmatic American capitalist would be used to promote economic justice and community uplift in eastern Nova Scotia. By the fall of 1931, Coady had visited the Carnegie offices twice and Tompkins, a good friend of its staff, had also solicited the corporation on behalf of extension. The corporation then commissioned Benson Y. Landis, a Protestant and an official of both the American Federal Council of Churches and the American Country Life Association, to review the extension program. Landis spent about one week in Nova Scotia, where he visited communities like Antigonish, Heatherton, St Andrews, Guysborough, and Canso, interviewed lay and clerical leaders alike, and examined the workings of Coady's nascent program at first hand. He estimated that about 60 out of 110 diocesan priests were actively cooperating with extension work, judged that most were of exceptional educational status and morale, and concluded that they were "in general the same group who worked for the federation plan of Dalhousie University."[142] Landis was very upbeat about the extension program. His enthusiastic report persuaded Carnegie officials, and, in 1932, they granted the program $35,000 over four years; by 1936 they had actually given $68,000.[143] They hoped extension work would be "a demonstration [in adult education] of what is needed in many sections of the United States"; its approach, they believed, fit the Carnegie philosophy of helping others to help themselves instead of depending on the state or volunteer agencies.[144] The announcement of Carnegie aid to St.F.X. was, in Dr Coady's words, "great, from the psychological as well as financial point of view." It injected an immense surge of encouragement into extension morale and immediately conferred a degree of prestige and legitimacy on the institution's new agenda for the people. In retrospect Coady concluded, "There is no doubt that without this help the Antigonish Movement could not have achieved in many decades (if it could have survived at all) what it has accomplished in the first ten years of its history."[145]

The Significance of the Extension Program
The St.F.X. leadership had made certain critical changes in faculty and programs between 1900 and 1930. Without doubt the founding of the department of extension transcended all others in long-range importance. The innovation represented a decisive move beyond the traditional classical and professional approaches in higher education into mass adult education. St.F.X. expanded its mandate beyond the Catholic formation of youth to include the uplift of the entire region through adult education and economic cooperation; in so doing, the college became ever more deeply rooted in the affections of its constituency. Coady and MacDonald had designed the extension department as an instrument of social action; thus they altered the character of the college. From then on, St.F.X. would define itself not only as "storehouse" of knowledge but also as "powerhouse" of social and economic change on behalf of the people.

The St.F.X. experiment in mass adult education was a unique Maritime and Canadian innovation. While other universities have established departments of extension, most often devoted to individual betterment,[146] St.F.X. pioneered the social reformist approach and tried to be an instrument of progress. For times of economic hardship, it provided an attractive and effective model, and has remained an inspiration as well as a spur in the side of adult educators.[147] Ian MacPherson, a student of Canadian cooperativism, has called Coady "perhaps the most profound Canadian Co-operator" and the Antigonish Movement "one of the most creative movements within the Canadian movement."[148] Coady claimed that the reformist approach was possible at St.F.X. because of its dependence on the people overall, and its non-alliance with a dominating social and financial elite.[149] He believed the large, privately endowed universities were too closely aligned with the vested interests to allow for anything but innocuous and respectable approaches to education. Finally, by putting into practice the social teachings of the church, rooted in Christian compassion, the call for justice, and convictions about the value and dignity of all people created in God's image, extension demonstrated, more daringly than other Canadian Catholics during the depression, that the church could be on the side of the poor.[150]

PART FIVE

Ordeal of War and Its Aftermath, 1936–54

· 12 ·

Stymied Plans,
1936–44

In the fall of 1936, when St.F.X. students returned to Antigonish, they found the Old Rector – a thirty-year stalwart of the St.F.X. community – in retirement. Ill health had finally forced his resignation at age sixty-nine and had brought to a close the longest presidential tenure in St.F.X. history. His close friend Bishop Morrison honoured him with the title "President-Rector Emeritus" and invited him to remain in residence at the college.[1] News of the Old Rector's retirement brought an avalanche of affectionate tribute from the humble and prominent for his many years of service. One friend astutely wrote, "You had become so much the institution itself, that to think of one without the other requires a new orientation."[2]

The MacPherson years had been three long decades of considerable action and advance at St.F.X.; they had encompassed the institution's growth from a small diocesan college to one of some national, even international acclaim because of its successful new adult education program. The most significant developments had included an affiliation with the Nova Scotia Technical College, two financial campaigns (1907 and 1920), the First World War, campus expansion, the inheritance of substantial Boston properties, the recruitment of capable faculty (some who would make historic contributions to the college), experiments with a people's school, the threat of university federation, the elimination of high school work, the establishment of the extension department, the ordeal of Depression, and the formation of a fruitful relation with the Carnegie Corporation of New York. Throughout, MacPherson had been a steady hand at the institutional tiller, perhaps a providential circumstance given the presence on board of some headstrong crew. Nearly one-half of the Old Rector's life had been spent at St.F.X. Not surprisingly, he accepted the bishop's offer to remain on campus and continued keen about college affairs until his death in 1949.

Rev. Dr Daniel J. MacDonald, president 1936–44

The New President

The students that fall of 1936 received the presidential greeting from a tall, physically striking individual and staff veteran of twenty-four years. President Daniel J. MacDonald, a native of Heatherton Parish, Antigonish County, had been appointed to the college back in September 1912, after doctoral studies in literature at the Catholic University of America. MacDonald had entered the priesthood in 1904 after completing the arts program at St.F.X. (1900) and theological training at the Urban College, Rome (1904), where he had to shorten his course for health reasons.[3] From 1912 to 1936 he had served St.F.X., mostly as professor of economics. He also gained administrative experience from 1925 to 1930 as vice-rector, and from 1930 to MacPherson's retirement as vice-president.[4] The notorious report of 1922, which condemned the proposal of university federation, had been his handiwork. An enthusiast for the extension program, MacDonald had been involved in the debates and conferences which led to its formation. Indeed, his brother "A.B." MacDonald was the assistant director to Coady. In most of his rather extensive public lecturing and publishing, President MacDonald had been preoccupied with the reform of Maritime rural life and economic relations.[5] Tompkins stated in the early 1920s that MacDonald was the most radical member of the faculty.[6] He certainly appeared much more active and public in his support for the Antigonish Movement than President MacPherson had been.

MacDonald was fifty-five years old when, at Bishop Morrison's request, he assumed the presidency of St.F.X. In some ways, his administration was to be dogged by frustration. By the mid-1930s, and in spite of the Depression, St.F.X. was riding high on the crest of a wave of optimism built up by its astonishing successes in extension work and the support of the Carnegie Corporation. The election of its alumnus Angus L. MacDonald as Liberal premier of the province in 1933 also contributed to the buoyant mood. President MacDonald and his college began to dream dreams of expansion and further educational conquest. Some of their plans were realized; however, much of the anticipated growth and expansion were stymied by the twin distractions of debt and war.

MacDonald's public utterances made clear his socially oriented educational philosophy and explain his interests as president. He stressed repeatedly that religion in college life had valuable consequences for society at large. With an anxious eye on Russian Communism and German Nazism, and their communist and fascist offspring in Canada, he emphasized that the religious principles underlying both classroom and extension work at St.F.X. would preserve freedom and promote justice. Universities, he insisted, were responsible for the tone and direction of society because they developed its leaders. He lectured, "The creative principle of our democratic society is Christian faith with its insistence on the dignity, rights and duties of the human person."[7] MacDonald pointed out that the fundamental philosophy of an institution has direct social consequences, and he prophesied that secular universities would ultimately destroy Christian civilization and encourage paganism and materialism. The small college, in President MacDonald's view, should largely be a transmitter of knowledge rather than an inventor of it; elaborate laboratories for the physical sciences were too expensive for them. His greatest interest lay in social life and theory; therefore, he promoted research in the social sciences (the laboratory is the social world all around, he claimed).[8] MacDonald believed universities should give their students "some conception of the whole field of knowledge, the connection between scientific and social knowledge, and above all, an awareness of the social world and the importance of understanding it."[9] The St.F.X. extension department, he judged, was perhaps most important for the impact it had on students at the university.[10] While MacDonald's interest in St.F.X.'s social impact was evident, the force of changing circumstances would determine how far his college could pursue these objectives.

College Expansion

In 1934 St.F.X. had appointed several faculty committees to review its program and facilities, and then to propose a blueprint for the future. Father Tompkins, by then parish priest in Reserve Mines, Cape Breton, was involved in the exercise; no doubt he stressed his favourite themes – expansion, progress, and higher standards.[11] The faculty committees concluded that the institution faced a critical turning point. Enrolments had gradually increased since the onset of Depression, the staff had expanded, and the extension department had made rapid strides while winning substantial financial support from the Carnegie Corporation. Nevertheless, the committees believed that "In college work, to stand still is to go back."[12] St.F.X. had erected no buildings since 1921; more faculty had only bachelors' degrees than before; the Sisters of St Martha's residence was overcrowded; dining and kitchen facilities were outdated; and the college had deferred urgent maintenance and repairs because of the Depression.[13] The faculty committees concluded, "[St.F.X.] stands in a less advantageous position among the institutions of higher learning and professional schools than it did ten or fifteen years ago."[14] They feared that McGill, the University of Toronto, and other professional schools would soon either demand advanced training of St.F.X. graduates, especially in the sciences, or reduce St.F.X. to the same junior college category occupied by unnamed other Maritime Catholic institutions.[15] The big American universities, the committee reports maintained, now considered St.F.X. graduates equivalent to those from junior colleges.

The administration, the board of governors, the faculty, and the alumni reached a consensus that St.F.X. should expand. Dr Nicholson, the dean of studies, reported in 1936 a "spirit of optimism" and "a better sentiment of solidarity" than he had known before.[16] At a special board meeting in May 1936, the faculty recommended the following: the establishment of scholarships, the construction of a library, a class-room building, and an auditorium, the formulation of a policy to ensure adequately trained faculty, the endowment of chairs of chem-istry, biology, physics, economics, English, and sociology, the endow-ment of the extension department, and scholarships to permit the training of community leaders.[17] For the mid-1930s, when the severe economic problems had brought Mackenzie King's Liberals back to replace R.B. Bennett's Conservatives, and many Canadians thought new parties like Social Credit and the Co-operative Commonwealth Federation offered better solutions, it was a most ambitious, even unrealistic program. The euphoria created by the conquests and vic-tories of extension inhibited sober judgment.

Morrison Hall

The immediate recommendations were for a laundry, which was built within the year, and, much more significantly, for an elaborate three-storey dining hall facility. The new building was to be constructed in Georgian style of native sandstone, to measure 162 by 74 feet,[18] and to contain the following: kitchen facilities, several dining rooms (one to accommodate about five hundred students), recreation rooms, a convent for the Sisters of St Martha, an infirmary, a chapel, and residence quarters for thirteen faculty.[19] Authorities expected the hall to free up space for classrooms and dormitories in the old administra-tion building. It would be located directly to the south of the old building, but facing west instead of north. The total cost of about $268,000, by far the largest sum yet paid for any structure erected on the campus,[20] was met through a bond issue[21] and donations to a building fund; the bishop and priests alone subscribed over $50,000 to the fund.[22] The college leadership named the edifice Morrison Hall in honour of the bishop who was its single most generous benefactor.

In retrospect, the construction and opening of Morrison Hall in the spring of 1938 had important consequences for the future development of St.F.X. First, it was the only substantial building erected since 1921 and symbolized the university's long-term commitment to expand and upgrade itself in spite of the realities of the Depression. Second,

Morrison Hall, built 1938

Morrison Hall was also the first of a series of new stone buildings completed by 1951 which would alter substantially the appearance of the campus. And finally, through the search for someone to design the new dining hall, St.F.X. obtained the services of a highly acclaimed New England architect, Jens F. Larson. He was the continuing architect for about twenty American colleges and universities and would eventually design twelve large buildings on the St.F.X. campus.[23] The building committee hired him "to make a general landscape development and perspective studies of the various contemplated buildings for the use of the University."[24] Not only had American money financed earlier campus expansion and new programs at St.F.X., but from 1936 American expertise would shape the material appearance of the developing college.

Financial Crisis

The immense debt incurred by the construction of Morrison Hall, along with several other developments, created a financial crisis at St.F.X. by the summer of 1938; the prospects dimmed for continued expansion along the lines of the optimistic plan of 1936. Donations from a private canvass were slower than anticipated and the annual Sunday college collection had, in Bishop Morrison's words, "languished with the course of time, and at present is about at the disappearing point."[25] Moreover, St.F.X. had not been able to sell its Boston properties, which were valued in 1936 at about $170,000.[26] Income from these properties had dropped considerably during the Depression,[27] and expenditures on them exceeded income in 1937–38 by $6405 because of needed repairs and a business recession in Boston.[28] And finally, the size of the Carnegie Corporation grants in aid of extension work was declining. Although Carnegie's support was substantial, amounting to $79,500 from 1932 to 1943,[29] the corporation refused to fund projects indefinitely. Thus, in the summer of 1938, the St.F.X. administration peered with dismay at the financial statement, which, for the second year running, showed a mounting deficit.[30]

The college had to restore its deteriorating finances. First, the board of governors approved an annual tuition fee increase.[31] Father Tompkins appealed unsuccessfully, along with others, for $125,000 over five years from the Rockefeller Foundation in New York.[32] In the Boston area, supporters of Extension work formed an organization in 1939–40 called Friends of the Antigonish Movement; they canvassed potential contributors, but with mediocre results.[33] In addition, the college began broadcasting through the calendar its serious financial needs and urging alumni and friends to remember St.F.X. in their wills.[34] The Alumni Association also aided the fund-raising cause; in 1936 it had enthusiastically supported the expansion program, and in 1940 it set up an alumni office at St.F.X. with a full-time secretary. The association appealed, through its new bulletin the *Alumni News*, far and wide for donations to an alumni fund.[35] Finally, the clergy also pledged to the college diocesan support by imposing for five years on all parish wage-earners a total annual quota of $20,000. The relative success of this latter scheme, no doubt highly popular with St.F.X. staff, ensured its renewal for another five years in 1943.[36]

In spite of these measures, the slide in finances continued, and President MacDonald's fear that the college programs would need to be curtailed became reality.[37] The board of governors examined the extension budget in 1939; its expenditures had run to about $250,000 between 1928 and 1939, and the cost to St.F.X. had been over $100,000.[38] Because of these mounting deficits, the board and chancellor required extension to reduce substantially its expenses.[39] This was a bitter pill for extension and the college to swallow, for the adult education program had achieved exhilarating results and widespread attention. In addition to a major expansion into educational and organizational work among Maritime fishermen in 1937 with federal funding, the department had also sponsored, a year later, an innovative cooperative housing project in Reserve Mines; it was a first in the province. The mastermind behind the scheme was an American, Mary Arnold.[40] About this time, Coady published a descriptive and inspirational account of the Antigonish Movement in a short book called *Masters of Their Own Destiny*.[41] And in March 1938 the Holy Father even saw fit to commend the Antigonish Movement and to bestow on its promoters the apostolic benediction.[42]

New Extension Organizations
The financial squeeze at St.F.X. contributed to the formation of several new organizations designed to shoulder some of extension's burden. The *Extension Bulletin*, renamed the *Maritime Co-operator* in June 1939, became the joint responsibility of the cooperatives and credit unions;[43] it would become "the most internationally oriented of the Canadian journals, featuring reports on many aspects of the movement in North America and Europe."[44] By August 1940, the Co-operative Educational Council for Nova Scotia was organized and made responsible for cooperative education.[45] However, these cost-cutting measures were not enough. Moreover, in 1941, wartime constraint reduced the federal grant for extension work among the Maritime fishermen.[46] Therefore, Coady had to severely curtail expenses, release some office staff and field-workers, and temporarily close the Glace Bay office in March 1941.[47] President MacDonald was embarrassed by these developments;

he stressed publicly that such stringent measures did "not imply that the University authorities are lukewarm towards the work of the Department."[48]

Radio Station CJFX

The financially distressed president understandably found attractive a proposal that St.F.X. establish a radio station as an instrument of extension work. Radio broadcasts promised to reach vast numbers of people, augment the work of extension, and ease the pressure on its limited staff. Such an idea was not new; it had been mentioned in the original plans for extension work in 1930[49] and had been urged on St.F.X. by the rural and industrial conference of 1936.[50] Apparently a small discussion group of Cape Breton priests and laity had become dissatisfied with the religious programming of station CJCB in Sydney. On the suggestion of Rev. James Boyle, the group recommended to President MacDonald that extension acquire its own radio station.[51] On 21 May 1941 the board of governors approved the project in principle, and by the end of the year Atlantic Broadcasters Limited had been formed to finance the station.[52] Its shareholders, mainly St.F.X. alumni, would pay in capital amounting to $45,000 by July 1945.[53] Rev. Daniel MacCormack, St.F.X. professor of commerce, became president of its board, and Clyde Nunn, a St.F.X. alumnus and experienced radio announcer from Sydney, who had some practice in educational broadcasting and a keen interest in extension work, became the station's first general manager. Nunn was extremely talented; he became a prominent local personality and would remain with the station for almost thirty years. While the application for a broadcasting licence inched through the bureaucracy in Ottawa, St.F.X. sent Nunn, thanks to a small grant from the Rockefeller Foundation, to study the use of radio in adult education in the United States.[54]

In its application for a licence, St.F.X., with the European conflict in mind, stated its plan to run programs of "a broadly educational character, which would be directed towards making the people it would serve better citizens and more appreciative of the spiritual, social and economic advantages of our democratic way of life."[55] Specific programs would be tailored for study clubs, farmers, fishermen, industrial workers, and women; and general entertainment programs would develop native talent and preserve and promote the culture of the region. The evident desire was for a "University of the Air" in service to the people of eastern Nova Scotia. However, financial constraints would require it to be a private, commercial station, supported by advertising revenue and with St.F.X. supplying materials for educational programming.[56] The application requested a one-thousand-watt licence so the station could broadcast over the eastern counties of Nova Scotia, Prince Edward Island, and the Magdalen Islands. After a period of delay, the station obtained its licence to broadcast. Father Ernest Clarke, professor of physics at St.F.X., did much of the station's technical design and construction.[57]

Premier A.S. MacMillan officially announced CJFX "on the air" on 25 March 1943, the Feast of the Annunciation. Its early programming, some of it live and much of it produced by volunteers, included music, talk shows, radio plays, sports broadcasts, religion, and news. In April, a St.F.X. professor of economics, Rev. Joseph A. MacDonald, initiated a weekly series called "Labour School of the Air," which involved organizing study groups in the industrial area of Cape Breton and supplying them with related study materials.[58] In 1945, faculty at St.F.X. cooperated to produce a program called "University of the Air." This program used a variety of formats to present information about nature, literature, health, home economy, science, and social and economic problems.[59] Rev. George L. Kane, professor of English, began a course at the college called "Radio Workshop," and, in cooperation with CJFX, introduced students to modern techniques of broadcasting. Students and faculty frequently worked as announcers at the studios on Main Street, and the station often covered important functions at St.F.X. It was an affiliate of the Canadian Broadcasting Corporation; therefore, in 1945 CJFX began carrying national programs. In 1946 its output was increased to five thousand watts, and in 1948 the station moved to permanent quarters in the Kirk House on St Ninian's Street, Antigonish.[60] CJFX, born during the Second World War and dedicated foremost to adult education, was partly a product of financial constraint at St.F.X. Although it eventually strayed from its original mandate, the station became a staple of local and regional culture, and retained a special relationship with St.F.X., its founding institution.

The Social and Cooperative Leadership Course

A radio station was one of two extension-related innovations at St.F.X. in the early 1940s. The college announced in 1941 a two-year diploma course in social and cooperative leadership. The new offering was a response to requests from students for such a course and to increasing interest from reformers in other countries.[61] The program was really an expansion of extension's short course offered since 1933. College officials designed the program "to develop social leadership and particularly to prepare future cooperator leaders among the rank and file."[62] The courses required were mostly ones already being taught: economics, sociology, the philosophy of cooperation, methods of adult education, accounting, home economics (for women), English, public

CJFX People's School broadcast, 1950.
J. Clyde Nunn on left, Allan J. MacEachen on right

St.F.X. faculty, 1936

speaking, religion (for Catholic students), contemporary social movements, education, political science, Canadian history, and home crafts.[63] Thus, virtually no extra expense would be incurred by offering it. Five weeks of practical field and office work were required each year. The program, which appeared quite flexible, was open to applicants under twenty-one who had junior matriculation; if over twenty-one, they were promised "special consideration."[64] The offering of this new diploma course in 1941, although widely advertised, was untimely. No diplomas were conferred until 1947, probably because of the distraction of war. Registrations remained low into the early 1950s, and those who did enrol were often international students.[65] However, the new program signalled increased confidence and expertise at St.F.X. in the complimentary areas of adult education, cooperativism, and social theory.

New Teaching Staff
Outside of the extension department, the 1930s had been for St.F.X. a decade of minimal expansion and change; financial constraint exacted its toll. A few alterations had been made in administration and faculty. The Old Rector, of course, had been replaced by President MacDonald in 1936. The new president was assisted by an extremely capable bursar, Rev. Dr Hugh J. Somers, priest-historian and son of a local merchant. An alumnus of St.F.X. and St Augustine's Seminary, Toronto, Somers had graduated with a PHD in history from the Catholic University of America; afterwards, in 1933, he had been appointed to guard the St.F.X. treasury and to introduce students to history. Two years later, another PHD from the Catholic University, Rev. Dr Malcolm MacLellan, had been appointed professor of education and secretary of the faculty. Several other staff who would enjoy lengthy careers at St.F.X. came on board in the 1930s: Rev. Dr Daniel MacCormack, commerce, economics, and sociology (1932), Donald F. MacDonald, geology (1932), Dr Cecil MacLean, French (1936), Sister St Veronica, history (1937),[66] Rev. George Kane, English (1938), Rev. Dr John H. Gillis, Latin (1938), and William T. Foley, chemistry (1938). Rev. R.K. MacIntyre, who had taught chemistry since 1907, left for a parish in 1936. The faculty had grown from twenty-three in 1931 (26 per cent with doctorates) to thirty-four (38 per cent with doctorates) in 1941; over one-half remained priests. Some of the staff increase was related to the burgeoning work of extension. Professors of Scottish lineage and St.F.X. graduates continued to predominate.[67]

The Issue of Academic Standards
As the Depression eased and enrolments increased, the college staff expressed concern about rising academic standards, keeping pace with

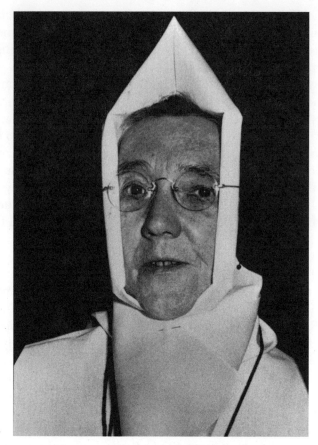

Sister Mary MacDonald (St Veronica), CND,
professor of history 1937–70 and first woman
appointed to the St.F.X. faculty

them at St.F.X., and obtaining the financial means to do so. Toward the end of the 1920s, St.F.X., along with other schools, apparently had been struck off the list of approved colleges recognized by the larger American universities. This development distressed St.F.X. students who hoped to pursue graduate studies in the United States. So, in 1936, St.F.X. authorities decided to seek accreditation through the Association of American Universities. Its standards required three years' graduate training of department heads and two years' graduate studies for college teachers. Bishop Morrison was a little sceptical about the need for his diocesan college to follow American standards, since its financial resources were limited, and its primary purpose, in his view, remained preparing "worthy candidates" for seminary training. He was lukewarm, therefore, about sending staff away for further preparation.[68] Nevertheless, St.F.X. asked Dr Roy J. Deferrari, general secretary of the Catholic University of America and a respected classicist, to conduct an informal inspection of the college as a first step toward seeking accreditation through the association of which Deferrari was a member.[69] Among other things, Deferrari recommended a clear statement of aims in the college calendar around which college curricula and life could be organized,[70] training of prospective faculty in the best American schools, research and publication by the St.F.X. faculty, the development of a constitution, a definite policy on the appointment and promotion of staff, and a complete reorganization and enlargement of the library. He did admit the generally excellent training of the staff and the adequacy of its admission standards.[71] Needless to say, some of his recommendations could not be achieved immediately; hence, the college had to postpone indefinitely formal application for accreditation in the association. It was another case, for St.F.X., of stymied plans.

Profile of the Student Body

In spite of the Depression, or perhaps because of it, students had come to St.F.X. in steadily increasing numbers through the 1930s. In 1930–31 registration had totalled 201; by 1939–40 it had climbed to 359. The proportion of females remained steady – around one-quarter of the student body. The highest proportion of students continued to be from working-class backgrounds in Cape Breton, but significant numbers also came from mainland Nova Scotia, New Brunswick, Quebec, and the United States.[72] As a proportion, those from outside the Diocese of Antigonish decreased from about one-half in 1930–31 to slightly over one-third in 1940–41.[73] The Depression, and then war, were probably responsible for this trend. A relatively even split existed between student numbers from rural backgrounds and those from urban areas.[74] Most students were Catholics (there were only six Protestants in 1939),[75] and the largest ethnic group predictable remained those of Highland Scottish descent. Generally, about two-thirds of the students lived in residence at St.F.X. and the remainder boarded in Antigonish. The largest number of students followed the arts program, but numbers in the sciences gradually mounted; fifteen graduated in 1941 with a bachelor of science degree, three with a diploma in engineering,[76] seven with a bachelor of science in home economics, and just two with a bachelor of science in nursing.[77]

Students commonly chose St.F.X. because of its Catholicism and its proximity to their homes. Sometimes cost, family tradition, or available programs were also factors in their choice.[78] Combined tuition and residency fees remained relatively stable from 1930 to 1938, when they rose from \$322 to \$342. Many students viewed the opportunity to attend St.F.X. as a great privilege; it opened up for them new horizons of culture, social life, and career possibilities. Compared to their home backgrounds, St.F.X. appeared as a dynamic centre of activity in touch with the wider world. At St.F.X. they found a small college with a strong sense of identity, a vigorous community life, a pervasive religious ethos, high ideals, an emphasis on social responsibility, and a rather exacting disciplinary regimen. Many of the students played sports – the most common were hockey, rugby, and boxing. Hockey games in the local Antigonish–Pictou County League were intensely competitive and at times too all-absorbing, at least from the professorial standpoint. Faculty, along with the Sisters of St Martha, were loyal fans of their own St.F.X. teams; they were known to supplicate regularly the highest authorities in heaven for St.F.X. victories.[79] The most popular student societies were drama, debating, and athletics; the more peripheral ones included the Cercle Français, Pre-Law, the Heather or Gaelic Society, the Canadian Catholic Student Mission Crusade, the American Club, and the University Band. Some of these latter regularly passed in and out of existence. Most alumni attest that participation in the student societies enriched their experience at St.F.X. The rich extracurricular life at St.F.X., like that at other Canadian universities, provided youth "with an outlet for their abundant physical and social energies."[80]

Nearly one-fifth of the St.F.X. students got involved with the *Xaverian Weekly*;[81] the remainder enjoyed its weekly offerings. During the 1930s, and in a newspaper format, it dutifully chronicled the comings and goings of college life, included short essays on diverse topics, advertised for local merchants in Antigonish, carried notes on its far-flung alumni, and usually spiced things up with a touch of humour. One issue carried "famous last words" like these: "Wonder if it's loaded?

I'll look down the barrel and see"; "The only way to manage a mule is to walk up behind him like this."[82] Another issue noted that "College bred does not mean a four year loaf."[83] Students circulated a slogan for the cows at Mount Cameron Farm: "You can whip our cream but you can't beat our milk."[84] The editors, besides entertaining, found the journal a useful tool to cajole, to chide, and, at times, to berate the students about all manner of perceived shortcomings – lack of spirit, neglect of the campus, poor support for the student societies, and ignorance about St.F.X.'s own extension department. The college regimen and its policies were rarely questioned or challenged. A *Xaverian* staple was sporting events, which composed a substantial part of its news coverage. Religious themes were important too; they were always treated with sobriety and within the clearly defined limits of Catholic orthodoxy. Finally, the student reporters commonly described developments of regional, national, and international significance, such as the Depression, the Antigonish Movement, and the Russian Communist and German Nazi threats in Europe.

Relations between St.F.X. students and the fairer sex residing at Mount St Bernard were sometimes closer than faculty and sisters desired, but rather too distant for the students encamped on opposite sides of the cathedral. The trend, although glacial, was toward integration. It had started in the classroom, even before the turn of the century; then came the annual junior prom, about 1923, which was "barely tolerated" by the bishop,[85] and afterwards, dances at the Celtic Hall on Main Street, all chaperoned, of course.[86] Graduation exercises were combined for the first time in the spring of 1927.[87] In college journalism things advanced, or regressed, depending on the perspective; the *Xaverian*'s October 1936 issue proudly declared a new role for itself: "to act for the students of Mount Saint Bernard College also."[88] A Mount student editor joined the staff, and the *Xaverian* columns were graciously opened to female journalists. In the final *Xaverian* issue that year, the editor exulted over the "union" and considered it "one of the greatest mile stones in our history." From then on, the journal was coeducational. In November 1940, the students also began a bi-monthly coeducational activity at Immaculata Hall. This was an open forum, with a coed slate of officers to govern its business, designed to improve public speaking skills and make students familiar with the parliamentary rules of procedure.[89] St.F.X. males occasionally registered dissatisfaction with the separation of the sexes. In 1944 one expressed "disgust toward the present unnatural setup." "A Mount girl," he complained, "is something like a mirage. A thing seen only under unusual conditions and only for a short time. If a dance is arranged the boys must beg for the girl's release. Once obtained the girl like a rented costume must be returned under a time limit, even before the dance is ended."[90]

Since the beginning of extension work in 1930, students had been aware of, or involved with, extension-related activities such as the Student's Co-operative Society and study clubs. It was impossible to be at St.F.X. and remain unaware of Coady and the St.F.X. social action agenda. Occasionally the *Xaverian* tried to tongue-lash the students into deeper interest and commitment to the Antigonish Movement. In early 1938 students organized a campus credit union to demonstrate the "practical aspect of the Co-operative Movement."[91] Membership was open to both students and faculty, and at the official opening on 26 March about forty joined.[92] Four years later a *Xaverian* editor concluded that the credit union had made an important contribution to student life by providing credit, encouraging savings, and educating in the principles of economic cooperation.[93] At an open forum sponsored by the credit union in early 1940, students discussed Coady's recently published book, *Masters of Their Own Destiny*; those present decided to petition the college administration for a sociology course on the history, theory, and philosophy of the Antigonish Movement.[94] The *Xaverian* also began in 1939 a column devoted to the Antigonish Movement called "The Co-operator."[95] Notwithstanding these cooperative projects, student interest in the extension's struggle for economic justice in Atlantic Canada waxed and waned through the decade.[96]

Origins of the Student Union
The first St.F.X. student union formed in the late 1930s. The various classes – freshmen, sophomore, junior, and senior – had elected officers before this, but the initial move toward general student government began in 1937 with the formation of a student council. The council was elected and was to be "the recognized means of communication between the Faculty and student body."[97] In the spring of 1938, students were working on a constitution, with the support of faculty, and in October 1939 held the first student union meeting. One of the union's major responsibilities was the approval of budgets for all the student societies.[98] The academic year 1939–40 was the first year of its operation. Although critics occasionally attacked the union, claiming excessive faculty supervision or control by a student elite, the student union became a permanent feature of campus life at St.F.X. The idea of student government was nothing new in 1937; its birth at St.F.X. in the late 1930s might have been related to trends at other Maritime universities, since St.F.X. students seemed to become more actively involved in the inter-campus scene during these years.

National Student Organizations

St.F.X. associations with other colleges came through intercollegiate sports and debating. In addition, St.F.X. also belonged to, or, at times, participated in, national and regional student organizations. The college's connections with both the National Federation of Canadian University Students (NFCUS) and the Canadian Student Assembly appeared to end in 1940.[99] These organizations lobbied for national scholarships, encouraged intercollegiate debating, and, in general, promoted student interests. NFCUS was temporarily disbanded during the Second World War and St.F.X. would not rejoin it until 1947.[100] In February 1939, St.F.X. was host to the first Annual Conference of Maritime University Students. The conference was preceded by a Model League of Nations which met at Dalhousie in 1937 and a Model Industrial Labour Organization which convened at the University of New Brunswick in 1938.[101] Seventy delegates from ten Maritime colleges gathered at St.F.X. for three days to discuss student life and government, college journalism, social, economic, and political issues, and foreign policy concerns; their conference closed after passing a variety of timely resolutions designed to promote student interests.[102]

St.F.X. students appeared cool about national student organizations, lukewarm about regional associations, but enthusiastic about Catholic federations. In 1937 they had tried unsuccessfully to form the Federation of Canadian Catholic Students.[103] So three years later, when a similar organization called the Canadian Federation of Catholic College Students was formed at the initiative of St Thomas University in New Brunswick, the St.F.X. student union voted unanimously to join.[104] Its representatives played an active part in the first conference held at St Dunstan's College, Charlottetown in March 1941, where delegates discussed topics like students and cooperation, family life, and Catholic social action.[105]

World War and the St.F.X. Campus

Canada declared war on Germany on 10 September 1939, shortly after Hitler's invasion of Poland. The war, finally drawn out for over five torturous years that witnessed a staggering loss of life, had a substantial impact on the campus. It contributed to the mounting debt, distracted St.F.X. from pursuing its 1936 plan for expansion, precipitated an outburst of war-inspired patriotism, and altered student life and program emphases. In addition to the deepening financial distress, war confronted President MacDonald with a second major frustration to any aspirations he had for St.F.X.

As in the First World War, the college, like the Maritime region itself, placed itself heart and soul behind the Allied cause. President Mac-

Donald on 16 September 1939, fully supported by the chancellor and board of governors, wrote Prime Minister Mackenzie King and Premier Angus L. MacDonald with a "comprehensive" offer of support from his college.[106] In the president's view, the war was a "noble cause" and victory would lay the foundation for universal peace.[107] St.F.X. would do its part: faculty members periodically lectured to troops; some enlisted in the services; the college assisted the Canadian Legion Educational Services; extension circulated books among troops in eastern Nova Scotia and encouraged credit unions to give easy credit to those contributing to the various war loan campaigns; the women's division of extension prepared pamphlets on the role of women in the war effort; and the students themselves undertook fund raising, donated blood, sent gifts to St.F.X. men overseas, and sold war savings stamps in their credit union. In 1942 college authorities formed a war services committee "to put the student war effort on an organized basis."[108] And that year, they offered two new courses with military application in radio and navigation.[109]

The St.F.X. campus was extensively militarized by the war effort. War news invaded the pages of the *Xaverian*,[110] and student journalists regularly reported the deaths of students or alumni missing or killed in action. In 1943 both St.F.X. and the Mount students established a memorial fund to finance a stadium dedicated to their war dead.[111] Student military organizations contributed most to campus militarization. Acting on the Federation of Canadian Universities and the department of national defence recommendations, St.F.X. made military training compulsory for all physically fit Canadian male students over eighteen years of age.[112] The Canadian Officers' Training Corp (COTC), which had organized on campus during the First World War, had been re-established at St.F.X. in 1938 by professors Dan Wallace and Gerry Blackburn.[113] As before, it provided elementary military and leadership training through demonstrations, gun drills, parades, inspections, and lectures; by 1940 it had 140 active members.[114] The college provided training and storage facilities in the gymnasium.[115] Other military organizations appeared before the war's end: the University Air Training Plan (UATP), which trained students wishing to serve in the Royal Canadian Air Force,[116] and the University Naval Training Division (UNTD), established for the development of navy personnel.[117] Considerable numbers of St.F.X. students joined these three campus organizations. At the conclusion of the war, compulsory military training ceased, so student interest waned in military affairs. Nevertheless, the college administration believed it "the part of prudence" to be prepared for a new outbreak of hostilities.[118] Thus, after

St.F.X. COTC contingent, Petawawa, 1939

the war, student military organizations would remain active at St.F.X. until the late 1960s.

War and the Extension Department

The war had a definite impact on the college's high-profile department of extension, which cooperated with government to increase food production and to educate among the soldiers.[119] In 1941 the annual short course, a staple on the campus since 1933, was shortened to one week, and, for the duration of the war, it itinerated across the Maritime provinces.[120] Extension staff did find it harder, as the war progressed, to organize people for formal study;[121] many of the most vigorous and best-trained leaders in the study clubs, in field-work, and in cooperative management joined the war effort. Alexander Laidlaw, who replaced extension's assistant director, A.B. MacDonald, in 1944,[122] claimed that the extension study program declined for two reasons: total war required first priority, and "war prosperity obscured the need for examination of basic social and economic problems."[123] On the other hand, the war stimulated commercial activity; thus many cooperative enterprises enjoyed unprecedented prosperity. Laidlaw estimated that the business of Nova Scotia's consumer cooperatives rose from about $2.5 million in 1939 to over $4.5 million in 1944.[124]

War affected another phase of the extension program: women's work. Dr Coady had placed this work under the capable supervision of Sister Marie Michael MacKinnon in 1933, assisted by Sister Irene Doyle from 1935. Their work had a rural life orientation; the main emphases had been on nutrition, home economy, handicrafts, and consumer education.[125] In 1941, Sister Irene Doyle concluded that women's work suffered from lack of funding. Therefore, extension convened in April 1942 a well-attended conference on handicrafts which successfully requested government to take over handicraft work; by the fall, the Nova Scotia department of industry had assumed control of the work.[126] Within a few years, Sister Doyle left extension to work with the postulants at the motherhouse of the Sisters of St Martha, and Sister Marie Michael had become more involved with library work. Extension work with women, which had never been a priority, was languishing. Moreover, a changed emphasis had emerged. This shift was signalled by a Maritime women's conference, sponsored by extension in the fall of 1942, which aimed "to awaken among women's groups throughout the country an active interest in adult education and cooperative work."[127] Leaders increasingly called for the full participation of women in the cooperatives. Retired field-worker Ida Delaney reports that women had a long struggle for full and equal participation in the consumer cooperatives.[128] By 1950, a subcommittee appointed by the Maritime Cooperative Services Planning Committee asserted, "Up to the present time we must conclude that men have dominated all phases of the Movement, and the women have been on the outside looking in, with no invitation or very little incentive to enter, and we believe this to be one of the major violations of the philosophy of the Cooperative Movement."[129] This "major violation" would be slow to change.

Faculty and Students in Wartime

During the Second World War, faculty numbers decreased; however, student registration increased. In all, six full-time faculty left the campus – two to join the Canadian Chaplaincy Service (Revs. Leo B. Sears and M.E. McLaughlin), three to serve in the military (Professors Wilfrid Garvin, Gerry Blackburn, and Duncan Hugh Gillis), and one to teach at the University of Toronto (Dr Egbert Munzer).[130] Before the end of the war, President MacDonald was complaining of a depleted and overworked staff. Students also enlisted, of course; those who chose otherwise obtained exemption from military service if they maintained a certain standing.[131] Nevertheless, the adventure and excitement promised by military service and the patriotic call to duty created a steady trickle of students away from the campus and into the services. On the other hand, certain developments encouraged increases in student numbers. The government Wartime Bureau of Technical Personnel, concerned about the needs of industry, controlled the transfer of students out of engineering and the sciences. Dr Nicholson, dean of studies during the conflict, also claimed that the war had put more money into circulation in eastern Nova Scotia. "Consequently," he reported, "families have sent boys to college who normally could not do so and our total registration has increased rather than the contrary."[132] In 1939–40, 359 students registered; the registration in 1944–45 was 513.[133] Some observers concluded that the enrolment trend showed that St.F.X. was harbouring draft dodgers, but President MacDonald claimed that the real problem was to persuade science students not to enlist.[134] Dr Nicholson estimated after the war that fully 176 of the registrants of 1939–40 alone eventually joined the service, and of these, 13 made the "supreme sacrifice." The total number of students and alumni who served during the Second World War was estimated at well over 749; of these, 49 lost their lives.[135]

While the war did not undermine enrolments at St.F.X., it definitely shifted the program interests of students. Early in the war, the federal government saw the massive technical demands created by highly mechanized military warfare. Hence, it inaugurated a massive war production scheme, and established the bureau of technical personnel in the fall of 1941 to supervise the supply of industrial workers in Canada. The bureau discovered that Canadian universities, in spite of their science and engineering programs, could then only supply about one-quarter of the required engineers and scientists. Thus government offered scholarships and loans to lure students into these fields. As a result, St.F.X., with the assistance of parish priests and alumni, vigorously recruited science and technical students.[136] Ever more students registered in the bachelor of science and diploma in engineering programs. For example, in 1939–40, 25 engineering students studied at St.F.X.; by 1944–45, 116 were enrolled. In November 1944, students formed an engineering society, and in the same year a female student from Moncton, New Brunswick registered in the program (she may have been the first woman engineering student at St.F.X.).[137]

Of course, the enlarged proportion of students in the sciences and engineering decreased enrolments in some of the liberal arts courses. The trend was evident at other Canadian universities, and it troubled some university staff. In a wartime rhapsody that camouflaged a substratum of anxiety, President MacDonald enthused, "the entire scholastic programme of the University has been adapted so that the greatest possible aid and assistance may be given to the training of skilled engineers and technicians for our war programme."[138] But still, he and other faculty were distressed by the utilitarian shift in emphasis created by the war effort. In public addresses the president reiterated time and again that the traditional Catholic liberal arts education was not a superfluous luxury; on the contrary, he asserted, it was essential to the preservation of civilization.[139] His anxiety was a reflection of "a crisis of confidence within the academic community in the Western liberal tradition."[140]

The Million-Dollar Campaign
The shift toward science and technology, along with the expanding enrolments, did nothing to ease the burden of debt St.F.X. had laboured under since the construction of Morrison Hall in 1937–38. Indeed, the college debt had climbed to $300,000 by 1944; furthermore, all educational and residence facilities were strained to the utmost, and on the post-war horizon loomed the daunting prospect of an influx of veterans. Therefore, it was no surprise that the idea of a fund-raising campaign should commend itself to the financially harried President MacDonald.[141] At his suggestion, the board of governors, in April 1944, decided to conduct a major campaign through the summer before other institutions entered the field, and before an anticipated post-war recession.[142] St.F.X. hired a professional American fund-raising firm,

appointed the bursar, Dr Somers, campaign committee chairman, and established the heady objective of $1 million.[143] The planners conducted the campaign in three phrases – an appeal first to the Diocese of Antigonish, then to the alumni outside the diocese, and finally to wealthy friends of St.F.X. It organized lay committees in all the parishes, and H.J. Kelly, president of Dominion Steel and Coal Company in Sydney, agreed to be diocesan chairman of the campaign.

The elaborate campaign drive machinery shifted into gear in July. The slick strategy for relaxing the constituency's grip on its purse strings included these tactics: high-profile public endorsations, media propaganda, laudatory speeches, and personal solicitation. Campaign literature underscored St.F.X.'s great needs as a progressive institution, and its value for developing Catholic leaders, for serving the community through extension education, and for defending the faith against the attacks of modern, subversive forces.[144] Bishop Morrison threw his considerable influence into the campaign by circularizing the clergy and laity. He promoted the effort both as part of the centennial celebration of the Diocese of Antigonish (1844–1944) and as "a great crusade in Catholic cooperation for our beloved youth."[145] The campaign of 1944 was remarkably successful. Apparently, about $1.1 million was subscribed, and by 1948, $800,000 had been paid in. The largest part, claimed Dr Nicholson, came from working people within the diocese;[146] this generosity doubtless revealed the goodwill St.F.X. had generated through its extension department and identification with the needs of the people. The proceeds of this most ambitious financial drive in St.F.X. history to that time were largely exhausted by disposing of the existing debt of $300,000 and by the construction of a new dormitory in 1946.[147] However, at a time when government funding was non-existent, it allowed St.F.X. to bail itself out of a deepening financial crisis. No doubt the success of the campaign resulted from an expanded and vigorous wartime economy as well as the skill of the professional fund-raising firm.

The President Resigns
While the financial drive in 1944 had President MacDonald's support, ill health unfortunately prevented him from directing it. Indeed, the president had been ailing for some time, plagued by high blood pressure and recurring nosebleeds. In 1944, before the campaign began, he had been forced to spend several months recuperating in the Canadian west. But on his return, he found himself unable to undertake much work and submitted his resignation effective 6 September.[148] Health was the central reason. He was sixty-three years old at the time and was to live only another four years.[149]

MacDonald's work at St.F.X., as both educator and administrator, creates an impression of neither brilliance nor dynamism; yet his thirty-two-year career had been solid. For twenty-four of those years he had served as professor of economics and sociology. In 1922, he had bolstered the anti-mergerite cause with his report on university federation. Moreover, he had lectured rather widely, and had been a strong supporter of St.F.X.'s move into extension work. He believed, along with many fellow priests, that St.F.X. should dedicate itself to serve the people of eastern Nova Scotia. MacDonald's presidency had been especially difficult and frustrating. His administration had faced a growing financial crisis at the end of the 1930s, and then war. Hence, the college's plans for upgrading and expansion had been stymied and postponed at nearly every turn. Nevertheless, the lasting contributions made during this time, and for which President MacDonald could justly claim partial responsibility, were Morrison Hall, Radio Station CJFX, a diploma course in cooperative leadership, and the financial campaign of 1944. At MacDonald's departure in the fall of 1944, St.F.X. was on the threshold of a new era, an era which would confront it with the challenge of soaring registrations.

· 13 ·

The Strain of Post-War Expansion, 1944-50

The conclusion of war in 1945 inaugurated a decade and more of rapid, stressful change for St.F.X. Climbing enrolments forced an expensive building program and required additional faculty; an influx of veterans brought a new seriousness of tone and challenged the disciplinary regulations; shifts in student interests brought curricular diversification; a new emphasis on research began to appear; and a change in diocesan administration infused the institution with fresh vigour and spawned a new educational experiment. Throughout, a new president, Rev. Dr Patrick J. Nicholson, stood resolutely at the helm, assisted in financial matters by his competent bursar, Dr Somers. During the first five years of President Nicholson's administration, trends appeared at St.F.X. which eventually transformed it from a small Catholic diocesan college into a larger, more professional university.[1]

St.F.X. was one small player on the broader provincial and federal stages. In Nova Scotia itself, Premier Angus L. MacDonald returned from Ottawa to lead the Liberal government from 1945 to 1954; on the federal scene the Liberals retained power, although Mackenzie King retired in 1948 and was replaced by Louis St Laurent. The parties were favoured with economic boom as both consumer demand and trade with the United States increased; the times seemed expansive and optimistic. However, there existed the sobering realities of the atomic age and the cold war, and then in the early 1950s, the Korean War. All these events had repercussions on the the St.F.X. campus.

President Nicholson
After accepting President MacDonald's resignation, Bishop Morrison appointed Dr Nicholson in early September 1944 to the presidency of St.F.X. for a six-year term.[2] By then, Dr Nicholson, already fifty-seven years old, had been at St.F.X for twenty-eight years and was known to generations of students as "Doc Pat." His credentials were impeccable[3] – eastern Nova Scotian, outstanding St.F.X. graduate (1909),[4]

doctorate in physics from Johns Hopkins University (1913), ordained a priest by Archbishop Neil McNeil of Toronto (1916), professor of physics at St.F.X. (1916–44), and experienced administrator (registrar 1920–36 and dean of studies 1936–44).[5] Dr Nicholson had gained a reputation for personal austerity, religious devotion, high academic standards, and lofty ideals. He was fully committed to the St.F.X. cause, and what he demanded of himself he expected of others. Although a stern taskmaster, he was usually congenial toward faculty and students; his memory of the names, faces, and genealogy of countless students was legendary.[6] To that time, Dr Nicholson was only the second Cape Bretoner to become president of the university (the first had been Archbishop Neil McNeil, 1884–91). He was hospitable in the tradition of the Old Rector and comfortable in the presence of the prominent; his outgoing and forceful personality left a sharper imprint on alumni memories than did his more withdrawn predecessor, President D.J. MacDonald.

President Nicholson's educational views were largely a restatement of the corpus of thought which had become the St.F.X. tradition of education. He liked to speak of education as "preparation for complete living"; this involved, he emphasized, lifelong development of the physical, mental, and spiritual capacities of the person.[7] The goal of education was to help students reach a stage of mental development where they could synthesize the various branches of knowledge. The development of the powers of thought, the strengthening of the will, and the adoption of ideals were more important, in Nicholson's view, than the mere acquisition of knowledge. He believed, moreover, that Catholic education had to keep alive the ideal of service. "Education, just as much as wealth and social position," he asserted, "is a sacred trust to be employed for the general welfare."[8] Although a scientist, Nicholson believed the liberal arts fundamental to the university's work, for therein was contained "the wisdom of the ages." He was troubled by the long-term trend away from the liberal arts and into the sciences and technologies, a trend which had been intensified by the war. St.F.X., he concluded, had to accommodate this trend, but he insisted that the liberal arts should never be weakened. "It devolves on such institutions as St Francis Xavier, on the one hand," he affirmed, "to keep abreast of all the achievements of the human mind, but on the other, to maintain its unshakable attachment to the eternal truth."[9]

President Nicholson believed that a university should hold faith and reason together in balance. Truth is one. There had been a divine revelation of "eternal truth," but this, he maintained, still leaves "an unlimited scope for intellectual browsing into all other questions."[10]

Rev. Dr Patrick J. Nicholson ("Doc Pat"), president 1944–54

The attitude of the liberally educated person should exemplify St Augustine's adage: "In essentials unity, in non-essentials liberty, in all things love." Nicholson firmly believed that knowledge of one's intellectual limitations should restrain a person from forcing his conclusions on others. Nonetheless, tolerance of others should not be based on an abandonment of the ideas of "absolute truth and of absolute goodness." He declared, "Genuine education develops a practical attitude of tolerance toward persons, unless they are really dangerous to the public weal, but an intellectual intolerance towards error and evil."[11]

St.F.X., in President Nicholson's view, was largely a minor seminary. Many students remember the "pre-sem grip," where the priest-president sidled up to them and counselled them to consider if they had a calling to the priesthood. On this practice he once wrote, "long experience has taught me that if suitable boys do not get the encouragement called for many excellent men would never get there. The world is so full of snares to stop good candidates that something of a counter-influence is needed."[12] Nicholson worked at being "a counter-influence." Shortly after appointing him the president, Bishop Morrison also made him chairman of a diocesan committee charged with promoting vocations to the priesthood and to religious communities.[13] Nicholson once wrote about his university: "St Francis Xavier was first organized as a seminary and although theological studies have been a part of its curriculum only during a very few years of its existence, the fact remains that its primary function is to direct young men to the priesthood."[14] Through his close contacts with youth at St.F.X., Nicholson succeeded in shepherding many toward the priesthood.[15] In 1952 he estimated that St.F.X. sent, on average, twenty to thirty men annually to various theological seminaries.[16]

Influx of Veterans

The first major challenge Nicholson and his staff faced was an influx of Second World War veterans. Under its Veterans' Rehabilitation training scheme, the federal government offered to finance, through monthly allowances and grants, the studies of ex-service men and women; many seized the opportunity.[17] In December 1945, 14,500 veterans were registered at Canadian universities, and the number had risen to 37,000 by 1947.[18] The first large group arrived at St.F.X. in September 1945.[19] Another wave registered in January 1946, and by 1947, they accounted for about one-third of the student population.[20] St.F.X. offered summer courses in 1946 so that these veterans could begin their sophomore year in the fall. Around one-quarter of them were married with children, and, in general, the veterans were older than the rest of the students. They had an impact on St.F.X. similar to that on other Canadian campuses.[21] Probably because of their maturity, their sense that they had to make up for lost time, and their need to maintain passing grades to retain government support, the veterans firmly applied themselves to their studies and improved the university's overall morale. They brought a wealth of experience to the campus, often broader than that of some faculty, and they undoubtedly enriched student life. The veterans also strained the disciplinary regimen of the university, which had hardly been designed for mature and war-hardened students.[22] In the fall of 1946, they formed a Students' Veteran Organization designed to unite the veterans on campus and to provide them with various types of assistance.[23] The society appointed a social committee, a sick committee, and an employment committee.[24] Moreover, the university provided the services of a veterans' counsellor. St.F.X. also discovered, at least for the early registrants, that the veterans were most interested in the engineering program; the pre-medical program ranked second to it in popularity.[25]

Demand for College Expansion

Along with the influx of veterans, a war-stimulated economy and increased opportunities in industry, commerce, and government created a surge in St.F.X. enrolments which continued from 1944 to the end of the decade.[26] There were 513 students in 1944–45 (17 per cent were female); numbers climbed steeply to 913 in 1949–50 with about the same proportion female.[27] Such expansion placed intense pressure on university facilities. The last residence had been built nearly thirty years before, and none were designed for married students. St.F.X. improvised by placing three students in rooms designed for two, by converting the basement of Mockler Hall into residence space, and by bringing two military buildings to the campus – one for use as a science hall annex with drafting and classrooms, and one for use as married students' quarters. In spite of these stopgap measures, some students had to find accommodation in the town.[28] A major part of the solution to residence space was the completion in 1946 of a new hall to house two hundred students.[29] St.F.X. again obtained the services of Jens Larson, the New England architect who had designed Morrison Hall. The attractive new structure was built of local sandstone in Georgian Colonial style, placed to the south of the old administration building, and named Cameron Hall in memory of the third bishop of the diocese.[30]

But the opening of Cameron Hall in the fall of 1946 was only a temporary solution. Students continued to pour onto the campus each autumn in ever-larger numbers. The needs for new classroom space, science laboratories, and a new library became more pressing. St.F.X.

was actually being forced to follow the plan of expansion outlined in 1936, a plan which had been blocked by war and debt. The student body had also outgrown the old Somers chapel which had been constructed in 1911. Hence, the board decided that a new structure should be built which would provide both a chapel and a basement auditorium to seat about 750.[31] The chapel, placed to the southwest of Cameron Hall and completed in 1949, was also built of sandstone and in the Georgian Colonial style.[32] It was hardly finished when the board, compelled by enrolments, built a residence to match Cameron Hall.[33] The architect Larson, whose monuments on the campus now included Morrison Hall, Cameron Hall, and the new chapel, donated to St.F.X. his plans for Cameron Hall.[34] The new residence, a twin to Cameron Hall, was located directly to the south of it. Named MacKinnon Hall after the bishop-founder of St.F.X., it opened in 1951. The administrative offices were transferred from the main building to the east wing of the new building.[35]

Institutional Growing Pains

The post-war flurry of building construction drained the university's coffers. The veterans' hall alone cost over $29,000.[36] Then there was the expense of Cameron Hall at about $350,000, MacKinnon Hall at about the same, University Chapel at around $400,000, and campus paving in 1951 at about $40,000.[37] In 1946 St.F.X. had loans amounting to $35,772 and in 1948 a deficit of $24,334;[38] by 1953 its debt had burgeoned to $1.2 million. In the late 1940s, the treasury was partly replenished through tuition fees, the diocesan quotas which had been levied for another five years beginning in 1943,[39] a supplementary grant from the government for the veterans, government grants for extension work, income on endowment investments, and private donations. But costs continued to escalate, the earning power of endowments decreased, and unfortunately, Dr Somers's urgent appeal to organizations south of the border, like the Carnegie Corporation and the Rockefeller Foundation, failed to draw a windfall.[40] Even regular hikes in residence and tuition fees (from $389 in 1945 to $620 by 1953) did little to slow the mounting debt. President Nicholson was compelled to take desperate measures to supplement the university's income. One such experiment was a short-lived experiment in mink farming.[41]

The university's financial plight was merely one presidential headache after the war. More faculty were urgently needed to man the classrooms and laboratories; no instant solutions to this problem were available. On the one hand, Dr Nicholson lamented that the supply of Catholic scholars was lean, and as a result the church, not to mention his university, was "suffering grievously."[42] On the other hand, St.F.X. was poverty-stricken and could hardly offer salaries which would attract outstanding scholars. Moreover, based on certain unpleasant past experiences, Dr Nicholson considered it a gamble to hire strangers. He stated, "We find it more desirable to have poorly qualified men who get along well with us than top notch scholars whose influence might be in the direction of disharmony."[43] As a short-term solution, he was forced to hire student assistants, especially in engineering and the sciences. Meanwhile, he followed the old practice of recruiting prospective priest-professors from within the student body. These would supply cheap labour, and he could be confident in their dispositions, abilities, and dedication. Occasionally, Dr Nicholson asked Bishop Morrison outright to appoint diocesan priests to the university. In September 1948, after he had received no satisfaction, the clerics on staff, repeating an action of five years before,[44] firmly lobbied the old bishop, noting the rising teacher-student ratio and the fact that ten new priests had joined the diocese that summer. Four days later Bishop Morrison assigned three new priests to St.F.X.[45]

For years, Dr Nicholson had been a strong advocate of higher standards at St.F.X.; thus, he was troubled about the decline of staff qualifications and believed it was undermining the university's prestige in the Maritimes. He lamented that St.F.X. was "getting loaded up with untrained personnel."[46] Dr Roy J. Deferrari, who returned from the Catholic University of America that year to inspect St.F.X., as he had done back in 1938, affirmed Nicholson's troubled conclusion.[47] Of the twenty-seven faculty members in 1946 (twenty of these were clerics), six had bachelors' degrees, eight had masters', and thirteen had doctorates; by 1951 only fourteen out of forty-nine had doctorates (twenty-nine of these were clerics), sixteen had masters', and sixteen had bachelors'.[48]

New Post-War Staff Appointments

Noteworthy newcomers joined the staff in the years immediately after the war. In 1947 these included Rev. Malcolm MacDonell in history, William Reid in physics, Rev. Charles R. MacDonald in philosophy, Allan J. MacEachen in sociology, and John Lee in music. Nicholson appointed more faculty in 1948 and 1949: Dr D. Hugh Gillis (political science), Dr Bernard J. Keating (geology), Rev. John Angus Rankin (religion), George G. Lent (education), Rev. Francis Edward Dolhanty (religion and economics), Rev. Roderick J. MacSween (English), Dr George Adamkiewicz (German, history, and commercial law), Dr Donald J. McIntosh (pre-medical and college physician), Dr John J. MacDonald (chemistry), Ambrose Gilmet (physical education), and

Rev. J. McMahon (sociology).[49] By this time, about one-third of the faculty were lay people, some of them married. Their plight included low salaries, high housing costs, eight-month contracts, little security of tenure, and few fringe benefits. After they lobbied for change in 1949 and complained periodically thereafter, their lot at St.F.X. gradually improved.[50] However, the administration was required by meagre resources to remain tight-fisted. Clergy and lay teachers carried an exacting load of four courses; prefecting and administrative duties added to the staggering burden of most priest-professors.

Post-War Curricular Adjustments
Many new staff at post-war St.F.X. filled positions in the sciences, engineering, and social sciences; such placements were forced by increasing student demands for these programs. For many years there had been a general trend, discouraging for classicists, of declining interest in the classical languages.[51] A report on the humanities sponsored in 1947 by the Humanities Research Council of Canada described this as "the flight from the classics which has been a mark of the twentieth century."[52] It paralleled the trend of increasing student interest in science and technology. Patricia Jasen writes, "Most university leaders favoured expansion in vocational fields and based much of their educational policy on the needs or wishes of provincial legislatures, professional associations, and farm and business groups."[53] At St.F.X. fewer bachelor of arts degrees were conferred in 1946 than in 1941; the combined number of bachelor of science degrees and diplomas in engineering conferred in 1951 far exceeded those awarded in the arts. These curricular shifts created anxiety among devotees of the liberal arts and evoked debates in higher education about the merits of cultural formation versus specialized vocational preparation.[54] For St.F.X. the continuing stress on utility and social service began to encroach on its earlier denominational aims and emphases.

To the end of the Second World War, St.F.X. had continued to offer the basic programs in arts and science, along with diploma programs in engineering, home economics, teacher training, and social leadership; it had also added professional degree programs in nursing and home economics. As well, preparatory, pre-dental, and pre-medical courses were offered.[55] All programs were highly prescriptive and included courses in public speaking and religion (for Catholic students only). In 1938, St.F.X. had introduced into the arts program the concept of a major area of study and a requirement for a senior-year essay.[56] The distinction between a bachelor of arts with a major and a pass bachelor of arts was first made in 1950. The pass BA still required a cluster of courses in one discipline and a smaller grouping in another subject, but a lower average for graduation and no senior-year essay.[57] From 1937 to 1955 students could also earn a BA or B SC with honours if they completed one extra year of study after graduation.[58] Finally, in 1945 officials replaced the unit measure of course value introduced in 1927–28 with the semester-hour rating. Most courses were rated at six semester hours, which involved three hours of class time each week during the full academic year.[59]

The expanding post-war enrolments, the changing interests of students, and the evolving needs of society evidently aroused considerable reflection among faculty about the adequacy of the St.F.X. curriculum. Faculty in the arts and sciences proposed more specific requirements for majors and higher standards.[60] Within five years they offered new courses, majors, or degree programs in political science (1947), psychology (1950), music (1947), commerce (1948), and education (1949).[61] President Nicholson desired to improve the French program[62] and, predictably, the courses in religion. He commented in 1949, "Religion courses have commonly been slipshod here just because they cannot be made more than a side issue, due to the heavy teaching load professors are carrying."[63] To bolster the preparation of pre-seminarians, the calendar in 1947–48 outlined a recommended pre-theology course and counselled "intensive training in Latin and Philosophy."[64] In 1951 the bishop tightened up the standards for pre-seminary training; he decided to accept, from then on, only those who had obtained commendable records of three years' university work in religion, philosophy, Latin, English, and French, along with a good grounding in Catholic social principles and the techniques of the extension department.[65]

New Graduate Programs
In 1948, and under the inspiration of a Canadian Social Science Research Council conference,[66] the university decided to offer the master's degree in selected social sciences and certain other departments. The master's degree had been dropped, back in 1938;[67] St.F.X. had then judged that it could no longer compete with larger institutions which had extended programs for the degree.[68] But the master of arts was reintroduced in 1948–49.[69] Much of the interest at St.F.X. in the social sciences after the war was apparently generated by students who registered to study the Antigonish Movement.[70] Sociology at St.F.X. had long been associated with the work of the extension department and Catholic social teachings. In the early 1950s Dr Doris Boyle, a graduate of the Catholic University of America, pressed for higher staff qualifications, more emphasis on research and methodology, and higher salaries to improve the social sciences at St.F.X.[71] Her criticisms would have applied to the social science disciplines at other

Canadian universities, for social science scholarship was "on the whole, meagre in the first half of the twentieth century."[72] The university also offered a master of social work from 1951,[73] and a master of arts in geology from 1953–54.[74] As the 1950s progressed, the social science offerings would be extended; under Rev. Dr Donald F. Campbell, psychology, a discipline which seemed to originate at St.F.X. with applied courses in education, would gradually achieve independence and legitimacy on its own. In the future, psychology would gain its own faculty and increasing popularity.[75]

New Emphasis on Research

Dr Nicholson anticipated that his augmented staff would undertake research in both the sciences and the humanities.[76] He could back his hope up with little more than moral support. Some research had been done before his presidency by faculty members like Dr C.J. Connolly (1911–24) and A. Chiasson in biology (1928–34), Dr Donald F. Mac-Donald in geology (1932–39), and Dr Daniel J. MacDonald in economics (1912–36).[77] Yet the impediments to research at St.F.X. were substantial. Before the war, little professional pressure was exerted to research and publish. Professional academic associations which tried to foster research, like the Canadian Social Science Research Council and the Humanities Research Council of Canada, only appeared in the early 1940s. Moreover, the St.F.X. community understood its primary responsibility to be teaching, and the teaching, prefecting, and administrative loads were so heavy that research and publication were almost impossible. Finally, the scarcity of cash and lack of adequate facilities created further barriers against research.

Nonetheless, certain faculty did conduct scientific research from 1942. Father Ernest Clarke, appointed professor of physics that year and awarded a doctorate from Laval University in 1956,[78] did work, with the aid of student assistants, in applied electronics for Radio Station CJFX, on the strength of wire ropes, on methods for measuring the water content of dried fish, and on methods of mapping rock structures.[79] No publications resulted. Dr Leo P. Chiasson, professor of biology from 1944, investigated, among other things, the blood groups and fingerprints of Micmacs. He was probably the first at St.F.X. to obtain National Research Council funding (an organization established in 1916 which came to play "a fundamental role in the development of Scientific research at Canadian universities"),[80] and he did publish the results of his research.[81] By the early 1950s, William T. Foley, professor of chemistry, was involved in a National Research Council project on the fundamentals of corrosion, Drs Donald J. Mac-Neil and J. Bernard Keating in geology had done considerable research

Rev. Dr Ernest M. Clarke, professor of physics 1942–c.1976.
"The nearest thing to a genius that was ever
around here"

on the geological resources of the region, and William Reid in physics was working on an electronic instrument for the detection of flaws in mine ropes.[82] Some of this work was funded by the Nova Scotia Research Foundation which Premier Angus L. MacDonald's Liberal government had established in April 1946. The foundation was a replacement for the Nova Scotia Economic Council, which had functioned from 1936 to 1942 but was disbanded under wartime constraints. It was to promote industrial development in the province through the use of scientific methods; this required cooperation with the universities and the National Research Council.[83] Hence the practical nature of the science projects funded at St.F.X. President Nicholson was one of the original governors of the new foundation.[84]

The funding agency soon became involved in a project which generated further interest in research at St.F.X. Along with the Nova Scotia Department of Mines and the Massachusetts Institute of Technology (MIT), the Nova Scotia Research Foundation established the Nova Scotia Centre for Geological Sciences at a place called Crystal Cliffs only nine miles north of Antigonish on St George's Bay. MIT, through the leadership of Dr Walter L. Whitehead, ran an eight-week Summer School of Geology at Crystal Cliffs from 1948 to 1957. The variety of rock structures in the region was a great lure for geologists. The MIT staff agreed to give regular undergraduate instruction in surveying, geological field-work, and associated sciences. Although only eight St.F.X. students studied with the summer school during its ten-year existence, the centre provided great opportunities to the St.F.X. geology staff through conferences, lectures, and collaboration with a wide field of scholars.[85] MIT found Dr Donald MacNeil, geology professor at St.F.X., a very useful instructor and efficient administrator for the summer school.[86] Dr Nicholson decided, because of the plans in 1947 for Crystal Cliffs, that his department of geology should be further developed, and so hired Dr Bernard J. Keating in 1948.[87] St.F.X. professor William T. Foley later commented, "the proximity of the MIT Summer School helped to enrich the outlook of the student and to enliven his course of studies."[88]

In spite of the summer school and the projects funded by the Nova Scotia Research Foundation and the National Research Council, research at St.F.X. was in its infancy during and immediately after the Second World War. Professors in the sciences complained about the heavy teaching loads, the absence of time for publishing their research, the lack of equipment, and the need for a new science hall, while President Nicholson prayed for the appearance of "a new Neil McNeil," the generous benefactor who had financed a science hall in

1910.[89] In its infancy, research at St.F.X. was sporadic, small-scale, and applied in nature.

The Legacy of the Veterans

By the early 1950s, most of the veterans who had streamed onto the campus after the war were gone. But their presence during the preceding years, along with expanding enrolments and certain social trends, had altered student life. A minority of students had always tried to buck the disciplinary regulations which required daily chapel, compulsory class attendance, permission for leaving campus, lights out at eleven p.m., no alcoholic beverages, and civilized and honourable conduct in public. Certain rules tended to rankle some of the veterans. Nonetheless, the St.F.X. administration tried to conserve the *status quo*; in a discipline statement in 1947, they reminded students that the good of the university community was of first importance, and that students could be expelled for consistent violation of the rules against gambling, cheating, drinking, any form of impurity, the use of profane or obscene language, theft, and habitual academic laziness.[90] However, President Nicholson admitted in retrospect that "disciplinary problems had to be treated differently" with the veterans.[91] For example, although prohibition remained the university rule, the exceptions to it were many, and prefects probably found themselves more often stressing the spirit of the law rather than the letter.[92]

Dr Nicholson also had to admit that, once the veterans left, it was difficult to "tighten up" the rules again.[93] In 1950 the senior class, or their self-appointed representatives, openly and harshly criticized the discipline and student government at St.F.X. Shrewdly borrowing certain democratic concepts from the extension department's philosophy, expressed in memorable Coady phrasing, the seniors charged that St.F.X. students existed under a "disciplinary dictatorship." The "great default" of the students was their toleration of a system which blocked them from becoming "masters of their own destiny." The seniors called for a "cooperative university" where the interdependence of administration, faculty, and students was acknowledged.[94] They accused St.F.X. of preaching one gospel to the people of eastern Nova Scotia through extension, and practising a very different one in their treatment of the students on the campus. What Dr Coady thought of this novel application of *Masters of Their Own Destiny* to his own university's regimen is uncertain. Some of the faculty reacted to the critique with considerable sympathy, while others judged it outrageous; President Nicholson remained rather non-committal.[95] The upshot was an investigation of university discipline and morale,[96] consultation with

Dorm life in the late 1940s

other universities about systems of discipline and student government, and a limited experiment in certain residences with student prefecting. Though it ultimately failed,[97] the *Xaverian Weekly* greeted this latter innovation with enthusiasm.[98]

The St.F.X. administration also made concessions about hazing or initiation. President Nicholson claimed in 1952 that for more than twenty years St.F.X. had tried to eliminate hazing. But, he reported, "We found the cure worse than the disease." To the dismay of officials, students organized unsupervised events off-campus or privately in the residences. Therefore, the administration decided to allow a "mild program" completely under the control of the student council. Nicholson concluded, "I still consider hazing intrinsically wrong; it is now a matter of tolerating a harmless amount of it to prevent greater evils."[99] Although a "mild program" of initiation was permitted, the practice of it, of course, remained controversial, as it always had been, among faculty and students both at St.F.X. and elsewhere.[100]

One close observer of the students at St.F.X. concluded by the mid-1950s that students overall had become milder. He stated, "Incidents of window smashing have decreased wonderfully. I would attribute this to the fact that there is more civilization among our boys. There is less broken furniture, students are quieter – I think this is because our youth are getting the war out of their systems."[101] This was the opinion of "Jack the Carpenter," the genial head carpenter at St.F.X., hired about 1932 and responsible for the upkeep of the university's expanding array of buildings. By 1956 Jack was seventy years old, the father of seven, and the grandfather of twenty-two. His real name was John H. MacDonald, and he, like many other craftsmen before and after, had a long and worthy association with the university.[102] Students considered him a witty, humorous gentlemen-philosopher and eulogized him affectionately: "For a word of wit, a word of wisdom or a word of good sound common sense, you will find all three conbined in personable 'Jack the Carpenter,' who is a most familiar and delightful figure here on the St.F.X. Campus."[103] Jack's headquarters were found behind the rink and gymnasium in a building which had once served as the college barn. For his part, Jack liked the students and found most of them worthy of the appellation; about the remaining small minority, he commented: "They are the ones who look upon St.F.X. bread as a four year loaf."[104]

Activities of the Student Union
The students had established formal student government at St.F.X. in 1939. Thereafter, the open meetings of the student union had regularly been vigorous and heated, ranging over such diverse topics as student

medical services, student elections, sports, college dining, discipline, rail service, and local haircut prices. Proceedings were ordered according to parliamentary rule and provided a marvellous training in public speaking and democratic procedure for those who chose to participate; and many did.[105] The student union decided to revise its constitution and by-laws in 1944. The union's stated objective was to "co-ordinate and direct" all student activities at St.F.X.; its functions included representation of the student body, promotion of cooperation between students and faculty in the interests of the whole, the administration of student funds, publication of the *Yearbook*, and the promotion of relations among universities. All registered male students became members automatically; the university president and faculty enjoyed honorary membership with no voting privileges. The senior class filled key executive positions, but other classes, the student societies, the *Xaverian*, and the faculty also had representation.[106] Up to 1950, the faculty had the right to veto decisions of the student union considered inimical to the interests of the university.[107]

The St.F.X. Student Union again adopted a new constitution in 1952. It provided for a student representative council designed to make the student union more orderly and efficient.[108] The council consisted of class presidents, one officer from each society, and representatives from each house on campus. It also had an inner executive composed of the president, secretary, and treasurer of the student union. From then on, the entire student body only met twice annually while the student representative council conducted the regular business of the union.[109] The expanding post-war student body had made necessary more complex machinery for self-government. About this time, the student union invited the Mount St Bernard student council executive to be honorary members of the student representative council.[110] Apparently, Mount students were already holding certain student union offices on campus,[111] and as early as 1943 had requested, without success, voting rights in the student union; they had argued for the privilege on the basis of real coeducation and democracy.[112]

Student Societies

The student societies were generally vigorous both during and after the war, and several new ones appeared. In 1941 students formed the *Exekoi* Society; its primary object was to provide academic assistance to other students. The society motto was *Non Solum Nobis*, "not for ourselves alone."[113] The Canadian Catholic Student Mission Crusade materialized in 1943 with the goal of supporting and promoting Catholic home and foreign missions.[114] Music lovers at St.F.X. began a Music Appreciation Club in 1945 and stated their purpose thus: "to

Cast for *Arsenic and Old Lace*, 1948

encourage an appreciation for great music, which transcends nationalities and expresses the fundamental elements and emotions that go to make up man."[115] The club started a collection of records and sponsored listening and live concerts; by 1954 a St.F.X. band was active as well as an orchestra.[116] Three years later the Gaelic Club, one of the earliest campus societies to appear, was revived. The *Xaverian* editor expressed delight: "The reorganization of such a society, fills a long felt need on the Xaverian campus where a great percentage of the students and faculty are of Scottish descent."[117] Actually, his claim of "a great percentage" was an exaggeration; by 1948–49 about 30 per cent of the students were of Scottish lineage.[118] Nevertheless, they still represented the largest ethnic group among the students. Of great moment for student life at St.F.X. after the war was the formation of the Students' Political Association in 1948 and thus the first appearance on campus of organized political activity. Interested students formed Liberal, Conservative, Cooperative Commonwealth Federation, and Social Credit clubs and sponsored all manner of lively political events – elections, model parliaments, debates, and speeches. Although some students opposed this development as a violation of campus neutrality, the Students' Political Association flourished, and politics became an important part of student life at St.F.X.[119]

The extension department and Antigonish Movement had always absorbed the interest of some St.F.X. students. Occasionally the co-op society, which ran the campus book store, and the credit union staged an upbeat co-op rally which helped to direct attention to extension work.[120] After the war, the appearance on campus of ever-larger numbers of international students from places like the Caribbean, India, and South America, who came to study the work of extension, also raised the interest and curiosity of students.[121] In the early 1950s, students formed the International Cooperative Club; those involved hoped to foster interest in adult education, provide a friendly place for foreign students, and promote social awareness and leadership.[122]

Post-War Sports at X
Several notable changes took place in the post-war sporting scene at St.F.X. Hockey received a considerable boost in 1947 through the generosity of the Alumni Association; with the assistance of Alumni Director Rev. Francis Smyth and the students, it purchased an artificial ice plant for the old Memorial Rink, built in 1921.[123] Under the reign of nature, hockeyists in the spring had sometimes found themselves playing in an unpleasant mixture of ice and mud. No more would the sacred sport depend on the uncooperative elements. President Nicholson expressed relief that his growing student body obtained

this timely diversion.[124] However, the president was unhappy with the "manly art"[125] of boxing which had been in vogue at St.F.X. for decades as both an intramural and intercollegiate sport. So in 1950, Dr Nicholson, bolstered by the confidence that he had the weight of current Catholic opinion on his side, banned the controversial sport. Some student backlash materialized.[126] However, the argument was clinched in the president's favour; soon after the ban was imposed a young man died in a locally sponsored boxing tournament.[127] Finally, early in the 1950s rugby was displaced by Canadian football, which had been gaining general popularity. By the fall of 1953, St.F.X. students were playing both intramural and intercollegiate Canadian football.[128]

Alterations in the Student Body
The profile of the St.F.X. student body changed in certain important respects between 1944 and 1950. The most evident alteration was in size: from 513 in 1944–45 to 913 in 1949–50. Females remained between 13 to 17 per cent of registrations. By 1950–51 the proportion of youth from outside the Diocese of Antigonish had increased to about 54 per cent from 41 per cent in 1945–46. The four largest groups came from New Brunswick (14 per cent), Quebec (11 per cent), Mainland Nova Scotia (11 per cent), and the United States (8 per cent). In 1949 President Nicholson thought the large numbers trekking north from New England would maintain the high enrolment levels even though the veterans were leaving. He wrote:

Next year I believe we can keep the total figure where it is if we are willing to fill up with Americans. We have the maximum U.S.A. registration of our history this year with a total of around 60, but of these one-half come from Portland, Maine. We feel we must continue playing ball with Maine, but other applicants from the U.S. must go through a sifting process. The Portland boys are really a superior group, and on the average the lads from the U.S. are really excellent.[129]

The higher numbers of international students, of whom almost one-half were priests, represented the following countries: Puerto Rico, Mexico, Columbia, England, Czechoslovakia, Poland, Austria, Korea, Japan, China, and India.[130] Most came to examine the workings of extension.[131] Of those students from within the diocese, about 75 per cent were Cape Bretoners, and of these, over 70 per cent lived in the Sydney–Glace Bay industrial area. This represented a complete reversal of the situation one hundred years before, when nearly all students at St.F.X. came from mainland Nova Scotia. Most students remained interested in programs outside of the arts, for of 236 degrees and diplomas conferred in 1951, only 62 were the bachelor of arts degree.[132] Protestants accounted for merely 5 per cent of the student body, but because of the overall increase in enrolments, enough of them attended to justify the formation of a chapter of the Student Christian Movement.[133] Veterans accounted for close to one-third of the students during this period and about 25 per cent of them were married.[134]

Certain aspects of the bigger St.F.X. troubled President Nicholson and his faculty. Nicholson labelled the problem of "bigness" a curse and stated: "In the larger institutions the organization becomes quite loose and the difficulty of exposing the average student to a genuine philosophy of life is insurmountable. Along with this goes the fact that it always becomes increasingly difficult to choose a staff of men who themselves have the right attitudes."[135] One of his faculty members concluded about the class of 1952, "we cannot say that we know these students."[136] In spite of these anxieties, St.F.X. made no plans to limit expansion.

The five years from 1945 to 1950 strained every element of university life at St.F.X. as they had never been strained before. These years were exhausting years for an overextended administration and faculty, alarming years for the university bursar, and dismaying years for those providing accommodation. However, it was timely that a president presided who was vigorous and tireless in his supervision and direction of the growing institution. St.F.X., like other universities in the Maritimes and Canada, had rapidly expanded because of the onset of higher enrolments under the Veterans' Rehabilitation program.[137] The tensions created by growth and the accommodations it required in every area of campus life did not subside in 1950. That year brought a change in diocesan administration, and hence a new, and even more expansive, era for higher education in eastern Nova Scotia.

·14·

Bishop and University, 1950–54

Bishop Morrison's Contribution

Bishop Morrison died on 13 April 1950; he was eighty-eight years old. Thus ended a dignified and staid thirty-eight-year episcopate. His diocesan college had undergone crucial change during his ecclesiastical reign. Throughout, the bishop-chancellor had been a faithful defender and advocate of the college. Perhaps his earlier experience as rector of St Dunstan's College, Charlottetown (1892–95) had made him sympathetic to the special needs of such institutions; of course, as bishop a healthy college favoured him with a steady supply of clerical candidates. Morrison had saved his college from the university federationists in 1922–23. Financially, he had done much to keep the college in business through appeals to the diocesan faithful, parish levies, and generous personal contributions. St.F.X. had shown its gratitude by naming a major building in his honour. Bishop Morrison had not been a dynamic, innovative leader; however, he had allowed room for such people at the college and in the diocese.[1] Rarely had he been heavy-handed or dictatorial toward St.F.X.[2] Caution, prudence, conservatism, and sober diligence had been his stock-in-trade. These had done little to harm the university and may indeed have been best for it in the long run. Only during his final years, when St.F.X. grew rapidly, had the old bishop appeared insensitive to the university's plight.

The "Bishop of Social Action"

Bishop Morrison's successor was Bishop John R. MacDonald, a fifty-nine-year-old native of Port Hood, Inverness County, Cape Breton and graduate of St.F.X. (1911). Before his appointment in 1945 as coadjutor to the aging Bishop Morrison, MacDonald had been bishop of Peterborough, Ontario (1943 to 1945). During the years from his ordination in 1916 to his first episcopal appointment in 1943, Father MacDonald had gained considerable experience in parish work. His longest periods of service had been at St Ninian's Parish in Antigonish (1916–22 and

Bishop John R. MacDonald,
fifth bishop of the Diocese of Antigonish 1950–59

1932-43). By the time of his return in 1945 to assist Morrison, he was known as a hurried activist. Since Bishop Morrison was unwilling to relinquish power or delegate responsibility, MacDonald had little free rein until the old bishop's demise.[3] In 1950, the new bishop initiated rapid organizational expansion within the diocese. His appointment inaugurated a new era in relations between the bishop of Antigonish and St.F.X. University.

President Nicholson was pleased with MacDonald's accession to power; he wrote to a friend: "We of the College can feel gratified over the fact that we know Bishop MacDonald's heart is completely with us. This is not intended as a criticism of [Bishop Morrison] who was such an outstanding benefactor, nevertheless I think it is not unfair to state that he never completely accepted our point of view."[4] Nicholson's optimism was justified; Bishop MacDonald immediately appointed two priests to the St.F.X staff and asked it to report on its future needs for priest-professors.[5] By April 1950, he had promised to the university five additional priests while requiring the release of two for other diocesan purposes (Rev. Jerome Chisholm in biology and Rev. George Kane in English). He also recommended that St.F.X. consider hiring a full-time director of fund-raising, drafting a constitution, and examining the status and weighting of its courses in religion.[6]

Bishop MacDonald was intensely interested in extension work at St.F.X. As a student he had come under the influence of Father Jimmy Tompkins. During the latter 1910s, MacDonald had helped him edit his *Casket* column "For the People" about the social and economic problems of the diocese. Later he had taught in Tompkins's people's school at St.F.X. in 1921-22; and through the years from 1918, he had participated in the vigorous diocesan conferences (educational, rural, and industrial) which had contributed to the formation of the extension department.[7] Indeed, in 1928 the new bishop had even been a member of the Alumni Association committee which had lobbied the St.F.X. board of governors to initiate extension work. His biographer claims that, through his work on social questions with the Canadian Conference of Catholic Bishops in the 1940s, Bishop MacDonald became known unofficially as the "Bishop of Social Action."[8] Therefore, extension department staff felt confident that his move to the episcopal helm promised them a great future.[9] He had high regard for Dr Coady and Coady was able to be frank with him.[10]

The Post-War Extension Department

After the war, the Antigonish Movement was the object of increasing international attention. The Caribbean region, which had historic

Dr Coady with visitors from Indonesia

links with Nova Scotia, faced similar problems in the fisheries and agriculture. Some of its countries – Jamaica, Puerto Rico, Trinidad, San Domingo, Dominica – as well as others in Central America, were among the first to send people to study the Antigonish Movement.[11] But visitors also came from South America, Asia, India, and Africa. As well, requests from such areas for information about the movement began to mount.[12] These demands placed increased strain on the staff and facilities of extension.[13] Dr Coady, his assistant director Alexander Laidlaw, who had replaced A.B. MacDonald in 1944,[14] and Bishop MacDonald began entertaining visions of promoting Catholic social movements in other parts of the world,[15] and were anxious to cooperate in 1950 with Canadian foreign aid programs. Extension conceived a plan to build an International House and call it "Democracy Insured."[16] But these ambitions were stymied by the perennial difficulty of inadequate financial resources. Between 1948 and 1954 extension incurred cumulative deficits which amounted to about $200,000; and there was "no compensating income of any kind."[17] Even schemes to gain further Carnegie assistance,[18] and to raise $1.25 million through an American organization called the International Friends of the Antigonish Movement, failed.[19]

Even though Bishop MacDonald was unable to solve the financial problems of extension, he did appoint more staff to the department and gave it strong moral support. Thus Coady and the extension staff began to dream even grander dreams. They requested staff for labour, urban, and rural education, for land settlement, and one as a director of publicity and finance. Coady advocated the appointment of union and cooperative representatives from central and western Canada to integrate the work of extension nationally.[20] He also hoped for the future appointment of experts in organic farming, forestry, fisheries, crops, housing, and colonization, as well as for the organization and education of the "maids and working girls" of the diocese.[21] The bishop satisfied some of these requests; by 1953 extension department full- and part-time staff included about twenty-five, consisting of directors, assistant directors, lecturers, consultants, secretaries, librarians, specialists, supervisors, and field-workers.[22] Bishop MacDonald was especially interested in land settlement, for he hoped that through immigration rural life in his diocese would be revitalized.[23] Meanwhile, Coady urged diocesan leaders who supported extension work to meet together regularly. This technique, he instructed them, had been used before extension began; it had helped to keep up morale, train leaders, create a "pressure group that will keep all our top leaders on the right track," and set the agenda for the St Joseph's Society, the clergy meetings, and the rural and industrial conferences.[24]

Antigonish and Sydney extension staff, 1950s

Dr Coady's Retirement

However, an era in extension's history was brought to a close in 1952 when ill health forced Dr Coady to resign as director.[25] He was seventy years old. Early in the year he suffered a serious heart attack and hence submitted his resignation effective 1 March.[26] Coady had planned to leave voluntarily later that year; he believed the old should teach the young all they know, then graciously shuffle aside and allow for young blood to pump fresh enthusiasm into the work. He left, full of his usual optimism, rejoicing in the success of extension work, and receiving the accolades of numerous cooperators and adult educators throughout Canada and the United States.[27] He would remain as "Director Emeritus" at St.F.X. with an office and full-time secretary, active, despite unstable health, in travelling, speaking, corresponding, and counselling until his death on 28 July 1959.[28]

Although Coady remained as a presence, his resignation was a hefty blow for extension. Much of the magic that it had exercised resided in his personality. It is surely rare to find so many leadership qualities – energy, oratory, imagination, vision, commitment, service, optimism, and courage – combined in one person. With the help of a capable, flexible, and cooperative office staff of men and women, along with field-workers and supporters in church and government, he made a historic contribution to St.F.X. and eastern Nova Scotia. His department had been dynamic and innovative; its teaching methods were varied, democratic, cooperative, and active, in contrast to the lecture method which exercised a virtual monopoly in the academic disciplines.[29] Dr Coady helped to inspire Catholic youth and colleagues with a sense of social responsibility, and he best epitomized the university's social conscience in action. Along with others committed to his agenda, he had introduced into the psyche of St.F.X. a tension between education to serve the *status quo* and education for social action.[30] Coady and extension also made a momentous, positive contribution to the reputation of St.F.X., a contribution which would be a valuable resource for public relations. Moreover, extension had generated good will among the people of eastern Nova Scotia who could see that the university was on their side. On the broader Maritime landscape, extension had encouraged the formation of a surprising number of credit unions and consumer, producer, and service cooperatives. On the side of intangibles, it had helped to overcome defeatism, to reduce religious intolerance, to inspire among the people more confidence in their own abilities, and to promote more careful thought about work, school, buying, housing, and public health.[31]

The Second Director of Extension

Bishop MacDonald replaced Dr Coady as director with a forty-six-year-old priest from Sydney Mines, Cape Breton.[32] Rev. Michael J. MacKinnon, the quiet and shy son of a coal miner, had spent most of his life in the rough and tumble of the industrial Cape Breton labour scene. From 1937 to 1950 he had been pastor of St Anthony's Parish, Glace Bay. In 1948 Coady appointed him director of labour classes in Cape Breton and then in 1950 head of the extension office, Sydney.[33] Apparently Father MacKinnon was popular with the labour unions, and Coady credited him with routing the Communists in the region.[34] A Carnegie official described him as "an intelligent and forceful person but without Coady's imagination and social graces."[35] He lacked Coady's fire and evident enthusiasm. However, he was a leader with the ability to pierce through to the heart of issues.[36] Shortly after his appointment, Coady suggested how he should work to retain the favour of all the regional groups served by extension, and what problems in the fisheries, forestry, and cooperatives were most urgent.[37] MacKinnon obviously had a tough act to follow and was occasionally troubled with a poignant sense of personal inadequacy.[38]

Xavier Junior College

On 8 January 1951 the St.F.X. board of governors resolved to establish a junior college in Sydney, Cape Breton.[39] The leading player in this development was none other than the energetic new bishop, John R. MacDonald.[40] The idea of an institution of higher education in Cape Breton was certainly not new. In 1905 King's College had tried to establish a school of engineering in Sydney; the Independent Labour Party had plans for a labour college in 1921; and suggestions for a junior college had also been made by churchmen and others in 1937–38 and again in 1947.[41] Moreover, the St.F.X. extension department, in 1932, had opened an office in Sydney, and in 1949 and 1950 St.F.X. had conducted a six-week summer school at the request of Cape Breton teachers.[42] In 1948 President Nicholson claimed that finances alone restrained St.F.X. from immediately opening an affiliated junior college in Sydney.[43] Actually, demographic trends in the diocese had made the existence of St.F.X. at Antigonish an anomaly. When St.F.X. had been opened in Antigonish County in the 1850s, the population had been close to 15,000, but by 1951 it was less than 12,000. In contrast, the population in Cape Breton County had jumped from 20,866 in 1861 to 120,306 by 1951, representing over 50 per cent of the diocesan population and about 58 per cent of its Catholics.[44] The main reason for the population shift, of course, had been the establishment of the Dominion Iron and Steel Company in Sydney at the turn of the

Rev. Michael J. MacKinnon,
second director of extension 1952–59

century. The population had more than tripled from about 3000 to 10,000, and Sydney had incorporated as a city within a few years. Steel and coal attracted workers and their families from rural areas and countries in Europe.[45] Thus the Sydney–Glace Bay area had developed as the key urban-industrial centre in the Diocese of Antigonish.

These facts, along with his commitment to a concept of St.F.X. as a "people's University,"[46] impelled Bishop MacDonald to press ahead with the ambitious project.[47] A joint committee worked out an initial plan; it recommended that the proposed college not compete with existing high schools in the area, that the old Sydney Lyceum be renovated and used, that a broad and flexible program of studies be offered at the freshman and sophomore levels, that an initial staff of two priests and four laymen be hired, that an annual budget of $26,000 be followed, that the college be administered by a principal who would report to the St.F.X. board of governors, that the college be opened in September 1951, that the new institution be known as Xavier Junior College (XJC), and that a public announcement be made immediately.[48] The joint committee plan was adopted.

The First Principal and His Trials

Bishop MacDonald requested, then insisted, that Rev. Dr Malcolm MacLellan, a forty-four-year-old education professor and dean of studies at St.F.X., be the college's founding principal.[49] MacLellan, a native of Inverness County, Cape Breton, had graduated from St.F.X. in 1926. After studies at St Augustine's Seminary, Toronto, he had been ordained to the priesthood in 1932 and had then earned a doctorate in education (1935) at the Catholic University of America.[50] His Cape Breton roots and experience in both teaching and educational administration made him a logical choice. However, MacLellan found it a daunting task – in his words, "a leap in the dark" – to organize a new college in Sydney where there existed neither campus, nor staff, nor college tradition, nor endowment.[51] Yet he entertained high hopes for what could be achieved through the advantages of close staff-student relations, small classes, improved guidance, and more individual attention.[52]

Early arrangements for the Sydney junior college were dogged by calamity, and its actual beginnings were primitive indeed. MacLellan would later call St.F.X.'s entrance onto the educational scene in Cape Breton "a veritable baptism of fire."[53] First, an arsonist did substantial damage to the Lyceum, which had been given to St.F.X. by Father R.C. MacGillivray of Sacred Heart Parish. The old building, located on George Street, had earlier been an impressive and popular theatre and community centre; it was gutted by fire on 7 March. After the

Rev. R.C. MacGillivray, Sacred Heart Parish, Sydney

The Old Lyceum and home of Xavier Junior College, Sydney, 1950s

St.F.X. board had decided to have it rebuilt,[54] using the insurance money ($50,000) generously offered by Father MacGillivray, a carpenters' strike delayed completion of the work. Therefore, Principal MacLellan was forced to start his new college venture close by, using two Second World War Navy League huts. He reflected later, "I doubt if any institution of higher learning ever started in such unpretentious conditions."[55] Not until January 1952 were the staff and students able to move into the renovated Lyceum. Perhaps the fire was a blessing in disguise, for MacLellan was able to alter the building more extensively, to better serve the purposes of his college.[56] Shortly after the college opened in September, the third calamity occurred: Xavier House in Westmount, purchased by St.F.X. as a residence for its priest-faculty, suffered considerable damage from fire.[57]

In spite of these calamities, XJC opened in September 1951. Five full-time members composed Principal MacLellan's founding staff, all St.F.X. graduates: Rev. Charles W. MacDonald, professor of Latin and philosophy, Rev. Francis J. Smyth, professor of economics and sociology, Yves Brunelle, professor of English and French, Elmer Britten, professor of chemistry and mathematics, and Rev. Michael J. MacKinnon, director of adult education.[58] The young staff were an intimate group who faced together the exciting and formidable challenge of making the junior college experiment a success. Through the early years, little complex organization was required, and close relations developed among staff, students, and parents.[59] On the occasion of the college's formal opening, Coady reminded them: "You are playing a significant historic role that we are sure will be to you a great source of future pride."[60]

In Service to the Community
While MacLellan had his own philosophy of education, imbibed at St.F.X., he promised to serve the educational needs of the Sydney area as they emerged and within the limits of his resources. The college aimed "to educate men and women intellectually, emotionally, and morally" and "to develop their ability to think clearly, to acquire wholesome attitudes towards life, and to strengthen their character and ideals."[61] A program of utility alone was not in the cards. Basic courses were offered, designed to lead into the arts, science,[62] commerce, home economics, nursing, and cooperative leadership programs at St.F.X.[63] MacLellan encouraged teachers and other vocational groups to make arrangements with the college for courses that interested them.[64] His watchword appeared to be flexibility.[65]

And flexibility was needed. From the start, local demands altered stated intentions. MacLellan planned to offer a full sophomore program,

First staff and students, Xavier Junior College, Sydney, 1951

but only remedial courses in the freshman year. By 1954 his college had been required to offer preparatory and freshman courses, as well as the sophomore level, along with first-year engineering. XJC also gave weekend preparatory and college-level courses, attended largely by teachers, and evening courses in accounting. The accounting classes were offered in conjunction with the Society of Industrial and Cost Accountants, and led to a certificate upon completion of four years' work. The staff also taught summer schools.[66] Finally, it became clear almost immediately that the college would have to expand rapidly to serve adequately the educational needs of the populous Sydney–Glace Bay area.

The First Students at "Little X"

Most students at the new junior college came from working-class families in the industrial area of Cape Breton – Sydney, North Sydney, Sydney Mines, Glace Bay, and New Waterford.[67] The 64 regular students in 1951–52 grew to 142 by 1953–54. Many came, encouraged by area pastors and high school principals.[68] No more than 10 per cent of these were female. However, of the considerable numbers who took weekend courses (102 in 1951–52), at least one-half were female. The tuition fees of $160 for a full program were equivalent to the St.F.X. fees; but Cape Breton students of the industrial area now had the chance to eliminate residence costs, since they could remain at home for the first two years of the St.F.X. program. MacLellan estimated that "nearly one-half of our student body would not attend college if Xavier Junior College had not been established."[69] During the first year, the students formed a student union, celebrated St.F.X. Day on 3 December, participated in a retreat,[70] organized a mid-year prom, held weekly debates, organized rugby, hockey, and basketball teams, and closed the academic year with a convocation and ball.[71] It was an energetic and enthusiastic start all around.

The Community Reception

The opening of XJC in 1951 was greeted warmly by people in the industrial area. Apparently labour, industry, the teaching profession, and civic leaders lauded its appearance.[72] Cooperative organizations were also enthusiastic; seven of them in 1952–53 contributed nine $50 entrance scholarships. MacLellan was highly impressed by this grass-roots support: "This is almost certainly," he declared, "one of the most significant and unique tokens of educational concern here or elsewhere and speaks volumes for the social responsibility that pervades the men and women of these organizations."[73] Professions of support, most of them merely verbal, came from others as well. The Sydney city council praised St.F.X. for establishing a junior college to serve the youth of industrial Cape Breton.[74] Of course, MacLellan made a careful public relations bid to gain the support of important and representative community leaders. The special guests at the official opening on 16 January 1952, attended by over five hundred, included school inspectors, high school principals, mayors, and the superintendent of Dominion Steel and Coal Company; and at the first convocation in May, St.F.X. conferred honorary degrees on two prominent local educational leaders.[75] Moreover, at the shrewd suggestion of Dr Somers, the St.F.X. board of governors formed an advisory board for the junior college, composed of community and college representatives, to "consider the manner in which the Junior College may be of greatest value in the industrial area of Cape Breton."[76] But public relations aside, the new college met an important need in the industrial area. And St.F.X. had established it at considerable cost when government funding was unavailable, and after the university's debt had burgeoned from forced post-war expansion.[77] Total capital costs to St.F.X. for the reconstructed Lyceum and staff residence were $154,796.[78]

Formalizing Public Relations
The post-war expansion at St.F.X., a result of rising enrolments and the new bishop's projects and plans, placed immense pressure on finances. Therefore, the administration in 1950 established a department of public relations and finance and placed it, appropriately, under the jurisdiction of Vice-President Somers.[79] To then, university publicity had been haphazard. The new department was responsible for publicity, fund-raising, and alumni activities,[80] as well as for organization of the approaching university centennial.[81] Somers was an excellent choice because of his experience in building construction and finance, and his abundant energy, vision, and ambition for St.F.X.[82] He drafted a brief which set forth strategies for achieving effective public relations, for making better use of alumni, and for acquiring more information on potential donors; he concluded with a call for a careful statement of the short- and long-term policies and plans of the university.[83] As a result of these suggestions, in May 1951 St.F.X. hired Brian O'Connell, a Haligonian with extensive radio and newspaper experience, for public relations work.[84] The new department of public relations and finance revealed St.F.X.'s intention to augment its influence as Canada's "leading English-speaking Catholic University."[85]

Federal Government Assistance
Some of the financial pressure at St.F.X. was relieved in 1951 when the federal government began giving grants to Canadian universities.

This would not be the first time St.F.X. had received government money, of course. Up to 1881, Nova Scotia had provided annual grants to its colleges; the St.F.X. high school had drawn the provincial county academy grant from 1882 to about 1928; the extension department had received federal funding through the department of fisheries from the late 1930s; and after the war, the national government gave annual supplementary grants for the education of the veterans. Then, in 1950, Premier Angus L. MacDonald's Liberal government made a one-time grant to its provincial universities; St.F.X. received $63,000.[86] In the late 1940s, Nova Scotia universities had complained that the federal supplementary aid for the education of veterans was declining, and that universities elsewhere enjoyed provincial government support.[87] Apparently universities throughout the British Commonwealth were likewise receiving government support by the late 1940s.[88] In 1949 Prime Minister Louis St Laurent appointed a Royal Commission on National Development in the Arts, Letters, and Sciences, popularly known as the Massey Commission. St.F.X. submitted a brief to the commission; it stressed the university's heavy financial burdens, which resulted from both its residential nature and its ambitious extension services. The brief concluded by urging the commission to recommend federal funding for Canadian universities.[89] After receiving similar advice across Canada, and concluding that the universities were increasingly critical to the nation's future, the commission concurred.[90]

The federal government was also lobbied by the National Conference of Canadian Universities (NCCU) to provide permanent university funding. President Nicholson, who had long cultivated contacts with other universities,[91] was president of the Conference from 1950 to 1951.[92] During this time, the NCCU orchestrated a national publicity campaign in favour of federal funding for Canadian universities. Nicholson fully supported the propaganda campaign.[93] In 1951, the government acceded to the demands and began making grants to Canadian universities. As McKillop has noted, "It was a measure applauded by universities and accepted by government and public like, that suited the expansive and generally optimistic atmosphere of postwar Canada."[94] In February 1952 St.F.X. received its first subsidy, which amounted to nearly $71,000.[95] It reduced the deficit that year from $110,000 to about $40,000.[96] In spite of the obvious benefit to the universities, the funding formula based on provincial populations rather than student enrolment was a disadvantage for certain regions of the country. For example, in Nova Scotia with its relatively small population and high university enrolments, the federal aid per student was much lower than in certain other parts of Canada.[97]

Centennial Celebrations

Just over the horizon loomed another opportunity for the St.F.X. administration to attack its debt – the centennial of the university's founding. The recently formed department of public relations and finance suggested that the public impact of the celebration be maximized by spacing the events over one year from St.F.X. Day 1952 to St.F.X. Day 1953. It recommended a series of events be held – an alumni homecoming, meetings of learned societies, a special fall convocation with high-profile speakers, an invitation to a representative of the Holy See, and a program celebrating the twenty-fifth anniversary of the extension department.[98] Vice-President Somers, the mastermind and supervisor of all the events, meticulously planned each one and ensured that protocol was observed on all occasions. The Alumni Association cooperated handsomely with Somers and company in organizing the year.[99] The two impelling motives behind the centennial year rush of activities were to gain public recognition for a century of achievement and to replenish the university's treasury.

An astonishing cast of eminent persons paraded across the campus that busy year.[100] Many had been charmed by President Nicholson's winsome personality at earlier meetings with him. On St.F.X. Day, 3 December 1952, His Eminence Cardinal James McGuigan celebrated solemn pontifical mass; it was the four hundredth anniversary of St Francis Xavier's death. The annual commencement week and family celebration of the centenary took place from 16 to 20 May. Then the National Conference of Canadian Universities met on the campus from 8 to 10 June, followed by the Regional Conference of the Canadian Association of Adult Education from the 10th to the 12th. On 7 and 8 July, St.F.X. celebrated the twenty-fifth anniversary of the founding of the extension department. A special ceremony was held on 19 July in Arichat, Isle Madame, Cape Breton, when Bishop John R. MacDonald, the chancellor of the university, unveiled a monument placed beside Our Lady of the Assumption Church; it commemorated the opening of St.F.X. and its first classes a century before on 20 July 1853.[101] Next followed a general alumni reunion (20–24 July), a first annual English-speaking Catholic Social Conference (2–4 August),[102] a diocesan eucharistic conference (5 August), and a conference of the Canadian Catholic Historical Association (6–7 August).

The frontispiece of the centennial year was the formal academic ceremonies with convocation on 1 and 2 September. An august group of luminaries assembled, which included the governor-general of Canada, His Excellency the Right Honourable Vincent Massey, the lieutenant-governor of Nova Scotia, Honourable Alistair Fraser, the Canadian prime minister, Right Honourable Louis St Laurent, the

Centennial Memorial at Arichat commemorating St.F.X.'s founding there in 1853

apostolic delegate to Canada, His Excellency the Most Rev. Ildebrando Antoniutti, the premiers of Nova Scotia, Prince Edward Island, and Newfoundland, and other government officials, both high and low. Twelve bishops and archbishops were present to represent the church. Moreover, 114 representatives from universities in Canada, the United States, Scotland, England, Ireland, and other Commonwealth and foreign countries attended, with delegates from thirty-eight learned societies, associations, and national organizations. At the formal academic assembly in the evening of 1 September, Sir Richard Livingstone, former vice-chancellor of Oxford, delivered a learned address; solemn pontifical mass followed the next morning, celebrated by the apostolic delegate, Most Rev. Ildebrando Antoniutti. At convocation in the afternoon honorary degrees were conferred on twenty-nine of the dignitaries.[103] The St.F.X. campus must have groaned under the sheer weight of such officialdom. Never had town or university witnessed such an array of personages. At a special dinner for these high-ranking guests, President Nicholson stated that their presence at St.F.X. conferred on it "undreamed, soul-stirring recognition as it completes the first century of its service."[104] For some reason, perhaps related to the university's humble origins and modest circumstances, its leaders appeared to hanker after the recognition and commendation of the leading lights of church, state, and academia.

The centennial year celebrations were undoubtedly a major public relations coup for St.F.X. Furthermore, the university succeeded, largely through the skill and drive of Vice-President Somers, in exploiting the historic year for financial profit. The board of governors had formed a centenary fund committee and a Montreal firm conducted a canvass for special gifts, especially in industry.[105] Premier Angus L. MacDonald, who was honorary chairman of the centenary and a renowned St.F.X. alumnus, participated enthusiastically in the campaign and apparently wrote personally to about eighty corporations.[106] Over $1.5 million was eventually raised.[107] The centennial also stimulated reflection on the history of the university, its origins among the Scottish Highland, Irish, and Acadian descendants who inhabited eastern Nova Scotia, and its significance for these people.[108] In a *Casket* article, President Nicholson stressed what the university had done for these oppressed peoples – prepared their young, both men and women, in a Catholic setting for careers in the church, the state, and the professions; then, with the founding of extension work and the opening of Xavier Junior College, it had directly responded to the needs of the people. He concluded, "One thing above all impresses an observer of the effort of the last half-century: the results achieved in view of the available means have regularly exceeded the expectations."[109]

The Departure of President Nicholson
In the year following the centennial, Nicholson's eventful and strenuous tenure as president of St.F.X. ended. His bishop appointed him, effective 31 March 1954, pastor of St Joseph's Parish, Sydney, where he remained until retiring back to the university campus in 1961.[110] Nicholson commented to a friend about his move from the university to a parish: "To be quite frank about the whole situation I have an acute consciousness of failing powers and I want to get out before I am pushed out."[111] Actually President Nicholson had tendered his resignation in 1950, but Bishop MacDonald had asked him to stay on until the end of the St.F.X. centennial year.[112] Nicholson then was sixty-seven years old and had been president for ten years. He also acknowledged a hankering after the active ministry. His era at St.F.X. had witnessed rapid expansion in enrolments, in faculty, and in buildings, as well as the episcopal appointment of a vigorous new champion of St.F.X., Bishop John R. MacDonald. The curriculum had diversified, discipline had moderated, and St.F.X. had undertaken a new educational venture in industrial Cape Breton. It was timely that Nicholson, a zealous, tireless worker, committed heart and soul to the cause of St.F.X., and with a vision for what it could become, had borne the presidential mantle through these years. Nicholson's valued secretary, Rebecca B. MacLean, retired at the same time. Her letter of resignation was as much an expression of her own good qualities as it was a tribute to Nicholson: "I cannot refrain from telling you how much I appreciate your tolerance of my incompetence on very many occasions. It has been a privilege all these years to be associated with a person who lives always so close to God, and I now thank you for all you have done for me."[113] Reflecting on his presidency, Nicholson found "most gratifying" the physical growth of the university and the improvement of staff qualifications.[114] On the eve of his departure, he remained fully aware that the achievements of the last ten years of St.F.X.'s first century resulted from the cooperative effort of students, faculty, support staff, board, alumni, and bishop.[115] However, "Doc Pat" himself had provided much of the remarkable leadership.

·15·

A Broadening Mandate, 1954–64

The seeds of change sown at St.F.X. after the Second World War grew with astonishing rapidity during the 1950s and would eventually lead to a striking institutional metamorphosis. During this decade diverse pressures forced St.F.X. to broaden its mandate. For most of its history, St.F.X. had served the Catholic constituency of eastern Nova Scotia as a small, residential, diocesan, undergraduate, liberal arts college. Now it was growing into a bigger, more professional university with a wider sense of responsibility for meeting the demands of a broader public interest. This stretching of its institutional mandate was caused by the combined pressures of burgeoning enrolments, student interests and program diversification, government and corporate funding, faculty professionalization, and mounting international interest in its extension work.

The New President
The person who occupied the office of president during the 1950s facilitated, even encouraged, the changes which were overtaking St.F.X. and making it into something new. Rev. Dr Hugh J. Somers was a fresh hand at the institutional helm, and one of Irish lineage at that, yet he was a veteran member of the administrative staff. His immediate roots were Catholic Antigonish. The St.F.X. of the 1920s had been his *alma mater*; then he had trained at St Augustine's Seminary, Toronto (1923–27), had been ordained in 1927, and had subsequently obtained a master's (1928) and then a doctorate in history (1931) from the Catholic University of America.[1] Because Somers revealed promising financial and administrative capabilities (his father had been a local merchant), the Old Rector had recruited him for bursar in 1933. He had subsequently served under Dr Nicholson as vice-president (1944–54) and as director of public relations and finance (1950–54). In these roles, his responsibilities had included general university finances, the campaign of 1944, the development of the campus,

307

President John Hugh Somers, 1954–64

and the centenary celebrations of 1953. By 1954, therefore, Somers had considerable experience in university finance and administration, had turned out to be a businessman *par excellence*, and had established wide-ranging connections with leaders in government, industry, academia, and church. Bishop John R. MacDonald, his long-time friend, believed Somers was best qualified to succeed President Nicholson. So after a consultative vote of the faculty and board of governors,[2] his bishop appointed him president on 31 March 1954. Somers was fifty-one years old at the time and claimed that he would have said "no" to the appointment if he had been given the chance.[3] He would be assisted in his new administrative duties by a devoted and efficient secretary, Betty MacDougall.

Like his predecessor Dr Nicholson, Somers was single-minded in his devotion to St.F.X. He was undoubtedly a tireless worker, a man of boundless nervous energy,[4] and a shrewd financier. However, his temperament was difficult and "consensus was not his game."[5] He was shy and appeared cool in his relations with most people. These weaknesses would dog his leadership. Nonetheless, the new president had a vision for what he thought St.F.X. should become, and he planned to see that vision realized. In his predecessor's opinion, Somers would "usher in the golden age of St Francis Xavier."[6] He believed strongly in the virtues of Catholic education and the need for all Catholic colleges to keep pace with the demands of the time or suffer absorption by the larger secular universities. His views of higher education, therefore, were at once conservative and progressive: conservative in their commitment to the Catholic heritage and ideal of education, yet progressive because he advocated adapting to contemporary change and demands. Somers expressed these twin emphases in a conference speech in 1955: "It is the duty of the university to preserve the knowledge of the past and pass that knowledge to its students as their spiritual and cultural heritage. It is also the duty of the university to apply the wisdom of the past and the brains of the present to the problems of the age in which we live. As well, the university must add to our store of knowledge by research."[7] These basic concepts would guide Somers's approach to university problems during the course of his presidency.

Soaring Enrolments

One central, perennial problem he confronted immediately was mounting enrolments. In 1950–51 the institution reported a total registration of 870; in 1959–60 it registered 1210.[8] By the end of the 1950s, it was not uncommon for the admissions office to turn away one hundred qualified students for lack of facilities.[9] The female proportion edged up from about 13 per cent in 1949–50 to nearly 20 per cent by 1960. And the proportion from outside the diocese also crept up to about 60 per cent of registrants, thus forcing St.F.X. to enlarge its sense of responsibility to include a far-flung constituency. The single largest group of students came from mainland Nova Scotia and the other Atlantic provinces (39 per cent); however, substantial numbers continued to come from Quebec (12 per cent) and the United States (14 per cent).[10] The enrolment pressures, which plagued all Canadian universities, resulted from a growing Canadian population, an increased birthrate since the early 1940s, and higher participation rates among the eighteen- to twenty-one-year-olds.[11]

Expanding student registrations also revealed the increasing need for further education in an urban-industrial economy which had been stimulated by the war and by the emerging welfare state. The war had revitalized industry and reduced poverty and unemployment. Expanding opportunities had prompted many in the country and the villages to forsake their homes and seek better things in the towns and cities of the region. By 1954 Nova Scotia was 54 per cent urban. Mackenzie King's Liberal government had created new social programs – unemployment insurance (1940), family allowance (1944), and Canada Mortgage and Housing (1946) – and the civil service at both levels of government grew by leaps and bounds. The 1950s appeared as a dynamic "decade of development" when "the forces of change would sweep away most of the remnants of the traditional way of life and replace it with highly bureaucratized and centralized structures from which few could escape."[12] State planning and federal government largesse attracted many Maritimers. And television appeared in living rooms to dispense the culture and ethics of mainstream North America.[13] The general prosperity created promising job prospects for university students everywhere and generated among them a feeling of optimism and confidence about the future. A St.F.X. student declared in the *Xaverian*: "That the 1957 graduate is calling his own shots is no secret. Industry, to keep pace with the [economic] boom, has its personnel and hiring departments going full tilt enlisting college grads at a phenomenal rate."[14]

Nonetheless, Atlantic Canadians in the 1950s grew more and more dissatisfied with their economic lot when they contrasted it to central Canada. There emerged "a groundswell of regional discontent" and demands for government action.[15] Leaders in the region formed joint agencies to further their cause – the Maritime Provinces Board of Trade (1951), the Altantic Provinces Economic Council (1954), the first Atlantic premiers' conference (1956), and the Atlantic Provinces Research Board (1958). Robert L. Stanfield, Conservative premier of

Nova Scotia (1956–67), and his provincial counterparts gained the attention of Ottawa, and regional equality was placed on the federal agendas of John Diefenbaker's Conservatives (1957–63) and of his Liberal successors led by Lester Pearson. Atlantic Canada began to reap the benefits of its lobby when equalization payments and federal services and development programs, such as the Atlantic Development Board (est. 1962), channelled large sums of money into the region. The growth in government and educational services and industry in Atlantic Canada provided a ready job market for university graduates in spite of continued regional disparities.

Student Life in the 1950s
During this "decade of development" much remained the same for the St.F.X. undergraduate. The disciplinary hand of the institution remained firm, religious rites were performed daily, the sense of community, signified by the phrase "Xaverian family," continued strong, and the priest-professor was omnipresent. Many alumni of the decade credit St.F.X. with building up their self-confidence, heightening their sense of social responsibility, broadening their horizons, and granting them the opportunity to make many new friends. They likewise recall a strong "X spirit," a combination of camaraderie, institutional loyalty, and sense of belonging.[16] The Sisters of St Martha were part of that X spirit. However, the rapid post-war expansion of the university overwhelmed their staff resources and more of their work was gradually relinquished to lay employees.[17]

While much remained constant for the Xaverian of the 1950s, he did experience several noticeable departures. Enrolment numbers made it more difficult for faculty to retain the old tradition of close faculty-student relations. To compensate for this, President Somers believed that counselling should be formalized through a counselling centre.[18] The Students' Political Association (SPA), formed in 1948, became a dynamic society giving many students, including such later notables as Senator B. Alasdair Graham (1950), Honourable Warren Allmand (1954), Senator Lowell Murray (1956), and Brian M. Mulroney (1959), the chance to develop and refine their political skills and establish political contacts. Brian Mulroney, a most capable student from Baie-Comeau, Quebec, later became St.F.X.'s most prominent political alumnus as leader of the Progressive Conservative Party (1983–1993) and prime minister of Canada (1984–93).[19] The *Yearbook* of 1951 commented on the new association, "From the status of a comparatively unknown organization the SPA has in a few years leapt into prominence as one of the most active, certainly one of the most colourful, campus activities, with a future that is indeed bright and promising."[20] The political activism and contribution of St.F.X. alumni has elicited public comment;[21] it can perhaps be partly explained by the existence of the SPA itself, the vigorous dramatic and debating societies, the involvement of St.F.X. in regional problems through its extension department, the political interest and involvement of certain faculty, and the strength of the political culture of Nova Scotia.[22] Students with a flair for things literary, and with the assistance of faculty members such as Fathers Roderick MacSween and Richard Bannon, occasionally published between 1954 and 1965 a short literary magazine called *X-Writes*.[23] The first economics society was formed in 1957,[24] and philosophy professor Rev. Charles R. MacDonald encouraged the formation two years before of a great books club which aimed "to encourage its members to read many of the classics which everyone wishes to read at some time in his life, but never does."[25] Finally, the students of the 1950s felt an increasing urgency to obtain a student union building for offices and recreational facilities.[26]

Relations Between Big and Little X

A student problem unique to the 1950s and 1960s at St.F.X. was the integration of Xavier Junior College (XJC) students into the student body. The difficulty was rooted in the separation of the students through the first and second years. When the "Capers," as Cape Breton students were called, arrived at the Antigonish campus, they naturally gravitated toward those students whom they had established friendships with already during their Sydney sojourn. Both the administration and the students tried to reduce the sense of separation through, for example, a special page in the *Xaverian* covering XJC news, exchange visits by student leaders, and occasional joint rallies and socials. However, no solution was entirely satisfactory for, in Principal MacLellan's words, "establishing a bond of unity between the two bodies of the one institution."[27] The formation of XJC in 1951 had definitely created a stronger sense at St.F.X. of a separate "Caper" contingent within the student body.[28]

Conquest in Sports

For a small university, St.F.X. achieved a surprising supremacy in certain sports through the 1950s and 1960s. It hired a permanent athletic director, Father Andrew Hogan, in 1954, and perhaps part of the explanation for its successes lies here. His task was to organize St.F.X.'s intramural and intercollegiate athletic program.[29] However, the "surprising supremacy" largely resulted from a winning combination of talented players and expert coaching. St.F.X. achieved special prominence in hockey under coaches Fathers Andy Hogan and George

St.F.X. hockey team, 1953 (university centennial year)

St.F.X. football team, eastern Canadian champions 1958–59

Kehoe, winning at least seventeen titles between 1950 and 1969. It was also exceptional in basketball; from 1950 to 1962 St.F.X. won about thirteen championships with coaches Father William Fogarty, Ambrose Gilmet, Alex MacAdam, and John "Packy" MacFarland. Finally, St.F.X. dominated Maritime inter-varsity football through the late 1950s and 1960s under coach Don Loney, a former CFL player. The decade and beyond was remembered by many alumni as a golden age of sports at St.F.X.

Athletics were central to campus life at St.F.X., and the leading athletes had standing among their peers. Furthermore, intercollegiate games supplied a rallying point for college spirit and an opportunity for faculty and students to mix informally outside the classroom and residences. However, sports at St.F.X. were not without their critics and the charge of overemphasis was sounded regularly.[30] In the 1960s, some critics believed St.F.X. was recruiting too few athletes from Atlantic Canada and too many outstanding ones from elsewhere.[31] President Somers claimed that the university opposed athletic scholarships; he stated, "to accept a student simply because he is a good athlete but not of university calibre would be against our principles."[32] During the 1950s many Canadian university leaders concluded that "professionalism" was starting to displace the traditional approach to college sports as a means to the end of forming the whole student. President Nicholson, in 1952, had declared that the St.F.X. faculty deplored "the deterioration of amateurism."[33]

Planning for Expansion
The key feature of student life during the 1950s, namely mounting enrolments, propelled rapid institutional growth. President Somers, who opposed the limitation of enrolments because he believed it would undermine St.F.X.'s service to church and state, sounded the alarm about registration trends in 1955. In the spring the National Conference of Canadian Universities had sponsored a symposium on enrolments where Dr E.F. Sheffield, director, educational division of the Dominion Bureau of Statistics, projected a doubling of university enrolments over the next decade. The symposium was followed in November 1956 by a national conference to consider "Canada's crisis in higher education." Somers presented a paper at the conference entitled "Private and Corporate Support of Canadian Universities."[34] At St.F.X. he convinced the board of governors that a joint committee of board and faculty members should be formed to investigate future expansion of the institution.[35] The following January, the committee noted the overtaxing of residential, dining, and science-engineering facilities at St.F.X.; hence it advocated an immediate program of

expansion. Based on both anticipated increasing emphasis on research and enrolment trends predicted by Sheffield and the National Conference of Canadian Universities, the committee report recommended allowing enrolments to rise during the next decade to at least 1500 at St.F.X. and to 250 to 300 at XJC. The expansion program called for three new buildings – one for chemistry and physics, one for student accommodation, and one for XJC – at a total cost of about $1.75 million. St.F.X. requested its university architect, Jens F. Larson, then of Reynolda, North Carolina, to develop preliminary short- and long-term building plans.

One influential voice sounded a protest against certain phases of the proposed expansion program. Board member Father Michael Gillis, an advocate in the early 1920s of university federation in Nova Scotia and an enthusiastic promoter of extension work by St.F.X., championed the cause of the people. In a provocative speech before the board, he described President Somers as "the brilliant student and professor who has spent his years of priesthood in the training of the small percentage of students selected to pursue higher studies on the university level."[36] Gillis criticized the Maritime universities for educating over the centuries a small minority for the religious and lay professions, and for leaving "work undone that hinders and keeps in quasi-slavery the great mass of the under-privileged today."[37] Since these institutions had produced the leaders of Maritime society, he blamed them for the deplorable conditions of the farms, the fisheries, the forests, and the mining towns. Father Gillis urged the increased hiring of lay staff,[38] a better supply of well-trained teachers, and the expansion of the social sciences and the extension department, as well as the equipping of XJC to meet the technical and scientific needs of the diocese. He pointedly concluded his speech,

So, on behalf of the common man who has loved St.F.X. for more than half a century and sacrificed much these past years, I appeal for a serious consideration of the expansion of the Extension Department for some years instead of intensifying the competition with sister institutions to enrol more and more students in the physical sciences. May we look for a little less vigor for the [social] apex, and a redoubling of effort directed towards enlightening and solidifying the base.[39]

Gillis evidently found unpalatable certain parts of President Somers's vision for St.F.X. About this time he wrote to Dr Coady, "Is not [Somers] planning a similar enslavement of the unemployed and poorly employed to meet the demands of the sons of the so-called elite and larger income class through the academic St.F.X. and Xavier College?"[40] In his protest,

Gillis, labelled privately as "one of the old mergerites" by President Somers,[41] echoed a traditional minority viewpoint, advocated by Father Jimmy Tompkins in the early 1920s, which pressed for the centralization of academic work at Halifax and specialization in extension at Antigonish.[42] However, this line of thought was to remain that of a small minority. The board apparently listened to Gillis's remarks with "stunned and respectful silence";[43] while all expressed sympathy with his views, they believed that expansion was necessary and that it need not exclude the extension department. Even the director of extension, Father Michael MacKinnon, praised President Somers's support for extension and offered the flattering and doubtful opinion that "The Governors of this University, acting collectively, do not make mistakes"! The board unanimously adopted the joint committee report which recommended expansion.

Expansion's Puzzle: University Finances
St.F.X. had never been wealthy. Therefore, President Somers and the board faced the central problem of funding the proposed expansion program. By the mid-1950s St.F.X.'s financial picture was improving. For the first time in years, it began reporting a surplus and its indebtedness was in decline. Student fees still composed the bulk of the university's income (about 82 per cent in 1956–57), but the federal grant was increasing in size ($147,938 in 1956–57, and $282,242 in 1959–60) at the collective urging of Canadian university presidents.[44] The diocesan quota, which had been initiated in 1938, had reached $20,000 annually and would remain at that level over the next decade.[45] However, funds needed for expansion had impelled the university to seek new sources of income. In 1956 it increased tuition and board. In addition, it joined other provincial universities in urging the provincial government to support higher education. The presidents submitted a petition for provincial funding in 1957 which underscored the private nature of all Nova Scotia universities, the laudable government support granted in other provinces, and the severe regional problems of inflation, burgeoning enrolments, small endowments, lack of facilities, and low professorial salaries.[46] Although they received limited funds in 1958, not until 1963 did Robert L. Stanfield's Conservative government resume the practice, abrogated eighty-two years before in 1881, of annual grants to the provincial universities.[47] Like other university leaders hard-pressed for funds to expand, Somers also eyed the corporations.[48] St.F.X. had undertaken its first major canvass of industry with its centenary campaign in the early 1950s, and it continued courting the corporations throughout the decade.[49] Eventually the university raised about $440,000.[50] However, the work was

difficult, hampered by St.F.X.'s distance from large industrial-urban centres, its lack of "a nucleus of economically successful alumni," and a persistent public perception of it as a "preparatory seminary."[51]

The conception of St.F.X. as a "preparatory seminary" for diocesan clergy had a long and honourable tradition. However, this conception and function were seriously eroded in the 1950s by, among other things, the university's search for new non-diocesan sources of funding. A Catholic college does not play up its denominational role when it appeals to government and industry for financial support. In his plea for government and corporate funding, President Somers had to stress the national and public character of the St.F.X. contribution to a strong democracy.[52] For St.F.X., the goals of the state and of industry were gradually eclipsing those of the church. Thus it began to take on more the aura of a public than a denominational or sectarian institution. President Somers, of course, believed St.F.X. had to remain competitive with other institutions in order to survive and continue to provide its unique brand of Catholic education. Yet he also recognized that the tradition of providing a philosophy of life based on the "eternal truths" could not be taken for granted. However, he appeared more sensitive to the issue of freedom from direct government control than to the more subtle implications of government or corporate funding.[53] At his installation in 1954, he repeated a warning which his predecessor Dr Nicholson had also intoned: "One of our great troubles is that we have been so busy trying to keep up with the demand for science and technology that we have failed to pay proper attention to the fundamentals – without which the preparation of our students too easily becomes training and not education."[54] Fresh in Dr Somers's mind was the experience of the German universities under the Nazi regime, where, in his view, religion had been divorced from the intellect with disastrous consequences for the human race. While he stressed the need to protect the autonomy of the university and its tradition of education for honourable living, he probably did not foresee the long-range implications of wooing the corporations and gaining substantial government funding.

Even though the state of the university's finances improved and St.F.X. exploited promising new sources of funding, its immediate problem was to raise a large sum for capital outlay to fund the proposed expansion. The board in January 1956 considered a bond issue to raise $1.75 million; however, Bishop John R. MacDonald, the chancellor, cautioned the board members that the current climate of economic optimism might be short-lived.[55] He eventually limited new debt to $1.1 million; hence, the board was only enabled to construct immediately a new physics and chemistry building, and the remainder of

Physics and Chemistry Hall, built 1957

the proposed expansion – a residence, an addition to Morrison Dining Hall, and an arts building at XJC – had to be postponed. The new science building, designed in Georgian Colonial style by the university architect and attached to the south side of the existing MacNeil Science Hall, reached completion in 1957. The final cost, which included equipment and an unanticipated hike caused by complications with quicksand, was nearly $1 million.[56] The new red brick building, the first permanent academic facility constructed at St.F.X. since 1910, became the home of the physics and chemistry departments; the engineering department moved into the old science hall, and the biology department acquired more space in Aquinas Hall.

A New Residence

Mounting enrolments over the next several years forced the university to obtain temporary residence space off campus,[57] and eventually, in 1961, to continue the expansion program with the construction of a new residence group. By then St.F.X. was able to draw on grants for capital expenses available through the Canada Council, established in 1957,[58] and on fifty-year loans from the Canada Mortgage and Housing Corporation, obtainable from 1961 for dining and residence facilities.[59] A brick residence group, composed of three sections each named after a bishop who had been of historical importance to the region – Joseph-Octave Plessis, Edmund Burke, and William Fraser – was completed in 1962 at a cost of nearly $885,000.[60] It could accommodate over three hundred students and was located on the west side of the campus between the university chapel and West Street. Renovations and additions to the laundry and to Morrison Hall were also completed in the early 1960s, since both facilities had been built in the 1930s for a much smaller student enrolment.[61]

Emerging Prominence of the Sciences

The construction of the physics and chemistry building in 1957 symbolized St.F.X.'s commitment to bolster its programs in the sciences. Since the Second World War, the rapid development of industry demanded curricular expansion in the sciences and engineering. By 1960 about 40 per cent of St.F.X. students were in the sciences and engineering.[62] Even though President Somers announced at the opening of the physics and chemistry building that the university had no intention of "departing from its century long approach to higher education ... to blend the Sciences and the Humanities, [and] to promote the development of character and responsibility," yet he fully supported the strengthening of the sciences so that St.F.X. could exercise a Catholic influence on fledging scientists.[63] By 1960 he had formed a short-lived twelve-member advisory council of Canadian industrial leaders to advise the science faculty "on the courses offered and their orientation to suit the needs of today; the research program of the university; and the changing needs for scientists and engineers."[64] Presumably, he was interested in more than just advice, but it is difficult to know if St.F.X. received any financial support through this shrewd arrangement.

Within the first year of his term, President Somers had shown his desire to update the overall work of the university's academic departments. In October 1954 he had asked each of the departmental groups – the arts, the sciences, engineering, commerce, and the social sciences – to present the status of work in their field, the future of undergraduate and graduate work, the place of research and scholarship, and the group's relation to the extension department. The science group concluded that the best science students were not challenged by the existing program and "barely achieve professional standing as scientists"; it recommended, therefore, a four-year honours course. The group also advocated the development of graduate programs in science and more time for "fundamental research."[65] The honours program in science materialized in 1955, and in 1960 a master's level course was available in chemistry, along with the one already advertised in geology.[66] The opening of the new science building facilitated more research at St.F.X. In 1955–56 only five scientists were engaged in research with total research funds of $16,400; by 1963–64, St.F.X. reported fifteen involved in research and receiving a total of $130,700 from such sources as the National Research Council, the Defence Research Board, the Nova Scotia Research Foundation, and Canadian industry.[67] With these developments, the sciences for the first time in the history of St.F.X. were emerging to a position of prominence, prestige, and dominance.[68]

The State of the Arts
Although the sciences appeared to be setting the pace at St.F.X. by the late 1950s, the arts faculty, of course, still considered their program central to the undergraduate educational experience. They had weighty historical reasons for believing so. However, they did acknowledge that there existed a lack of respect for the arts course; therefore they aspired to enlarge their teaching staff and to offer, eventually, an honours degree and even graduate programs.[69] Few arts faculty engaged in research leading to publication, perhaps because of the excessive workload carried by the priest-professors.[70] A four-year honours program in selected arts disciplines would not be offered until 1966,[71] and only after a general BA and a BA with a major were

Rev. R.V. Bannon, professor of English 1924–31 and 1933–72

instituted in 1959. Undoubtedly the trend set by the sciences stimulated the arts faculty to upgrade themselves, to undertake research, and to better prepare their students for graduate studies.[72]

St.F.X. made a unique and important addition to its arts curriculum in 1958 – one which was long overdue – namely a program in Celtic studies. Since 1894, interested faculty had offered, sporadically, courses in Gaelic, and some enthusiasts in 1919 had pressed for an endowed chair. These things happened against a backdrop of steady decline in the use of the language and of the cultural assimilation of eastern Nova Scotia Celts.[73] Given the roots of St.F.X. among the descendants of the Highland Scots, the Gaelic offerings were one means to preserve and to examine their cultural legacy. The small numbers of students who took the courses usually came from families where Gaelic was spoken.[74] By the 1950s, only a tiny minority of staff and students had a working knowledge of the language. President Nicholson, a fluent Gaelic speaker himself who had contacts with people such as John Lorne Campbell, a folklorist in Scotland, was anxious that St.F.X. preserve the Celtic traditions in Nova Scotia.[75] During his presidency (1944–54), an ambitious proposal was made to create a Gaelic Folklore Archive at St.F.X.[76] It was also during his administration that the Liberal Premier, Angus L. MacDonald, a champion of Scottish tradition in Nova Scotia,[77] was approached by Sir James Dunn, a leading industrialist and another Celtic enthusiast, with an offer to resign the premiership and fill at St.F.X. a proposed chair of Celtic studies at Dunn's expense.[78] It seems that the idea for such a chair originated with the premier, and apparently, at Somers's invitation, he planned to fill it, but he died beforehand.[79] However, "Angus L." did acquire $5000 from the MacDonald Tobacco Company to encourage student research on the early history of the Scots in Nova Scotia,[80] and he also recommended that a new library at St.F.X., which would bear his name, call its main reading room "the Hall of the Clans."[81]

President Somers was enthusiastic about the idea of Celtic studies and believed such a program would be popular. In 1957 he wrote, "St.F.X. is more indebted, probably than any university in Canada, to the Celts and especially to those who come from the Highlands of Scotland. This university was founded by a great Highlander and through the years its leadership and support have come to a great degree from the Scottish people."[82] Somers was able to hire Major C.I.N. MacLeod, a Gaelic-speaking native and Presbyterian of Dornie, Kintail, Ross-Shire, Scotland, who had been educated at the Universities of Glasgow and Edinburgh. MacLeod had come in 1949 as a Gaelic lecturer to the Gaelic College in St Ann's, Cape Breton. However, from 1950 to 1958 he served as Gaelic advisor to the Nova Scotia

C.I.N. MacLeod,
professor of Celtic studies 1958–77

department of education.[83] At St.F.X. MacLeod was named associate professor of Celtic studies; he continued the courses in Scottish Gaelic, added new ones in Celtic history and literature, published about eight books which dealt with the Gaelic language and Celtic literature, and instructed in piping.[84] Until his sudden death in June 1977, he would remain the mainstay of the department and a "colourful figure" who embellished many formal university functions with his expert piping.[85] His department's offerings remained of interest to a minority of students.

Faculty Expansion and Laicization

No expansion of enrolments, programs, and facilities at St.F.X. during the 1950s would have been possible without a parallel development of the faculty. President Somers sweated at this task, both convincing the board to allow for more hirings and finding or developing[86] qualified people to bring on staff.[87] In 1950–51 fifty-two professors composed the faculty; by 1960–61 there were ninety-one. Women faculty numbers climbed from one to fourteen; most employed were sisters. Some of those hired in the 1950s would have long and prominent careers at St.F.X.: Rev. Edo Gatto (philosophy), Rev. Andrew Hogan (Latin/economics), Sister Mary Byrne (music), Sister Catherine MacNeil (home economics), Randall Cormier (geology), Walter Kontak, William Woodfine, and Rev. Philip Mifflen (economics), Rev. Gregory MacKinnon (religion), Sister Carmel Losier and Rev. Murdoch MacLean (education), Sister Marion Power and John T. Sears (commerce), Etalo A. Secco (chemistry), and Antonio Olmos-Weingartshofer (physics).

Somers's recruiting efforts were hampered by financial restraint, the isolation of Antigonish from the larger urban centres, and the lack of affordable housing. Traditionally, St.F.X. had partially resolved the problem of its low, unappealing salaries by hiring priest-professors, by giving them room and board on campus, and then by expecting them to be satisfied with minimal wages. In 1956 the administration increased the priest-professors' annual salary scale by $100 to between $500 and $800 depending on years of service.[88] Most of the lay professors were then earning annual salaries of $3000 to $4500. However, during the 1950s no inexhaustible supply of qualified priests was available to meet the need for new faculty, especially in the sciences. Somers had to compete with the needs of the parishes, which grew in number from eighty-five to eighty-nine between 1953 and 1959,[89] and with Bishop John R. MacDonald's need for priests to undertake his many new projects.[90] The St.F.X. demand far outstripped the diocesan supply.

Therefore President Somers went searching for more and more lay faculty. The result was an inexorable and irreversible trend of faculty laicization. In 1951 nineteen lay professors were on staff; by 1961 there were forty-nine, 46 per cent of the total faculty. In that year alone, thirteen laymen were appointed and only three priests.[91] Because Somers wanted to retain the lay staff he had, as well as to lure new ones to St.F.X., he became solicitous for their circumstances. In 1958 he professed, "The matter of professors' salaries has been foremost in my mind since I became president"; he claimed to have raised lay salaries by 50 per cent over four years, yet acknowledged they remained below the norm found outside the Maritimes.[92] That same year he adopted a recommendation of a faculty committee on public housing to provide mortgages for lay faculty using university funds.[93] By 1967 sixteen faculty members had been helped to build their own homes.[94] Somers also gained in 1958 the unanimous agreement of the lay faculty for an improved pension plan.[95] In spite of these improvements, he shared a predicament faced by other Maritime universities. The president of Acadia University, Watson Kirkconnell, put it this way: "The raiding of Nova Scotia's faculties by the more affluent universities of the other nine provinces has already begun and replacements are increasingly difficult to secure in the light of our lower salary range."[96]

Professionalization of the Lay Faculty
The increase of lay staff during the 1950s led to the professionalization of the lay faculty, symbolized by the formation on campus of a chapter of the Canadian Association of University Teachers (CAUT). This national association had been formed in 1951 so that the Canadian professorate could improve its employment conditions and status in the post–Second World War period of rapidly expanding enrolments and surging inflation. CAUT organizers believed a professional association, rather than militant unionization, would be most compatible with Canadian university life and their own professional status.[97] University administrators generally shared their concerns. In 1956 St.F.X. remained one of the few Canadian universities without a local association of CAUT. Therefore in 1957 the faculty formed one to promote "the welfare of the university and its academic staff."[98] They called their new organization the St.F.X. Association of University Teachers (STFXAUT). It adopted a constitution and elected a slate of officers with professor Walter Kontak of economics the first president. The priest-professors remained apart from the association; the bishop established their salary levels and pension arrangements.[99] President Somers firmly supported the new association at St.F.X.

The early concerns of the STFXAUT centred on salaries, sabbaticals, fringe benefits, and rank and tenure. Toward the close of the decade, CAUT examined the salaries of university teachers in all the Atlantic provinces. Its report concluded that the economic lot of professors in the region had deteriorated rapidly in relation to general academic salaries elsewhere; the institutions of eastern Canada, CAUT predicted, faced the possibility of "a mounting exodus of their underpaid staffs to the scarcely lush but certainly greener fields of Central and Western Canada."[100] In December 1959, the STFXAUT requested that "the faculty scale at St Francis Xavier University be raised to and *maintained* at the median level of faculty salaries in Canadian universities."[101] Thereafter a steady rise in faculty salaries occurred through the 1960s.[102] The STFXAUT also obtained a clear statement on sabbatical leave and a full waiver of tuition for the dependents of St.F.X. employees.[103] Moreover, it convinced the administration in 1959 to establish the academic qualifications and experience required for the four ranks of lecturer and assistant, associate, and full professor.[104] St.F.X. rationalized its rank, tenure, and promotion provisions in 1964 when the STFXAUT accepted a revised report heavily influenced by CAUT regulations. The provisions, apparently agreed to by the administration, established the criteria for appointment and promotion (academic credentials, teaching experience and ability, scholarship, and exceptional service), recommended the formation of a committee on promotions, set forth the principles and purposes governing tenure, identified specific grounds for dismissal, and clarified two types of appointment: temporary and permanent.[105] While the provisions governing these issues were undergirded by legitimate concerns for quality, fairness, security, and academic freedom, they eroded the authority of the administration over the lay faculty. The president in 1964, Dr Malcolm MacLellan, saw the implications of the new provisions, and wanted at least to preserve the right to dismiss faculty "who, after due warning, persist in teaching or acting in a manner which is contrary to the aims and objectives of the university."[106] His suggestion was not accepted; neither did St.F.X. retain the explicit right to hire on the additional basis of the religious, philosophical, or educational commitments of prospective faculty. Thus the president's ability to form a cohesive institution dedicated to furthering his own vision of education was lessened and the conditions established for increasing philosophical and educational pluralism at St.F.X. The increase of lay faculty also decreased the control of the bishop-chancellor over the institution, since lay professors, in contrast to priest-professors, owed no direct allegiance to the bishop of the diocese.[107]

A Changing Mandate
The trends of faculty laicization and professionalization, along with rising enrolments, appeals for financial support to government and

industry, and the expansion of the sciences, further altered the mandate of the university. Lay faculties' daily concerns were not the objectives of the church but the advancement of both their disciplines and their careers. At best these had been secondary concerns for the priest-professors, who were priests first and professors second. Professionalization reinforced among the lay faculty a sense of identification with the wider university teaching profession and especially with other practitioners of their own disciplines. Such shifts in identity and loyalties among the faculty gradually altered the institutional ethos.

On 18 December 1959 Bishop John R. MacDonald died suddenly in his Antigonish residence. He had led the diocese for nearly ten years and at a rather hurried pace.[108] The diocesan historian wrote, "In the work of the Diocese, Bishop MacDonald set and maintained a pace which exhausted some of his subordinates and finally took its toll of his own health."[109] With his passing, President Somers lost a close friend and St.F.X. lost a great champion, for, as bishop of the diocese and chancellor of the university, he had taken a close and keen interest in its advancement. Although a conservative churchman in doctrinal and ecclesiastical matters, he had been especially interested in social issues throughout his long priestly career. As a young priest in the 1920s, Bishop MacDonald had been a leading participant in the rural and industrial conferences, and had strongly supported the formation of an extension department at St.F.X., the setting up of Xavier Junior College in Sydney, and the establishment of the Coady International Institute. Pending Rome's appointment of a new bishop, Father Joseph N. MacNeil administered the diocese (18 December 1959 to 10 August 1960).

Somers's Presidency Challenged

During Father MacNeil's interim administration, Dr Somers completed his six-year term as president of St.F.X. He received a severe blow about then, one which had been flexing for some time, when a number of the priest-professors at St.F.X. petitioned that he not be reappointed for a second term. Most likely a combination of factors, which had increased in significance through the 1950s, explain this unusual move by those St.F.X. priests who appeared alienated from Somers and generally demoralized. Somers's personality was undoubtedly difficult: he was cool and aloof, except with a few intimates, and appeared to be part of a developing "administrative elite."[110] Moreover, some believed he acted in a high-handed fashion and failed to communicate and consult.[111] In addition, before the very eyes of the faculty, he had been redefining the university by a massive program of expansion, by bolstering the sciences, by wooing the corporations, by hiring lay faculty in unprecedented numbers, and by working conscientiously on their behalf. The so-called "Priests' Revolt" in 1960, although a quiet affair, did not serve to strengthen relations between the priests and lay faculty, who had not been consulted about the move against Somers.[112] Neither did it succeed in ridding the institution of its president or in resolving the issues forthrightly. A new bishop was installed at Antigonish on 10 August 1960. Rev. William E. Power was a forty-four-year-old native of Montreal.[113] He asked Somers to remain as president for one more year, and then, in June 1961, at the bishop's request and after a consultative vote of the faculty, Somers reluctantly agreed to a further three-year term.[114]

Constitutional Adjustments

The vast changes at St.F.X. during Somers's presidential tenure demanded revisions to the act of incorporation and the constitution. Even before Somers became president, St.F.X. had made several important post-war adjustments. By 1952 the St.F.X. administration included a university council composed of university officials and two elected faculty representatives. The council's responsibilities included advising the president, formulating disciplinary policy, acting as a final court of appeal in disciplinary matters, and recommending to faculty candidates for honorary degrees.[115] Authorities made several important innovations in 1953: the faculty were given the right to have three representatives on the board of governors, three of the laymen elected by the diocesan priests to the board had to be representative of farming, fishing, and labour,[116] the heads of XJC and the extension department became *ex officio* board members, and the teaching staff was divided into three departmental groups – the humanities, the natural and applied sciences, and the social sciences and commerce.[117]

In 1956 the St.F.X. constitution again came under scrutiny. An amended act of incorporation (1957) and a revised constitution were the results. The constitutional revision was largely driven by the expansion of the sciences and the eccentricity of the departmental groups arrangement. In place of this latter set-up, the faculty accepted (twenty-three for and fifteen against), after extensive discussion, a new division of the faculty into arts and sciences.[118] This faculty reorganization was undoubtedly the most important provision in the constitution of 1959. However, the revisionists made other important provisions: faculty representation on the board had to include two laymen; the president was granted the right to designate departments and appoint department heads;[119] the president could appoint vice-presidents and deans of faculties; and the university council was expanded and charged with the planning and coordination of key phases of university life, i.e, expansion, enrolment, training and recruitment of faculty, discipline, honorary degree candidates, and recommendations for curricular changes.[120]

The new constitution both revealed and promoted the increasing complexity of St.F.X. The division of the faculty into arts and sciences required the appointment now of two deans instead of a single dean of studies. The first dean of science was also the first lay administrator at St.F.X. Dr John J. MacDonald, a graduate of St.F.X., had been a professor of chemistry since 1949 and would eventually occupy several prominent administrative posts before retiring in 1991.[121] Already in 1958 Somers had needed to reduce the rigours of his office by appointing an executive vice-president.[122] In 1960, after the death of Rev. Michael MacKinnon, he appointed Rev. Cyril H. Bauer executive vice-president in charge of the "internal, current, academic and business administration of the university."[123] Like MacDonald, Father Bauer would have a long career of distinguished service to St.F.X., working quietly in the administrative trenches of the expanding institution and receiving little public recognition. That same year the board of governors also formalized the practice of appointing an executive committee to attend to matters of an "emergent nature" and to carry out the instructions of the board.[124] Other new university offices, such as the offices of placement and development, likewise showed the growth of St.F.X.'s administration.[125]

President Somers's Exit
President Somers retired from St.F.X. on 30 June 1964 at the age of sixty-two. His contributions, spanning a thirty-six-year career at the university, were substantial.[126] Along with his predecessor, Dr Nicholson, and his successor, Dr MacLellan, Somers ranks as one of the chief architects of the modern St.F.X. With the aid of many competent and dedicated staff, he was able to expand the campus with impressive new buildings, bolster the sciences, multiply the number of lay staff and advance their conditions of employment, and increase the financial resources of the institution. Furthermore, during his term the constitution was updated, the faculty was reorganized into arts and sciences, and a professional association of lay faculty was formed.

Dr Somers's contributions to higher education extended far beyond his work at St.F.X.; neither did they end with his retirement from the university. While at St.F.X., he had remained keen about educational developments both nationally and internationally.[127] In 1958 he had become a director of the National Conference of Canadian Universities, and from 1958 to 1961 the national chairman of the Canadian Universities Foundation established to distribute federal funding to

Dr John J. MacDonald, professor of chemistry
and first dean of science

Rev. Cyril H. Bauer, professor of modern
languages, dean of studies, first dean of arts,
and executive vice-president

Canadian universities. From 1961 to 1962 he had been appointed the first national chairman of the Canadian University Service Overseas (CUSO).[128] His major post–St.F.X. contribution, though, was his role as a leading founder and first executive director of the Association of Atlantic Universities (AAU), the first regional voluntary association of universities in Canada. Beginning in 1961 at the instigation of Archbishop Berry of Halifax, several Catholic college officials from the region had occasionally met to discuss ways of cooperating.[129] Soon other universities joined the discussions; eventually eleven universities formed in 1964 an association of Atlantic universities.[130] It aimed to help coordinate higher education in the Atlantic provinces, to protect high academic standards in a period of escalating costs, and to avoid duplication of facilities and courses of study.[131] The permanent secretariat was located in Halifax, and there Dr Somers became the founding executive director in 1964.[132] That Dr Somers had attained the status of a statesmen of higher education by the 1960s was symbolized by the six honorary doctorates he received from Canadian universities between 1961 and 1969.[133]

Somers had overseen the growth and transition of St.F.X. from a small diocesan, clerically dominated liberal arts college toward a larger, more professionalized, quasi-denominational public university. Its administration followed the lead of other universities which "enhanced their social and economic relevance by engaging increasingly in scientific research, by providing degrees in such fields as agriculture, and by teaching business and commerce."[134] St.F.X.'s broadened mandate and changing identity resulted from larger numbers of students drawn from a wider constituency, their changing program interests, the strengthening of the sciences, the cultivation of non-diocesan sources of funding, and the gradual laicization and professionalization of the faculty. Through the 1950s and 1960s St.F.X. was likewise altered by its endeavours beyond the campus in Antigonish. President Somers had been deeply involved in these projects; in fact, he was largely responsible for initiating one of them which, in a way, brought the world to the doorstep of Antigonish.

·16·

Campus Extensions, 1954–70

"For the people" had been an important emphasis in the work of St.F.X. from its beginning. The extension department and Xavier Junior College best symbolized this Xaverian sense of responsibility for serving the whole constituency of eastern Nova Scotia. By 1960 there would be another offspring added to the existing Xaverian family of institutions. Through the 1950s and 1960s the development of these incarnations of St.F.X. would be fascinating in themselves; moreover the interplay between them would prove intriguing. The extension department would experience a rather prolonged sense of anticlimax in its adult education mission; the junior college would rapidly grow to adolescence and struggle to sally forth more independently; and the latest addition, the Coady International Institute, would be born and learn to stand on its own.

Origins of the Coady International Institute
Four years before his retirement, President Somers announced, on 2 December 1959, the eve of St.F.X. Day, the inauguration of the Coady International Institute.[1] The announcement signalled the administration's decision to formalize an ambitious international "extension of the St.F.X. Extension Department."[2] From then on at St.F.X., "for the people" would include working for the betterment of the people not only in the Canadian Maritime provinces but also in the less developed regions of the world. It was a lofty new undertaking, a substantial challenge from every angle, and an additional burden for an institution then wrestling to meet its existing responsibilities.

The idea of an international institute to promote development work in less developed countries was nothing new in 1959. Clyde Nunn, the founding manager of Antigonish radio station CJFX and a stalwart member of the St.F.X. board of governors, remembered Coady boasting to him in the 1930s: "Nunn, one day you will see a great building on this campus, and over its main doorway there will be the superscription

'International House!'"[3] By the conclusion of his book *Masters of Their Own Destiny* (1939), Coady could no longer contain his expansive vision for cooperation; he urged the creation of "a people's research institute" which would be "international in scope and application."[4] In addition, as more and more internationals appeared in small-town Antigonish in order to get a glimpse of the extension department in action and meet its chief apostle, the extension leaders were forced to respond to their demands for information and advice. With just a touch of exasperation, Coady wrote, two years after the war, to his close confidant, Father Michael Gillis, "We have definitely decided that our only hope here is to raise about a million or more, build an International House, and staff the place with competent professors to take care of courses, short and long, for people from everywhere."[5] However, neither St.F.X. nor Coady found any million-dollar pot of gold, in spite of considerable searching,[6] so the extension staff had to struggle on, supplying the mounting requests for help as best they could.

The international demands proved relentless. The assistant director of extension, Alexander Laidlaw, was asked in 1949 by a United Nations organization to address a conference in Costa Rica on agriculture and rural education. He found Latin American delegates keenly interested in the Antigonish Movement and returned firmly convinced that St.F.X. had much to offer the Latin American republics.[7] During the 1950s, both the Canadian government (through various technical assistance programs)[8] and other agencies[9] got further into foreign aid and sponsored a stream of international visitors to Canada, some of whom studied at St.F.X.[10] Well over one hundred internationals (excluding students from the United States) registered at St.F.X. during the decade.[11] In addition, requests came for help overseas in places such as Africa, India, South America, and the Caribbean.[12] Evidently, many people in underdeveloped nations found attractive the grass-roots methods of the Antigonish Movement, which appeared inexpensive, effective, supportive of democracy, and self-sustaining.[13]

The interest of the western democracies in international development work was heightened by the atmosphere of cold war between the east and the west, and the fear of a world-wide expansion of Communism. Coady was especially concerned about Central and South America. In 1956 he wrote, "I am saddened to say that I am forced to the conclusion that South America will go Communist. We could save it but we won't."[14] Extension, he was convinced, had the "formula" which could save the world from Communism; and eastern Canada could be "a great social laboratory for the undeveloped parts of the world."[15] Later in the 1960s, fund-raising for the Coady Institute

333

would appeal directly to the fear of Communism; one brochure declared that, by then, it had "blunted the thrust of Communist subversion and shored up the ramparts of free enterprise democracy."[16] The Diocese of Antigonish became increasingly interested in Latin and South America during the 1950s, and especially so in 1960 when Pope John XXIII entrusted to the hierarchies of Canada and the United States a special responsibility "to use every possible means to increase the number of priests and militant Catholics in these countries."[17] Bishop John R. MacDonald had visited Panama in 1955 and was anxious to help his Latin and South American colleagues.[18] He had also successfully urged the Knights of Columbus to aid priests from economically underdeveloped countries to study the Antigonish Movement.[19]

In late March 1959, President Somers suggested to Bishop John R. MacDonald that the former bishop's residence, situated immediately to the southeast of the campus, be taken over by St.F.X. and used as an "International House for Priests" or an "International Institute or Coady Institute." He also proposed rudimentary organizational steps, such as the appointment of a director, the recruitment of full-time staff, and the offering of special courses. His letter declared, "Accordingly, this service to the Church, and we believe it to be a most important service, must be placed on a fully organized basis, with residence, special courses to suit the needs of the students, and with individual attention that only a full time staff can give."[20] The bishop was predictably enthusiastic; however, his former residence was not made available. Neither was the plan realized to have foreign priests study separately under a new director, and laypersons work under the supervision of Executive Vice-President Msgr Michael MacKinnon.[21] MacKinnon died suddenly at the age of fifty-three on 16 October. Actually, two other pioneers of extension work died that year before the proposed international institute appeared – Dr Coady on 28 July and Bishop John R. MacDonald himself on 18 December. So, in the fall, after the St.F.X. board of governors embraced Somers's suggestion to establish the "Coady International Institute" (the Coady) in memory of the late Dr Coady, the founding director faced the full task of providing residence space and the entire training program for both clerical and lay students from overseas.[22]

The Founding Director
The founding director, whose appointment Bishop John R. MacDonald supported, was the Very Rev. Francis J. Smyth. He was a forty-two-year-old Sydney native and a St.F.X. alumnus (1941) who had been a member of the St.F.X. staff (1946–51) and a pioneer faculty member

Msgr Francis J. Smyth, first director of the
Coady International Institute 1959–70

of Xavier Junior College (1951–53). In 1955 his graduate studies in sociology at Notre Dame University, Indiana were interrupted when Bishop John R. MacDonald appointed him to work for the Canadian Catholic Conference, Ottawa, as director of the English-language section of the social action department.[23] He held this position until his appointment as director of the Coady on 1 February 1960.[24] Smyth's long-standing interest and experience in social action issues, along with other leadership abilities, fitted him well for the daunting new assignment. He was charged with the responsibility for financing a permanent building for the Coady, for finding scholarship assistance for the students, for creating a centre which could handle requests for information and assistance from overseas, and for developing a specialized training program in social leadership.[25] The founding director had a lofty conception of the importance of his task,[26] and convened a number of committees – executive, local and international – composed of an impressive array of talent to help him plan the program and establish international contacts.[27]

From the start, Smyth appeared untiring in his efforts, especially among the Catholic hierarchy, to gain support for the new institute.[28] Almost immediately he struck gold with Richard Cardinal Cushing, archbishop of Boston. Cardinal Cushing, an admirer of Bishop John R. MacDonald and recipient of a St.F.X. honorary in 1950,[29] pledged $200,000 for a priests' residence in memory of the recently deceased bishop of Antigonish.[30] The gift was a marvellous boost for the new program; it financed the largest part of a new four-storey brick building completed in 1961 and located, at Smyth's insistence, on the south side of the campus next to the proposed Trans-Canada bypass.[31] Actually, Smyth had ambitious plans for a complex of three buildings; however, at that time only enough money for one was obtainable.[32] The opening of the Bishop John R. MacDonald Building on 17 October 1961 marked the official opening of the Coady International Institute.[33]

The Coady Program and Pioneer Staff
The original Coady program was succinctly described by the college calendar as "essentially an extension to the international field of the traditional philosophy and techniques of the Antigonish Movement."[34] Smyth wanted the new institute to honour the Xaverian extension tradition by being "as orthodox as possible."[35] Because the Coady's constituency embraced the world, religion was kept low-key, although lectures in Catholic social teachings were delivered to those who wanted them.[36] For the previous two decades, St.F.X. had offered both a short and a longer course in social leadership.[37] The Coady staff adopted the substance of these courses and compressed the new

diploma course in social leadership into the university's eight-month academic year.[38] The program involved classroom and library work, discussions, and supervised field work. The subject matter embraced the philosophy and principles of cooperation, cooperative service organizations, economics, management, communications, and community development. The first lecturers decided that the students should write, as a culmination of their work, a major paper "dealing with the definition and solution of a major problem of their area in light of the information derived from the course."[39] Out of the need for flexibility, practicality, and adjustable admission standards, the social leadership course was made a non-credit program.[40] The Coady also offered a short certificate course in adult education each summer.[41]

It was a great advantage for the new Coady project that it could draw on the extensive faculty resources of the university to operate its innovative program. The founding staff included only four full-time persons: Very Rev. Francis J. Smyth, director, J. Frank Glasgow, assistant director, George Wicks, registrar and house manager, and Ellen Arsenault, secretary. Glasgow had been an inspector of schools in Cape Breton, Wicks was an Englishman experienced in international refugee work who had been Smyth's assistant in the social action department, Ottawa, and Arsenault had been Dr Coady's personal secretary from 1947 to 1959. The various lecturers were largely drawn from the extension and social science departments of the university. They included people such as Rev. Andrew Hogan, Walter Kontak, Dr Daniel MacCormack, and Norman Riley. None of the staff, full- or part-time, were novices in the work of adult education and economic cooperation. Smyth was fortunate to be able to draw on such a fund of experience and talent for his new institute.

Financing the Coady
Smyth's fund-raising duties were burdensome, for university funds were limited and his institute had no founding endowment. Nonetheless, he did succeed in securing substantial annual scholarship assistance for the students. Through the decade the largest amount came from the federal Department of External Aid; however, Smyth also acquired significant assistance from Misereor, a German bishops' fund set up after the war to sponsor international development work. Misereor was administered from Aachen, Germany and would faithfully support the Coady for the next thirty-one years. Lesser contributors included the Canadian Catholic Conference, the Knights of Columbus, the Catholic Women's League, the Canadian Catholic organization Development and Peace, and the Coady International Associates.[42] This latter organization was the brain-child of Malcolm F. MacNeil,

337

a member of the St.F.X. board of governors and a businessman resident in Watertown, Massachusetts. A small number of dedicated St.F.X. alumni undertook the work of the associates, canvassing other alumni, industry, and the foundations.[43] By 1970 it had made important contributions to three new facilities at the Coady. In the mid-1960s climate of ecumenicity, two prominent Jews from Montreal also became firm supporters of the Coady and helped it financially.[44] At this time, Smyth urged the need for an endowment fund to place the Coady on a more stable financial basis. Bernard and Louis Bloomfield generously helped plan a $2 million campaign.[45] Through its first decade, the Coady acquired over $1.6 million in donations for scholarships and buildings.[46]

The Coady Students
The students who joined the Xaverian family at the Coady were literally a colourful group, representing a multitude of nations. Staff admitted men and women who had a working knowledge of English and experience or interest in helping their people "through a democratic program of self-help."[47] By 1968 Smyth described the types who attended: "All of our graduates are associated in one way or another with community development – missionaries, teachers, youth workers, nurses, co-operative employees, government administrators in departments of co-operation, education, agriculture, fisheries and extension generally."[48] Enrolments climbed steadily between 1960 and 1965, and then levelled off at around eighty to ninety annually. Between 1959 and 1970, 753 students had registered in the eight-month social leadership program and 491 in the summer short courses. These represented ninety countries with the largest proportions coming from Africa, Asia, Canada, Latin America, and the Caribbean. Eighty per cent of the Coady students were male and nearly 30 per cent were clerics and sisters. About one-third of the students of the 1960s had to live off-campus in the town; on-campus residence space was severely restricted. However, St.F.X. opened a twenty-nine-room International House in 1965 and provided an additional sixty-six rooms with a large four-storey brick residence, constructed in 1969 and named in honour of the lately deceased benefactor, Malcolm F. MacNeil.[49]

The Coady's international students gave a cosmopolitan flavour to the town and campus. Sometimes they could be seen dressed in native costume, and the lack of accommodation on campus required many of them to mingle closely with the townspeople. The internationals often faced special problems of language, finance, climate, and homesickness. For many of them who had never travelled outside their native lands, the overseas trip to Nova Scotia was the first trauma. Then

First class, Coady International Institute, 1959–60

Coady students in native costume

there was the intimidating, indeed, sometimes overwhelming, experience of being in a strange land which had a harsh climate and among strangers of alien customs. However, the Coady staff were imbued with a sense of missionary zeal for their project, and people like Sister Marie Michael and George Wicks and his wife, Nora, made outstanding efforts, far beyond the call of duty, to help the students adjust.[50] Moreover, Smyth had arranged in 1961 for the presence at the Coady of three Marthas – Sisters Justina, Daniel Marie, and Donalda – a community well known at St.F.X. for their sensitivity, hospitality, and motherly care. A folk school at the beginning of each year helped to develop rapidly a sense of family.[51] The Coady staff tried to handle prudently potential student conflicts rooted in religious, nationalistic, ethnic, and tribal divisions.[52] A tiny sampling of names of those who came to the Coady between 1960 and 1970 reveals the cultural diversity and richness of the student body: Lim Eng Chuan (Taiping, Malaya), Abbas K. Shyjah (Bagdad, Iraq), Rev. Noel A. Garcia, SJ (Nicaragua), Vincent Kagambirwe (Uganda), Sister Ola Evaristus (Ireland), Ramon Almont (Dominican Republic), and Alexius Kerketta (India).[53] Such students grappled at the Coady with the "Antigonish Way" in adult education and then returned to their homelands, often inspired with high hopes and elaborate plans for social change through economic cooperation.[54] Their hopes found expression in their major essays which bore titles such as "Nyasaland Yesterday, Today and Tomorrow," "Adult Education: The Key to Progress and Prosperity," and "Weep No More, My Beloved Mother Basutoland."[55]

Mounting Demands

The Coady staff's primary work was the eight-month diploma course in social leadership. However, requests came for direct assistance overseas which they also tried to satisfy. Over the years, the director established broad international contacts with church and government agencies. Both the Coady and extension were closely associated through the 1960s with the establishment and work of an extension department at Pius XII University College in Basutoland, Africa.[56] Early in the decade, some of the institute staff gave a series of lectures in Rome, and in 1966 Smyth travelled on a UNESCO fellowship to India, Ceylon, Malaysia, the Philippines, Korea, Formosa, Hong Kong, and Japan in order to explain the Antigonish Movement.[57] Coady personnel also assisted with projects in Tanzania, Venezuela, Ireland, Antigua, Hong Kong, the Philippines, Costa Rica, and Ecuador.[58] Through both the work of the staff overseas and the Coady graduates, the institute established centres of influence in many parts of the less developed world.[59]

Institutional Interrelations

While the Coady's work continued through the 1960s, there remained an undercurrent of dissatisfaction among some St.F.X. administrators and faculty about the institute's relations to both the extension department and the university in general. Some Xaverians expressed scepticism about the separation of the two extension programs, both organizationally and physically, and the alleged lack of cooperation between them. Smyth had recommended to the president in 1960 that the Coady program be a "distinct institute" and that its director be a vice-president and *ex officio* member of the board of governors.[60] President Somers stated in 1961 that "St.F.X. must present to the world one program of adult education and end all reports of disunity within our ranks."[61] St.F.X. experimented with suggested ways to unify or bring the extension and Coady into closer collaboration. In 1961 the university had the remarkable need, apparently, for three vice-presidents: an executive vice-president, a vice-president and director of the Coady International Institute, and a vice-president and director of extension. That year the president concluded that one official should be finally responsible for both the domestic and the international phases of extension work; hence, he appointed Rev. Joseph N. MacNeil director of extension and vice-president for adult education.[62] However, this directive was never implemented; Smyth and MacNeil observed "an unspoken, unwritten entente," and the Coady remained independent.[63] A committee appointed in 1965 to examine the interrelations among the Coady, the extension, and the social sciences at St.F.X. again recommended that definite advantages would accrue if the two programs were unified under a single director, but to no avail.[64] The Coady's director remained convinced that notions of division caused by his institute existed more in the minds of "outsiders" than in the real affairs of the university.[65] Moreover, he believed that others at St.F.X. bore some responsibility for not being better informed and better informing the faculty and students of its work.[66] The interrelations among these programs remained a topic for discussion in 1969–70, but both phases of extension work at St.F.X. – the international and the domestic – would ultimately remain organizationally and physically separate.[67]

Achievements of the First Decade

The Coady celebrated its tenth anniversary in 1970, and that same year its founding director retired. By then Smyth, who had visited fifty-three countries during his directorship and was undoubtedly the "most travelled man of the St.F.X. staff," had concluded that the institute needed "someone fresh, with new ideas and a new orientation."[68] Moreover, the constant travel up and down the globe had taken its toll on his health, and he was not accorded extra help needed both to direct the Coady and to raise funds on behalf of the university.[69] Smyth must be credited with the drive and ambition to build the institution from the ground up. He had been its tireless fund-raiser and persuasive promoter. Of course, he had the expert help of both a dedicated staff, which had grown from four in 1960 to about eighteen full-time teaching, administrative, and secretarial members, along with the rich faculty resources of the university.[70]

By 1970, over twelve hundred internationals had been trained in the Coady programs. A study of Coady graduates in 1968 discovered that most had been employed by governments, cooperatives, churches, universities, and voluntary organizations. They worked most frequently in rural communities addressing problems of poverty, illiteracy, rudimentary technologies, exploitation, unemployment, and health. Many of them were applying the Antigonish Movement techniques – study clubs, short courses, and public meetings – and its philosophy to local problems. However, the role of government in other countries, as well as economic and social conditions, differed greatly from eastern Nova Scotia. These factors at times hindered the work of the Coady graduates and made it less effective than it might otherwise have been.[71] Nonetheless, a demand continued for the Coady program through the following decades, while the institute also evolved greatly in philosophy and approach.[72] The Coady International Institute has been a small yet high-profile part of St.F.X. since its founding in 1960. It is arguably the most distinctive and visionary work ever begun by the university. While it gave St.F.X. a presence on the international scene, it also gave the international scene a very obvious presence on the campus of a small university in eastern Nova Scotia.

St.F.X. Extension in a New Era
The oldest and most widely acclaimed St.F.X. campus extension during the 1950s was the extension department itself. Since the war it had confronted circumstances vastly altered from those of the 1930s. Now it shared the field of economic and social development with numerous other educational agencies – the Nova Scotia Credit Union League, the Nova Scotia Cooperative Union, the Adult Education Division of the Nova Scotia Department of Education, the Nova Scotia Housing Commission, the labour unions, the farm forums, and the *Maritime Co-operator*. Some of these agencies were extension's very own offspring. In the economic field, formidable new competitors, such as the Dominion stores and Simpsons-Sears, challenged the consumer cooperatives. Government was constructing the welfare state, rapidly

developing bureaucratized and centralized structures, engaging in state planning on an unprecedented scale, and offering state aid for development projects. The economy was experiencing continued rapid growth, and television and local organizations competed with the study clubs. Carmen Miller claims that after the war, "in radio, as elsewhere, service, social concern, and criticism gave place to reassurance, consumerism, and escapism."[73] The economic depression and localism of the 1930s, which had made many people in eastern Nova Scotia highly receptive to the extension program, were history. The extension staff now faced the challenge of finding their way in a new era.

Review of Staff and Programs

Dr Coady's successor, Father Michael MacKinnon, directed the department from 1952 to 1958, although Coady himself loomed as a large presence in the immediate background. MacKinnon's staff included Alexander Laidlaw, associate director, directors of radio education, land settlement, rural education, and urban education, an agricultural consultant, a field supervisor, a librarian, and eleven field workers assigned to fisheries, labour, and cooperatives.[74] Rev. George Topshee directed the Sydney office of extension. Ex-miner Joseph Laben led the program in cooperative housing concentrated in the Cape Breton industrial region; by 1958, 763 families were living in cooperative housing groups.[75] Extension in 1954–55, using the federal department of fisheries annual grant, extended its fisheries field-work into western Nova Scotia and Charlotte County, New Brunswick; it also reported revived enthusiasm for cooperative methods among Victoria County fishermen in Cape Breton.[76] Unfortunately, the cooperative fish processing plants faced imposing difficulties after the war. For example, along New Brunswick's eastern shore twelve cooperative canneries closed between 1945 and 1956; only six remained in operation. Stiff competition from private firms, obsolete methods and equipment, and incompetent management appeared to be at the root of their demise.[77] The extension staff continued to offer short courses during the winter in Antigonish or in the field. The Sydney extension office worked closely with labour, promoted cooperative housing, conducted people's schools which involved a series of weekly classes in the industrial districts, a radio program over CJFX, and the distribution of relevant literature,[78] and ran programs over CJCB-TV. From 1950 extension occasionally organized rural and industrial conferences to generate ideas and enthusiasm for the Antigonish Movement.[79]

An event of significance for extension occurred in 1956 when existing regional cooperative wholesales in Antigonish and Cape Breton amalgamated to become Eastern Co-operative Services (ECS). Coady,

Extension office staff: Kay Desjardins (on left), first secretary in extension, 1931 and later editor of the *Maritime Co-operator*; Ellen Arsenault, Dr Coady's secretary, 1947–59 and then secretary to the director of the Coady

MacKinnon, and his director of rural education, John Chisholm, were strong proponents of the project, which was located close to Sydney. The plant, opened in September 1959, included administrative headquarters, a poultry processing plant, an egg grading station, fruit and vegetable grading and packing, and cold storage facilities. Chisholm, since coming on staff in 1954, had obtained support in eastern Nova Scotia for an ambitious agricultural program involving small fruits, vegetables, poultry, and hogs. An integrated wholesale marketing program was part of his agenda. In Coady's opinion, ECS was "the synthesis of all the things we have been working at in the past twenty-eight years."[80] Chisholm became general manager of the new organization, which did almost $5 million in business through its first year of operation.[81]

Unfortunately, the formation of ECS damaged relations between extension and the provincial department of agriculture. Coady had always acknowledged the important contribution that department had made to the success of extension work, so he hoped to retain good relations with its staff.[82] However, his successor, Father MacKinnon, failed to do so. One extension worker claimed that MacKinnon exhibited a "bulldozing fighting spirit" in his relations with the department of agriculture and a "disregard for the point of view of other institutions."[83] Perhaps his long experience on the tough Cape Breton labour scene had ill prepared him for the skilful diplomacy necessary to maintain positive inter-institutional relations. Anyway, Bishop John R. MacDonald, a keen supporter of extension work, was dissatisfied with his performance as director and in 1958 directed President Somers to replace him. Somers made MacKinnon executive vice-president of St.F.X., a new position apparently required by the "constantly increasing burden and ever diversifying character of the president's office."[84] As noted above, within two years he would die suddenly of a heart attack at the age of fifty-four.[85] Two years before MacKinnon was removed as director, the associate director, Alexander Laidlaw, left extension. Following the same path as his predecessor, A.B. MacDonald, Laidlaw became general secretary of the Co-operative Union of Canada and eventually obtained the stature of a national leader in cooperatives and adult education.[86]

Director MacKinnon Replaced

Bishop John R. MacDonald pressured President Somers to replace Msgr MacKinnon with Rev. John A. Gillis, a man who had potential for healing the rift between extension and the department of agriculture.[87] Gillis was a forty-seven-year-old native of New Waterford, Cape Breton who had limited experience with extension work. However, he had been associated, as Father Jimmy Tompkins's curate in Reserve Mines, with the first cooperative housing project in Nova Scotia, and had broad experience in rural and industrial parishes, where he had participated in cooperative activities among farmers, fishermen, and labourers.[88] Most recently, from 1956 to 1958, Father Gillis had competently managed, evidently to the satisfaction of his bishop, the local college farm, Mount Cameron. At Gillis's request, Mount Cameron Farm had come under the direct jurisdiction of the extension department. Before this the farm had been operated for about four years by the Priests of the Congregation of the Sacred Heart of Jesus, a Dutch order which had a strong heritage of teaching agriculture.[89] At the time of his appointment to the directorship of extension, Father Gillis had strong ties to the agricultural community through his work at Mount Cameron Farm and his membership on the boards of the Nova Scotia Co-operative Abattoir and the Nova Scotia Federation of Agriculture.

As the new director of extension in 1958, Gillis believed it was time for the department to reappraise its traditional program. Therefore he canvassed the key players in the department for their views on its work overall, and for recommendations about how extension could more effectively contribute to adult education and the cooperative movement in eastern Nova Scotia. In his reply, Coady railed against the results of exploitation by private-profit business and praised the fruits of the extension program of adult education and economic cooperation. He also warned Gillis of those enemies of the people who hoped to water down the extension philosophy. In his view, strategies would need to change occasionally, but never the fundamental philosophy. Coady vowed that if anyone interfered with the program of helping the people to own and control their own economic affairs, "it matters not who he is or what his position, we will fight him to the death."[90] Even though Coady had entered the final year of his life, he was still capable of considerable fire and passion. The gist of the other replies to Gillis's survey warned that he would alter fundamental extension policies at his own peril. Father Gillis apparently embraced the basics of the program; yet he hoped to update its approaches and provide more effective leadership in adult education.[91] To help revitalize extension, he hired Dr Remi Chiasson as associate director, a St.F.X. alumnus and inspector of schools in Cape Breton who had a strong interest in extension.

New Extension Programs

The extension staff, under Gillis's leadership, continued with extension's traditional programs in cooperative housing, consumer and producer cooperatives, labour education, fisheries, short courses, and conferences. They also undertook some new work. With funding from the department of Indian affairs, and after a request in 1957 from parish clergy, Rev. William Roach of the Sydney extension office began adult education work on native reservations. Since the Second World War, seven reservations had been established in eastern Nova Scotia – Membertou, Eskasoni, Whycocomagh, Barra Head, Nyanza, Afton, and Pictou Landing.[92] In 1959 Gillis hired a full-time field worker, E.W. Coldwell, to help organize the woodlot owners in the six eastern counties of Nova Scotia.[93] A Swedish firm, Stora Kopperberg, attracted by generous government inducements, constructed a pulp mill at the Strait of Canso in 1959 which precipitated the organizing effort. While an association of woodlot owners rapidly formed, it almost as rapidly vanished, a fate experienced by earlier organizations.[94] St.F.X. decided to get further involved with television in 1960 by sponsoring a station. It had established a precedent for media work with the founding of radio station CJFX in 1943. President Somers hoped the new TV station would make "a significant contribution" in "educational and cultural telecasts."[95] At the university's initiative, the Atlantic Television Company incorporated and struck an agreement with Cape Breton Broadcasters to provide the facilities and equipment in exchange for advertising rights. Unfortunately, CFXU-TV failed to fulfil its promise and in 1965 it was sold.

Resignation of a Troubled Director

Even more short-lived than the television station was Father Gillis's directorship of extension. From its start, his appointment had been unpopular, and he confronted pronounced opposition from some of his own staff. President Somers was unhappy with the bishop's selection of Gillis, and Somers and Gillis remained at loggerheads. Dr Coady predicted that Gillis would be "a great success" as head of extension, but Gillis claimed that Coady "waned hot and cold" in his outward attitude toward him.[96] Father George Topshee in the Sydney office complained that Gillis kept Sydney ill informed of policy decisions and did not "uproot our main cancer," which he believed was lack of teamwork.[97] Then there were also the criticisms about lack of appropriate cooperation with the newly established Coady International Institute.[98] Gillis's failure to support certain extension policies in agriculture and the fisheries, policies which he considered "untenable" and "rigid," also created resentment from the start.[99] In the face of these conflicts, he contemplated resigning more than once. Certain university people, he came to believe, were interested only in the university's public image and a whitewash of all extension problems. Finally, Gillis had registered dissatisfaction with the way Eastern Co-operative

Services had been founded and managed. In his view, "It was a furtive, panicky attempt to build something to show for extension's twenty-five year efforts in agriculture."[100] Apparently, Nova Scotia cooperative movement leaders were ignored in the planning and development of ECS, and agricultural representatives considered ECS an example of clerical domination – imposing a program on the people without their approval.[101]

Plagued by these and other distressing problems, Father Gillis resigned as director in the spring of 1961.[102] Although his leadership had been unpopular, he had maintained the traditional extension programs, had nurtured new ones among the natives and woodlot owners, and had worked "to consolidate existing co-operative enterprises and to co-ordinate [the] work with that of other agencies in the field."[103] He had also laboured successfully to bring two Prince Edward Island fisheries cooperatives into the United Maritime Fishermen, to establish a central cannery for the Maritimes, and to help form an abattoir in Halifax.[104]

Extension's Fourth Director

A young priest replaced Father Gillis in 1961: Father Joseph N. Mac-Neil, a native of Sydney and graduate of St.F.X. (1944). Most recently he had served as diocesan administrator, after the death of Bishop John R. MacDonald, and as pastor of St Ninian's Parish, Antigonish. Mac-Neil had limited experience with extension work and confessed that he undertook the directorship "with considerable fear and trepidation"; he thought there were others better qualified than himself.[105] Nonetheless, he was evidently a capable administrator who believed in the general philosophy of extension and the need for the department to adjust to changing circumstances. He reappointed the two associate directors, Dr Remi Chiasson to St.F.X. and Rev. George Topshee to Sydney. Between the two offices his staff numbered about thirteen full-time and eleven fisheries fieldworkers.[106] Perhaps because of the recent passing of several pioneers of extension – Dr Coady (1959), Msgr MacKinnon (1959), Bishop John R. MacDonald (1959), Dr Hugh ("Little Doc") MacPherson (1960), and Dr Daniel MacCormack (1961) – the university appointed an advisory board to extension, composed of people of long experience in the field. A new generation was assuming responsibility for the extension project; by 1969, out of twenty-five extension staff members, about twenty did not know personally the founding fathers of the Antigonish Movement – Dr Coady, Father Jimmy Tompkins, and A.B. MacDonald.[107]

During MacNeil's directorship, extension continued with its programs in the fisheries, rural development, labour education, credit

Rev. Joseph N. MacNeil,
director of extension 1961–69

unions, cooperatives, native community development, forestry, and housing. In addition, MacNeil promoted more research and data collection on regional problems, since he observed that much of the traditional work undertaken by extension had been assumed by other agencies. In 1964 he wrote, "Extension is firmly committed to the promotion of economic co-operation but its actual involvement, in certain circumstances, is tending toward participating in training programs and giving guidance in policy decisions."[108] He hoped to establish a research institute at St.F.X. which would employ sociologists and economists trained in community research and development.[109] In addition, he advocated the provision of a master's program in adult education,[110] a labour-management relations institute, and a residential program in adult education.[111] He harboured reservations about the type of education undertaken by the cooperatives and credit unions, believing it to be preoccupied with management techniques while neglecting philosophical principles.[112] During the mid-1960s, in the heady new climate of ecumenism, extension helped the Nova Scotia Agricultural College in Truro run Rural Clergy Institutes which aimed to further the resolution of rural problems. MacNeil observed in 1968, "Throughout the area one finds a great spirit of common purpose and a casting aside of old quarrels and prejudices."[113]

Social Changes and Program Adjustments
There emerged other developments of significance for MacNeil's extension department through the 1960s. The decade has been characterized as one of optimism and "egalitarian idealism." Wide-ranging development was undertaken, much of it funded by massive federal equalization revenues. Councils and development agencies sought economic salvation for the Atlantic provinces: APEC promoted the economic well-being of Atlantic Canada; the province completed the Canso Causeway in 1955; the Atlantic Development Board researched, advised, and distributed grants; and the Agriculture and Rural Development Act (ARDA) was instituted as a cost-sharing program to improve poor rural areas.[114] However, the number of people employed in the primary industries greatly decreased. In agriculture, fewer farmers cultivated larger farms. Inshore fishermen experienced decreasing catches, low incomes, and underemployment, while governments promoted and subsidized the offshore fishery.[115] Atlantic Canada witnessed a growing shift "to manufacturing, mining, construction, and public service employment."[116] These shifts had major implications for extension's traditional programs.

MacNeil saw the invasion of governments into Atlantic Canada's social and economic development as a confirmation of what extension had been doing since the 1930s. Yet he feared that civil servants were ignoring extension, which was a veteran in the field. He stated in 1964, "A major problem for Extension is that of adapting ourselves to this exuberant interest in the Atlantic Provinces by so many government departments and agencies."[117] As director, he stressed the need for governments to collaborate with extension and to exploit its expertise and experience. MacNeil did realize that collaboration could threaten extension's independence, its integrity, and its freedom to criticize. Yet isolation from government promised, in his view, to render extension obsolete and irrelevant. MacNeil's stress on collaboration allowed his department to influence government funding and policy decisions in the region.[118]

The Pressures of Prestige

During MacNeil's directorship, extension had continued to make useful contributions to the region's social and economic life; however, the department suffered a growing public image problem. People inevitably compared extension in the 1960s to the department's "glory days" of the 1930s and 1940s and found it wanting; to them, it appeared more and more a rather humdrum sideshow. MacNeil found frustrating the question: "What is Extension doing now?" and informed the St.F.X. board of governors in 1966: "it should be obvious that a great deal is being done." It was "unreasonable to expect the same public attention that was engendered in the Thirties and Forties when Extension was new and was such a dynamic force."[119] Such criticisms would persist long after MacNeil left to accept an ecclesiastical promotion in New Brunswick as bishop of Saint John.[120] Notwithstanding the irksome murmurs of criticism, his leadership had been effective. In contrast to his predecessors, Msgr Michael MacKinnon and Father John Gillis, he had revealed more diplomacy in his relations with staff and external agencies. His cooperation with government and other organizations had retained extension's presence and influence in the field of regional development. And finally, the director had maintained a strong staff, had granted them considerable freedom, and had backed worthy causes.[121]

MacNeil's replacement as director of extension, appointed 2 June 1969, was Rev. George Topshee; he had managed the Sydney office of extension since 1952. Topshee had concluded that extension, in light of the decline of traditional industries in the region, such as coal mining and fishing, should emphasize "educational upgrading and retraining of adult workers." Low-cost housing, he believed, along with community development projects would also help to raise the economic and social standards of the area.[122] Within one year of his appointment as director, the long-standing fisheries program, which had been funded by the federal government since the late 1930s, as well as work on the native reservations, came to an halt with the withdrawal of federal funding.[123] However, extension staff remained active in offering adult evening courses, fostering co-op housing, consulting with governments and cooperative organizations, educating labour, producing films and the People's School TV programs, and planning a graduate program in adult education. Although extension was required to terminate certain important programs, it adjusted to the changes, and Father Topshee continued as director through the following decade.[124]

The Growth of Xavier Junior College
Xavier Junior College (XJC) had been founded in 1951 by Dr Malcolm MacLellan, its first principal, as an extension of the St.F.X. campus designed to increase higher educational opportunities for the people of industrial Cape Breton. This offspring's subsequent astonishing growth in Sydney paralleled that of its parent institution in Antigonish. XJC rapidly became a vigorous member of the Xaverian family of institutions. Its story during the 1950s and 1960s is largely a story of struggle to provide adequate facilities and staff in order to satisfy the ever-increasing demands made upon it by the local urban-industrial community. Its growth would generate aspirations among both college and community members for an institution accorded greater educational scope and powers of self-determination. Its growth would also place it in competition with the Antigonish campus for the already strained resources of the university, and would pit it against those who expected it to remain a feeder college for St.F.X.

Dr MacLellan and his young faculty were annually amazed by the acceleration of enrolments at their busy two-year college in downtown Sydney. About 60 full-time students had enrolled in 1951; by 1961 the number had reached 265. Nearly 80 per cent of these were male, over 60 per cent were freshmen, and 86 per cent were Catholics. Close to 80 per cent registered in the arts and commerce; the remainder pursued science and engineering. Part-time students in 1961 numbered 376 and fully 77 per cent were teachers upgrading their qualifications; in 1951–52 only about 125 had been registered for part-time studies. Indeed, teacher upgrading became a most significant phase of the program.[125] Those who attended the summer school at XJC in 1961 (first held in 1957) numbered 417. Most students lived in the industrial area – Sydney, North Sydney, Glace Bay, and New Waterford.[126] Close to one-half of them had fathers who worked for the Dominion Steel and Coal Corporation.[127] Commonly they had studied at these high schools:

Sydney Mines High, St Ann's High, Sydney Academy, Holy Angels High, and St Agnes High.

Students at "Little X"

The "Capers" who attended "Little X," as XJC was known, generated a vigorous extra-curricular program, even though their college was not residential. It included hockey, basketball, skating, debating, dramatics, socials, student government and politics, and journalism. From 1955, the first year a junior college yearbook appeared, the students produced their own newspaper called the *Junior College Bi-Weekly* (renamed *Excalibur* in 1959). From that same year, when Dr MacLellan appointed Sister Margaret Beaton librarian, the students found library discipline rigorous; the faculty had to request several years later that the stacks be opened to students![128] Capers faced the more imposing difficulty of financing their education at the college. Dr MacLellan remained keenly aware of the economic disabilities which plagued working-class families; his constant refrain became the need for scholarship and loan assistance for college students of the area. Each year some help was forthcoming from individuals or from local cooperative organizations, and in 1962, through the generosity of William Mac-Donald and Margaret Walker, the Xavier Foundation was established to provide scholarship assistance.[129]

Expanding Faculty and Campus

The startling rise in student enrolments at XJC within one decade of its founding forced Dr MacLellan and the St.F.X. administration to meet the demands with more faculty. In 1951 the principal began with a full-time staff of six; in 1961 MacLellan had a staff of eighteen full-timers and nine part-timers. Four of the full-time faculty had doctorates, eight had masters' degrees, and six had attained the bachelor's. Pillars of the XJC faculty in 1961 included Dr Donald F. Arseneau (chemistry), Gerald E. Aucoin (French), Elmer F. Britten (mathematics), Rev. A. Brooks Campbell (economics and sociology), Owen Carrigan (history), Rev. Dr Charles W. MacDonald (philosophy), Rev. Everett J. MacNeil (history), John A. MacPherson (English), William Reid (physics), and Sister Margaret Beaton, PH D (librarian). In spite of the rigour of her ways with students, Sister Beaton developed the library and made an especially important contribution to the heritage of the region with her Cape Bretoniana Collection.[130] A healthy sense of collegiality characterized the junior college staff, and their relations with the comparatively small student body were intimate.

Another measure of the college's growth during its first decade was its soaring operating expenditures. In 1951 they amounted to $23,000 and by 1961 they had climbed to $192,000.[131] Dr MacLellan referred to this first decade at XJC as "Operation Shoestring," as years when "balancing the budget was a feat of magic."[132] In spite of the financial difficulties, the mounting enrolments and expansion of the staff made larger facilities ever more urgent as the decade progressed. These facts gave weight to Dr MacLellan's argument for expansion, which he presented both to the local community and to the St.F.X. board of governors.[133] In 1955 he urged, "we need a new junior college building immediately, to take care not only of what we are doing, but of what can be done as well."[134] The board agreed and purchased, in 1956, the "Navy League Property" opposite the college on George Street, and three years later constructed on it a new arts building. The facility was designed by the university architect, funded jointly by the Canada Council and gifts from William and Mary MacDonald, after whom it was named, and officially opened on 19 September 1960. The new MacDonald Arts Building, constructed of red brick, accommodated a larger library, five classrooms, about ten offices, a canteen, and a book store.[135] It was an excellent start toward a more adequate educational facility.

Nonetheless, the need remained for further expansion, especially in the sciences. Up to the early 1960s, XJC only offered the first year of science in chemistry and physics. Based on local interest and need, Dr MacLellan urged more offerings and improved facilities in the sciences, as well as an even larger library, a student centre, and better quarters for administrative and extension offices.[136] However, before his dreams could be realized, in 1964 his bishop appointed him president of St.F.X.[137] The appointment came as a rude jolt; the junior college had become his "pride and joy."[138] MacLellan was its founding father who had organized the college from the ground up, had tried to satisfy the needs of his constituency, and had reached out to Catholics and non-Catholics alike. By the time of his transfer to Antigonish, Dr MacLellan had acquired considerable stature in the community. At a dinner in his honour, an occasion for an outpouring of accolades from community leaders who gave him a standing ovation, the president-elect informed the gathering that his years in Cape Breton had been "the happiest days of his life" and he "left for his new position with some regrets."[139]

The Second Principal – Dr Donald F. Campbell

Dr MacLellan's successor as principal of XJC was another Cape Bretoner and priest, Father Donald F. Campbell. Dr Campbell was a Sydney native who had deep family roots in the area. His connections to St.F.X. also ran deep: both his parents were graduates, as was he

Rev. Dr Donald F. Campbell, principal of
Xavier College 1964–74, then president of the
College of Cape Breton 1974–82

(1945). Campbell had been appointed to the faculty of St.F.X. in 1949 as instructor in education. In 1956 he obtained his doctorate in education from the Catholic University of America.[140] Before his appointment by the bishop as the second principal of XJC, Dr Campbell had founded the department of psychology at the university and had served as dean of arts (1962–64). He was enthusiastic about the new challenge in Sydney, and his leadership at the college would prove to be more collegial and democratic than Dr MacLellan's.[141] He would remain at its institutional helm for nearly twenty years – a period of rapid and profound change – first as principal (1964–74) and then as founding president of the College of Cape Breton (1974–82).[142] His first measures at XJC included the appointment of a vice-principal, a bursar, a dean, and a new registrar; as well, he planned and initiated a financial campaign for a new building.[143]

Within one year of Dr Campbell's appointment, the St.F.X. board of governors, on the recommendation of a committee which had examined the college's needs, approved the construction of a new science hall in Sydney.[144] Biology courses had only recently been added to the existing science courses in physics and chemistry. And out of a full-time registration in 1963–64 of 302, close to 30 per cent of the students had enrolled in the sciences or engineering.[145] So the science hall, completed in 1966, was a godsend. It was designed as a match to the MacDonald Arts Building, was located adjacent to it, and accommodated the courses in physics, chemistry, biology, and engineering. By then the junior college had grown into a cluster of three substantial buildings.

Rising Aspirations and Tensions
Two events at the official opening of the science hall were portentous for the college's future. First, the mayor of Sydney in his speech "endorsed the proposed expansion of this institution to a degree-granting university."[146] Second, for the first time in the college's short history, it conferred degrees on behalf of St.F.X. The mayor's comments signalled the rising level of community aspiration for their college. And the hearty response of local business and industry to the "Science for Xavier Campaign" in 1964 revealed how intensely the area had come to identify and "own" the institution.[147] In the mid-1960s, the idea of a degree program at XJC was nothing new; as early as 1953 a student had requested permission to complete his degree requirements in Sydney, and in 1959 a junior college debating team won a unanimous decision over St.F.X. arguing that XJC become a distinct degree-granting institution.[148] However, the only extension to its program which XJC secured in the mid-1960s was the second year of courses leading to the bachelor of science degree.[149]

Nevertheless, the pressure for an extension of program offerings in Sydney was mounting. Many in the community supported the idea. In 1966 St.F.X.'s announcement that it had hired a consulting firm – Taylor, Lieberfeld and Heldman Limited – to study future expansion of the college, along with the pending opening of the new science hall, elicited a lobby by certain Sydney businesses and organizations for a full degree program. The *Cape Breton Post* reported in late summer, "Grass-roots support was growing this week for a speed-up in raising Sydney's Xavier College to degree-granting university status. St Francis Xavier University of Antigonish, the College's parent, has already commissioned a study on the question by a United States consulting firm. So far, the public support has been spontaneous and unorganized, but it was expected to develop into a full-fledged campaign."[150] The Sydney board of trade surveyed over one hundred of its members, who almost unanimously favoured the four-year program.[151] The public lobby placed both Dr MacLellan, then president of St.F.X. and the founding principal of XJC who had overseen its first decade of rapid growth, and Dr Campbell, then principal of the college, in an awkward position. At his appointment to Sydney, Campbell's bishop had warned him of the aspirations of some there for the four-year program; however, Campbell discovered that neither staff qualifications nor facilities then justified such a step.[152] In the fall, both administrators released a joint statement which underscored the complexity of the degree program issue and noted that the St.F.X. board of governors had hired a consulting firm to study the question of expansion.[153] Drs MacLellan and Campbell seemed most immediately concerned with "developing a first rate two-year College possessing the highest standards in staff and facilities."[154] The stand of the board and faculty in Antigonish was this: "Any expansion of programs and courses in Sydney ... should not jeopardize the common good of the institution as a whole."[155]

Mounting tension between Sydney and Antigonish was exacerbated by the difficulties of communication rooted in geographical separation. Within two years of the college's founding, the faculty had wrestled with means to promote unity.[156] In 1957, when St.F.X. deliberated over constitutional revisions, the XJC faculty successfully moved that one of their members be elected, along with the three from Antigonish, to the board of governors, that the principal be an *ex officio* member of the university council, and that the XJC faculty have representation on the executive of the proposed association of university teachers (STFXAUT).[157] Furthermore, the minutes record, "Improved communication between the Junior College and St.F.X. were [*sic*] urged by several faculty members, the others readily agreeing. A direct telephone line and a two-way short wave radio were suggested as possible solutions to the problems."[158] And the students from XJC faced the perennial problem of integrating with a student body at Antigonish which had already lived together for one or two years. Students from both campuses sometimes stooped to rather low levels of mutual recrimination over the difficulties; more positively, they also experimented with various ways to overcome them, for example, with a student liaison officer and better orientation programs.[159]

The Lieberfeld Reports and the Future

The consulting firm hired to examine the present and future needs of the college reported in March 1967.[160] Notwithstanding the unstable economic situation in Cape Breton during the 1960s, occasioned by the decline of the mining and steel industries, the Lieberfeld Report, as it was known, predicted a continuous climb in enrolments. Because the George Street site in downtown Sydney was inadequate to accommodate such growth, it recommended either the purchase of nearby Victoria Park (an eighteen-acre site owned by the department of national defence and used for reserve training) for purposes of expansion, or the outright relocation of the college to a new site.[161] Most of the college faculty preferred a completely new site next to the Sydney bypass called "Cossitt's Lake," a site which the St.F.X. board of governors eventually purchased for the proposed expansion.[162] The college faculty also supported a degree program in Sydney and urged the board to investigate the feasibility of this proposal.[163] An early indication of the faculty's hopes for their college had been symbolized by their move in 1962 to change its name from "Xavier Junior College" to "Xavier College" (XC).[164]

President MacLellan asked Lawrence Lieberfeld to study the degree program proposal; he reported in January 1969. The expanding enrolments and higher education aspirations of the Sydney–Glace Bay region, he concluded, could best be resolved by "a more flexible two-campus university, structured so that degree programs in certain specific and limited subject fields, would be offered at the Sydney campus."[165] Several university committees, composed of members from both the Sydney and Antigonish campuses and appointed to examine Lieberfeld's findings, failed to attain a consensus and divided on geographical lines.[166] However, the pressure continued to mount from the community, the XC faculty, and even the students.[167] In 1969, a group of mature students, many of them married, including coal miners on Cape Breton Development Corporation retraining scholarships, requested that St.F.X. allow them to complete their degree program requirements while remaining at home.[168] Another factor which favoured the degree program in Sydney was the likely prospect that Nova Scotia would

shortly require grade twelve for admission to university; such a requirement promised to reduce the college to a one-year institution unless it
could also offer the junior and senior years.[169] Even though the St.F.X.
university council, board of governors, and faculty did approve in 1970
the idea of a general bachelor of arts program in Sydney, several hurdles
prevented its immediate implementation.[170]

Nevertheless, the hurdles would prove temporary. By 1970 Xavier
College had attained a considerable level of maturity. Full-time enrolment stood at 559, part-time at 645, and non-credit adult studies at
980 for a total of nearly 2200 students. The faculty had grown to fifty-
four with forty-three of them full-time, separate departments had
developed, and the library then contained fifty thousand volumes.[171]
Principal Campbell was convinced that Sydney required the degree
program and he worked diplomatically toward this goal. Furthermore,
students who did not want to go to Antigonish were obtaining their
junior- and senior-level courses through the part-time offerings.[172]
During the next fifteen years the institution would grow through two
more important stages. In 1974 it merged with the Nova Scotia Eastern
Institute of Technology (established in 1968) on the latter's campus
situated on the Sydney–Glace Bay Highway to form an independently
incorporated institution called the College of Cape Breton. Yet, while
it could then offer the degree program, it did so in affiliation with
St.F.X. Complete independence came in 1982, when the College of
Cape Breton attained the power to grant its own degrees; it was then
renamed the University College of Cape Breton.[173] The parting of ways
with St.F.X., its parent institution, would be painful; indeed, a legacy
of bitterness remained on both campuses among those involved in the
move by the college to increasing autonomy and final independence.
However, the success of Xavier College by 1970, and the crucial
contributions it had by then made to the educational, cultural, and
intellectual life of Cape Breton, revealed the wisdom of those who
founded it in 1951 as well as the vision, competence, and commitment
of those who developed it thereafter.

·17·

Institutional Metamorphosis, 1964–70

Webster's dictionary defines metamorphosis as "a striking alteration in appearance, character, or circumstances." The definition accurately describes the transition St.F.X. underwent between 1945 and 1970. Its president from 1964 to 1970, Dr Malcolm MacLellan, oversaw the initiation and culmination of changes which had great consequence for the institution's future. The key phases of university life were substantially modified. These changes altered the university's identity and radically transformed the St.F.X. undergraduate experience. The local transitions occurred against an eventful national backdrop which witnessed Canada's centennial celebrations, the Quiet Revolution in Quebec, a royal commission on bilingualism and biculturalism, and the appearance of a young and dynamic Liberal prime minister, Pierre Elliott Trudeau.

It was also an eventful decade for universities in the Atlantic region. Memorial College, Newfoundland, which had been chartered to grant degrees in 1949, moved to a new, expansive campus; in New Brunswick, after a royal commission on higher education (1962), the University of New Brunswick opened a campus in Saint John, St Thomas University moved from Chatham to the UNB's Fredericton campus, and a single French-language university was established at Moncton; on Prince Edward Island, Prince of Wales and St Dunstan's universities were merged to form the new University of Prince Edward Island; and in Nova Scotia St Mary's came under the control of a lay board and the denominational regulation of Acadia ended.[1] Driven by climbing enrolments, all university campuses expanded rapidly.

President Malcolm MacLellan

Dr MacLellan was both surprised and dismayed by his appointment to the presidency of St.F.X. in 1964. He had found his assignment as founding principal of Xavier College (1951–64) quite congenial indeed. As principal, he had become a respected member of the community

President Malcolm MacLellan, 1964–70

and was deeply involved in the educational affairs of his native Cape Breton. Moreover, at age fifty-eight, MacLellan felt he was losing some of his vigour.[2] However, Bishop William Power concluded, given MacLellan's extensive educational and administrative experience, that he was best qualified for the St.F.X. presidency. He came to Antigonish anticipating a hectic and difficult time; he would not be disappointed.

From the perspective of St.F.X.'s educational philosophy, Dr MacLellan was a strong appointment. He had reflected on the fundamentals of higher education and had formed basic convictions about the dignity of the person, the critical nature of the relation between faith and learning, and the need for students to develop a practical philosophy of life. In 1966, he declared before convocation, "What a University graduate believes in and values ... is more fundamental than the extent of his knowledge. Unless this University has enabled you graduates to fashion such a philosophy, education has failed."[3] Within six months of his appointment, MacLellan selected the practical priorities which would guide his leadership. He was committed to the institution's continued growth, to ecumenism, to cooperation with the recently formed Atlantic Association of Universities, to extended student counselling services, to teacher in-service education, to improving the liberal arts program, to graduate programs in selected disciplines, to strengthening the relations between the Coady, extension, and the social sciences, to re-examining the relation between St.F.X. and Mount St Bernard College, and to the development of Xavier College as "a full-fledged" two-year institution.[4] This was a full slate of commitments; MacLellan's pursuit of them would be complicated by the inevitable contingencies of life.

Physical Expansion Continued
One predictable development was the continued, urgent need for expansion. In May 1965 a committee on needs and means presented an important report to the board of governors which became a blueprint for university physical expansion over the next ten years. The report recommended that St.F.X. retain its traditional role as a primarily residential liberal arts undergraduate institution stressing the intellectual formation of students while not neglecting the development of their characters and leadership abilities. It also called for the following new facilities – as finances would permit: a new classroom building, a new gymnasium, a student centre, new residences, new accommodations for the department of biology, and the purchase of more land for further expansion.[5]

One building, central to the work of the university, which was long overdue for replacement was the library.[6] It had been built in 1916 when St.F.X.'s enrolment stood at about 135 and its faculty numbered twenty. By 1960, student numbers had reached nearly ten times what they had been in 1916. Of course, the administration and faculty had long been painfully aware of the utter inadequacy of their library.[7] Initial plans for a new one had been prepared in the early 1950s, but excessive demands on the university treasury forbade its construction. Finally, in 1964 the university decided to build; the university architect, in consultation with the head librarian, Sister Madeline Connolly, a decisive, no-nonsense Martha who had served faithfully since 1942,[8] designed a new library facility which cost nearly $1 million. At an auspicious occasion on 17 July 1965, Prime Minister Lester B. Pearson received a honorary degree and officially opened the building. The four-storey brick structure was located directly south of the Physics and Chemistry Building, completed eight years before. It could accommodate five hundred students and nearly two hundred thousand volumes. A distinctive and attractive feature, in keeping with one dimension of the region's cultural heritage, was the main reading room, called the "Hall of the Clans" to honour the Celtic settlers of eastern Nova Scotia who had been so important for the founding and development of St.F.X.[9] The late Liberal premier, Angus L. MacDonald, had made this suggestion before his death in 1954; St.F.X. named the new library in honour of its eminent son.[10]

As with the library, the cash-strapped St.F.X. had too long delayed the updating of its recreational facilities. Indeed, the existing gymnasium in 1964 had been built in 1916, the same year as the original library. Dr MacLellan believed the need was urgent to provide better arrangements which would also accommodate the expanding annual convocations and bolster student morale.[11] Again the university architect, Jens F. Larson, was called upon to design a modern recreational structure. Colonel Sydney Oland of Oland's Limited, Halifax, generously pledged, over a period of twenty years, a considerable sum toward its cost; St.F.X. drew the remainder from the coffers of government.[12] The new, impressive athletic-recreation complex, which provided office space, classrooms, multiple courts, and two gymnasia, officially opened in May 1967. It occupied the southwest side of the expanding campus, could accommodate three thousand students, and was named the Oland Centre.[13]

Along with the new library and athletic facility, an academic centre made a highly significant addition to the St.F.X. campus during the later 1960s. Surprisingly, since 1910 nearly all expansion at St.F.X. had been in residential capacity. By the 1960s, with the growth of both enrolments and faculty, a new office-classroom complex was a most pressing need. A planning committee in 1966 recommended a combination three-storey classroom structure along with an eight-storey

363

office tower. The board of governors approved the plan, and construction began in 1967.[14] After unfortunate delays and problems with the construction firm, including its removal from the site and replacement by another company, the facility opened in the fall of 1969.[15] The new academic centre was the first high-rise on campus, apparently representing "a new trend in university construction"; it offered a rather stark contrast in appearance – a commercial-industrial one – to the earlier buildings designed by the university architect.[16] However, it was a most necessary addition to the existing facilities, providing seventy-seven offices for faculty and administration, twenty-six classrooms, and several auditoria. Officials named the centre in honour of the recently deceased past-president of St.F.X., Dr Patrick J. Nicholson, and located it on a rising slope to the southeast side of the campus where it loomed above the entire university.[17]

As it opened Nicholson Hall, St.F.X. also completed two other substantial brick residences, both located on the south periphery of the university property. MacNeil Hall served as a Coady residence. The other residence, which provided accommodation for 230 students, was named in honour of D.F. MacIsaac, an alumnus and generous benefactor.[18] St.F.X. not only built rather frantically during these years, but it also purchased new properties.[19] Its bid, eventually realized, to purchase the Antigonish High School located to the east of the campus evoked considerable ill will among the townspeople. Public relations difficulties, along with cost considerations and the need to expand the heating plant, also explain St.F.X.'s shift from the use of coal to oil around 1967. Soot fall-out from the university stack had done little to promote better relations with Antigonish neighbours.[20] St.F.X. authorities recognized the need to work closely with the town to ease tensions caused by the university's rapid expansion.[21]

The new buildings constructed in the 1960s were the last ones designed by Jens F. Larson and his son Nils; the Larsons had been closely associated with St.F.X. campus planning and architecture since 1936. In all, they had designed twelve of its buildings.[22] From then on St.F.X. would use Nova Scotia architects. However, the 1960s witnessed the near-completion of the final phase of rapid post-war expansion at St.F.X.[23] In 1945 the university had been composed of nine rather modest buildings; in 1970, the number was twenty and most of the new facilities were imposing brick structures built on a scale noticeably more ambitious than before.

Dependence on Government
The post-war expansion placed immense stress on the university budget, both capital and operating. Authorities, therefore, mounted several

Aerial view of St.F.X. during the construction boom of the 1960s

financial campaigns and regularly increased tuition and board. However, St.F.X.'s traditional funding sources were utterly inadequate to finance its operation and growth. Governments became the university's primary source of funding. In 1945 government funding for the academic program was nil; St.F.X.'s revenues of $202,040 came from tuition fees (66 per cent), room rents, endowment income, and an annual diocesan quota.[24] By 1970 government funding was cardinal. That year the annual revenues reached nearly $7.3 million; government grants accounted for 56 per cent of this total and tuition only 28 per cent.[25] The state had likewise become the cardinal financier of the capital costs of construction. Between 1964 and 1971 St.F.X. received capital loans amounting to about $8.5 million.[26] Of course, the university's leadership strongly favoured government funding, a fact made abundantly clear by its many public pronouncements on the issue since the late 1940s, including its brief in 1964 to the so-called Bladen Commission on the financing of Canadian higher education.[27]

For governments, such funding raised issues about the proper and efficient use of public monies. Not long after the formation of the Nova Scotia University Grants Committee to advise the province on the financing of higher education, Premier Robert L. Stanfield spoke in Antigonish at the installation of President Malcolm MacLellan. He warned, "Academic freedom will not justify to the hard-pressed taxpayer what he may regard as a waste of money. Any attempt to convert the legitimate and supremely important concept of academic freedom into an academic curtain to hide empire-building or expensive duplication of effort or incompetence could lead only to disaster. The Nova Scotia taxpayer will not support sacred cows from the public treasury."[28] This hard-nosed comment signalled that, for universities, heavy dependence on one financial source could threaten institutional autonomy. Shortly after the inauguration of federal government funding in 1951, Dr Hugh Somers had warned, "Our task as citizens is to see that the universities have enough private support to remain independent. If our universities should lose their autonomy, if control of the thinking of our nation passes into the hands of the state – no matter how benign the state may be – our freedom will not survive long." Whatever the dangers, real or imagined, by 1970 St.F.X. was more beholden than ever before to one source of funding.[29]

A Complex Institution
Not only had St.F.X.'s budget and funding sources changed dramatically by 1970, but so had its administrative and constitutional complexity. In 1945 ten university administrative positions existed, nearly all filled by clerics – a chancellor, president, dean of studies, director

of extension, registrar, directors of religious activities, bursar, directors of discipline, and librarian;[30] by 1970 over twenty university officials held appointments, excluding Xavier College, and the administrative offices had expanded significantly. Important new positions included an executive vice-president, a dean of arts, a dean of science, a dean of admissions, a comptroller, an administrative assistant to the president, academic department heads, a business manager, student services personnel, and a university archivist;[31] the administration had also appointed directors of athletics, public relations, development, and student activities. Most of the principal administrative positions remained in the possession of clerics; however, lay people were represented. A noticeable predominance of administrators of Highland descent was evident, and almost all were male.[32] The university council, which did not even exist in 1945, numbered twenty-five in 1970, and the board of governors had grown from twenty to thirty-seven. The problems of communication caused by increasing institutional complexity convinced President MacLellan of the need to publish from his office a monthly bulletin called *Inter-X*, which aimed "to improve communications at all levels of University affairs."[33]

In 1968 a committee revised the constitution of 1959; its key recommendation, strongly influenced by the Sir James Duff and Robert A. Berdahl investigation of 1964-65 into university government,[34] called for the replacement of the university council by a senate. This crucial proposal was accepted – although not without some trepidation and second thoughts by certain faculty members – and the senate, from 1970, became the supreme academic governing body of the university. All these administrative and constitutional changes vastly increased St.F.X.'s institutional complexity, and increasingly diffused authority from the president's office to the constituent parts of the university.[35]

Enrolment Trends
Compared to the student enrolments at the conclusion of the Second World War, those in 1970 revealed startling contrasts. In 1945, 460 regular undergraduates attended the college; by 1970 the number had mounted to 2347 at the Antigonish campus alone. The explanation for the increase lay in the growing population,[36] the rise in the number of college-age young people (the first wave of the post-war generation), and the higher proportion of college-age youth choosing to attend college.[37] Many people had come to believe that "a university education represented an almost certain path to economic growth and individual prosperity."[38] Over 60 per cent of St.F.X. students continued to come from working-class homes, the vast majority (86 per cent) were from the Atlantic region, and most were natives of Nova Scotia (70 per

cent).[39] Roman Catholics accounted for 86 per cent of all Xaverians in 1970.[40] The number of married students was on the increase (6 per cent); the number of American students was on a slide (4 per cent). The arts faculty claimed 73 per cent of student enrolments and the sciences 26 per cent. Some students in 1970 registered in programs which were non-existent twenty-five years before: business adminis-tration, theology, bachelor of secretarial arts, bachelor of nursing, bach-elor of science in physical education, bachelor of education, master of arts in guidance, and master of arts in teaching.[41]

One striking trend in enrolments was the large increase in female students. In 1970 close to 40 per cent of the students were females (906); twenty years before, they represented only 13 per cent of all Xaverians. Their rapidly mounting numbers during the 1960s, a trend experienced on other campuses, created a special problem of residential space for St.F.X.'s affiliated Mount St Bernard College. Since the Mount's affiliation with St.F.X. in 1894, it had provided all the resi-dential accommodation for women enrolled in college-level studies at the university, along with instruction in freshman arts and other pro-grams in home economics, secretarial arts, art, music, and library science. By 1968 the Mount had forty-nine sisters in residence; of these, twenty-five were administrators or St.F.X. faculty members. In 1960, 235 students lived in residence; in 1968 there were 634. This dramatic rise placed an enormous stress on facilities, staff, and finances. The Mount, therefore, added two new impressive residences in the 1960s – the Camden-Marguerite Complex (1963) and Lane Hall (1968) – which could accommodate about five hundred more students. However, the Mount faculty only increased from seventeen to eighteen between 1960 and 1968.[42]

The Mount administration and faculty, therefore, faced two options: either bolster its financial and academic capacity and remain an auton-omous women's residential college in affiliation with St.F.X., or inte-grate with the university and become "a mere dormitory."[43] By the 1960s, the Mount had a more than seventy-year tradition of college-level instruction, and some members of the community hoped to con-tinue this tradition.[44] However, changing ideas about coeducation and the problem of resources – academic and otherwise – forced the Mount's college program to become, gradually, an integral part of St.F.X.[45] The Mount had found that, as St.F.X. expanded after the war, it became more and more difficult, and perhaps less desirable, to retain its distinct academic identity. Sister St Winnefride wrote Presi-dent Somers in 1956 that "the pressure from the common campus tends to an increasing degree to absorb the activities of our students, and to make more difficult our efforts to give a more feminine direction to their education."[46] After 1969, St.F.X. would no longer be able to leave the problem of the accommodation of female students to its affiliated women's college.[47]

The End of In Loco Parentis

The student experience at St.F.X. of both males and females was deeply altered, indeed transformed, during the 1960s. Two key developments materialized; both would contribute weightily to institutional metamorphosis – the dismantling of the traditional regimen of *in loco parentis*, and the right to student participation in university administration. The old ways of automatic student deference to authority and contrite obedience to the college hierarchy passed into oblivion. The traditional disciplinary regulations had been strict – morning chapel virtually required, unexcused class absences forbidden, alcohol on campus prohibited, females barred from the male residences, no operation of cars on or off campus by students, required participation in spiritual retreats, permission required for off-campus evening excursions, and lights out at a set evening hour. Under the general supervision of a head prefect or dean of students, in-residence priest-prefects had enforced this order, at times inconsistently. During Dr MacLellan's presidency there arose a frontal assault on this old order.

The veterans at St.F.X. after the Second World War, along with certain students both before and after, had chafed under the disciplinary regime.[48] However, a direct attack on it did not take place until the 1960s. Perhaps the first clear sign of an impending onslaught appeared when students boycotted classes for two days in the late fall of 1961. They were angered by the administration's unilateral and uncompromising decision to shorten the Christmas vacation. Most students supported the two-day walkout.[49] Predictably, the faculty and administration were opposed; they condemned the strike as "an infringement on the legitimate authority of the institution."[50]

Gradually the students succeeded in redefining St.F.X.'s "legitimate authority" over them. The general trend was to constrict the authority of the priests and to expand the personal responsibility of the students. Student residences gained the right to "all night lights" in 1961;[51] students assumed control of their own supervision at athletic and social events when they established a campus police force in 1963;[52] two years later the priest-prefects, responsible for discipline in the residences (there were twenty-four of them), became priest-counsellors. Students were then granted the right to form house committees chaired by student-prefects with powers to formulate and enforce residence rules. Students achieved another shift in policy in 1968 when the administration formed student and university disciplinary committees. The priest-counsellor participated in neither of these two bodies.[53] These developments drastically reduced the authority of the priests, demoralized some (especially the older ones), and precipitated their exit from the student residences through subsequent years. The priest-professor was no longer a disciplinarian at St.F.X.; and less and less often would he be a counsellor. A symbol of his declining pastoral role was, perhaps, the establishment at this time of a professional counselling centre.[54]

The president of St.F.X., Dr MacLellan, favoured the priest as pastor and counsellor above that of prefect and "policeman"; however, he recognized that the relation between priest-professor and student had been "an outstanding characteristic" of the traditional structure of St.F.X., and he neither contemplated nor hoped for what eventually happened, namely its slow but sure disappearance.[55] Rev. George Kehoe, the dean of men (1961–68), also favoured the move toward student responsibility for discipline.[56] The new order, its proponents argued, would be superior for developing mature, responsible, independent, open, and honest students. Student reformers made effective use of the student newspaper to argue, plead, badger, lecture, tongue-lash, and cajole the students and faculty to accept their point of view. One rhetorical question summed up their agenda: "Do you want to change this archaic institution into something that bears at least a half decent resemblance to a modern university?"[57]

Student Power

The students' agenda to change the "archaic institution" embraced their participation in its administration. In 1967, the president permitted student representation on the university council,[58] the committee on students' activities, and the athletic committee. That same year X-men gained the right to present their ideas and concerns to the board of governors, a first in the institution's history,[59] and in 1969 they gained the legal right to elect annually three students to the board.[60] When a senate was formed at St.F.X. in 1970, the student union president and four other students were included in its composition.[61] Therefore, by 1970 students had substantially democratized St.F.X., then having the privilege of representation on eleven councils and committees; by doing so, they overturned their earlier allegation to be merely "passive instrument[s] of the administration."[62]

Along with assuming responsibility for their own discipline and gaining a voice in institutional administration, St.F.X. students also worked to de-regulate their spiritual and moral lives. The on-campus use of alcohol and open housing (visiting privileges for females in the male residences) became two volatile issues. In 1968 and in response to student demands for change, Dr MacLellan set up a president's

Student unrest in the 1960s

commission to investigate the personal and social conditions of the student body and to recommend improvements to the university council at the beginning of each semester.[63] The commission worked hard to propose various supposed improvements. By March of 1970, the long reign of "prohibition" had ended at St.F.X.: the student union had acquired a liquor licence from the Nova Scotia Licensing Board to serve liquor, beer, and wine to those age twenty-one and over in a campus club located, suprisingly, in the old chapel.[64]

Open housing became a more explosive issue, eventually provoking a student referendum, briefs, negotiations, demonstrations, sit-ins, endless *Xaverian Weekly* harangues, and a strike. Female students, who resided at the Mount unless they were day students, yearly were becoming a larger presence. It was perennial for male students to attack the Mount's restrictions on the female students; one particularly inflammatory article in 1969 was called "Mount St Bernard: A Closed Society."[65] And, of course, the ban against females in the St.F.X. residences became galling to many male students. In 1969 the student council declared it "a basic and natural right" that students control their own environment as much as possible.[66] However, many faculty, though not all,[67] feared the possible consequences of open housing for privacy, morale, academic life, and sexual behaviour, including its implications for the university's Catholicity.[68] The administration also mused over its potential impact on public relations. Many parents opposed open housing and some hoped that St.F.X. would buck the trends, "dare to be different and remain loyal to basic Christian principles of morality."[69] President MacLellan also noted the age range of the student body, the prevalent use of alcohol, and the design of the residences. He likewise underscored the moral implications: "To assume that there are no moral overtones is to assume that there are no irresponsible students."[70] Because of stern opposition from both faculty and administration, the students failed to obtain open housing until the next decade, in spite of their overwhelming support for it.[71]

Curricular Reform
Students also took aim at the curriculum in their attempts to reform the "archaic institution." They urged the dean of arts, Father Malcolm MacDonell, to introduce more choice and flexibility in the arts program.[72] One critic claimed that St.F.X. had "the least flexible course of all" universities in the Atlantic provinces; moreover, the trend at most universities, in response to a widespread student critique of the arts curriculum,[73] was toward less compulsion and more freedom in the selection of courses.[74] The traditional St.F.X. arts curriculum had been largely prescribed; it had required for a degree about fifteen

courses out of twenty.[75] After studying the curricular regulations at other universities and receiving input from a committee on curricular policy,[76] Dean MacDonell proposed the elimination of all specific requirements for the bachelor of arts with major and the general bachelor of arts. It was his position that the old policy should be replaced by a required distribution of five courses in each of two related subjects, three pairs of courses, and four free electives.[77] In this way, the student would be liberated from curricular compulsion in order to shape his own academic program; yet he would also be forced by the distribution requirements to obtain a general education with some depth in selected disciplines. The new curricular plan was an attempt to resolve a persistent dilemma in higher education: "to combine speciality of function with generality of culture."[78]

The faculty's reaction to the dean's proposal was divided but largely favourable. President MacLellan stated, expressing a common view, that the suggested revision would eliminate compulsion but preserve "the principle of general and liberal education" for St.F.X.[79] On the other hand, some faculty predicted that the proposed curriculum would suffer from a lack of coherence and would fail to reflect the traditional St.F.X. Catholic educational philosophy. They believed that philosophy and theology should be integral to the intellectual and ethical formation of all students.[80] In addition, fears were voiced of drastic enrolment reductions in theology and philosophy. However, the winds of change were blowing in the direction of individual choice, both at Catholic and more secular institutions, and by the late 1960s they were sweeping through Antigonish.[81] The general faculty accepted Dean MacDonell's proposal in April 1968, and St.F.X. instituted the new curriculum in September of that year.[82]

It was a milestone in the curricular history of the institution. Some resultant decline of demand appeared in philosophy, theology, modern languages, and mathematics, but no radical changes in departmental teaching loads.[83] However, the implications of these changes for curricular coherence and exposure of the entire student body to the basics of the Catholic religious and intellectual tradition were another matter. The revision exchanged prescribed content for a prescribed distribution of courses, instituted a democracy of the disciplines in place of a hierarchy of knowledge, and admitted the right of students above that of the institution to decide what should be learned. The 1960s democratization of St.F.X. thus included reform not only of its administrative structures but also of its curriculum. St.F.X. subsequently effected curricular revisions in the direction of more choice in the sciences and professional programs.[84] Of course, a gradual expansion of program offerings had likewise contributed to the amount of curricular choice

Rev. Malcolm MacDonell, professor of history 1945–64,
dean of arts 1964–70, president 1970–78

at St.F.X.: in 1945 it offered twelve separate programs; the offerings numbered twenty-four by 1970.[85]

Changing Times

The forces in student life at St.F.X., both social and academic, which so starkly changed the institution during the 1960s reflected developments on university campuses elsewhere in Canada, the United States, and Europe.[86] It was an era of coffee houses,[87] folk music, and civil rights, a decade of optimism and "egalitarian idealism."[88] In Canada a new Liberal prime minister, Pierre Elliott Trudeau, projected a younger, more dynamic image for the nation. University students everywhere pressed for more personal responsibility, more participation in decision making, more open housing; in all, they campaigned for more power, personal freedom, and democracy. Student strikes and demonstrations became commonplace, the militancy apparently influenced by the American Civil Rights Movement and the hope for social justice. A sexual revolution also took shape as inhibitions between the sexes were relaxed and traditional standards were discarded by many. By the mid-1960s, the "New Morality" of open discussion about sex and advocacy of artificial forms of birth control edged onto the pages of the *Xaverian*.[89] In 1967, a student survey at St.F.X. revealed that a substantial majority of students supported birth control, sex education, and the abolition of capital punishment, while surprising minorities favoured abortion.[90] More open discussion occurred about selected moral and social issues, and more toleration was evident for diversity of opinion and dissent from traditional Catholic teachings. Although some observers criticized St.F.X. students of the 1960s for ignoring important social issues and focusing on internal, campus concerns,[91] some students' horizons extended beyond Antigonish. From its founding in 1965, they participated in the X-Project, "a student-oriented social action group," which held "Teach-Ins" on blacks, natives, and the non-medical use of drugs, and offered a volunteer tutoring program for depressed communities in the area.[92] Furthermore, students discussed and debated the Cuban Missile Crisis, the Viet Nam War, the Civil Rights Movement, Vatican II, Quebec separatism, and the Antigonish Movement.[93] For most undergraduates, the 1960s proved a time of flux, of exhilarating hope, and of some disquiet as old verities crumbled underfoot. As in the 1930s, student radicals definitely made campus life "more vital, engaged, and interesting."[94]

Altering Faculty Profile

By 1970 the undergraduate experience, as well as the ethos of St.F.X., had been deeply altered, not only by the dismantling of *in loco*

375

parentis, democratization, and revision of the curriculum, but also by the laicization of the faculty.[95] In 1945 twenty out of twenty-seven faculty members were clerics, as were all eleven university officials.[96] The entire faculty was Roman Catholic. The ubiquitous priest-professor was almost always a native of the Diocese of Antigonish and a graduate of St.F.X., frequently recruited from among the students because of his academic talents and religious propensities. Many were of Highland Catholic descent. As a child, he probably learned the rudiments of the faith in a devout, modest Catholic home and under the careful instruction of the parish priest. After receiving a general liberal arts undergraduate preparation at St.F.X., he usually proceeded to the seminary,[97] and then finally to graduate studies in a chosen or assigned discipline. Often he had an earned doctorate, but sometimes only a master's or bachelor's degree. This background formed a professor with deep, ingrained loyalties to his region, to his church, and to his *alma mater*; he was a product of all three. His professional aspirations rarely aimed beyond the diocesan horizons, and his professional rewards were obtained within its institutions. His interests centred on the advance of religion as much as, or more than, they did on the progress of his academic discipline. In 1945, the St.F.X. undergraduate lived and moved and had his being in an institution whose tone was set by such a priest-professor.

Rapid post-war growth at St.F.X. had made urgent the need for more faculty in the classrooms and laboratories. However, the supply of Catholic scholars was lean, and successive bishops, who were responsible for the pastoral needs of the diocese, did not have an inexhaustible supply of priest-professors to assign to the university.[98] Indeed, after 1965, the supply of priests became increasingly problematic as vocations declined and some resigned from the priesthood.[99] Thus began an irreversible trend at St.F.X. of faculty laicization. In 1945, 83 per cent of the faculty of 27 were clerics or sisters; by 1970 the percentage had plummeted to 36 per cent of 147 faculty members.[100]

Transformation of the Undergraduate Experience
The changes this implied for the undergraduate experience will escape those who fail to consider the differences between clerical and lay faculty, and other shifts in the backgrounds of the St.F.X. teaching staff. First, lay faculty had a different set of priorities; they were not committed to a career within the church or to celibacy. Neither did they owe a dual allegiance to university president and diocesan bishop. Priestly pastoral concerns about the religious and ethical development of their students and the advance of Catholicism were displaced by concentration on their discipline and advance of their own academic

careers. Professional concerns about rank, tenure, research, and publication were given impetus by the formation of the STFXAUT in 1957.
The administration supported these trends, for it was one way a small,
relatively isolated university like St.F.X. could gain academic credibility
for itself.[101] For those with an envious eye on developments elsewhere,
it became important to shuck the supposed image of a backward,
obsolete Catholic college of inferior status and standards. From 1964
to 1967 the St.F.X. faculty of science reported seventy scientific publications and symposia presentations.[102] The faculty of arts was also
publishing, although its output was much less impressive.[103] By 1967-
68 a university council for research had been established which provided some internal funding for both faculties.[104] Starting in 1963, the
university published a journal called the *Contemporary and Alumni
News*, which, although promotional in purpose, included short articles
by faculty on their academic specialties; from 1970 a literary journal
entitled the *Antigonish Review* would be published.[105] Although the
soaring faculty interest in research and publication may occasionally
have detracted from teaching responsibilities,[106] the institution's professed priority – the heavy teaching and prefecting loads of priest-
professors – was probably no less detrimental.

The lay staff lived off campus and, of course, they had no prefecting
duties. Therefore, their social relations with students were much more
limited and largely centred around academic concerns. For better or
for worse, their chances to shape and guide the personal, social, vocational, and spiritual lives of students were fewer. A student advisor in
1967 believed that "the lay faculty could be enticed into showing more
interest and concern in student activities," and a veteran priest-professor observed that "a good many of the faculty are cut off from the life
on the campus."[107] The fact that lay faculty were much more specialized in their academic backgrounds and interests undoubtedly affected
the way they presented subject matter in the classroom and the role
in that presentation played by religion. Finally, the replacement of
priests by laymen no doubt influenced the fertility of St.F.X. for
priestly vocations. Many priests in the diocese had been inspired
toward the priestly life by the priests-professors they came to know at
St.F.X. This relation, as well as the pervasive religious ethos and
rigorous practice of the institution, explains why it had such an impressive record of vocations. In the future, things would be different.[108]

By 1970 other changes in the St.F.X. faculty also altered the undergraduate experience. The faculty was much larger, of course. Moreover, immediately after the war, nearly the entire faculty were native
to the region; in 1970 only about 44 per cent of the faculty had roots
in eastern Nova Scotia. The number of X-men had also decreased from

about 90 per cent to around 61 per cent by 1970. This latter trend was partly caused by the decline in the 1960s of the traditional recruitment of promising students from among the graduates for further training and eventual placement on the St.F.X. faculty.[109] Moreover, the faculty as a male preserve (only two women were on faculty in 1945) was eroding: by 1970 females, most of them sisters, accounted for over one-quarter of the St.F.X. professorate. Lastly, because it was difficult to find qualified staff in the 1960s,[110] and religious commitment became a matter of indifference in hiring decisions,[111] the proportion of Catholic faculty had decreased to 80 per cent by the end of the decade.[112] In 1970 the St.F.X. faculty had much less knowledge of the region, of the traditions of St.F.X., and of the Catholic faith than any which had staffed the institution in its history. Some of them, trained in large, secular, research-oriented institutions, found it difficult to accept and adjust to what they found at St.F.X.;[113] they lacked respect for its traditions and perhaps hoped to remake it in the image of their own *alma mater*. Even though many lay faculty continued to be Catholic, they appeared to belong "to a more socially-assimilated post-war generation and had imbibed more of the atmosphere of secular higher education than earlier cohorts of Catholic academics."[114] The cumulative result of this change in the faculty profile was a greatly altered experience for St.F.X. undergraduates, an altered relation between the university and its constituency, and a different institutional mission.

Changing Institutional Mission
Throughout its history St.F.X., like all other educational institutions, has had to adjudicate among the sometimes conflicting demands made on it by the church, the public, the students, the faculty, the alumni, and its own heritage. Up to the Second World War, the church's interests were dominant, guarded by successive bishop-chancellors, reinforced by the predominance of clerical faculty, clerical administrators, Catholic students, and Catholic financial support, and buttressed by a social ethos of deference to hierarchy and authority. As a product of these influences, St.F.X.'s mission was to provide clerical candidates and Catholic lay leaders formed through a residential, Catholic, liberal arts education. This stressed the development of the whole person, emphasized a sense of social responsibility, reproduced attitudes of deference, allegiance, and conformity to the Catholic hierarchy and its traditions, and provided some limited vocational training. The successful students obtained from the institution socially recognized credentials – degrees, certificates, and diplomas. Religion, that is, Roman Catholic orthodoxy, was truly the "central and unifying force on the campus."[115]

However, as Canadian society increased in social and economic complexity, the demands for utilitarian and scientific training became more persistent.[116] Such demands have existed in increasing tension with both the aims of religion and traditional liberal education. George Marsden, in his wide-ranging study of the relation between religion and the academy, observed, "there is the increasing growth of practical disciplines and sub-disciplines that do not concern themselves with the big questions but rather engage in technical research or teach technical skills."[117] This trend, along with those described above – government funding, faculty laicization, faculty professionalism and specialization, the dismantling of *in loco parentis*, institutional democratization, curricular reforms, (all attempts to conform to changes and standards elsewhere) – began to disestablish religion at St.F.X. and contribute to the university's institutional metamorphosis.[118]

Religion at X during the 1960s
The Second Vatican Council (1962–65) also contributed to the changing role of religion at St.F.X. The purpose of the council was to update and renew the church.[119] It effected important changes in the liturgy, the role of the laity, attitudes toward non-Catholics, and attitudes toward church authority. At St.F.X. renovations were made in the university chapel – the altar was shifted forward, the sanctuary rail was removed, and contemporary art work was incorporated.[120] The breezes of change also brought more openness among Catholics and made diversity of opinion on religious and social questions more acceptable. Theological and philosophical pluralism appeared at St.F.X. Before, faculty and students accepted Catholic belief and practice as a given; if theological and philosophical criticism was practised, it was fired in the direction of Protestantism, non-Christian religions, and modern movements of philosophy. In the new climate inaugurated by Vatican II, the recently formed department of theology[121] hired two Protestant theologians (Rev. Jan Huntjens and John M. Berridge). Speakers and chaplains from Protestant denominations were welcomed onto the campus and ecumenical discussions organized.[122] Broad religious consensus became an important ideal, and Catholics, like most Protestants, believed it best "to be low-key, entirely civil, and inclusive" about their faith.[123]

In the midst of these developments, it became evident on campus during the 1960s that all was not well with religion among the students. In 1966, the spiritual director at St.F.X. reported "considerable indifference" about religion and predicted that "Religion as a University influence is in for difficult times."[124] Two years later the president informed the board of governors, "The students evidence to some degree the disenchantment and disinterest in 'organized religion' that is typical of their generation." Seminary candidates were becoming a rare breed, the practice of confession infrequent, and religious retreats or conferences rather unpopular.[125] Some observers expressed concern that "the Catholicity of St.F.X. [was] on the wane to the point of maybe 'no return.'"[126] Most students elsewhere at Canadian Catholic colleges and universities, apparently, had only a vague idea of what it meant for their college to be Catholic and rarely enrolled because it was Catholic.[127] Little reason exists to doubt that the same generalization held for the students at St.F.X. in the 1960s.

Mixed Reactions to the New St.F.X.

By the end of the decade, an undergraduate's educational experience at St.F.X. was less and less rooted in a Catholic consensus about the meaning of life and the purpose of education. In 1969–70, in its official statement of purpose, St.F.X. elevated for the first time the intellectual development of students as the "principal objective of the University."[128] Statements about the development of student "character and integrity" still registered, officially at least, continued respect for the traditional St.F.X. way in education. However, the new ranking of aims revealed deep changes within the institution. Of course, some members of the Xaverian community seemed oblivious to the new direction and ethos, some were indifferent, some were enthusiastic, and others were troubled.[129] In the summer of 1969, a small number of faculty and administrators met together to discuss such questions as these: "Are we moving too deliberately and too rapidly from our former policy of total education of the student, morally as well as intellectually? Does our 'constituency' impose a peculiar responsibility in this regard? Is there a way in which we should be different?"[130] One veteran professor was dismayed by the alleged obsession with academic strength alone and condemned it as a betrayal of the past.[131] The president himself expressed uneasiness with certain results of the changes he had overseen; in the last year of his presidency he contemplated the need for something like an "Institute of Human Concern," which would be, in his words, "one kind of interdisciplinary and integrating program that seems to be very urgently needed, even if it caught only one-quarter of the students."[132] The post-war trends which had caught St.F.X. up in a rapid process of change leading to institutional metamorphosis had precipitated for it a crisis of identity and mission. The institution was caught between the claims of the old ways and the demands of the new; its future challenge would be how to satisfy both with integrity.

Institutional Metamorphosis

The cumulative result of the changes from 1945 to 1970 meant that St.F.X. presented a very different image and offered a transformed experience to the undergraduate of 1970 compared to his 1945 counterpart. In 1970 the freshman discovered a campus with over twice as many buildings and the most recent ones imposing indeed. In place of a small, intimate, Catholic, liberal arts college, the undergraduate now entered a growing university, with a more specialized and professional faculty who were discipline-oriented and increasingly involved in research and publication. For many, their backgrounds did not predispose them to institutional or regional loyalty. Faculty laicization meant the undergraduate was less likely to rub shoulders with a priest-professor – indeed, with any professor outside of the confines of academic course work. Neither was he likely to have much to do with the Sisters of St Martha, whose numbers had increased little since the 1940s while the student numbers, by contrast had virtually exploded.[133] Faculty-student relations now largely developed on a formal-professional basis. The administration was more distant and impersonal because of bureaucratization. Since *in loco parentis* had been dismantled, the undergraduate enjoyed considerable personal liberty. Among the faculty and students he observed diversity of opinion about religious and ethical issues. He could now select freely from a broad range of programs, with the sciences and pre-professional courses boasting, if not the most prestige, then at least the most utility for employment in the technological society. If so inclined, he could avoid altogether courses in religion and philosophy. The undergraduate in 1970 also saw opportunities to participate on important administrative councils and committees. The male undergraduate noted, doubtless with some delight, that women were a substantial minority of the student body and commonly found occasion to socialize with the opposite sex. He also discovered enthusiasm for religious observances noticeably lacking; in the calendar no retreats were scheduled or any student religious organizations listed.[134] His university was less certain about its Catholicism, and therefore, less sure about its educational mandate. The old "Xaverian family-styled institution" was no more.[135]

President MacLellan's term ended 30 June 1970. He had led the institution through a harrowing transition period, rampant with surprises, challenges, and changes. MacLellan was a product of the old St.F.X.; however, circumstances had forced him, his colleagues, and his faculty to adjust to new social and academic trends. While uneasy about certain developments, MacLellan had tried to preserve what he judged best in the institution's heritage. He stands out as an administrator in St.F.X.'s history who had a clear philosophy of education, a profound conviction about the dignity of each person, and a sympathy for the interests of all; yet he also stands out as the president to 1970 least able to command institutional allegiance to his own principles. His tenure at St.F.X. was one of the longest; during it he had occupied key positions in the academic life of the institution – professor of education, dean of studies, founding principal of Xavier Junior College, and president of St.F.X. The institution he left behind in 1970 was a world away from the one he had entered in 1920 as a young, rural freshman student from Inverness County, Cape Breton.[136] It was now embarking on a new phase of its existence.

Conclusion

By 1970 St.F.X. had travelled nearly twenty years into its second century. If the first rectors and students had revisited their institution that year, it would have appeared to them a place alien except in name. Succeeding generations of eastern Nova Scotia Catholics had altered and adjusted the original project until they had fashioned something quite new. After almost 120 years, only a faint whisper of the old St.F.X. remained. What Bishop Colin MacKinnon had begun in 1853 as a small, intimate, classically oriented, liberal arts, Catholic, diocesan seminary/college had become a much more elaborate, professional, residential, semi-public university. Its original mission to develop a native priesthood, prepare a select group for the "learned professions," and achieve a higher social standing and influence for its modestly endowed constituency of Scots, Irish, and Acadians was likewise transformed. In 1970 St.F.X. still provided a basic undergraduate preparation for students who wished to enter the professions, and indeed, had itself developed an array of pre-professional and professional programs; however, no longer was it a nursery for vocations to the priesthood and much less forcefully was it an instrument of religious propagation for the Roman Catholic Church. Now, as a government-funded institution, its service to the state and the industrial-consumer society had eclipsed its earlier objectives. Moreover, a professional and increasingly specialized faculty found it a useful institutional nexus to pursue their own professional aims. Likewise a larger, liberated student body had learned to exact more attention from the university to their own interests. The new St.F.X., a product of changes it experienced between 1945 and 1970, discovered the claims of its heritage increasingly problematic.

By 1970 St.F.X. had an admirable heritage of identification with and educational service to the Diocese of Antigonish; it had worked to be "for the people." The college had been born of regional, denominational interests, and therefore was the offspring of the people of eastern Nova Scotia. It had identified with them, perhaps most widely and effectively, through its extension department and then its Xavier

Junior College in Sydney. The extension department, under the directorship of Dr Coady, had heightened the social conscience of the university, and the Coady International Institute had extended service to the people of underdeveloped countries.

However, with rapid post-war expansion, changes in the origins of the faculty, developments in the social and economic life of eastern Nova Scotia, and the eventual institutional independence of the junior college, St.F.X.'s keen identification with its constituency began to erode. The university faced the challenge of retaining a strong regional identity and effective service at the grass-roots level. Moreover, the loss of the traditional practice of recruiting prospective faculty from among its students meant that St.F.X. would less often help to develop a native intellectual leadership; more often it would import its intellectuals. As the Celtic legacy of the region disintegrated under the onslaught of modern social trends, St.F.X. also faced the question of its responsibility for preserving and exploring the cultural heritage of its people.

Moreover, at the end of the 1960s, St.F.X. found problematic its heritage of forming Catholic young people through a liberal arts residential program. Expanding enrolments, the imitation of trends elsewhere, the increasing religious pluralism of the faculty, the elimination of a prescriptive curriculum, and the dismantling of *in loco parentis* fractured the university's traditional vision of education and its image of the ideal person. Pre-professional, professional, and expanding science programs challenged the dominance of the liberal arts. St.F.X. began to face the question of whether to preserve, salvage, or abandon the traditional approach to education which had been founded on a Catholic consensus about the meaning of life and the nature of the person.

In 1970, St.F.X. was less at the heart of the diocese than it had been before. State and professional interests were more often setting its agenda. As a professional lay faculty replaced the traditional priest-professors, so denominational aims were displaced by secular ones. Research, publication, learned presentations, and equipping students with useful skills for the market-place became central emphases. St.F.X. was becoming less a coherent institutional expression of the faith and culture of a people and more the product of competing groups with divergent interests and priorities. Democratization and new hiring practices meant the church would have less say or influence on institutional ideals and goals. However, St.F.X. remained a Catholic institution, although in a much looser sense, and did not experience the fate of St Mary's University, Halifax, Acadia University, Wolfville, Mount Allison University, Sackville, and St Dunstan's University,

Charlottetown. All four of these Maritime denominational institutions, born, like St.F.X., in mid-nineteenth-century Atlantic Canada, had been secularized and their traditional identities transformed.[1]

Like other universities, St.F.X. had forged, from the beginning, its own identity; it was not merely a copy of some imported institutional type.[2] As in the past, it would have to decide, in constructing its future, the relative importance of its own heritage to that of developments, models, and trends existing elsewhere.

While acknowledging the problems bequeathed to St.F.X. by the post-war changes, and the challenge it faced of adjusting to the present and future without utterly abandoning or betraying its past, the university's contribution to eastern Nova Scotia and beyond should not be ignored. St.F.X. had helped create a social, spiritual, and intellectual leadership for the diocese and had supplied ecclesiastical, political, and professional leaders for regions beyond. Many of its alumni who followed careers in the Roman Catholic Church or its network of regional and national institutions contributed to what has been called the "conspicuous influence" of the Diocese of Antigonish.[3] St.F.X.'s arts courses and activities contributed to the culture of the area; its extension program, Xavier Junior College, and Coady International Institute stimulated community development both locally and internationally; and its undergraduate programs provided access to higher education for the region and enriched the intellectual lives of many. In 1970, after nearly 120 years of higher educational work, St.F.X. had a venerable record of service to the people of eastern Nova Scotia.

St.F.X. University Hallmarks

A. PATRON: ST FRANCIS XAVIER

Born: Kingdom of Navarre (northern Spain), 7 April 1506.

Education: early tutelage under local priests; University of Paris, 1525–36 (MA in philosophy, 1530).

Ordained: June 1537.

Work: teacher of philosophy 1530–34; secretary of the Jesuits c. 1538–40; missionary in Goa, India, May 1542; in Malabar, Travancore, Ceylon, 1542–45; in East Indies 1545–47; in Goa, March 1548–49; in Japan 1549–51.

Died: Island of Sancian (off coast of China) 3 December 1552; body taken in 1554 to Goa, India, where it was enshrined and venerated.

Comments: co-founder of the Jesuits; main activities: pioneer missionary, apostolic nuncio, and Jesuit superior; canonized in 1622; designated Patron of all Catholic missions in 1927; annual liturgical feast celebrated on 3 December; other universities have been named after him, e.g., Xavier University in Cincinnati, Ohio and Xavier University of Louisiana; President Patrick J. Nicholson (1944–54), a great devotee of St Francis Xavier, obtained relics of the Saint c.1951 and placed them in the main altar of the college chapel.

Sources: The Encyclopedia of Religion (1987), Presidential papers, and James Brodrick, SJ, *Saint Francis Xavier (1506–52)* (Garden City, NY: Doubleday, 1957).

B. UNIVERSITY MOTTO

The University motto, *Quaecumque sunt Vera* (Whatsoever things are true), is from the Latin Vulgate version of the Bible, the Epistle of St Paul to the Philippians, chapter 4, verse 8:

Finally Brethren, whatsoever things are true, whatsoever things are honest, whatsoever things are just, whatsoever things are pure, whatsoever things are lovely, whatsoever things are of good report; if there be any virtue, and if there be any praise, think on these things.

The earliest discovered reference to the motto is in a letter of 1914 from President H.P. MacPherson to Archbishop M.F. Howley of St John's, Newfoundland on the subject of a coat of arms for St.F.X. President MacPherson wrote, "We think of taking for our motto the text of St Paul Phil. 4:8 *"Quaecumque sunt vera."* Who suggested the motto and what occasioned the search for one are now probably impossible to discover.

Since adopting this motto, Xaverians have used it regularly to inspire and to chastise one another.

Sources: President H.P. MacPherson to Archbishop M.F. Howley, 21 July 1914, RG 5/9/5033, PMP, STFXUA; and *Xaverian,* 30 March 1946, 4; 2 March 1951, 4–5; and 4 December 1953, 1.

C. THE UNIVERSITY COAT OF ARMS

The current university coat of arms seemed first to appear in May 1933 on the alumni number of the *Xaverian.* The arms are composed of a blue St Andrew's cross on a silver background (the arms of Nova Scotia) with the supposed shield of the patron saint, Xavier of Navarre, superimposed on this. A scroll at the top contains the university motto; the mayflower and maple leaf below represent emblems of Nova Scotia and Canada respectively.

This coat of arms was not the original used at St.F.X. A very simple one appeared on St.F.X. calendars from 1898, and President H.P. MacPherson (1906–36) made several attempts to have a new coat of arms designed around 1914. Finally, a sister at Ville Marie in Montreal, the motherhouse of the Congregation of Notre Dame, designed one which was used in the 1920s and 1930s. Along with other university arms, it was hung, as a three-foot stone tablet carving, in the Memorial Tower, Halifax in 1916. Elements common to this one and the current coat of arms include the university motto, the cross of St Andrews, the mayflower, and the maple leaf.

Sources: St.F.X. calendars, 1898–99, 1924–25, 1937–38, *Xaverian,* May 1933 (alumni number).

D. THE X-RING

The distinctive St.F.X. X-Ring symbolizes membership in the Xaverian family. It is awarded to the graduating class in a special investiture ceremony, a custom which originated in October 1958. The X-Ring was copyrighted in 1957 under the Industrial Designs Act. After several years of debate, the student union that year passed legislation which defined the ring, designated who could wear it, and granted a joint student-faculty committee power to control its production.

The use of the X symbol appeared on athletic uniforms early in this century. The St.F.X. Amateur Athletic Association registered the "X" as their official symbol in 1920 and decided in 1929 to engrave it on a pin to be awarded to varsity champions. Of course, the X appeared on an early St.F.X. coat of arms in 1916. It was customary for St.F.X. graduating classes to design their own emblem, often a ring. So it was no great leap of the imagination to conceive of an X-Ring. The received explanation for the origins of the current ring goes like this: William J. MacDougall of the class of 1942 was designated to design a class ring but failed to do so until the last minute when he drew a circle and placed an X within. Subsequent classes liked the design and so the X-Ring tradition was born.

The X-Ring was the subject of considerable debate through the 1950s and again in 1967. Students found it difficult to agree on who should wear the ring. Engineering students have sometimes conceived of their own design. Faculty and students also frequently waxed eloquent on the symbolism of the ring. By the 1990s it had become an enduring university hallmark.

Sources: Xaverian, February 1921, 39, 20 November 1948, 1, 13 March 1953, 8, 25 February 1955, 1, 1 November 1957, 1, 2, and 5, 9 October 1958, 3.

E. THE UNIVERSITY COLOURS: BLUE AND WHITE

The only explanation discovered for the origin of the St.F.X. colours appeared in an undocumented *Xaverian* article in 1938:

When [St.F.X.] was transferred to Antigonish in 1855 a move was made to adopt colors. Many, of course, fell under consideration. It was suggested that the colors of St Andrew be used. This suggestion was prompted by the fact that many of the students were from the parish of St Andrews and again these colors symbolized Nova Scotia. It was accepted and from that time onward blue and white has stood for St.F.X.

Source: *Xaverian*, 22 October 1938, 2.

F. XAVERIAN'S PRAYER

This prayer appeared in the *St.F.X. Prayerbook* of 1949 and the *Xaverian*, 7 May 1949. It came from the pen of Rev. Dr John Hugh Gillis, faculty member from 1938 to 1974. Editors subsequently updated the Old English.

O Lord Jesus Christ, Who in Thy perfect love for the Eternal Father didst always conform Thy human actions to His will, graciously look down upon the Xaverian family which seeks to follow in Thy footsteps.

Inspire those in authority with devotion to truth and justice; fill them with zeal that they may faithfully discharge their noble trust. In Thy Providence help them to obtain the means whereby they may effectively advance Thy Kingdom.

Instill into those whose minds and wills are now being moulded an ardent desire to take advantage of their opportunities. Grant that as they advance in age they may grow in wisdom and in grace and that in their individual and social lives they may bear fruit in keeping with the talents given to them and the sacrifices made for them.

Inflame the hearts of those who have passed beyond the halls of Alma Mater with the ideals of Catholic education and of Catholic Action.[1] Hasten to bestow on the souls of those who have passed beyond this life a place of rest in the eternal vision of Thy presence.

Grant strength to all Xaverians, wherever we may be, that our lives may be symbolized by the colours we cherish: white for purity and blue for courage; and may we go forward, like the Apostle of the Indies, to promote whatsoever things are true.

Sanctify Thy Xaverian family in truth and keep us one in Thee, so that we may be found worthy to take our place in the family of Thy Saints, Thou Who livest and reignest world without end. Amen.

Source: St.F.X. Prayerbook (1949), 199, *Xaverian*, 7 May 1949, 2, and interview with Rev. Dr John Hugh Gillis, 4 February 1993, St.F.X.

G. XAVERIAN HYMN

Several college songs have been composed for St.F.X. The earliest extant one was by Professor W.P.M. Kennedy in 1913. Although English professor Rev. R.V. Bannon wrote at least two, his most enduring one appeared in 1936. A former student, Stephen MacGillivray of Glace

1 The phrase "and of Catholic Action" was apparently dropped at the direction of President Hugh J. Somers.

Bay, wrote the music for the song. Here are the words of the original published in 1936:

ST.F.X. HYMN

1. Hail and health to Alma [Mater],
   On for St.F.X.'s fame;
   Leading, trailing, vim unfailing –
   Play the game!
   Life's the goal that gleams before us;
   Faith and honor free.
   Swell the old Xaverian chorus
   Sing for victory:

CHORUS
   Sons of old St Francis Xavier,
   Manly hearts and true;
   Years may creep but still we keep
   Loyal to the White and Blue.

2. Sing for friends no longer near us,
   Sing for happy days of yore.
   Onward striving, forward driving
   Get that score!
   Memories of high endeavour
   Stir our spirits still;
   Here's to St.F.X. forever,
   Sing it with a will.

CHORUS

3. Here's a health to merry Mockler,
   Here's a toast to M.S.B.
   Science, Arts-men, play your parts men,
   Faculty!
   Strong Xaverian lights to guide us,
   Golden as we sing:
   Whatsoever fates betide us,
   Let the old song ring:

CHORUS

Sources: Xaverian, December 1903, 49, January–February 1914, 5, 25 April 1936, 8, and 12 February 1965, 5.

Enrolments, Finances, and Population Statistics

Table 1: St.F.X. Enrolments, 19th Century

	1853–54	1857	1870–71	1880–81	1890–91	1900–1
Seminary	14[a]	9[b]				
College		43	55	38		77
Public Schools[c]						
males		57		45		39[d]
females		22				
Totals		131		83	108[e]	c.120

Sources: St.F.X. College Reports, 1857, 1860–61, *St.F.X. Calendars*, 1891–92 and 1901–2, *Annual Reports of the Superintendent of Education*, 1871, 1881, and *The Calendar of the Collegiate School of St. John the Baptist*, 1902–3.

a These first students were training for the priesthood at the Arichat Seminary, but not all had begun formal studies in theology.

b Full theological training at St.F.X. was discontinued about 1861. However, around twelve priests ordained in the diocese had by then received their complete theological course at St.F.X. From then on until the end of the nineteenth century, pre-seminarians occasionally took part of their theology course at St.F.X.

c To about 1878, St.F.X. provided common school through to college-level instruction. From then until 1928 it offered a high school program.

d This figure is from the year 1902–3. It was the only figure available close to the year 1900–1.

e The St.F.X. calendar for this year supplied only a composite total for the college and academy. From 1883 the academy was male only; the sisters of the Congregation of Notre Dame conducted a female academy in Antigonish from 1886.

Table 2: St.F.X. Enrolments, 20th Century

	1910–11	1920–21	1930–31	1940–41	1950–51	1960–61	1969–70
College							
male	114	167	178	224	657	993	1441
female	18	30	54	80	97	337	906
totals	132	197	232	304	754	1330	2347
High-School-Preparatory[a] department	119	118[b]	36	14	15		
Graduate students[c]			9	18	59		
Special students[d]				15	57		
Non-Catholics							329
Totals	251	315	277	351	885	1330	2347

Sources: *St.F.X. Calendars*, 1911–12 to 1961–62, and statistical summaries from presidential papers.

a The high school or county academy was eliminated in 1928 and replaced by a preparatory department.

b The St.F.X. high school in 1920–21 included only grades ten and eleven.

c Figures are unavailable for 1960–61 and 1969–70.

d Special students were enrolled in a course but not in a regular degree program.

Table 3: Ethnic Background of St.F.X. Students (College Level), 1857–1951

	1857		1900–1		1950–51	
	No	%	No	%	No	%
Totals	52	100	77	100	870	100
Scottish	38	73	44	57	263	30
Irish	5	10	16	21	152	17
English	6	11	11	14	220	25
French	2	4	5	7	109	13
Other[a]	1	2	1	1	126	15

Sources: St.F.X. College Report, 1857–58, *St.F.X. Calendars*, 1901–2 and 1951–52.

Note: Since this table is, by necessity, based on the surnames of fathers only, it does not reveal the number of students who came from a mixed ethnic background. However, the figures indicate general trends.

a A substantial proportion of these were children of immigrant families from Europe who came to work in the industrial area of Cape Breton after 1900.

Table 4: Geographical Origins of St.F.X. Students (College Level), 1857–1970

	1857 No	1857 %	1886 No	1886 %	1900–1 No	1900–1 %	1930–31 No	1930–31 %	1950–51 No	1950–51 %	1969–70 No	1969–70 %
Totals	52	100	61	100	77	100	241	100	870	100	2347	100
A. From diocese[a]	51	98	51	84	58	75	145	60	416	48		
Antigonish Town	4	8	11	18	15	19	42	17	44	5		
Antigonish Co.[b]	32	61	32	52	27	35	52	21	61	7		
Cape Breton	13	25	17	28	25	32	79	33	317	37		
Pictou/Guysb.	2	4	2	3	6	8			14	6		
B. From Outside Diocese	1	2	10	16	19	25	96	40	454	52		
Maritime Provs.			3	5	13	17	56	23	211	24		
Newfoundland			6	10	1	1	7	3	33	4		
Quebec							9	4	98	11		
Ontario							4	2	15	1.5		
Western Canada							2	1	4	0.5		
United States			1	2	4	5	18	7	77	9	94	4
Overseas	1	2			1	1			16	2		

Sources: College Report, 1861, St.F.X. Calendars, 1886, 1900–70.

a The Diocese of Antigonish includes the seven counties of eastern Nova Scotia, three on the mainland – Pictou, Antigonish, and Guysborough – and four on Cape Breton Island – Richmond, Inverness, Cape Breton, and Victoria.

b This includes the town of Antigonish.

Table 5: St.F.X. Program Enrolments 1855–1970

	1855	1900	1961	1970
Arts				
general			466	1148
business admin.			189	306
education			67	173
secretarial arts				78
total arts	38	77	722	1705
Sciences				
general		n/a	247	315
engineering			161	110
home econ.			n/a	93
nursing			n/a	47
physical ed.				77
total science			580	642
Total	38	77	1302	2347

Sources: St.F.X. Calendars, and registrar's and presidential papers.

Note: Statistical summaries of program enrolments were woefully inadequate up to the 1950s.

Table 6: St.F.X. Alumni: Occupational Distribution, 1952

	No
Teachers	147
Clergy	265
Nurses	56
Doctors	209
Dentists	51
Lawyers	75
Engineers	200
Total	1003

Source: St.F.X. "History and Development," April
1952, RG 5/12/14599, PSP, STFXUA.
Note: St.F.X. authorities estimated there were
about 5000 alumni in 1952; they had addresses
for 4500. Information on the activities of alumni
was very incomplete.

Table 7: St.F.X. Alumni: Geographical Distribution, 1964

	No	%
By province		
Nova Scotia	3,133	42
New Brunswick	910	12
Prince Edward Island	86	1
Newfoundland	291	4
Quebec	755	10
Ontario	901	12
Saskatchewan	55	0.7
Manitoba	25	0.3
Alberta	171	2
British Columbia	90	1
Outside of Canada	1,126	15
Total	7,543	100

Source: St.F.X. Brief to Bladen Commission, 24 October 1964, RG 5/13/3145, PMMP, STFXUA.

Table 8: St.F.X. Faculty Profile 1861–1971

	1861 No	1861 %	1901 No	1901 %	1931 No	1931 %	1951 No	1951 %	1971 No	1971 %
Totals	7[a]	100	15	100	23	100	47	100	167	100
lay	4	57	9	60	8	35	20	43	109	65'
cleric	3	43	6	40	15	65	26	55	38	23
sister							1	2	20	12
female	1	14					2	4	30	18
Scottish descent	6	86	7	44	9	39	17	36	54	32
St.F.X. grad.	3	50	9	56	19	83	39	83	102	61
Urban College grad.	2	29	5	31	2	9			1	0.5
Catholic Univ. of Amer. grad.					3	13	6	13	6	4
Terminal degree										
bachelor's			4[b]	25	3	13	16	34	25	15
master's			2	13	13	57	15	32	75	45
doctorate[c]	2	29	5	31	7	30	15	32	65	39
Catholic							47	100	133	80

Sources: St.F.X. College Report, 1861, *St.F.X. Calendars*, 1900–71, and Rev. A.A. Johnston, "Diocesan Priests."

Note: The data for 1951 and 1971 do not include the extension department, Xavier Junior College, or the Coady International Institute.

a This figure includes the teachers in the public school.

b The terminal degree of four faculty members for this year is undetermined.

c This includes earned doctorates only.

Table 9: Xavier Junior College Enrolments, 1951–70

	1951–52	1960–62	1969–70
Full-time	64	248	557
male	c.57	198	344
female	c.7	50	213
Part-time	107	361	631
Adult (non-credit)	53		969
Non–Roman Catholic	n/a		109
Totals	219	629	2157

Sources: Xavier College reports and registrar's office statistical summaries.

Note: These figures do not include summer schools. The figure for non-Catholic enrolment in 1969–70 is full-time.

Table 10: Coady International Institute Enrolments, 1960, 1965, 1970

	1960	1965	1970
Diploma course	20	79	81
male	16	60	62
female	4	19	19
cleric/sister	8	16	28
Summer course	12	77	65
Totals	32	156	146

Source: Coady International Institute student lists.

Table 11: St.F.X. Sources of Revenue, 1855–1970

	1855		1900		1942		1960		1970	
Revenues	$	%	$	%	$	%	$	%	$	%
Fees	240	19			104,188	72	761,652	69	2,270,448	39.5
Investment income					12,772	9	15,558	1	27,799	0.5
Donations					7,022	5	10,416	1	334,815	6
Government grants	1000	81					280,862	26	3,109,298	54
Diocesan quota					18,608	13	20,000	2		
Other					1,601	1	12,468	1	6,919	0.1
Totals	1240	100	12,000		144,190	100	1,100,956	100	5,749,299	100

Sources: St.F.X. College Report, 1855 and selected financial statements in presidential papers.
Note: This data is for St.F.X., Antigonish campus only. Some of the data was unavailable.

Table 12: St.F.X. Annual Tuition, Board and Fees – Selected Years: 1890–1970

Year	Tuition Alone ($)	Tuition, Board, & Fees ($)
1890–91	c. 16.00	c. 88.00
1895–96	31.50	99.00
1900–1	35.00	160.00
1905–6	35.00	160.00
1937–38	109.00	322.00
1939–40	129.00	342.00
1949–50	154.00	519.00
1959–60	250.00	908.00
1969–70	548.00	1408.00

Sources: St.F.X. Calendars, 1890–1970.

Table 13: St.F.X. Endowment Fund – Selected Years: 1886–1970

Year	General ($)	Special ($)	Total ($)
1886[a]	21,070	none	21,070
1900	n/a	n/a	73,262
1920	26,000	n/a	n/a
1930	50,000	174,750	224,750
1940	50,000	174,750	224,750
1950	85,000	411,000	496,000
1960	85,000	491,000	576,000
1970	650,752	366,706	1,017,458

Sources: *St.F.X. Calendars* and financial statements in presidential papers.

a The first endowment fund was formed in 1881 after the provincial government withdrew funding from all denominational colleges.

Table 14: Maritime Catholic University Enrolments, 1960–61

University	Totals
St.F.X. University	1330
Mount Saint Vincent College (Halifax)	378
Le Collège St.-Anne (Church Point, NS)	97
Université Saint-Joseph (Moncton, NB)	563
Université Saint-Louis (Edmunston, NB)	206
St Mary's University (Halifax)	475
St Thomas College (Chatham, NB)	115
St Dunstan's College (Charlottetown, PEI)	–

Source: Statistical returns from colleges in President Somers Papers, RG 5/12/21318–52, STFXUA.

Note: These numbers represent students eligible for the federal government grant.

Table 15: Selected Maritime University Enrolments, 1923, 1960, 1970

Year	St.F.X.	Mt.A.	UNB	Acadia	King's	Dal.	St Mary's
1923	201	238	138	278	83	752	–
1960	1330	1160	1837	884	182	1758	475
1970[a]	3087[b]	–	–	2352	285	5545	2296

Sources: C. Fred Pearson, "Statistical Studies of the Colleges Situated in the Maritime Provinces" (Halifax, NS: reprint from the *Morning Chronicle*, 1923), University Grants Committee, *Higher Education in Nova Scotia* (Halifax: January, 1971), and statistical reports in St.F.X. presidential papers.

a These are full-time totals including arts, sciences, professional, and postgraduate.

b This includes Xavier College enrolments.

Table 16: Religious Denominations of Students at Maritime Universities, 1923

Denomination	Mt.A.	UNB	Acadia	King's	St.F.X.	Dal	NST	Total
Anglican	22	38	16	64	2	102	11	255
Baptist	8	33	211	2	–	71	15	340
Methodist	149	19	18	7	1	68	8	270
Presbyterian	53	29	31	10	6	380	17	526
Roman Catholic	1	18	1	–	192	97	6	315
Others	5	1	1	–	–	34	–	41
Total	238	138	278	83	201	752	57	1747

Source: G. Fred Pearson, *Statistical Studies of the Colleges Situated in the Maritime Provinces* (Halifax, NS: reprint from the *Morning Chronicle*, 1923), 3.

Table 17: Diocese of Antigonish Population Trends, 1861–1961

	1861	1901	1931	1961
Cape Breton Co.	20,866	49,166	92,419	131,507
Antigonish Co.	14,871	13,617	10,073	14,360
Total Diocese	119,452	163,001	197,115	241,407
Catholic	52,097	75,277	97,887	133,169
Scottish	13,591[a]	98,373	93,552	n/a

Source: *Census of Nova Scotia, 1861* and *Census of Canada*, 1901, 1931, and 1961.

a Unlike the remaining figures in this row, this number represents those who were born in Scotland. The 1861 census did not give the numbers of native-born of Scottish descent.

Contributors to the History of St.F.X. Project

The following people kindly granted interviews or submitted documents or written recollections for the History of St.F.X. Project:

Arsenault, Ellen, Antigonish

Arseneau, Dr Donald, UCCB, Sydney

Balawyder, Dr Aloysius, Antigonish

Bauer, Msgr C.H., St.F.X.

Blackburn, Gerald, Ottawa

Bruce, George, Delhi, Ontario

Brunelle, Yves G., Antigonish

Cameron, Zita, Antigonish

Campbell, Dr Donald F., Sydney

Campbell, Rev. John V., St.F.X.

Capstick, Rev. John, Sydney

Carty, Ed, St.F.X.

Chiasson, Joseph, Antigonish

Chiasson, Leo P., St.F.X.

Cormier, Dr Randy, St.F.X.

Currie, Dr Sheldon, St.F.X.

Curtis, Redmond, Sydney

Desjardins, Kay, Antigonish

Doyle, Sister Irene, Antigonish

Foley, William T., Antigonish

Gillis, Rev. Dr John H., St.F.X.

Goff, James R., Calgary, Alberta

Hutton, R.K., Gravenhurst, Ontario

Langley, J. Thomas, St.F.X.

MacDonald, Dr A.A., St.F.X.

MacDonald, Rev. Bernard A., St.F.X.

MacDonald, Brian, St.F.X.

MacDonald, Dr Burton, St.F.X.

MacDonald, Dr Charles W., UCCB, Sydney

MacDonald, Dr J.J., St.F.X.

MacDonald, Rev. Dr R.B., St.F.X.

MacDonald, Ronald A., Antigonish

MacDonell, Rev. Malcolm, Antigonish

MacDonell, Sister Margaret, Mount St Bernard College, Antigonish

MacDougall, John H., Antigonish.

MacInnes, Dr Daniel, St.F.X.

MacIsaac, Peggy, Antigonish

MacKinnon, Dr Ronald, St.F.X.

MacKinnon, Rev. Dr Gregory, Antigonish

MacLean, Judy, St.F.X.

MacLean, Rev. Dr Murdock, Antigonish

MacLean, T.L., Beaton Institute, UCCB, Sydney

MacLean, Dr Raymond,
  Antigonish
MacLellan, J.A., St.F.X.
MacLellan, Rev. Dr Malcolm,
  Antigonish
MacLellan, Rev. Vincent, St.F.X.
MacPherson, Dr John, St.F.X.
McMullin, Dr J.D., St.F.X.
MacNeil, Archbishop Joseph N.,
  Edmonton, Alberta
MacNeil, Kevin J., St.F.X.
Morgan, Dr Robert, Beaton
  Institute, Sydney

Nearing, Frank, Eugene,
  Oregon
O'Donnell, Dr J.C., St.F.X.
Pluta, Dr Leonard, St.F.X.
Power, Bishop William,
  Antigonish.
Roach, Tom, St.F.X.
Sears, Dr John T., St.F.X.
Secco, Dr E.A., St.F.X.
Smyth, Msgr Francis, Antigonish
Weingartshofer, Dr Antonio,
  St.F.X.
Wicks, George, Antigonish

Abbreviations

For the sake of economy, the abbreviations below are used in the endnotes to indicate archives, documentary collections, institutions, associations, and serial publications.

ARCHIVES

AAH	Archives of the Archdiocese of Halifax
AAQ	Archives of the Archdiocese of Quebec
ADA	Archives of the Diocese of Antigonish, Antigonish
APF	Archives of the Propaganda Fide, Rome
BI	Beaton Institute of Cape Breton Studies, Sydney, NS
CCA	Carnegie Corporation Archives, Rare Book and Manuscript Room, Butler Library, Columbia University, New York
CDPM	Centre de Documentation des Oeuvres Pontificales Missionnaires, Lyon, France
DUA	Dalhousie University Archives, Halifax
MSBA	Mount St Bernard Archives, Antigonish
NAC	National Archives of Canada, Ottawa
PANS	Public Archives of Nova Scotia, Halifax
RAC	Rockefeller Archive Centre, New York State
SSTMA	Sisters of St Martha Archives, Motherhouse, Antigonish
STFXUA	St.F.X. University Archives, Antigonish

DOCUMENTARY SOURCES

AAR	Alumni Association Records
AMP	Archbishop McCarthy Papers
BMP	Bishop James Morrison Papers
BOG	Board of Governors
CPP	Dr Moses Coady Personal Papers
DCP	Dr Moses Coady Director's Papers
DSP	Msgr Francis J. Smyth Director's Papers
EC	Extension Collection

ESBK	Extension Department Scrapbook
FEPP	Father W.X. Edwards Personal Papers
JCPP	Bishop John Cameron Personal Papers
LADP	Alexander Laidlaw Assistant Director Papers
MACLPP	Dr Malcolm MacLellan Personal Papers
MADP	Angus B. MacDonald Assistant Director's Papers
MPP	Dr H.P. MacPherson Personal Papers
MSU	Minutes of the St.F.X. Student Union
PCP	President Daniel Chisholm Papers
PMCDP	President Daniel J. MacDonald Papers
PMMP	President Malcolm MacLellan Papers
PMP	President H.P. MacPherson Papers
PNP	President Patrick J. Nicholson Papers
PNPP	Dr Patrick J. Nicholson Personal Papers
PSP	President Hugh J. Somers Papers
PTP	President Alexander Thompson Papers
RFC	Rockefeller Foundation Collection (RAC)
RJPP	Rev. Angus Anthony Johnston Personal Papers
SPP	Dr Hugh J. Somers Personal Papers
SRC	Scriture Riferite Nei Congressi (APF)
TPP	Rev. Jimmy Tompkins Personal Papers, Beaton Institute, Sydney
VPSP	Vice-President Hugh Somers Papers
VPTP	Vice-President Jimmy Tompkins Papers

INSTITUTIONS

AML	Angus L. MacDonald Library, St.F.X.
CII	Coady International Institute
MSB	Mount St Bernard College
St.F.X.	St Francis Xavier University
UCCB	University College of Cape Breton, Sydney, NS
XC	Xavier College
XJC	Xavier Junior College

ASSOCIATIONS

AAU	Atlantic Association of Universities
CAUT	Canadian Association of University Teachers
CCHA	Canadian Catholic Historical Association
NCCU	National Conference of Canadian Universities
STFXAUT	St Francis Xavier Association of University Teachers

SERIAL PUBLICATIONS

CHR	*Canadian Historical Review*

ABBREVIATIONS

CJHE   *Canadian Journal of Higher Education*
DR   *Dalhousie Review*

GOVERNMENT DOCUMENTS

Journal and Proceedings   *Journal and Proceedings of the House of Assembly of the Province of Nova Scotia*

Notes

INTRODUCTION

1 This description of Highland Catholic life is based on Christine Johnson, *Developments in the Roman Catholic Church in Scotland 1789–1829* (Edinburgh: John Donald, 1983), 1–31.

2 Bonnie and Vern Bullough, "Intellectual Achievers: A Study of Eighteenth Century Scotland," *American Journal of Sociology* 76 (1970–71):1052.

3 Roman Catholics are rarely mentioned in R.D. Anderson's excellent study, *Education and Opportunity in Victorian Scotland* (Oxford: Clarendon Press, 1983).

4 George E. Davie, *The Democratic Intellect: Scotland and her Universities in the Nineteenth Century* (Edinburgh: University of Edinburgh Press, 1961).

5 Ibid., 251.

6 Johnson, *Developments in the Roman Catholic Church* and Alexander Stuart MacWilliam, "The Highland Seminaries" (thesis, n.p., n.d.).

7 Only three Catholics were represented in Bonnie and Vern Bullough's sample of 375 intellectual achievers in eighteenth-century Scotland. See "Intellectual Achievers," 1048–63.

8 Stephen Hornsby, "Scottish Emigration and Settlement in Early Nineteenth-Century Cape Breton," in *The Island: New Perspectives on Cape Breton History 1713–1990*, ed. Kenneth Donovan (Fredericton and Sydney: Acadiensis Press and the University College of Cape Breton Press, 1990), 49.

9 See J.M. Bumsted, *The People's Clearance: Highland Emigration to British North American 1770–1815* (Winnipeg: University of Winnipeg Press, 1982), appendix A, table 2.

10 Ibid., 95.

11 J.M. Bumsted, "The Scottish Catholic Church and Prince Edward Island, 1770–1810," in *Religion and Identity: The Experience of Scottish and Irish Catholics in Atlantic Canada*, ed. Terrence Murphy and Cyril J. Byrne (St John's: Jesperson Press, 1987), 18–33.

12 See Andrew H. Clark, "Old World Origins and Religious Adherence in Nova Scotia," *Geographical Review* 50, no. 3 (July 1960):323 and 327.

13 Bumsted, *The People's Clearance*, appendix B.

14 James Hunter, *The Making of a Crofting Community* (Edinburgh: John Donald Publishers, 1976), 6–14.

15 See the reasons given for emigrating in the passenger lists cited in Bumsted, *The People's Clearances*, appendix B, in the emigrant poetry in Margaret MacDonell, *The Emigrant Experience: Songs of Highland Emigrants in North America* (Toronto: University of Toronto Press, 1982), and in Marianne MacLean, *The People of Glengarry: Highlanders in Transition, 1745–1820* (Montreal and Kingston: McGill-Queen's University Press, 1991), 5 and 8–9.

16 A helpful overview of the settlement, early development, and cultural characteristics of these three Scottish Catholic enclaves is given in Raymond MacLean, "The Highland Catholic Tradition in Canada," in *The Scottish Tradition in Canada*, ed. W. Stanford Reid (Toronto: McClelland and Stewart, 1976), 93–117.

17 Ibid., 103–4.

18 Hornsby, "Scottish Emigration," 59–60, Rusty Bitterman, "The Hierarchy of Soil: Land and Labour in a 19th Century Cape Breton Community," *Acadiensis* 18, no. 1 (Autumn 1988):34, Neil MacNeil, "A Reconsideration of the State of Agriculture in Eastern Nova Scotia, 1791–1861" (MA thesis, Queen's University, 1985), Charles W. Dunn, *Highland Settler: A Portrait of the Scottish Gael in Cape Breton and Eastern Nova Scotia* (Wreck Cove, Cape Breton: Breton Books, 1991), 108–11, 114, MacLean, "Highland Catholic Tradition," 104–5, and R. Louis Gentilcore, "The Agricultural Background of Settlement in Eastern Nova Scotia," *Annals of the Association of American Geographers* 46 (December 1956):378–404.

19 Raymond MacLean, "The Scots – Hector's Cargo," in *Banked Fires: the Ethnics of Nova Scotia*, ed. Douglas C. Campbell (Port Credit, Ont.: Scribbler's Press, 1978), 118. The colony itself had by this time reached a level of overall development sufficient to produce an "intellectual awakening." D.C. Harvey, "The Intellectual Awakening of Nova Scotia," *DR* 13 (1933):1–22 and Kenneth Donovan, "'May Learning Flourish': Beginnings of a Cultural Awakening in Cape Breton During the 1840s," in *The Island: New Perspectives on Cape Breton History 1713–1990*, ed. Kenneth Donovan (Fredericton and Sydney: Acadiensis Press and University College of Cape Breton Press, 1990), 89–112.

20 Clark, "Old World Origins," 322.

21 *Census of Canada 1871*, 1:328–33.

22 Ibid.

23 Ibid.

24 John Reid, *Six Crucial Decades: Times of Change in the History of the Maritimes* (Halifax: Nimbus, 1987), 97–117.

25 John Garner, "The Enfranchisement of Roman Catholics in the Maritimes," *CHR* 34, no. 3 (September 1953):204, 206, and 215–18.

26 A.J.B. Johnston, "The 'Protestant Spirit' of Colonial Nova Scotia: An Inquiry into Mid-Nineteenth Century Anti-Catholicism" (MA Thesis, Dalhousie University, 1977).

27 Bishop MacKinnon to the Propaganda Fide, 12 January 1860, SRC, vol. 7, APF.

28 Terrence Murphy, "The Emergence of Maritime Catholicism, 1781–1830," *Acadiensis* 13, no. 2 (1984):29.

29 Rev. Angus Anthony Johnston, *A History of the Catholic Church in Eastern Nova Scotia*, 2 vols. (Antigonish: St.F.X. University Press, 1960, 1971), 2:205–15.

30 Lilian Toward, "The Influence of the Scottish Clergy on Early Education in Cape Breton," *Collections of the Nova Scotia Historical Society* 29 (1951):153–77.

31 For an overview of this process in eastern Nova Scotia, see D. Campbell and R.A. MacLean, *Beyond the Atlantic Roar: A Study of the Nova Scotia Scots* (Toronto: McClelland and Stewart, 1974), 120–68.

32 A vicar apostolic is a titular bishop, possessing nearly the same powers as a diocesan bishop. He acts in the name of and with the authority of the Holy See.

33 "An Act to consolidate and amend the Acts relating to the Roman Catholic Episcopal Corporation of Arichat," *Statutes of Nova Scotia*, 1887, cap. 86, 300–1.

34 *Casket*, 14 February 1978.

35 The Palazzo which housed the offices of the Congregation, "Propaganda Fide," included the residence of the cardinal prefect, the archives, the library, a printing press, and the Church of the Epiphany. *Casket*, 19 March 1903.

36 About 155 students from British North America, and later Canada, attended the Urban College between 1829 and 1922. Many became leaders in the Canadian Roman Catholic Church. About thirty-five of this total were from the Diocese of Arichat/Antigonish. Giovanni Pizzorusso, "Documents d'interest Canadien dans les archives du College Urbain de Propaganda Fide a Rome (1829–1922)," 1992, Manuscripts Division, NAC.

37 "Colleges and Seminaries, Roman," *New Catholic Encyclopedia*, 3:1009.

38 Johnston, *A History*, 2:437.

39 "Pontifical Universities, Roman," *New Catholic Encyclopedia*, 11:558. I have no information on the requirements which had to be met to earn these advanced degrees. Based on his own research, C. Joseph Nuesse states that in the nineteenth century the licentiate and doctorate in theology stood "not so much for specialized knowledge, as for 'a general, yet profound training in the whole field of theology.'" C. Joseph Nuesse, *The Catholic University of America: A Centennial History* (Washington, DC: Catholic University of America Press, 1990), 33.

40 Dr John Schulte, "The Doctrine of Happiness," (1890), partial copy of manuscript, MG 31/2/10–17, box 81, Father Charles Brewer Personal Papers, STFXUA.

41 Dr Coady to Rev. Cornelius Costello, 20 July 1956, RG 30-2/1/1134–5, DCP, EC, STFXUA.

CHAPTER ONE

1 Since St.F.X. functioned as both a liberal arts college and a seminary during its first decade, the term "college/seminary" most accurately describes it.

2 Terrence Murphy, "The Emergence of Maritime Catholicism, 1781–1830," *Acadiensis* 13, no.2 (Spring 1984):32–4.

3 Ibid., 35. See, for example, the case of Edward Phelan in Terrence Murphy, "James Jones and the Establishment of Roman Catholic Church Government in the Maritime Provinces," CCHA, *Study Sessions* 48 (1981):26–42.

4 Edward MacDonald, *The History of St Dunstan's University 1855–1956* (Charlottetown: Board of Governors of St Dunstan's University and Prince Edward Island Museum and Heritage Foundation, 1989), 6–7.

5 Laurence K. Shook, *Catholic Post-Secondary Education in English-Speaking Canada: A History* (Toronto: University of Toronto Press, 1971), 11–13.

6 Rev. A.A. Johnston, *A History of the Catholic Church in Eastern Nova Scotia*, 2 vols. (Antigonish: St.F.X. University Press, 1960), 1:264–8.

7 Ibid., 413–17.

8 MacEachern to Bishop Plessis, 21 February 1821, AAQ.

9 MacDonald in chap. 2 of *The History of St Dunstan's* gives an excellent account and assessment of the work of this predecessor to St Dunstan's.

10 MacDonald, *The History of St Dunstan's*, 13–14 and 23.

11 Fraser to Angus MacDonald, 28 December 1831, Vicar Apostolic, 15, Archives of the Scots College, Rome.

12 MacDonald, *The History of St Dunstan's*, 20 and n. 5, 39.

13 Johnston, *A History*, 2:89–93 discusses this as "Bishop Fraser's School at Antigonish." There are few extant sources so little is known about who taught, who attended, and how long it survived.

14 Rev. A.A. Johnston, "The Right Reverend William Fraser, Second Vicar Apostolic of Nova Scotia, First Bishop of Halifax, and First Bishop of Arichat," CCHA, *Report* (1935–36):24.

15 J. Brian Hanington, *Every Popish Person: The Story of Roman Catholicism in Nova Scotia and the Church of Halifax, 1604–1984* (Halifax: Archdiocese of Halifax, 1984), 82–3. Hanington notes further that "even when the operations [at the seminary] were firmly under way, Fraser took little interest in the project." This view is confirmed by Johnston, *A History*, 2:166–7.

16 Msgr P.J. Nicholson has noted that Fraser's residence, built in Antigonish in 1846, may have been made so palatial because he was planning to imitate Bishop MacEachern on PEI and put most of his residence at the disposal of students. Nicholson claims, "There has been a tradition ... that from the beginning Bishop Fraser had planned to share his residence with young men aspiring to the priesthood." *Casket*, 20 July 1961. See Bishop Walsh to the Propaganda Fide, 2 August 1850, SRC, 6:215–24, for comments on Fraser's lack of interest in episcopal functions, and also Johnston, *A History*, 2:61.

17 Petition of Bishop Fraser and others against the plurality of colleges and the establishment of one university, March 1844, MG 17, vol. 1, no. 81, PANS.

18 Johnston, *A History*, 2:153.

19 An apt phrase used by Johnston, *A History*, 1:479.

20 Ibid., 1:480.

21 Using what little evidence there is, Johnston has given an account of this school in *A History*, 1:479–81.

22 Johnston, *A History*, 2:89. In 1991 an historical marker was placed in front of the East Bay Church. It states, in part: "This cairn was raised to the memory of our ancestors who in 1824–1828 established on these shores the College of East Bay."

23 Johnston, *A History*, 2:156–9 gives an account of the academy. He claims that Chisholm opened it "at the direction of Bishop Fraser," but provides no evidence for this claim; the documents he does use give credit for the academy's founding to Father Chisholm.

24 MacKinnon to the Society for the Propagation of the Faith, 19 October 1852, #9238, CDPM.

25 *Casket*, 3 March 1892.

26 E.R. Forbes and D.A. Muise, eds, *The Atlantic Provinces in Confederation* (Toronto and Fredericton: University of Toronto Press and Acadiensis Press, 1993), 8–9.

27 *Casket*, 3 March 1892.

28 Rev. A.A. Johnston, *Antigonish Diocese Priests and Bishops 1786–1925*, ed. Kathleen M. MacKenzie (Antigonish: Casket Printing and Publishing Co., 1994), 81, and Raymond A. MacLean, "MacKinnon, Colin Francis," *Dictionary of Canadian Biography*, 1871–1880, 10:479–80.

29 A coadjutor is appointed by the Holy See to assist a bishop governing a diocese and has the right of succession.

30 Walsh to Cardinal Fransoni, 2 August 1850, SRC, vol. 6, fol. 215–24, APF.

31 MacKinnon to the Society for the Propagation of the Faith, 19 October 1852, #9238, CDPM.

32 "First Pastoral Letter to the Clergy and Laity of the Diocese of Arichat," 27 February 1852, MG 75/1, RJPP, STFXUA.

33 MacKinnon and Rev. Neil MacLeod to the prefect of the Propaganda Fide, Autumn, 1850, SRC, vol. 6, APF. The whole English-speaking Catholic Church in Canada remained heavily dependent on Quebec for the training of its priests during the nineteenth century. See John S. Moir, "The Problem of a Double Minority: Some Reflections on the Development of the English Catholic Church in Canada in the Nineteenth Century," *Social History* 7 (1971):60.

34 MacKinnon to Bishop Alexander Smith, 20 January 1854, MG 75/1, RJPP. It must have been a serious problem in the diocese which also prompted Bishop Walsh's comment: "nearly one-half of the entire are clergymen of broken reputations." Walsh to Propaganda Fide, 2 August 1850, SRC, vol. 6:215–24.

35 The monument was unveiled and blessed by Bishop John R. MacDonald on Sunday, 19 July 1953 as part of the St.F.X. centennial celebrations. Nearly two thousand people were present to witness the unveiling and hear the principal speaker, Archbishop John Hugh MacDonald of Edmonton. *Casket*, 23 July 1953 and St.F.X. *Alumni News* 11 (October 1953):3.

36 The *Casket* is a weekly newspaper published almost continuously at Antigonish since 24 June 1852. Its perspective has been Catholic. The original proprietor and publisher was John Boyd, an alumnus of the St Andrews Grammar School.

37 MacKinnon, "Third Pastoral Letter," 10 July 1853, MG 75/1, RJPP.

38 MacKinnon to Cardinal Fransoni, 26 April 1853, SRC, vol. 6, APF.

39 *Census of Nova Scotia 1861*, 27.

40 MacKinnon to Cardinal Fransoni, 9 May 1853, SRC, vol.6, APF.

41 A phrase used by Remi Benoit, a student at Arichat Seminary. He also called it "Mother Hubert's big house." Letter to the editor, *Casket*, 5 September 1918.

42 MacKinnon to Mr John, 2 July 1853, MG 75/1, RJPP. For an account of the later use of this building as a residence for the Christian Brothers,

then as a parish residence, and finally as a rectory, see P.J. Nicholson's article in the *Casket*, 11 January 1962.

43 MacKinnon to the Prefect, 12 April 1852, SRC, vol. 6:462–5, APF.

44 MacKinnon, "Pastoral Letter," 10 July 1853, MG 75/1, RJPP.

45 MacKinnon to Cardinal Fransoni, 21 June 1853, SRC, vol. 6, APF and Johnston, *A History*, 2:270, 289, and 295. Five francs were equal to about one dollar.

46 This lay association had originated in early-nineteenth-century France, had been authorized by Pope Pius VII in 1823, and supported a proliferating number of missions around the world. Its Central Councils in Paris and Lyons collected and allocated the money for the needy missions. In 1922 the association was transferred to Rome and became a pontifical society governed by the Congregation for the Propagation of the Faith. "Propagation of the Faith, Society for The," *New Catholic Encyclopedia*, 11:844–6.

47 Quoted in Johnston, *A History*, 1:392. The almost singular dependence of St Dunstan's University on this association in the nineteenth century is noted in MacDonald, *The History of St Dunstan's*, 109.

48 MacKinnon to Charles Choiselat, 29 June 1855, CDPM.

49 Father John Chisholm had established the Arichat Academy in 1833, but it had closed in 1841. See D.C. Harvey, "Early Academies in Nova Scotia, 1841–1850," *Journal of Education*, Halifax, NS (April–May 1936):366.

50 MacKinnon to Joseph Howe, 15 July 1853, MG 75/1, RJPP.

51 Johnston, *A History*, 2:299 and *Journal and Proceedings*, 1854, appendix no. 73:368. The pound was equal to about $5.00 in 1860. Donald H. Flick, "Early Money in Nova Scotia. A Short History of Currency, Exchange and Finance," *Nova Scotia Historical Review* 1, no. 2 (1981):13.

52 Johnston, *A History*, 2:330.

53 MacKinnon to Cardinal Fransoni, 12 April 1852, SRC, vol. 6, APF.

54 Thus began a long tradition of priest-rectors or priest-presidents at St.F.X., an enduring symbol of the church's abiding interest in its work. The first lay president, Dr David Lawless, was not appointed until 1990.

55 MacKinnon to Cardinal Fransoni, 21 June 1853, SRC, vol. 6, APF.

56 Johnston, *Antigonish Diocese*, 110.

57 Ibid., 44.

58 H.M. MacDonald, *Memorable Years in the History of Antigonish* (Antigonish: Casket Printing and Publishing Company, 1964), 15–19.

59 *Casket*, 30 December 1886.

60 Johnston, *A History*, 2:301.

61 MacKinnon to Bishop Thomas Connolly of Saint John, NB, 12 December 1854, MG 75/1, RJPP.

62 Martin Gillis to his brother, 6 December 1853, MG 45/2/275, box 79, Father W.X. Edwards Personal Papers, STFXUA.

63 Hugh Cameron, a Cape Bretoner who taught for a short time at St.F.X. in Antigonish, later claimed, I think wrongly, that the seminary would still have been in Arichat if it had not been for the Arichat fogs, "obnoxious to professors and seminarians from Nova Scotia proper." Historical notes to the editor, *Casket*, 17 June 1909.

64 Johnston, *Antigonish Diocese*, 21.

65 Cameron to his father John Cameron, 12 August 1846, MG 75/1, RJPP.

66 Raymond A. MacLean, *Bishop John Cameron – Piety and Politics* (Antigonish: Casket Printing and Publishing, 1991), 9.

67 Bishop MacKinnon claimed in 1863 that Cameron knew Gaelic, English, Italian, French, and Latin, and was versed in Greek, Hebrew, and Syrian. MacKinnon to the Cardinal Prefect, March, 1863, Acta of 1870, 263:161, APF.

68 MacLean, *Bishop John Cameron*, 35. A Propaganda Fide report of 13 February 1870, Acta of 1870, 234:162, APF, states that Cameron assisted the vice-rector of the Urban College for one month while the rector was ill.

69 Giovanni Pizzorusso, "Documents d'intérêt Canadien dans les archives du Collège Urbain de Propaganda Fide a Rome (1829–1922)," 1992, 11, Manuscripts Division, NAC.

70 MacKinnon to Bishop Thomas Connolly, 12 December 1854, MG 75/1, RJPP.

71 See MacLean, *Bishop John Cameron*, for a fine biographical study of Cameron.

72 Daniel MacGregor to his uncle, 18 November 1854, MG 75/1, RJPP.

73 Uncertainty surrounds this staff member's identity and the spelling of his name.

74 MacKinnon to Rev. William MacLeod, 25 March 1855, MG 75/1, RJPP.

75 Student records for this early period are non-existent and anecdotal material is sparse.

76 MacKinnon to Charles Choiselat, 7 December 1853, MG 75/1, RJPP, and Johnston, *A History*, 2:296.

77 Martin Gillis to John Gillis, 21 August 1853, MG 45/2/275, box 79, Father W.X. Edwards Personal Papers, STFXUA.

78 *Halifax Catholic*, 29 July 1854 and MacKinnon to Rev. Louis J. Casault, Rector of Laval University, 3 July 1854, MG 75/1, RJPP.

79 *Xaverian*, March 1908, 220. The three surviving early graduates had distinguished careers. William Chisholm, ordained with Thomas Sears by Bishop MacKinnon on 21 September 1856, could preach fluently in English, Gaelic, and French. He served the Acadians in Cheticamp (1857–66), and then in Pomquet, along with the Micmac mission (1866–84). Chisholm died 15 February 1884. Sears ministered in several diocesan parishes, but then was sent to serve his fellow Gaels on the west

coast of Newfoundland, becoming the first prefect apostolic in that region (1871–85). He died nearly two years after Chisholm, 7 November 1885. Kenneth MacDonald was ordained 8 December 1856 and then served various parishes, spending the longest at Mabou (1868–94). His Highland parishioners discovered him to be vigorous in the cause of total abstinence and in the confiscation of fiddles. MacDonald brought the Sisters of the Congregation of Notre Dame to Mabou. He died 17 August 1910. Johnston, *A History*, 2:412 and 528–9, and *Antigonish Diocese*, 29, 63, and 111.

80 John Cameron to Cardinal Fransoni, 16 October 1854 and MacKinnon to Cardinal Fransoni 20 November 1854, SRC, vol. 6, APF.

81 *Xaverian*, March 1908, 220.

82 MacGregor to his uncle, 18 November 1854 and 12 March 1855, MG 75/1, RJPP.

83 Duncan Grant to Rev. Alexander MacDonald, 11 January 1856, MG 1, vol. 564, #43, PANS.

84 MacGregor to his uncle, 17 December 1855, MG 75/1, RJPP.

85 Johnston, *A History*, 2:303 and Cameron to Cardinal Fransoni, 16 October 1854, SRC, vol. 6, APF.

86 This "intolerable grievance" was attacked unsuccessfully by Bishop Cameron in 1877 and 1879 when he petitioned the legislature to provide a bonus for teachers who prepared themselves in French. He claimed that Acadian children were "condemned from the outset to grope in the dark" and thus come to view school as a "penitentiary rather than a house of education." Cameron to John Thompson, 3 March 1879, MG 75/1, RJPP.

87 MacGregor to his uncle, 24 September 1854, MG 75/1, RJPP.

88 The educational work of the academy in Arichat was soon supplemented by a convent school. In 1856 Bishop MacKinnon obtained three sisters from the Congregation of Notre Dame, Montreal to establish and run it. Johnston, *A History*, 2:330–2.

89 MacKinnon to Rev. William MacLeod, 25 March 1855, MG 75/1, RJPP.

90 MacKinnon to John Cameron, November 1853, MG 75/1, RJPP and MacKinnon to Cardinal Fransoni, 20 November 1854, SRC, vol. 6, APF.

91 Ibid.

92 Ontario also experienced the same pattern of early Anglican exclusivism and the subsequent proliferation of denominational colleges. See A.B. McKillop, *Matters of Mind: The University in Ontario 1791–1951* (Toronto: University of Toronto Press, 1994), 3–25.

93 W.S. MacNutt, "The Universities of the Maritimes – A Glance Backward," *DR* 53 (1973–74):447 and Gerald T. Rimmington, "The Founding of the Universities in Nova Scotia," *DR* 46 (1966):319–37.

CHAPTER TWO

1 Even though St.F.X. continued to function as a seminary and college until 1861, for the sake of simplicity it will be referred to hereafter as a college.

2 *Halifax Catholic*, 19 September 1855.

3 Rev. Dr John Cameron to Cardinal Fransoni, 16 October 1854, MG 75/ 1, RJPP.

4 *Casket*, 16 July 1857 and MacKinnon, First Pastoral Letter, 27 February 1852, MG 75/1, RJPP.

5 Henry was a native of Halifax, a Presbyterian and Liberal MLA for Antigonish County who would later become a Father of Confederation.

6 "Petition of Bishop Colin Francis MacKinnon ... ," MG 100, vol. 124, #24, PANS.

7 An editorial in the *Casket*, 13 April 1855 complained that favouritism had been shown every other denomination "while we poor Catholics were constrained to struggle on with the tyrant foot of ignorance, hate, and bigotry pressing and cramping our exertions for an equality with our fellow men."

8 MacKinnon to James W. Johnston, 19 March 1855, MG 75/1, RJPP.

9 MacKinnon to Joseph Howe, 5 February 1855, Joseph Howe Papers, 2:354–6, NAC.

10 *Journal and Proceedings*, 1854–55, appendix #81, 286, 605 and 695.

11 On 29 June 1853, MacKinnon had purchased a two-acre lot for the college site at the corner of College and Main streets from Edward and Anne Kenny. The price was 200 pounds. *Land Registry Book*, 13:531–2, Registrar of Deeds, Antigonish.

12 College Report, 1857, STFXUA.

13 Before the college had officially opened, Roderick MacDonald, first professor of mathematics in Arichat, had begun holding public school classes in the basement from October 1854. Letter to the editor from Hugh Cameron, *Casket*, 17 June 1909, and *Journal and Proceedings*, 1854–55, appendix #81, 286. Other schools existed in the town; a school return for 31 October 1854 reports that Jesse MacPhie and Mary Irish both operated schools. About twenty were attending the MacPhie school and forty-one the Irish school. School Papers, RG 14, vols. 3 and 4, 1854, #479 and 480, PANS.

14 *Casket*, 23 July 1936.

15 *Casket*, 16 July 1857 and MacKinnon to Alexander MacDonald, 23 June 1855, MG 75/1, RJPP.

16 MacKinnon to Alexander MacDonald, 23 June 1855, MG 75/1, RJPP.

17 Cameron to editor, *Casket*, 17 June 1909 and *Halifax Catholic*, 29 July 1854.

18 School Papers, RG 14, vols. 47–8, #232, PANS.

19 School Papers, RG 14, vol. 45, #32 and #33, PANS.

20 The second Presbyterian minister in the town, Rev. Thomas Trotter, opened a grammar school in the 1820s. Catholics were unhappy with Trotter's control of the school and called it "the Presbyterian Schoolhouse." Trotter often hired schoolmasters who were young Pictonians headed for the Presbyterian ministry. Thus the discontented Catholics decided to open an academy in 1841, which lasted through until 1849 and then became a grammar school in 1850. Where it met before this is uncertain, but in the early 1850s it was in private rooms under the direction of Roderick MacDonald. For further evidence of local Protestant-Catholic conflict over education, see a Catholic petition of 1839 against the Protestant composition of the Board of School Commissioners in the district. School Papers, RG 14, vol. 45, #38, PANS and D.C. Harvey, "Early Academies in Nova Scotia, 1841–50," *Journal of Education*, Halifax, NS (April–May, 1936):365–6.

21 Ronald A. MacDonald, "The Squires of Antigonish," *Nova Scotia Historical Review* 10, no. 1 (1990):63.

22 *Census of Nova Scotia 1861*, 18 and 190–9.

23 MacDonald, "The Squires of Antigonish," 63.

24 D.G. Whidden, *History of the Town of Antigonish* (n.p., n.p., 1934), 109–23.

25 St.F.X. College Report, 1 January 1857–1 January 1858, STFXUA.

26 Cameron to Cardinal Barnabo, 9 September 1856, SRC, vol. 6, APF. Barnabo became prefect of the Propaganda after the death of Cardinal Fransoni in 1856. He would hold this position until his death on 24 February 1874. *Casket*, 26 March 1874.

27 MacKinnon to Schulte, 30 April 1855, MG 75/1, RJPP.

28 St.F.X. College Report, 1861, 2, STFXUA, describes the duties of the director of studies. By 1858 the director was holding a bi-monthly meeting with the teaching staff to "arrange matters concerning the discipline, method, and arrangement of the different philosophical, mathematical, classical, and English Departments of the college; the conduct, proficiency, and transferments of the pupils." St.F.X. College Report, 1858, 2, STFXUA.

29 There is no evidence about Schulte's place of residence when he first came to Antigonish, but he probably lived with Cameron in the seminary. According to Dr P.J. Nicholson, he did live for a time in what came to be called the Schulte Oratory. Nicholson writes: "It had been erected on an elevation adjoining the cemetery road, approximately flanking the university power house, where traces of its foundation may still be found." Apparently it was used, in Schulte's time, as a chapel and was a centre of religious processions in honour of the Virgin Mary. After his

departure, it was transferred to a site behind the original St Martha's Convent and was used as an ice house for a "considerable time." *Casket*, 1 February 1962 and Rev. A.A. Johnston, *A History of the Catholic Church in Eastern Nova Scotia*, 2 vols. (Antigonish: St.F.X. University Press, 1971), 2:317–18.

30 I am indebted to Ronald A. MacDonald, Antigonish, for information on the lay trustees. Chisholm invented a mathematical scale, apparently a forerunner to the modern slide ruler. Johnston, *A History*, 2:324 claims that Roderick MacDonald in 1861 began to use it in the mathematical department of the college.

31 *Statutes of Nova Scotia*, 1845, cap. 25, 31–40.

32 "An Act to Incorporate the Roman Catholic Bishop of Arichat," *Statutes of Nova Scotia*, 1854, cap. 74, s. 1–5 and Johnston, *A History*, 2:311.

33 Johnston, *A History*, 2:321 claims that his tenure was interrupted for one year in 1858, but gives no documentation.

34 St.F.X. College Report, 1855, STFXUA.

35 Cameron to editor, *Casket*, 17 June 1909. This account has been confirmed by no extant source other than this letter, which was written long after the incident occurred; but neither has any contradictory evidence been discovered.

36 Ibid.

37 The early aims of education at St.F.X. – character formation, mental training, and social utility and uplift – were common to all nineteenth-century Canadian colleges. The main features of the colleges' programs were also similar, such as a prescribed curriculum, a general rather than specialized approach, an emphasis on the classic languages and literature, a focus on mental training based on the assumptions of faculty psychology, and the view that moral and spiritual formation were as important as the mastery of content. See chap. 1 of Patricia Jasen, "The English-Canadian Liberal Arts Curriculum: An Intellectual History From 1800 to 1950" (PHD thesis, University of Manitoba, 1987).

38 Gaelic language and literature were not taught at St.F.X. until 1894, and they always remained an insignificant part of the university's educational program. Later proponents of Gaelic studies based their case on its literary rewards, not on its practical usefulness. *Casket*, 29 November 1894 and *Excelsior*, November 1897, 4. A recent study of the fate of Scottish Gaelic in Eastern Canada overstates the importance of "pressure directed from above" by the anglophone majority and understates the willingness of the Scottish descendants to relinquish their language and culture in exchange for material and social advantages. See Gilbert Foster, *Language and Poverty: The Persistence of Scottish Gaelic in Eastern Canada* (St John's: Institute of Social and Economic Research, 1988), 8.

39 C.W. Dunn, *Highland Settler: A Portrait of the Scottish Gael in Cape Breton and Eastern Nova Scotia* (Wreck Cove, Cape Breton: Breton Books, 1991), 146.

40 A disproportionately large number of notable Canadians have come from Pictou compared to other counties in Nova Scotia. Douglas F. Campbell and Gary D. Bouma, "Social Conflict and Pictou Notables," *Ethnicity* 5 (1978):76–88.

41 R.A. MacLean, *Bishop John Cameron: Piety and Politics* (Antigonish: Casket Printing and Publishing Co., 1991), 70.

42 See the following for perceptive comments on this: President Thompson to R.S. Conage, 30 October 1900, RG 5/8/3407, PTP, President H.P. MacPherson, Commencement Exercises Address, c. 1919, RG 5/9/12467, PMP, and President MacPherson to Neil McNeil, 20 May 1948, MG 1/1/ 1820, MPP, STFXUA.

43 This is a phrase used by David O. Levine to characterize the American drive for economic and social mobility in his study *The American College and the Culture of Aspiration, 1915–1940* (Ithaca and London: Cornell University Press, 1986).

44 A term used by his bishop. MacKinnon to Cardinal Barnabo, 2 October 1856, SRC, vol. 6, APF.

45 The following analysis of educational philosophy at early St.F.X. recognizes that there is a difference between institutional theory and practice. However, the lack of documentation makes it most difficult to assess the difference between the ideal and the real.

46 John Schulte, "How to Study: A Lecture" (Halifax: Compton and Bowden, 1861), 6, RG 5/12/25479, STFXUA. Rev. Ronald MacDonald in an opening lecture in 1878 argued a similar point about the thrust of studies at St.F.X. The best way of acquiring a useful education, he stressed, was through a general cultivation of the intellect guided by religious truth: "a course of studies realizes my ideal of *utility*, which imparts knowledge of such character as can be turned into account in any one of the legitimate avocations of life, gives in its acquisition a healthy development to the mental powers, and a Christian direction to the moral faculties, is in a word cast in a Catholic mould, and comes out bearing the impress of religion stamped on its every feature." See "Catholic Higher Education," in *Prospectus and Course of Studies*, 1878, 12–14, RG 5/12/25195, STFXUA.

47 Ibid., 32.

48 MacDonald, "Catholic Higher Education," 16.

49 Ibid., 17.

50 Ibid., 21.

51 Ibid., 23.

52 Schulte, "How to Study," 24–5.

53 *Journal and Proceedings*, 1867, appendix no. 13, 40.

54 St.F.X. College Report, January 1856 to March 1857, 1, STFXUA. Because Highland Catholics had been excluded from higher education in Scotland, it is doubtful that Scottish emphases – the centrality of philosophy, the openness to all classes of society, the concern for the development of the whole person, and the enmeshing of religion and education – were directly imported from there. Scottish approaches certainly had a direct impact at other Maritime educational institutions like Pictou Academy and Dalhousie. See anon., "Scottish Influence on Higher Education in Nova Scotia," *Scottish Tradition* 3/4 (Fall–Spring 1973–74):46–8, Anne B. Wood, "Thomas McCulloch's Use of Science in Promoting a Liberal Education,"*Acadiensis* 17, no. 1 (Autumn 1987):56–73, and John G. Reid, "Beyond the Democratic Intellect: The Scottish Example and University Reform in Canada's Maritime Provinces, 1870–1933," in *Youth, University, and Canadian Society: Essays in the Social History of Higher Education*, ed. John Reid and Paul Axelrod (Montreal and Kingston: McGill-Queen's University Press, 1989), 275–300.

55 A.B. McKillop, *Matters of Mind: The University in Ontario, 1791–1951* (Toronto: University of Toronto Press, 1994), 85.

56 St.F.X. College Report, 1 January 1856–15 March 1857, STFXUA.

57 The *Halifax Catholic*, 8 December 1855 reported that a certain well-known Protestant had written bigoted and malicious letters to "gentlemen of the highest respectability in Pictou and other places," attacking the president and professors, and trying to dissuade parents from sending their children to St.F.X.

58 *Casket*, 13 April 1855.

59 MacKinnon to Mr Creamer, Halifax, May or June, 1853, MG 75/1, RJPP.

60 Johnston, *A History*, 2:300–1.

61 *Casket*, 13 December 1888. In an important speech at the Jubilee celebrations in 1905, Rector Alexander Thompson would also credit John Cameron with naming the college. *Xaverian*, October 1905, 6.

62 John Cameron to Duncan Cameron, 2 November 1845, MG 75/1, RJPP. I found no confirmation for another explanation of the origin of the name, namely that it was early proposed that the college at Antigonish be given to the Jesuits; hence the name "St Francis Xavier's." Notes taken by Rev. Dr Dougald C. Gillis in conversation with Rt Rev. John Cameron and others, RG 5/12/25263, STFXUA. An additional explanation has been reported by Malcolm MacDonell in "The Early History of St Francis Xavier University," *Canadian Catholic Historical Association Report*, (1947–48):85 that the French Association for the Propagation of the Faith suggested the name when it made its first contribution to the diocese in 1853.

63 For some decades uncertainty continued over the pronunciation and spelling of the college name. An article in the *Casket*, 19 October 1893 noted the variety of common usage, but favoured the possessive "St Francis Xavier's" rather than "St Francis Xavier" because of similar usage at Saint Francis Xavier's College in New York, usage in the Charter of 1866, analogous usage with other names, e.g., St Dunstan's College on PEI, and the stronger implication of the idea of the saint's patronage when the possessive is used. The surname, apparently, was pronounced in a "bewildering variety of ways" at this time. The anonymous author appealed to Webster and Worcester to support a short "a" as in "fat."

64 *Casket*, 11 December 1862.

65 St.F.X. College Report, 1858 and the *Casket*, 16 July 1857.

66 *Casket*, 28 June 1861.

67 Ibid., 1 January 1856 to 15 March 1857, STFXUA.

68 Petition of the Trustees of the College at Antigonish, 7 February 1856 and *Journal and Proceedings*, 1856, 185, 187, 197 and appendix #71, 247.

69 McKillop, *Matters of Mind*, 111.

70 Schulte, "How to Study," 39.

71 MacGregor to his uncle, 5 March 1857, MG 75/1, RJPP.

72 *Casket*, 17 June 1909.

73 St.F.X. College Report, January 1856–March 1857, STFXUA.

74 MacGregor to his uncle, 19 February 1857, MG 75/1, RJPP.

75 *Casket*, 5 August 1858 and Schulte, "How to Study," 15–16.

76 Cameron to John S.D. Thompson, 4 March 1881, MG 73/1/1630–1, and Cameron to L.G. Power, 29 April 1881, MG 73/1/1643–6, JCPP, STFXUA.

77 Hugh Cameron then decided to go to Boston, and he eventually earned a degree in medicine through the University of Pennsylvania. MG 45/2/631, FEPP. St.F.X. College Report, 1857, STFXUA.

78 Hugh Cameron's later claim that this development "demoralized the Higher English Department" and forced the trustees to return to the original arrangement may be true, since a regular teacher was hired for this department at least from 1860 and few students thereafter were used as teachers. Hugh Cameron to editor, *Casket*, 17 June 1909.

79 MacLean, *Bishop John Cameron*, 29.

80 Bishop Alexander MacDonald to President H.P. MacPherson, 29 September 1921, RG 5/9/6211, PMP, STFXUA.

81 *Casket*, 18 June 1857.

82 Title to this land passed to the Roman Catholic Episcopal Corporation of Arichat on 22 August 1855. *Land Registry Book*, 14:283, Registrar of Deeds, Antigonish. MacKinnon was so gratified by the gift that he mentioned it, on his Rome trip in 1855–56, to Cardinal Fransoni, who

pronounced the donors *Bene Meriti de Ecclesia* (to have well deserved of the church). Pope Pius IX approved of the reward; the names of the MacDonald brothers were engraved on tablets of the Propaganda and two medals were issued to them on 7 November 1858. Bishop MacKinnon, Pastoral Letter of 1 October 1856, MacKinnon to Angus and Samuel MacDonald, 7 November 1858, MG 75/1, RJPP and the *Casket*, 9 October 1856 and 18 November 1858.

83 Excerpts from Notebooks of Rev. Dr Dugald C. Gillis, MG 45/2/642, box 80, FEPP, STFXUA.

84 Diocesan Report to the Propaganda, SRC, 1858–61, vol. 7, APF.

85 *Land Registry Book*, 19:534–6, Registrar of Deeds, Antigonish. Johnston, *A History*, 2:321 quotes the Historical Notebooks of Rev. Dugald C. Gillis, ca 1908: "the land was sold by Bishop MacKinnon to start the College." Evidently it was not. The bishop may have needed the money for a trip to the first Vatican Council.

86 Excerpts from Notebooks of Rev. Dr Dugald Gillis, MG 45/2/642, box 80, FEPP, STFXUA and Duncan Grant to Rev. Alexander MacDonald, 11 January 1856, MG 1, vol. 564, #43, PANS.

87 Bishop Walsh of Halifax became angry at Fraser's inaction. In 1850 he complained to a Rome official: "Monsignor Fraser promised me to give one-half of John Ryan's pious bequest but has always evaded the fulfilment of said promise. People and clergy of Halifax are extremely indignant that this city, the native place of the deceased and place so dear to him had been defrauded of the share they expect from the said pious legacy." Walsh to Rector of the Irish College, Rome, April 1850, and Walsh to Propaganda, 2 August 1850, SRC, 6:181 and 215–24, APF. What portion of the legacy the Diocese of Halifax eventually received is unclear.

88 *Decree Book A*, 1844–78, 13ff. and file A-166, Registry of Deeds and Probate, Antigonish.

89 MacKinnon used some of the money to finance his trip to Rome in 1855–56. Duncan Grant to Rev. Alexander MacDonald, 11 January 1856, MG 1, vol. 564, #43, PANS and MacKinnon to Grant, 16 August 1855 and 5 March 1857, MG 75/1, RJPP. Johnston, *A History*, 2:295 writes that MacKinnon acquired none of the legacy until 1857, but the extant correspondence reveals that he occasionally acquired instalments before this from both Duncan Grant and Daniel Creamer, the legacy administrators.

90 St.F.X. College Report, 1 January 1856–15 March 1857, STFXUA. In the same year, a student, Daniel MacGregor, stated that the library holdings included three or four hundred volumes "on all subjects, religious, political and moral." MacGregor to his uncle, 19 February 1857, MG 75/1, RJPP.

91 *St.F.X. Calendar 1890–91*, 9, STFXUA.

92 *Casket*, 29 July 1858.

93 In his farewell address to the Catholics of Arichat, MacKinnon informed them that "The sacred canons and discipline of the Church forbid a residence elsewhere, save in the Episcopal See." Ibid. Evidently, both Bishops Fraser and MacKinnon took these particular "sacred canons" rather lightly.

94 Cameron to the Propaganda, 19 October 1858, Acta of 1859, vol. 228, APF.

95 Johnston, *A History*, 2:320.

96 Schulte to Cardinal Barnabo, 24 December 1859, MacKinnon to Cardinal Barnabo, 12 January 1860, SRC, vol. 7, APF.

97 MacKinnon to Duncan Grant, 5 March 1857, MG 75/1, RJPP. The house and one-half-acre lot belonged to George and Ann Brenan. It cost MacKinnon three hundred pounds. *Land Registry Book*, 15:59–61, Registrar of Deeds, Antigonish. Apparently he even had the house renovated to suit his educational purposes. Daniel MacGregor to his uncle, 11 May 1858, MG 75/1, RJPP.

98 MacKinnon, Pastoral Letter of 1 October 1856, MG 75/1, RJPP and the *Casket*, 9 October 1856.

99 MacKinnon sold the land to Honourable Edward Kenny on 17 November 1859 for 375 pounds. The property renovations probably account for the increased selling price. *Land Registry Book*, 16:31–2, Registrar of Deeds, Antigonish.

100 Johnston, *A History*, 2:332–3 makes this connection between the bishop's failure to staff a convent and the opening of a female department in the college.

101 *Casket*, 4 November 1858. Local school boards had been permitted since 1838 to hire female teachers. In 1851 they accounted for merely 20 per cent of Nova Scotia's public school teachers; by 1880 they made up about 66 per cent of the whole. This "feminization" of public schooling was a trend elsewhere in Canada, the United States and the British Isles. Janet Guildford, "'Separate Sphere': The Feminization of Public School Teaching in Nova Scotia, 1838–1889," *Acadiensis* 22, no. 1 (Autumn 1992):44–64.

102 Narcissa died in 1907 at the age of seventy-six. These details from Ronald A. MacDonald, Antigonish.

103 Johnston, *A History*, 2:433. The School Act of 1845 provided the legal basis for incorporating a female department into an academy. The teacher and her pupils were to be under the "control and superintendence" of the principal teacher in the academy. The female teacher was entitled to receive the ordinary tuition charged in common schools and a portion of the provincial grant, as determined by the trustees. *Statutes of Nova Scotia*, 1845, cap. 25, 31–40.

104 *Casket*, 2 September 1858.

105 John Cameron to Cardinal Barnabo, 29 October 1860, SRC, vol. 7, APF and MacKinnon to A. Certis, 7 January 1869, #9293, CDPM.

106 *Xaverian*, January 1911, 127–8.

107 *Xaverian Weekly*, 28 January 1928, 3.

108 *Casket*, 20 September 1860. MacKinnon to Cardinal Barnabo, 12 January 1860, SRC, vol. 7, APF.

109 Rev. A.A. Johnston, *Antigonish Diocese Priests and Bishops 1786–1925*, ed. Kathleen M. MacKenzie (Antigonish: Casket Printing and Publishing Co., 1994), 65.

110 Shirley B. Elliott, ed., *The Legislative Assembly of Nova Scotia 1758– 1983: A Biographical Dictionary* (Halifax: Province of Nova Scotia, 1984), 126.

111 MacKinnon to Cardinal Barnabo, 12 January 1860, SRC, vol. 7, APF.

112 Cameron to Cardinal Barnabo, 12 January 1860, SRC, vol. 7, APF. In all, about fourteen priests received their exclusive training for the priesthood at St.F.X. Based on a review of Rev. A.A. Johnston, *Antigonish Diocese*.

113 *Casket*, 15 November 1860.

114 Rev. John Schulte, "How to Study," 1.

115 MacKinnon to Cardinal Barnabo, 9 December 1861, SRC, 8:296–303, APF.

116 MacKinnon to Cardinal Barnabo, 18 August 1862, SRC, 8:422–3, APF.

117 In addition to noting his outstanding talent, conscientiousness, piety, and progress, Schulte's Urban College student report recorded that he was "perhaps too philosophical." Johnston, *Antigonish Diocese*, 110.

118 John Schulte, "The Doctrine of Happiness" (1890), 3–4, partial copy of manuscript, MG 31/2/10–17, box 81, Father Charles Brewer Personal Papers, STFXUA.

119 Both MacKinnon and an anonymous article in the *Casket*, 5 March 1863, stated that intemperance was a possible explanation for his departure from the church. Another false explanation gained currency: that he had left Nova Scotia with a woman who later became his wife. Dr Patrick Nicholson to Rev. Malcolm MacDonell, 1 March 1954, MG 2/1/157, PNPP, STFXUA.

120 Rev. J.T. Wagner to Bishop MacKinnon, 14 October 1862, SRC, 8:444, APF.

121 This news occasioned an extremely uncharitable article in the *Casket*, 5 March 1863, called "Apostasy of Dr. Schulte." One quote indicates the caustic tone of the anonymous remarks: "The unfortunate doctor having proved himself so utterly unworthy of the dignity of a Catholic priest as to betray the cause of his divine master for worldly considerations, we feel no loss to be rid of him." The writer proceeded to develop an

uncomplimentary analogy between Schulte and Judas, his "infamous prototype," and attacked the *Presbyterian Witness* for "an extravagant estimate of the doctor's superior learning."

122 Justice Chisholm used this phrase in a letter about Schulte to President H.P. MacPherson, 18 February 1935, RG 5/9/1824, PMP, STFXUA.

123 Schulte, "The Doctrine of Happiness," 4.

124 MacLean, *Bishop John Cameron*, 30.

125 *Casket,* 26 December 1895 and Lenore E. Schulte to Charles M. Tierney, 12 February 1954, MG 45/2/694-5, box 80, FEPP, STFXUA. William Meikle has noted Schulte's possible influence, in his post-Antigonish career, on the evangelical religious convictions of an important Canadian historian at the University of Toronto, George Wrong. Before going to Toronto, Wrong had attended Wycliffe College (founded in 1878 by supporters of Canadian evangelical Anglicanism) instead of Trinity College. Meikle remarks that Wrong had grown up in Huron Diocese, where Schulte, a strong supporter of evangelical Anglicanism, had been rector of Port Burwell and Vienna from 1866 to 1878. See Meikle, "'And Gladly Teach': G.M. Wrong and the Department of History at the University of Toronto" (PHD thesis, Michigan State University, 1977), 20-1. H.M. MacDonald has published a short, useful, although somewhat speculative and undocumented, biography of Schulte called *The Rector* (Antigonish: n.p., 1976). For a short examination of the Antigonish period in his life, see James D. Cameron, "The Shock of Apostasy: St.F.X. and Its First Rector," *Alumni News*, Fall 1992, 3-7.

126 The St.F.X. College Report, 1862-63 does not list him as faculty or administration. It is possible, but unconfirmed, that Cameron's assumed support in the May 1863 provincial election for his cousin, who had run against the bishop's brother, was related to his transfer to Arichat in July. MacLean, *Bishop John Cameron*, 35.

127 Johnston, *A History*, 2:432. Theological studies would occasionally be revived during the next forty-five years. Dr P.J. Nicholson, untitled typescript, 3, RG 5/12/25352, STFXUA. Apparently the last class of theology was taught in 1906-7 by Rev. Dr Dougald C. Gillis. *Casket,* 12 October 1961.

128 MacKinnon to the Catholics of the Mission of Pictou, 5 March 1862, MG 75/1, RJPP.

CHAPTER THREE

1 Bishop MacKinnon to M. Gaudry, 15 December 1865, #9332, CDPM.

2 Unfortunately it is impossible to do little more than infer what student life was like during this period. The university records are thinnest for these years, and thus the students remain largely invisible.

3 Rev. A.A. Johnston, *Antigonish Diocese Priests and Bishops 1786–1925*, ed. Kathleen M. MacKenzie (Antigonish: Casket Printing and Publishing Co., 1994), 73.

4 MacKinnon to Cardinal Barnabo, 1 August 1860, SRC, vol. 7, 476–7, APF.

5 Giovanni Pizzorusso, "Documents d'intérêt Canadien dans les archives du Collège Urbain de Propaganda Fide à Rome (1829–1922)," 18, 1992, Manuscripts Division, NAC.

6 Daniel MacGregor, *The Evils of a Superficial Education* (Halifax: Compton and Company, 1866), passim, RG 5/12/25641, STFXUA.

7 Bishop John Cameron to Hugh Gillis, 11 July 1877, MG 75/1, RJPP.

8 John J. Power to President MacPherson, 28 January 1918, RG 5/9/10499–500, PMP, STFXUA.

9 Moses Coady to Evelyn and Helen [?], 25 May 1955, MG 52/1/18, Sister Anselm Personal Papers, STFXUA.

10 In 1868 MacKinnon reported to the Propaganda, "I myself live under the same roof as the students of the Diocesan Seminary and fulfil to the best of my ability the double office of Rector of the Seminary and President of the College of St Francis Xavier." MacKinnon to Cardinal Barnabo, 18 November 1868, SRC, vol. 11, 163–4, APF.

11 *Casket*, 27 February 1862.

12 MacKinnon to Rome, Acta of 1870, vol. 236, 165–6, APF.

13 Rev. A.A. Johnston, *A History of the Catholic Church in Eastern Nova Scotia*, 2 vols. (Antigonish: St.F.X. University Press, 1960, 1971), 2:402–3 speculates that MacKinnon's apparent use of Archbishop Connolly of Halifax as a scapegoat in 1865 over the publication of a pamphlet libellous against the Diocese of Arichat "may have been an early indication of MacKinnon's waning mental powers." See MacKinnon's embarrassingly blunt and bold letter to the archbishop, 1865, MG 75/1, RJPP.

14 Johnston, *Antigonish Diocese*, 38.

15 Johnston, *A History*, 2:435 claims, without documentation, that the English and Female Departments were "evidently two classes of the public school on Main Street in Antigonish" from 1865 onward.

16 Johnston, *Antigonish Diocese*, 43.

17 Douglas Somers Ormond, ed., *A Century Ago at Arichat and Antigonish* (Hantsport, NS: Lancelot Press, 1985), 51–2.

18 Johnston, *A History*, 2:438.

19 MacGregor noted his need for help in a letter to the Propaganda, 9 November 1865, SRC, vol. 8, 1485–6, APF.

20 Johnston, *A History*, 2:390.

21 MacKinnon to the Propaganda, 20 January 1873, SRC, vol. 12, 292–4, APF.

22 *Xaverian*, October 1911, 12.

23 Pizzorusso, "Documents d'intérêt Canadien," 17.

24 St Dunstan's College in Charlottetown decided to go for affiliation with Laval University rather than obtain a charter to grant its own degrees, an action it deferred until 1917.

25 Petition of Bishop MacKinnon, 26 April 1866, MG 27/1/11–12, box 13, Dr Raymond MacLean Personal Papers, STFXUA.

26 *Journal and Proceedings*, 1866, 88, 95, 101, 102, and 107. In addition, the bishop had the government amend his 1854 bill, "An Act to Incorporate the Roman Catholic Bishop of Arichat," so that the diocese could hold real estate valued up to $3000 in each of the counties of Pictou, Guysborough, Inverness, Victoria, and Cape Breton, and up to $6000 in Antigonish and Richmond. The amendment also invested all real estate "considered and used as the property of the Roman Catholic Church" in the Roman Catholic Episcopal Corporation of Arichat. See "An Act to amend the Act to Incorporate the Roman Catholic Bishop in Arichat," *Statutes of Nova Scotia*, 1866, cap. 92, 136.

27 "An Act to enable the College of Saint Francis Xavier, at Antigonish, to confer Degrees," *Statutes of Nova Scotia*, 1866, cap. 93, 136–7.

28 Laurence K. Shook, *Catholic Post-Secondary Education in English-Speaking Canada* (Toronto: University of Toronto Press, 1971), 24.

29 Ibid. While the British North America Act reserved educational affairs for the provincial legislatures, it did protect in section 93(1) the rights of denominational schools existing "by law" at the time of Confederation.

30 Shirley B. Elliott, ed., *The Legislative Assembly of Nova Scotia 1758–1983: A Biographical Dictionary* (Halifax: Province of Nova Scotia, 1984), 140–1.

31 P.L. McCreath, "Charles Tupper and the Politics of Education in Nova Scotia," *Nova Scotia Historical Quarterly* 1, no. 3 (September 1971):203–22. Nova Scotia was the second colony in the Maritimes to achieve free schools; PEI was the first with its Free Education Act of 1852, perhaps inspired by the Island tenants' need for basic literacy in order to protect their interests against those of the landowners. See Ian Ross Robertson, "Reform, Literacy, and the Lease: The Prince Edward Island Free Education Act of 1852," *Acadiensis* 22, no. 1 (Fall 1990):52–71.

32 B. Anne Wood, "The Significance of Evangelical Presbyterian Politics in the Construction of State Schooling: A Case Study of the Pictou District, 1817–1866," *Acadiensis* 22, no. 2 (Spring 1991):62–85.

33 *Statutes of Nova Scotia 1865*, cap. 28, s. 44(5).

34 Johnston, *A History*, 2:421–2.

35 Sister Francis Xavier, "Educational Legislation in Nova Scotia and the Catholics," CCHA, *Report* 24 (1957):69.

36 The depth of bitterness which characterized the debates over religion and education in other provinces, like Prince Edward Island, seemed absent in Nova Scotia. For example, see Ian Robertson, "Religion, Politics, and

Education in Prince Edward Island, from 1856–1877" (MA thesis, McGill University, 1968).

37 His colleague in Charlottetown, Bishop James McIntyre, also coveted separate Catholic schools and fought hard for them only to be defeated with the passage in 1877 of the PEI Public Schools Act, which entrenched state-financed non-sectarian education. Robertson, "Reform, Literacy, and the Lease," 57, n. 20.

38 MacKinnon was understandably disturbed by the agenda of the normal school, which appeared to exclude educational diversity. Forrester apparently hoped to raise the moral tone of the colony and believed that "a common moral code was best reinforced by a uniform system of teacher training, common sets of authorized texts, a centrally controlled organization and set of procedures, and compulsory schooling financed by direct assessment." B. Anne Wood and Donald Soucy, "From Old to New Scotland: Nineteenth Century Links between Morality and Art Education," in *Framing the Past: Essays on Art Education*, ed. Donald Soucy and Mary Ann Stankiewicz (Reston, Virginia: National Arts Education Association, 1990), 50.

39 MacKinnon to Howe, 1 October 1856 (taken from a note by Father W.X. Edwards), STFXUA.

40 Petition of the Bishop of Arichat, Magistrates, Clergy and other Inhabitants of Eastern Nova Scotia, August, 1868, MG 17, vol. 1, #82, PANS. Johnston, *A History*, 2:422–3 wrongly implies that MacKinnon was fully in favour of the new free public school system, but he wasn't; he wanted separate schools supported through general assessment.

41 Bishop MacKinnon to Cardinal Barnabo, 12 January 1860, SRC, vol. 7, APF and *Journal and Proceedings*, 1865, sppendix no. 9, 26. John S.D. Thompson, a judge of the Supreme Court of Nova Scotia and a Catholic, informed MacKinnon's successor that Catholic schools, i.e., those attended by Catholics only, could use Catholic textbooks and teach Catholic doctrine during school hours without violating any existing law. Bishop John Cameron believed this to be a "most important lever" for achieving religious education in the diocese. Cameron to Thompson, 29 November 1882, MG 75/1, RJPP.

42 *Journal and Proceedings*, 1867, appendix no. 13, 39–40. This report claims that "On one pupil only has the degree of MA been conferred." I found no other information to verify this report.

43 Ibid., 1868, appendix no. 14, 55.

44 Ibid.

45 Ibid., appendix no. 5, y.

46 E.R. Forbes and D.A. Muise, eds., *The Atlantic Provinces in Confederation* (Toronto and Fredericton: University of Toronto Press and Acadiensis Press, 1993), 80.

47 MacKinnon to his clergy and laity, 10 April 1866, in *Halifax Evening Express*, 16 April 1866. MacKinnon's archbishop, Thomas Connolly of Halifax, appeared to be an even stronger champion of confederation. F.J. Wilson, "The Most Reverend Thomas L. Connolly, Archbishop of Halifax," CCHA, *Report* (1943–44):55–108.

48 MacKinnon to Cameron, 24 February 1875, MG 75/1, RJPP.

49 See a series of letters from the Central Councils to MacKinnon, MG 73/1/1199–1207, JCPP, STFXUA.

50 See the statistical summaries of the college returns in the *Journal and Proceedings*, 1867–77, appendices on education, and Forbes and Muise, *The Atlantic Provinces*, 61.

51 MacKinnon realized the need for maintenance and repairs to the buildings, since he was living in the seminary and close to the college. Indeed in 1870 he appealed to the Propaganda for help to undertake some required work. MacKinnon to Cardinal Barnabo, 7 February 1870, SRC, vol. 2, 607–8, APF. The government summaries of the St.F.X. College returns indicate that small-scale improvements were made to one or both buildings in 1869 and in each year from 1873.

52 MacKinnon to Cardinal Barnabo, July 1870, SRC, vol. 11, 572, APF.

53 MacKinnon to Cardinal Barnabo, 17 October 1871, SRC, vol. 11, 1059–60, APF.

54 Bishop Cameron to Archbishop Donatus Sbarretti, 22 November 1904, MG 73/1/2222–3, JCPP, STFXUA. Bishop Cameron, because of later conflicts over other issues, may have retrospectively exaggerated MacGregor's faults; but MacGregor's drinking problem was serious.

55 MacKinnon to the Propaganda, 27 February 1872, SRC, vol. 12, 33–4, APF.

56 MacKinnon to the Propaganda, 20 January 1873, SRC, vol, 12, 292–4, APF.

57 MacKinnon did let MacGregor go for part of the summer of 1873. MacKinnon to the Propaganda, 20 June 1873, vol. 12, SRC, APF.

58 All college statistics for the period 1865 to 1881 require a cautionary note. Few college registers exist for the early history of St.F.X. up to 1889–90. From 1865, the primary source of information on enrolments is government summaries of the college returns. But at times the reported figures are either not credible or confusing. For example, 1867 was the first year that the report on colleges began listing students who were in a "partial course." Presumably it meant part-time students, but this is not made explicit. In certain years the partial category seems also to be included in the total number of students enrolled, but in other years this was not the case. The St.F.X. student enrolment figures for these years must, therefore, be treated as suggestive only and far from precise.

59 *Census of Canada, 1871,* 1:81 and 243.

60 Alan Brooks, "Out-Migration from the Maritime Provinces 1860–1900: Some Preliminary Considerations," *Acadiensis* 5, no. 2 (Spring 1976):26–55 and Patricia Thornton, "The Problem of Out-Migration from Atlantic Canada, 1891–1921: A New Look," *Acadiensis* 15, no. 1 (Autumn 1985):3–34.

61 Bishop John Cameron commented in 1879: "the Gaelic is fast dying out and giving way to English." Cameron to John Thompson, 3 March 1879, MG 73/1/1564, JCPP, STFXUA.

62 D.C. Harvey, *An Introduction to the History of Dalhousie University* (Halifax: McCurdy Printing, 1938), 95.

63 Minutes of the Dalhousie University Board of Governors, 14 May 1874, MS-1–1, A-3, DUA. The Dalhousie invitation to St.F.X. is no longer extant.

64 Harvey, *An Introduction*, 95–6 and John G. Reid, *Mount Allison University, A History to 1963. Vol. 1: 1843–1914; Vol. 2: 1914–1963* (Toronto: University of Toronto Press, 1984), 1:130–2.

65 Peter B. Waite, *The Lives Of Dalhousie University. Volume One, 1818–1925. Lord Dalhousie's College* (Montreal and Kingston: McGill-Queen's University Press, 1994), 118.

66 *Journal and Proceedings*, 1867, 16.

67 W.S. MacNutt, "The Universities of the Maritimes – A Glance Backward," *DR* 52 (1973–74): 431–48, passim.

68 *Journal and Proceedings*, 1875, appendix no. 14, 16.

69 *Statutes of Nova Scotia*, 1876, cap. 27, 46–7.

70 Quoted in Denis Healy, "The University of Halifax, 1875–1881," *DR* 53 (1973–74):40. This article gives a useful account of the university.

71 "An Act to Establish a Provincial University," *Statutes of Nova Scotia*, 1876, cap. 28, 47–57.

72 *Journal and Proceedings*, 1876, 97–100, 108, and 143.

73 *Journal and Proceedings*, 1876, 108–10.

74 Anonymous letter, January 1877, published as "The University of Halifax criticized in a letter addressed to the Chancellor," V/F, vol. 31, #11, PANS.

75 Waite, *The Lives of Dalhousie*, 1:119–20.

76 See "An Act to Establish a Provincial University," *Statutes of Nova Scotia*, 1876, cap. 28, sections 29 and 30.

77 The dearth of nineteenth-century documents renders it difficult to determine with certainty the attitude of St.F.X. authorities toward the new university. Presidential papers exist only for the years following 1891. The St.F.X. perspective had to be pieced together, and then inadequately, from the scanty correspondence of bishops and priests.

78 University of Halifax Papers, Minutes of Senate, 235, MG 17, vol. 104, PANS.

79 No examinations were held in 1876, the year the University of Halifax was created, since the senate first met in September of that year.

80 F.C. Sumichrast to Rev. Alexander Chisholm, 11 May 1877, University of Halifax Papers, Letterbook, MG 17, vol. 106, PANS.

81 Cameron to the Central Council of the Association, 30 November 1876, MG 75/1, RJPP.

82 Annual Diocesan Report to the Association for the Propagation of the Faith, 1878, MG 75/1, RJPP.

83 When Cameron took over the diocese in 1877, he inherited a debt of about $36,600 with annual interest payments of $1856. Cameron to Msgr J.V. Agnozzi, 13 February 1879, SRC, vol. 20, APF. Apparently Cameron made a public statement at a later date that the debt in 1877 was just over $42,000.

84 Cameron to the Propaganda, 13 May 1876, SRC, vol. 14, APF.

85 Cameron to the Propaganda, 23 September 1876, SRC, vol. 14, APF.

86 In July 1877, Rev. Hugh Gillis reiterated Cameron's conclusion; he stated, "Its reputation is down to nil." Gillis to Cameron, 20 July 1877, MG 75/1, RJPP.

87 Cameron to the Propaganda, 23 September 1876, SRC, vol. 14, APF.

88 Gillis to Cameron, 20 July 1877, MG 75/1, RJPP.

89 Father Gillis told Cameron, in July 1877, that if "Rory" MacDonald was not removed from the college, his presence would discourage students from coming. Gillis to Cameron, 20 July 1877, MG 75/1, RJPP. A comment twenty-seven years later by Bishop Cameron implied that MacDonald's problem was "intoxification." Cameron to Archbishop Donatus Sbarretti, 22 November 1904, MG 73/1/2222–23, JCPP, STFXUA.

90 MacKinnon to Cameron, 28 August 1877, MG 75/1, RJPP. Johnston, *A History*, 2:498 records six boarders. The state of both Bishop MacKinnon's mental condition and his college makes it difficult to determine the veracity of his observation in 1877: "the priestly vocation is not so common as it was twenty-six years ago." MacKinnon to George Conroy, 12 August 1877, MG 75/1, RJPP.

91 Father Hugh Gillis to Cameron, 20 July 1877, ibid., complained that the plaster was breaking in the college and that the sills were becoming rotten.

92 Cameron to the Propaganda, 25 April 1877, SRC, vol. 15, APF.

93 Gillis to Cameron, 30 June 1877, MG 75/1, RJPP.

94 Johnston, *Antigonish Diocese*, 19.

95 Cameron to MacGregor, 5 July 1877, MG 73/1/352, JCPP, STFXUA.

96 Cameron to Father Hugh Gillis, 11 July 1877, MG 75/1, RJPP.

97 Gillis to Cameron, 30 June and 20 July 1877, MG 75/1, RJPP.

98 MacGregor's activities during the next few years are uncertain; but from 1881 he served successively in several different parishes – Harbour Grace, Newfoundland, Thorburn, Nova Scotia, and Bridgeport, Cape Breton. He died at Marble Mountain on 24 January 1918, aged eighty-

one. Johnston, *Antigonish Diocese*, 73. MacDonald's course after leaving St.F.X. is unclear, but he only lived another nine years. His "comparatively premature demise" at the age of fifty-six came on 21 December 1886. *Casket*, 30 December 1886.

99 *Aurora*, 20 April 1882.

100 Hannan to Bishop John Cameron, 8 July 1877, MG 75/1, RJPP.

101 MacKinnon's Resignation, 17 July 1877, MG 75/1, RJPP. Archbishop Hannon described the difficult task in a letter to Cameron, 20 July 1877, ibid.

102 Ibid. and Father Gillis to Bishop Cameron, 20 July 1877, MG 75/1, RJPP.

103 Gillis to Bishop Cameron, 8 August 1877, MG 75/1, RJPP. It seems that two of MacKinnon's brothers were in sympathy with his decision to stay while two others were opposed.

104 Hannan to Cameron, 17 August 1877, MG 45/2/92, STFXUA.

105 MacKinnon to Cameron, 28 August 1877, MG 75/1, RJPP.

106 Johnston, *A History*, 2:542.

107 Rev. R. MacGillivray, "Remember Your Prelates: A Sermon, Preached at the Solemn Requiem of Colin Francis MacKinnon, Archbishop of Amydo," St Ninian's Cathedral, 30 September 1879, 13, RG 5/12/25194, STFXUA. Johnston, *A History* 2:497 gives figures which are somewhat different.

108 MacGillivray, "Remember Your Prelates," 4–5. MacLean concludes his biographical sketch of MacKinnon in the *Dictionary of Canadian Biography*, 10:480: "His work in the promotion of higher education in Nova Scotia stands as his greatest achievement."

CHAPTER FOUR

1 *The Golden Jubilee 1905* (pamphlet), 6, MG 45/2/688, box 81/1, FEPP, STFXUA.

2 E.R. Forbes and D.A. Muise, eds., *The Atlantic Provinces in Confederation* (Toronto and Fredericton: University of Toronto Press and Acadiensis Press, 1993), 116.

3 D.G. Whidden, *History of the Town of Antigonish* (Antigonish: Casket Printing and Publishing Co., 1934), 145–55, R.A. MacLean and D.F. Campbell, *Beyond the Atlantic Roar: A Study of Nova Scotia Scots* (Toronto: McClelland and Stewart, 1974), 77–8, and Kris E. Inwood, "Maritime Industrialization from 1870–1910: A Review of the Evidence and Its Interpretation," *Acadiensis* 21, no. 1 (Autumn 1991):132–55.

4 *Casket*, 29 October 1896.

5 Rev. A.A. Johnston, *Antigonish Diocese Priests and Bishops 1786–1925*, ed. Kathleen M. MacKenzie (Antigonish: Casket Printing and Publishing Co., 1994), 43.

6 Father Gillis's day-to-day work remains rather obscure because his personal and presidential papers are not extant. Neither are those of the two subsequent rectors, Drs Angus Cameron and Neil McNeil. Because of the existing documentation, Bishop Cameron's role through these decades is much easier to chart. Furthermore, the bishop played a more prominent part in college affairs than would subsequent bishops. The style and contribution of the early St.F.X. rectors is difficult to identify except on the basis of the sometimes unreliable testimony of external witnesses.

7 *Excelsior*, November 1896, 4 and William Chisholm to Bishop Cameron, 12 April 1979, MG 45/2/108, box 79, FEPP, STFXUA.

8 Gillis to Bishop Cameron, 20 July and 10 August 1877, MG 75/1, RJPP.

9 Chisholm to the Propaganda, 19 February 1880, ASC, vol. 20, #83, APF. Cameron contacted typhoid fever when he was in Rome and in 1880 almost died from inflammation of the lungs. Cameron to Cardinal Simeoni, 20 May 1880, MG 73/1/1263, box 126, JCPP, STFXUA.

10 *Prospectus and Course of Studies, 1878*, RG 5/12/25195, PSP, STFXUA.

11 Bishop Cameron to Msgr J.V. Agnozzi, 13 February 1879, SRC, vol. 20, APF.

12 "Reminiscences of St Francis Xavier's," anon., *Xaverian*, January 1911, 128.

13 In September 1877 Cameron extended this debt to over $44,000 when he purchased for about $2000, from Adam Kirk, a farm of about 110 acres located south of St Ninian's Cathedral. For the first few years the farm failed to yield a profit. *Casket*, 26 November 1896 and Bishop Cameron to J.S.D. Thompson, 27 October 1880, MG 73/1/1598–1602, JCPP, STFXUA.

14 Some Catholics believed that St Ninian's Parish, Antigonish, alone was responsible for the debt, since much of it had been incurred in the construction of their cathedral. Others harboured a "well-founded prejudice," claimed Bishop Cameron, that diocesan contributions in the past had been diverted from their intended purposes. Cameron, "Circular to the Clergy, 1879," MG 75/1, RJPP and Cameron to the Central Councils of the Association for the Propagation of the Faith, 10 November 1877, MG 73/1/77, JCPP, STFXUA.

15 Cameron to the Association for the Propagation of the Faith, 23 July 1879, MG 75/1, RJPP. Cameron would later claim that over one-half of the heavy debt incurred in the construction of the cathedral was paid with money received from the Association. *Casket*, 25 November 1897.

16 Peter Smyth, a merchant of Port Hood, willed $4000 to the support of St.F.X. in 1879 and Father Drummond gave over $3000 in 1880. Extract from the Last Will of Honourable Peter Smyth, 16 January 1889, and Bishop Cameron to James Wallace, 17 October 1882, MG 75/1, RJPP.

17 For example, in 1880–81 three priests teaching at St.F.X. received each $200 annually plus board and washing. Cameron to J.S.D. Thompson, 27 October 1880, MG 73/1/1598–1602, JCPP, STFXUA.

18 Hannan to Cameron, 28 June 1877, MG 45/2/91, box 79, FEPP, STFXUA.

19 Rev. A.A. Johnston, A History of the Catholic Church in Eastern Nova Scotia, 2 vols. (Antigonish: St.F.X. University Press, 1960, 1971), 2:505 and Rev. Neil MacLeod to Cameron, 14 March 1879, MG 45/2/107, box 79, FEPP, STFXUA.

20 The Jesuits were reorganizing their North American missions in the late 1870s, and their visitator to Canada in September 1879 got wind of Archbishop Hannan's scheme and responded enthusiastically about a Jesuit administration. Ultimately, the Jesuits assumed control of St Dunstan's in 1880, but for only one year. G. Edward McDonald, History of St Dunstan's University 1855–1956 (Charlottetown: Board of Governors of St Dunstan's University and Prince Edward Island Museum and Heritage Foundation), 1989, 124–45.

21 Hannan to Cameron, 31 January 1879, MG 45/2/95, box 79, FEPP, STFXUA.

22 MacDonald to Cameron, 11 and 22 February 1879, MG 45/2/97–8, box 79, FEPP, STFXUA.

23 Not all the correspondence generated by Bishop Cameron's canvass of his priests survived, but the following give a fair indication of existing sentiment toward the plan: Rev. John J. Chisholm to Cameron, 13 March 1879, Rev. Daniel J. MacIntosh to Cameron, 25 February 1879, Rev. Hugh Gillis to Cameron, 24 February 1879, Rev. William Chisholm to Cameron, 12 April 1879, Rev. John MacDougall to Cameron, 6 March 1879, and Rev. Hubert Girroir to Cameron, 3 and 5 March 1879, MG 45/2/99–104, 106, 108, 110, box 79, FEPP, STFXUA.

24 Hannan to Cameron, 6 August 1879, MG 75/1, RJPP. Johnston, A History, 2:510 believed that advice about the inadequacy of the grounds at Pictou brought negotiations on the proposal to an end. While this may have been one factor, the financial considerations appeared to have clinched the case for Hannan.

25 Giovanni Pizzorusso, "Documents d'intérêt Canadien dans les archives du Collège Urbain de Propaganda Fide a Rome (1829–1922)," Manuscript Division, NAC, 21.

26 Cameron to Cardinal Simeoni, 20 May 1880, MG 73/1/1263, box 126, JCPP, STFXUA, Casket, 16 and 30 July 1908, and Johnston, Antigonish Diocese, 19.

27 The new wing cost $7200 and was built by contractors from New Glasgow and Stellarton. See Articles of Agreement, 30 May 1880, MG 62/6/220, box 134/1, SPP, STFXUA.

28 Bishop Cameron to J.S.D. Thompson, 27 October 1880, MG 73/1/1598–1602, box 126, JCPP, STFXUA.

29 "Diocesan Report to the Association for the Propagation of the Faith, 1880," MG 75/1, RJPP.

30 Bishop Cameron to J.S.D. Thompson, 27 October 1880, MG 73/1/1598–1602, box 126, JCPP, STFXUA.

31 The selling price was $1750. *Land Registry Book*, 33:349–54, Registrar of Deeds, Antigonish. Around 1907 the old college building was relocated directly behind the court house, where it housed municipal offices until fire destroyed it in 1943. Anonymous typescript, MG 73/1/2869, JCPP, STFXUA.

32 The common school students might have moved to the new Main Street school a few years before. In 1883 Catholic coeducation in the town ended when the Mount St Bernard convent school opened for females.

33 Johnston, *A History*, 2:549.

34 Cameron to the Prefect of the Propaganda, June 1880, SRC, vol. 21, APF and Johnston, *A History*, 2:549.

35 *Casket*, 23 September 1886.

36 Denis Healy, "The University of Halifax, 1875–1881," *DR* 53 (1973–74):47.

37 Minutes of Senate, 396, MG 17, vol. 104, University of Halifax Papers, PANS.

38 Such divisions were only slightly less insurmountable in nineteenth-century Ontario, where the withdrawal of government funding in 1868 helped federation at the University of Toronto achieve partial success. A.B. McKillop provides an excellent account of this problem in Ontario of "the one and the many" in *Matters of Mind: The University in Ontario 1791–1951* (Toronto: University of Toronto Press, 1994), 26–55.

39 The two students were Angus J. Chisholm and Alexander MacDonald, who later became a professor of philosophy and vice-rector at St.F.X., then bishop of Victoria, British Columbia. They had tried in a four- or five-month period to master a two-year course in chemistry in preparation for the University of Halifax examinations. But as MacDonald would put it later, they unfortunately found that "William's Inorganic Chemistry was too big a mouthful, and too difficult of digestion." Right Rev. Alexander MacDonald, "A Bit of Autobiography," MG 31/5/2, box 92/3, Father Charles Brewer Personal Papers, STFXUA. The students actually did well in their other exams.

40 First Bachelor of Arts Examination Report, 5 August 1879, University of Halifax Papers, MG 17, vol. 103, PANS.

41 George Hill to Dr Alex. Chisholm, 7 August 1879, MG 73/1/2779, JCPP, STFXUA.

42 MacDonald to Bishop Cameron, 3 December 1880, MG 75/1, RJPP.

43 Cameron to Senator L.G. Power, 29 April 1881, MG 73/1/1643–46, JCPP, STFXUA.

44 Cameron to J.S.D. Thompson, 27 October 1880, MG 73/1/1598–1602, JCPP, STFXUA.

45 Cameron to J.S.D. Thompson, 7 February 1881, MG 75/1, RJPP.

46 Minutes of Senate, 236, University of Halifax Papers, MG 17, Vol. 104, PANS.

47 Mount Allison, which was uniquely cooperative with the University of Halifax, apparently brought its curriculum into line with the university; this resulted in "a more vigorous requirement." John G. Reid, *Mount Allison University: A History to 1963. Vol. 1:1843–1914; Vol. 2:1914–1963* (Toronto: University of Toronto Press, 1984), 1:141.

48 Minutes of Senate, 324, 364, and 410, University of Halifax Papers, MG 17, vol. 104, PANS.

49 Bishop Cameron to J.S.D. Thompson, 24 February 1881, MG 73/1/1626– 27, JCPP, STFXUA.

50 Healy, "The University of Halifax," 51.

51 *Journal and Proceedings*, 1881, 61.

52 J. Murray Beck, *Politics of Nova Scotia*, 2 vols. (Tantallon: Four East Publications, 1985), 1:207.

53 J.S.D. Thompson to Cameron, 29 November 1880, MG 75/1, RJPP.

54 Cameron to J.S.D. Thompson, 12 March 1881, MG 73/1/1632–3, JCPP, STFXUA.

55 Cameron to J.S.D. Thompson, 28 January 1881, MG 73/1/1622–3, JCPP, STFXUA.

56 Dr Daniel MacGregor, whom Cameron had dismissed from St.F.X. in 1877, was partial to Premier Holmes's plan. The bishop considered MacGregor's support of Holmes "a sort of idolatry." Cameron to J.S.D. Thompson, 26 December 1880, MG 73/1/1607–8, JCPP, STFXUA.

57 At this point, he offered this interesting observation on the souls of Nova Scotians: "The supernatural has not yet been so completely banished from the souls of Nova Scotians that the proper advocacy of theology as an essential and far-reaching branch of knowledge will be resented." Cameron to J.S.D. Thompson, 7 February 1881, MG 75/1, RJPP.

58 Peter Waite has published an excellent biographical study of Thompson called *The Man from Halifax: Sir John Thompson Prime Minister* (Toronto: University of Toronto Press, 1985).

59 D. Hugh Gillis, "Sir John Thompson's Elections," *CHR* 37 (1956):26. See Thompson's acknowledgment of the bishop's support in Thompson to Cameron, 28 December 1877, MG 73/1/1547–8, JCPP, STFXUA.

60 P.B. Waite, "Thompson, Sir John Sparrow David," *Dictionary of Canadian Biography*, 1891–1900, 12:1040 and "Annie and the Bishop: John S.D. Thompson Goes to Ottawa, 1885," *DR* 57 (Winter 1977–78):614.

61 *Journal and Proceedings of the Legislative Council of the Province of Nova Scotia,* 1881, 61–2.

62 Cameron to Thompson, 24 March 1881, MG 73/1/1637–38, JCPP, STFXUA. In the summer of 1881, reformers started an association called the Society for Promoting University Consolidation. Apparently the advocates of such a scheme were figures of some consequence. See the pamphlet, "A Short Statement of the Advantages of University Consolidation" (Halifax: Nova Scotia Printing Co., 1881), V/F, vol. 201, #15, PANS.

63 Bishop Cameron, "Pastoral Letter," (1881), 9–11, MG 73/1/20, box 123, JCPP, STFXUA.

64 In Ontario, government aid to denominational colleges had been withdrawn in 1868. McKillop, *Matters of Mind,* 32–3.

65 An Act for the better Encouragement of Education, *Statutes of Nova Scotia, 1866,* cap. 29, schedule B, 94.

66 Thompson to Cameron, 12 April 1881, MG 75/1, RJPP.

67 Thompson to Cameron, 8 August 1881, MG 75/1, RJPP. Although Antigonish had separate Catholic and Protestant high schools at this time, there was a degree of cooperation between them. During Rev. Dr Neil McNeil's rectorship 1884–91, McNeil allowed the Protestant St Ninian Street High School Teacher $50 out of the academy grant which his pupils helped the Academy to draw. This was a personal arrangement between McNeil and the teacher. Bishop McNeil to Rev. A. Thompson, 7 August 1899, RG 5/8/1164, PTP, STFXUA.

68 *Journal and Proceedings,* 1882, appendix 5, xii.

69 Laurence K. Shook, *Catholic Post-Secondary Education in English-Speaking Canada* (Toronto: University of Toronto Press, 1971), 62.

70 Cameron to the Association for the Propagation of the Faith, 13 November 1881, MG 75/1, RJPP.

71 Bishop Cameron, Pastoral Letter, 24 May 1881, MG 73/1/20, box 123, JCPP, STFXUA.

72 Cameron to Thompson, 14 April 1881, MG 73/1/1041–2, JCPP, and Thompson to Cameron, 22 June 1881, MG 75/1, RJPP, STFXUA.

73 Bishop Cameron to the Association for the Propagation of the Faith, 16 November 1883, MG 75/1, RJPP, Memo: Moneys invested by Governors of St.F.X. College, 1 October 1885, MG 73/1/2865, JCPP, STFXUA, and *St.F.X. Calendar 1886,* 3. These early practices of investing and loaning to parishes and private individuals would continue. For example, the board bought shares in *Casket* stock in 1895. Rev. James Quinan to Chisholm, 16 December 1895, RG 5/7/774, PCP, STFXUA. Between 1886 and 1898 the board granted thirty-two mortgages. The loans ranged from $100 to $500 for one to five years, usually at an annual rate of interest of 7 per cent. Rarely did borrowers default on their loans. Based on a review of St.F.X. mortgages, 1886–98, Registrar of Deeds, Antigonish.

74 Cameron to Thompson, 5 September 1881, MG 73/1/?, JCPP, STFXUA.
According to *The Prospectus and Course of Studies, 1878*, there was a
board of directors composed of twenty priests, politicians, and professionals. It was not incorporated and its function remains elusive. See
Prospectus, RG 5/12/24195, PSP, STFXUA.

75 He also asked Thompson to obtain a seal for the college with an engrav-
ing of St Francis Xavier holding a parchment containing the words
Initium Sapientiae, Timor Domini. Cameron to Thompson, 14 and 21
March 1882, MG 73/1/1672–3, 1676–7, JCPP, STFXUA.

76 P.B. Waite, "Thompson," *Dictionary of Canadian Biography*, 1891–1900,
12:1039–48.

77 An announcement of the incorporation by the *Aurora*, 13 April 1882,
made these points.

78 Shirley B. Elliott, ed., *The Legislative Assembly of Nova Scotia 1758–
1983: A Biographical Dictionary* (Halifax: Province of Nova Scotia,
1984), 134.

79 *Land Registry Book*, 33:488–90, Registrar of Deeds, Antigonish.

80 "An Act to Incorporate the Governors of Saint Francis Xavier's College,"
Statutes of Nova Scotia 1882, cap. 77, 202.

81 The proceedings and decisions of the board of governors through its first
decades remain elusive because of the lack of records. A close associate
of St.F.X. claimed that the rectors through the 1880s and 1890s irregu-
larly convened the board. A.J.G. MacEchen to President H.P. MacPherson, 24 September 1907, RG 5/9/24079–80, PMP, STFXUA.

82 Cameron to Thompson, 17 November 1881, MG 75/1, RJPP, STFXUA.

83 Sister St Victor to Cameron, 16 and 24 March 1880, MG 75/1, RJPP,
STFXUA.

84 "Congregation de Notre Dame, Sisters of," *New Catholic Encyclopedia*,
4:171.

85 See Sister St Miriam of the Temple, "The Congregation of Notre Dame
in Early Nova Scotia," *CCHA Report* (1953):67–80.

86 A problem with licensing the sisters arose in Nova Scotia. The council
of the congregation forbade all sisters to submit to examinations for
school licences. Yet the School Act of 1865 required that school trustees
only hire licensed teachers, and only licensed teachers could draw on
government funds. In 1881, Cameron asked Thompson "to use your
influence to get a minute of council passed that will give the needed legal
qualification to the Sisters." Cameron to Thompson, 17 November 1881,
MG 75/1, RJPP. Thompson must have been successful, for the *Casket*, 20
March 1884, reported that the teachers at St Bernard's Convent held
provincial licences. And Sister John Baptist wrote in 1950: "Sir John
[Thompson] also helped in having the Novitiate period of the Congregation

de Notre Dame recognized by the Department of Education as a substitute for Normal School training." Sister John Baptist to Hugh MacPherson, 8 March 1950, MG 45/2/561, box 80, FEPP, STFXUA.

87 A John McDonald built it for $8188 and the bishop paid for it. McDonald's receipts issued to Bishop Cameron, MG 75/1, RJPP, STFXUA.

88 *Mount Saint Bernard Centennial Booklet* (1883–1983), 17 and MSB House Annals, 1858, 3, MSB.

89 *Aurora*, 10 October 1883.

90 *Aurora*, 7 November 1883.

91 *Casket*, 3 September 1885. *The Catholic Diocesan Directory of Nova Scotia 1936*, 133.

92 *St.F.X. Calendar 1894–95*, 62.

93 *Mount Saint Bernard Centennial Booklet 1883–1983*, 19 and Mount St Bernard House Annals, 1886, 41, MSB. Since the government would only grant support for one academy in each county, for reporting purposes St Bernard's was considered a department of the St.F.X. County Academy. The administration of the two academies, however, remained fully separate.

94 *Journal and Proceedings*, 1887, appendix 5, 32.

95 *Mount Saint Bernard Centennial Booklet 1883–1983*, 34.

96 Pizzorusso, "Documents d'intérêt Canadien," 26.

97 Johnston, *Antigonish Diocese*, 57, *Xaverian*, December 1908, 4, and Alexander MacDonald, "Evolution and the Origin of Species," n.d., STFXUA. Darwin's theory of evolution, set forth in his *Origins of Species* (1859), provoked extensive controversy at the Canadian Protestant colleges in the latter part of the nineteenth century. It challenged biblical revelation and orthodox science. See McKillop, *Matters of Mind*, 114–23. Little evidence exists to show how Darwin's ideas fared at St.F.X. Shook's study of Canadian Catholic colleges, *Catholic Post-Secondary Education*, does not even mention Darwin's name.

98 George Boyle, *Pioneer in Purple: The Life and Work of Archbishop Neil McNeil* (Montreal: Palm, 1951), 26.

99 McNeil to Cardinal Franchi, 1 January 1880, American Sett. Canada, vol. 21, APF.

100 McNeil seemed to do an excellent job of editing this paper. The first issue appeared in December 1881. It carried regular items on church history, Roman Catholic teachings, local news, and commercial and agricultural information. Although it had a circulation of 2500 by 1885, its publisher, W.H. Buchanan, decided to end its career because of numerous unpaid subscriptions, slow renewals, and "the cool indifference with which the paper is regarded in some quarters." *Aurora*, 20 May 1885. In light of a later controversy with McNeil over his editorial policy at the *Casket*, it

is ironic that Bishop Cameron indirectly complimented him when he commended the *Aurora* for its rule of avoiding party politics. *Aurora*, 13 December 1882. Bishop Cameron's reasons for wanting a second newspaper in Antigonish are unclear.

101 Johnston, *Antigonish Diocese*, 88.

102 McNeil to Judge Meagher, 20 April 1906, MG 75/1, RJPP, STFXUA.

103 Bishop Cameron, Circular to Clergy, 28 September 1885, MG 75/1, RJPP, STFXUA.

104 Bishop Cameron, Circular, 24 August 1888, printed in the *Casket*, 7 November 1889.

105 *Aurora*, 20 June 1883.

106 Bishop Cameron, Circular, 24 August 1888. The president of the Association for the Propagation of the Faith encouraged him to build and contributed to Cameron's revenues. Cameron to Alexander Guasco, 19 November 1890, #9459, CDPM.

107 Ledger, MG 45/2/160, box 79/2, FEPP, STFXUA.

108 *St.F.X. Calendar 1890–91*, 9. No information remains on its location. It measured thirty feet by fifty-five feet.

109 Some time later, the *Casket* offices were located here and remained until 1898. Then the building, which had occupied these grounds since 1846, was sold to a local citizen, who divided it into two sections and then moved them to West Street where they were renovated as apartments. *Casket*, 17 October 1898 and 11 January 1962.

110 Bishop Cameron to J.S.D. Thompson, 5 March, 16 October, and 4 December 1888, MG 75/1, RJPP, STFXUA.

111 *Casket*, 9 February 1888.

112 *St.F.X. Calendar 1890–91*, 14. Up to the 1890s, the activities and ethos of St.F.X. student life remain largely in the shadows. Nearly all pre-1890 student records have been lost, and a student journal was not begun until 1896.

113 Bishop Cameron, Circular to Clergy, 28 September 1885, MG 75/1, RJPP, STFXUA.

114 *St.F.X. Calendar 1890–91*, 12–14.

115 See A.G. MacDonald's reflections on the curricular changes at St.F.X. through the 1880s. *Casket*, 20 June 1895 and *St.F.X. Calendar 1886*, 4–5.

116 Bishop Cameron, Circular, 24 August 1888; printed in the *Casket*, 7 November 1889.

117 Roberto Perin, *Rome in Canada: The Vatican and Canadian Affairs in the Late Victorian Age* (Toronto: University of Toronto Press, 1990), 17.

118 *Sadlier's Catholic Directory*, 1877 and 1887, MG 75/1, RJPP, STFXUA.

119 Bishop Cameron, Observations on the State of the Mission, 1886, MG 75/1, RJPP, STFXUA.

120 *Casket*, 20 June 1895.

CHAPTER FIVE

1 *Casket*, 16 January 1890.

2 Bishop Cameron to J.S.D. Thompson, 31 December 1889, MG 75/1, RJPP.

3 Angus J. Chisholm to Bishop Cameron, 31 March 1890, MG 73/1/2131–33, JCPP, STFXUA.

4 Cameron to J.S.D. Thompson, 1 April 1890, MG 73/1/1822, JCPP, STFXUA.

5 *Casket*, 10 April 1890.

6 Cameron to Thompson, 16 and 27 December 1890, MG 73/1/1845, 1847, JCPP, STFXUA. This dispute was not the first that Cameron had with the *Casket* over its coverage of political affairs. Months before the federal election of 1887, he had brought pressure to bear on its proprietor, Angus Boyd, in order to "improve" the paper. Cameron to Thompson, 1 November 1886, MG 73/1/1723, JCPP, STFXUA.

7 Cameron to Thompson, 30 December 1890, MG 73/1/1849, JCPP, STFXUA.

8 Cameron to Dr Angus Chisholm, 14 January 1892, MG 73/1/2081, JCPP, STFXUA.

9 McNeil to the Propaganda Fide, 1 November 1891, vol. 32, #562, ASC.

10 *Casket*, 10 September 1891.

11 Cameron to Thompson, 3 February 1892, MG 73/1/1891, JCPP, STFXUA. Apparently McNeil had become, next to Michael Donovan, the new publisher and the most important shareholder in the *Casket*. He was also elected some time in late 1891 one of the three directors of the company who had the power to appoint the editor. Cameron to Father MacGillivray, February, 1892, MG 75/1, RJPP.

12 The letter is not extant, but the bishop's reply to it is. See Cameron to Neil McNeil, 22 March 1892, MG 73/1/2099, JCPP, STFXUA.

13 Quoted in George Boyle, *Pioneer in Purple: The Life and Work of Archbishop Neil McNeil* (Montreal: Palm, 1951), 35 and 37.

14 Rev. Angus J. Chisholm to Bishop Cameron, 12 January 1892, MG 73/1/2129–30, JCPP, STFXUA.

15 *Casket*, 27 August 1891.

16 At this point he resigned from the St.F.X. board of governors and was replaced by Rev. James M. Quinan, vicar-general to Bishop Cameron. Rev. Daniel Chisholm to the board of governors, 23 July 1895, RG 5/7/31, PCP, STFXUA.

17 Rev. A.A. Johnston, *Antigonish Diocese Priests and Bishops 1786–1925*, ed. Kathleen M. MacKenzie (Antigonish: Casket Printing and Publishing Co., 1994), 88.

18 *Casket*, 11 September 1991, 3–4.

19 He also replaced McNeil as secretary-treasurer of the board of governors. McNeil himself recommended this in October 1891; he believed that it

was to the college's advantage for the rector to hold this position. McNeil to Bishop Cameron, 16 October 1891, MG 73/1/2782, JCPP, STFXUA.

20 Chisholm to the Propaganda Fide, 30 July 1890, vol. 31, #916, ASC, APF. Johnston, *Antigonish Diocese*, 25.

21 *Casket*, 9 March 1905.

22 *Casket*, 16 March 1905, 2.

23 Chisholm's presidential papers are the earliest extant collection of such papers for St.F.X. Their usefulness is marred by two facts: there are almost no letters by Chisholm himself, as he failed to keep copies of his own letters (his presidential papers, therefore, are filed correspondence received from others); second, there are few letters related to the first two years of his presidency, 1891–93.

24 *Casket*, 27 August 1891 and Thompson to the Propaganda, 4 September 1891, vol. 32, #468, ASC, APF.

25 Johnston, *Antigonish Diocese*, 24.

26 For a brief history of public speaking at St.F.X., see Msgr C.H. Bauer, *The History of Public Speaking at St Francis Xavier University; The Early Years 1853–1903* (St.F.X. 1990), STFXUA.

27 Joseph P. McCarthy, *Times of My Life* (n.p: n.p., n.d.).

28 Horrigan to Neil McNeil, 16 December 1892, MG 45/2/387, box 80, FEPP, Horrigan to Daniel Chisholm, 14 August 1893, 29 August 1894, and 15 July 1895, RG 5/7/230, 231, and 233, PCP, STFXUA.

29 *Casket*, 29 September 1892.

30 *Casket*, 14 July 1892, and 13 April 1899.

31 *Casket*, 29 November and 6 December 1894, and 2 December 1897.

32 *Casket*, 29 November 1894.

33 I am indebted to Dr Raymond MacLean for drawing this pattern to my attention.

34 A.B. McKillop, *Matters of Mind: The University in Ontario 1791–1951* (Toronto: University of Toronto Press, 1994), 88.

35 *St.F.X. Calendar 1890–91*, 10.

36 It appears that only four students took advantage of the program from 1890 to 1900; thereafter, numbers increased, but to no more than one or two each year.

37 P.A. MacDonald to Chisholm, 25 June 1896, RG 5/7/1221, PCP, STFXUA.

38 *St.F.X. Calendar 1894–95*, 15.

39 Ibid., 16.

40 President Thompson to E.P. Rice, 24 January 1903, RG 5/8/2770, PTP, STFXUA.

41 In addition to the dominant academic and religious aims, the college also believed it necessary to teach such things as "proper deportment" at mealtimes. See President Thompson to John Chisholm, 11 July 1900, RG 5/8/1721, PTP, STFXUA.

42 *St.F.X. Calendar 1897–98*, 21. At times, people expressed concern about the prefects' influence on the younger students; it was not always praiseworthy. F.A. Roman to President Chisholm, 24 November 1894, RG 5/7/804, PCP, STFXUA.

43 *Casket*, 8 December 1898. See also the baccalaureate sermon by Rev. D.M. MacAdam in the *Casket*, 26 June 1902.

44 *St.F.X. Calendar 1894–95*, 18.

45 Ibid.

46 *Casket*, 20 September 1894.

47 Keith Walden, "Hazes, Hustles, Scraps and Stunts: Initiations at the University of Toronto, 1880–1925," *Youth, University and Canadian Society: Essays in the Social History of Higher Education*, ed. Paul Axelrod and John G. Reid (Montreal and Kingston: McGill-Queen's University Press, 1989), 94–121.

48 *Casket*, 9 October 1890.

49 *Casket*, 28 September 1893.

50 *Casket*, 5 October 1893.

51 *St.F.X. Calendar 1893–94*, 45.

52 Ibid.

53 The "Act to Incorporate the Governors of St Francis Xavier's College" was amended in 1894 to accommodate this election of two additional representatives annually to the board of governors. *Statutes of Nova Scotia 1894*, cap. 103.

54 The executive committee obtained the right to hold the annual meeting on another day, but from the beginning it became a tradition for the association to meet during the college closing exercises.

55 The Alumni Association's constitution and by-laws were published in the *St.F.X. Calendar 1898–99*, 57–61.

56 An Act to Incorporate "The Alumni Association of St Francis Xavier's College, Antigonish," *Statutes of Nova Scotia 1894*, cap. 105. The act was passed on 12 February 1894.

57 *St.F.X. Calendar 1893–94*, 51–4.

58 *Casket*, 19 October 1893.

59 *Casket*, 21 June 1894.

60 *St.F.X. Calendar 1901–02*, 61.

61 *Casket*, 22 June 1899. I found no information on how much of this total was actually collected.

62 *St.F.X. Calendar 1898–99*, 61.

63 Ibid., 33–5.

64 A.J.G. MacEchen to William McDonald, 13 May 1897, RG 5/7/443, PCP, STFXUA.

65 See the alumni statements in RG 5/8/3590–4 and RG 5/8/3606–8, PTP, STFXUA.

66 "Report of the Committee on College Extension," 1897, STFXUA.

67 *St.F.X. Calendar 1897–98*, 36–40. Honours courses were added in the classical languages, mathematics, and the sciences from around 1905 to 1915; the honours offering was not resumed until 1937–38.

68 *St.F.X. Calendar 1891–92*, 18

69 MSB House Annals, 1887, 61, MSB and *St.F.X. Calendar 1890–91*, 28.

70 *St.F.X. Calendar 1894–95*, 60–1.

71 The MSB House Annals record nothing about the affiliation. *Mount Saint Bernard Centennial Booklet, 1883–1983*, 21, gives a brief account of the negotiations. Apparently the affiliation agreement was merely verbal.

72 Donna Y. Ronish, "Sweet Girl Graduates: The Admission of Women to English-Speaking Universities in Canada in the Nineteenth Century" (PH D thesis, University of Montreal, 1985), 8–23 and McKillop, *Matters of Mind*, 124–46.

73 See the 1947 recollections of a graduate of 1898 who credited Sister St Margaret of the Cross with successfully pressing St.F.X., in the face of opposition, for college-level courses. Item 64, Heritage Room, MSB. See also Mary Cameron Hartigan to George Boyle, 14 August 1953, MG 45/ 2/277–8, FEPP, STFXUA. *The Nexus*, 1924, 179, the *Mount Saint Bernard Centennial Booklet, 1883–1893*, 21, and Ronish, "Sweet Girl Graduates," 537–47. Sister St Leonard had high academic potential and ambitions. In 1912 she earned an MA from St.F.X. and then fulfilled all the requirements at the Catholic University of America for a PH D but tragically died in 1914. Sister St Margaret to Father J.J. Tompkins, 20 February 1914, MG 10,2, TPP, BI.

74 R.A. MacLean, *Bishop John Cameron: Piety and Politics* (Antigonish: Casket Printing and Publishing Co., 1991), 80–5.

75 Cameron to Lady Aberdeen, 19 March 1895, MG 73/1/2050, JCPP, STFXUA.

76 Ronish, "Sweet Girl Graduates," 539.

77 The four young women awarded the bachelor of arts degrees were Florence MacDonald, Bailey's Brook, Mary Elizabeth Bissett, River Bourgeois, Cape Breton, Margaret Frances MacDougall, Antigonish, and Lillian E. MacDonald, Antigonish. *Casket*, 24 June 1897. By 1901, ten women had been awarded the St.F.X. BA.

78 *Excelsior*, June 1897, 4.

79 This was Notre Dame in Baltimore, Maryland. Chartered in 1896, it would grant six BAs to female graduates in 1899. S.J. Hennesey, *American Catholics: A History of the Roman Catholic Community in the United States* (New York: Oxford University Press, 1981), 187. From the overall perspective of higher education for women in the Maritimes, Mount St Bernard was not ahead of its time: twenty-two years before, Mount

Allison College in Sackville, New Brunswick had been the first institution in the British Empire to confer a bachelor's degree on a woman. John G. Reid, "The Education of Women at Mount Allison, 1854–1914," *Acadiensis* 12 (Spring 1983):3. Canadian English-speaking universities, in 1896, alone conferred 103 degrees in arts, music, letters, and science on women. Donna Y. Ronish, "Sweet Girl Graduates," 576.

80 Rev. Duncan J. Rankin, "Rev. Dr Dan A. Chisholm" (1949), unpublished, MG 75/1, RJPP, and Sister John Baptist Cameron, "History of the Sisters of St Martha, 1894–1948", n.d., SSTMA.

81 The rector of the Quebec Seminary recommended that Dr Chisholm follow their example and found a community to meet the college's special needs. Rev. Louis A. Paquet to Chisholm, 6 January 1894, A/100/2/1/23, SSTMA. For an account of the early work of the Marthas at St.F.X., see Kathleen M. MacKenzie, "Deo Soli – For God Alone: The Sisters of St Martha (1894–1921)," *Alumni News* (Spring and Summer 1988):4–6.

82 The Sisters of Charity were indebted to Bishop Cameron for his support in their dispute with Archbishop Hannan. In August 1880 they had been withdrawn from the archbishop's jurisdiction and made directly subject to the holy see with Bishop Cameron as the apostolic delegate. This arrangement continued until 5 December 1882. MacLean, *Bishop John Cameron*, 80–5.

83 Sister May Mulvihill, CSM, "Origin and Early History: History of Sisters of St Martha of Antigonish, 1894–1917," 1981, 6, 12–13, and 15, SSTMA.

84 Bishop Cameron, Circular, 22 May 1893, MG 75/1, RJPP.

85 *Casket*, 20 September 1894. Miss Agnes Dugan of Meteghan, Nova Scotia was the first recruit; she adopted the name Sister M. Cecilia. Miss Elizabeth MacAdam was the first from the Diocese of Antigonish; she became Sister M. Francis.

86 *St.F.X. Calendar 1894–95*, 23–6.

87 Chisholm to Governors of St.F.X., 19 October 1894, MG 73/1/2811, JCPP, STFXUA.

88 A.H. MacKay, Superintendent of Education, to Chisholm, 21 July 1894, RG 5/7/658, PCP, STFXUA.

89 Bishop McNeil of St George's, Newfoundland loaned about $5000 in 1896. N. Meagher to Chisholm, 28 October 1896, RG 5/7/1379, PCP. A. McKenna, a tobacco manufacturer in Pictou, loaned $6000 in 1896 and another $2000 in 1897. A. McKenna to Chisholm, 6 April 1896, 8 February and 27 March 1897, RG 5/7/489–91, PCP, STFXUA.

90 *Casket*, 14 March 1895.

91 The farm was located immediately to the south of Xavier Hall and supplied St.F.X. with some of its required food.

92 The *Casket*, 6 February 1896, carried a detailed description of the newly completed wing. J.C. Dumaresq of Halifax was the architect, J.F. Teed

of Dorchester, NB was the contractor, and G.A. Wootne of Antigonish installed the heating.

93 Chisholm to Blouin correspondence, 1896, RG 5/7/1–19, PCP, Chisholm to the Propaganda, 6 November 1892, vol. 32, #1221, ASC, APF, and *Casket*, 30 September 1897.

94 *Excelsior*, November 1897, 6.

95 Mother Fidelis to Chisholm, 3 March, 30 June, and 2 July 1897, MG 45/2/246–7a,b, box 79/2, FEPP. See also RG 5/7/1071–5, PCP, STFXUA.

96 Sarah MacPherson, "Religious Women in Nova Scotia: A Struggle for Autonomy. A Sketch of the Sisters of St Martha of Antigonish, Nova Scotia, 1900–1960," CCHA, *Study Sessions* (1984):89–106.

97 Mother Fidelis to Chisholm, 7 and 15 July 1897, MG 45/2/248–51, box 79/2, FEPP, STFXUA.

98 *Calendar of the Collegiate School of St John the Baptist, 1902–1903*, 5, STFXUA.

99 *Casket*, 16 January 1890.

100 *Casket*, 1 November 1894, 11 June 1896, and 9 June 1904. See also President Thompson to Alex. Campbell, 6 May 1899, RG 5/8/1680, PTP, STFXUA.

101 *Casket*, 29 November 1894. Msgr C.H. Bauer has written a useful chronicle of drama at St.F.X. which describes the plays performed from 1889 to 1945, identifies and profiles the actors, provides excerpts from reviews, and notes the waxing and waning of the Drama Society. See *Drama at St Francis Xavier University*, vols. 1 and 2 (Antigonish: St.F.X., 1987 and 1989), STFXUA.

102 *Excelsior*, December 1897, 3.

103 Alyce Taylor Cheska, "The Antigonish Highland Games: A Community's Involvement in the Scottish Festival of Eastern Canada," *Nova Scotia Historical Review* 3, no. 1 (1983):55–6.

104 *Casket*, 21 September 1892.

105 *St.F.X. Calendar 1894–95*, 44.

106 *Excelsior*, May 1897, 5 and the *Casket*, 13 May 1897.

107 *Casket*, 4 January 1906.

108 A point made by Paul Axelrod, "Student Life in Canadian Universities: The Lessons of History," *CJHE* 20–3 (1990):17.

109 *Casket*, 8 and 15 October 1896. Unfortunately, the first edition of the paper is missing.

110 This was one theory expressed in the paper on the reason for its establishment. *Excelsior*, January 1900, 8–11.

111 *Casket*, 5 November 1896.

112 *Excelsior*, June 1897.

113 *Excelsior*, October 1899, 13–14.

114 *Xaverian*, November 1903, 15–16.

115 The grant of $600 had been increased in 1894. Under the school act, the academy department received the grant, but a number of the St.F.X. professors taught at both the academy and college levels; hence, the editor's charge that the grant was subsidizing the work of the college had some legitimacy.

116 *Eastern Chronicle*, 29 April, 20 May, 3, 10, and 24 June, 8 July, and 11 September 1897.

117 Apparently, Rector Chisholm's family had a tradition of firm Tory loyalty. I'm indebted to Ronald A. MacDonald, Antigonish for this information.

118 *Casket*, 24 June 1897.

119 *Eastern Chronicle*, 3 and 10 June 1897.

120 A.G. MacDonald to Chisholm, 11 May 1897, RG 5/7/340, PCP, STFXUA.

121 Bishop Cameron, Memo, 20 June 1896, MG 73/1 2522, JCPP, STFXUA.

122 Archbishop D. Falconio to Bishop Cameron, 27 May 1900, MG 73/1/2567–9, JCPP, STFXUA and MacLean, *Bishop John Cameron*, 155–6 and 159. After a permanent delegation from Rome was established in Ottawa, Archbishop Falconio was the first apostolic delegate appointed.

123 *Casket*, 10 February 1898.

124 *Casket*, 23 June 1898.

125 *Casket*, 16 March 1905, 2.

126 Chisholm to Cameron, 27 November 1898, A/100/2/1/6, SSTMA.

127 Chisholm to Cameron, 17 January 1899, MG 73/1/2788–92, JCPP, STFXUA. The extant sources fail to clarify if or why a rift appeared between the rector and the bishop before Chisholm left, why the bishop did not make it clear to Chisholm that his rectorship was finished, or why Chisholm continued to believe that he was still officially the rector one year after he had left the college.

128 Johnston, *Antigonish Diocese*, 25.

129 *Casket*, 30 June 1898.

130 *Casket*, 8 July 1897.

CHAPTER SIX

1 Rector A. Thompson, Rectorial Address, in *The Golden Jubilee 1905* (pamphlet), 7, MG 45/2/688, box 81/1, FEPP, STFXUA.

2 *Casket*, 30 June 1898.

3 Rev. A.A. Johnston, *Antigonish Diocese Priests and Bishops 1786–1925*, ed. Kathleen M. MacKenzie (Antigonish: Casket Printing and Publishing Co., 1994), 42.

4 *Casket*, 1 September 1898 and Johnston, *Antigonish Diocese*, 65.

5 Johnston, *Antigonish Diocese*, 91.

6 Johnston, *Antigonish Diocese*, 101.

7 *Casket*, 29 March 1900.

8 *Excelsior*, October 1899, 19 and *Casket*, 9 October 1899.

9 *Journal and Proceedings*, 1900, appendix #5.

10 A.B. McKillop, *Matters of Mind: The University in Ontario 1791–1951* (Toronto: University of Toronto Press, 1994), 56–79.

11 P.B. Waite, *The Lives of Dalhousie University. Volume One, 1818–1925. Lord Dalhousie's College* (Montreal and Kingston: McGill-Queen's University Press, 1994), 1:137–41 and 164–8.

12 T.W. Acheson, "The National Policy and the Industrialization of the Maritimes," *Acadiensis* 1, no. 2 (Spring 1972):3–28.

13 Del Muise, "'The Great Transformation': Changing the Urban Face of Nova Scotia, 1871–1921," *Nova Scotia Historical Review* 11 (1991):1–42.

14 Muise, "'The Great Transformation,'" 2.

15 The process of professionalization and its relation to the universities in the United States has been examined by Burton Bledstein in *The Culture of Professionalism: The Middle Class and the Development of Higher Education in America* (New York: Norton, 1976).

16 *Census of Nova Scotia 1861*, 190–9 and *Census of Canada 1911*, 6:154–6 and 249.

17 *St.F.X. Calendar 1899–1900*, 19.

18 Ibid., 46–7.

19 *Casket*, 13 July 1899.

20 Thompson to Andrew Carnegie, 18 March 1901, RG 5/8/130–33, PTP, STFXUA. Actually, Dalhousie had been offering some courses in engineering from 1893 or earlier. *Dalhousie Calendar 1893–94*, DUA. Perhaps St.F.X. could lay claim to be the first Maritime college to officially establish a school or department in applied science.

21 Thompson to A.G. Macdonald, 25 May 1899, RG 5/8/644–5, PTP, STFXUA.

22 This fortitude was undoubtedly galvanized by support from alumni and members of the board of governors who believed that St.F.X. had to respond to the needs of a changing society. However, the meagre sources do not reveal the role of the alumni and board in initiating the new program of applied science.

23 This had been the case at other colonial colleges. Only toward the end of the nineteenth century did some universities follow the German model of producing scientists through research, lectures, and laboratory work. The establishment of engineering programs was often the catalyst for developing research laboratories. Richard A. Jarrell, "Science at the University of New Brunswick in the Nineteenth Century," *Acadiensis* 2, no. 2 (Spring 1973):55–79.

24 This trend in the approach to science at the Maritime colleges has been described by Paul A. Bogaard, ed., *Profiles of Science and Society in the*

Maritimes Prior to 1914 (Fredericton and Sackville, NB: Acadiensis Press and Centre for Canadian Studies, Mount Allison University, 1991), 18.

25 Thompson to MacPherson, 13 May 1899 and MacPherson to Thompson, 6 September 1899, RG 5/8/1183, and 1184a, PTP, STFXUA. Johnston, *Antigonish Diocese*, 90.

26 *St.F.X. Calendar 1899–90*, 38.

27 Thompson to *Halifax Herald*, 4 August 1900, RG 5/8/457–8, PTP, STFXUA.

28 Thompson to L. Insurance Company, 23 January 1900, RG 5/8/482–4, PTP, STFXUA.

29 *Casket*, 28 September 1899 and *St.F.X. Calendar 1900–1901*, 32–3.

30 *Casket*, 31 August 1899.

31 *Casket*, 12 October 1899.

32 Thompson to J.B. Currie, 16 August 1899, RG 5/8/3070, PTP, STFXUA. Some priests were also generous with donations and bequests to their *alma mater*: Rev. Neil MacLeod gave $4000 in 1884, Very Rev. James Quinan granted $4000 in 1902, Rev. Colin Chisholm donated $727 in 1903. Lay people granted funds too. Most often these bequests and donations were to finance the training of ecclesiastical or pauper students.

33 Thompson to Joseph A. Chisholm, 25 August 1901, RG 5/8/200, PTP, STFXUA. *St.F.X. Calendar 1899–1900*, 26.

34 Some parish priests viewed these solicitations as rude intrusions. Thompson to Rev. Colin T. MacKinnon, 1 February 1901, RG 5/8/1067–70, PTP, STFXUA.

35 *Casket*, 11 October 1900 and Rev. Neil MacDonald to Thompson, 22 April 1901, RG 5/8/4395, PTP, STFXUA. Thompson made a second appeal to Carnegie in 1902. Carnegie probably did not donate to St.F.X. at this time. Thompson to F. Schueman, 22 December 1902, RG 5/8/1447–50, PTP, STFXUA. But already his largesse was reaching the area: he gave $15,000 to the town of Sydney for a library building in 1901. *Casket*, 14 March 1901.

36 *Casket*, 13 August 1903.

37 *Casket*, 22 June 1899.

38 Resolution of the Special Committee, 22 July 1903, RG 5/8/21–3, PTP, STFXUA.

39 *Casket*, 6 August 1903 and Bishop Cameron, Circular to the Clergy, n.d., MG 73/1/2783, JCPP, STFXUA.

40 *St.F.X. Calendar 1903–04*, 78.

41 Thompson, of course, assumed they were capable of greater support; some probably were not.

42 Thompson to R.S. Cronage, 30 October 1900, RG 5/8/3407, PTP, STFXUA.

43 *Casket*, 21 March 1901.

44 Petition for Grant in Aid of Engineering School, 20 March 1901, MG 45/ 2/477, box 80, FEPP, STFXUA.

45 Unsigned statement, RG 5/8/3609–12, PTP, STFXUA.

46 Thompson to Premier Murray, 9 April 1901, RG 5/8/14773–5, PTP, STFXUA.

47 *Journal and Proceedings*, 1902, appendix #5, xxxii, Rev. Charles Scholfield to Thompson, 25 August 1905, RG 5/8/1444, PTP, STFXUA, and P.B. Waite, *The Lives of Dalhousie. Volume One, 1818–1925. Lord Dalhousie's College* (Montreal and Kingston: McGill-Queen's University Press, 1994), 191.

48 Donald MacLeod, "Practicality Ascendant: The Origins and Establishment of Technical Education in Nova Scotia," *Acadiensis* 15, no. 2 (Spring 1986):66.

49 McKillop, *Matters of Mind*, 166–79. A School of Practical Science had been established at the University of Toronto in 1878 and a School of Mining and Agriculture at Queen's in 1893.

50 The superintendent of education, A.H. MacKay, was one such advocate. *Journal and Proceedings*, 1900, appendix #5, lxvi. See also a citizens' petition which asked the government to establish an Engineering School independent of "all direct ecclesiastical control" with an endowment of $75,000. Petition for Engineering School, n.d., RG 5/8/621, PTP, STFXUA.

51 A.A. Hayward to President MacPherson, 7 March 1907, RG 5/9/4715, PMP, STFXUA.

52 *St.F.X. Calendar 1909–10*, 51.

53 The Technical Education Act, *Statutes of Nova Scotia 1907*, cap. 1, 1–5.

54 *St.F.X. Calendar 1909–10*, 51.

55 Frank Adams to J.J. Tompkins, 21 December 1914, RG 6/5/463–4, VPTP, STFXUA.

56 *Casket*, 19 May 1904. Three BSC degrees were conferred.

57 MacLeod, "Practicality Ascendant," 54.

58 Patricia Jasen, "The English-Canadian Liberal Arts Curriculum: An Intellectual History, 1800–1950" (PHD thesis, University of Manitoba, 1987), 70.

59 *Casket*, 20 February 1902. *Journal and Proceedings*, 1903, appendix #5, 115.

60 See the lecture by Professor Kidner, Principal of the MacDonald Manual Training School in Truro, published in the *Casket*, 13 December 1900.

61 One author claims that the schools were promoted as a complement and support to strictly academic training and as a means to inculcate skills and habits required in an industrial society. MacLeod, "Practicality Ascendant," 63–5.

62 D.C. Chisholm, Secretary of the School Board, to Thompson, 4 March 1902, RG 5/8/178–9, PTP, STFXUA. At first, the local school board officials expressed concern about the cost of the school. *Casket*, 24 December 1901.

63 Thompson to J.M. Almon, 31 July 1902 and 23 August 1903, RG 5/8/4, 20 and Almon to Thompson, 3 September 1902, RG 5/8/14, PTP, STFXUA.

64 *St.F.X. Calendar 1903–04*, 41–5.

65 *Casket*, 6 June 1901 and *Calendar of the Collegiate School of St John the Baptist 1904–05*, MG 75/1, RJPP.

66 *Casket*, 4 October 1900.

67 Thompson to B. McKittrick, 2 March 1901, RG 5/8/1091, PTP, STFXUA.

68 *St.F.X. Calendar 1894–95*, 15.

69 Thompson to Capt. D.H. Mahoney, 6 September 1901, RG 5/8/1236, PTP, STFXUA.

70 One mother who had a young son at the college wrote to Thompson: "I am also very thankfull to ... dear Sr. Gregory who was the first who showed Jack that he could allways relie on Her as Mother, and I am glad to say that he respects her as mother." Mrs R.F. Hope to Thompson, 29 June 1899, RG 5/8/2092, PTP, STFXUA. The first rules of the Marthas required them to have "a maternal care of the small pupils of the College, without however showing any familiarity." First Rules and Constitutions of the Sisters of St Martha, 48, B/200/1/1, SSTMA.

71 F.A. Roman to President Chisholm, 24 November 1894, RG 5/7/804 and [name removed] to President Chisholm, 12 February 1895, RG 5/7/601, PCP, STFUXA.

72 *Collegiate School Calendar, 1904–05*, 15–16, MG 75/1, RJPP.

73 Thompson to Mother Fidelis, 11 August 1899, RG 5/8/306a,b, PTP, STFXUA.

74 Sarah MacPherson, "Religious Women in Nova Scotia: A Struggle for Autonomy. A Sketch of the Sisters of Saint Martha of Antigonish, Nova Scotia, 1900–1960," CCHA, *Study Sessions* (1984):92.

75 Sister John Baptist Cameron, "History of the Sisters of St Martha, 1894–1948," n.d., 6, SSTMA.

76 Mother Fidelis to Thompson, 17 August 1899, RG 5/8/306c, PTP, STFXUA. Perhaps as many as twenty-five had entered the order from outside the Diocese of Antigonish. Sister May Mulvihill, "Origin and Early History: History of Sisters of St Martha of Antigonish, 1894–1917," 1981, 10, SSTMA.

77 Apparently, some of the Charities were distressed by their superior's lack of cooperation with Cameron. Sister Mary Regis to Cameron, 6 July 1900, and Sister de Sales to Cameron, 20 June 1902, and Sister May Mulvihill, "New Theory for the Origins of the Sisters of St Martha," 19 March 1980, SSTMA.

78 Some controversy arose between Thompson and Mother Fidelis over the freedom of choice allowed the sisters. Thompson to Mother Fidelis, 24 July 1900, RG 5/8/309–13, PTP, STFXUA.

449

79 Rules and Constitutions of the Sisters of St Martha, 1900, 1–2, ch. 2, article 1, ch. 2, articles 3 and 4, B/200/1/2, SSTMA, MacPherson, "Religious Women in Nova Scotia," 93–4, and *Casket*, 25 December 1902.

80 The early work of the Marthas outside St.F.X. included management of St Joseph's Hospital, Glace Bay (1901), a hospital for Antigonish (1905–), the foundation and training of domestic service for St Augustine's Seminary, Toronto (1913), and the initial training of a new congregation of Marthas for St Dunstan's College, Charlottetown (1918–).

81 Bishop Cameron, Circular, 22 May 1893, MG 75/1, RJPP.

82 Sister M. Immaculata to Rev. Dr D.J. MacDonald, 2 January 1938, RG 5/10/1778, PMCDP, STFXUA.

83 Dissidents at other Nova Scotia Colleges believed the utilitarian trend in higher education was narrow and materialistic; in their judgment, the central aim of character development was being undermined. MacLeod, "Practicality Ascendant," 77.

84 MacDonald to Bishop Cameron, June 1901, MG 45/2/111–17, FEPP, STFXUA.

85 Thompson to Bishop Cameron, 6 August 1901, MG 73/1/2799–2804, JCPP, Alex MacDonald to Bishop Cameron, n.d., MG 45/2/111–13, box 79/2, FEPP, STFXUA.

86 Rev. Alex MacDonald to Bishop Cameron, n.d., MG 45/2/141–45, box 79/2, FEPP and Thompson to Bishop Cameron, 21 April 1903, MG 73/1/2808–10, JCPP, STFXUA.

87 Joseph A. Wall to Alex MacDonald, 1 October 1902, MG 73/1/2806–7, JCPP, STFXUA.

88 A.J.G. MacEchen to Thompson, 22 September 1902, RG 5/8/826–31, PTP, STFXUA.

89 MacEchen to Thompson, 31 July 1905, RG 5/8/868–71, PTP, STFXUA.

90 Thompson to John Cronan, 23 June 1901, RG 5/8/1781, PTP, STFXUA.

91 Thompson to the Propaganda, 23 November 1903, NS vol. 245, 1903, #569, ASC, APF.

92 Thompson to Dr Macdonald, 16 September 1903, RG 5/8/2375, and Thompson to Father Neil MacDonald, 29 June 1901, RG 5/8/4407, PTP, STFXUA.

93 *Excelsior*, October 1897, 4.

94 Thompson to J.J. Tompkins, 13 June 1905, MG 10, 2, TPP, BI.

95 Thompson wrote to President Charles Eliot in the summer of 1901. Eliot had been the president of Harvard for thirty-two years and he informed Thompson that by statute he was forbidden to act independently. The changes he had achieved through his long presidency he won through extended discussions with the university's various governing boards. He added, "I am inclined to believe that only those educational reforms persist and succeed which commend themselves to the judgement of the

men and women who have to put them into execution. Therefore, debate, experiment, and time are needed to bring about this consensus of opinion in favour of reform." Eliot to Thompson, 22 August 1901, RG 5/8/287–9 and Thompson to Eliot, 16 August 1901, RG 5/8/284–6, PTP, STFXUA.

96 Thompson to J.C. Fraser, 5 November 1900, RG 5/8/4055, PTP, STFXUA.

97 *St.F.X. Calendar 1894–95*, 18.

98 An Urban College official considered Thompson, the student, admirable for his mercy. Giovanni Pizzorusso, "Documents d'intérêt Canadien dans les archives du Collège Urbain de Propaganda Fide a Rome (1829–1922)," 1992, 32, Manuscripts Division, NAC.

99 "Bosco, John, St," *New Catholic Encyclopedia*, 2:714–15.

100 In July 1901, Thompson wrote to the superior of the Salesian Fathers in San Francisco for a copy of the rules prescribed by Don Bosco for his schools. He had also been reading articles on Bosco's system of education and had copies of the *Salesian Bulletin*, the official organ of the Salesian Cooperators. Thompson to Superior of the Salesian Fathers, 19 July 1901, RG 5/8/4928–30, PTP, STFXUA.

101 Rev. Ronald MacDonald to Thompson, 8 October 1902, RG 5/8/715, PTP, STFXUA.

102 Johnston, *Antigonish Diocese*, 42 and 101.

103 Alex MacDonald to the Propaganda, 31 October 1902, NS vol. 220, #9, ASC, APF. Johnston, *Antigonish Diocese*, 57. MacDonald, interestingly, received an honorary doctorate from St.F.X. at its jubilee celebrations in 1905. In 1908 he became the bishop of Victoria.

104 St.F.X. actually began in 1853 in Arichat; the jubilee celebrations were probably held in 1905 because certain college officials believed the Arichat School had been separate from the college/seminary opened in Antigonish in 1855. The centennial celebrations would be held in 1953 with the appropriate credit given to the Arichat beginnings in 1853.

105 *Annual Report of the Superintendent of Education 1906*, xxxix–xl.

106 *Xaverian*, October 1905, 48.

107 The quotations in this paragraph are taken from his speech found in *The College Jubilee 1905* (pamphlet), 4–11, MG 45/2/688, box 81/1, FEPP, STFXUA.

108 For an account of St.F.X.'s contribution to the social advance and cultural integration of the Highland Catholics of eastern Nova Scotia, see James D. Cameron, "'Erasing forever the brand of social inferiority': Saint Francis Xavier University and the Highland Catholics of Eastern Nova Scotia," CCHA, *Historical Studies* 59 (1992):49–64.

109 Scots have been ambivalent about their Highland traditions in eastern Nova Scotia. But like other ethnic groups, they have been caught on the horns of a dilemma. Jack Bumsted describes their predicament, namely a tension between the drive for "a full sharing in economic prosperity

and social equality" and the concern to maintain a "separate sense of identity." See "Ethnic Studies in Atlantic Canada: Or, Some Ethnics Are More Ethnic Than Others," *Acadiensis* 14, no. 1 (Fall 1989):204.

110 For a nineteenth-century Maritime example of a quicker and more complete loss of ethnic identity among an immigrant community, see T.M. Punch, "The Irish in Halifax, 1836–1871: A Study in Ethnic Assimilation" (MA thesis, Dalhousie University, 1976).

111 *Casket*, 14 November 1907, 1.

112 The tendency for the St.F.X. alumni to associate Bishop Cameron with the founding and growth of the college, and to neglect the role of Bishop MacKinnon, was probably related to: (1) the golden jubilee anniversary, which set the date of origin at 1855 when Cameron was rector and officially opened the college in Antigonish (Bishop MacKinnon had departed for Rome); (2) the fact that Bishop Cameron was still alive at the time of the jubilee in 1905 and his flock was probably tempted to praise him excessively in his old age, and (3) the memory that Bishop Cameron had saved St.F.X. in 1877 from probable extinction.

113 *The College Jubilee 1905* (pamphlet), 9, MG 45/2/688, box 81/1, FEPP, STFXUA.

114 Ibid., 14–27.

115 Circular to the Alumni and Other Friends of the University of St Francis Xavier, *Casket*, 17 August 1905, 2.

116 *Xaverian*, October 1905, 1–64.

117 *Casket*, 7 September 1905.

118 The list was published in *The College Jubilee 1905*, STFXUA. The sources used to compile it were not cited. In addition, much of the information was incomplete, especially the listing of occupations. Nevertheless, the list is a reliable indicator of the ethnicity of the student body and the types of occupations which many graduates entered.

119 A comparison of student lists found in the St.F.X. calendars of 1876–77 and 1911–12 shows that, as a proportion of the student body, those of Scottish lineage steadily declined from 70 per cent in 1876 to 51 per cent in 1911.

120 Based on a survey of Shirley B. Elliott, *The Legislative Assembly of Nova Scotia 1758–1983: A Biographical Directory* (Halifax: Province of Nova Scotia, 1984) and Ronald R. Chisholm, "A Biographical Survey of the Members of Parliament for Antigonish 1867–1982" (BA thesis, St.F.X., 1982).

121 *Casket*, 28 September 1893.

122 This important point is made by Daniel W. MacInnes, "Clerics, Fishermen, Farmers and Workers: The Antigonish Movement and Identity in Eastern Nova Scotia, 1928–1939" (PHD thesis, McMaster University, 1978), 95. For Canada overall, Catholics were much less likely than

Presbyterians to make a name for themselves in industry and commerce. The former most often strove for social advance through the professions. T.W. Acheson's "collective portrait" of the Canadian industrial elite in the early 1880s revealed that Presbyterians accounted for 36 per cent of the elite while they made up only 16 per cent of the population; Catholics represented 42 per cent of the population but only 12 per cent of the industrial elite. See "The Social Origins of the Canadian Industrial Elite, 1880–1885," in *Canadian Business History: Selected Studies, 1497–1971*, ed. David S. MacMillan (Toronto: McClelland and Stewart, 1972), 158.

123 Between 1876 and 1911 students who advanced to the priesthood became a smaller proportion of the student body. In 1876, 24 per cent of the student body became clergy; by 1911 the proportion had dropped to 7 per cent. Based on St.F.X. calendar student lists and alumni files in STFXUA.

124 Some of the trends mentioned above – an increasing shift from the provision of priests to the supply of lay leaders, a conscious awareness of degrees, the admission of women, and the move from a classical to an elective program – were also developing in other English-speaking Catholic colleges during the last half of the nineteenth century. See Laurence K. Shook, *Catholic Post-Secondary Education in English-Speaking Canada* (Toronto: University of Toronto Press, 1971), 31.

125 Johnston, *Antigonish Diocese*, 113. Rev. Dr Thompson's great capabilities and foresight heightened the tragedy of his later struggle with alcohol and drug abuse. After leaving Glace Bay in disgrace in 1924, he apparently spent most of his final years in New Orleans. He died at St Martha's Hospital, Antigonish on 6 August 1936, shortly after his return from the south. Bishop James Morrison to Rev. Dr A. Thompson, 15 May 1924, #11279, Archbishop of New Orleans to Bishop Morrison, 22 June 1934, #20457, BMP, ADA.

126 Cameron to Thompson, 19 October 1906, MG 23/1/4, box 13/3, Kay Desjardins Personal Papers, STFXUA.

127 *Xaverian*, January 1907, 49–50.

128 *Casket*, 26 April 1906, 4 and *Xaverian*, January 1907, 49–50.

129 *Xaverian*, January 1907, 49–50.

CHAPTER SEVEN

1 The name "rector" had been used at St.F.X. up to this time. Then the awkward phrase "president-rector" was used for the next three decades until it was replaced by "president." For simplicity's sake, "president" will be used in the narrative from here on.

2 Rev. W.X. Edwards labelled part of this period (1906–22) the "MacPherson-Tompkins Era" and has given a good overview of it in "The

MacPherson-Tompkins Era of St Francis Xavier University," CCHA, *Report* (1953):49–65.

3 Cameron to MacPherson, 13 October 1906, MG 1/1/1, 110, MPP, STFXUA.

4 Rev. A.A. Johnston, *Antigonish Diocese Priests and Bishops 1786–1925*, ed. Kathleen M. MacKenzie (Antigonish: Casket Printing and Publishing Co., 1994), 90.

5 *Casket*, 10 January 1907.

6 Giovanni Pizzorusso, "Documents d'intérêt Canadien dans les archives du Collège Urbain de Propaganda Fide à Rome (1829–1922)," 1992, 42, Manuscripts Division, NAC.

7 Johnston, *Antigonish Diocese*, 113. Tompkins's biography has been written by George Boyle, and is entitled *Father Tompkins of Nova Scotia* (New York: P.J. Kennedy, 1953).

8 *St.F.X. Calendar, 1897–98*, 6.

9 *St.F.X. Calendar, 1885–86*, 6–7 and *1905–06*, 57–9.

10 E.R. Forbes and D.A. Muise, eds., *The Atlantic Provinces in Confederation* (Toronto and Fredericton: University of Toronto Press and Acadiensis Press 1993), 167.

11 *Census of Canada, 1901*, 1:22.

12 *St.F.X. Calendar 1905–06*, 57–9.

13 Both regional economic shifts and stagnation, as well as expanding opportunities in the New England states and central and western Canada, fuelled the exodus. See Alan Brooks, "Out-Migration from the Maritime Provinces, 1860–1900: Some Preliminary Considerations, *Acadiensis* 5 (Spring 1976):26–55 and Patricia A. Thornton, "The Problem of Out-Migration from Atlantic Canada, 1871–1921: A New Look," *Acadiensis* 15 (Autumn 1985):3–34.

14 Andrew H. Clark, "Old World Origins and Religious Adherence in Nova Scotia," *Geographical Review* 50, no. 3 (July 1960):340.

15 *Aurora*, 28 May 1884.

16 Clark, "Old World Origins," 335.

17 Paul Axelrod, "Student Life in Canadian Universities: The Lessons of History," *CJHE* 20, no. 3 (1990):19.

18 In Antigonish County alone, the school inspector in 1902 reported twelve sections which did not operate schools. *Annual Report of the Superintendent of Education on the Common, Academic, Normal and Model Schools of Nova Scotia, 1881*, 31–47.

19 See the *Annual Report of the Superintendent*, 1881, 31–47, and 1891, 86–103.

20 *St.F.X. Calendar 1890–91*, 28.

21 President Thompson to Joseph A. Chisholm, 25 August 1901, RG 5/8/200, PTP, STFXUA.

22 *Calendar of the Collegiate School 1902–03*, 6.

23 Ramsey Cook, *The Regenerators: Social Criticism in Late Victorian English Canada* (Toronto: University of Toronto Press, 1985), 228–32.

24 A.B. McKillop, *Matters of Mind: The University in Ontario 1791–1951* (Toronto: University of Toronto Press, 1994), 204–31.

25 *Excelsior*, February 1901, 7–10.

26 *Casket*, 20 September 1894.

27 *St.F.X. Calendar 1897–98*, 5.

28 For examples, see Rev. James Morrison to Rector Chisholm, 22 November 1894, RG 5/7/633, PCP and President Thompson to Neil MacDonald, 10 April 1901, RG 5/8/4394, PTP, STFXUA.

29 G. Edward MacDonald makes this point in *The History of St Dunstan's University 1855–1956* (Charlottetown: Board of Governors of St Dunstan's University and Prince Edward Island Museum and Heritage Foundation, 1989), 184–5.

30 *Excelsior*, January 1897, 8.

31 *Land Registry Book*, 67:151–3, Registrar of Deeds, Antigonish.

32 Minutes of Meeting, August 1907, RG 5/9/12288a, PMP, STFXUA, and the *Casket*, 15 August 1907, 1.

33 In 1900 the college was already providing living space for retired priests, but little information remains about the arrangement. See K.J. MacDonald to President Thompson, 1 February 1900, RG 5/8/2352, PTP, STFXUA.

34 Boyle, *Father Tompkins*, 34–40 and *Casket*, 19 August 1919, 8.

35 Bishop Cameron, Circular Letter to the Clergy and Laity of the Diocese of Antigonish, 28 October 1907, MG 73/1/2784, JCPP, STFXUA. Cameron reported that the proposal for an endowment fund campaign emanated from some of the diocesan societies, for example, the Knights of Columbus. It is unclear why they advocated such a campaign at that time.

36 *Casket*, 5 December 1907, 4.

37 "An Act to Incorporate the Officers of St Francis Xavier's College Endowment Fund Association," *Statutes of Nova Scotia*, 1908, cap. 174, 498–501.

38 St Francis Xavier's College Endowment Fund pamphlet, February 1908, RG 5/9/27428, PMP, STFXUA.

39 *Casket*, 30 May and 14 November 1907, and 3 July 1913.

40 See "An Act to Consolidate and Amend the Acts and Amendments to the Acts Relating to the Governors of St Francis Xavier's College," *Statutes of Nova Scotia*, 1909, cap. 126, 5–15.

41 MacPherson to Miller, 27 December 1909, MG 10-2, 4d (f1), TPP, BI.

42 *Xaverian*, January 1909, 8–13.

43 *Casket*, 24 October 1907, 5 and E. Arthur Betts, *Maritime Presbyterian Ministers* (Halifax: Maritime Conference Archives of the United Church of Canada, 1983), 118–19.

44 *St.F.X. Calendar 1909–10*, 18.

45 *Xaverian*, October 1909, 44.

46 *Casket*, 21 May 1908, 4 and 14 September 1961.

47 *Casket*, 18 June 1908, 8.

48 *St.F.X. Calendar 1909–10*, 48.

49 President MacPherson to Reginald V. Harris, 7 July 1921, RG 5/9/20691, PMP, STFXUA.

50 McKillop, *Matters of Mind*, 149–66.

51 *Xaverian*, October 1909, 35.

52 *St.F.X. Calendar 1909–10*, 64–5.

53 *Casket*, 19 August 1909, 5. The identity of the prime mover behind this experiment is unclear, although Tompkins is a prime suspect. Neither is it clear why the school was held then and for only two successive years.

54 St.F.X., especially through the leadership of one of its engineering professors, John W. MacLeod of Pictou, promoted the campaign against tuberculosis and financed the publication and distribution of *Consumption: Its Cause, Prevention, and Cure*, ed. George H. Cox and John W. MacLeod (London: Eyre and Spottiswoode, 1912). This book contained summaries of its contents written in Micmac, Gaelic, French, and Italian.

55 *Casket*, 12 March 1914, 8.

56 Respondents' Brief in *Isaiah R. Clarke v Murdock H. McNeil*, n.d., STFXUA.

57 McNeil kept the cost secret, but two tenders in PMP are for $38,715 and $40,830. RG 5/9/25278, PMP, STFXUA.

58 In April 1910, the Roman Catholic Episcopal Corporation granted the required property. *Land Registry Book*, 69:174, Registrar of Deeds, Antigonish.

59 *St.F.X. Calendar 1911–12*, 42 and *Xaverian*, October 1913, 31–2.

60 The benefactor spelled his own name "McNeil" while the name on the building was spelled "MacNeil."

61 *Casket*, 7 September 1911, 4, 6, and 7.

62 MacPherson to the Apostolic Delegate, 4 July 1910, MG 1/2/1098–1104, Rev. H.P. MacPherson Administrator's Papers, STFXUA.

63 *St.F.X. Calendar 1914–15*, 55.

64 *Xaverian*, October 1911, 17–20.

65 Boyle, *Father Tompkins*, 45.

66 Bishop Cameron's later years were plagued by "diocesan disputes." See Rev. Dr R.B. MacDonald's three-part article "Diocesan Disputes" in the *Casket*, 2, 9, and 16 September 1992.

67 *Casket*, 11 September 1991, 3–4.

68 Rev. Donald M. MacAdam to President MacPherson, 23 January 1911, MG 1/2/495, Rev. Dr H.P. MacPherson Administrator's Papers, STFXUA.

69 Bishop Morrison to Rev. Miles N. Tompkins, 17 November 1921, # 8804, BMP, ADA.

70 Tompkins to Neil McNeil, 31 August 1912, MG 10-2, 4c (f1), TPP, BI.

71 *Xaverian*, October 1912, 1–2.

72 Much later, a friend of the bishop reflected that he was gregarious before he came to the diocese but found it necessary to distance himself from the factionalism; thereafter he maintained a decided air of aloofness in his relations with others. Interview with Msgr H.J. Somers by Rev. P.A. Nearing, October 1964, St.F.X., MG 62/6/185, box 131, PSP, STFXUA.

73 See the *Casket*, 12, 19, and 24 December 1907, 9 January 1908, 29 April, 17 June, 18 and 25 November 1909, and 10 March 1910. The *Casket*, 5 June 1913, 8 reported that the endowment fund campaign had received and invested $26,185.

74 H.F. McDougall to Duncan Curry, 25 June 1913, RG 5/9/24059–63, PMP, STFXUA. Father Edwards suggests the failure resulted from lack of experience and inadequate organization at the parish level. "The MacPherson-Tompkins Era," 55.

75 This is a claim now impossible to verify.

76 Rev. Ronald MacDonald to Bishop Morrison, 6 April 1913, MG 45/2/535–51, box 80, FEPP, and Bishop Alexander MacDonald to Father Lachlan, 25 January 1911, RG 5/9/6200, PMP, STFXUA.

77 Cormier to Bishop Morrison, 19 April 1913, BMP, ADA.

78 *Casket*, 24 October 1918, 1.

79 Tompkins to John C. MacNeil, 11 May 1913, MG 10-2, TPP, BI.

80 MacPherson to Very Rev. N. Gariepy, Laval University, 16 February 1911, RG 6/5/119–20, VPTP, STFXUA. I found no evidence that Tompkins ever pursued a doctorate at Laval.

81 Tompkins to McNeil, 6 November 1913, MG 10-2, 4e, (F1), TPP, BI.

82 Tompkins to Neil McNeil, 29 September 1914, MG 10-2, 4e, (F2), TPP, BI.

83 *Casket*, 6 November 1913, 8. This progressive movement featured a drive to resolve labour conflicts through peaceful means, the application of science to social and moral problems, effective public health care, more state intervention, and crusades for social regeneration. Forbes and Muise, eds., *The Atlantic Provinces*, 156–7.

84 *Casket*, 21 December 1911, 8.

85 *Casket*, 12 July and 8 August 1912 and 10 July 1913, 8.

86 *Casket*, 5 March 1914, 4.

87 For example, see the *Casket*, 20 and 27 November 1913, 29 January and 9 April 1914.

88 Practical results of the Forward Movement included the formation of a local board of trade, an information and immigration bureau, a civic improvement league, the government appointment of an agricultural representative for the county, countless public lectures on social and

economic progress, the appointment of an immigration and publicity agent for the seven eastern counties of eastern Nova Scotia, and the publication by the board of trade and town council of a pamphlet promoting the county. Based on a review of the *Casket* for this period.

89 Tompkins to Dr Moses Coady, 29 October 1914, MG 10,2, TPP, BI.

90 Tompkins to Henry Somerville, n.d., MG 10-2, 1a (f6), TPP, BI.

91 *St.F.X. Calendar 1910–11*, 105–6. Various bursaries had been established to support seminarians at ecclesiastical schools, and a new one was formed in May 1906 called the Dr Daniel A. Chisholm Memorial Fund. *Casket*, 7 June 1906, 4.

92 For an excellent history, see C. Joseph Nuesse, *The Catholic University of America* (Washington, DC: Catholic University of America Press, 1990).

93 These would include Dr Joseph Nelson Rice (mathematics), Rev. Dr Eugene Mullins (chemistry), Dr Thomas George Foran (education), Rev. Dr Donald Alexander MacLean (philosophy), and Rev. Dr Cornelius J. Connolly (psychology/anthropology). See Richard T. Joy, "St Francis Xavier Students at the Catholic University of America," c. 1934, RG 5/ 9/27431, PMP, STFXUA.

94 MacPherson to Neil McNeil, 20 July 1912, RG 5/9/2291, PMP, STFXUA.

95 St.F.X. had hired a Trinity College, Dublin graduate, W.P.M. Kennedy, in 1913 to teach history and English, but, in President MacPherson's words, he had "a loose screw in his mechanism" and left after the first year. The college was more cautious the following year and decided to interview prospective professors before hiring them. MacPherson to John E. Somers, 18 May 1914, RG 5/9/22047, PMP, STFXUA. Ironically, Kennedy went on to a productive career at the University of Toronto. His publications included *The Constitutional History of Canada* (Oxford, 1922).

96 *St.F.X. Calendar 1914–15*, 8–9.

97 *St.F.X. Calendar 1918*, 36.

98 *Xaverian*, March 1917, 54. In practice, the affiliations probably meant little, since few St.F.X. graduates continued their studies in England. Moreover, by 1928 a St.F.X. Rhodes Scholar found that Oxford did not recognize St.F.X. degrees. W.J. Maynes to President MacPherson, 13 January 1928, MG 45/2/597–614, FEPP, and John Read to MacPherson, 5 January 1928, RG 5/9/21101, PMP, STFXUA.

99 President MacPherson to Lord Strathcona, 27 October 1913, RG 5/9/ 16181 and MacPherson to John A. White, 29 July 1914, RG 5/9/16251, PMP, STFXUA.

100 Bishop Morrison to M.J. O'Brien, 5 October 1917, #4578, BMP, ADA.

101 President MacPherson to Neil McNeil, 20 July 1912, RG 5/9/22921, PMP, STFXUA.

102 Warren H. Manning to President MacPherson, 20 February 1913, RG 5/ 9/8644, PMP, STFXUA and the *Casket*, 7 November 1912, 8.

103 *St.F.X. Calendar 1913–14*, end of volume.
104 W.P.M. Kennedy, "Song of St Francis Xavier's College," 1913. University Historian Files, STFXUA.

CHAPTER EIGHT

1 In 1905 an artillery company was established in the county; St.F.X. students formed a unit of this company and drilled at the college rink. *Casket*, 30 November 1905. *St.F.X. High School Calendar 1909–1910*, 18–19 and President MacPherson to A.H. Borden, 15 and 16 November 1910, RG/9/4723 and 4729, PMP, STFXUA. In 1912 the federal government formed a Canadian universities regiment so that college students could acquire elementary military training and join the militia. I found no evidence that it organized at St.F.X.

2 University contingents of Officers' Training Corps had been formed in Britain as early as 1908 and by the First World War were apparently in "a flourishing state." W.S.B. Gunn, "The Army and the Universities," *Canadian Army Journal* 15, no. 1 (Winter 1961):74.

3 *Casket*, 4 February 1915, 8.

4 Ibid.

5 President MacPherson to Honourable Major General Samuel Hughes, 15 March 1915, RG 5/9/4730, PMP, STFXUA. See Desmond Morton, *Canada and War: A Military and Political History* (Toronto: Butterworth, 1981), 52.

6 *St.F.X. Calendar 1915–16*, 78–9.

7 *Xaverian*, April 1910, 49.

8 *Xaverian*, December 1915, 29–30.

9 P.W. Thibeau to Rev. Jimmy Tompkins, 10 July 1916, MG 10-2, TPP, BI.

10 *Casket*, 19 August 1915, 8 and President MacPherson to J.N. Keynes, 15 November 1916, RG 5/9/5497, PMP, STFXUA.

11 President MacPherson to Harriet S. Arnold, 10 June 1916, RG 5/9/131, PMP, STFXUA. By 1917 few young men were left to enlist; many had already enlisted or had moved to the United States or the Canadian West. MacPherson to Captain G.M. Campbell, 14 February 1917, RG 5/9/4746, PMP, STFXUA.

12 President MacPherson to H.M. Tory, 10 January 1918, RG 5/9/11754, PMP, STFXUA.

13 Duff Crerar, "Bellicose Priests: The Wars of the Canadian Catholic Chaplains 1914–1919," CCHA, *Historical Studies* 58 (1991):36–8.

14 President MacPherson to Donald MacLennan, 19 April 1920, RG 5/9/7992, PMP, STFXUA. Dr Hugh MacPherson acted as "substitute manager" during this time, but he was also a full-time government agricultural representative for the county; therefore he could do little for the college

farm. Rev. A.A. Johnston, *Antigonish Diocese Priests and Bishops 1786–1925*, ed. Kathleen M. MacKenzie (Antigonish: Casket Printing and Publishing Co., 1994), 114.

15 *St.F.X. Calendars*, 1914–19, student lists.

16 *Casket*, 2 May 1918, 4.

17 Tompkins to Neil McNeil, 20 September 1915, MG 10-2, 4e, (f2), TPP, BI.

18 Laurence K. Shook, *Catholic Post-Secondary Education in English-Speaking Canada* (Toronto: University of Toronto Press, 1971), 249. See also H.A. MacDougall, "St Patrick's College (Ottawa) (1929–1979) Ethnicity and the Liberal Arts in Catholic Education," CCHA, *Study Sessions* 49 (1982):55–6.

19 Tompkins to Neil McNeil, 20 September 1915, MG 10-2, 4e, (f2), TPP, BI.

20 McNeil to Tompkins, 20 June 1914, MG 10-2, 4e, (f2), TPP, BI.

21 Mockler to President MacPherson, 16 July 1914, RG 5/9/22088–9, PMP, STFXUA.

22 R.V. Bannon, "Mockler Speaking," STFXUA.

23 *St.F.X. Calendar 1916–17*, 41.

24 See Dr Somers–President MacPherson correspondence, RG 5/9/11184–242, PMP, STFXUA.

25 *Casket*, 11 July 1918, 4. By the time the bequest was paid in June 1921, it had been reduced to about $7000. The endowment was stock in American Tel. and Tel., which began to net $2000 annually from 1918. President MacPherson to Neil McNeil, 24 October 1918, Bursar's Papers, STFXUA.

26 MacPherson to Miss MacGillivray, 22 July 1918, RG 5/9/7056, PMP, STFXUA. For a student eulogy, see the *Xaverian*, November 1918, 29.

27 Somers to President MacPherson, 18 December 1915, RG 5/9/11188, PMP, STFXUA.

28 May C. MacDonald to President MacPherson, 24 June 1920, Bursar's Papers, STFXUA. I am indebted to Ronald A. MacDonald, Antigonish for bringing the family connection to my attention.

29 Waite describes the stationary hospital as "the stage between a field hospital and one back in Britain or in Canada." P.B. Waite, *The Lives of Dalhousie. Volume One, 1818–1925. Lord Dalhousie's College* (Montreal and Kingston: McGill-Queen's University Press, 1994), 226.

30 President MacPherson to Crosby, 9 May 1916, RG 5/9/15761–3, PMP, STFXUA.

31 David B. Hogan, "History of the No. 9 Stationary Hospital (St Francis Xavier University), 1916–1919," 7–8 (unpublished manuscript, n.d.), STFXUA. This is a thorough and careful account of the unit's experience, written from a doctor's point of view. I have depended on it for much of my information about the unit. The STFXUA sources on the hospital unit are very incomplete. One document called "Diary of No. 9 Stationary

Hospital" is really a historical sketch of the first year of its operation; it is of value for the nominal roll of its personnel at embarkation from Halifax in June 1916. The hospital unit's correspondence did not remain at St.F.X. See President MacPherson to J. Higgins, 5 May 1920, RG 5/9/4848, PMP, STFXUA.

32 *Xaverian*, January 1917, 31–2.

33 *Casket*, 30 March 1916, 4.

34 *Casket*, 4 May 1916, 8.

35 Diary of No. 9 Stationary Hospital, MG 45/2/79–83, FEPP, STFXUA.

36 Hogan, "History of the No. 9 Stationary Hospital," 13. A comparison of the list of original personnel to the St.F.X. student list for 1915–16 reveals only about 28 St.F.X. students enlisted in the unit. Others may have been earlier graduates, both male and female.

37 President MacPherson claimed that Major (Dr) Carruthers, at first appointed second in command, had to be demoted to adjutant because of his unpopularity with the medical profession. MacPherson to Colonel Ronald St John MacDonald, 30 June 1920, Bursar's Papers, STFXUA. The following *Xaverian* articles chart the unit's organization: March 1916, 40, April 1916, 45–7, November 1916, 44–5, and January 1917, 31–2.

38 MacPherson to A.B. Crosby, 20 January 1916, RG 5/9/2348, PMP, STFXUA.

39 Tompkins to Neil McNeil, 20 January 1916, MG 10-2, 4e, (f2), TPP, BI.

40 President MacPherson to Rev. John J. Burke, 18 October 1916, RG 5/9/25834, PMP, STFXUA.

41 President MacPherson to W.F. Chisholm, 18 August 1916, RG 5/9/1874, PMP, STFXUA.

42 H.E. Kendall to President MacPherson, 16 August and 18 October 1917, RG 5/9/5454, 5452 and MacPherson to Kendall, 24 November 1917, RG 5/9/5455, PMP, STFXUA.

43 *Casket*, 1 February 1917, 8.

44 President MacPherson to Lieutenant-Colonel Grant, 13 February 1917, RG 5/9/4270, PMP, STFXUA.

45 Hogan, "History of the No. 9 Stationary Hospital," n.p. Oswin Mac-Donald states that four were killed and fifteen seriously wounded. See "St Francis Xavier Unit No. 9 Stationary Hospital," in *Catholics of the Diocese of Antigonish, Nova Scotia, and the War, 1914–1919* (Antigonish: St.F.X. University Press, 1919), 56.

46 Hogan, "History of the No. 9 Stationary Hospital," n.p.

47 *Casket*, 10 July 1919, 1 and 4.

48 Apparently a group of hospital unit members called "the literary and social staff" produced a little magazine entitled *Camouflage*. It was a souvenir item which appears to be lost. *Casket*, 29 May 1918, 8.

49 Waite, *The Lives of Dalhousie*, 226.

50 Hogan comes to this conclusion in "History of the No. 9 Stationary Hospital," n.p.

51 Hogan, "History of the No. 9 Stationary Hospital," n.p.

52 Duff Crerar, in "Bellicose Priests," 21, contends that "English-speaking Roman Catholic churchmen fought to establish a public identity as both Catholics and Canadian nationalists."

53 Father Charles Brewer has examined the war efforts of the diocese in "The Diocese of Antigonish and World War I" (MA thesis, University of New Brunswick, 1975).

54 MacDonald, *Catholics of the Diocese of Antigonish*, foreword, n.p.

55 At his next visit south, a Boston friend had promised "to stage a thriller representing 'a man with money getting away from J.J. [Tompkins] with a whole skin.'" H.H. MacDonald to Tompkins, 6 November 1917, MG 10-2, TPP, BI.

56 H.H. MacDonald to Tompkins, 6 November 1917, MG 10-2, 2, TPP, BI.

57 W.J. White to Tompkins, 19 October 1917 and Tompkins to Dr Donald F. MacDonald, 4 December 1917, MG 10-2, 4d, (f3), TPP, BI.

58 President MacPherson to Henry Somerville, 21 June 1918, RG 5/9/16846, PMP, STFXUA.

59 Bishop Morrison to President MacPherson, 19 March 1921, RG 5/9/9075, MacPherson to Rev. R. McInnis, 14 November 1918, and Morrison to McInnis, 1 April 1913, RG 5/9/10856, PMP, STFXUA.

60 President MacPherson to A.H. Atwood, 21 January 1920, RG 5/9/275, PMP, STFXUA.

61 Tompkins to Archbishop Neil McNeil, 16 November 1916, MG 10-2, 4d, (f2), TPP, BI.

62 Rev. William B. MacDonald granted $14,000 worth of investments and $2000 cash to endow a chair of history in his name. Professors G. Humphrey and W.H. Bucknell had developed a proposal for a department of history at St.F.X., in May 1916, which called for the endowment of three chairs. See "A Department of History for St.F.X.," 8 May 1916, MG 45/2/567, FEPP, STFXUA. Tompkins acquired a $10,000 endowment for a chair of geology in the fall of 1917 from M.J. O'Brien, a wealthy and prominent "son of Antigonish." President MacPherson to M.J. O'Brien, 2 October 1917, RG 5/9/10134, PMP, STFXUA.

63 Bishop Morrison Circular, 1 September 1915, #2373, BMP, ADA and the *Casket*, 14 August 1919, 8. In 1919, sixty-five parishes contributed a total of $4821 to St.F.X. through the revived college collection. College Collection Statement, #7117, ibid.

64 *Casket*, 20 February 1919, 8 and E.R. Forbes and D.A. Muise, eds., *The Atlantic Provinces in Confederation* (Toronto and Fredericton: University of Toronto Press, 1993), 194–228.

65 *Xaverian*, December 1918, 33.

66 *Xaverian*, May 1919, 41.

67 See *Catholics of the Diocese of Antigonish*, 179–88. President MacPherson to President Falconer, 20 October 1919, RG 5/9/3447, PMP, STFXUA reports slightly lower figures. A plaque commemorating the dead was later placed in the university chapel. *Casket*, 14 December 1922, 1.

68 St.F.X. students heard the rumble and felt the shaking of the buildings in December 1917; later they discovered it was the Halifax Explosion. Preparations were made to accommodate some of the wounded, but a violent snowstorm blocked train transportation between Truro and Antigonish. Joseph P. McCarthy, *Times of My Life* (N.p.: n.p., 1969), 59–60.

69 The government only provided educational funding for those disabled, hence unable to resume their civilian jobs; those who had enlisted in the military before their eighteenth birthday were granted one year's university tuition. Gwendoline E. Pilkington, *Speaking with One Voice: Universities in Dialogue with Government* (Montreal: History of McGill Project, McGill University, 1983), 13 and 36.

70 *Census of Canada 1921*, 1:384–98.

71 Forbes and Muise, *The Atlantic Provinces in Confederation*, 221.

72 Tompkins to Bishop Morrison, 24 November 1919, #6319, BMP, ADA.

73 In 1911 Andrew Carnegie had established the foundation in order "to promote the advancement and diffusion of knowledge." Most grants for the British Commonwealth between 1912 and 1927 went to Canada and Newfoundland because of their proximity to the Corporation. Stephen H. Stackpole, *Carnegie Corporation: Commonwealth Program 1911–1961* (New York: Carnegie Corporation of New York, 1963), 3.

74 Review of *St.F.X. Calendars*, 1891, 1901, 1911, and 1921.

75 Tompkins to James Bertram, 29 October 1919, RG 6/5/32, VPTP, STFXUA.

76 By this date, he had literature on the corporation and had suggested to Rev. Dr Moses Coady, who was studying education at the Catholic University of America, to write a thesis on the foundation and perhaps "get something out of Carnegie." Tompkins to Coady, 5 October 1914, MG 10-2, 4d, (f1), TPP, BI.

77 From 1911 to 1921 Maritime universities received $700,000 from these funds. Robert M. Lester, *Review of Grants in the Maritime Provinces of Canada and in Newfoundland* (New York: Carnegie Corporation, 1934), 8.

78 Tompkins to Bishop Morrison, 23 December 1919, #6869, BMP, ADA. Tompkins was anxious that Morrison know about the corporation's openness to religion. In a long article about the endowment, published in the *Casket*, 4 March 1920, 10, Rev. James Boyle also assured the Catholic public of this fact.

79 James Bertram to Tompkins, 28 November 1919, RG 6/5/34, VPTP, STFXUA and the *Casket*, 18 December 1919, 4. St.F.X. officials wanted

to call the new chair "The Carnegie Chair of French," but the Carnegie Corporation trustees advised against it. Dr Henry Pritchett to Tompkins, 21 May 1921, St.F.X. file, Carnegie Collection, CCA.

80 *Casket*, 18 December 1919, 4.
81 *Casket*, 5 January 1922, 4.
82 *Xaverian*, November 1921, 28.
83 *Casket*, 4 March 1920, 10.
84 Patricia Lotz, "Scots in Groups: The Origin and History of Scottish Societies with Particular Reference to Those Established in Nova Scotia" (MA thesis, St.F.X., 1975), 48.
85 This sentiment was echoed by President MacPherson in 1929. MacPherson to Bishop Morrison, 12 March 1929, RG 5/9/9190, PMP, STFXUA.
86 *Casket*, 7 May 1925, 2.
87 Resolution of the Highland Society, n.d., RG 5/9/6288, PMP, STFXUA.
88 F.A. Cameron to President MacPherson, 31 May 1920, Bursar's Papers, STFXUA. A priest offered $2000 toward the endowment of a chair in Celtic literature if others would raise $1000. *Casket*, 6 February 1919 and *Xaverian*, February–March 1919, 46.
89 *Casket*, 18 December 1919, 1.
90 *Xaverian*, February–March 1919, 46 and February 1921, 17. D.A. MacDonald to President MacPherson, 1 March 1920, RG 5/9/6371, PMP, STFXUA. *Casket*, 7 May 1925, 2.
91 *Xaverian*, 21 February 1925, 1 and 4.
92 *Census of Canada, 1921*, 1:606–18.
93 D.F. Campbell and R.A. MacLean, *Beyond the Atlantic Roar: A Study of Nova Scotia Scots* (Toronto: McClelland and Stewart, 1974), 169, *Casket*, 15 September 1904, and E.R. Forbes, *The Maritime Rights Movement* (Montreal: McGill-Queen's University Press, 1979).
94 *Casket*, 5 September 1912, 8.
95 *Casket*, 14 December 1911, 8, and 16 June 1913, 5
96 *Casket*, 16 May 1912, 8, and 1 August 1912, 4 and 7.
97 *Casket*, 7 June 1917, 3 and President MacPherson to Rt Rev. A.S. Barnes, 10 April 1917, RG 5/9/394, PMP, STFXUA.
98 Leo XIII, *Rerum Novarum* (New York: Paulist Press, 1939).
99 *Casket*, 14 June 1917, 4.
100 Tompkins, manuscript, n.d., MG 10-2, 1a, (f6), TPP, BI.
101 Tompkins to D. MacGillivray, 3 May 1917, MG 10-2, TPP, BI.
102 President MacPherson, Commencement Exercise Address, 1919, RG 5/9/12467, PMP, STFXUA.
103 *Casket*, 24 and 31 January 1918, 2 and 4. The column lasted around two years and was later replaced by one called "For Social Betterment." It was occasionally resurrected. See the *Casket*, April, May, and June 1922.

104 For examples, see the *Casket*, 7 February 1918, 2, 25 April 1918, 2, and 25 July 1918, 2.

105 Tompkins to Somerville, 4 July 1915, MG 10-2, 4b, (f2), TPP, BI.

106 Jeanne M. Beck, "Henry Somerville and Social Reform: His Contribution to Canadian Catholic Thought," CCHA, *Study Sessions* (1975):91–108.

107 *Casket*, 8 August 1918, 4 and the *Xaverian*, February–March 1919, 44.

108 *Casket*, 18 July 1918, 4 and J. Frank Glasgow, "The Role of Educational and Rural Conferences in the Development of the Extension Department of Saint Francis Xavier University" (BA thesis, St.F.X., 1947).

109 See *Proceedings of the Second Annual Educational Conference*, 11–13 August 1919, Antigonish, STFXUA. "Educational and Social Conference," fourth annual meeting, MG 10-2, 5f, TPP, BI.

110 *Casket*, 24 February 1921, 6 and C. Joseph Neusse, *The Catholic University of America: A Centennial History* (Washington, DC: Catholic University of America, 1990), 178–9 and 195.

111 See subsequent conference reports in the *Casket*, 26 February 1920, 1, 12 August 1920, 6, and 4 August 1921, 6.

112 McArthur to Tompkins, 19 October 1920, MG 10-2, 4c, (f2), TPP, BI.

113 George Boyle, *Father Tompkins of Nova Scotia* (New York: P.J. Kennedy and Sons, 1953), 79 and 82.

114 *Casket*, 29 July 1920, 6.

115 Tompkins to Bishop Morrison, 13 June 1920, #7109, BMP, ADA.

116 Father Jimmy Tompkins, *Knowledge for the People* (Antigonish: n.p., 1921).

117 Tompkins to R.F. Phalen, 22 November 1920, RG 30–2/110/71, EC, STFXUA.

118 *Casket*, 23 December 1920, 1.

119 For some years the *Casket* had been the object of considerable criticism about its alleged localism, etc. Its manager, Michael Donovan, had also had occasional disagreements with the college over printing jobs. The diocese was able to gain, in 1919, a controlling interest in the paper. Unfortunately, Donovan was unhappy with his loss of control and the ensuing nasty dispute with Bishop Morrison eventually came before the apostolic delegate. See Federation of Catholic Societies, Glace Bay, 1 March 1915, (circular letter) BMP, ADA, Bishop James Morrison to clergy, 19 March 1919, MG 10-2, 2a (fi), TPP, BI, and Morrison to Most Rev. P. Di Maria, 7 November 1921, #8775–6, BMP, ADA.

120 *Casket*, 2, 16, and 30 December 1920.

121 *St.F.X. Calendar 1921*, 59–61 and 67.

122 *Proceedings of the Second Annual Educational Conference*, 11–13 August 1919, 90, STFXUA.

123 *Casket*, 2 February 1922, 6. Some evidence shows that it was also held at St.F.X. from 15 January to 10 March in 1923 under the direction of

Rev. Dr Hugh MacPherson. See the *Casket*, 4 January 1923, 2 and 25 January 1923, 8.

124 After the first people's school, the college published a pamphlet which contained glowing testimonials by the bishop, faculty, and students who had participated, as well as tributes from the public. "The People's School" (St.F.X.: n.p., n.d.). President MacPherson to Dr Louis Hunt, 2 March 1923, RG 5/9/5076, PMP, STFXUA. Bishop Morrison, who was familiar with the Danish type of people's school, was cautiously supportive of Tompkins's project. Bishop Morrison to Tompkins, 16 December 1919, #6960, BMP, ADA.

125 Johnston, *Antigonish Diocese*, 17.

126 *Casket*, 25 January 1923, 4, 8 February 1923, 8, 10 January 1924, 6, 17 January 1924, 11, 7 February 1924, 6, and 28 February 1924, 6.

127 *Xaverian*, November 1921, 19–20 and February 1922, 35.

128 *Casket*, 9 June 1921, 12.

129 *Casket*, 13 January 1921, 10.

130 BOG Minutes, 18 December 1919, #7229, BMP, ADA.

131 Bishop Morrison to St.F.X. faculty, 19 April 1920, RG 5/9/9064, PMP, STFXUA. See also the campaign pamphlet "St Francis Xavier's University, 1853–1920," RG 5/9/27427, PMP, STFXUA.

132 BOG Minutes, 18 December 1919, STFXUA.

133 *Casket*, 4 November 1920, 4.

134 *Casket*, 12 May 1920, 6, 17 and 24 June 1920, 6, 5 and 12 August 1920, 1.

135 *Casket*, 20 May 1920.

136 The brief which the provincial council submitted to the St.F.X. board of governors is a fascinating window on social and educational attitudes and aspirations at the Mount. It is uncertain how the board responded. See Provincial Council of CNDs to the St.F.X. Board of Governors, 23 January 1920, RG 5/9/4195, PMP, STFXUA.

137 *Casket*, 25 November 1920, 6.

138 *St.F.X. Calendar 1927–28*, 12.

139 *Xaverian*, 2 April 1954, 3.

140 Interview with Father Gregory MacKinnon, 8 March 1995, St.F.X.

141 *Casket*, 1 April 1954.

142 MacPherson to Bishop Morrison, 23 February 1919, RG 5/9/9043–4, PMP, STFXUA.

143 Trust Deed of Neil McNeil, 1 February 1919, RG 5/9/23447–79, PMP, STFXUA.

144 *Casket*, 8 December 1921, 3.

145 *Casket*, 15 December 1921, 12, and 16 February 1922, 8.

146 Neil R. McArthur to President MacPherson, 14 March 1924, RG 5/9/15890–1, PMP and Neil MacNeil to Kathleen MacKenzie, University Archivist, St.F.X., 27 January 1988, Vertical File, STFXUA.

147 President MacPherson reported to Bishop Morrison at the time McNeil made the trust deed that he was "in good bodily and mental health." MacPherson to Morrison, 23 February 1919, BMP, ADA. See also MacPherson to I.R. Clark, 27 February and 9 March 1922, RG 5/9/22228 and 22232, PMP, STFXUA.

148 A.E. Little to President MacPherson, 16 December 1926, RG 5/9/22566–74, PMP, STFXUA.

149 I.R. Clark to President MacPherson, 2 November 1922, RG 5/9/22282–3, PMP, STFXUA.

150 By 1925, St.F.X. had paid $15,000 in legal fees. Clark, Vanderhoof and Little, Itemized Bills, RG 5/9/22453–81, PMP, STFXUA.

151 In 1930 they would still own thirty-four properties in Boston. A.A. McIntyre and Rev. H.D. Barry to President MacPherson, 16 January 1930, RG 5/9/72228, PMP, STFXUA. It was unfortunate that McNeil had not fulfilled his plan to sell off his properties after the war and place the proceeds in personal securities so the college would not have to administer the Boston properties. McNeil to MacPherson, 29 October 1918, Bursar's Papers, STFXUA.

152 A.B. McKillop, *Matters of Mind: The University in Ontario 1791–1951* (Toronto: University of Toronto Press, 1994), 291.

153 Interview with Rev. Dr Malcolm MacLellan, 12 November 1987, Antigonish, by Kathleen MacKenzie, University Archivist, St.F.X.

154 Compare the proportions listed in the *St.F.X. Calendars*, 1913–14 (12 per cent), 1917–18 (25 per cent), and 1920–24 (15 per cent). Female college students boarded at the Mount but attended many classes on the St.F.X. campus, accompanied by the CNDs. The president of Acadia referred to the upsurge of women on the campuses during the First World War as "the feminine invasion of the colleges." George B. Cutten to President MacPherson, 18 May 1917, RG 5/9/2455, PMP, STFXUA.

155 President MacPherson to Hugh F. Hamilton, 29 November 1920, RG 5/9/25243, PMP, STFXUA.

156 *Xaverian*, March 1920, 25–7.

157 The Students of Arts and Sciences to the Board of Governors, 31 January 1921, RG 5/9/4205–6, PMP, STFXUA.

158 Senior Class Resolution, 21 February 1922, RG 5/9/3755 and President MacPherson to James Friel, 22 and 25 February 1922, RG 5/9/3756, 3757. See also the student petition, n.d., RG 5/9/2102–4, PMP, STFXUA.

159 *Xaverian*, 28 November 1925, 2.

160 The estimated damage was $13,000; fortunately, it was covered by insurance. President MacPherson to Neil McNeil, 2 October 1919, Bursar's Papers, STFXUA. *Casket*, 2 October 1919, 4, and 13 and 27 November 1919.

161 President MacPherson to John C. MacNeil, 24 November 1919, RG 5/9/8240, PMP, STFXUA.

162 It is remarkable that in November 1919 three students were expelled from Mount Allison Academy for setting fire to the academy residence. J.M. Palmer to President MacPherson, 8 November 1919, RG 5/9/10281, PMP, STFXUA. The St.F.X. student was Edward Francis of Sydney Mines. MacPherson to John W. Francis, 10 November 1919, RG 5/9/3699, PMP, STFXUA.

163 President MacPherson to Neil McNeil, 13 and 24 November 1919, RG 5/9/8240, PMP, STFXUA.

164 *Casket*, 20 October 1919, 4.

165 *Casket*, 3, 10, and 24 November 1921, 12.

166 Rev. Dr C.J. Connolly to the Board of Governors, 18 June 1921, RG 5/9/2188, PMP, STFXUA.

167 President MacPherson to Captain Patrick Mockler, 24 October 1921, RG 5/9/8906–7, PMP, STFXUA.

CHAPTER NINE

1 *Census of Canada, 1921*, 1:606–18.

2 John Leefe, "King's and Dalhousie: An Early Attempt at University Consolidation in Nova Scotia," *Nova Scotia Historical Quarterly* 2 (March 1972):41–54 and W.S. MacNutt, "The Universities of the Maritimes: A Glance Backwards," *DR* 53 (1973–74):431–48.

3 P.B. Waite, *The Lives of Dalhousie University. Volume One, 1818–1925. Lord Dalhousie's College* (Montreal and Kingston: McGill-Queen's University Press, 1994), 22–4 and 146–7.

4 Denis Healy, "The University of Halifax, 1875–1881, *DR* 53 (1973–74):39–56.

5 A.D. Tremaine to the St.F.X. Board of Governors, 22 March 1902, RG 5/8/1519–22, PTP and P.B. Waite to author, 2 August 1991, University Historian Files, STFXUA.

6 *Xaverian*, April 1909, 27–30 and 45–7.

7 Report of the Committee on College Extension, 1897, STFXUA and the *Casket*, 7, 14, and 21 November 1907, and 5 December 1907.

8 A.B. McKillop, *Matters of Mind: The University in Ontario 1791–1951* (Toronto: University of Toronto Press, 1994), 322–61.

9 E.R. Forbes, *The Maritime Rights Movement, 1919–1927* (Montreal and Kingston: McGill-Queen's University Press, 1979).

10 Henry S. Pritchett to President MacPherson, 4 January 1921, RG 5/9/383, PMP, STFXUA, Robert M. Lester, *Review of Grants in the Maritime Provinces of Canada and Newfoundland, 1911–1933* (New York, 1934), 8, and James R. Angell to Pritchett, 10 August 1922, Maritime Provinces Educational Federation File, 30 January 1922, CCA.

11 Of seventeen faculty in 1921, all had some postgraduate training, seven had PH DS, and eight held masters' degrees. *St.F.X. Calendar 1921*, 8–9. The recent development of the campus was, of course, the five buildings recently constructed through the generosity of Neil McNeil, Dr John Somers, and Patrick Mockler.

12 William S. Learned and Kenneth C.M. Sills, *Education in the Maritime Provinces of Canada* (New York: Carnegie Foundation for the Advancement of Teaching, 1922), 25.

13 Ibid., 16.

14 Ibid., 42–3.

15 Ibid., 46.

16 Ibid.

17 C.B. Sissons, "University Federation at Toronto: A Canadian Experiment," *CHR* 31, no. 2 (June 1950):168.

18 *Casket*, 20 and 27 April 1922, 8.

19 Howard Murray, Secretary of the Senate, Dalhousie University, to Tompkins, 25 August 1919, MG 10-2, TPP, BI. Tompkins might have been the first Catholic to receive an honorary doctorate from Dalhousie, a college often viewed by Catholics as a Presbyterian stronghold. Tompkins to President MacPherson, 3 February 1920, RG 6/5/380, VPTP, STFXUA.

20 Tompkins to Learned, 7 April 1922, MG 10-2, TPP, BI.

21 John Reid, "Health, Education, Economy: Philanthropic Foundations in the Atlantic Region in the 1920s and 1930s," *Acadiensis* 14, no. 1 (Autumn 1984):74. Also see his article, "Beyond the Democratic Intellect: The Scottish Example and University Reform in Canada's Maritime Provinces, 1870–1933," in *Youth, University and Canadian Society: Essays in the Social History of Higher Education*, ed. John Reid and Paul Axelrod (Montreal and Kingston: McGill-Queen's University Press, 1989), 288–91.

22 Tompkins to William Learned, 1 May 1922, MG 10-2, 6b(1), TPP, BI. Learned was certainly open to this possibility and stressed that the proposed university was intended for "all the people." Learned to Tompkins, 13 May 1922, STFXUA.

23 Tompkins to Learned, 4 and 5 October 1922, MG 10-2, 6b(1), TPP, BI. Tompkins's interest in a labour college had probably been stimulated by Henry Somerville, who taught at the St.F.X. people's school in early 1922 and had recently become director of a new labour college at Oxford. *Casket*, 15 December 1921, 8, 22 December 1921, 6, and 8 July 1926, 8. In 1938, Tompkins and Coady would be discussing the idea of a labour college for Cape Breton. Coady to Rev. Michael Gillis, 16 November 1938, MG 20/1/932, CPP, STFXUA.

24 Tompkins to (?), 12 May 1922, MG 10-2, 1a (f7), TPP, BI and *Canadian Forum* 3, no. 36 (September 1923):363.

25 Carr to Tompkins, 13 May 1922, RG 5/9/16210, PMP, STFXUA. See Laurence K. Shook, *Catholic Post-Secondary Education in English-Speaking Canada* (Toronto: University of Toronto Press, 1971), 29 and 149–65 for an account of Carr's contribution to St Michael's College.

26 McNeil to President MacPherson, 5 February 1922, RG 5/9/15977, PMP, STFXUA.

27 Professor Smith even took issue with an article in the *Casket* on the future of small colleges which claimed that an Oxford pupil graduated from a virtually self-sufficient college instead of from the university. *Casket*, 6 July 1922, 4.

28 The resolution was moved by Dr Hugh MacPherson (professor of geology) and seconded by Dr Moses Coady (professor of education). Dr D.J. MacDonald to Learned, 31 January 1922, St.F.X. University 1921–55 File, CCA and Learned to President MacPherson, 28 February 1922, RG 5/9/5790, PMP, STFXUA.

29 Tompkins to Learned, 9 January 1922, Maritime Provinces Educational Federation File, 30 June 1922, CCA.

30 In 1920 Tompkins had expressed the opinion that "no progress of any kind can be made at St.F.X. so long as Dr MacPherson is in charge here." Rev. Ronald MacDonald to Bishop James Morrison, 29 February 1920, #7275, BMP, ADA. See also Tompkins to Rev. Michael Gillis, 24 February 1918, MG 10-2, TPP, BI.

31 A statement of his views had been printed as early as 1913 in both the *Halifax Herald* and the *Casket*, 2 January 1913, 4.

32 MacPherson to Di Maria, 26 January 1922, RG 5/9/2748, PMP and Di Maria to MacPherson, 4 February 1922, uncatalogued file, STFXUA.

33 MacPherson to Rev. R. Bourque, 30 June 1922, RG 5/9/814, PMP, STFXUA.

34 MacPherson to McNeil, 18 January 1922, RG 5/9/8399–8400, PMP, STFXUA.

35 MacPherson to Edward J. O'Brien, 26 June 1922, RG 5/9/10094, PMP, STFXUA. There is no indication whether the affiliation arrangement St.F.X. had with the adjacent women's college, Mount St Bernard, was a factor in President MacPherson's opposition to federation. The removal of St.F.X. would have had serious implications for Mount St Bernard's degree program, which had been established in 1894. Tompkins had always supported improved staff qualifications and college-level courses at the Mount. Presumably he thought Catholic women from the diocese should, from henceforth, acquire their college education in Halifax.

36 Copy of King's Board of Governors Resolution, 11 May 1922, RG 5/9/918, PMP, STFXUA.

37 President Byron Borden to H.S. Pritchett, 27 May 1922, RG 5/9/725, PMP, STFXUA.

38 MacPherson to Dr T.S. Boyle, 30 June 1922, RG 5/9/922, PMP, STFXUA.

39 Walker to MacPherson, 8 July 1922, RG 5/9/11934–6, PMP, STFXUA and Minutes of a Conference of Representatives of Maritime Provinces Universities and Colleges, 7 July 1922, Maritime Provinces Educational Federation File 1 July–31 December 1922, CCA.

40 Tompkins to Learned, 19 July 1922, MG 10-2, 6b(1), TPP, BI. This was the only source found to reconstruct developments at the clergy retreat. It is, quite clearly, a one-sided account of the proceedings.

41 Morrison to MacPherson and Tompkins, 24 July 1922, #9441, BMP, ADA.

42 Morrison to Rev. G.J. MacLellan, 3 June 1922, #9368, BMP, ADA.

43 *Casket*, 8 September 1921, 6, 23 March 1922, 6, 3 August 1922, 2. The issue of public funding for the Catholic schools of Pictou County would simmer and occasionally boil for years. See, for example, the *Casket*, 2 May 1929, 4, 8 March 1932, 4, and 19 March 1936, 2.

44 Morrison to Premier George H. Murray, 28 February 1918, #4996 and Morrison to Honourable C.P. Chisholm, 24 April 1917, #4117, BMP, ADA. The "squalid old building" was the old Main Street School; Catholics succeeded in replacing it at that time with a new brick school located directly behind St Ninian's Cathedral and named after Bishop Morrison.

45 Duff Crerar, "Bellicose Priests: The Wars of the Canadian Catholic Chaplains 1914–1919," CCHA, *Historical Studies* 58 (1991):21.

46 Bishop Morrison, notes on university federation, 15 July 1922, #9347, BMP, ADA.

47 Morrison to Robert Phalen, 15 April 1915, BMP, ADA. The diocese had acquired a majority interest in the *Casket* in 1919, so the bishop had every legal right to influence editorial policy. However, even when the *Casket* was privately owned, Phalen acknowledged the right of the bishop to advise him on editorial matters.

48 McCarthy to Morrison, 11 October 1922, #9502, BMP, ADA.

49 Morrison to Whom It May Concern, 7 August 1922, RG 5/9/9094, PMP, STFXUA.

50 St.F.X. BOG Minutes, 1 August 1922, #9335, BMP, ADA.

51 McCarthy to Morrison, 11 October 1922, #9502, BMP, ADA.

52 Morrison to McCarthy, 12 October 1922, #9694, BMP, ADA.

53 G. Edward MacDonald, in *The History of St Dunstan's University 1855–1956* (Charlottetown: Board of Governors of St Dunstan's University and Prince Edward Island Museum and Heritage Foundation, 1989), 296 concluded that Charlottetown Bishop Louis O'Leary's "role in the Maritime hierarchy deliberations about university federation is unclear." There is evidence that he thought each diocese should have been free to act on its own.

54 The presidents of St Mary's College, Halifax, St Dunstan's College, Charlottetown, and St Thomas College, Chatham, NB supported federation; St Joseph's College, Memramcook, NB was opposed. See Rev. G.J. MacLellan to Vice-President Tompkins, 26 May 1922, L. Guertin to President MacPherson, 9 February 1923, RG 5/9/4290, STFXUA, and G.D. Meader to Archbishop McCarthy, 18 October 1922, #171a, AMP, AAH, Halifax. For an examination of a debate over federation in the west, see Alphonse de Valk, CSB, "Independent University or Federated College?: The Debate among Roman Catholics during the Years 1918–1921," *Saskatchewan History* 30, no. 1 (Winter 1977):18–32.

55 Minutes of the Conference of the Catholic Hierarchy, Halifax, 19 October 1922, #171 (b), AMP, AAH.

56 Morrison to President MacPherson, 12 October 1922, #9693, BMP, ADA.

57 *Casket*, 26 May 1921, 11.

58 MacPherson to Morrison, 17 October 1922, #9496, BMP, ADA.

59 St.F.X. BOG Minutes, Special Meeting, 20 October 1922, RG 5/9/12362 and President MacPherson to G. Fred Pearson, 20 October 1922, RG 5/9/10351, PMP, STFXUA.

60 Morrison to Neil McArthur, 21 October 1922, #9699, PMP, STFXUA.

61 Tompkins claimed that Dr D.J. MacDonald was the most radical member of the faculty and that MacDonald did not believe a word of the report he (MacDonald) had written after three months of research for it in the United States. Tompkins to Cartwright, 30 July 1924, Maritime Provinces Educational Federation File, 1924, CCA. For some reason, extant copies of the report do not reveal the author's name.

62 A Report on the Proposed Federation of the Maritime Universities, 1922, 16, RG 5/12/25204, PMP, STFXUA.

63 Ibid., 8.

64 Ibid., 19.

65 It was mailed, unsolicited and anonymous, to J.L. MacDougall of Inverness County, Cape Breton; he decided to publish it as an appendix in his *History of Inverness County, Nova Scotia* (n.p., n.p., 1922), 642–84, because "it is interesting and deals with a public question of exalted importance."

66 Morrison to Most Rev. Peter Di Maria, 15 December 1922, #9864, BMP, ADA.

67 R. Phalen to Bishop Morrison, 3 June 1923, #10158, BMP, ADA.

68 Tompkins to William Learned, 20 September 1922, MG 10-2, 6b (1), TPP, BI.

69 For example, H.R. Smith was granted a one-year leave to pursue graduate studies in England, Dr C.J. Connolly was also given leave to conduct research in the United States, René Gautheron left for France in order to write a thesis, and Rev. James Boyle had been on study leave at

Columbia University, New York in 1921–22 and was placed in a parish on his return.

70 Waite, *The Lives of Dalhousie*, 1:269–70.

71 Report of the Archdiocese of Halifax to the Congregation of Seminaries and Universities, 17 January 1923, #176 (a), AMP, AAH.

72 *Halifax Chronicle*, 31 October 1922, 8 and Gerald W. Lyons to President MacPherson, 19 December 1922, RG 5/9/15878, PMP, STFXUA.

73 Morrison to Most Rev. Peter Di Maria, 5 March 1923, #10148, BMP, ADA.

74 MacPherson to Rt Rev. Paquet, 31 October 1922, RG 5/9/16095, PMP, STFXUA.

75 Morrison to Msgr W.R. Clapperton, 26 January 1923, #10045, BMP, ADA.

76 *Casket*, 26 October 1922, 6.

77 *Casket*, 30 November 1922, 1, 7 and 14 December 1922, 1, 11 and 18 January 1923, 1, 1 and 22 February 1923, 1, 1 and 8 March 1923, 1 and 4.

78 Catholic mergerites found this "muzzling" of discussion galling, and some bitterly criticized the editor for adopting such a policy. R. Phalen to Angus L. MacDonald, 15 and 20 December 1922 and MacDonald to Phalen, 22 December 1922, RG 6/5/193–201, STFXUA.

79 *Casket*, 18 January 1923, 1.

80 A.S. MacKenzie to Henry S. Pritchett, 21 December 1922, RG 5/9/10355, PMP, STFXUA.

81 Carnegie Corporation to A.S. Stanley, 17 January 1923, RG 5/9/10357, PMP, STFXUA.

82 R. MacDonald to MacPherson, 13 December 1922, RG 5/9/15931, PMP, STFXUA.

83 Morrison to Cardinal Merry Del Val, 11 November 1922, #9766 and #9767, BMP, ADA.

84 Morrison to Tompkins, 13 December 1922, #9855, BMP, ADA.

85 Morrison to Most Rev. Peter Di Maria, 24 September 1923, #12524, BMP, ADA. Somehow a rumour spread about Tompkins's removal from the college which gained amazing and enduring currency. The false idea was that Tompkins had been ejected because his economic ideas were too radical for his bishop.

86 Tompkins to William Learned, 21 December 1922, MG 10-2, TPP, BI. At one point, Tompkins developed a plan to obtain a scholarship for study at the University of Wisconsin and afterwards to propagandize throughout the Maritimes in favour of university federation and adult education. Bishop Morrison to Rev. J.W. MacIsaac, 18 December 1922, #9885, BMP, ADA and Tompkins to Learned, 8 January 1923, Maritime Provinces Educational Federation File, January–December 1923, CCA.

87 Tompkins to Learned, 24 December 1922, MG 10-2, TPP, BI and Tompkins to Learned, 8 January 1923, Maritime Provinces Educational Federation File, January–December 1923, CCA.

88 Tompkins to President F.P. Keppel, 28 May 1929, Maritime Provinces Educational Federation January 1927–29 File, CCA.

89 *Contemporary and Alumni News* 4, no. 2 (15 June 1966):10–11.

90 For tributes in the *Casket* which emphasize these contributions, see 18 September 1919, 4 and 16 October 1919, 4.

91 Morrison to Most Rev. Peter Di Maria, 24 September 1925, #12529, BMP, ADA.

92 MacPherson to Morrison, 17 October 1922, #9496, BMP, ADA. Dr Coady appeared to give a balanced assessment of his strengths and weaknesses in "Dr J.J. Tompkins – An Appreciation," May 1953, RG 25-3/4/5617, Faculty Files #194, STFXUA.

93 Roche to McCarthy, 10 January 1923, #175b, AMP, AAH.

94 McCarthy to Roche, 5 January 1923, #175a, AMP, AAH.

95 Report of the Archdiocese of Halifax to the Congregation of Seminaries and Universities, 19 January 1923, #176a, AMP, AAH.

96 Morrison to Cardinal Merry Del Val, 23 January 1923, #10043 and Morrison to Msgr W.R. Clapperton, 26 January 1923, #10045, BMP, ADA.

97 Morrison to Most Rev. Peter Di Maria, 5 March 1923, #10148 and William R. Clapperton to Morrison, 2 April 1923, #10044, BMP, ADA.

98 Morrison to Msgr W.R. Clapperton, 7 March 1923, #10157, BMP, ADA.

99 Tompkins to Learned, 8 June 1923, Maritime Educational Federation File, January–December 1923, CCA.

100 McNeil to Rev. John R. MacDonald, 25 May 1923, uncatalogued, Bishop John R. MacDonald Papers, ADA.

101 Peter Di Maria to Archbishop McCarthy, 15 May 1923, MG 75/1, RJPP, STFXUA.

102 Morrison to Diocesan Clergy, 25 May 1923, RG 5/9/12627, PMP, STFXUA and the *Casket*, 31 May 1923, 4.

103 Morrison to Most Rev. Peter Di Maria, 25 May 1923, #10356, BMP, ADA.

104 Tompkins to Cardinal Gasquet, 27 May 1925, MG 10-2, 1b, TPP, BI.

105 Tompkins to Learned, 14 May 1923, Maritime Provinces Educational Federation File, January–December 1923, CCA.

106 Moses Coady, Comments on Manuscript for George Boyle, 28 August 1951, RG 30-2/1/4796–7, DCP, EC, STFXUA.

107 Tompkins blamed a Catholic exclusivism rooted in Quebec nationalism for allegedly influencing the Acadian bishops against federation. Tompkins to Learned, 4 June 1923, Maritime Provinces Educational Federation File, January–December 1923, CCA.

108 Morrison to Most Rev. Peter Di Maria, 8 April 1924, #11174, BMP, ADA.

109 Learned, when he heard of the wording of the question, thought that it assured Rome's opposition. The scheme he claimed to have proposed was for a central university subsisting on state aid in affiliation with several religiously independent colleges. Learned to Tompkins, 31 May

1923, Maritime Provinces Educational Federation File, January–December 1923, CCA.

110 I am following, here, the argument made by Alphonse de Valk in "Catholic Higher Education and University Affiliation in Alberta, 1906–1926," CCHA, *Study Sessions* 46 (1979):42–3. A full treatment of the varied Catholic institutional arrangements in Canadian higher education must await the opening of Vatican Archives beyond the current closure date of 1922.

111 Tompkins to Learned, 8 June 1922, Maritime Provinces Educational Federation File, 30 June 1922, CCA.

112 Ironically, while the federation debate continued in the Maritimes, one of Bishop Morrison's own priests, and the one who succeeded him as bishop of the diocese, Rev. John R. MacDonald, helped Archbishop O'Leary establish an affiliated college on the campus of the University of Alberta and obtained, in May 1923, $100,000 from the Carnegie Corporation to support the project. Carnegie officials hoped the grant would encourage "sound educational policy" throughout the dominion and "give impetus" to the Maritime University federation movement. See Peter Nearing, "Rev. John R. MacDonald, St Joseph's College and the University of Alberta," CCHA, *Study Sessions* (1975):71–90 and University of Alberta Notes, n.d., Alberta, University of, St Joseph's College File, CCA.

113 De Valk, "Catholic Higher Education," 42–3.

114 Ibid., 42–4.

115 Shook, *Catholic Post-Secondary Education*, 66–7 and Morrison to Most Rev. A. Cassulo, Apostolic Delegate, 6 October 1927, #14382, BMP, ADA.

116 Dr T.S. Boyle to President MacPherson, 6 October 1923, RG 5/9/21220, PMP, STFXUA. For an account of the negotiations and final arrangements, see Waite, *The Lives of Dalhousie*, 272–6.

117 John G. Reid, "Mount Allison College: The Reluctant University," *Acadiensis* 10 (Autumn 1980):37 and 66.

118 F.P. Keppel to President MacPherson, 5 July 1929, RG 5/9/1388, PMP, STFXUA.

119 Learned to Tompkins, 31 May 1923, Maritime Provinces Educational Federation File, January–December 1923, CCA.

120 James Bertram to President Keppel, 5 August 1926, Maritime Provinces Educational Federation File, January 1925–December 1926, CCA.

121 W.A. Cartwright to President MacPherson, 7 July 1923 and MacPherson to Cartwright, 16 July 1924, RG 5/9/384,386, PMP, STFXUA.

122 Central Advisory Committee of the Carnegie Corporation, Minutes, 27 February 1925, RG 5/9/15697–8, PMP, STFXUA.

123 R.W. Kane, "The Atlantic Provinces Examining Board," *Canadian Education* 13, no. 2 (1958):25–34.

124 Lester, *Review of Grants*, 26–9. Its financial support of the committee's work continued until 1941.

125 Bishop Morrison to Benefactors of St.F.X., 22 July 1916, MG 10-2, 4e, (f2), TPP, BI.

126 Clergy Eulogy to President MacPherson, c. 1917, MG 1/1/1, 1202, MPP, STFXUA.

127 Bishop Morrison to Most Rev. Peter Di Maria, 24 September 1925, #12529, BMP, ADA.

CHAPTER TEN

1 George Boyle, *Father Tompkins of Nova Scotia* (New York: P.J. Kennedy and Sons, 1953), 79.

2 Rev. Dr Malcolm MacLellan interview, 16 September 1991, Antigonish, STFXUA.

3 Rev. A.A. Johnston, *Antigonish Diocese Priests and Bishops 1786–1925*, ed. Kathleen M. MacKenzie (Antigonish: Casket Printing and Publishing Co., 1994), 90.

4 *Casket*, 9 January 1919, 1, 26 March 1931, 6, 16 April 1931, 8, and 30 April 1931, 10.

5 President MacPherson, speech on education to graduates, May 1928, RG 5/9/12474, PMP, STFXUA.

6 MacPherson to Captain Patrick Mockler, 24 October 1921, RG 5/9/8906, PMP, STFXUA.

7 Johnston, *Antigonish Diocese*, 60 and Rev. Dr Malcolm MacLellan, "At Age Fourteen – A Freshman," 11–12, STFXUA.

8 Johnston, *Antigonish Diocese*, 59.

9 Joseph P. McCarthy, *Times of My Life* (n.p.: n.p., 1969), 56 and Johnston, *Antigonish Diocese*, 75.

10 *Xaverian*, November 1919, 42, *Casket*, 18 February 1954, Johnston, *Antigonish Diocese*, 97 and Rev. Dr Malcolm MacLellan interview, Antigonish, 1991.

11 The new motherhouse was completed by the fall of 1921. It replaced the old one on the St.F.X. campus, which had been built in 1896–97. *Casket*, 22 September 1921, 6.

12 MacLellan, "At Age Fourteen," 19–20, STFXUA and McCarthy, *Times of My Life*, 57.

13 Morrison to President MacPherson, 6 September 1924, RG 5/9/9121–2, PMP, STFXUA.

14 Johnston, *Antigonish Diocese*, 17.

15 After his departure from the college, he unfortunately continued for some years with bouts of excessive drinking. A Reply by Bishop James

476

Morrison to a statement prepared by Rev. Thomas O'R. Boyle, 6 April 1936, #21869, BMP, ADA.

16 For a concise biography by a former student and fellow professor, see Rev. Dr Malcolm MacLellan, *Coady Remembered* (Antigonish: Casket Printing and Publishing Co., 1985).

17 Rev. Moses Coady, "My Story," CBC-TV transcript, 2, 8 July 1957, MG 75/1, RJPP, *Casket*, 25 November 1920, 4, 23 December 1923, 12, and 9 June 1921, 6.

18 Johnston, *Antigonish Diocese*, 30, Coady to President MacPherson, 14 May 1915, RG 5/9/15731, PMP, and MacLellan, "At Age Fourteen," 45, STFXUA.

19 President MacPherson to Bishop Morrison, 12 March 1929, RG 5/9/9190, PMP, STFXUA.

20 Rev. Dr Malcolm MacLellan interview, Antigonish, 1987, STFXUA and Johnston, *Antigonish Diocese*, 105.

21 President Nicholson to Honourable L.D. Currie, 21 October 1944, RG 5/11/2884, PNP, STFXUA.

22 He became well known in scientific circles, especially for his study *External Morphology of the Primate Brain* (1950). Johnston, *Antigonish Diocese*, 31 and Rev. Dr Malcolm MacLellan interview, Antigonish, 16 September 1991.

23 Johnston, *Antigonish Diocese*, 90 and *Casket*, 7 October 1920, 12.

24 *St.F.X. Calendar 1922*, 20–3.

25 *St.F.X. Calendar 1931–32*, 76–7 and 96–105.

26 Dalhousie Faculty of Law to St.F.X. Registrar, 22 May 1922, RG 5/9/21072–3, PMP, STFXUA.

27 *Casket*, 20 October 1927, 12, Mary A. Lynch, "Speech Training: 1926–1968, St.F.X.," MG 4/1/1–50, box 5/1, Dr Mary A. Lynch Personal Papers, STFXUA, and *St.F.X. Calendar 1927–28*, 33.

28 *Casket*, 29 April 1926, 12.

29 *Xaverian*, 24 April 1926, 2 and *St.F.X Calendar 1927–28*, 38–9.

30 In the face of some opposition from college officials and clergy, the Marthas had achieved autonomy in 1917. By 1921 they had erected a new motherhouse, aptly called Bethany, on a hill to the north of town, but retained the convent at St.F.X. for sisters who were working there. College officials wanted to ensure that the Marthas continued to serve adequately St.F.X.'s domestic needs. See Articles of Agreement, 7 August 1917, BMP, ADA, Sister May Mulvihill, "Origin and Early History. History of Sisters of St Martha of Antigonish, 1894–1917," 1981, 35–40, A/100/3/14, case #3c, SSTMA, and Sarah MacPherson, "Religious Women in Nova Scotia: A Struggle for Autonomy. A Sketch of the Sisters of Saint Martha of Antigonish, Nova Scotia, 1900–1960," CCHA, *Study Sessions* (1984):97–8.

31 *St.F.X. Calendar 1927-28*, 18 and Provincial Council of CNDs to St.F.X. BOG, 23 January 1920, RG 5/9/4198, PMP, STFXUA.

32 Sister St Margaret of the Cross to the Rector and Faculty of St.F.X., 10 December 1926, RG 12/6/32, Rev. J.C. Chisholm Registrar's Papers, STFXUA.

33 RG 5/10/1736-7, PMP, STFXUA.

34 A.B. McKillop, *Matters of Mind: The University in Ontario 1791-1951* (Toronto: University of Toronto Press, 1994), 420.

35 Ibid., 407.

36 *St.F.X. Calendar 1923*, 26.

37 *Casket*, 16 and 23 September 1926, 12.

38 Munro to President MacPherson, 21 August 1926, RG 5/9/9407, PMP, STFXUA.

39 Minutes of Conference of Presidents of the Universities with the Superintendent of Education, 10 September 1926, RG 5/9/9413, PMP, STFXUA.

40 *St.F.X. Calendar 1923*, 14.

41 *St.F.X. Calendar 1927-28*, 40-1.

42 *St.F.X. Calendar 1927-28*, 25.

43 President MacPherson to D.C. Chisholm, 6 February 1929, RG 5/9/1666 and MacPherson to Superintendent Henry Munro, 23 September 1929, RG 5/9/9418, PMP, STFXUA.

44 Thompson to President MacPherson, 16 May 1907, RG 5/9/11593, PMP, STFXUA.

45 Staff Survey Summary, 1920, #7169, BMP, ADA.

46 President MacPherson to Bishop Morrison, 30 August 1922, RG 5/9/9100 and MacPherson to Neil McArthur, 1 May 1929, RG 5/9/6074, PMP, STFXUA.

47 See *Annual Report of the Superintendent of Education*, 1883 and 1921.

48 *St.F.X. Calendar 1927-28*, 25.

49 *St.F.X. Calendar 1931-32*, 96-105.

50 McKillop, *Matters of Mind*, 406. Some historians are casting doubt on this popular conception of 1920s youth as hedonistic materialists.

51 *St.F.X. Calendar 1931-32*, 21. The college deficit in 1922 alone was $28,552. St.F.X. Financial Statement, 30 June 1922, STFXUA.

52 *St.F.X. Calendar 1931-32*, 13. The Nova Scotia Knights of Columbus began the scholarship program in 1921. The amounts were for $200 yearly, to be acquired through competition and held for four years at a Catholic institution by "deserving young men," especially those who needed financial assistance. Knights of Columbus regulations, 1921, #8216, BMP, ADA.

53 *St.F.X. Calendar 1931-32*, 13.

54 MacPherson to W.J. Brown, 21 March 1932, RG 5/9/21910, PMP, STFXUA.

55 *Xaverian*, 26 November 1932, 4.

56 *Xaverian*, December 1919, 43–4.

57 *Xaverian*, May 1921, 91–3.

58 *St.F.X. Calendar 1926–27*, 51. The Athletic Association formally registered the "X" as their official symbol on 23 November 1920 at the Patent and Copyright Office, Ottawa, under the Trade Mark and Design Act. The *Xaverian*, February 1921, 39 described it as "an Industrial Design of a badge of proficiency in athletics.

59 President MacPherson to G. Bonno, 7 August 1923, RG 5/9/695 and Wilfrid Bovey to A. Gordon Bagnall, 8 May 1925, RG 5/9/325a, PMP, STFXUA.

60 President MacPherson to Percy Davies, 7 October 1930, RG 5/9/2546, PMP, STFXUA.

61 *Xaverian*, December 1923, 47 and March 1924, 37.

62 Minutes of the Freshmen Society, RG 5/9/27402, PMP, STFXUA.

63 *Xaverian*, November 1922, 17–19.

64 Harvey Steele, *Dear Old Rebel: A Priest's Battle for Social Justice* (Lawrencetown Beach, NS: Pottersfield Press, 1993), 33.

65 *Xaverian Supplement 1930*, 134–5 and the *Casket*, 26 February 1931, 12.

66 *Xaverian*, 10 March 1950, 1.

67 President MacPherson to Mrs Martin Daley, 11 January 1912, RG 5/9/2523, PMP, STFXUA.

68 Rev. Dr Malcolm MacLellan, "At Age Fourteen – A Freshmen," 2, STFXUA.

69 *St.F.X. Calendar 1927–28*, 20.

70 Rev. Dr Malcolm MacLellan interview, 16 September 1991, Antigonish.

71 MacPherson to Mary L. Bollert, 27 May 1924, RG 5/9/21801, PMP, STFXUA.

72 He claimed that it had started during the First World War. Actually initiation was already being practised at St.F.X. in the 1890s.

73 *Xaverian*, November 1925, 2.

74 *Xaverian*, 15 October 1927, 1.

75 *Xaverian*, 11 October 1930, 8.

76 MacPherson to James Friel, 22 February 1922, RG 5/9/3756, PMP, STFXUA.

77 Mr Proctor, Chief Commissioner, to President MacPherson, 19 August 1930, RG 5/9/9921, PMP, STFXUA.

78 MacPherson to Mr Fleming, 23 March 1936, RG 5/9/13409, PMP, STFXUA.

79 MacPherson to Bishop Morrison, 2 July 1925, BMP, ADA.

80 *Xaverian*, May 1921, 95.

81 *St.F.X. Calendar 1931–32*, 3.

82 MacPherson to Rev. T.M. Gillis, 2 March 1929, RG 5/9/3849, PMP, STFXUA.

83 *Xaverian*, 5 February 1927, 2.

84 Faculty Regulations, RG 5/10/990, President MacDonald Papers, STFXUA.

85 Bishop Morrison to Nicholson, 31 August 1927, #14276, BMP, ADA.

86 Ernest R. Forbes, *The Maritime Rights Movement, 1919-1927: A Study in Canadian Regionalism* (Kingston and Montreal: McGill-Queen's University Press, 1979), viii.

87 Ibid., 54. Chapter 4, "The Impact of the Depression," 54-72, does an excellent job charting the decline in each sector of the economy.

88 David Alexander, "Economic Growth in the Atlantic Region, 1880-1940," *Acadiensis* 8, no. 1 (Autumn 1978):59.

89 *Report of the Duncan Commission*, 8 January 1926 and David Frank, "The Election of J.B. McLaughin: Labour Politics in Cape Breton, 1916-1935," in *The Island: New Perspectives on Cape Breton History 1713-1990*, ed. Kenneth Donovan (Fredericton, NB and Sydney, NS: Acadiensis Press and the University College of Cape Breton Press, 1990), 187-219.

90 L.D. McCann, "The Mercantile-Industrial Transition in the Metal Towns of Pictou County, 1857-1931, *Acadiensis* 10 (Spring 1981):29-64.

91 Forbes, *Maritime Rights*, 65.

92 *Census of Canada 1931*, 1:348.

93 MacPherson to Eric F. MacNeill, 23 September 1926, RG 5/9/14592, PMP, STFXUA. For a good first-hand grass-roots account of the problems many people in eastern Nova Scotia faced keeping body and soul together during the twenties, see Ida Delaney, *By Their Own Hands: A Field Worker's Account of the Antigonish Movement* (Hantsport, NS: Lancelot Press, 1985), chapter 1.

CHAPTER ELEVEN

1 The offspring of the St.F.X. extension department, the Antigonish Movement, has been the college's main claim to fame throughout and far beyond the diocese. It has received the lion's share of attention from scholars interested in St.F.X. The following are selected descriptions and interpretations of the movement: Moses Coady, *Masters of Their Own Destiny* (New York: Harper and Brothers, 1939), Alexander Laidlaw, *The Campus and the Community: The Global Impact of the Antigonish Movement* (Montreal: Harvest House, 1961), Ida Delaney, *By Their Own Hands: A Field Worker's Account of the Antigonish Movement* (Hantsport, NS: Lancelot Press, 1985), Francis J. Mifflin, "The Antigonish Movement: A Revitalization Movement in Eastern Nova Scotia" (PHD thesis, Boston College, 1974), Daniel W. MacInnes, "Clerics, Fishermen, Farmers and Workers: The Antigonish Movement and Identity in Eastern Nova Scotia, 1928-1939" (PHD thesis, McMaster University, 1978), R. James Sacouman, "Underdevelopment and the Structural

Origins of Antigonish Co-operatives in Eastern Nova Scotia," *Acadiensis* 7 (Autumn 1977):66–85, and Anne MacDonald Alexander, "The Meaning of Liberation in Adult Education as Revealed by Moses Coady and the Antigonish Movement" (PH D thesis, University of Alberta, 1985).

2 After his removal from the college, Tompkins organized a series of lectures on educational problems for the people in his parish of Canso. *Casket*, 24 and 31 January 1924, 2. Perhaps in connection with the people's school in Cape Breton in 1922, Bishop Morrison had directed professor T. O'R. Boyle to form some type of study clubs and then to expand them into various parts of the diocese in order to assist those not benefiting from current educational efforts. The nature and extent of these study clubs is unclear. Morrison to Boyle, 17 and 21 February 1922, #9126 and #9082, BMP, ADA.

3 *Casket*, 4 November 1920, 4.

4 *Casket*, 6 July 1916, 8, 25 July 1918, 8, 5 October 1916, 5, 8, and 9 November 1916, 8.

5 *Casket*, 11 August 1927, 12, and 18 August 1927, 6.

6 See John Francis Glasgow, "The Role of Educational and Rural Conferences in the Development of the Extension Department of Saint Francis Xavier University" (BA thesis, St.F.X., 1947).

7 Coady to Gillis, 31 August 1951, MG 20/1/954–5, CPP, STFXUA.

8 Morrison to Clergy, 21 December 1925, MG 10-2, 2a (f2), TPP, BI and Rev. A.A. Johnston, *A History of the Catholic Church in Eastern Nova Scotia*, 2 vols. (Antigonish: St.F.X. University Press, 1960, 1971), 2:555.

9 E.R. Forbes and D.A. Muise, eds., *The Atlantic Provinces in Confederation* (Toronto and Fredericton: University of Toronto Press and Acadiensis Press, 1993), 194–228.

10 *Casket*, 18 December 1924, 12, 25 December 1924, 8, and 20 October 1927, 6.

11 Minutes of the Fourth Annual Rural Conference of the Diocese of Antigonish, 10–11 November 1926, RG 30-3/28/17, EC, STFXUA.

12 Rev. John R. MacDonald to Coady, 12 February 1938, MG 20/1/1366–8, CPP, STFXUA.

13 *Casket*, 15 September 1927, 12, and 6 October 1927, 6 and 8.

14 Rev. H.J. MacDonald to Tompkins, 29 October 1928, MG 10-2, 4e(1), TPP, BI.

15 Alexander Laidlaw, "Silver Jubilee Review of the St.F.X. Extension Department," 1953, RG 30-3/25/1503, EC, STFXUA.

16 Constitution and By-Laws of the Scottish Catholic Society of Canada, 1920, MG 6-26, C(1), BI and the *Casket*, 8 January 1920, 8.

17 S.B. McNeil to President MacPherson, 11 October 1928, RG 5/9/12700, PMP, STFXUA and the *Casket*, 26 July 1928, 8.

18 Coady to R.J. MacSween, 24 March 1953, RG 30-2/1/2963–6, EC, STFXUA.

19 Scottish Catholic Society of Canada Record Book, 74, STFXUA.

20 *Casket*, 21 August 1930, 6, 20 August 1931, 6, and 25 August 1932, 2.

21 R.J. MacSween, "The Part Played by the Scottish Catholic Society of Canada in the Establishment of the St.F.X. Extension Department," n.d., RG 30-3/25/1586–1600, J.H. McNeil to Rev. Michael Gillis, 18 January 1938, RG 30-2/1/1414–15, DCP, EC, STFXUA, and Daniel MacInnes, "The Role of the Scottish Catholic Society in the Determination of the Antigonish Movement," *Scottish Tradition* 7/8 (1977–78):25–46.

22 Scottish Catholic Society of Canada Record Book, 41–2, STFXUA.

23 Coady to R.J. MacSween, 24 March 1953, RG 30-2/1/2963–6 and Coady to Rev. Mother St Aidan, 14 July 1954, RG 30-2/1/4543, DCP, EC, STFXUA. See also Coady, *Masters*, 7.

24 McArthur was a St.F.X. graduate and had been member of the board of governors from 1921. In 1924 he was referred to as one of Cape Breton's "leading legal lights." At that time he was town solicitor and legal adviser to the United Mine Workers. *Casket*, 8 May 1924, 11. In 1934 he was appointed a county court judge. *Casket*, 1 November 1934, 12. His correspondence with President MacPherson on legal and other university affairs was extensive.

25 *Casket*, 24 May 1928, 4.

26 *Casket*, 19 May 1927, 11 and BOG Minutes, 18 August 1927, STFXUA.

27 Alumni Association Minute Book, 1927, RG 25-1/1/7, AAR, and Coady Address before the Royal Fisheries Commission at Halifax, 1927, RG 30-2/1/14–15, EC, DCP, STFXUA.

28 Coady, "Brief to Royal Commission on Taxation of Cooperatives, 1945," in Extension Department, *The Antigonish Movement Yesterday and Today* (Antigonish: Extension Department, 1976), 8.

29 Tompkins's involvement with the committee is unclear. His name did not appear on the final report. It is apparent from later evidence that Tompkins, after being removed from the college in 1922 by Bishop Morrison for his advocacy of university federation, did not initially support the move by St.F.X. into extension work. Neither did he conceive of the study club or of the application of economic cooperation to adult education. However, because of his work with the early St.F.X. summer schools, his *Casket* column "For the People," his pamphlet *Knowledge for the People*, his People's School, and his work in Canso, he is rightly considered a pioneer in Canadian adult education. After the St.F.X. extension department got started, Tompkins became one of its most ardent supporters. Coady to Rev. Mother St Aidan, 14 July 1954, RG 30-2/1/4543, DCP, EC, STFXUA.

30 Alumni Association Minute Book, 1929, RG 25-1/1/7, AAR, STFXUA.

31 Alumni Association Committee Proposal to the Board of Governors, August 1928, RG 5/9/12384–9, PMP, STFXUA.

32 BOG Minutes, 19 November 1928 and Alumni Association Book, 1929, RG 25-1/1/7, AAR, STFXUA. Coady claimed that their reluctance to act had been rooted in financial stringency and the fear of alienating big supporters of the college. Coady, *Masters*, 14.

33 Coady at first objected to his appointment on the grounds that he was too old. Later he reflected, "I learned later that the job called for a lot of experience that probably a young man could not have." His confidence that a general program of adult education would work was based, he reported, on an "educational and cooperative experiment" he had begun in his home territory of Margaree in 1926, where about twelve farmers met in a study group to examine problems of production and marketing. Coady to R.J. MacSween, 24 March 1953, RG 30-2/1/2965, DCP, EC, STFXUA.

34 Through the first part of his trip he headed a delegation of coal people who lobbied the government in Ottawa. *Casket*, 24 January 1929, 12.

35 Coady to President MacPherson, 19 February 1929, RG 5/9/2034 and printed statement by Coady, n.d., RG 5/9/12504-5, PMP, STFXUA.

36 *Casket*, 18 July 1929, 8.

37 *Casket*, 26 September 1929, 6.

38 *Casket*, 3 July 1930, 11.

39 Rev. Moses Coady, "My Story," CBC-TV transcript, 8 July 1957, 4, MG 75/1, RJPP, STFXUA.

40 BOG Minutes, 5 August 1929 and 31 January 1930, STFXUA.

41 Notice of Meeting, 14 January 1930, RG 5/12/25635, PSP, STFXUA and the *Casket*, 23 January 1930, 6.

42 MacDonald to Tompkins, 2 June 1916, MG 10-2, f5, d(1), TPP, BI. Rev. Dr D.J. MacDonald, professor of economics at St.F.X., was A.B. MacDonald's brother.

43 Biographic Profile, RG 25-3/4/2751-2, Faculty Files, STFXUA.

44 St.F.X. Extension Department, *The Antigonish Way* (Regina: Co-operative Union of Canada, 1947), 6.

45 However, extension followed a policy of strict neutrality in politics. The left-wing Cooperative Commonwealth Federation (CCF), founded in 1932 as a national party, tried to establish some connection or identification with it. See A.B. MacDonald to J.S. Woodsworth, 11 March 1935, RG 30-2/2/2545-6, also 3549-2552, MADP, EC, STFXUA. The policy of non-alignment was designed to prevent extension's work from being identified with any one segment of the population, and to prevent the people from expecting a quick political fix to their problems. Extension tried to be universal in its approach by rising above divisions of politics, religion, gender, ethnicity, and occupation.

46 The conferences did exactly this. New experiments, such as work among women, the short leadership courses, and the *Extension Bulletin*, were

ideas apparently hatched at the conferences. See the *Casket*, 3 September 1931, 7, and 15 September 1932, 2.

47 Possible Activities of Extension Department, 1930, ESBK, July 1930–December 1942, EC, STFXUA.

48 By the end of October, extension had established study clubs in Cape Breton. *Casket*, 20 October 1930, 12.

49 Delaney, *By Their Own Hands*, 34.

50 Study Clubs pamphlet, ESBK, July 1930–December 1942, 5, EC, STFXUA.

51 First Study Club Lesson, 23 October 1930, ESBK, July 1930-December 1942, 5, EC, STFXUA. In retrospect, Coady thought the early study clubs were "sickly things and the education that was carried on through them was often superficial and inapplicable to the needs of individuals." The mistake was, he stated, a lack of direction for developing specific economic ventures. Coady, *Masters*, 44.

52 Coady, *Masters*, 35.

53 Coady to Rev. A. MacDonell, 16 January 1932, RG 30-2/1/2538, DCP, EC, STFXUA.

54 Ibid.

55 Anonymous, "Mobilizing for Enlightenment," c. 1940, 24, EC, STFXUA.

56 Ibid., 24.

57 For example, see the *Casket*, 25 February 1915, 1, and 6 December 1917, 7.

58 *Casket*, 26 January 1933, 10, and 2 February 1933, 10.

59 Extension form letter, 23 October 1930, ESBK, July 1930-December 1942, 5, EC, STFXUA.

60 Both Sister Irene Doyle and Judith F. MacLean drew my attention to the important role played by women in the extension office.

61 Interview with Sister Irene Doyle, CSM, 24 February 1993, St.F.X.

62 Coady to Kay Thompson, 17 October 1941, uncatalogued, STFXUA.

63 *Casket*, 29 December 1932, 6.

64 Course Materials, 1932, RG 30-3/27/1–8, EC, STFXUA.

65 Course Materials, 1934, RG 30-3/27/15–16, EC, STFXUA.

66 Coady to Rev. James Boyle, 20 January 1936, MG 20/1/155, CPP, STFXUA.

67 Course Materials, 1934, RG 30-3/27/15–16, EC, STFXUA.

68 Delaney, *By Their Own Hands*, 64.

69 Course Materials, 1932–40, RG 30-3/27/1–80, EC, STFXUA.

70 Course Materials, 1933, RG 30-3/27/9–13, EC, STFXUA.

71 Minutes of the Ninth Rural Conference, 1–2 September 1931, ESBK, July 1930–December 1942, 11, EC, STFXUA and the *Casket*, 3 September 1931, 7.

72 For a good overview of women and the Antigonish Movement, see Judith F. MacLean and Daniel MacInnes, "'What Can the Women Do?': The Antigonish Movement and Its Programs for Women, 1918–1945," paper

presented to the Canadian Association for Studies in Co-operation, 1 June 1992, University of Prince Edward Island, Charlottetown, Prince Edward Island.

73 Report of Extension, May 1934, ESBK, July 1930–December 1942, 15, EC, STFXUA.

74 *Casket*, 22 February 1934, 10.

75 Report on Women's Work, c. 1934, RG 5/9/25132–3, PMP, STFXUA.

76 Sister Irene Doyle, "My Experience as an Extension Worker Over Fifty Years Ago," speech to the Antigonish Heritage Association, 8 March 1993, STFXUA.

77 Coady to W.H. Frost, 7 February 1933, RG 30-2/1/1266–7, DCP, EC, STFXUA.

78 The Canadian cooperative movement has been charted in Ian MacPherson, *Each for All: A History of the Co-operative Movement in English Canada, 1900–1945* (Toronto: Macmillan, 1979).

79 Ibid., 1, 8, 22, and 28.

80 Coady, "My Story," 4–5.

81 ESBK, July 1930–December 1942, EC, STFXUA.

82 Coady to Rev. Michael Gillis, 6 March 1932, RG 30-2/1/1389, DCP, EC, STFXUA and the *Casket*, 8 December 1932, 12, and 11 May 1933, 6.

83 *Casket*, 19 January 1933, 2.

84 Report of Extension, May 1932, RG 5/9/25138, PMP, STFXUA. MacIntyre had been a Communist Party member.

85 *St.F.X. Calendar 1933–34*, 110–11.

86 Bergengren presented a paper on credit unions at the diocesan rural conference in 1931. He returned in late 1932 to help organize four credit unions in Cape Breton.

87 Delaney, *By Their Own Hands*, 67.

88 Apparently Bergengren helped A.B. MacDonald draft credit union legislation for Nova Scotia; Coady and Tompkins pressed for its passage and the "Credit Union Societies Act" was enacted by the provincial government in April 1932. *Casket*, 3 September 1931, 7, 24 November 1932, 6, 22 December 1932, 6, and "Credit Union Societies Act," *Statutes of Nova Scotia*, 1932, cap. 11, 190–209.

89 "An Act to Incorporate the Nova Scotia Credit Union League," *Statutes of Nova Scotia*, 1938, cap. 72, 3–6.

90 She has given a superb first-hand account of life on the front lines of extension work. Her book is a marvellous, vivid, and often humorous description of how the program worked or didn't work in the local communities of the region. Ida Delaney, *By Their Own Hands*.

91 *St.F.X. Calendar 1940–41*, 89–94. Apparently fisheries had asked extension in the fall of 1938 to take on thirty-two workers; they had trouble finding suitable candidates. A.B. MacDonald to L.A. Wolfe, 23 February

1939, RG 30-2/2/655, MADP. Coady claimed that they took on thirty-six new workers in the fall of 1938. Coady to Very Rev. Vincent J. Ryan, 10 March 1939, RG 30-2/1/3672, DCP, EC, STFXUA. For a helpful visual depiction of the Antigonish Movement, see plate 44 by Dr Daniel MacInnes in *Historical Atlas of Canada*, vol. 3, ed. Donald Kerr and Deryck W. Holdsworth (Toronto: University of Toronto Press, 1990).

92 By 1943 the Sydney branch had been reorganized as an independent wholesale and renamed Cape Breton Co-operative Services, Limited. Shortly thereafter, the Canadian Livestock Co-operative in Moncton became Maritime Co-operative Services Limited.

93 See Mark G. McGowan, "Conspicuous Influence: The Diocese of Antigonish and the Development of the Canadian Catholic Church, 1844–1994," 20–3. Paper presented at the Rev. A.A. Johnston Memorial Conference, 19–20 August 1994, St Francis Xavier University.

94 Father Andrew MacDonell, OSB, Report of the Scottish Immigrant Aid Society, 1933, RG 12/5/230–7, Registrar's Papers, STFXUA, and the *Casket*, 25 January 1924, 12, 18 October 1934, 12.

95 George Kane to President MacPherson, 21 March 1936, RG 5/9/5384, PMP, STFXUA and the *Casket*, 20 February 1936, 6, 26 March 1936, 1, and 11 June 1936, 11.

96 See Ronald L. Faris, *The Passionate Educators: Voluntary Associations and the Struggle for Control of Adult Educational Broadcasting in Canada 1919–1952* (Toronto: Peter Martin Associates, 1974) and Michael Welton, "'On the Eve of a Great Mass Movement': Reflections on the Origins of the CAAE," in *Choosing Our Future: Adult Education and Public Policy in Canada*, ed. Frank Cassidy and Ron Faris (Toronto: OISE Press, 1987), 17–18.

97 Report of the National Convener of Study Clubs, Catholic Women's League of Canada, June 1937, RG 30-2/1/1475–83, DCP, EC, STFXUA.

98 *Casket*, 31 October 1935, 1. G. Edward MacDonald's *History of St Dunstan's University 1855–1956* (Charlottetown: Board of Governors of St Dunstan's University and Prince Edward Island Museum and Heritage Foundation, 1989), 344–9, describes some of the early connections between St.F.X. and the Island Catholic college.

99 Coady to Rev. James E. Byrne, 19 June 1936, RG 30-2/1/851, DCP, EC, STFXUA. See also the *Casket*, 14 June 1934, 12, and 28 June 1934, 10. In 1936 a St.F.X. graduate began to organize Newfoundland fishermen cooperatively. *Casket*, 18 June 1936, 6.

100 Roy Bergengren to Coady, 30 January 1940, RG 30-2/1/413, DCP, EC, STFXUA.

101 *Casket*, 27 August 1936, 1.

102 For example, see the notes on outstanding speakers who were invited to the rural and industrial conference in 1935, and the report on world-wide

interest in the movement. *Casket*, 8 August 1935, 10, 9 May 1936, 5, and 24 December 1936, 12.

103 *St.F.X. Xaverian Yearbook*, May 1934, 27.

104 Rev. Thomas O'R. Boyle to Coady, 30 October 1936, RG 30-2/1/780, DCP, EC, STFXUA.

105 MacPherson, *Each for All*, 168.

106 Alexander Laidlaw, Silver Jubilee Review of the St.F.X. Extension Department, 1953, RG 30-3/25/1503, EC, STFXUA.

107 Dr Alexander Laidlaw, "The Antigonish Movement in Retrospect," An Address to the Royal Canadian Institute, 9 December 1967, RG 30-3/8/217, EC, STFXUA.

108 Program of Catholic Social Action, 5, in ESBK, July 1930–December 1942, 14, EC, STFXUA.

109 St Francis Xavier University, Extension Work in Nova Scotia, Report 31 May 1933, 2, St.F.X. Extension File, 1940, CCA.

110 Rev. Ronald MacDonald to President MacPherson, 11 January 1924, MG 45/2/411, FEPP, STFXUA.

111 Coady to Rev. Charles H. Foote, 1 December 1943, RG 30-2/1/1225–6, DCP, EC, STFXUA.

112 Coady to Rev. Michael Gillis, 29 January 1953, RG 30-2/1/1367, DCP, EC, STFXUA.

113 *Maritime Co-operator*, 15 November 1954.

114 Coady to Rev. Charles H. Foote, 1 December 1943, RG 30-2/1/1223–6, DCP, EC, STFXUA.

115 Coady to Rev. Cornelius Costello, 20 July 1956, RG 30-2/1/1125–36, DCP, EC, STFXUA.

116 Ibid.

117 For an example, see A.B. MacDonald's description of how a female merchant in Terence Bay opposed the work of extension. MacDonald to W.H. Dennis, 20 August 1941, RG 30-2/2/613e, MADP, EC, STFXUA.

118 Coady to Edward J. Meehan, 2 June 1945, MG 20/1/1633–4, CPP, STFXUA.

119 *Maritime Co-operator*, 15 November 1954.

120 Coady to Andrew S. Wing, 26 January 1938, RG 30-2/1/4521, DCP, EC, STFXUA.

121 MacDonald to P.M. Dewar, 29 December 1933, RG 30-2/2/619a, MADP, EC, STFXUA.

122 Coady, *Masters*, 17.

123 Coady to J.J. Harpell, 28 November 1938, RG 30-2/1/1511, DCP, EC, STFXUA.

124 For example, see Coady to Dr J.G. Cormier, 13 October 1947, RG 30-2/1/1128–30, DCP, EC and Coady to J.A. Morris, 8 February 1956, MG 20/1/1717, CPP, STFXUA. From the vantage point of the 1990s, early extension

can easily be criticized for its neglect of all minorities in its constituency; the fairness of such criticism is another question.

125 Interview with Rev. J.N. MacNeil by Rev. P.A. Nearing, 11 October 1964, St.F.X., RG 30-2/6/1283, EC, STFXUA.
126 Ian MacPherson, "Patterns in the Maritime Co-operative Movement 1900–1945," *Acadiensis* 5 (Autumn 1975):68.
127 *Casket*, 23 July 1936, 13.
128 Some of the British and central and southern Europeans who had immigrated to work in the mines and steel mill from about 1900 brought with them radical ideas which Coady claimed "proved a great source of trouble during the past three decades." Program of Catholic Social Action, 25 September 1933, in ESBK, July 1930–December 1942, 14, EC, STFXUA. For an example of a radical leader, see David Frank, "The Election of J.B. McLaughlin," in *The Island: New Perspectives on Cape Breton History, 1713–1990*, ed. Kenneth Donovan (Sydney and Fredericton: University College of Cape Breton and Acadiensis Press, 1985), 187–219.
129 McIntyre to Dr D.J. MacDonald, 24 October 1935, RG 30-2/7/267–8, EC, STFXUA.
130 Coady to the Director, Catechetical Guild, 2 March 1951, RG 30-2/1/1015, DCP, EC, STFXUA.
131 Coady to Neil W. Arnett, 13 October 1937, RG 30-2/1/76, DCP, EC, STFXUA.
132 President MacPherson to J.J. Young, 6 March 1934, RG 5/9/1222, PMP, STFXUA.
133 *Casket*, 23 July 1936, 13–16.
134 Coady, *Masters*, 68.
135 *Xaverian Weekly*, 11 October 1930, 1, 3, 3 October 1931, 1, 3, and Dr Dan MacCormack to Dr W.V. Longley, 11 September 1946, RG 30-2/1/2066–7, DCP, EC, STFXUA.
136 *Xaverian Weekly*, 21 February 1931, 7.
137 *Xaverian Weekly*, 2 November 1935, 7–8.
138 For example, see Harvey Steele's autobiography, *Dear Old Rebel: A Priest's Battle for Social Justice* (Lawrencetown Beach, NS: Pottersfield Press, 1993). He attended St.F.X. in the early 1930s and claimed that extension was "to prove one of the most important influences in my life" (34).
139 *Casket*, 28 February 1935, 6.
140 *Xaverian Weekly*, 29 February 1936, 5. At least, no evidence shows that the project succeeded; not even a subsequent trace of its mention was discovered.
141 Suggested Budget for Extension Department, August 1930, ESBK, July 1930–December 1942, 3, EC, STFXUA.

142 Benson Y. Landis, Memorandum of Benson Y. Landis for the Carnegie Corporation, 14 December 1931, St.F.X. Extension File, 1940, CCA.

143 Summary of Progress Reports for Carnegie Corporation Trustees, February 1938, 107, RG 30-2/1/1963, DCP, EC, STFXUA.

144 James Bertram, Secretary of the Carnegie Corporation, Memo to F.P. Keppel, re Extension Department of St Francis Xavier University, 12 December 1931, St.F.X. Extension File, 1940, CCA.

145 Coady, "Mobilizing for Enlightenment: St Francis Xavier University Goes to the People," c. 1940, 14–15, STFXUA.

146 By 1936 many organizations in Nova Scotia alone were sponsoring various forms of extension work. Summary of Adult Education Activities in Nova Scotia, n.d., RG 5/9/25099–106, PMP, STFXUA.

147 See, for example, Alexander, "The Meaning of Liberation in Adult Education." Faris, in *The Passionate Educators*, identified two elements within the Canadian adult education movement: those who promoted "enlightenment within a existing social order" and others who promoted "social action for social change" (xv).

148 MacPherson, *Each for All*, 202.

149 Coady, *Masters*, 162.

150 Baum, in his study of Canadian Catholicism and socialism in the 1930s and 1940s, concluded that "The Antigonish Movement was certainly the most daring response of Canadian Catholics to the social injustices during the Depression." See Gregory Baum, *Catholics and Canadian Socialism: Political Thought in the Thirties and Forties* (Toronto: J. Lorimer, 1980), 202.

CHAPTER TWELVE

1 President MacPherson to Morrison, 3 June 1936, MG 1/1/1,918, MPP and Morrison to MacPherson, 9 June 1936, RG 5/9/16059–60, PMP, STFXUA.

2 Rev. J.M. Kiely to MacPherson, 20 June 1936, MG 1/1/1,539, MPP, STFXUA.

3 Giovanni Pizzorusso, "Documents d'intérêt Canadien dans les archives du Collège Urbain de Propaganda Fide à Rome (1829–1922)," 1992, 44, Manuscripts Division, NAC.

4 Rev. A.A. Johnston, *Antigonish Diocese Priests and Bishops 1786–1925*, ed. Kathleen M. MacKenzie (Antigonish: Casket Printing and Publishing Co., 1994), 59.

5 For examples, see "Poverty, Its Causes and Remedies," *Casket*, 29 March 1917, 4, "The Catholic Church and Social Work," *Casket*, 17 March 1921, 10, "Labour and the Social Economic Problem of the Day," *Casket*, 24 January 1924, 5, and "Country Life Versus City Life" (pamphlet), RG 30-3/21/517, EC, STFXUA.

6 Tompkins to Dr Cartwright, 30 July 1924, Maritime Provinces Educational Federation File, 1924, CCA.

7 President MacDonald, Graduation Address, 1941, RG 30-2/111/36,37a, EC, STFXUA.

8 President MacDonald, Commencement Exercises Address, 18 May 1937, RG 5/111/742–4, PMCDP, STFXUA.

9 President MacDonald, Graduation Address, 1938, RG 30-2/111/9, EC, STFXUA.

10 Because of its social activism in the 1930s, St.F.X. does not quite fit Paul Axelrod's characterization of Canadian universities as institutions merely aiming to produce "respectable middle-class citizens, armed with a 'disciplined intelligence' and ready to assume positions of professional and community responsibility." Axelrod, *Making a Middle Class: Student Life in English Canada During the Thirties* (Montreal and Kingston: McGill-Queen's University Press, 1990), 50.

11 Tompkins to Dr Benson Y. Landis, 22 December 1934, MG 10-2, 1b, TPP, BI. Tompkins was appointed to the board of governors for the first time after his departure from St.F.X. in 1937; he remained a member until December 1948, five years before his death.

12 *Casket*, 23 July 1936, 13.

13 Rev. Hugh J. Somers, "As I Remember," n.d., STFXUA.

14 Faculty Recommendations Concerning the Development of St.F.X., 1936, RG 5/10/1304–9, PMCDP, STFXUA.

15 Ibid.

16 Nicholson to Cyril Burchell, 24 November 1936, RG 5/10/4446, PMCDP, STFXUA.

17 BOG Minutes, 18 May 1936, RG 5/9/12411–13, PMP, STFXUA.

18 The laundry was built and equipped at a cost of about $13,950. President MacDonald, Commencement Exercises Address, 18 May 1937, RG 5/10/742, PMCDP, STFXUA.

19 *Casket*, 5 and 12 November 1936.

20 BOG Minutes, 1 February 1937, RG 5/10/125–9, 370, PMCDP, STFXUA.

21 "An Act to Amend Chapter 190, Acts of Nova Scotia 1921, relating to St Francis Xavier University," *Statutes of Nova Scotia*, 1937, cap. 121, 382–3.

22 Bishop Morrison to President MacDonald, 8 May 1940, RG 5/10/3301 and Contributions to New Building, 18 June 1941, RG 5/10/384–5, PMCDP, STFXUA.

23 Somers recorded the story of his trip with President D.J. MacDonald to about fifteen colleges in the United States, and their meeting with Larson, who only agreed to undertake architectural work for St.F.X. when he realized that his best friend in the Canadian Army during the First World War was a St.F.X. alumnus and that this alumnus had a brother at the

college whose name was Rev. Jerome C. Chisholm. See "As I Remember," n.d., STFXUA. For an overview of Larson's contribution to St.F.X. (1936–68), see James D. Cameron, "An American Imprint on St.F.X.," *Alumni News* (Winter/Spring 1994):13–14.

24 St.F.X. Building Committee Minutes, 18 May 1936, RG 5/12/25 240–9, PSP, STFXUA.

25 Morrison to President MacDonald, 29 January 1937, RG 5/10/3252, PMCDP, STFXUA.

26 Report on the Boston Properties, July 1936, RG 5/10/230–9, PMCDP, STFXUA. About thirty-two properties remained in 1936; apparently the management of them was inadequate and the college, on the recommendation of the bursar, Dr Somers, assumed direct management of them. The board tried to sell the properties off as fast as the market permitted. By 1945 almost all of the Boston properties had been sold and the proceeds invested in Canadian bonds. The Neil McNeil Endowment then totalled about $230,000 and was subsequently listed in the college calendar under this name. President Patrick J. Nicholson to A.B. Moffatt, 8 September 1945, RG 5/11/11933, PNP, STFXUA.

27 President MacPherson to N.B. Vanderhoof, 25 January 1935, RG 5/9/23412, PMP, STFXUA.

28 Financial Report for Year Ending 31 May 1938, RG 5/10/205, PMCDP, STFXUA.

29 Steven H. Stackpole, *Carnegie Corporation and Commonwealth Program, 1911–1961* (New York: Carnegie Corporation of New York, 1963), 47.

30 The deficit in 1937–38 amounted to $24,461, over double that of the year before. Financial Report for the Year Ending 31 May 1938, RG 5/10/203, PMCDP, STFXUA.

31 BOG Minutes, 15 August 1938, RG 5/10/209, PMCDP, STFXUA and *St.F.X. Calendar 1938–39*, 31.

32 David H. Stevens to President MacDonald, 22 March 1938, RG 5/10/4054, and Finances, 1938, RG 5/10/1368–9, PMCDP, STFXUA.

33 May G. Cavanagh, a social worker, was a key person who helped form this group made up of alumni and New England cooperative leaders. See pamphlet entitled "The Story of the Antigonish Movement," n.d., n.p., and Cavanagh to Charles Dollard, 30 July 1940, in St.F.X. Extension File, 1940, CCA, New York.

34 *St.F.X. Calendar 1938–39*, 20.

35 Alumni Association Minute Book, 1936, RG 25-1/1/7, AAR, and *Alumni News*, 1 May 1940, 4, STFXUA.

36 Bishop Morrison to Clergy, 11 November 1938, MG 10-2, 2a, f3, TPP, BI, Morrison to Clergy, 9 February 1943, RG 5/10/987–8, PMCDP. At the end of the first five years, $79,480 of the targeted $100,000 had been collected. Parish Levies Statement, June 1943, ibid., STFXUA.

37 Extension only succeeded in retaining its very capable assistant director by obtaining external financial help. In 1938, A.B. MacDonald had been asked by the Ontario Department of Agriculture to organize extension services in that province. St.F.X. found it impossible to increase his salary enough for him to stay. However, W.H. Dennis, a Halifax publisher who was a keen supporter of St.F.X. extension work, began to contribute $1000 annually to MacDonald's salary. A.B. MacDonald to Bishop Morrison, 8 February 1939, #23509, BMP, ADA and MacDonald to Tompkins, 18 January and 25 February 1938, RG 5/10/4156–7, PMCDP, STFXUA.

38 Anonymous pamphlet, "Mobilizing for Enlightenment," c. 1940, EC, STFXUA.

39 Committee Minutes, 11 September 1939, RG 5/10/218–19 and BOG Minutes, 8 July 1940, RG 5/10/220–1, PMCDP, STFXUA.

40 Mary E. Arnold, *Story of Tompkinsville* (New York: Co-operative League of New York, 1940).

41 Coady was ill when he conceived *Masters of Their Own Destiny* (New York: Harper and Row, 1939) and required the assistance of others – for example, his private secretary, Zita O'Hearn Cameron – to complete it. In 1938 the Rockefeller General Education Board granted him $2,500 over eight months to write it. They hoped the study would be a means of informing people doing similar cooperative work, especially in the southern United States. David H. Stevens to Coady, 20 January 1938, MG 20/1/1925, CPP, STFXUA.

42 *Xaverian*, 23 April 1938, 3.

43 ESBK, 1930–42, n.p., EC, STFXUA.

44 Ian MacPherson, *Each for All: A History of the Co-operative Movement in English Canada, 1900–1945* (Toronto: Macmillan, 1979), 182.

45 *St.F.X. Calendar 1941–42*, 94 and A.B. MacDonald to W.H. Dennis, 10 August 1940, RG 30-2/2/610, MADP, EC, STFXUA. Within five years' time, this organization would be succeeded by the Nova Scotia Co-operative Union in affiliation with the Co-operative Union of Canada. *Casket*, 23 July 1944.

46 J.R. Kirk to President MacDonald, 12 March 1941, RG 5/10/2019–20, PMCDP, STFXUA.

47 Coady to A.B. MacDonald, 6 March 1941, RG 30-2/1/2133, DCP, EC, STFXUA. It is unclear how long the office remained closed.

48 President MacDonald, Graduation Address, 1941, RG 30-2/111/35–6, EC, STFXUA.

49 In 1930 President MacPherson had expressed hopes of using radio to make St.F.X. "more useful to the people whom it tries to serve." MacPherson to C.H. Mercer, 23 May 1930, RG 5/9/8860, PMP, STFXUA.

50 *Halifax Chronicle*, 22 August 1936.

51 MacDonald to Alex Johnston, 25 September 1940, RG 5/10/1882, PMCDP, STFXUA and Bruce Nunn, "Life Was His Podium: A Biography of J. Clyde Nunn" (BA thesis, St.F.X., 1984), 2–3.

52 Rev. John R. MacDonald to Rev. H.P. MacPherson, 15 December 1941, MG 1/1/1,655, MPP, STFXUA. The board decision called for St.F.X. to own 51 per cent of the stock. BOG Minutes, 21 May 1941, RG 5/10/223, PMCDP, STFXUA.

53 MacCormack to Friends, 15 July 1945, #27691, BMP, ADA.

54 Grant in Aid, 3 June 1942, RG 1.1, series 427R, box 28, file 282, RFC, RAC, New York State.

55 Application for a License to Build and Operate a Transmitter Station by St Francis Xavier University, 16 November 1940, RG 5/10/9745–8, PMCDP, STFXUA.

56 Rev. A.A. Johnston states that St.F.X. at first obtained a licence for educational broadcasts alone, which allowed for no revenues. It later exchanged this for a licence to operate a private station. Johnston, Transcript of Talk for twentieth Anniversary of Atlantic Broadcasters, 10 June 1963, MG 75/1, series A, file 12, RJPP, STFXUA.

57 *Xaverian*, 27 March 1943, 1.

58 *Xaverian*, 3 April 1943, 1.

59 *Xaverian*, 17 February 1945, 1 and 13 October 1945, 1 and 2.

60 Clyde Nunn, Report on Radio Station CJFX, October 1948, RG 1.1, series 427R, box 28, file 282, RFC, RAC and *Xaverian*, 3 April 1948, 1.

61 The following resolution of the St.F.X. credit union might have encouraged the college to inaugurate the course: "That a full year's course be given to the study of the Co-operative Movement, its history and its running" so that a St.F.X. graduate would have a greater background and "a comprehensive knowledge of the movement sponsored by his own Alma Mater." Henry J. Crochetiere to President MacDonald, 11 March 1940, RG 5/10/810, PMCDP, STFXUA.

62 President MacDonald, Graduation Address, 1941, RG 30-2/111/32–3, EC, STFXUA.

63 School for Leadership (pamphlet), RG 30-3/27/81, EC, STFXUA.

64 Ibid.

65 *St.F.X. Calendars*, 1947–48 to 1953–54 and course file, RG 30-3/27/81–7, EC, STFXUA.

66 Sister St Veronica was the first female faculty member at St.F.X. She belonged to the Congregation of Notre Dame and was the sister of Premier Angus L. MacDonald.

67 Analysis of *St.F.X. Calendars*, 1931–41.

68 Rev. Dr P.J. Nicholson to Morrison, 1 March 1938 and Morrison to Nicholson, 3 March 1938, RG 10/6/457–9, Dean Nicholson Papers, STFXUA.

69 Nicholson to Deferrari, 22 November 1937, RG 10/6/145, ibid.

70 Such a statement appeared for the first time in the *Calendar 1938–39*, 20–1.

71 Dr Roy Deferrari, Report of Inspection, 17–19 May 1938, RG 5/10/891–3, PMCDP, STFXUA.

72 Paul Axelrod in *Making a Middle Class*, chap. 7, claims that most Canadian students in the 1930s came from modest, middle-class backgrounds. At St.F.X. most came from modest working-class backgrounds. However, the university remained a means of social advance into the middle class for most students.

73 *St.F.X. Calendars*, 1931–32, 1936–37, and 1941–42.

74 *Alumni News*, October 1940, 2 and selected college calendars.

75 President MacDonald to Arthur Compton, 31 January 1939, RG 5/10/6491, PMCDP, STFXUA.

76 The numbers in engineering were much larger than this; it appears that most engineering students did not remain at St.F.X. for the full three-year diploma course.

77 *St.F.X. Calendar 1941–42*, 81–3.

78 In addition to documentary research and interviews, some of the following description of student life is based on a student alumni survey conducted in October 1991. Eight hundred and twenty surveys were sent to St.F.X. alumni of selected classes from 1915 to 1971. Two hundred and fifty-five surveys were completed and returned (a 31 per cent rate of return). Of these, 76 per cent had been done by males and 21 per cent by females (gender was left unidentified in 3 per cent of the surveys). The questionnaire asked both closed and open-ended questions. Recollections of university life tended to be positive. The results are suggestive rather than incontrovertible. St.F.X. Student Alumni Survey, written responses and computer analysis, October 1991, University Historian Files, STFXUA.

79 Faculty Minutes, 21 November 1939, 487, STFXUA.

80 Axelrod, *Making a Middle Class*, 98.

81 The *Xaverian Supplement* evolved into the *Yearbook* in 1938 and was published by the students annually from that year. *Xaverian*, 26 March 1938, 5.

82 *Xaverian*, 31 October 1942, 5.

83 *Xaverian*, 10 October 1936, 5.

84 Ibid.

85 President Nicholson to Stillman S. Smith, 22 March 1947, RG 5/11/13730, PNP, STFXUA.

86 *Xaverian*, 10 November 1939, 1, 5.

87 *Xaverian*, 16 April 1927, 1.

88 *Xaverian*, 24 October 1936. The Mount students had published their own quarterly journal called the *Memorare* from 1914 to 1929.

89 *Xaverian*, 9 November 1940, 3.

90 *Xaverian*, 11 November 1944, 3.

91 *Xaverian*, 19 February and 26 March 1938.

92 *Xaverian*, 2 April 1938, 1, 3.

93 *Xaverian*, 29 March 1941, 4.

94 *Xaverian*, 3 February 1940, 1, 7. A course called "The Cooperative Approach to Maritime Problems" had been listed since 1939, and from about 1930 one on contemporary social movements, which included the cooperative approach.

95 *Xaverian*, 14 October 1939, 3.

96 No organized political activity appeared among St.F.X. students during the 1930s as it would with a flourish after the war. Axelrod discovered that nationally only a minority were politically active, notwithstanding the fact that economic and political conditions were conducive to student activism. He attributes this to students' preoccupation with future economic security and claims that there existed a "campus culture of conformity." Axelrod, *Making a Middle Class*, 128, 135, and 137.

97 *St.F.X. Calendar 1938–39*, 35. The student council was first mentioned in the *Xaverian*, 9 October 1937, 4.

98 Faculty Minutes, 6 April 1938, 463–4, 12 January 1939, 476, 27 March 1939, 479–80, 4 April 1940, 493, STFXUA, *Xaverian*, 7 October 1939, 1 and 10 October 1942, 2.

99 *Xaverian*, 24 February 1940, 1, 8.

100 *Xaverian*, 22 November 1947, 1.

101 *Xaverian*, 21 June 1939, 4.

102 *Xaverian*, 18 February 1939, 1, 3, 7, and 8.

103 President Nicholson to Bernard de Hoog, 21 March 1949, RG 5/11/3113, PNP, STFXUA.

104 *Xaverian*, 14 December 1940, 1, 4.

105 *Xaverian*, 8 March 1941, 1–2.

106 President MacDonald to Prime Minister Mackenzie King, 16 September 1939, RG 5/10/1995 and President MacDonald to Premier Angus L. MacDonald, 16 September 1939, RG 5/10/2253, PMCDP, STFXUA.

107 President MacDonald, Graduation Address, 1942, RG 30–2/111/39, EC, STFXUA.

108 *Xaverian*, 7 October 1944, 3.

109 Faculty Minutes, 13 April 1942, 523, STFXUA.

110 For example, see the Len Bardsley column "Progress of the War – A Résumé," *Xaverian*, 12 October 1940, 1.

111 *Xaverian*, 13 February 1943, 1 and 8.

112 President MacDonald, Graduation Address, 1941, RG 30-2/111/31–2, EC, STFXUA and the *Xaverian*, 12 October 1940, 2.

113 Gerry A. Blackburn, *Mainly a Fun Run: Memories of a Public Servant* (Ottawa: Commoners' Publishing Society, 1991), 100–2.

114 *Xaverian*, 27 February 1937, 4, 20 March 1937, 4, 12 February 1938, 1, 14 October 1939, 1, and 2 December 1939, 1 and 3.

115 President's Report, 1940, RG 5/10/8951–4, PMCDP, STFXUA.

116 President MacDonald to Commanding Officer, Montreal, 11 June 1943, RG 5/10/580, PMCDP, STFXUA and the *Xaverian*, 31 October 1942, 4–5.

117 President MacDonald to Captain A.C. Wurtele, 11 June 1943, RG 5/10/4218, PMCDP, STFXUA and the *Xaverian*, 9 October 1943, 1 and 8.

118 RG 25-3/4/4755, AAR, STFXUA.

119 *St.F.X. Calendar 1940–41*, 89.

120 *St.F.X. Calendar 1941–42*, 95.

121 Report of the St.F.X. Extension Department, 1 June 1940–31 March 1942, RG 30-3/25/1017–19, EC, STFXUA.

122 MacDonald resigned from St.F.X. to become national secretary of the Co-operative Union of Canada. He helped to reorganize and revitalize the organization. MacPherson, *Each for All*, 209.

123 Alexander Laidlaw, "The Antigonish Movement in Wartime," in *American Cooperation, 1942–1945* (Philadelphia: American Institute of Cooperation, n.d.), 361.

124 Ibid., 363.

125 Irene Doyle, CSM, "My Experience as an Extension Worker over Fifty Years Ago," 5, Antigonish Heritage Association Speech, 8 March 1993, STFXUA.

126 Synopsis of the Minutes of Handicraft Conference, 14 and 15 April 1942, RG 30-3/30/111, EC, STFXUA.

127 Quoted in Doyle, "Women of the Antigonish Movement," Speech to the Atlantic Institute, 21 July 1982, STFXUA.

128 Ida Delaney, *By Their Own Hands: A Field Worker's Account of the Antigonish Movement* (Hantsport, NS: Lancelot Press, 1985), 117–28.

129 Quoted in Doyle, "Women of the Antigonish Movement," 9. Judith MacLean and Daniel MacInnes concluded that, by the mid-1940s, the women's program ended with "unfulfilled expectations." See Judith F. MacLean and Daniel MacInnes, "'What Can the Women Do?': The Antigonish Movement and Its Programs for Women, 1918–1945," 23. Paper presented to the Canadian Association for Studies in Co-operation, 1 June 1992, University of Prince Edward Island, Charlottetown, Prince Edward Island.

130 President Nicholson to A.W. Lea, 29 August 1944, RG 5/11/7277, PNP, STFXUA.

131 *St.F.X. Calendar 1942–43*, 33.

132 Nicholson to J. Wilfrid Brophy, 14 September 1944, RG 5/11/1227, PNP, STFXUA.

133 *St.F.X. Calendars*, 1940–41, 1943–44, 2, and 1945–46. The decrease in faculty and the rising enrolments during the Second World War evoked probably the first and last suggestion in St.F.X history that there be a religious test for admission. The board of governors apparently recoiled in horror at the prospect for public relations when Dr Nicholson suggested that Protestants be excluded because of the great difficulty of accommodating even Catholics. Nicholson to Dr Watson Kirkconnell, 9 May 1953, RG 5/11/6928, PNP, STFXUA.

134 President MacDonald, "Canadians in the War Effort," RG 30-3/23/51–8, EC, STFXUA.

135 President Nicholson, newspaper clipping, RG 25/3/4/4755, Alumni Collection, AAR, STFXUA.

136 Rev. Hugh Somers to the Clergy, 2 June 1942, RG 6/7/1047–8, VPSP, Dr Nicholson to Dr Alan E. Cameron, 15 September 1942, RG 10/6/32, Dean Nicholson Papers, President MacDonald, "Canadians in the War Effort," RG 30-3/23/51–8, EC, and Alumni Minutes, 19 May 1942, RG 25-1/1/12, X box 69/2, AAR, STFXUA.

137 *Xaverian*, 25 November 1944, 2 December 1944, 1 and 24 March 1945.

138 MacDonald to Dr W.J. Dunlop, 23 December 1942, RG 5/10/1074, PMCDP, STFXUA.

139 President MacDonald, Graduation Address, 1943, RG 30-2/111/50a–54, EC, STFXUA.

140 A.B. McKillop, *Matters of Mind: The University in Ontario 1791–1957* (Toronto: University of Toronto Press, 1994), 538. See also 529 and 531–47.

141 The bursar, Dr Somers, later stated that the bishop of Peterborough, Ontario and a native priest of the Diocese of Antigonish, John R. MacDonald, kept "blasting" him about St.F.X.'s unpreparedness for the postwar era and urging a financial campaign by the college. Interview with Msgr Hugh J. Somers by Rev. Peter A. Nearing, October 1964, St.F.X., MG 62/6/185, box 131, SPP, STFXUA.

142 MacDonald to J.A. Walker, 4 April 1944, RG 5/10/4255, PMCDP, STFXUA.

143 BOG Minutes, 26 August 1943 and 11 April 1944, and H.J. Somers, Memorandum Presented to a Special Meeting of the Board of Governors of St.F.X. University, 11 April 1944, ibid., STFXUA.

144 Plan of Diocesan Fund Campaign for St Francis Xavier University, BOG Minutes, 10 May 1946, STFXUA.

145 Bishop Morrison, "To the Reverend Clergy and Laity of the Diocese of Antigonish," 19 June 1944, ADA and "Some Reasons Why You Should Support St.F.X. University" (pamphlet), RG 5/10/431, PMCDP, STFXUA.

146 Nicholson to M.E. Tansey, 29 November 1948, RG 5/11/15531, PNP, STFXUA. Somers reported that almost $900,000 was collected. See Somers, "As I Remember," 10. Apparently much of the money from within the diocese was "derived by the check-off system from coal-miners who contributed 50 cents a week for two years." John Price Jones Co., "A Survey, Analysis and Plan for St Francis Xavier University," May 1952, 1–6, RG 5/12/14961–15059, PSP, STFXUA.

147 Nicholson to Dr David H. Stevens, 18 January 1946, RG 5/11/15387, PNP, STFXUA.

148 MacDonald to Bishop Morrison, 9 May and 12 August 1944, #30464 and #30672, BMP, ADA.

149 MacDonald to J.L. Kenny, 5 September 1944, RG 5/10/1958, PMCDP, STFXUA. In May 1945 the governors granted him board and a $500 pension. BOG Minutes, 25 May 1945, STFXUA.

CHAPTER THIRTEEN

1 Up to 1945 St.F.X. did not consistently use the title "college" or "university" to designate itself. However, legal documents most commonly used the word "college". In 1945, St.F.X. amended its act of 1921 and called itself a university. See An Act to Amend Chapter 190 of the Acts of 1921, *Statutes of Nova Scotia* 1945, cap. 115, s. 1, 495. Hereafter, the narrative will normally use "university" in conformity with the statutory amendment.

2 Morrison to Nicholson, 9 September 1944, RG 5/11/12123, PNP, STFXUA.

3 The only possible blemish on his record was his support of university federation in 1922.

4 Father Jimmy Tompkins had recommended Nicholson to Johns Hopkins University as a student of "exceptional ability" who had won the medal for four successive years as the student with the highest class standing in his course. Tompkins to the Board of University Studies, Johns Hopkins University, n.d., RG 6/12/413, VPTP, STFXUA.

5 Rev. A.A. Johnston, *Antigonish Diocese Priests and Bishops 1786–1925*, ed. Kathleen M. MacKenzie (Antigonish: Casket Printing and Publishing Co., 1994), 97.

6 Interviews with Msgr Cyril H. Bauer, 30 June 1992, Msgr Malcolm MacLellan, 16 September 1991, and Rev. Malcolm MacDonell, 9 November 1992, St.F.X.

7 *Casket*, 4 March 1954.

8 Nicholson, "Education in the Modern World," 1951, RG 5/11/6423, Presidential Address to the National Conference of Canadian Universities, "The Universities as Custodians of Western Civilization," 31 May 1951, McGill University, RG 5/11/25239–48, PNP, and "To the Graduates of Notre Dame," 31 May 1955, MG 2/1/297a, PNPP, STFXUA.

9 Nicholson, President's Report, 23 May 1945, RG 5/11/14073–4, PNP and RG 25-3/4/4754, n.d., AAR, STFXUA.

10 Nicholson, "To the Graduates of Notre Dame," 31 May 1955, MG 2/1/297a, PNPP, STFXUA.

11 Ibid., 5–6.

12 Nicholson to Daniel Brown, 22 August 1948, RG 5/11/1238, PNP, STFXUA.

13 Morrison to Nicholson, 19 June 1945, RG 5/11/12132, PNP, STFXUA.

14 Nicholson to Rev. Rod. MacNeil, 18 June 1954, RG 5/11/11130, PNP, STFXUA.

15 Interview with Rev. Malcolm MacDonell, 9 November 1992, St.F.X.

16 Nicholson to Finlay Beaton, 24 January 1952, RG 5/11/615, PNP, STFXUA.

17 The period of government support at a university was generally based on the veteran's length of service in the military. A veteran could forfeit his grant by failing in more than two courses in an academic year. Maintenance grants were also available for graduate study and vocational and technical training. The monthly allowance for a married person was $80 and for a single person $60. *St.F.X. Calendar 1945–46*, 98–101.

18 Gwendoline E. Pilkington, *Speaking with One Voice: Universities in Dialogue with Government* (Montreal: McGill University, 1983), 38.

19 Nicholson to Andrew Merkel, 20 February 1946, RG 5/11/11751, PNP, STFXUA.

20 *Herald*, 31 December 1947.

21 Charles M. Johnston, *McMaster University: The Early Years in Hamilton, 1930–1957*, 2 vols. (Toronto: University of Toronto Press, 1981), 2:142.

22 Interviews with Msgr Cyril Bauer, 30 June 1992, Rev. Malcolm MacDonell, 9 November 1992, Rev. Vincent MacLellan, 7 December 1992, and Dr Italo Secco, 6 June 1993, St.F.X.

23 *Xaverian*, 2 November 1946, 1.

24 *Yearbook 1947*, 61.

25 President Nicholson to Andrew Merkel, 20 February 1946, RG 5/11/11751, PNP, STFXUA.

26 The federal and provincial civil services expanded, and governments supported public improvements and private-sector development. See E.R. Forbes and D.A. Muise, eds., *The Atlantic Provinces in Confederation* (Toronto and Fredericton: University of Toronto Press and Acadiensis Press, 1989), 332.

27 *St.F.X. Calendars*, 1945–46 and 1950–51.

28 President Nicholson to S.R. Arnold, 22 January 1947, RG 5/11/389–91, PNP, STFXUA.

29 BOG Minutes, 18 November 1944, STFXUA.

30 *St.F.X.Calendar 1946–47*, 16.

31 BOG Minutes, 10 May 1946, STFXUA. Closing exercises were first held in the auditorium in May 1948. In the future it would be used for countless dramatic and concert performances.

32 *St.F.X.Calendar 1949–50*, 14.

33 BOG Minutes, 26 August 1949, STFXUA.

34 Building Committee Minutes, 27 June 1948, STFXUA.

35 The university authorities in 1951, after consulting the faculty and board of governors, decided to name the old main or administration building "Xavier Hall." Its southern and western extremities were called respectively Aquinas and Augustine. President Nicholson to the Board and Faculty, 26 February 1951, RG 5/11/3914 and Nicholson to Rev. Francis Xavier, 27 March 1951, RG 5/11/9543, PNP, STFXUA.

36 St.F.X. did recoup $12,600 from the government for this facility. President Nicholson to J.S. Hodgson, 13 March 1947, RG 5/11/5760, PNP, STFXUA.

37 President Nicholson to W.P. Gillespie, 28 September 1948, RG 5/11/4615, PNP and BOG Minutes, 8 January 1951, STFXUA.

38 Financial Statements of St.F.X., 1946, RG 5/11/25778 and 1948, RG 5/11/25780, PNP, STFXUA.

39 Bishop Morrison to Rev. Jimmy Tompkins, 10 February 1943, MG 10-2, 2a, file 3, TPP, BI. As in 1938, the diocesan levy was for $20,000 annually. From 1945 to 1947 $44,057 was collected. Statement of Payment of Diocesan Quotas, June 1, 1945 to June 30, 1948, RG 5/11/25765–7, PNP, STFXUA.

40 Somers to President Nicholson, 11 January 1947, RG 5/11/880, PNP, STFXUA.

41 The project failed because of poor management, lack of expertise, and a drop in pelt prices. See Nicholson to Honourable Harold Connolly, 4 July 1945, RG 5/11/2547 and selected correspondence, RG 5/11/2571–2620, PNP, STFXUA. See also *Contemporary-Alumni News* 2, no. 3 (15 September 1964):5.

42 RG 25-5/4/4775, AAR, STFXUA. In 1952 he commented, "I feel that scholarship as a career has not been sold to our people in the East up to the present. This is a point in which I am deeply concerned." Nicholson to D.R. Michener, 25 November 1952, RG 5/11/11774, PNP, STFXUA.

43 Nicholson to Rev. R.L. Baines, 30 April 1947, RG 5/11/498, PNP, STFXUA.

44 M.A. MacEachern to Morrison, 21 May 1943, #30901, BMP, ADA.

45 President Nicholson to Morrison, 5 June 1948, RG 5/11/12178 and St.F.X. Priest-Professors to Morrison, 13 September 1948, RG 5/11/12179a and b, PNP, STFXUA.

46 Nicholson to Rev. Michael Gillis, 11 May 1948, RG 5/11/4836, PNP, STFXUA.

47 Nicholson to Deferrari, 28 August 1948, RG 5/11/3092, PNP, STFXUA.

48 *St.F.X. Calendars*, 1946 and 1951.

49 *St. F.X. Calendars*, 1947–50 and *Xaverian*, 2 October 1948, 1.

50 Suggested Regulations Re Lay Members of Faculty, n.d., RG 5/11/3901–2, PNP and Dr Leo P. Chiasson to Dr Somers, 1 June 1952, RG 6/7/107–10, VPSP, STFXUA.

51 The number of years of Latin study required for the bachelor's degree was reduced from three to two in 1938–39; Nicholson unsuccessfully tried in 1942 to return to the three-year requirement. Part of his concern was to equip pre-seminarians for seminary work. *St.F.X. Calendars*, 1937–38, 43 and 1938–39, 39, and Faculty Minutes, 13 April 1942, 525 and 8 May 1942, 526, STFXUA.

52 Quoted in A.B. McKillop, *Matters of Mind: The University in Ontario 1791–1951* (Toronto: University of Toronto Press, 1994), 463.

53 Patricia Jasen, "The English-Canadian Liberal Arts Curriculum: An Intellectual History, 1800–1950" (PH D thesis, University of Manitoba, 1987), 203.

54 *Xaverian*, 16 February 1946, 4 and Jasen, "The English-Canadian Liberal Arts Curriculum," 262–306.

55 *St.F.X. Calendar 1945–46*, 40.

56 *St.F.X. Calendar 1938–39*, 39–40.

57 *St.F.X. Calendar 1950–51*, 33.

58 *St.F.X. Calendar 1937–38*, 53. Note that the bachelor's degree with honours was a rigorous program, as described in the calendar, requiring graduation with distinction, a major, a thesis, one year's residence, a language, and an average of at least 75 per cent.

59 *St.F.X. Calendar 1945–46*, 40. Units had been equivalent to hours of instruction per week. Most courses had been worth three units. *St.F.X. Calendar*, 32.

60 For example, see Rev. R.V. Bannon, "Recommendations regarding the majoring in English," 20 October 1947, RG 5/11/525, anonymous statement on requirements for a major in biology, 22 October 1947, RG 5/11/812, and Drs J.J. MacDonald and E.M. Clarke to Dr Malcolm MacLellan, Proposed Schedule for Chemistry and Physics Majors, 20 January 1950, RG 5/11/478, PNP, STFXUA.

61 *St.F.X. Calendars*, 1945–53.

62 Not everyone either at St.F.X. or among Acadians in the region had been satisfied with the French courses. Nicholson had no success in finding an Acadian student, preferably a seminarian, to train for his staff. In 1948 he appealed for help to the bishop of Edmunston, New Brunswick. Nicholson to Bishop Marie-Antoine Roy, 28 May 1948, RG 5/11/14393–4, PNP, STFXUA. Interview with Dr Leo P. Chiasson, 4 November 1992, St.F.X.

63 Nicholson to Rev. Donald F. Campbell, 22 March 1949, RG 5/11/1540, PNP, STFXUA.

64 *St.F.X. Calendar 1947–48*, 41–2.

65 Bishop John R. MacDonald to Nicholson, 17 December 1951, RG 5/11/8803, PNP, STFXUA.

66 Report to the Faculty on Social Science Meeting at Sackville, 29–30 August 1947, RG 5/11/3904–6, PNP, STFXUA.

67 It was last offered in the *St.F.X. Calendar 1937–38*, 53–4.

68 President Nicholson to James J. Leightizer, 22 June 1938, RG 5/10/5042, PMCDP, STFXUA.

69 The requirements for the degree were first laid out in the *St.F.X. Calendar 1950–51*, 42–3.

70 RG 5/11/14024, PNP, STFXUA.

71 Doris Boyle, Report of the Social Science and Commerce Departments, 1952–53, MG 2/1/23–9, PNPP, STFXUA.

72 McKillop, *Matters of Mind*, 484.

73 Before this, a social service course had been offered, consisting merely of a number of recommended courses in the BA program which prepared students to enter the Maritime School of Social Work in Halifax; the school had been founded in 1941. The master of social work degree was only available to those students who had fulfilled the requirements for the two-year graduate program in Halifax. *St.F.X. Calendar 1951–52*, 42.

74 *St.F.X. Calendar 1953–54*, 62–3.

75 In addition to Campbell, early teachers of psychology at St.F.X. would include Herman Timmons, Rev. F.X. MacNeil, and Oonagh MacDonald. Stimulus for the Mental Health Clinic at St Martha's Regional Hospital, Antigonish, originated with Dr D.F. Campbell and the nascent psychology department at St.F.X. Interview with Dr D.F. Campbell, 12 April 1994, Sydney.

76 In the humanities, Nicholson especially hoped that St.F.X. would take the lead in historical work on the Scottish pioneers and Celtic traditions. He had a long-standing personal interest in Celtic history; he spoke and read Gaelic, had edited a Gaelic column in the *Casket* for about twenty-five years, corresponded frequently with an eminent Gaelic scholar and folk-song collector, John Lorne Campbell of the Isle of Canna, and had developed his own substantial collection of Celtic materials. In the early 1950s, plans appeared to establish at St.F.X. a Gaelic Folklore Archive, but they remained unfulfilled. *Casket*, 22 January 1953, Nicholson to Colin S. MacDonald, 25 February 1953, RG 5/11/8332–3, and Memorandum Concerning the Creation of a Gaelic Folklore Archive at St Francis Xavier University, n.d., RG 5/11/4396–4400, PNP, STFXUA.

77 Dr Hugh MacPherson, appointed to St.F.X. in 1900, was one of the first scientists at St.F.X. I found no evidence that he conducted formal research or publication in the contemporary sense. However, he did

promote "scientific" agriculture and cattle breeding through his work at Mount Cameron Farm and as a government agricultural representative for the County of Antigonish.

78 Rev. A.A. Johnston, "Antigonish Diocesan Priests," #450, unpublished, STFXUA.

79 Summary of Research, 1942–52, RG 5/11/2324–5 and 6288, PNP, STFXUA.

80 Yves Gingras, "Financial Support for Post-Graduate Students and the Development of Scientific Research in Canada," in *Youth, University and Canadian Society: Essays in the Social History of Higher Education*, ed. John G. Reid and Paul Axelrod (Montreal and Kingston: McGill-Queen's University Press, 1989), 316.

81 For example, Dr Leo P. Chiasson, "Fingerprint Pattern Frequencies in the Micmac Indians," *Canadian Journal of Genetics and Cytology* 2, no. 2 (June 1960):184–8. See also Scientific Contributions and Interests of the Department of Biology, n.d., RG 5/11/13734, PNP, STFXUA.

82 William T. Foley, Report to the University President from the Science Group, 23 October 1953, MG 2/1/30–6, PNPP, and Publications by Members of the Science Faculty, St.F.X., n.d., RG 5/11/13735, PNP, STFXUA.

83 *Nova Scotia Research Foundation, First Annual Report 1947* (Halifax: King's Printer, 1948).

84 The minutes of the foundation's board of governors are in his Presidential Papers, RG 5/11/12570–674, PNP, STFXUA.

85 Robert R. Shrock, et al., *Ten Years in Nova Scotia: The Massachusetts Institute of Technology Summer School of Geology, 1948–1957* (Cambridge, Mass.: Department of Geology and Geophysics, MIT, 1957).

86 W.L. Whitehead to President Nicholson, 23 December 1949, RG 5/11/16181, PNP, STFXUA.

87 Nicholson to Keating, 27 January 1948, RG 5/11/20697 and Nicholson to Archbishop John H. MacDonald, 18 October 1948, RG 5/11/8625, PNP, STFXUA.

88 William T. Foley, "Report to the University President from the Science Group, 23 October 1953, MG 2/1/30–6, PNPP, STFXUA.

89 President Nicholson, Annual Report, 1948, RG 5/11/25166, PNP and William T. Foley, Report to the University President from the Science Group, 23 October 1953, MG 2/1/30–6, PNPP, STFXUA.

90 Discipline Statement, 1947, RG 5/11/3326 and Nicholson to Joseph P. Connolly, 13 December 1947, RG 5/11/2566, PNP, STFXUA.

91 Nicholson to Very Rev. L.J. Bondy, 9 May 1950, RG 5/11/921, PNP, STFXUA.

92 Interview, Dr Donald F. Campbell, 12 April 1994, Sydney.

93 Ibid.

94 Anon., To the Faculty, Administration and Students, St Francis Xavier University, n.d., RG 5/11/3278–3303, PNP, STFXUA.

95 D. Hugh Gillis to Nicholson, n.d., RG 5/11/4655–7 and Nicholson to the Senior Class, 31 March 1950, RG 5/11/3305a, PNP, STFXUA.

96 Report of Faculty Committees on Student Discipline and Morale, n.d., RG 5/11/3314–20, PNP, STFXUA.

97 President Nicholson to Rt Rev. William T. Dillon, 4 April 1950, RG 5/11/3259, PNP, and Student Discipline Committee, December 1954, RG 5/12/24248–51, PSP, STFXUA.

98 *Xaverian*, 23 February 1951, 1 and 28 September 1951, 5.

99 Nicholson to Sydney C. Mifflin, 4 October 1952, RG 5/11/11860, PNP, STFXUA.

100 *Xaverian*, 7 October 1944, 4–5, 29 September 1950, and interview with Rev. Dr Roderick B. MacDonald, 6 August 1992, St.F.X. Hazing appeared to decrease when the veterans came on campus; it was hardly appropriate that veterans should be subjected to indignities imposed by younger students. Keith Walden, "Hazes, Hustles, Scraps and Stunts: Initiations at the University of Toronto, 1880–1925," in Reid and Axelrod, eds., *Youth, University and Canadian Society*, 94–121.

101 *Xaverian*, 17 February 1956, 5.

102 Interview with Father Gregory MacKinnon, 8 March 1995, St.F.X.

103 *Xaverian*, 14 February 1952, 4.

104 Ibid. Off campus, St.F.X.'s head carpenter was known as "Jack the Piper," since he was, for many years, the official piper of the Antigonish Highland Society. *Casket*, 2 December 1971.

105 MSU, 1945–55, STFXUA.

106 Constitution and By-Laws of Student Union, 1944, St.F.X., RG 5/10/1927, PMCDP, STFXUA.

107 MSU, 30 April 1950, STFXUA.

108 MSU, 20 April 1952, 185 and *Yearbook 1953*, 111.

109 *Yearbook 1954*, n.p.

110 *Xaverian*, 9 October 1953, 1.

111 MSU, 26 April 1953, 221–2, 7 October 1953, 231, and 18 November 1953, 241 and 243.

112 *Xaverian*, 13 February 1943, 7 and 27 February 1943, 4.

113 *Xaverian*, 17 February 1945, 1 and 7. This was probably the most elitist of societies at St.F.X. Members had to be above the freshmen level and have a course average over 75 per cent. They were selected for membership by a faculty committee and one representative of the *Exekoi* executive. *Xaverian*, 15 March 1947.

114 Canadian Catholic Mission Crusade Society Minutes, 2 and 8 February 1943, MG 62/4/9–11, SPP, STFXUA.

115 *Xaverian*, 24 February 1945, 1 and 4, and 20 October 1945, 3 and 8.

116 MSU, 16 October 1954, 285–6, STFXUA.

117 *Xaverian*, 21 February 1948, 1.

118 *St.F.X. Calendar 1949–50*, 88–109.

119 *Xaverian*, 27 November 1948, 1, 17 February 1950, 1 and 2, 17 November 1950, 2 and 17 October 1952, 1.

120 See for example, the *Xaverian*, 3 March 1945, 3.

121 President Nicholson, Annual Report, 1950, RG 5/11/25180, PNP, STFXUA.

122 *Xaverian*, 2 February 1951, 3 and *St.F.X. Calendar 1954–55*, 28.

123 Alumni Association Minutes, 21 May 1946, RG 25-1/1/12, X box 69/2, AAR, STFXUA, *Herald*, 31 December 1947, and interview with Msgr Francis J. Smyth, 8 April 1994, Antigonish.

124 Nicholson to Dr A.E. Kerr, 18 August 1948, RG 5/11/6674, PNP, STFXUA.

125 This phrase was used in a *Xaverian* editorial which praised the sport. *Xaverian*, 22 March 1941, 4.

126 Frank J. Burke to Nicholson, n.d., RG 5/11/1318, and Nicholson to Burke, 7 March 1950, RG 5/11/1319, PNP, STFXUA. See also the *Xaverian*, 10 March 1950, 1.

127 President Nicholson to A.L. Livingstone, n.d., RG 5/11/7474, PNP, STFXUA.

128 *Xaverian*, 16 November 1951, 24–5, 16 October 1953, 7 and 6 November 1953, 7.

129 Nicholson to Rev. Donald F. Campbell, 22 March 1949, RG 5/11/1541, PNP, STFXUA.

130 *St.F.X. Calendar 1951–52*, 78–100.

131 President Nicholson, Commencement Speech, 1947, RG 5/11/14028, PNP, STFXUA.

132 *St.F.X. Calendar 1951–52*, 103–9.

133 *Xaverian*, 23 February 1945, 1 and President Nicholson to Rev. C. Ritchie Bell, 30 October 1952, RG 5/11/672, PNP, STFXUA.

134 *Herald*, 31 December 1947.

135 Nicholson to F.W. Walsh, 9 March 1948, RG 5/11/16046, PNP, STFXUA.

136 Alumni Association Minutes, 21 May 1952, RG 25-1/1/12, X box 69/2, AAR, STFXUA.

137 Forbes and Muise, eds., *The Atlantic Provinces in Confederation*, 329 and Pilkington, *Speaking with One Voice*, 48.

CHAPTER FOURTEEN

1 Coady, reflecting in 1950 on Bishop Morrison's relation to reform in the diocese, noted that he had long been criticized for not providing leadership. But Coady himself concluded that Bishop Morrison had been "broad-minded" in the sense of allowing others the freedom to work as they saw fit. Coady to Rev. Adolphus Gillis, 16 January 1950, MG 20/1/917, CPP, STFXUA. Rev. Dr Malcolm MacLellan reached a similar conclusion: "his greatest claim to fame was the dexterous manner in which

he tolerated progressive movements." MacLellan, "Xavier Junior College 1951–1964," 1988, MG 57/7, MACLPP, STFXUA. See also Rev. A.A. Johnston, *A History of the Catholic Church in Eastern Nova Scotia*, 2 vols. (Antigonish: St.F.X. University Press, 1960, 1971), 2:553–7 and the *Xaverian*, 11 January 1963, 10 and 12.

2 Outstanding examples of direct intervention had been his transfer in 1922 of Father Jimmy Tompkins from St.F.X. to Canso, and his veto of the faculty decision to grant an honorary degree to Premier Angus L. MacDonald in the late 1930s.

3 Peter A. Nearing, *He Loved the Church: The Biography of Bishop John R. MacDonald* (Antigonish: Casket Printing and Publishing Co., 1975), 62.

4 Nicholson to Dr Alex Johnston, 3 February 1950, RG 5/11/6218, PNP, STFXUA.

5 MacDonald to Nicholson, 30 January 1950, RG 5/11/8718, PNP, STFXUA.

6 MacDonald to Nicholson, 3 April 1950, RG 5/11/8732, PNP, STFXUA.

7 As a young priest, Bishop MacDonald had supported Tompkins's losing side in the controversy over Maritime university federation and had probably landed in a rather isolated parish for his impertinence. Nearing, *He Loved the Church*, 24 and interview with Msgr H.J. Somers by Rev. P.A. Nearing, October 1964, St.F.X., MG 62/6/185, box 131, PSP, STFXUA.

8 Nearing, *He Loved the Church*, 15, 17, 35, and 64.

9 Coady to Ildebrando Antoniutti, apostolic delegate, 10 February 1950, MG 20/1/15, CPP, STFXUA.

10 Interview with Msgr H.J. Somers by Rev. P.A. Nearing, October 1964, St.F.X., MG 62/6/185, box 131, PSP, STFXUA.

11 Somers, "The Antigonish Movement: The Early Years to 1959," n.d., 8–14, STFXUA.

12 Coady to Rev. S. Miranda, 26 November 1951 and Coady to Rt. Rev. L.G. Ligutti, 12 May 1954, RG 30-2/1/2038 and 3186, DCP, STFXUA.

13 For example, see the attempts to work out adequate arrangements in 1953 with the federal department of trade and commerce. President Nicholson to J.A. MacDonald, 9 January 1953, RG 5/11/600b, PNP, STFXUA.

14 Laidlaw, a native of Port Hood, Cape Breton, was thirty-two years old when he joined extension in 1944. He had both a BA (1929) and an MA (1933) from St.F.X. and would eventually obtain a DED from the University of Toronto in 1958. Before coming to St.F.X. he had gained considerable experience in public school education. At extension he proved scholarly, orderly, articulate, and dedicated. Interview with Zita Cameron, 23 March 1993, Antigonish.

15 President Nicholson to Rev. Dr C.J. Connolly, 12 February 1947, PNP, STFXUA. A conference trip in 1949 to Costa Rica bolstered Laidlaw's

enthusiasm for extension possibilities in Latin America and the need at St.F.X. for an International Centre. Alexander Laidlaw, Report to President Nicholson, 9 September 1949, St.F.X. Extension Department File, Laidlaw's Attendance at the Conference of the Food and Agricultural Organization, CCA.

16 D.V. LePan to Coady, 11 August 1950, RG 6/7/856–7, VPSP and Coady to LePan, 22 August 1950, RG 30-2/1/1930, DCP, EC, STFXUA.

17 Rev. Daniel MacCormack to Alex Laidlaw, 22 October 1954, RG 30-2/3/1038, LADP, EC, STFXUA.

18 Between 1947 and 1953, St.F.X. made at least five appeals to the Carnegie Corporation. The delegations included people like Bishop MacDonald, Coady, Somers, and, on one occasion, even Premier Angus L. MacDonald. But the corporation's basic position was to help an enterprise get on its feet and then move on to other projects. Record of Interview, 24 February 1947, Whitney H. Shephardson–Coady Interview, 29 September 1947, Shephardson–Somers Interview, 17 March 1950, St.F.X. Extension Department File, and Somers to Robert M. Lester, 23 December 1953, St.F.X. 1921–55 File, CCA. The only request to which the corporation acceded was Coady's for $2500 in 1949 to fund a biography of Father Tompkins. George Boyle undertook this project and the result was *Father Tompkins of Nova Scotia* (New York: Kennedy and Sons, 1953). Lester to Coady, 22 November 1949, St.F.X. File, Biography of Rev. J.J. Tompkins, CCA.

19 This organization was the brain-child of the fund-raising firm of Raymond T. Rich Associates, New York City. Rich to Bishop MacDonald, 25 April 1949, RG 5/11/15571–90, PNP and BOG Minutes, 25 May 1949, STFXUA. It did come through with at least $6000. Financial Statement, 1951, RG 6/7/187, VPSP, STFXUA. For its presentation in the United States of extension as a means to combat international Communism, see the pamphlet *If You Want to Do Something about Communism* (New York: International Friends of the Antigonish Movement, n.d.), EC, STFXUA.

20 Coady to Bishop MacDonald, 23 February 1950, and Extension Staff to MacDonald, 8 September 1951, MG 20/1/1371 and 1378, CPP, STFXUA.

21 Ibid.

22 *St.F.X. Calendar 1951–51*, 11.

23 Nearing, *He Loved the Church*, 74. The bishop appointed Rev. Frank N. MacIsaac to organize land settlement. During the next several years, and with the assistance of the provincial government, about 110 Dutch families were settled in the diocese.

24 Coady to Rev. Michael Gillis, 31 January 1951, MG 20/1/954–5, CPP, STFXUA. The first rural and industrial conference since 1939 was held at St.F.X. in August 1950. *Casket*, 17 August 1950.

25 One year later, on 5 May 1953, Rev. Jimmy Tompkins, who had been ailing for some years, died.

26 Coady to Bishop MacDonald, 15 February 1952, RG 5/11/8807, PNP, STFXUA.

27 Coady to Teresa Coady, 7 March 1952, MG 20/1/704–5, CPP, STFXUA. From his American friends, Coady received a bound volume of tribute letters, 1952, RG 30-2/1/4711, DCP, EC, STFXUA. These reveal the breadth of contacts he had in the United States and the many there he had inspired.

28 Apparently, in the spring of 1959 he was working on an autobiography which he planned to call "In Search of Possibilities." Coady to David H. Stevens, 9 April 1959, RG 30-2/1/3905, DCP, EC. His successor reported that he rarely remained absent from the extension office and continued as "the idea man" of the department. Rev. Michael MacKinnon, Report on Extension, n.d. RG 30-3/25/1075–6, EC, STFXUA.

29 The department held regular staff meetings to assess their programs and chart out the future. Visitors and associates were frequently invited to participate.

30 By 1952 Coady had concluded that most university extension departments did innocuous work because educators in general were enslaved to the "vested interests" and "afraid to call their souls their own." Coady, "Some Reflections on the Experience of the St.F.X. Extension Department," 5 August 1952, RG 5/11/2406, PNP, STFXUA.

31 Some of these observations on the intangible impact of the Antigonish Movement were made by Edward A. Corbett, director of the Canadian Association of Adult Education from 1936 to 1951, who knew and sometimes worked with Dr Coady and other members of the extension department. See Corbett, *We Have with Us Tonight* (Toronto: Ryerson Press, 1957), 137–38.

32 MacDonald to Coady, 23 February 1952, RG 30-2/1/2488, DCP, EC, STFXUA.

33 Rev. A.A. Johnston, "Antigonish Diocesan Priests," #411, unpublished, STFXUA.

34 Coady to Dr Stewart Bates, Deputy Minister of Fisheries, 3 March 1952, MG 20/1/116, CPP, STFXUA.

35 Memo, 8/13–14/55, St.F.X. 1931–55 File, CCA.

36 I am indebted to Msgr Cyril Bauer for this observation.

37 Coady to MacKinnon, 14 March 1952, and "Some Extension Problems Calling for Consideration," MG 20/1/1525–32, CPP, STFXUA.

38 MacKinnon to Somers, 13 May 1953, RG 6/7/577–9, VPSP, STFXUA.

39 BOG Minutes, 8 January 1951, STFXUA. At the time, the board consisted of twenty members; almost one-half were from Cape Breton and all but two of these were from its industrial region. *St.F.X. Calendar 1951–52,*

3. The following essays have been written on what later became the University College of Cape Breton. They are all unpublished and written by people who have been involved in the institution. Rev. Dr Malcolm MacLellan, "Xavier Junior College, 1951–1964," 1988, MG 53/7, series A, file 10a, MACLPP, Dr Donald F. Campbell, "What's in a Name – University College of Cape Breton," May 1989, pamphlet #137, and "An Idea Whose Time Had Come," 17 October 1990, pamphlet #136, Catherine Arseneau, "The Founding of Xavier Junior College," 10 April 1990, BI, and Dr Robert J. Morgan, "UCCB – The Vision of the Founders," 5 December 1991, pamphlet #135, STFXUA.

40 Rev. Dr Malcolm A. MacLellan, "Xavier Junior College, 1951–1964," 3–5. Dr Hugh J. Somers's account of who should be given credit for the early plans for a college in Sydney contradicts MacLellan's account. See interview with Msgr H.J. Somers by Rev. P.A. Nearing, October 1964, St.F.X., MG 62/6/185, box 131, PSP, STFXUA.

41 D.S. Morrison, Diary 1938, MG 12,46, A31, D.S. Morrison Papers, BI, and *Sydney Post-Record*, 23 September 1947.

42 M. MacEachern, Summer School Report, 1950, RG 10/7/755, MacLellan's Dean of Studies Papers, STFXUA. See also an undated report, RG 10/7/715–16, ibid.

43 Nicholson to Dr Alex Johnston, 3 March 1948, RG 5/11/6189, PNP, STFXUA.

44 *Census of Nova Scotia 1861*, 7 and *Census of Canada 1951*, 1:2–1, and 41–6 to 41–9.

45 R.J. Morgan, "The Changing Face of Sydney," address to the Old Sydney Society, 27 February 1975, MG 12, 82 (9), BI.

46 This was a phrase he used at the dedication of the college. Bishop John R. MacDonald, "Dedicatory Address – Xavier Junior College," 16 January 1952, 4, MG 53/7, series A, file 10a, MPP, STFXUA.

47 Rumours that other universities had plans to set up "feeder colleges" in Sydney may have precipitated the bishop's moves. MacLellan, "Xavier Junior College," 3. However, Dr Somers recollected that only after the junior college plans had been finalized did St.F.X. authorities learn that Dalhousie had made a survey the year before but had concluded that the time was not "ripe" for a community college in Sydney. Interview with Msgr H.J. Somers by Rev. P.A. Nearing, October 1964, St.F.X.

48 Joint Committee Minutes, 24 January 1951, STFXUA and interview with Rev. Dr Malcolm MacLellan, 24 October 1991, St.F.X.

49 MacDonald to MacLellan, 17 February 1951, RG 5/11/10100, PNP, STFXUA. MacLellan, "Xavier Junior College, 1951–1964," 9–11.

50 Johnston, "Diocesan Priests," #425, STFXUA.

51 Interview with MacLellan, 24 October 1991, St.F.X. and "Xavier Junior College, 1951–1964," 10.

52 MacLellan, "The Realization of Our Capacities," Sydney Academy, 14 June 1951, MG 13-59, 2C, MPP, BI.

53 MacLellan, "Xavier Junior College, 1951–1964," 33.

54 Junior College Committee Minutes, 12 March 1951, STFXUA.

55 MacLellan, "Xavier Junior College, 1951–1964," 25.

56 Junior College Committee Minutes, 28 March 1951, STFXUA.

57 *Xaverian*, 28 September 1951, 1. Apparently the fire was started accidently by a blow-torch when the exterior was being renovated.

58 *Official Bulletin of Xavier Junior College, May 1951*, 7. Only MacLellan had a PH D. Three staff members had bachelors' and two had masters' degrees.

59 The faculty minutes reveal the challenges and the often mundane work required by the founding faculty. XJC Faculty Minutes, 16 October 1951f, BI.

60 Coady to MacLellan, congratulatory telegram, 16 January 1952, *Xavier Scrapbook 1951–1960*, BI.

61 *Official Bulletin 1951*, n.p. MacLellan's educational ideals are set forth in a seventy-seven-page booklet he wrote to help Xavier Junior College students get the most out of their course. See "Orientation Notes for Students," MG 13-59, 2C, MACLPP, BI.

62 The courses in physics and chemistry were not at first accepted by Dalhousie; this seriously inconvenienced students who wanted to transfer from XJC into its pre-medical or pre-dental programs. MacLellan to Alex S. Mowat, Dalhousie Secretary of Senate, 28 September 1953, RG 5/12/20479, PNP, STFXUA.

63 The extension department hoped to make the college "a real centre of adult education." Alex Laidlaw to Rev. Michael Gillis, RG 30-2/3/646, LADP, EC, STFXUA.

64 *Official Bulletin 1951*, n.p., STFXUA.

65 MacLellan frequently stated publicly his intention to try to respond to the expressed educational needs of the area. See "Education for Democracy," 15 April 1951, and "The Realization of Our Capacities," 14 June 1951, MG 13-59, 2C, BI. Of course, there were clear limits to the flexibility. Although local industry would have been well served by a vocational or technical institute, St.F.X. was constrained by finances and philosophy to remain aloof from such a program. MacLellan knew a "dire need" existed for such an institute and claimed that XJC had examined the Ryerson Institute programs, but costs were prohibitive. MacLellan, "A College is Born," MG 13-59, 2d, f2, MACLPP, BI.

66 MacLellan, Report to the St.F.X. BOG, 25 August 1954, MG 53/7, series A, file 10a, MACLPP, STFXUA.

67 *Xaverian*, 28 September 1951, 1 and interview with MacLellan, 24 October 1991, St.F.X.

68 MacLellan, "Xavier Junior College, 1951–1964," 26.

69 MacLellan, Report to the St.F.X. BOG, 25 August 1954, 2, MG 53/7, series A, file 10a, MACLPP, STFXUA.

70 MacLellan recalled that some Protestants in the area saw XJC as strictly Catholic and were slow to realize that the college was open to all. Interview with MacLellan, 24 October 1991, St.F.X. He also noted that the "proximity of Sacred Heart Church to the college was a real asset, enabling us to respect the religious tradition of the University." MacLellan, "Xavier Junior College, 1951–1964," 30.

71 *St.F.X. Yearbook 1952*, 152–5.

72 Yves Brunelle, "A Centenarian's Progeny Makes Good," *Cape Breton Mirror*, July 1952, 23. MacLellan reports that the *Cape Breton Post* and *Halifax Herald* wrote laudatory articles. MacLellan, "Xavier Junior College, 1951–1964," 45.

73 Principal MacLellan, General Report for Xavier Junior College 1951–52, MG 1, 1, A–Z, box 3, file 1, BI.

74 H. Reid McPherson, City Clerk, to President Nicholson, 7 February 1951, RG 5/11/11228, PNP, STFXUA.

75 XJC Opening Program, 16 January 1952, MG 53/7, series A, file 10a, MACLPP, STFXUA and the *Post-Record*, 17 January 1952.

76 Somers to Dr MacLellan, 20 April 1953, RG 5/12/120574, PSP, and BOG Minutes, 19 May 1953, STFXUA.

77 Business leaders in the area approached for support failed to come through with funding as hoped. MacLellan, "Xavier Junior College, 1951–1964," 19.

78 MacLellan, "Xavier Junior College, 1951–1964," 39. Dr Somers reported that St.F.X. borrowed about $175,000 to finance Xavier Junior College and the staff residence in Westmount. Somers to Dr H.R. Corbett, 31 July 1956, RG 5/12/1399, PSP, STFXUA. St.F.X. enrolments dipped for a few years, a result no doubt of the founding of XJC and the disappearance of veterans from campus. Nicholson also believed that a new requirement in New Brunswick of grade twelve for university entrance and a compulsory military service law in the United States contributed to the enrolment decline. President Nicholson, Annual Report, 1951, RG 5/11/25185, PNP, STFXUA.

79 Coady to Bishop MacDonald, 23 February 1950, MG 20/1/1371, CPP. Coady thought such a department should be headed by an extension department person who would send money their way. His department had been the most expensive and the most restricted by finances since its founding in 1928. Coady to Rev. Michael Gillis, 27 August 1951, RG 30-2/1/1434–5, DCP, EC, STFXUA

80 Greater attention had been given to alumni affairs during the late 1930s. Rev. Michael Gillis was the first full-time secretary; he served from

6 June 1937 to 5 July 1938. In 1939, an alumni office opened at St.F.X. Somers was the secretary from about 1940–45. Then in 1946 the first permanent secretary was appointed – Rev. Francis J. Smyth; he remained secretary until after his assignment to the staff of XJC in 1951.

81 BOG Minutes, 29 September 1950, STFXUA.

82 Somers had been bursar from 1933 to 1950, responsible for the day-to-day management of St.F.X., which included purchasing, payment of bills, building repairs, the expenses of extension, the management of Mount Cameron Farm, superintendence of the support staff, and responsibility for university investments. He recommended to Bishop MacDonald in 1950 that a full-time bursar be hired to replace him. Somers to Bishop MacDonald, 16 August 1950, RG 5/11/8749–51, PNP, STFXUA.

83 Untitled statement, n.d., RG 5/11/872–8, PNP, STFXUA.

84 Somers to Murray G. Ballantyne, 7 November 1951, RG 6/7/19, VPSP, STFXUA.

85 Anonymous Planning Statement, n.d., RG 5/11/872–8, PNP, STFXUA.

86 Henry Hicks to President Nicholson, 5 May 1950, RG 5/11/5709, PNP, STFXUA.

87 Nicholson to Premier Angus L. MacDonald, 12 March 1949, RG 5/11/8235, PNP, STFXUA.

88 Nicholson to Dr Alex. Johnston, 2 August 1949, RG 5/11/6215–16, PNP, STFXUA.

89 Brief Submitted to the Royal Commission on National Development in the Arts, Letters, and Sciences, December 1949, RG 5/11/14402–7, PNP, STFXUA.

90 David A.A. Stager, "Federal Government Grants to Canadian Universities, 1951–66," *CHR* 54, no. 3 (September 1973):292.

91 Nicholson maintained congenial working relationships with other university presidents. From about 1940 to 1945 he had been secretary of the central advisory committee on Atlantic Canada education; in 1946 he was its president. Between May 1950 and August 1957, Nicholson received honorary doctorates from seven universities. Johnston, "Diocesan Priests," #361, STFXUA.

92 Along with two other delegates, Nicholson represented the NCCU in December 1950 at the founding conference in Nice, France of the International Association of Universities. Its permanent secretariat was the International Bureau of Universities established in Paris the year before at the initiative of UNESCO. Nicholson to Jacques Lambert, 4 October 1950, RG 5/11/7149, PNP, STFXUA.

93 During his tenure, the NCCU compiled a "Manual of Facts for use in Furthering Federal Aid to Canadian Universities," April 1951, RG 5/11/24009, PNP, STFXUA.

94 McKillop, *Matters of Mind: The University in Ontario 1791–1951* (Toronto: University of Toronto Press, 1994), 564.

95 D.C. Abbott to Nicholson, 26 February 1952, RG 5/11/46, PNP, STFXUA. The grants were distributed on a per capita basis; in the view of Nova Scotia university presidents, this tended to penalize their universities on account of the high ratio of college students to the total provincial population. Dr A. Kerr to Nicholson, 29 November 1951, RG 5/11/6656, PNP, STFXUA.

96 Nicholson to Paul Berry, 5 March 1953, RG 5/11/787, PNP, STFXUA.

97 Gwendoline E. Pilkington, *Speaking with One Voice: Universities in Dialogue with Government* (Montreal: McGill University, 1983), 67–8.

98 Anonymous Statement, n.d., RG 5/11/872–8, PNP, STFXUA.

99 Alumni Association Minutes, 15 October 1952, RG 25-1/1/12, X box 69/2, AAR, STFXUA.

100 For a pictorial and literary review of the centennial year, see the *Xaverian*, 4 December 1953, special section.

101 The fiftieth anniversary of St.F.X. was held in 1905, the jubilee of its opening in Antigonish. The choice of 1953 for the centennial was more historically accurate, since the university did begin in Arichat in 1853 and then transferred two years later to Antigonish.

102 Somers estimated that about six hundred alumni attended the reunion. Alumni Association Minutes, 20 April 1954, RG 25-1/1/12, X box 69/2, AAR, STFXUA.

103 *Academic Assembly Program*, RG 5/11/21610, PNP, STFXUA.

104 Nicholson, Reply to Toast to the University, 2 September 1953, RG 5/11/21640, PNP, STFXUA.

105 BOG Minutes, 20 August 1951 and 16 January 1952, STFXUA.

106 BOG Minutes, 20 May 1952, STFXUA.

107 Somers, "As I Remember," 19, n.d., STFXUA. Substantial contributions came from companies like the Bank of Nova Scotia, Moosehead Breweries, and Canada Packers. Somers to D.H. MacDougall, 19 December 1952, RG 6/7/514, VPSP, STFXUA.

108 The following papers were presented at the conference of the Canadian Catholic Historical Association which met at St.F.X. in August: Rev. William X. Edwards, "The MacPherson-Tompkins Era in the History of Saint Francis Xavier University," Rev. Sister Mary Liguori, "Some Aspects of Catholic Emancipation in Nova Scotia," Rev. Sister St Miriam of the Temple, "The Congregation of Notre Dame in the Diocese of Antigonish," and Rev. Dr Hugh Somers, "The Church in Canada – The Great Struggle for Freedom, 1759–1827." Program, Twentieth Annual Meeting of the Canadian Catholic Historical Association, 6–7 August 1953, RG 5/11/1789, PNP, STFXUA. The *Xaverian*, 3 December 1952,

printed a special section on the history of St.F.X. The St.F.X. centennial year was also an important one for the history of the diocese, for Bishop John R. MacDonald appointed Rev. A.A. Johnston official diocesan historian. His conscientious, meticulous, and painstaking work eventually resulted in the publication of the two-volume study *A History of the Catholic Church in Eastern Nova Scotia.*

109 *Casket,* 21 May 1953. See also Nicholson, "The Significance of St Francis Xavier University," 1953, RG 5/11/25218–22, PNP, STFXUA.

110 Johnston, "Diocesan Priests," #361, STFXUA. Nicholson died on 4 November 1965. He was seventy-eight years old. For an evocative two-article reflection by Rev. R.J. MacSween (his nephew) on Nicholson's departure from St.F.X. in 1954 and his return in 1961, see *Contemporary and Alumni News,* 15 March 1966, 4–6 and 15 June 1966, 7–8.

111 Nicholson to Rev. James McMahon, 19 March 1954, RG 5/11/10782, PNP, STFXUA.

112 Bishop MacDonald, Comments at a Faculty Dinner for President Nicholson, 28 March 1954, tape, STFXUA.

113 MacLean to Nicholson, 8 March 1954, RG 5/12/5334, PSP, STFXUA.

114 *Casket,* 18 February 1954.

115 *Casket,* 1 April 1954.

CHAPTER FIFTEEN

1 Somers's doctoral thesis was entitled "The Life and Times of the Honourable and Right Reverend Alexander Macdonell, First Bishop of Upper Canada (1762–1840)" (1931). His minor subjects at the Catholic University were education and economics. While Somers was a competent historian, maintained a life-long interest in history, and even published occasionally, his administrative responsibilities at St.F.X. restricted his chances to pursue his original academic interest.

2 BOG Minutes, 6 August 1953, STFXUA.

3 Rev. A.A. Johnston, "Antigonish Diocesan Priests," #398, unpublished, and Interview with Monsignor Hugh J. Somers by Rev. Peter Nearing, October 1964, St.F.X., MG 62/6/185, box 131, PSP, STFXUA.

4 Somers appeared to live on the edge. Dr Nicholson sometimes feared he would have a breakdown. Nicholson to Dr Leddy, 1 March 1954, RG 5/11/7355, PNP, STFXUA.

5 Interview with Rev. Malcolm MacDonell, 8 December 1992, St.F.X.

6 Nicholson to Dr Leddy, 1 March 1954, RG 5/11/7355, PNP, STFXUA.

7 Dr Hugh J. Somers, "Private and Corporate Support of Canadian Universities," 1956, RG 5/12/8094, PSP, STFXUA.

8 This includes enrolments at Xavier Junior College.

9 BOG Minutes, 19 May 1959.

10 The substantial American contingent was partly a result of recruitment efforts in New England by faculty and alumni. Students from certain Catholic high schools – for example, Cheverus in Portland, Maine – came no doubt attracted by the Catholicity of St.F.X., low tuition rates, and the chance for some adventure in a foreign country. Interview with Professor J.C. O'Donnell, 29 January 1993, St.F.X.

11 In 1952–53, 9.8 per cent of Nova Scotia youth enrolled at university; by 1962–63 the participation rate had climbed to 16.6 per cent. University Grants Committee, *Higher Education in Nova Scotia* (Halifax: University Grants Committee, 1964), 39.

12 E.R. Forbes and D.A. Muise, eds., *The Atlantic Provinces in Confederation* (Toronto and Fredericton: University of Toronto Press and Acadiensis Press, 1993), 382.

13 Ibid., 336 and 396.

14 *Xaverian*, 22 February 1957, 4.

15 Forbes and Muise, *The Atlantic Provinces*, 403.

16 St.F.X. Student Alumni Survey: Written Responses, October 1991, 29–33 and 52–5. Some respondents defined the X spirit more objectively as the institutional ethos – religion and a set of moral standards, and dedication to helping others.

17 The number of Marthas at St.F.X. declined from twenty-six to twenty between 1942 and 1955. As more lay workers were hired (forty-two were on staff in 1955), the Marthas more frequently occupied supervisory roles. See *Xaverian*, 30 November 1946, 2 and 25 January 1947, 1. At the instigation of Dr John H. Gillis, who knew some of the founding Marthas, a Sisters' Appreciation Society existed at St.F.X. from 1953 to 1966. In a variety of ways, it expressed the gratitude of the students for the Marthas' past and present contribution to St.F.X. See Record Book of the Sisters Appreciation Society, BX 4261 M3 R4, and *X-Owes*, May 1955.

18 Somers to Rev. F.X. MacNeil, 26 May 1959, RG 5/12/5516, PSP, STFXUA.

19 St.F.X. would become indebted to these alumni for their fund-raising assistance and service on the board of governors.

20 *St.F.X. Yearbook*, 113. At the provincial election of 8 October 1963, nine St.F.X. alumni were elected as members of the Conservative government. Premier Robert L. Stanfield to President Somers, 12 October 1963, RG 5/12/7932, PSP, STFXUA.

21 The CAUT *Bulletin*, November 1962, editorial. See also Harry Bruce, "Where Politicians Are Made," *Atlantic Insight*, July 1989, 31.

22 Such explanatory factors were suggested in the *Contemporary and Alumni News*, 1, no. 2 (15 June 1963):6.

23 *Xaverian*, 3 February 1964, and RG 5/12/26727–35, PSP, STFXUA.

24 *Xaverian*, 1 March 1957, 1.

25 *Xaverian*, 18 November 1955, 1.

26 Student Union Minutes, 15 November 1953, 241 and BOG Minutes, 15 May 1957, STFXUA.

27 *Xaverian*, 1 March 1957, 5, 5 March 1954, 6, and Student Union Minutes, 9 December 1953, 250, 2 and 28 February 1954, 257–8.

28 One result of the establishment of XJC was the dominance thereafter of St.F.X. student government by students from outside the diocese. Between 1951 and 1970 only four student union presidents came from the diocese and other student union executive positions were generally filled by those "from away." Based on review of St.F.X. yearbooks, 1951–70.

29 Student Union Minutes, 4 April and 7 October 1954, 261 and 278–9, President Somers to Hogan, 20 May 1954, RG 5/12/24021–2, PSP, STFXUA.

30 For example, see Rev. George Kehoe to Dr William Woodfine, 12 February 1969, box 40, PMMP, STFXUA.

31 George Kehoe, John McFarland, and Don Loney had to defend themselves against this charge, which had been laid before the president, box 40, PMMP, STFXUA.

32 Somers to Dr W.H. MacKenzie, 9 December 1961, RG 5/12/5230, PSP, STFXUA.

33 Nicholson to W.W. Judd, 2 October 1952, RG 5/11/6362, PNP, STFXUA.

34 Claude T. Bissell, ed., *Canada's Crisis in Higher Education* (Toronto: University of Toronto Press, 1957), 200–14.

35 BOG Minutes, 14 August 1955, STFXUA.

36 BOG Minutes, 9 January 1956, STFXUA.

37 Ibid.

38 He believed the day of the lay apostolate had dawned and that the priests were overworked.

39 BOG Minutes, 9 January 1956, STFXUA.

40 Gillis to Coady, n.d., RG 30-2/1/1363, DCP, EC, STFXUA.

41 Interview with Msgr H.J. Somers by Rev. Peter A. Nearing, October 1964, 17, St.F.X., MG 62/6/185, box 131, PSP, STFXUA.

42 Rev. James J. Tompkins, "Knowledge for the People" (Antigonish: n.p., 1921).

43 Interview with Msgr H.J. Somers by Rev. Peter A. Nearing, October 1964, 17, St.F.X., MG 62/6/185, box 131, PSP, STFXUA.

44 BOG Minutes, 15 May 1957, STFXUA. In 1957 Somers recommended that the federal government increase the total grant "by an amount sufficient to bring the per capita grant in any province up to the national average." Dr Somers, "The Annual Federal Grant to Canadian Universities," 15 November 1957, RG 5/12/21243–5, PSP, STFXUA.

45 In 1946 it had amounted to only $13,102 and from 1947 to 1951 the financial statements reported no diocesan quota as income. See RG 5/12/26770–4 and RG 5/12/26763–9, PSP, STFXUA.

46 A Petition, 21 November 1957, RG 5/12/21046–8, PSP, STFXUA.

47 Of course, the province had been providing annual grants in aid of teacher training, and in support of the Nova Scotia Teachers' College, the Agricultural College, and the professional schools at Dalhousie University.

48 The Industrial Foundation on Education, established in 1956 and dismantled in 1963, tried to promote corporate support of the Canadian universities. See RG 5/12/3837–84, PSP, STFXUA.

49 This courting of the corporations is revealed by the honorary degrees offered and conferred during this period on such leaders as Sir James Dunn, president of Algoma Steel (1953), Donald F. MacIsaac, president of the Industrial Machine Company (1954), William J. Bennett, president of Eldorado Mining and Refining Company and president of Atomic Energy of Canada (1956), O.M. Solandt, vice-president of Research and Development for Canadian National Railways (1956), Henry Ford II (1959), Malcolm F. MacNeil, president of Ark-Les Switch Company (1960), Alex. G. Sampson, president of Chateau-Gai Wines (1960), and Henry Borden, president of Brazilian Traction, Light and Power Company (1960).

50 BOG Minutes, 4 April 1961, 2.

51 Somers to Senator Harold Connolly, 29 February 1956, RG 5/12/1355 and BOG Minutes, 4 April 1961, 6, and 19 October 1966, 15, STFXUA.

52 Dr Somers, "Private and Corporate Support of Canadian Universities," 1956, RG 5/12/8094, PSP and BOG Minutes, 9 January 1956, 3, STFXUA.

53 President Somers, Installation Address, 1 September 1954, RG 5/12/7863, 2–3, PSP, STFXUA.

54 Ibid., 5.

55 BOG Minutes, 9 January 1956, 11–12, STFXUA.

56 BOG Minutes, 20 October 1958, STFXUA.

57 See Master Questionnaire, 25 January 1961, RG 5/12/25388, PSP, STFXUA.

58 A.W. Trueman to President Somers, 18 September 1957, RG 5/12/20879, PSP, STFXUA.

59 Through the CMHC scheme, universities could apply for up to 90 per cent of the cost of any building. BOG Minutes, 4 April 1961, 4, STFXUA.

60 BOG Minutes, 13 May 1963, 2. Eventually this residence group was called "Bishops Hall."

61 BOG Minutes, 19 May 1959 and 13 May 1963, 2, STFXUA.

62 Dr J.J. MacDonald, Science Faculty Report, April 1961, RG 5/13/2041–7, PMMP, STFXUA.

63 President Somers, Address at the Opening of the Chemistry and Physics Building, 29 August 1957, RG 5/12/26101, and Somers to Paul Berry, 12 December 1956, RG 5/12/620–1, PSP, STFXUA.

64 See Somers to Dr W.J. Bennett, 23 April 1958, RG 5/12/8, a draft letter, RG 5/12/66, and a List of Council members in October 1960, RG 5/12/32, PSP, STFXUA.

65 Committee Reports, 1955, RG 5/12/24999–25042, PSP, STFXUA.
66 *St.F.X. Calendar 1956–57*, 46–7, Faculty Minutes, 20 January 1960, RG 5/12/23011, PSP, STFXUA, and *St.F.X. Calendar 1960–61*, 59.
67 National Research Council Survey, box 4, PMMP, and News Release, 17 June 1960, RG 5/12/6889, PSP, STFXUA.
68 This trend was occurring at most other Canadian universities. Charles M. Johnston claims that at McMaster University in Hamilton, Ontario, it was both "acclaimed and lamented, acclaimed because it promised to make for growth and sophistication, lamented because it threatened the generality of the traditional curriculum and the cohesiveness of the small university." Johnston, *McMaster University: The Early Years in Hamilton, 1930–1957* (Toronto: University of Toronto Press, 1981), 1:xi.
69 Committee Reports, 1955, RG 5/12/24999–25042, PSP, STFXUA.
70 Interview with Dr D.F. Campbell, 12 April 1994, tape #2, Sydney.
71 *St.F.X. Calendar 1966–67*, 52–4. For the preparatory work, see Rev. Dr Donald F. Campbell, Report on Honours Program, 2 April 1963, RG 5/12/25123–5, PSP, STFXUA.
72 Rev. Dr Donald F. Campbell, Rev. Gerald Power, and John Stewart to Very Rev. C.H. Bauer, 18 April 1962, RG 5/14/17,361–7, President Malcolm MacDonell Papers, and Faculty Minutes, 4 November 1959, RG 5/12/23005 and 23030–7, PSP, STFXUA.
73 John Edwards, "Gaelic in Nova Scotia," *Linguistic Minorities, Society and Territory*, ed. Collin Williams (Clevedon, England: Multi Lingual Matters, 1991), 269–97.
74 Dr D.J. MacDonald to R.W. Regan, 7 February 1938, RG 5/10/3764, PMCDP, STFXUA.
75 Nicholson to Colin S. MacDonald, 25 February 1953, RG 5/11/8332–3, PNP, STFXUA.
76 Whoever made the proposal hoped that it would become "a centre of Scottish Gaelic culture ... for the whole world" and an encouragement to Scottish folklorists who were suffering from "official and private indifference." Memorandum Concerning the Creation of a Gaelic Folklore Archive at St Francis Xavier University, c. 1953, RG 5/11/4396–4400, PNP, STFXUA.
77 See Ian McKay, "Tartanism Triumphant: The Construction of Scottishness in Nova Scotia, 1953–1954," *Acadiensis* 21, no. 2 (Spring 1992):5–47, a highly critical and provocative article which argues that Premier "Angus L." (1933–40; 1945–54) was largely responsible for creating a false image of Nova Scotia as essentially Scottish.
78 Sir James Dunn had been an old friend of the late Alexander Johnston, a St.F.X. alumnus. After Johnston's death in 1951, Dunn, then president of Algoma Steel, established at St.F.X. the Dr Alexander Johnston Foundation designed to promote the arts, including Celtic culture especially.

His company paid in $10,000 annually over twenty-five years. St.F.X. conferred an honorary LL D on Dunn in 1953. *St.F.X. Calendar 1953–54*, 16–17 and bibliographic material, RG 25-3/4/1488–1507, X box 76, STFXUA.

79 Somers to Lady Beaverbrook, 16 August 1963, RG 5/12/508, and Somers to Judge A.H. MacKinnon, 22 November 1957, RG 5/12/5240–2, PSP, STFXUA.

80 Dr Nicholson to Angus L. MacDonald, 16 February 1954, RG 5/11/8269, PNP, STFXUA.

81 Somers to Lady Beaverbrook, 16 August 1963, RG 5/12/508, PSP, STFXUA.

82 Somers to A.H. MacKinnon, 22 November 1957, RG 5/12/5240–3, PSP, STFXUA.

83 *Xaverian*, 26 September 1958, 4.

84 *St.F.X. Calendar 1959–60*, 64–5.

85 *Alumni News and Contemporary* (15 September 1977):7.

86 Some faculty were granted leaves each year to upgrade their qualifications. For example, in 1962–63 out of fifty-nine full-time members of the arts faculty, twelve were on leave. BOG Minutes, 13 May 1963, 7, STFXUA.

87 BOG Minutes, 17 January 1955, STFXUA.

88 Clergy Salaries, 1955–56, RG 5/12/7503, 7506, PSP, STFXUA.

89 *Diocese of Antigonish Yearbook*, 1953 and 1959.

90 The number of diocesan priests increased from 175 to 206 between 1953 and 1959; however, the proportion of diocesan priests serving at St.F.X. remained constant. *Diocese of Antigonish Yearbooks*, 1953, 76 and 1959, 86.

91 BOG Minutes, 18 October 1961, 7, STFXUA.

92 Somers to Dr Doris Boyle, 24 March 1958, RG 5/12/743, PSP, STFXUA.

93 Report of the Faculty Committee on Public Housing, 13 December 1957, RG 5/12/25066–72, PSP, STFXUA.

94 BOG Executive Committee Minutes, 3 February 1967, 7, STFXUA.

95 The new scheme was taken under the Teachers' Insurance and Annuity Association, a group closely connected with the Carnegie Corporation. It sponsored the pension plan of about 350 universities.

96 Watson Kirkconnell, "The Predicament of Nova Scotia Universities," 1960, RG 5/12/21105–6, PSP, STFXUA.

97 Frank Abbott, "Founding the Canadian Association of University Teachers, *Queen's Quarterly* 93, no. 3 (Autumn 1986):516.

98 Faculty Minutes, 18 February 1957, RG 5/12/22953, and introductory letter and constitution, 6 December 1957, RG 5/12/4118–20, PSP, STFXUA.

99 Interview with Msgr Cyril Bauer, 21 December 1993, St.F.X.

100 CAUT, Salaries of University Teachers in the Maritime Provinces, n.d., RG 5/12/24980–9, PSP, STFXUA.

101 Dr Leo P. Chiasson to President Somers, 1 December 1959, RG 5/12/1203, PSP, STFXUA.

102 See documents, box 38 PMMP, STFXUA.

103 University Council Minutes, 21 April 1959, RG 5/12/23092 and Leo P. Chiasson to Somers, 9 July 1959 and Somers to Chiasson, 9 September 1959, RG 5/12/1199–1200, PSP, STFXUA.

104 See Statement of Rank, January 1959, RG 5/12/7512, PSP, STFXUA.

105 STFXAUT, Revised Report of the Committee on Rank and Tenure, 21 February 1964, box 38, PMMP, STFXUA.

106 Ibid.

107 In 1966 James Duff and Robert Berdhal remarked, "There is an inevitable and continuing conflict between the President's interest in creating and maintaining the unity of the institution (centralizing tendency) and the faculty's interest in obtaining the maximum possible decentralization." See *University Government in Canada, Report of a Commission Sponsored by the AUCC and the CAUT* (Toronto: University of Toronto Press, 1966).

108 Interview with Dr Malcolm MacLellan, 24 October 1991, St.F.X.

109 Rev. A.A. Johnston, *A History of the Catholic Church in Eastern Nova Scotia*, 2 vols. (Antigonish: St.F.X. University Press, 1960, 1971), 2:558.

110 Interview with Dr Donald F. Campbell, 12 April 1994, Sydney.

111 Rev. Daniel MacCormack to Somers, 29 April 1961, RG 5/12/23921–2, PSP, STFXUA.

112 Interview with Dr Leo P. Chiasson, 5 November 1992, St.F.X.

113 Johnston, "Antigonish Diocesan Priests," #591, STFXUA.

114 Power to Somers, 1 August 1960, RG 5/12/7129, Power to Somers, 23 May 1961, RG 5/12/7152, PSP, and Somers to Power, 22 May 1961, MG 62/6/194, box 134, SPP, STFXUA.

115 Report of Special Committee, June 1949, RG 5/12/24236, PSP and Dr Nicholson to the Department of Finance, 21 February 1952, RG 5/11/3195, PNP, STFXUA.

116 In his 1956 research on Canadian university governance, Donald C. Rowat commented directly on the relatively unique arrangements at St.F.X.: "It appears to be a most interesting combination of hierarchical control, representation of the outside community, and internal 'grass roots' democracy." He was especially impressed by the unusual right of faculty to representation on the board, their right to be consulted about the appointment or reappointment of a president, and the provision for laymen representing farmers, fishermen, and labourers to be elected to the board. Rowat, "The Government of Canadian Universities," *Culture* 17 (1956):276–7 and 375.

117 *Xaverian*, 13 March 1953, 1 and 8. This rather unique idea of departmental groups was apparently based on McGill University's constitution and was merely "a non-academic device" to facilitate the arrangement of meetings. Faculty Minutes, 12 December 1958, RG 5/12/22986, PSP, STFXUA.

118 Faculty Minutes, 18 January 1957, RG 5/12/22951 and 13 February 1959, RG 5/12/22990, PSP, STFXUA.

119 The term "department head" was an appropriate title, given the powers he received to plan and allocate courses of instruction, to "supervise" departmental research and instruction, and to supervise students who were majoring in his department. St Francis Xavier University Constitution, 26 October 1959, RG 5/12/22414–49, 24, STFXUA.

120 Ibid.

121 Interview with Dr John J. MacDonald, 19 October 1992, St.F.X. and *Campus News* 2 July 1991, 1 and 3. The president of the STFXAUT thought a layman should be appointed to the position primarily because he would be able to make more effective contacts with outside agencies. Dr Leo P. Chiasson to President Somers, 25 March 1960, RG 5/12/1204–6, PSP, STFXUA.

122 BOG Minutes, 13 May 1958, STFXUA.

123 Somers to Bauer, 24 August 1960, RG 5/12/24346, PSP, STFXUA.

124 BOG Minutes, 17 May 1960, 11, STFXUA.

125 Don Loney became the first placement officer and Kingsley Brown appeared to be the first development officer. BOG Executive Committee Minutes, 17 January 1962, STFXUA.

126 Harry Bruce has written a brief and useful article on Dr Somers based on an interview with him in the late 1980s. See *Alumni News* (Fall/Winter 1988–89):4–6.

127 Dr Somers retained scrapbooks of media articles on a broad range of educational issues. These are retained in the STFXUA.

128 CUSO was established at McGill in 1961 to coordinate the work of placing Canadian university graduates in short-term work overseas. It was a privately sponsored organization connected with bodies such as the Canadian Association of Medical Students and Internes, Canadian Overseas Volunteers, the World University Service of Canada, and the National Conference of Canadian Universities and Colleges.

129 Dr Somers to Dr W.J. MacNally, 24 April 1967, RG 30-3/7/6658–63, EC, STFXUA.

130 Minutes of the Associated Atlantic Universities, 26 January 1963, MG 62/1/9286–8 and Notes re Meeting of University Presidents, 6 December 1963, MG 62/1/9292–5, SPP, STFXUA.

131 President Somers, President's Address, May 1964, RG 5/12/22397–9, PSP, STFXUA.

132 For his own description of the AAU, see Somers, "The Atlantic Provinces," in *Changing Patterns of Higher Education in Canada*, ed. Robin S. Harris (Toronto: University of Toronto Press, 1966).

133 Johnston, "Antigonish Diocesan Priests," #398 and Faculty File, STFXUA. Somers eventually died in Antigonish in 1989 at the age of eighty-seven years. In his later years he had also served as a member of the Nova Scotia University Grants Committee (1965–74) and as a member of the Maritime Provinces Higher Education Commission (1974–80).

134 Paul Axelrod, *Making a Middle Class: Student Life in English Canada during the 1930s* (Montreal and Kingston: McGill-Queen's University Press, 1990), 11.

CHAPTER SIXTEEN

1 *Xaverian*, 4 December 1959, 1.

2 An apt phrase used by Very Rev. Francis J. Smyth in Smyth to Rev. Father, 31 May 1960, RG 50-1/1/40, DSP, STFXUA.

3 Talk by Clyde Nunn, 3 December 1963, RG 50-1/1/136, DSP, STFXUA.

4 Moses Coady, *Masters of Their Own Destiny* (New York: Harper and Row, 1939), 164–5.

5 Coady to Rev. Michael Gillis, 14 February 1947, MG 20/1/941, CPP, STFXUA.

6 St.F.X. delegations made at least two visits to the Carnegie Corporation in 1947.

7 Alexander Laidlaw, Report to President Nicholson, 9 September 1949, St.F.X. Extension Department File, CCA, NY.

8 The programs supported by Canada included the Technical Assistance Programme, the United Nations Fellowship Programme, and the Commonwealth Programme for the Economic Development of South and South-East Asia (the Colombo Plan).

9 These included the UNESCO, the International Labour Association, the International Co-operative Alliance, and some agencies sponsored by the government of the United States. See President Somers to Rt Rev. A.S. MacKenzie, 6 February 1960, RG 5/12/5179–81, PSP, STFXUA.

10 Dr Coady to D.V. Le Pan, 22 August 1950, RG 6/7/858, VPSP, STFXUA.

11 This total, based on a review of student lists for the 1950s, does not include those many inquirers who came for short periods but did not formally register in a program.

12 Dr Coady to Rt Rev. L.G. Ligutti, 12 May 1954, RG 30-2/1/2038, DCP, EC, STFXUA. St.F.X. developed a relatively long-standing relationship from 1945 with cooperators in Puerto Rico. Rev. Joseph A. MacDonald, who was on the extension staff from 1945 to 1950, did considerable work

in that country. Msgr Francis J. Smyth, "The Social Contributions of Co-operative Education," 27 June 1967, box 50, PMMP, STFXUA.

13 Allan J. MacEachen, "Canadian Approaches to Co-operation: The Antigonish Movement and Canada's International Responsibilities," *Human Development through Social Change*, ed. Philip Milner (Antigonish: Formac, 1979), 13–15.

14 Coady to Gregory T. Feeney, 13 April 1956, RG 30-2/1/4578, DCP, STFXUA.

15 Coady to Jane M. Hoey, 13 January 1958, MG 20/1/1075, CPP, STFXUA.

16 Coady brochure, "Mutual Aid and World Trade," c. 1968, RG 50-1/1/306, DSP, STFXUA.

17 M.J. Lemieux, archbishop of Ottawa and president of the episcopal commission on Latin America, to Superiors of Major Seminaries, Universities and Colleges, 30 March 1960, box 49, PMMP, STFXUA.

18 Peter A. Nearing, *He Loved the Church: The Biography of Bishop John R. MacDonald* (Antigonish: Casket Printing and Publishing Co., 1975), 97. The bishop had attended the International Rural Life Conference, where he read a paper entitled "The Mystical Body of Christ and the Co-operative Movement."

19 Knights of Columbus Supreme Council Aid to St.F.X. University, n.d., RG 5/13/1279–81, PMMP, STFXUA. The KOC granted at least $15,000 to sponsor visiting priests.

20 Somers to MacDonald, 29 March 1959, RG 5/12/4861a,b, PSP, STFXUA.

21 Interview with Msgr Francis J. Smyth, 14 April 1994, Antigonish.

22 BOG Minutes, 26 October 1959, and Executive Committee Minutes, 29 November 1959. See also Dr Somers, "The Antigonish Movement: The Early Years to 1959," n.d., 18–20, STFXUA.

23 The office of social action director had been established by the Canadian bishops in 1948 with Bishop John R. MacDonald playing a prominent part. The first director, Father Francis Marrocco, had been influenced by Bishop John R. MacDonald and the Antigonish Movement. Both directors were involved in developing the Catholic Social Life Conference, which was first held at St.F.X. in 1953. Brian F. Hogan, CSB, "The Institute of Social Action and Social Catholicism in Canada in the 1950s," CCHA, *Historical Studies* 54 (1987):126 and Nearing, *He Loved the Church*, 64–5.

24 Rev. A.A. Johnston, "Antigonish Diocesan Priests," #461, unpublished, STFXUA.

25 President Somers to Smyth, 17 March 1960, box 49, PMMP, STFXUA.

26 Smyth Report in BOG Minutes, 17 May 1960, STFXUA.

27 Interview with Msgr Smyth, 14 April 1994, Antigonish.

28 On a trip to Rome in the spring of 1960, Smyth canvassed an amazing array of church officials in Germany, Rome, Geneva, Paris, Oxford,

London, and Ireland. See Smyth, "Notes on European Trip – May 31 to July 4, 1960," box 49, PMMP, STFXUA. It is of interest that he approached, without success, the Carnegie Corporation, which had funded extension so generously in its early years.

29 *Casket*, 25 May 1950.

30 Cardinal Cushing to President Somers, 15 February 1960, box 49, PMMP, STFXUA.

31 Its approximate cost was $365,730. BOG Minutes, 18 October 1961, 4. The required right-of-way for a boulevard type of highway was deeded by the St.F.X. board of governors to the province early in 1962. Ibid., 14 May 1962, 4, STFXUA. It cut across the lower, south end of the campus.

32 Announcement of Cardinal Cushing gift, 10 March 1960, box 49, PMMP, STFXUA.

33 Convocation Program, 17 October 1961, box 50, PMMP, STFXUA.

34 *St.F.X. Calendar 1961–62*, 13.

35 Interview with Msgr Francis Smyth, 14 April 1994, Antigonish.

36 The first Coady brochure quoted Dr Coady on this issue: "Truth is non-denominational and at the disposal of all. Co-operation in itself is a good thing. It is a body of natural truths acquired by the light of reason." See Coady brochure, 1960, RG 50-1/1/42, DSP, STFXUA.

37 The original course in social and cooperative leadership, offered annually from 1941, had been reduced from two years to one in 1954. It combined eight months of course work and four months of field work. Faculty Minutes, 15 December 1954, RG 5/12/22915, PSP, STFXUA.

38 This arrangement was followed until 1972 when the program's schedule was set for the period from June through to November.

39 Minutes of the Social Leadership Lecturers' Meeting, 5 May 1960, RG 50-1/1/14, DSP, STFXUA. See also the *St.F.X. Calendar 1962–63*, 58.

40 Smyth to Bauer, 14 November 1960, box 49, PMMP, STFXUA.

41 Short Course Outline, 1960, RG 50-1/1/16, DSP, STFXUA.

42 Smyth to Dr Malcolm MacLellan, 25 October 1969, box 49, PMMP.

43 The Coady International Associates was chartered by Massachusetts in 1963. It eclipsed an earlier, rather ineffective, fund-raising organization established in New York about 1949 called the International Friends of the Antigonish Movement. This latter organization was closed out around 1967. C.R. Chadwick to Mrs J.F. Larson, 13 September 1967, box 40, PMMP, STFXUA.

44 Bernard M. Bloomfield, Memorandum re: Coady International Institute, Antigonish, Nova Scotia, 23 November 1965, box 49, PMMP, STFXUA. Bernard Bloomfield and his brother Louis were directors of the Eldee Foundation. Money which they offered for the construction of a third Coady building around 1969 was used, at Msgr Smyth's recommendation, for a student centre eventually opened in 1971 and named in their honour.

45 Minutes of Meeting held at the Coady, 11 December 1965, box 49, PMMP, STFXUA.

46 Notes on the Coady International Institute's Program, c. 1970, RG 50-1/1/10399, DSP, STFXUA.

47 Smyth to Bishop M.M. Otunga, Kenya, 30 June 1961, box 49, PMMP, STFXUA.

48 Smyth to Romeo Marione, 30 May 1968, box 49, PMMP, STFXUA.

49 BOG Executive Committee Minutes, 31 August 1965 and BOG Minutes, 16–17 October 1969, Campus Construction and Planning Summary, RG 5/13/2709, President Malcolm MacLellan Papers, STFXUA. Since 1954 or earlier, after he had been appointed to the board of governors, MacNeil had been an ardent supporter of St.F.X., generous with both his time and his money. The university had awarded him an honorary doctorate in 1960, and in 1969 Smyth recommended that the new building be named in his honour. Smyth to Dr Malcolm MacLellan, 14 July 1969, box 16, PMMP, STFXUA.

50 There was one major tragedy in 1967 when a student from Kenya committed suicide. *Xaverian*, 19 January 1968, 5.

51 Interview with Msgr Francis J. Smyth, 14 April 1994, Antigonish.

52 Interview with George Wicks, 30 March 1994, Antigonish.

53 These names are taken from the Student Lists, Social Leadership Diploma Course and Summer Course, University Historian's Files, STFXUA.

54 A.A. MacDonald characterizes this first decade of the Coady's existence as "the Adult Education and Economic Cooperation phase," which produced graduates who became "apostles or visionaries of economic self-reliance as the approach to social change." MacDonald, "The Coady International Institute: A Perspective on Integral Development," unpublished, January 1984.

55 A complete collection of these fascinating and informative major essays is on file at the Sister Marie Michael Library, the Coady International Institute, St.F.X.

56 BOG Minutes, 31 October 1960, 12. By 1970 that university proposed a "twinning arrangement" with St.F.X. which had important implications for assistance in technical areas in addition to Antigonish Movement ideas. J.G. Brossard to Dr Malcolm MacLellan, 26 April 1966, and Memorandum Re: Lesotho University, 25 October 1968, and MacLellan to the University Council and Faculty, 23 October 1969, box 48, PMMP, STFXUA.

57 Smyth, Report on Itinerary and Activities, 20 June 1966, box 50, PMMP, STFXUA.

58 Smyth to Dr MacLellan, 25 October 1969, RG 50-1/1/8047–56, DSP, STFXUA.

59 A.A. MacDonald developed a selected list which identified forty-eight development centres and agencies with Coady linkages. See appendix 1 in "The Coady International Institute," 1984.

60 Smyth to Somers, 16 March 1960 and Somers to Smyth, 16 March 1960, box 49, PMMP, STFXUA.

61 Somers to Smyth, 5 September 1961, box 49, PMMP, STFXUA.

62 Ibid.

63 Interview with Msgr Francis Smyth, 4 May 1994, Antigonish.

64 Review of Inter-Relationships of Coady International Institute, Extension Department and Social Sciences, 12 August 1965, box 48, PMMP, STFXUA.

65 Smyth to Dr William M. Reid, 9 May 1967, uncatalogued, and Smyth to George Wicks, 26 March 1969, box 49, PMMP, STFXUA.

66 Smyth to George Wicks, 26 March 1969, RG 50-1/1/15,580–15,583, DSP, STFXUA.

67 Coady International Institute, Report of Activities, June 1969–May 1970, RG 50-1/1/335, DSP, STFXUA.

68 Smyth to John A. MacNeil, 28 March 1969, box 49, PMMP, STFXUA.

69 *Halifax Herald*, 3 December 1970 and interview with Msgr Francis Smyth, 4 May 1994, Antigonish.

70 Coady, Report of Activities, 30 June 1969–May 1970, RG 50-1/1/334–5, DSP, STFXUA.

71 For a study of the transference of the Antigonish Movement to Africa, see Leonard A. Pluta and Walter J. Kontak, "Transfer of a Development Program to Africa: The Case of the Antigonish Movement," *Focus* 1 (1976): 12–16.

72 For a recent description of the Coady program, see W. Bean and A.A. MacDonald, "Institution Strengthening and the Program of the Coady International Institute," Paper Presented at the Annual Conference of the Comparative and International Education Society of Canada of the Canadian Society for the Study of Education, 6 June 1992, University of Prince Edward Island, Charlottetown.

73 In E.R. Forbes and D.A. Muise, eds., *The Atlantic Provinces in Confederation* (Toronto and Fredericton: University of Toronto Press and Acadiensis Press, 1993), 338.

74 *St.F.X. Calendar 1953–54*, 9–10.

75 Report of the Director, 1958, RG 30-3/25/1130–1, EC, STFXUA.

76 BOG Minutes, 14 August 1955 and Extension Department Fisheries Report, 31 March 1955, EC, STFXUA.

77 Extension Department Report for New Brunswick, 1956–57, RG 30-3/25/1071–94, EC, STFXUA.

78 In 1950–51 extension claimed that seven hundred adults registered in the people's schools. Its report stated, "We regard this as one of the most

valuable efforts in adult education in which we are engaged. Extension Report, 1950–51, RG 30-3/25/1038–9, EC, STFXUA.

79 Alexander Laidlaw to Rev. Michael MacKinnon, 22 October 1953, RG 30-2/3/1727, Laidlaw's Papers, EC, STFXUA.

80 Coady to E.R. Bowen, 5 November 1957, RG 30-2/1/717, DCP, EC, STFXUA.

81 BOG Minutes, 26 October 1959, STFXUA.

82 Coady to Clyde Nunn, 27 January 1954, RG 30-2/1/3384–5, DCP, EC, STFXUA.

83 W. Brandeis to Rev. J.A. Gillis, 2 November 1958, RG 30-3/25/1801–6, EC, STFXUA.

84 BOG Minutes, 13 May 1958, STFXUA.

85 Johnston, "Antigonish Diocesan Priests," #411, STFXUA.

86 Coady was ambitious for Laidlaw and had recommended that he apply for the position of general secretary of the Co-operative Union of Canada in 1952 (after the death of A.B. MacDonald), so that he could "give us in the Maritime Provinces a chance to put across our complete co-operative philosophy." Coady to Laidlaw, 17 September 1952, MG 20/1/1162, CPP, STFXUA. Laidlaw wrote extensively on the Antigonish Movement. His doctorate on the subject was published in 1961 under the title *The Campus and the Community: The Global Impact of the Antigonish Movement* (Montreal: Harvest House, 1961), and in 1971 he published a selection of Coady's writings entitled *Man from Margaree: Writings and Speeches of M.M. Coady* (Toronto: McClelland and Stewart, 1971).

87 Rev. Peter Nearing interview with President Somers, October 1964, St.F.X., MG 62/6/185, box 131, SPP, STFXUA.

88 Johnston, "Antigonish Diocesan Priests," #432, STFXUA and the *Casket*, 26 June 1958.

89 Mount Cameron had been owned by St.F.X. since 1907. Over the decades it had supplied the college with produce. Yet the farm almost always ran a deficit. In June 1952 St.F.X. had invited the Priests of the Congregation of the Sacred Heart of Jesus, under the supervision of Father Peter Renders, to manage the farm and correlate its program with that of extension. However, the order had to relinquish the farm in 1956, apparently because the fathers were needed more urgently elsewhere. In 1961, on the recommendation of a committee of the St.F.X. board of governors, the farm was sold to Dr A. George, a local physician. See T.M. MacIntyre, Report of a Study of Mount Cameron Farm, 1947 and BOG Executive Committee Minutes, 15 September 1961, STFXUA.

90 Coady to Gillis, 30 September 1958, RG 30-3/25/1810–12, EC, STFXUA.

91 Gillis, Report on Extension, June 1960, RG 30-3/25/1142–43, EC, STFXUA.

92 BOG Minutes, 17 May 1960, STFXUA. For a review of this program, see A.A. MacDonald, "Community Development Program: Eastern Nova Scotia Indian Reserves 1957–1970," unpublished, October 1986, STFXUA.

93 BOG Minutes, 19 May 1960 and E.W. Coldwell, "Nova Scotia Woodlot Owners' Association," December 1960, RG 30-3/14/73–5, EC, STFXUA.

94 Waldo Walsh, *We Fought for the Little Man* (Moncton: Co-op Atlantic, 1978), 142–55. For an examination of the Nova Scotia woodlot owners' struggle for bargaining power, see A.A. MacDonald, "Organization of Woodlot Owners for Market Power," seminar presentation, University of Reading, 4 February 1986.

95 Somers to Hon. George Nowlan, 8 May 1959, RG 5/12/6726–7, PSP, STFXUA.

96 Coady to Loran E. Baker, 2 July 1958, RG 30-2/8/262, EC and Gillis, My Side of the Story, c. 1961, MG 74/1/1, MG box 88/3, Rev. John Allan Gillis Personal Papers, STFXUA.

97 Topshee to Gillis, 8 April 1960, box 49, PMMP, STFXUA.

98 Minutes of the Policy Committee on the Extension Department, 4 October 1960, RG 30-2/8/287–90, EC, STFXUA.

99 Gillis, Report to the Board of Governors, 31 October 1960, [not given], RG 30-2/8/341f, EC, STFXUA.

100 Gillis, My Side of the Story, c. 1961, MG 74/1/1, MG box 88/3, Rev. John Allan Gillis Personal Papers, STFXUA.

101 Gillis, Notes, RG 30-2/8/362, EC, STFXUA.

102 Gillis to Bishop William Power, 6 June 1961, RG 3-3/25/1832, EC, STFXUA.

103 BOG Minutes, 31 October 1960, STFXUA.

104 Peggy MacIsaac, "Coady's Shadow Proved Too Much for Gillis," *Atlantic Cooperator*, April 1990, 10. The bishop appointed Father Gillis to Mabou Parish, where he remained until his death on 28 December 1973 at the age of sixty-two years.

105 Rev. Joseph N. MacNeil, Interim Report to the Board of Governors, 18 October 1961, RG 30-3/25/1148–55 and Profile, RG 30-2/6/564, EC, STFXUA. Interview with Archbishop Joseph N. MacNeil, 7 October 1994, St.F.X.

106 Ibid.

107 Rev. George Topshee to Dr Malcolm MacLellan, 19 September 1969, box 41, PMMP, STFXUA.

108 Rev. Joseph N. MacNeil, Memorandum on St Francis Xavier Extension Department, 13 October 1964, RG 30-3/25/1283–93, EC, STFXUA.

109 Rev. Joseph N. MacNeil, Extension Report, 1961–62, 11, RG 30-3/25/1180, EC, STFXUA. Dr Somers favoured upgrading the qualifications of extension staff. He claimed that Bishop John R. MacDonald thought extension workers could get all the training they needed in Antigonish.

In Somers's opinion, "the day had passed when a person trained in the Antigonish Movement here could give the new direction necessary for the new day." Interview with Msgr H.J. Somers by Rev. P.A. Nearing, October 1964, St.F.X., MG 62/6/185, box 131, SPP, STFXUA.

110 This graduate program was eventually advertised in 1970–71. *St.F.X. Calendar 1970–71*, 96–7.

111 Rev. Joseph N. MacNeil, Memorandum on St Francis Xavier Extension Department, 13 October 1964, RG 5/13/887–96, PMMP, STFXUA.

112 Interview with Archbishop Joseph N. MacNeil, 7 October 1994, St.F.X.

113 Rev. Joseph N. MacNeil, Interim Review, Extension Activities, 1967–68, RG 30-3/25/1433, EC, STFXUA.

114 Forbes and Muise, eds., *The Atlantic Provinces in Confederation*, 421–32.

115 Ibid., 386 and 432.

116 Ibid., 453.

117 J.N. MacNeil, Report of St.F.X. Extension Department to Priests' Meeting, 8 June 1964, 1, University Historian Collection.

118 Interview with Archbishop Joseph N. MacNeil, 7 October 1994, St.F.X.

119 BOG Minutes, 18 and 19 October 1966, 9–10, STFXUA.

120 He eventually became in 1973 archbishop of Edmonton. Johnston, "Antigonish Diocesan Priests," #487, STFXUA.

121 Peggy MacIsaac, "MacNeil Trained as Canon Lawyer; Known for Diplomacy," *Atlantic Cooperator*, June 1990, 8.

122 Rev. George Topshee, Interim Report, St.F.X. Extension Department, 1969–70, RG 30-3/25/1435, EC, STFXUA.

123 The Union of Nova Scotia Indians negotiated with government so that they could assume the work of extension among their own people. St.F.X. Extension Report, 1969–70, 10–11.

124 BOG Minutes, 17 April 1970, President's Interim Report, 1969–70, 8, RG 5/13/2710, PMMP, STFXUA and Johnston, "Antigonish Diocesan Priests," #454.

125 BOG Minutes, 31 October 1960, STFXUA.

126 XJC Annual Report, 1961–62, RG 5/12/20489–92, PSP, STFXUA.

127 Note, anon., Xavier Junior College, 1959, RG 5/12/20368–71, PSP, STFXUA.

128 XJC Faculty Minutes, 25 September 1959, MG 1,1,A.3, b(10), file 1b, BI, UCCB.

129 Dr MacLellan, Report of the Principal, 1958, MG 1,1,A.2, box 3, file 1, BI. At the recommendation in 1955 of a committee on educational assistance, a loan fund was set up. However, it is unclear if and how the fund functioned. Committee on Educational Assistance Minutes, 13 February 1955, RG 5/12/20427–8, PSP, STFXUA.

130 This collection eventually formed the basis for the Beaton Institute of Cape Breton Studies, an archive and research centre which was named in her

honour after her death in 1975. It is now a part of the University College of Cape Breton. Sister Beaton was devoted to things Scottish, promoted the revival of the Celtic heritage, and taught Gaelic language classes.

131 Report of the Principal, May 1961, MG 1,1,A.2, box 3, file 1, BI.

132 Dr MacLellan, Address at the Opening of the Science Building, 3 December 1966, *Xavier Scrapbook 1966*, BI.

133 Dr MacLellan, Kiwanis Speech, 1956, MG 13-59, 2d (f2), Dr Malcolm MacLellan Personal Papers, and Annual Report of XJC, 1956–57, STFXUA.

134 Dr MacLellan, XJC Report, 1955–56, MG 1,1,A.2, box 3, file 1, BI.

135 Agreement of Sale, 1956, RG 5/12/20392, PSP and BOG Minutes, 19 May 1959, STFXUA.

136 Dr MacLellan, the Report of the Principal, May 1964, MG 1,1,A.2, box 3, file 1, BI.

137 President Somers to MacLellan, 13 June 1963, RG 5/12/20644, PSP, STFXUA. The year before, he had been reappointed to a third term as principal of XJC.

138 Interview with Msgr Cyril Bauer, 2 July 1992, Antigonish.

139 Newspaper clipping, Dr MacLellan's alumni file, STFXUA.

140 Johnston, "Antigonish Diocesan Priests," #492, STFXUA.

141 Interview with Dr Robert Morgan, 3 March 1994, BI.

142 Dr Campbell would also become the first president of the University College of Cape Breton in 1982. Then he would serve another ten years (1983–93) there in the department of psychology until his retirement.

143 Interview with Dr D.F. Campbell, 12 April 1994, Sydney.

144 BOG Minutes, 11 May 1965, 5 and Preliminary Report of the Sub-Committee Studying the Needs and Means of Xavier College, n.d., RG 5/13/879–82, PMMP, STFXUA.

145 BOG Minutes, 11 May 1964, 2, STFXUA.

146 *Excalibur*, December 1966, 1.

147 Dr MacLellan, Address at Science Hall Opening, Xavier College, 3 December 1966, *Xavier College Scrapbook*, 1966, BI. By November 1964, $345,000 had been pledged or donated during the campaign for the new science building. See also Dr D.F. Campbell, Report of the Principal, May 1965, MG 1,1,A.2, box 3, file 1, BI.

148 Minutes of the Committee on Studies, 30 October 1953, MG 1,1,A.3, b(10), file 1a, BI and *Xaverian*, 4 December 1959, 1.

149 University Council Minutes, 8 November 1965, RG 5/14/24809, President Malcolm MacDonell Papers, STFXUA.

150 Undated clipping in *Xavier Scrapbook 1966*, 150–4, BI.

151 James A. Wright to Dr MacLellan, 26 September 1966, box 19, PMMP, STFXUA.

152 Interview with Dr D.F. Campbell, 12 April 1994, Sydney.

153 Dr MacLellan and Dr Campbell, Statement with Regard to Xavier College Expansion, 8 November 1966, box 19, PMMP, STFXUA.

154 MacLellan to James A. Wright, 5 October 1966, box 19, PMMP and BOG Minutes, 19 October 1966, 12–13, STFXUA.

155 Report of the Committee on Needs and Means, 11 May 1965, STFXUA.

156 Faculty Minutes, 15 September 1953, RG 44/2/26914, STFXUA.

157 "An Act to Consolidate and Amend the Acts and Amendments to Acts Relating to the Governors of St Francis Xavier University, Antigonish, Nova Scotia," *Statutes of Nova Scotia 1957*, cap. 101, 313 and St.F.X. University Constitution, 1959, RG 5/12/22414–49, PSP, STFXUA.

158 XJC Faculty Minutes, MG 1,1,A.3,b(10), file 1.b, BI.

159 See the sociology class research project on XC–St.F.X. student relations, RG 5/13/2174–7, PMMP, STFXUA. In a nasty exchange in 1966, students locked horns in the *Xaverian* over whether XC was inbred and locally oriented, whether "Capers" at St.F.X. were "close and exclusive," whether academic standards at XC measured up, and whether it siphoned too much money and staff from the parent campus. *Xaverian*, 30 September 1966, "Kaper Korner," and 7 October 1966, 1, 4 and 8.

160 Taylor, Lieberfeld and Heldman were headquartered in New York City. They were a reputable "Planning Services" organization hired by St.F.X. in the summer of 1966 at a fee of $22,000 to report in five months on the present and future needs of Xavier College. BOG Minutes, 18 and 19 October 1966, 5, STFXUA.

161 Taylor, Lieberfeld and Heldman Limited, "A Physical Plant Development Program for Xavier College," March 1967, STFXUA.

162 Submission to the Sub-Committee of the Board of Governors on Xavier College Development from Xavier College Faculty, n.d., RG 5/13/2502–8, PMMP, STFXUA and *Chronicle-Herald*, 12 May 1969, 17.

163 Over 80 per cent of thirty-one faculty surveyed supported a four-year degree program in Sydney and believed it would cause "no permanent adverse effects on our Antigonish campus." BOG Minutes, 5 May 1967, 12–18, STFXUA and Summary of Faculty Opinions from a Circulated Questionnaire, c. 1966, *Xavier College Scrapbook 1966*, 227, BI.

164 Draft Constitution, Xavier College, April 1962, RG 5/12/20410–24, PSP and BOG Minutes, 13 May 1963, 5, STFXUA.

165 Rev. C.W. MacDonald, Digest of the Lieberfeld Report, n.d., RG 11/1, series E, file 21, Library Collection, STFXUA.

166 For example, a six-member university council committee divided clearly along geographical lines. The three members from Sydney reported in favour of a general bachelor's degree program at the college and the three members from Antigonish recommended retaining the two-year program. University Council Minutes, 14 April 1970, RG 50-1/1/11489–94, DSP, STFXUA.

167 See the *Cape Breton Post*, 17 February 1969 and 13 January 1970.
168 Xavier College Report to the St.F.X. Board of Governors, 3 October 1969, RG 5/13/3034–5, PMMP, STFXUA.
169 President's Interim Report, 1969–70 in BOG Minutes, 17 April 1970, 5–9, RG 5/13/2710, PMMP, STFXUA.
170 *Alumni News and Contemporary* 8, no. 3 (November 1970):2.
171 Annual Report of the Principal, 1970–71, MG 1,1,A.2, box 3, file 1, BI.
172 Interview with Dr D.F. Campbell, 12 April 1994, Sydney.
173 See "An Act to Establish the College of Cape Breton and Incorporate Its Board of Governors," *Statutes of Nova Scotia 1974*, cap. 4, 21–30, and "An Act to Change the Name of the College of Cape Breton and to Amend Chapter 4 of the Acts of 1974," *Statutes of Nova Scotia 1982*, cap. 59, 301–2.

CHAPTER SEVENTEEN

1 E.R. Forbes and D.A. Muise, eds., *The Atlantic Provinces in Confederation* (Toronto and Fredericton: University of Toronto Press and Acadiensis Press, 1993), 438–9.
2 Interview with Dr Malcolm MacLellan, 29 October 1991, Antigonish.
3 Dr Malcolm MacLellan, Convocation Report #2, 18 May 1966, STFXUA.
4 Dr MacLellan, Installation Address, 12 January 1965, box 1, PMMP, STFXUA.
5 BOG Minutes, 11 May 1964, 14, 15 October 1965, and Report of the Committee on Needs and Means, 11 May 1965, RG 5/13/977, PMMP, STFXUA.
6 BOG Minutes, 17 May 1960, STFXUA.
7 For example, see the Inspection Report, 1938, RG 5/10/891f, PMCDP, STFXUA.
8 Sister Madeline Connolly's religious name was Sister Regina Clare. St.F.X. conferred on her an honorary LL D in 1986 for her great contribution to its library services.
9 Fifty coats of arms representing those clans, both Scottish and Irish, which had settled eastern Nova Scotia were obtained from a firm in Scotland and used to adorn the walls of the Hall of the Clans. Angus L. MacDonald hoped that the Hall of the Clans "would remind generations of students of their forebears and of the qualities and virtues of these early pioneers – their honesty, faith, thrift, courage." Msgr Hugh J. Somers to Lady Beaverbrook, 16 August 1963, RG 5/12/508–9, PSP, STFXUA. The library plan also included a room for a special collection of Celtic history and literature.
10 *St.F.X. Calendar 1965–66*, 20.

11 MacLellan to Commission on Aid to the Universities of Nova Scotia, 26 November 1964, RG 5/13/610, PMMP, STFXUA.

12 BOG Minutes, 15 October 1965, 8, STFXUA. The final cost was over $2.2 million; the Olands pledged $500,000 over twenty years. See MacLellan to Honourable M. Wallace McCutcheon, 21 June 1965, box 22 and note, RG 5/13/652, PMMP, STFXUA.

13 *St.F.X. Calendar 1967–68*, 17.

14 BOG Executive Committee Minutes, 3 February 1967, 6.

15 St.F.X. awarded the initial contract of $3,144,954 to Inspiration Limited of Montreal; because of the legal tangle which ensued, construction was completed by Fraser-Brace. BOG Executive Committee Minutes, 16 January 1969, RG 5/13/2971–82, PMMP, STFXUA.

16 *Contemporary and Alumni News* 5, no. 3 (1 October 1967):7.

17 Notes, box 30, PMMP, STFXUA.

18 BOG Minutes, 13 May 1963, 8–9, STFXUA.

19 Around this time, and within five years of selling Mount Cameron, the college farm, St.F.X. purchased from the provincial government another farm called Crystal Cliffs. University officials believed the farm, which had several buildings on about one hundred acres, held promise for a variety of uses. BOG Executive Committee Minutes, 17 March 1965, STFXUA. Crystal Cliffs had been used from 1948 to 1957 for a joint venture sponsored by the Nova Scotia Department of Mines and the Massachusetts Institute of Technology called the Nova Scotia Centre for Geological Sciences, which held annual summer schools. See p. 276.

20 President MacLellan to Berton Robinson, 19 July 1968, RG 5/13/1196–7, PMMP, STFXUA.

21 BOG Minutes, 2 May 1966, 7 and 2–3 October 1967, appendix #1, RG 30-3/25/2741, EC, STFXUA.

22 See James D. Cameron, "An American Imprint on St.F.X.," *Alumni News* (Winter/Spring 1994):13–14.

23 The final two substantial additions to the St.F.X. campus included the Bloomfield Centre in 1971, which serves as a student centre, and J. Bruce Brown Hall in 1976, the home of the departments of biology, human nutrition, and nursing.

24 Auditors' Report 1945, RG 5/12/26763, X box 152, PSP, STFXUA.

25 St.F.X. President's Report 1971–72, pamphlet #31, table #2, STFXUA.

26 University Grants Committee, *Higher Education in Nova Scotia* (Halifax: University Grants Committee, 1972), table 5.

27 St.F.X. Bladen Commission Brief, 24 October 1964, RG 5/13/3144, PMMP, STFXUA.

28 Address by Honourable Robert L. Stanfield, QC, at installation dinner, 12 January 1965, box 1, PMMP, STFXUA.

29 The University Grants Committee itself recommended that the universities not rely too much on any one source of income. However, it believed that, in accepting public funding, the universities had new responsibilities toward government, "in particular those of efficient and economical operation of the individual university and of co-operation and co-ordination among the universities as a group." University Grants Committee, *Higher Education in Nova Scotia* (Halifax: University Grants Committee, 1968), 13. Somers, "Academic Freedom and National Survival," 1953, RG 44/1/7754–9, Public Relations Papers, STFXUA.

30 *St.F.X. Calendar 1944–45*, 4.

31 Dr MacLellan, who had a keen interest in history, especially the Celtic heritage, appointed Rev. Dr John Hugh Gillis the first university archivist on 2 September 1967. Dr Gillis had been on the faculty of St.F.X. since 1938, first as professor of classics (fourteen years), and then as professor of philosophy (fifteen years). He then established the St Francis Xavier University Archives. See Rev. Dr J.H. Gillis, "The St Francis Xavier University Archives," CCHA, *Study Sessions* (1971): 67–9 and Kathleen MacKenzie, "St Francis Xavier University Archives," CCHA, *Bulletin* (Fall 1993): 7–9.

32 *St.F.X. Calendar 1970–71*, 12–13.

33 *Inter-X*, October 1968, 1, STFXUA.

34 CAUT, Press Release, 11 September 1964, box 24 and Rev. Sydney Mifflin, Recommendations for the Revision of St.F.X. Governing and Administrative Structures, May 1968, box 18, PMMP, STFXUA.

35 Jeffrey Holmes wrote in 1977, "The presidential authority has been steadily eroded as institutions have grown in size and complexity. The department, especially, has emerged as a key decision centre on each campus. Changes in the composition of boards and senates have tended to diffuse authority further." Jeffrey Holmes, "Systems of Higher Education in Canada: A Critical Review, Atlantic Region," 1977, 3–20 to 3–21, MG 62/1/9025–59, MG box 105, SPP, STFXUA.

36 The population within the seven counties of eastern Nova Scotia increased from 216,952 in 1941 to 245,795 in 1971. The percentage of Roman Catholics increased from 51 per cent to 57 per cent. *Census of Canada, 1941*, 2:522–5 and 1.3:12–1 and 12–3.

37 In 1952–53, the proportion of college age youth (eighteen to twenty-one years) who enrolled at university was 9.8 per cent. Within ten years it had mounted to 16.6 per cent. University Grants Committee, *Higher Education in Nova Scotia* (Halifax: University Grants Committee, 1964), 39.

38 David M. Cameron, *More Than an Academic Question: Universities, Governments and Public Policy in Canada* (Halifax: Institute for Research on Public Policy, 1991), 67.

39 St.F.X. Student Alumni Survey, 1992, University Historian Files, and Statistics Summary, 1969–70, RG 5/13/2200–1, PMMP, STFXUA.

40 Registrar's Office, Enrolment Figures (Religion) 1969–70, 8 April 1970, RG 5/13/2203, PMMP, STFXUA.

41 Enrolment Statistics, 1969–70, RG 5/13/2205–07, PMMP, STFXUA.

42 Six were then pursuing graduate training. Report for the Community Research Committee. Mount Saint Bernard College Historical Sketches and Data File, MSBA.

43 Sister Cecelia MacAulay, superior from 1964 to 1968, hoped to avoid this fate and instead to retain the "Mount College image." Her plan to build an academic centre for the Mount was never realized. Advisory Board Minutes, 20 January 1967, box 43, PMMP, STFXUA. Under both presidents, Dr Somers and Dr MacLellan, an advisory board discussed and advised on the relations between the two institutions.

44 In 1951, under Sister St Catherine Martyr, Superior, the Mount had tried to expand this tradition by adding the sophomore level arts to its program, but the St.F.X. faculty was suspicious of such expansionist ambitions. Sister St Catherine Martyr to Dr Nicholson, 29 April 1951, RG 5/12/22841, Nicholson to Sister St Catherine Martyr, 11 May 1951, RG 5/12/22844, PSP, and St.F.X. Faculty Minutes, 9 May 1951, RG 44/2/26882–5, Public Relations Papers, STFXUA. The faculty did approve a major in library science, which was offered from 1953 to 1963. *Mount Saint Bernard Centennial Booklet 1883–1983*, 37.

45 The following departments were transferred to the university over the next two decades: art (1976), home economics (1976), secretarial arts (1979), and music (1987). The calendar description of the Mount was fully integrated into the St.F.X. calendar in 1968–69, admissions were unified in one central office in 1969–70, and in 1969 the St.F.X. board of governors accepted that the principal of the Mount should be an *ex officio* member. Lane Hall was purchased by St.F.X. in 1976.

46 Sister St Winnefride to Somers, 10 October 1956, RG 5/12/22881, PSP, STFXUA.

47 MSB Report, October 1969, in BOG Minutes, 16–17 October 1969, RG 5/13/2709, PMMP, STFXUA.

48 *Xaverian*, 25 March 1960, 1, 14 April 1961, 6 and 10 November 1961, 4.

49 *Xaverian*, 1 December 1961, 1, 2, and 8.

50 President Hugh J. Somers and Cyril H. Bauer, To the Students of St Francis Xavier University, 5 December 1961, RG 5/12/24945–6, PSP, STFXUA. The strike precipitated a rather wide-ranging study into university morale which concluded that student morale was generally high; but it urged, among other things, that the students have a student union building. Report of the Morale Committee to Council and Faculty, St.F.X., 3 May 1962, RG 5/12/26595–623, PSP, STFXUA.

51 *Xaverian*, 14 April 1961, 6.

52 *Xaverian*, 18 October 1963, 1 and 4.

53 *Xaverian*, 1 October 1965, 1 and 4, and 14 February 1969, 2.

54 *St.F.X. Calendar 1966–67*, 4 and 38.

55 President Malcolm MacLellan, Convocation Report 2, 13 May 1965, STFXUA.

56 Kehoe to MacLellan, 20 April 1965, RG 5/13/1138–9, PMMP, STFXUA.

57 *Xaverian*, 22 November 1968, 1.

58 The university council was responsible for university policy on registration, programs, the constitution, discipline, and for selecting honorary degree candidates.

59 *Xaverian*, 6 October 1967, 1 and 7.

60 BOG Minutes, 2–3 October 1967, 18–20 and "An Act to Amend Chapter 101 of the St.F.X. Acts of 1957," *Statutes of Nova Scotia 1969*, cap. 142, 531–2.

61 *Act of Incorporation and By-Laws*, May 1969 and October 1970, STFXUA.

62 *Xaverian*, 10 February 1967, 3 and *St.F.X. Calendar 1969–70*, 44.

63 Minutes of the Special Meeting of the University Council, 28 November 1968, RG 5/13/1912–13, PMP, STFXUA.

64 *Xaverian*, 13 March 1970, 1.

65 *Xaverian*, 17 October 1969, 4 and 8.

66 Student Union to the Faculty, 20 October 1969, MG 53/3/823, box 90, MPP, STFXUA.

67 After a lengthy discussion on open housing on 2 December 1968, faculty voted eighty-eight against and twenty for. Faculty Minutes of Special Meeting, 2 December 1968, RG 5/14/24,853, President Malcolm MacDonell Papers, STFXUA.

68 Faculty Statement, 28 November 1968, RG 5/13/1817–18, PMMP, STFXUA.

69 A.J. MacIsaac to Dr MacLellan, n.d., MG 53/3/ 814f, box 90, MPP, and Sociology Department Survey of Parental Attitudes, 1969, RG 5/13/1862–4, PMMP, STFXUA.

70 Dr MacLellan, "The Complexity of the Issue of Open House," 1969, RG 5/13/1781–3, PMMP, STFXUA.

71 BOG Executive Committee Minutes, 1 November 1969, RG 5/13/3061–2, PMMP, STFXUA. The president's commission, after a great deal of debate and consultation with other universities, eventually advised limited open housing on a trial basis. However, the three women on the commission did not support the recommendation. President's Commission, Report to the University Council on Open Housing by the President's Commission on Social Life, 31 March 1970, RG 5/13/1885–1913, PMMP. The university council rejected the recommendation of the president's commission

nineteen to one. University Council Minutes, 14 April 1970, RG 50-1/1/
11489–94, DSP, STFXUA.

72 Academic Board of the Student Union to Father Malcolm MacDonell,
Dean of Arts, Memo re Course Changes and Improvements, n.d., uncatalogued, STFXUA and *Xaverian*, 29 September 1967, 5.

73 See Patricia Jasen, "'In Pursuit of Human Values (or Laugh When You
Say That)': The Student Critique of the Arts Curriculum in the 1960s,"
in *Youth, University and Canadian Society: Essays in the Social History
of Higher Education*, ed. John G. Reid and Paul Axelrod (Montreal and
Kingston: McGill-Queen's University Press, 1989), 247–71. Student
reformers attacked the sharp boundaries between disciplines, the high
proportion of American content, the neglect of low-status groups in the
curriculum, and the lack of student input in curricular decision-making.
Jasen notes the legitimacy of the criticisms, as well as the fact that many
curriculum problems – "the conflict between job training and general
culture, between research and teaching, between the inculcation of values
and the quest for objectivity, and between curricular pluralism and
curricular order" – remained unsolved (264).

74 Notes, RG 5/14/17,416–17, President Malcolm MacDonell Papers,
STFXUA.

75 These courses included philosophy (3), theology (2), English (2), modern
language (2), history, mathematics, Latin, physical education, public speaking, music appreciation, and orientation. *St.F.X. Calendar 1966–67*, 55–7.

76 The Curriculum Committee Report, 25 September 1967, RG 30-3/23/983–
94, EC, STFXUA. This committee had been established by the university
council. After examining the curricula of other small liberal arts colleges
and the writings of leading authorities in higher education, it recommended, among other things, more flexibility in course requirements.

77 *St.F.X. Calendar 1969–70*, 58–64.

78 Patricia Jasen, "The English-Canadian Liberal Arts Curriculum: An
Intellectual History, 1800–1950" (PHD thesis, University of Manitoba,
1987), 333.

79 BOG Minutes, 15 May 1968, addendum #1, RG 30-3/25/2742, EC, STFXUA.

80 Faculty Minutes, 13 March 1968, RG 5/14/16,682–4, President Malcolm
MacDonell Papers, STFXUA.

81 See Commission of Inquiry on Forty Catholic Church-Related Colleges
and Universities, *A Commitment to Higher Education in Canada*
(Ottawa: National Education Office, 1970), 155–7. This report noted the
curricular trend toward increased election but warned of the need for "a
core of different courses that together will constitute an essential minimum of general cultural formation and also permit philosophy and
religious studies to continue to play the important role that is properly
theirs in the intellectual formation of students" (157).

82 Faculty Minutes, 22 April 1968, RG 5/14/16,686, President Malcolm Mac-Donell Papers, STFXUA. See *St.F.X. Calendar 1969–70*, 58–62.

83 BOG Minutes, 6 May 1969, RG 5/13/2708, PMMP, STFXUA.

84 Science Faculty Minutes, 6 May 1968, RG 6-2/1/5639–42, STFXUA.

85 *St.F.X. Calendar 1945–46*, 40 and 1969–70, 58–89. New programs included masters' programs in selected subjects, such as chemistry (1960), physics (1966), education (1959), adult education (1970), teaching, guidance, and counselling (1966), and bachelor level programs in commerce, education, theology, Celtic studies, psychology, Russian, political science, physical education (1966), nursing (1966), and secretarial arts (1967).

86 See Cyril Levitt, *Children of Privilege: Student Revolt in the Sixties* (Toronto: University of Toronto Press, 1984).

87 In 1963 two young professors, Edo Gatto (philosophy) and Robert Thompson (biology), sponsored a coffee house called "Abelard's" which encouraged informal discussion and the display of musical, literary, and dramatic talent. *Contemporary and Alumni News* 1, no. 4 (15 December 1963):16 and interview with Professor Thomas Roach, 19 June 1992, St.F.X.

88 Forbes and Muise, eds., *The Atlantic Provinces*, 421.

89 *Xaverian*, 10 February 1967, 3.

90 *Xaverian*, 20 October 1967, 8.

91 Dr D. Hugh Gillis commented in 1971, "One would have thought that the question of how, and where, and under what conditions boy meets girl was the paramount social issue of our time." Gillis, Talk to Graduating Class, Mabou Consolidated School, 11 June 1971, RG 50-1/1/14,604, STFXUA.

92 Report of St.F.X. Volunteer Group, n.d., box 41, PMMP, STFXUA, "The Black Man in Nova Scotia: Teach-In Report," AML, and "Review of the Work of the Extension Department, June 1969–June 1970," 12–13, STFXUA.

93 St.F.X. Student Alumni Survey: Written Responses, 5–8, University Historian Files, STFXUA, and *Xaverian*, 19 March 1965, 1.

94 Paul Axelrod, *Making a Middle Class: Student Life in English Canada during the 1930s* (Montreal and Kingston: McGill-Queen's University Press, 1990), 148.

95 By laicization I mean the expanding proportion of lay faculty.

96 Of the remaining seven, two were sisters. *St.F.X. Calendar 1945–46*, 8–9.

97 The most common seminaries attended by St.F.X. graduates in the twentieth century were Holy Heart, Halifax and St Augustine's, Toronto.

98 Moreover, after Vatican II the church began to stress more the lay apostolate, and young priests were not always willing to be placed in the demanding role of priest-professor by the bishop's fiat alone. Interview with Bishop William Power, 14 March 1994, St.F.X.

99 Elizabeth Weber and Barry Wheaton, "Atlantic Area Resignations from Diocesan Priesthood after Vatican II," *Studies in Religion* 17, no. 3 (Summer 1988):315–28.

100 *St.F.X. Calendars* 1945–46, 8–9 and 1969–70, 13–15.

101 Interview with Dr J.J. MacDonald, 23 October 1992, St.F.X.

102 Scientific Publications and Symposia Presentations by Faculty Members for the Period October 1964 to December 1967, RG 6-2/1/5620–5, STFXUA.

103 BOG Minutes, 13 May 1963, 7, STFXUA.

104 University Council for Research 1967–68, RG 5/13/2171, PMMP, STFXUA.

105 *Contemporary and Alumni News* 1, no. 1 (April 1963) and 8, no. 2 (August 1970):2.

106 The Nova Scotia University Grants Committee in 1966 concluded that the emphasis on the PHD as a requirement for hiring regrettably led to some "decline in emphasis on teaching and on the importance of undergraduates." University Grants Committee, *Higher Education in Nova Scotia, Annual Report* (Halifax: University Grants Committee, 1966), 55–6.

107 Bernard J. Keating to President MacLellan, 20 April 1967, RG 5/13/2248–52, PMP, STFXUA and *Alumni News* (Summer 1980):7.

108 Between 1950 and 1960, thirty to thirty-five Xaverians annually entered seminaries, and about 95 per cent of priests ordained to the Diocese of Antigonish had attended St.F.X. See Vernon R. Boutilier, "A Study of Priestly Vocations in the Diocese of Antigonish during the Period 1950–1960" (MA thesis, University of Ottawa, 1961), 73–4 and 148.

109 The loss of this faculty recruitment policy was important. Apparently some administrators and faculty believed that St.F.X. was too parochial and should only bring in staff "from away." However, the policy had ensured intimacy among faculty with Xaverian traditions, a Catholic presence on the staff, and the development of local intellectual leaders. Interviews with Msgr Cyril Bauer, 2 July 1992, and Dr Malcolm MacLellan, 5 November 1991, Antigonish.

110 Interview with Dr MacLellan, 5 November 1991, Antigonish.

111 The STFXAUT established these hiring and promotion criteria – academic credentials, teaching ability and experience, and scholarship. Interview with Dr Antonio Weingartshofer, 27 January 1993, St.F.X.

112 After surveying Canadian Catholic colleges in the late 1960s, the Commission of Inquiry in its report, *A Commitment to Higher Education*, raised the issue of the relation between non-Catholic faculty and Catholic institutional identity: "the Commission questions whether the colleges and universities are taking sufficient pains to recruit the professional services of a greater number of competent Catholic professors" (56).

113 Interview with Dr Raymond MacLean, 27 July 1992, St.F.X.

114 George Marsden and Bradley J. Longfield, eds., *The Secularization of the Academy* (New York: Oxford University Press, 1992), 244.

115 *St.F.X. Calendar 1966–67*, 19.

116 Mario Creet, "H.M. Tory and the Secularization of Canadian Universities," *Queen's Quarterly* 88, no. 4 (Winter 1981):718–36 and Paul Axelrod, "Higher Education, Utilitarianism, and the Acquisitive Society: Canada, 1930–1980," in *Modern Canada, 1930s–1980s: Readings in Canadian Social History*, ed. Greg Kealey and Michael Cross (Toronto: McClelland and Stewart, 1984), 179–203.

117 Marsden and Longfield, eds., *Secularization of the Academy*, 33.

118 These factors closely parallel those which promoted increased secularization at St Dunstan's University in Charlottetown, Prince Edward Island. See G. Edward MacDonald, *The History of St Dunstan's University 1855–1956* (Charlottetown: Board of Governors of St Dunstan's University and Prince Edward Island Museum and Heritage Foundation, 1989), 442.

119 Bishop William Power to Priests, Religious and Laity of the Diocese of Antigonish, 21 November 1965, box 17, PMMP, STFXUA.

120 Earl Neiman and Angus MacGillivray were responsible for much of the renovations and art work. *Xaverian*, 18 November 1966, 4 and 10 November 1967, 9.

121 In the early 1960s, St.F.X. decided for academic and pastoral reasons that the traditional offerings in religion should be strengthened. The aim was "to produce graduates whose competence in theology would be that expected of educated Catholic laymen." The university sent several young priests away for further graduate studies and started the new department in 1964. Rev. Gregory MacKinnon, Report to the President from the Department of Religion, 13 September 1965, RG 5/13/1941–5, PMMP, STFXUA. For an overview of the history of religion at St.F.X., see Rev. R.B. MacDonald, "Theology/Religion/Theology at St.F.X" (1992), University Historian Files, STFXUA.

122 Rev. H.F. Gardiner to Dr MacLellan, 19 November 1965, RG 5/13/1947, PMMP, STFXUA.

123 Marsden and Longfield, eds., *The Secularization of the Academy*, 24.

124 BOG Minutes, 2 May 1966, 17, STFXUA.

125 President's Interim Report to the Board of Governors, 1968–69, 8–9, RG 5/13/2708, PMP, STFXUA.

126 William Connolly to President MacLellan, 13 April 1967, box 39, PMMP, STFXUA.

127 Commission of Inquiry, *A Commitment*, 222.

128 *St.F.X. Calendar 1969–70*, 3.

129 The Commission of Inquiry which collected data at St.F.X. in 1967–68 commented about the faculty: "Many of the faculty are uncertain about

the aims and purposes of the University as a Catholic Church–related institution." The commissioners discovered a spectrum of opinion about the importance of religion; at one extreme were those who believed it was insignificant, and at the other those who believed it was crucial. Their report also observed, "Though evolution started earlier and has taken place more gradually than in most other institutions of this kind, much of it seems to have gone on without being consciously planned or even noticed. The nature and role of the University is changing considerably without many in the University being completely aware of what is happening." Commission of Inquiry, Private Report, RG 5/13/1717–58, PMMP, STFXUA.

130 Minutes of Ingonish Conference, 7–8 August 1969, box 13, PMMP, STFXUA. Five priest-professors and eight laymen attended this seminar.

131 Rev. William P. Fogarty to Bishop William Power, 12 December 1969, MG 53/3/378–9, box 89, MPP, STFXUA.

132 Dr MacLellan to Rev. Paul J. Berry, 4 December 1969, box 8, PMMP, STFXUA.

133 In 1950–51 thirty Marthas lived at the convent on campus; by 1970–71 the numbers had declined to twenty. Active Marthas, toward the end of the 1960s, generally filled supervisory roles in St.F.X.'s household affairs. St.F.X. Deanery Minutes, 3 April, 1967, box 42, PMMP, STFXUA. By 1994, the centennial of the origins of the Marthas, about 235 sisters had served at St.F.X.

134 St.F.X. Calendar 1969–70, 44–5.

135 A phrase used in James K. Reed to Dr MacLellan, 8 October 1966, uncatalogued, STFXUA.

136 Rev. A.A. Johnston, "Antigonish Diocesan Priests," #425, unpublished, STFXUA. Dr MacLellan remained active in diocesan and civil affairs after his retirement in 1970. The University of Western Ontario conferred an honorary degree on him in 1970, St.F.X. did likewise in 1982, and so did the University College of Cape Breton in 1989. He died on 26 May 1992 at the age of eighty-six years. See Campus News, 10 June 1992, 1–2.

CONCLUSION

1 The same fate was shared by Catholic colleges outside Atlantic Canada, such as the Catholic classical colleges in Quebec, St Patrick's in Ottawa, and Assumption University in Windsor, Ontario. Of course, other Catholic colleges have retained their Catholic identity, e.g., St Thomas More at the University of Saskatchewan, St Thomas at the University of New Brunswick, the University of St Anne, Church Point, Nova Scotia, and the University of St Michael's College at the University of Toronto. See Alexander Reford, "St Michael's College at the University of Toronto,

1958–1978: An Ontario Solution" and Margaret F. Sanche, "A Matter of Identity: St Thomas More College at the University of Saskatchewan 1961–1977 – A Saskatchewan Solution" (both papers presented at the sixty-first Canadian Catholic Historical Association Meeting, University of Calgary, 15 June 1994).

2 John G. Reid, *Mount Allison University: A History, to 1963*, 2 vols. (Toronto: University of Toronto Press, 1984), 2:358.

3 Mark G. McGowan, "Conspicuous Influence: The Diocese of Antigonish and the Development of the Canadian Catholic Church, 1844–1994." Paper presented at the Rev. A.A. Johnston Memorial Conference, 19–20 August 1994, St Francis Xavier University.

Index

X = St Francis Xavier University

MacDonald, Roderick: pioneer faculty member, 31, 55, 57

MacDonald, Rev. Ronald (later bishop of Harbour Grace, Newfoundland): pioneer faculty member, 31, 33, 40; transferred to Pictou, 42–3; involved with University of Halifax, 54, 71; reacts to Maritime Catholic College proposal, 66

MacDonald, Rev. Dr Ronald (vice-rector), 113, 128, 150

MacDonald, Ronald, professor of geology, 115

MacDonald, Ronald St John (Major), 161

MacDonald, Samuel: early college benefactor, 38, 419n82

MacDonald, Rev. William B., 462n62

MacDonald, Sir William C., 120

MacDonell, Rev. Malcolm, 271; dean of arts, 372–5

MacDougall, Betty, 309

MacDougall, William J., 389

MacEchen, A.J.G., 91, 96, 141

MacEachen, Allan J. (senator), 271

MacEachern, Bishop Angus B. (bishop of Charlottetown), 5, 12

MacEachern, Rev. Malcolm, 199

MacFarland, John "Packy," 314

MacGillivray, Angus, 85, 114, 134

McGillivray, Archibald: early college trustee, 31

MacGillivary, Rev. R.C., 294, 296

MacGillivray, Rev. Ronald, 30–1, 59

MacGillivray, Stephen, 390

MacGregor, Rev. Dr Daniel: student days in Arichat, 23; appointed to X, 42, 44–5; drinking problems and dismissal, 50–1, 57

McGuigan, Cardinal James, 301

MacIntosh, Alexander: early trustee, 40

MacIntosh, Rev. D.J., 134, 271

MacIntyre, A.S., 226

McIntyre, Michael J., 134

MacIntyre, Rev. R.K., 152, 197, 251

MacIsaac, Angus, 94

McIsaac, Colin: founding board member, 75

MacIsaac, D.F.: benefactor of X, 364

MacIsaac, Rev. Frank N., 507n23

MacKay, Rev. D.C., 198

McKenna, Rev. Leo G., 199

McKillop, A.B., 174

MacKinnon, Alexander, 45

MacKinnon, Bishop Colin F. (bishop of Antigonish), xviii, 32, 38, 41, 49, 50; appointed bishop, 7; career, 14–16; relocates to Arichat, 17; role in early life of X, 14–22; relocates to Antigonish and becomes rector of X, 39; mental instability, 45, 55; petitions for college charter, 47; builds St Ninian's

Cathedral, 50; decline, resignation and contributions, 55–9

MacKinnon, Rev. Dr Gregory, 324

MacKinnon, John, 48

MacKinnon, Rev. Michael J.: second director of extension, 292, 296, 316, 343, 351; character and replacement, 345; death, 334

MacKinnon, Sister Marie Michael, 222, 224, 260, 340

McLaughlin, Rev. M.E., 261

MacLean, Cecil, 251

MacLean, Donald Alexander, 458n93

MacLean, Rev. Murdoch, 324

MacLean, Rebecca, 173, 304

MacLellan, Malcolm: classical scholar, 13

MacLellan, Rev. Dr Malcolm (president): appointed to X, 251; appointed principal of Xavier Junior College, 294, 296, 298; appointed president of X, 354, 360–3; concerns about X, 326, 380; retirement and contribution, 381–2, 541n136

MacLeod, C.I.N. (Major), 322–4

MacLeod, John W., 456n54

MacLeod, Roderick C. (Commanding Officer), 159, 161

MacLeod, Rev. William B.: pioneer of Catholic higher education, 13, 30

McMahon, Rev. J., 271

MacNeil, Rev. F.X., 502n75

MacNeil, Donald J., 274, 276

MacNeil, Rev. Everett J., 353

MacNeil, Rev. Joseph N.: director of extension, 341, 348–51

MacNeil, Malcolm F., 337–8, 525n49

McNeil, Archbishop Neil (archbishop of Toronto): founding board member of X, 75; appointed rector of X, 79; editor of Casket, 84; dispute with Bishop John Cameron, 84–7; on university federation, 183, 192

McNeil, Neil: early benefactor of X, 144–6, 157, 173–4

MacNeil, Sister Catherine, 324

MacPherson, Rev. Dr Hugh ("Little Doc Hugh"): early years at X, 115, 166, 201, 502n77; manages Mount Cameron Farm, 459n14

MacPherson, Rev. Dr Hugh P. (president): appointed rector of X, 132–4; appointed diocesan administrator, 148; on university motto and coat of arms, 388; opposes university federation, 183; character and educational views, 196–7; retirement, 239

MacPherson, Ian, 229, 231, 234

MacPherson, John A., 353

MacPherson, Rev. Lauchlin, 113

MacSween, Rev. Alexander: early college trustee, 31

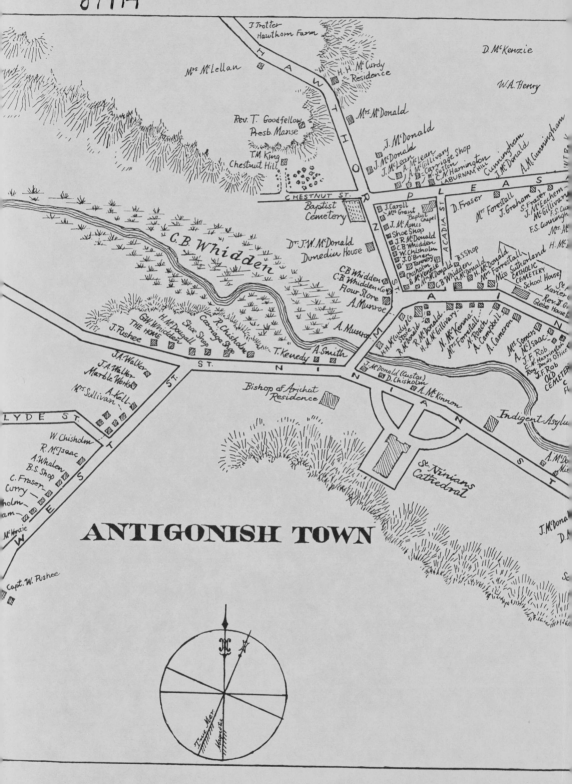

ANTIGONISH TOWN